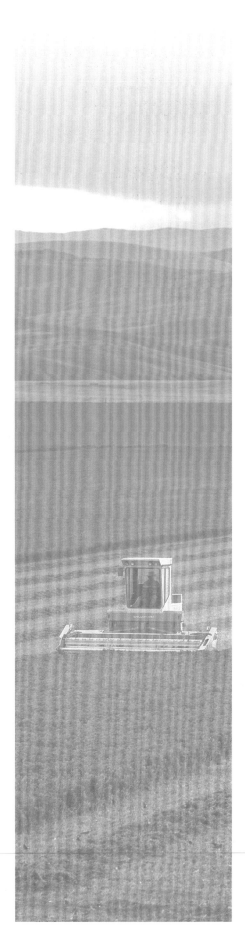

Irrigated Alfalfa Management

for Mediterranean and Desert Zones

DATE DUE

Edited by

Charles G. Summers

Daniel H. Putnam

University of California

Agriculture and Natural Resources

Publication 3512

To order or obtain ANR publications and other products, visit the ANR Communication Services online catalog at http://anrcatalog.ucdavis.edu or phone 1-800-994-8849. You can also place orders by mail or FAX, or request a printed catalog of our products from

University of California
Agriculture and Natural Resources
Communication Services
6701 San Pablo Avenue, 2nd Floor
Oakland, California 94608-1239

Telephone 1-800-994-8849
510-642-2431
FAX 510-643-5470
E-mail: danrcs@ucdavis.edu

Publication 3512
ISBN-13: 978-1-60107-608-3
Library of Congress Control Number: 2008908449

Photo credits are given in the acknowledgments.
Cover and book design: Will Suckow

UC PEER REVIEWED This publication has been anonymously peer reviewed for technical accuracy by University of California scientists and other qualified professionals. This review process was managed by the ANR Associate Editor for Agronomy and Range Management.

PRECAUTIONS FOR USING PESTICIDES

Pesticides are poisonous and must be used with caution. READ THE LABEL CAREFULLY BEFORE OPENING A PESTICIDE CONTAINER. Follow all label precautions and directions, including requirements for protective equipment. Use a pesticide only on crops specified on the label. Apply pesticides at the rates specified on the label or at lower rates if suggested in this publication. In California, all agricultural uses of pesticides must be reported. Contact your county agricultural commissioner for details. Laws, regulations, and information concerning pesticides change frequently, so be sure the publication you are using is up to date.

Legal Responsibility. The user is legally responsible for any damage due to misuse of pesticides. Responsibility extends to effects caused by drift, runoff, or residues.

Transportation. Do not ship or carry pesticides together with foods or feeds in a way that allows contamination of the edible items. Never transport pesticides in a closed passenger vehicle or in a closed cab.

Storage. Keep pesticides in original containers until used. Store them in a locked cabinet, building, or fenced area where they are not accessible to children, unauthorized persons, pets, or livestock. DO NOT store pesticides with foods, feeds, fertilizers, or other materials that may become contaminated by the pesticides.

Container Disposal. Dispose of empty containers carefully. Never reuse them. Make sure empty containers are not accessible to children or animals. Never dispose of containers where they may contaminate water supplies or natural waterways. Consult your county agricultural commissioner for correct procedures for handling and disposal of large quantities of empty containers.

Protection of Nonpest Animals and Plants. Many pesticides are toxic to useful or desirable animals, including honey bees, natural enemies, fish, domestic animals, and birds. Crops and other plants may also be damaged by misapplied pesticides. Take precautions to protect nonpest species from direct exposure to pesticides and from contamination due to drift, runoff, or residues. Certain rodenticides may pose a special hazard to animals that eat poisoned rodents.

Posting Treated Fields. For some materials, reentry intervals are established to protect field workers. Keep workers out of the field for the required time after application and, when required by regulations, post the treated areas with signs indicating the safe reentry date.

Harvest Intervals. Some materials or rates cannot be used in certain crops within a specific time before harvest. Follow pesticide label instructions and allow the required time between application and harvest.

Permit Requirements. Many pesticides require a permit from the county agricultural commissioner before possession or use. When such materials are recommended in this publication, they are marked with an asterisk (*).

Processed Crops. Some processors will not accept a crop treated with certain chemicals. If your crop is going to a processor, be sure to check with the processor before applying a pesticide.

Crop Injury. Certain chemicals may cause injury to crops (phytotoxicity) under certain conditions. Always consult the label for limitations. Before applying any pesticide, take into account the stage of plant development, the soil type and condition, the temperature, moisture, and wind direction. Injury may also result from the use of incompatible materials.

Personal Safety. Follow label directions carefully. Avoid splashing, spilling, leaks, spray drift, and contamination of clothing. NEVER eat, smoke, drink, or chew while using pesticides. Provide for emergency medical care IN ADVANCE as required by regulation.

3m-pr-11/08-MR/WS

Dedication to
Dr. Vern Marble

This manual is dedicated to Dr. Vern L. Marble, Extension Agronomist Emeritus, University of California, Davis. We can think of no one who has contributed more to the scientific basis of California alfalfa production than has Vern.

Dr. Marble has been known for many years as "Mr. Alfalfa" in California and has a tremendous depth of knowledge about this crop, about the history of alfalfa in the West, breeding, genetics, pest management, forage quality—just about any subject related to forage crops.

He is a true leader for forages. He was instrumental at promoting the introduction of multiple pest-resistant varieties, particularly CUF 101 in the 1970s and 80s, which had a tremendous impact on California producers and on alfalfa producers worldwide. In some countries, the introduction of CUF 101 was so revolutionary that growers mark the history of alfalfa in those countries as "before CUF101" and "after CUF101," particularly in Argentina, the Middle East, and Australia. He exhibited leadership in introducing forage testing to the industry and promoting standardization, cofounding the National Forage Testing Association (NFTA) in the 1980s. Dr. Marble has served as a mentor to countless numbers of farm advisors and Agricultural Experiment Station scientists. For 50 years, everyone working with alfalfa in California has benefited from Vern's gentle guidance and council.

Vern was born in Tremonton, Utah, on September 27, 1928, and moved with his family four years later to Fillmore, Utah, where his father taught vocational agriculture. In 1936, the family moved to Gustine, California, then to Chino and subsequently Salinas, where his father taught vocational agriculture and mathematics at Salinas Junior College, now Hartnell College. Vern had his first introduction to farm life at the beginning of WWII when, at the age of 13, he went to work for his grandfather and uncle on the 3,000-acre dryland family farm near the Utah-Idaho border. He was paid the handsome sum of $3 per day plus room and board, the same wages paid for the hired man who was drafted to serve in the army. While on the farm, he drove a D-6 tractor, combining wheat, ploughing, and harrowing. He engaged in weeding, treating planting seed with fungicides, planting wheat, running and repairing combines, cutting, raking, and baling dryland alfalfa, milking cows, and running a large herd of horses and mules.

Vern graduated with a B.S. and M.S. degree from Utah State Agricultural College, now Utah State University, in Logan, Utah. He served in the U. S. Army, and at the end of the Korean War returned to California. In 1957 he completed his PhD in plant physiology at the University of California, Davis. He worked for a short time as a regional agronomist for Chevron Chemical Company and in late 1957 accepted a position as extension agronomist at UC Davis.

Dr. Marble has been author or coauthor of over 230 popular and technical publications during his career, while providing statewide leadership to the important alfalfa hay and seed production industry. He devised the alfalfa hay quality evaluation system used by hay growers and dairymen in California. He also chaired the National Alfalfa Hay Testing Association, a program aimed at eliminating test differences among states. An important part of his applied research was on alfalfa varietal evaluation and production of high-quality hay and seed.

With the cooperation of UC farm advisors, researchers, and members of industry, Dr. Marble organized the California Alfalfa Symposium in 1971. This important annual gathering rapidly became the premier forage meeting for California, if not the West. This symposium continues today to provide critical and timely information to alfalfa producers, dairymen, and industry representatives, a well-appreciated University meeting begun by Dr. Marble.

Additionally, Vern saw the need for greater cooperation between UC Cooperative Extension farm advisors and campus-based researchers and organized the California Alfalfa Workgroup in the early 1970s. This was one of the first UC workgroups organized, a model that was subsequently followed by the UC Office of the President for many other subject areas. Dr. Marble developed funding for workgroup members for cooperative projects that provided new information to benefit the alfalfa industry.

During his career, Dr. Marble has been a consultant in more than a dozen foreign countries. He completed an FAO evaluation of alfalfa research capabilities in the Near and Middle East, as well as a book on alfalfa production for the region. He has served on various university committees concerned with programs and policies in agricultural research and extension. In recognition for his work, Dr. Marble has received numerous awards, and in 1990, received the Outstanding Alfalfa Extension Specialist Award for the USA from the American Society of Agronomy.

Dr. Vern L. Marble retired September 30, 1991, after 34 years of service with the University of California, Davis, as Cooperative Extension forage specialist. Vern believes that his greatest fulfillment and personal reward has come from working with the many UC Cooperative Extension farm advisors, with their unique ability to identify and solve problems of great importance to the agricultural community. The farm advisors would tell you that much of their ability to do that comes from the teachings of Dr. Marble.

We can think of no one more deserving of this dedication and honor than Vern Marble. He is truly the leader of alfalfa production in California. Vern, we salute you and thank you for your tremendous contribution to our field of study. Congratulations.

Charles G. Summers,
Daniel H. Putnam, and
Steve B. Orloff,
with the help of Mary Marble

Contents

vi

Preface

Alfalfa was one of the first crops planted during California's early history, and it currently leads the state in number of acres in cultivation. Over the past 150 years, alfalfa has progressed from a relatively low-value pasture, hay, and rotation crop to a high-value, highly managed cash crop worth over $1 billion per year. Scientific research and grower knowledge about stand establishment, irrigation, pest management, harvest management, and end use have been critical to its success in the state. This publication represents a compilation of many aspects of this knowledge, which can be of benefit both to existing growers and those new to the crop.

The purpose of this publication is to provide detailed, comprehensive, scientifically accurate information about the growth, production, management, and use of alfalfa grown under irrigation, particularly as appropriate for the Mediterranean and desert zones of California. Although it is intended for use by growers, farmworkers, managers, consultants, agents, and advisors in irrigated regions, anyone with an interest in alfalfa will find something of value herein.

This book is simultaneously published online as a series of independent, stand-alone chapters at the UC Alfalfa and Forage Systems Workgroup Web site, http://alfalfa.ucdavis.edu. Readers should consult this Web site for updates of individual chapters and for other resources related to alfalfa.

This publication is a product of the University of California Alfalfa and Forage Systems Workgroup, a coordinated working group of University of California scientists from many disciplines who have interest in alfalfa. The workgroup has been operational since 1970 and has sponsored the California Alfalfa Symposium and national conferences each year for 38 years (see the above Web site for proceedings from these conferences). In this publication, we have tapped the interdisciplinary expertise of members of the University of California Agricultural Experiment Station and Cooperative Extension, as well as colleagues from neighboring states. We have made every attempt to make statements that are derived from scientific research or from years of observation and grower experience.

This book is the culmination of efforts that began over 10 years ago. We are grateful for the herculean efforts and patience of authors, reviewers, the editorial committee, and production staff who have made this publication possible. On behalf of our colleagues, we are pleased to offer *Irrigated Alfalfa Management for Mediterranean and Desert Zones*.

—Charles G. Summers and
Daniel H. Putnam, Editors

For updates to these chapters and for further information about alfalfa, please see the

**UC Alfalfa Workgroup Web site,
http://alfalfa.ucdavis.edu/.**

Contributing Authors

Khaled M. Bali
Farm Advisor, University of California Cooperative Extension, Holtville, CA

Mick Canevari
Farm Advisor, University of California Cooperative Extension, Stockton, CA

Carlos A. Cangiano
Research Scientist, INTA EEA Balcarce, Provincia de Buenos Aires, Argentina

Alejandro R. Castillo
Farm Advisor, University of California Cooperative Extension, Merced, CA

R. Michael Davis,
Extension Specialist, Department of Plant Pathology, University of California, Davis

Ed DePeters
Professor of Ruminant Nutrition, Department of Animal Science, University of California, Davis

Carol A. Frate
Farm Advisor, University of California Cooperative Extension, Tulare, CA

Larry D. Godfrey
Extension Entomologist, Department of Entomology, University of California, Davis

Juan N. Guerrero
Farm Advisor, University of California Cooperative Extension, El Centro, CA

Blaine R. Hanson
Irrigation Specialist, Department of Land, Air, and Water Resources, University of California, Davis

Gerald E. Higginbotham
Farm Advisor, University of California Cooperative Extension, Fresno, CA

Karen Klonsky
Cooperative Extension Specialist, Department of Agricultural and Resource Economics, University of California, Davis

Rachael F. Long
Farm Advisor, University of California Cooperative Extension, Woodland, CA

Daniel B. Marcum
Farm Advisor, University of California Cooperative Extension, McArthur, CA

Marsha Campbell Mathews
Farm Advisor, University of California Cooperative Extension, Modesto, CA

Roland D. Meyer
Cooperative Extension Specialist Emeritus, Department of Land, Air, and Water Resources, University of California, Davis

Shannon C. Mueller
Farm Advisor, University of California Cooperative Extension, Fresno, CA

Eric T. Natwick
Entomology Farm Advisor, University of California Cooperative Extension, Holtville, CA

Steve B. Orloff
Farm Advisor, University of California Cooperative Extension, Yreka, CA

Nyles G. Peterson
Farm Advisor, University of California Cooperative Extension, Riverside, CA

Daniel H. Putnam
Forage Extension Specialist, Department of Plant Sciences University of California, Davis

Barbara A. Reed
Farm Advisor, University of California Cooperative Extension, Orland, CA

Peter Robinson
Extension Nutritionist, Department of Animal Science, University of California, Davis

Anne V. Rodiek
Professor, California State University, Fresno

Terrell P. Salmon
Wildlife Specialist, University of California Cooperative Extension, San Diego, CA

Blake L. Sanden
Farm Advisor, University of California Cooperative Extension, Bakersfield, CA

Jerry L. Schmierer
Farm Advisor, University of California Cooperative Extension, Colusa, CA

Carolyn L. Stull
Extension Specialist, University of California School of Veterinary Medicine, Davis

Charles G. Summers
Entomologist, University of California Kearney Agricultural Center, Parlier, CA

Larry R. Teuber
Professor, Department of Plant Sciences, University of California, Davis

Dan J. Undersander
Extension and Research Forage Agronomist, Department of Agronomy, University of Wisconsin, Madison

Ron N. Vargas
Farm Advisor Emeritus, University of California Cooperative Extension, Madera, CA

Becky B. Westerdahl
Extension Nematologist, Department of Nematology, University of California, Davis

Desley A. Whisson
Lecturer in Wildlife and Conservation Biology School of Life and Environmental Sciences, Faculty of Science and Technology, Deakin University, Burwood, Victoria, Australia

Acknowledgments

This manual was produced through the collaborative efforts of the University of California Division of Agriculture and Natural Resources Alfalfa Workgroup. We are grateful to the editorial committee, Carol A. Frate, Shannon C. Mueller, W. Michael Canevari, Ronald N. Vargas, Steve B. Orloff, Rachael F. Long, and Larry R. Teuber, for their thoughtful insight and wise counsel in the preparation of this manual. Their guidance and support through some very difficult times and decisions is greatly appreciated. We are appreciative of the efforts and contributions made by a legion of anonymous peer reviewers from across the United States. Their unselfish efforts contributed to significant improvements in each of the chapters in this manual. We thank Will Suckow for his outstanding layout and design of each chapter and Mary Rodgers for her copyediting. We are grateful to Larry Strand for supplying a great number of photographs from the IPM collection that add significantly to the value of this manual. Mary Lou Flint served as the associate editor for chapters 8 through 12 and chapter 24, and her assistance is greatly appreciated.

We wish to express our sincere thanks to our sponsors, who are listed on a separate page, for their generous contributions without which this manual could not have gone forward. Bob Sams, Ann Senuta, and Stephen Barnett of ANR Communication Services provided valuable information and input throughout this entire process and we are grateful for their help. Finally, we are grateful to the authors and coauthors without whom this manual could not have become a reality. These individuals represent the best and broadest range of knowledge available regarding alfalfa production. Their willingness to accept this assignment on top of all of their other responsibilities and duties and share this information is to be commended.

Photo Credits

Angel Barrenechea: Page 265, 281. **James H. Cane**: Fig. 22.9C. **Mick Canevari**: Fig. 1.21, 12.6, 12.9B, 15.1, 15.5; Plate 8.1, 8.2, 8.4, 8.12. **Jack Kelly Clark**: cover; Page 113, 131, 155, 187, 343 inset, 357 inset; Fig. 1.19, 1.20, 1.23, 6.3, 9.4, 9.5, 10.3, 11.6, 12.1, 12.3, 12.7, 12.8, 12.9A, 15.4, 16.7 inset, 22.6A, 22.9A; Plate 6.2, 6.6, 6.7, 8.11, 8.6, 8.7, 8.8, 8.9, 9.1, 9.10, 9.11, 9.12, 9.13, 9.14, 9.15, 9.16, 9.17, 9.18, 9.19, 9.2, 9.21, 9.22, 9.23, 9.24, 9.3, 9.4, 9.5, 9.6, 9.7, 9.8, 9.9, 10.1, 10.10, 10.13, 10.15, 10.2, 10.20, 10.22 , 10.3, 10.4, 10.6, 10.8, 1A1, 1A2a(A), 1A2bi, 1A3, 1B2a, 1B2bii, 1B2c, 2A1ai, 2A1aiii, 2A1aiv(B), 2A1biai, 2A1biaii, 2A1bibi, 2A1bibii, 2A2b, 2A3a, 2A3b, 2B1, 2B2b(A), 2C1a, 2C1b, 2C2b(A), 2D1ai, 2D1aii, 2D1bi, 2D1bii, 2D2ai, 2D2aii, 2D2aiii, 2D3a, 2D3b, 2D3c(B), 2D4, 2E2b, 2E2e. **Jerry P. Clark**: Fig. 12.4A. **Robert J. Coleman**: Fig. 17.7. **Joseph M. DiTomaso**: Plate 8.3. **Dan Drake**: Fig. 17.4. **Donald C. Erwin**: Plate 2E2c. **Bill Fischer**: Plate 2A1biia. **Carol Frate**: Plate 10.3, 10.12, 2A1aiv(A). **David G. Gilchrist**: Fig. 2.4; Plate 10.5, 10.7, 10.9, 2D3c(A), 2E1, 2E2a. **Dennis H. Hall**: Plate 10.14, 10.19. **Jeffrey Hall**: Plate 10.18. **Blaine Hanson**: Page 89. **Gerald E. Higginbotham**: Fig. 17.3. **B. A. Jaffee**: Fig. 11.4. **J. Kuhn**: Fig. 1.27, 1.30. **Rachael F. Long**: Page 313, 343, 357; Fig. 17.5,

21.1, 21.2. **Mary Marble**: Page iii. **Vernon L.Marble**: Fig. 22.7A, 22.8; Plate 10.11, 10.17, 10.21, A2bii, 2A1biib(B), 2E2d. **Marsha Campbell Mathews**: Fig. 4.4; 20.1. **Roland Meyer**: Page 73, 305; Fig. 20.2; Plate 6.1, 6.3, 6.4, 6.5, 2C2a, 2C2b(B). **Shannon C. Mueller**: Page 39, 299, 327; Fig. 19.2, 22.4, 22.6B, 22.7B, 22.9B. **Eric Natwick**: Plate 1B1, 2C1c. **Steve Orloff**: Page 31, 175; Fig. 1.22, 2.2, 14.6, 15.3; Plate 1B2bi, 2A1aii, 2A1biib(A), 2B2b(B), 11.1B. **Suzanne Paisley**: Page 227; Fig. 19.1. **Richard Peaden**: Plate 10.16; Plate 2A2a. **Nyles G. Peterson**: Fig. 17.6. **Dan Putnam**: Page 1, 19, 59, 197, 209, 241; Fig. 1.15, 1.16, 1.17, 1.18, 1.24, 1.25, 1.26, 1.28, 1.29, 1.31, 2.6, 4.2, 4.3, 4.5, 4.6, 4.7, 4.8, 5.7, 16.7, 16.8. **Oklahoma State University Cooperative Extension**: Fig. 5.8A, 5.8B. **San Joaquin Valley Haygrowers**: Fig. 1.4, 1.5, 1.6. **Blake Sanden**: Fig. 2.5. **Thomas A. Schultz**: Page 305 inset. **Larry Strand**: Fig. 2.1. **Charles G. Summers**: Plate 9.20, 1A2a(B), 2B2a. **Larry Teuber**: Fig. 5.8C. **UC Alfalfa Workgroup**: Fig. 7.4, 15.2, 21.3, 22.5. **UC Davis Department of Nematology**: Page 175 inset; Fig. 11.3, 11.5; Plate 11.1A. **UC Vertebrate Pest Management Program**: Fig. 12.2, 12.4B, 12.5., 12.10. **Ron Vargas**: Plate 8.5, 8.10.

Acknowledgment of Sponsors

Many thanks to the contributors who have stepped forward to sponsor this important educational project.

PLATINUM SPONSORSHIP ($5,000)

Bowles Farming Company, Inc.
Los Banos, CA

National Alfalfa & Forage Alliance
St. Paul, MN

GOLD SPONSORSHIP ($2,500)

Ag-Seeds Unlimited
Woodland, CA

California Alfalfa & Forage
Association, Novato, CA

CROPLAN GENETICS®
St. Paul, MN

Dairyland Seed
Sloughhouse, CA

Farm Science Genetics/
Allied Seed LLC, Nampa, ID

Lockwood Seed & Grain
Chowchilla, CA

Monsanto
St. Louis, MO

New Mexico Hay
Association, Dexter, NM

Pioneer Hi-Bred
Johnstown, IA

Producer's Choice Seed
Woodland, CA

WL Research
Madison, WI

SILVER SPONSORSHIP ($500)

Americas Alfalfa, Los Banos, CA
Bayer CropScience CA/AZ District Team, Kingsburg, CA
Dr. Vern L. & Mary H. Marble, Davis, CA
Eureka Seeds, Woodland, CA
Gillespie Ag Service, Porterville, CA
Hastings Island Land Company, Rio Vista, CA
Imperial Valley Seeds, Inc., Holtville, CA
Inland Tarp & Cover, Inc., Moses Lake, WA

Kuhn Farms, Seeley, CA
NK/Syngenta Seeds, Minneapolis, MN
Ranier Seeds, Davenport, WA
Silverado Ranch Supply, Yerington, NV
S&W Seed Company, Five Points, CA
TS&L Seeds, Woodland, CA
Valent-Chateau Herbicide Stewardship Program, Walnut Creek, CA
Verdegaal Brothers Inc., Hanford, CA

GREEN SPONSORSHIP ($250)

Amvac Chemical Corporation, Los Angeles, CA
Cal Poly Pomona - College of Agriculture
Chemtura Corporation, Fresno, CA
Ferguson Farms, Inc., Stockton, CA
Imperial Valley Milling Co., Holtville, CA

Irrometer Company, Riverside, CA
Stinger, Ltd., Hanes, KS
T-L Irrigation, Hastings, NE
Zen-Raku-Ren, San Francisco, CA

Listing of these company sponsors does not imply endorsement by the University of California or its affiliates.

 This publication has been anonymously peer reviewed for technical accuracy by University of California scientists and other qualified professionals. This review process was managed by the ANR Associate Editor for Agronomy and Range Management.

1

Alfalfa Production Systems in California

Daniel H. Putnam
Forage Extension Specialist, Department of Plant Sciences,
University of California, Davis

Charles G. Summers
Entomologist, University of California Kearney Agricultural Center,
Parlier, CA

Steve B. Orloff
Farm Advisor, University of California Cooperative Extension, Yreka, CA

Alfalfa is considered the "Queen of Forages" worldwide and is unrivaled among forage crops due to its combination of high quality, high yield, stand persistence, wide adaptation, biological nitrogen (N) fixation, and soil benefits. Alfalfa is one of the most palatable forages, providing high energy and protein for dairy cows as well as other types of livestock. It is an "engine of human food production," eventually transformed into milk, cheese, meat, wool, and even honey. It provides a livelihood to thousands of farmers, contributes to wildlife habitat, protects the soil, and provides open spaces. It is the first choice of many farmers and ranchers as the premier perennial forage legume.

California's agriculture is most often identified with high-value specialty crops, such as lettuce, tomatoes, fruits, almonds, and grapes. In 2005 the state's agricultural value was over $31 billion per year—first in the nation—and these crops were leading commodities. However, California also produces over 21 percent of the nation's milk and has become the leading dairy producer. As a result, alfalfa is the state's highest acreage crop, and California is the leading alfalfa hay-producing state in the United States. The dairy-forage continuum is the state's most important agricultural enterprise, with dairy ranked as the state's number-one commodity, exceeding $5 billion per year in recent years. There are also significant numbers of other alfalfa-consuming livestock, including beef cattle, horses, goats, and sheep. The linkage with dairy production and other animal enterprises has caused alfalfa and forage crops to play a significant role in the state.

This chapter provides an overview of alfalfa history and production methods, describes its role in cropping systems, and provides a context for alfalfa production in irrigated regions of California.

Alfalfa Growing Regions

The state of California is highly diverse in its climates and soils, but alfalfa is important in most of the agricultural regions in the state. The primary production areas are the Central Valley and the Low Desert, High Desert, Coastal, and the Intermountain Regions.

Central Valley

Alfalfa is produced throughout California, but the major growing areas are the rich alluvial plains of the Sacramento and San Joaquin Rivers, collectively called the Great Central Valley of California. This region, considered one of the most important agricultural regions of the world, has a Mediterranean climate and is characterized by mostly deep, alluvial soils, but with significant salt-affected soils in the western portion of the San Joaquin Valley. The Central Valley is characterized by hot, dry summers (daily maximum temperatures over 100°F [38°C]) and cool winters (daily maximum temperatures of 60° [16°C]). Rainfall ranges from 8 to 18 inches (20–46 cm) south to north and occurs mostly from November through March, but supplies of irrigation water from rivers, streams, canals, and reservoirs originating from the Sierra Nevada Mountains to the east and north are significant. Over 70 percent of California's alfalfa is produced in the Central Valley (Fig. 1.1). Nearly 100 percent of the state's alfalfa is irrigated.

FIGURE 1.1

Map of production zones in California. The major production zones are the San Joaquin Valley (61% of the state's production), followed by the Low Desert (17%), Sacramento Valley (9.7%), Intermountain (9.5%), High Desert (1.7%), and Coastal (0.5%) Regions. Percentages are from 2005 USDA National Agricultural Statistics Service. Green marks indicate acreage.

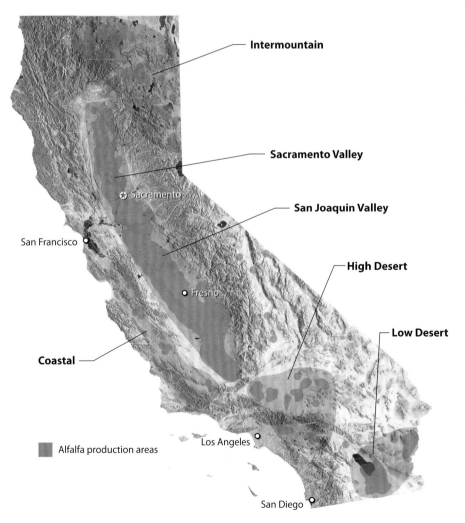

Low Desert

The southern Low Desert Region, consisting primarily of the Imperial and Palo Verde Valleys, is an area with searing hot summers (daily maximum greater than 105°F [41°C]) and warm winters (daily maximum 75°F [24°C]) enabling crop growth throughout the year. This region receives less than 3 inches (8 cm) of rain per year, but receives large allocations of irrigation water originating from the Colorado River. Soils are generally heavy, but some sandy regions can be found, and salts are a significant management issue. Surface flood irrigation systems are the most common. About 17 percent of the state's production is from this region (Fig. 1.1).

High Desert

The High Desert Region is north and east of the Los Angeles Basin and is characterized by high elevation (1,500 to 3,000 feet [457 to 914 m]) and very low rainfall (less than 5 inches [13 cm] per year). Unlike the Low Desert, winters are cold (mean low of 37°F [3°C]), sometimes even snowy, limiting winter growth. Soils tend to be light sandy loams to clay loams, prone to wind erosion, and most water sources are from groundwater. Salinity is a problem in some areas, and water is primarily pumped from aquifers. Less than 2 percent of the state's production is from this region (Fig. 1.1).

Coastal Region

The cool coastal valleys of California can grow alfalfa, but much of the production has been displaced by urbanization and higher value crops in recent years. Less than 0.5 percent of the state's alfalfa is located here (Fig. 1.1).

Intermountain

Alfalfa is a significant crop in the more temperate high-elevation Intermountain Regions of California, which experience freezing winters and clear, warm summers. Summer highs average 86°F (30°C), and winter lows average 26°F (–3°C). Rainfall averages about 20 inches (51 cm) per year. A detailed description of Intermountain alfalfa production can be found in *Intermountain Alfalfa Management* (Orloff and Carlson, eds.). Approximately 10 percent of the state's alfalfa crop is produced in this region (Fig. 1.1).

Production

Statewide, average dry-matter (DM) yields are 7.0 to 7.5 tons per acre (15–17 Mg ha^{-1}) (Fig. 1.2). Growers harvest up to 12 times per season in the southern deserts of California (the average is 6 to 7 through most of the state), producing about 7 million tons (6.3 Mg) per year in California.

FIGURE 1.2

Average yields (to convert t/acre to Mg/ha, multiply by 2.24) for selected production zones in California, 2004–2005 (County Agricultural Statistics Reports).

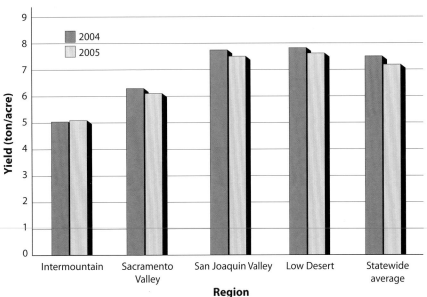

History of Alfalfa

Alfalfa's history spans more than 4,000 years, originating from the very early history of agriculture (Fig. 1.3). California has played a special role in its history in North America. Alfalfa was likely domesticated near present-day Turkemnistan, Iran, Turkey, and the Caucasus. The earliest written reference to alfalfa was from Turkey in 1300 BC.

Alfalfa was important to the early Babylonian cultures, the Persians, Greeks, and Romans. Aristotle and Aristophanes wrote about it, as did early Roman writers. Alfalfa was reportedly brought to Greece in 500 BC by invading Median armies to feed their chariot warhorses. The forage culture that included alfalfa enabled Roman and other Mediterranean empires to expand, due to the linkage with horses and military might, as well as its role in milk and meat production. Alfalfa was introduced into China in 126 AD, accompanying prized Persian horses given to the Chinese Emperor. Alfalfa moved across the Alps into Northern Europe acquiring the name "lucerne," as it is currently known in many countries. Similarly, the Arab empires in the Middle Ages spread alfalfa throughout many areas of Europe and the Middle East. The word "alfalfa," meaning "best horse fodder," has Arabic, Persian, and Kashmiri roots.

The first recorded attempt to cultivate alfalfa in the United States was in Georgia in 1736. Presidents Washington and Jefferson, as well as others, grew alfalfa, but these early efforts were largely unsuccessful. The important introductions into the United States came during the California Gold Rush around 1850. Unlike many crops that were important in the east and then moved west, alfalfa gained its first foothold in the United States in California and other western states and subsequently moved eastward.

Alfalfa and the Gold Rush

Historians have said that it is impossible to overemphasize the importance of the California Gold Rush of 1849–1860 as it influences the history of the West, and the same can be said for the history of alfalfa, which was linked to the Gold Rush. Although exact dates are unknown, the first alfalfa seed probably entered California from South America between 1847 and 1850. Alfalfa had been cultivated in Chile for more than 20 years prior to this time and was originally promoted to California farmers as "Chilean clover." Although a vast majority of prospectors failed at mining, many were successful in agriculture, and alfalfa was an important component of early California farms. In just a few years, alfalfa spread north and eastward to Nevada, Utah, Oregon, Kansas, and Oklahoma.

Alfalfa was a natural fit with livestock in the expanding West. It readily adapted to the warm sun and deep soils of California where irrigation water was available. While non-irrigated wheat was dependent on far-away markets, and methods for processing vegetables and fruits were not yet developed, there was always a steady, local demand

FIGURE 1.3

Alfalfa was one of the earliest domesticated crops and was an important component of early Mediterranean cultures of Europe and the Near East. It plays an important role today in the regions of California with a Mediterranean climate.

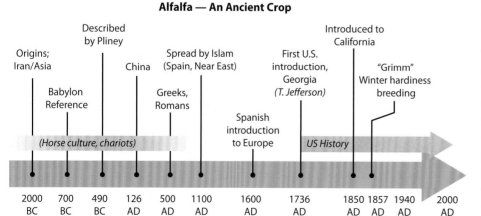

Alfalfa — An Ancient Crop

Apasti ➡ Alfalfa, "best horse fodder"

for alfalfa hay. Hay production in California increased from about 2,000 tons (1,814 Mg) in 1850 to 550,000 tons (498,850 Mg) by 1870. This was accompanied by a rise in the dairy industry around cities, particularly San Francisco.

Alfalfa—A Traded Crop

Alfalfa hay has been a traded crop since its first introduction. The availability of river transportation (Fig. 1.4) and the new rail lines built in the 1880s greatly enhanced the viability of alfalfa as a cash crop. The San Joaquin and Sacramento Rivers provided a water highway from the agricultural areas of the Central Valley to San Francisco and other coastal regions. Transportation of hay required baling mechanisms, such as the Petaluma Hay Press (Fig. 1.5). In Southern California, alfalfa hay was raised in the deserts around Los Angeles and was the key first crop in the newly irrigated desert areas of the Imperial Valley in the early 20th century.

Alfalfa—A Western Crop

Alfalfa's sweep across the farming areas of the West was completed shortly after 1900, and alfalfa became one of the key irrigated crops in most western agricultural areas. By the turn of the 19th century, alfalfa acreage west of the Mississippi River accounted for over 98 per-

cent of the total U.S. alfalfa production. In the 1920s, the leading alfalfa states were Kansas, Nebraska, Colorado, California, and Idaho. Most early methods required much hand labor (Fig. 1.6). Later introductions and the spread of "Grimm" and other winter-hardy cultivars assisted in the development of alfalfa for northern midwestern states and eastern states, and by 1940, midwestern and eastern production exceeded western production.

Yield and Quality Changes

Since the early 1920s, alfalfa yields have increased about two-fold in California (Fig. 1.7). This amounts to an average increase of nearly 0.5 ton per acre (1.1 Mg ha^{-1}) each decade. The primary factors for this increase were (1) expansion of alfalfa into higher-yielding districts like the Imperial Valley, (2) mechanization techniques that enable more cuttings per year, (3) techniques leading to improved irrigation management, such as laser leveling and better sprinklers, (4) new varieties

FIGURE 1.5

The Petaluma Hay Press was an early baler developed in Petaluma, California, (near San Francisco) to bale hay from stationary stacks.

FIGURE 1.4

Hay was transported in the late 1800s and early 20th century on the many waterways of California's San Joaquin and Sacramento Valleys. Alfalfa hay was a traded commodity from the earliest periods in California.

with higher yield and pest resistance, (5) new pest management methods, (6) increased use of fertilizers, and (7) better agronomic techniques, such as time of seeding and harvest scheduling.

In recent years, intensification of management for quality, particularly shorter cutting

schedules (e.g., < 28–30 days), have likely had the effect of slowing yield increases (Fig. 1.7). Cutting schedules in the 1950s through the 1970s were clearly longer than current practice, thereby resulting in lower-quality hay. Thirty- to 40-day schedules were normal in this period, while currently, 22- to 28-day schedules are more typical to achieve higher quality. Petaluma Hay Testing Service in Petaluma, California, has shown a gradual increase in quality of the samples received from about 53 percent total digestible nutrients (TDN) to above 55 percent TDN (90% DM) since 1970 (Fig. 1.8), a measurement based upon fiber concentration. Since cutting for quality almost always sacrifices yield, this may explain a large portion of the yield "plateau" that some observers say has occurred over the past 20 years.

FIGURE 1.6

Early methods of western alfalfa cultivation included field stacking of hay in large units, with the use of the Jackson Fork, using horse-drawn derricks.

FIGURE 1.7

Yearly average alfalfa yields (to convert t/acre to Mg/ha, multiply by 2.24), California, 1912–2006 (USDA National Agricultural Statistics Service).

FIGURE 1.8

Changes in forage quality analysis since 1970. Each point is the average of thousands of samples received each year by Petaluma Hay Testing Service, Petaluma, California (data courtesy of Don Waite).

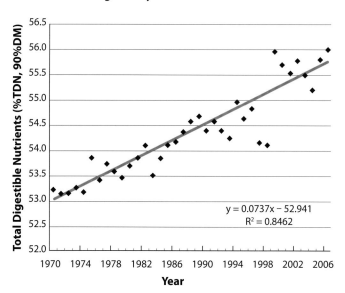

Variety Improvement

In the early 20th century, there were only five alfalfa variety groups known to U.S. researchers, mostly by their country of origin or land races, such as "California Common" and "Kansas Common" and "Peruvian." In the late 1920s, breeders discovered that they could select for improved performance and disease resistance, beginning with bacterial wilt. By the 1950s, a greater number of alfalfa strains were available, mostly selections made by the U.S. Department of Agriculture (USDA) and State Experiment Station researchers. Key milestones have been the development of aphid resistance, nematode resistance, and resistance to root diseases, particularly phytophthora, and the development of "nondormant" lines (such as CUF 101), which are much higher yielding in long-season regions like California. By the 1970s, the private sector began to dominate alfalfa breeding, and since that time dozens of new alfalfa varieties have been released each year (see Chapter 5, "Choosing an Alfalfa Variety").

Current Status and Statistics

Worldwide, alfalfa is grown on approximately 79 million acres (32 million ha), 70 percent of which comes from the United States, Russia, and Argentina. In the United States, alfalfa competes with wheat as the third most important crop in value, depending on year (Table 1.1). Alfalfa is California's highest acreage crop, and California is currently the leading producer of alfalfa hay in the United States (Fig. 1.9). Alfalfa is the dominant forage grown in the western United States under irrigation (Fig. 1.10), and is first either in acreage or value of agronomic crops in all western states.

Acreage

Alfalfa acreage in California reached a maximum of over 1.2 million acres (486,000 ha) in the 1960s, and has ranged from 950,000 to 1.15 million acres (385,000 to 466,000 ha) since

TABLE 1.1

Top six value crops in the United States, including value of milk produced for reference. Alfalfa is included in the "all hay" category and competes with wheat for the third or fourth place in value, depending on year. (USDA National Agricultural Statistics Service)

Crop	2003	2004	2005	Rank
	Value in Billions ($ × 1,000,000,000)			
Corn	24.5	24.4	21.0	(1)
Soybean	18.0	17.9	16.9	(2)
Hay (all)	12.0	12.2	12.5	(3)
Hay (alfalfa)	6.7	6.9	7.3	(3–4)
(Milk)	*21.4*	*27.5*	*26.9*	
Wheat (all)	7.9	7.2	7.1	(3–4)
Cotton	5.5	4.8	5.6	(5)
Potato	2.7	2.6	2.9	(6)
All Field Crops	**82.3**	**80.7**	**76.8**	

FIGURE 1.9

Leading alfalfa-producing states in the United States (USDA National Agricultural Statistics Service). Note: haylage is omitted from this total, which is significant in several states, especially Wisconsin.

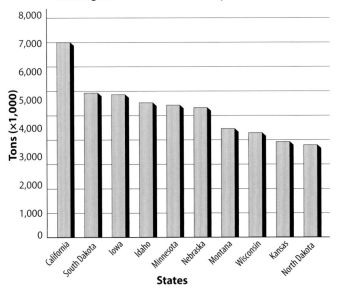

Leading U. S. States in Alfalfa Hay Production

FIGURE 1.10

Irrigated alfalfa production in the United States (USDA National Agricultural Statistics Service).

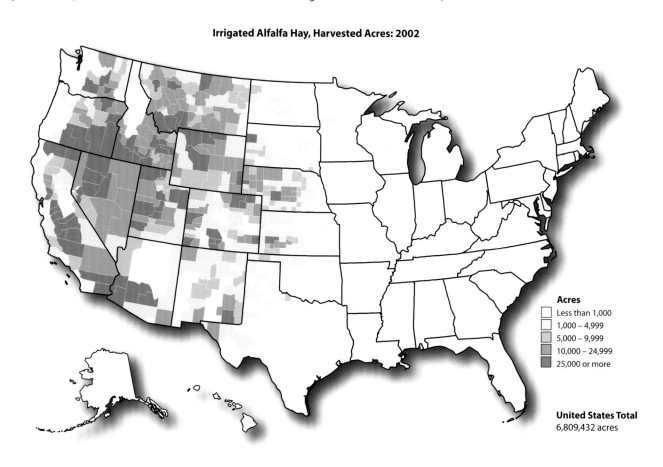

Irrigated Alfalfa Hay, Harvested Acres: 2002

Acres

☐ Less than 1,000
☐ 1,000 – 4,999
▨ 5,000 – 9,999
▨ 10,000 – 24,999
■ 25,000 or more

United States Total
6,809,432 acres

FIGURE 1.11

Trends in California acreage and production, 1920–2005.

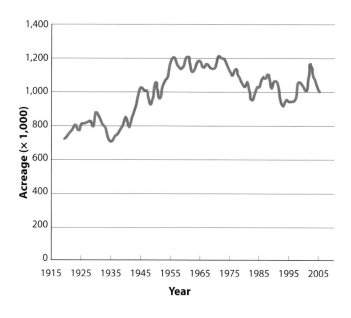

that time (Fig. 1.11). However, due to higher yields (Fig. 1.7), overall production has continued to increase slightly. Conversion of alfalfa acreage to higher-value specialty crops, urban conversion, and limitations of water supply have been factors limiting California's alfalfa acreage during the late 20th century and early 21st century. Countervailing these trends has been the phenomenal increase in California dairy cow and recreational horse numbers, thus increasing the demand for forages. As a result, acreage has remained fairly constant for decades. All forages (alfalfa, irrigated pasture, corn silage, small grain forages, and miscellaneous hays) occupy over 2 million (810,000 ha) of the 9.4 million irrigated acres (3.8 million ha) in the state.

Dairying in California

The growth of the dairy industry in California has been a major factor influencing alfalfa production in this region. California surpassed Wisconsin as the number-one dairy state in 1993 (Fig. 1.12), and now produces more than 21 percent of the nation's milk. The growth of western dairying, particularly in California, was a major trend during the last quarter of the 20th century. In 2005, California milk production was about four times that of 1975 production (Fig. 1.13). Milk cow numbers have increased an average of over 3 percent per year, and production per cow has increased an average of 2.2 percent per year over this period in California. At least 75 percent of the alfalfa in the state goes to the dairy industry. This trend for growth in dairying has also occurred in several other western states, particularly Idaho, New Mexico, and Arizona. By 2005, western states accounted for over 40 percent of the nation's milk supply, up from 15 percent in the 1970s (Fig. 1.14).

A typical California dairy farm currently averages over 800 milking cows, and this number increases every year. In 2007, there were approximately 1.8 million dairy cows in California on less than 2,100 dairy farms. Growth in dairying is driven by growth in western populations, lower costs of production than in other regions, availability of

FIGURE 1.12

Top 10 milk producing states in the United States, 2005.

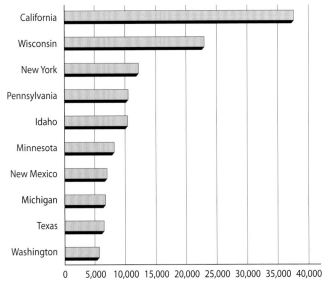

FIGURE 1.13

Total milk production, dairy cow numbers, and production per cow, expressed as a percentage of 1975 (USDA National Agricultural Statistics Service).

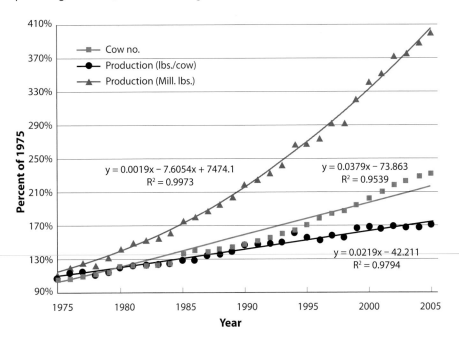

high-quality forages and by-products for feeding (such as whole cottonseed, citrus pulp, and tomato pomace), availability of labor, and reinvestment by dairies displaced by urbanization.

California dairy units consist of large corrals with open shelters and large milking parlors, and are characterized by high capital investments, high culling rates, and confinement housing. Grazing of alfalfa or other forages is a minor component of most California dairies, but grazing occurs on some Coastal and Northern California dairies.

Unlike many other dairy regions, the vast majority of the feed consumed by California dairy farms is purchased, including the majority of the alfalfa hay. Although dairy farms produce sizeable quantities of corn silage, small grain silage, and some alfalfa, the majority of alfalfa in this region is traded on the open market. The segregation of the alfalfa hay producer (seller) from the dairy producer (buyer) is a unique feature of western forage systems. This has large implications for alfalfa production, since forage quality testing plays an important role in setting price, and storage and transportation are important economic factors.

Alfalfa Production Methods

In many respects, much of California presents an ideal location for growing alfalfa. Plentiful sunshine and warmth; lack of excessive rain during the growing season; fertile, well-drained soils; and the availability of sufficient irrigation water enable production of high-quality, high-yielding alfalfa in many California regions. Water, however, is increasingly a key limiting resource.

Alfalfa as a System

Established alfalfa crops interact in complex ways with other crops, farming activities, and many other organisms in the surrounding ecosystem. Alfalfa's dense canopy and crown structure afford a wide variety of habitats for exploitation by a diverse array of organisms. Alfalfa's deep and extensive root systems create a biologically rich belowground environment. In addition to the symbiotic relationship with *Rhizobium* bacteria that fix atmospheric nitrogen in alfalfa roots, root exudates create a rich rhizosphere and a favorably crumbly soil structure. The vigorous canopy and roots support herbivores of various types, from vertebrates to a wide range of arthropods.

Alfalfa is most often grown in pure stands in California, but sometimes it is grown in mixed culture with various forage grasses. Alfalfa stands in California average 3 to 4 years in longevity, but in some cases stands may remain in production for up to 8 years. Such longevity provides a temporal stability that is uncommon with most agricultural crops and provides ample time for the establishment and development

FIGURE 1.14

Change in milk production, 27 eastern states, 12 midwestern states, and 11 western states as a percent of U.S. production (USDA National Agricultural Statistics Service).

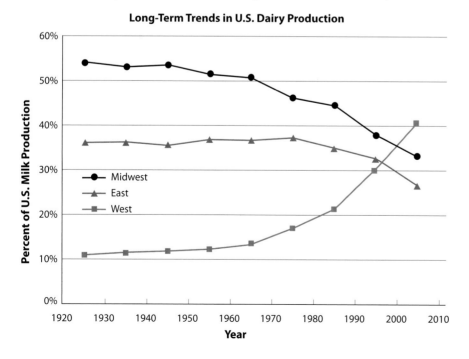

Long-Term Trends in U.S. Dairy Production

of a diverse community of organisms, including many types of wildlife.

Crop Rotation

Alfalfa is highly valued by farmers for its rotational benefits, including soil improvement and benefits to subsequent crops. Alfalfa is most often grown in rotation with wheat, corn, cotton, sugar beets, and processing tomatoes. Given the diversity of California agriculture, it is common to have individual farms producing walnuts, almonds, or rice on some fields, and tomatoes, cotton, wheat, or corn rotated with alfalfa on others. Growers of vegetable or specialty crops especially value the rotational benefits of alfalfa, since it improves water infiltration and soil fertility and can provide a less weedy environment for subsequent crops.

In the regions surrounding dairy farms, corn silage has increased significantly in recent years, grown in rotation with alfalfa and small grain forage. This is an important fact for alfalfa producers, since corn silage has replaced alfalfa in many dairy rations over the years. The benefits of alfalfa in rotation with corn include its provision of nitrogen to the corn crop; a range of 40 to 120 pounds per acre (45–134 kg ha) N is typically credited to the alfalfa in an alfalfa–corn rotation.

Alfalfa has unique production features in the desert and Mediterranean areas of the West that are distinct from higher rainfall areas. The obvious differences are related to the need for irrigation water, but a range of other factors are also unique to arid production systems, including cutting schedules, stand establishment methods, pest management, and variety selection. Alfalfa is a very adaptable plant and can be grown under a wide range of soil and climatic conditions. Although a wide variety of methods are used to produce alfalfa, the following represents an overview of the typical methods used in many parts of the state.

Soil Types and Site Selection

Alfalfa can be grown on a wide range of soil types, but a key requirement is good internal drainage and lack of subsoil impediments. Soil types chosen vary from sands and sandy loams to clay loams, loamy clays, and deep cracking clays. Alfalfa is frequently produced on heavy soils in California, which is not true of higher-rainfall regions. A key reason is the ability to control water applications, avoiding saturated soil conditions (see Chapter 2, "Choosing Appropriate Sites for Alfalfa Production").

Stand Establishment

To establish an alfalfa crop, growers must first consider subsoil impediments and correct those with deep tillage, if necessary. "Deep ripping" using deep chisel plows or other implements is common. Soil amendments of gypsum or sulfur for salt-affected soils are sometimes used, and fertilizer problems are addressed before planting. Lime is used occasionally, but acid soils are not common. Since check-flood irrigation and other surface irrigation methods are dominant in these regions, land leveling utilizing laser technology is often preferred to assure uniformity of irrigations (Fig. 1.15). Sprinklers are frequently used for stand establishment, followed by flood irrigation during production. Seeding is accomplished utilizing grain drills, broadcast air planters, Brillion seeders, aircraft, or no-till planters. Fall planting, mid-September through mid- to late October, is recommended. Growers can plant in winter or spring in most regions, usually with less success, but rarely in midsummer due to excessive heat. Companion crops are rarely used, and herbicides are usually used to control weeds while young seedlings are developing. Optimization of stand establishment techniques is critical to ensure the long-term success of alfalfa production (see Chapter 4, "Alfalfa Stand Establishment").

FIGURE 1.15

Land leveling during stand establishment.

Varieties

California is unique compared with other regions of the United States in that the full range of fall dormancy (FD) classifications of varieties are utilized. Nondormant varieties (those that grow actively in the winter, FD 8–11) dominate the desert zones, and semidormant to nondormant varieties (FD 4–9) are grown in the Central Valley, whereas dormant varieties (FD 3–4) are grown in the Intermountain north. Growers sometimes choose dormant varieties that yield less but produce higher-quality forage, even in "nondormant" areas. Plant breeders have been successful at developing varieties with a wide range of resistance to diseases, nematodes, and insects—more so than any other agronomic crop (Fig. 1.16). In recent years, genetically engineered Roundup Ready varieties have been introduced. Variety selection is an important component of both profitability and a successful pest management program for alfalfa (see Chapter 5, "Choosing an Alfalfa Variety").

FIGURE 1.16

Variety selection.

Irrigation

One of the most important aspects of alfalfa production in the arid West is the need for irrigation water. Nearly 100 percent of California's alfalfa crop is irrigated, although some dryland alfalfa is produced in coastal and mountain regions. Management of irrigation to match crop needs is often the most yield-limiting factor for California alfalfa production. Alfalfa requires 5 to 6 acre-feet (1550-1800 mm) of water per year in the Imperial Valley, and about 4 acre-feet (1200 mm) per year in the San Joaquin Valley, and 2.5–3.0 acre-feet (760 - 900 mm) in the Intermountain area. However, frequently more water is needed to leach salts and to compensate for irrigation inefficiencies. The majority of water comes from surface-water sources (rivers, streams, canals, and reservoirs), but pumped groundwater is used in some regions. More water is applied to alfalfa in California than to any other crop, accounting for nearly 20 percent of the state's agricultural water use. However, alfalfa is one of the most water-use efficient crops and produces more dry matter per unit of water than many crops. In the Central Valley and Imperial Valley, check-flood surface irrigation is most common, while sprinklers are common in high desert and mountain regions. Sprinklers are commonly used for stand establishment (Fig. 1.17), followed primarily by flood irrigation for forage production (Fig. 1.18). Timing of irrigations is highly influenced by cutting schedules, since the soil must dry for harvests, approximately every 28 days. Growers typically irrigate once, twice, or sometimes three times between harvests in surface-irrigated systems. Alfalfa grown on heavier clay-containing soils is irrigated less frequently but with more water applied per irrigation than alfalfa grown on light-textured, sandy soils (see Chapter 7, "Irrigating Alfalfa in Arid Regions").

FIGURE 1.17

Sprinkler irrigation during establishment.

FIGURE 1.18

Gravity-fed surface flood irrigation is the most commonly used in California.

Insects

Alfalfa supports an incredible diversity of insects, most of which have little or no impact on the plant itself. Alfalfa has been called an "insectary" since it is home to many predators and beneficial insects (Fig. 1.19) that move among crops and provide biological control of pests in diverse cropping systems as well as in alfalfa itself. For example, while over 1,000 species of arthropods have been identified from alfalfa, fewer than 20 are pests and fewer still are serious pests. These serious pests include the alfalfa weevil in the spring (Fig. 1.20), a complex of caterpillar larvae (alfalfa caterpillar and armyworms) in the warmer months, and a complex of aphids throughout the year. Most growers use pesticides to control these insect pests based on IPM (Integrated Pest Management) principles. Numerous management strategies, including resistant varieties, biological control, chemical control, and cultural control, have been devised to mitigate pest impact on alfalfa yield and quality (see Chapter 9, "Managing Insects in Alfalfa").

FIGURE 1.19

Beneficial insects are common in alfalfa (lady beetle feeding on aphids).

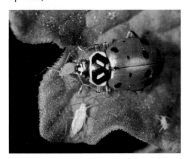

FIGURE 1.20

Alfalfa weevil larvae , a major pest in alfalfa.

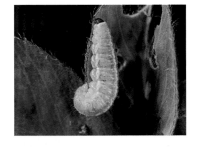

Weeds

Weeds have a tremendous effect on forage quality and significantly lower the economic value of alfalfa (Fig. 1.21). Weeds have less effect on yield, and actually sometimes increase yield, but can make the hay unmarketable. Herbicides are frequently used to control weeds during stand establishment, since alfalfa seedlings are slow to develop and susceptible to weed competition. This is the most critical period in which to control weeds. After alfalfa plants are well established and vigorously growing, weed intrusion is less common. It's often said that the best defense against weeds is a vigorous competitive stand of alfalfa. After establishment, herbicides and sometimes grazing are used to control winter annual weeds and summer annual grasses (see Chapter 8, "Weed Management in Alfalfa").

Diseases and Nematodes

In California's dry climate, diseases are generally not the most important yield-limiting factor, but several diseases and nematodes can be found. Seedling diseases often kill young seedlings on wet, heavy soils during cold periods. Root diseases can damage or kill established plants. Stem nematode (Fig. 1.22) and root knot nematodes are important pests in several areas of California. Selection of varieties to resist diseases and nematodes is the major control strategy available to growers (see Chapter 10, "Alfalfa Diseases and Management," and Chapter 11, "Parasitic Nematodes in Alfalfa").

Vertebrate Pests

Gophers, ground squirrels, and voles are serious pests (Fig. 1.23) in alfalfa fields in most areas of California. Flood irrigation helps keep gopher populations in check, but numbers can still reach damaging levels under some conditions. Meadow

FIGURE 1.21

Chickweed in alfalfa.

FIGURE 1.22

Stem nematode in alfalfa.

FIGURE 1.23

Pocket gopher in alfalfa.

voles have cyclic populations that reach damaging levels in some years (see Chapter 12, "Vertebrate Pests").

Cutting Schedules

Cutting frequency has a very important effect on both forage quality and yield; longer cutting schedules result in higher yield and lower quality, while shorter cutting schedules result in lower yields but higher quality. After the first harvest in the spring, and through the long, hot summer, alfalfa is typically harvested every 26 to 28 days to maintain the high quality demanded by the dairy industry. Short cutting schedules reduce stand, vigor, and persistence and favor weed intrusion (see Chapter 13, "Harvest Strategies for Alfalfa").

Harvest Methods

Greater than 98 percent of California's alfalfa is baled as dry hay, not ensiled or grazed. Alfalfa is most frequently harvested with a "swather" (Fig. 1.24), or mower-conditioner, which cuts off the plant and crushes the stems to speed drying. Both sickle-bar and disc-type mowers are used. The hay is placed in windrows, and after a few days is raked to enhance drying. Baling occurs from 3 to 10 days after cutting, depending on time of year, soil type, size of windrow, temperature, and humidity. Bale size ranges from "small," three-tie square bales (80 to 140 pounds [36–64 kg]) to "large," rectangular bales (750-pound [340-kg] to 1-ton [907-kg] bales). The latter has become more popular in recent years due to handling and shipping advantages. Some smaller (60-pound [27 kg]) bales are occasionally used for retail markets for horses. Round bales are rare due to difficulty in transportation. Alfalfa hay is frequently baled at night, since dew is needed for leaf retention. Square

FIGURE 1.24

Swathing alfalfa.

bales are collected using a bale wagon, or harrow-bed, which automatically stacks the hay on a platform and deposits the hay on the roadside for loading (Fig. 1.25). A "squeeze" (modified forklift) stacks bales on flatbed trucks for hauling, so that hay is nearly entirely mechanically handled. Hay is usually stored outside for short or long periods, but moved to open-sided barns or tarped for protection from sun and rain (see Chapter 14, "Harvest, Curing and Preservation of Alfalfa").

FIGURE 1.25

Alfalfa hay is frequently "roadsided" in the field before movement to dairies (Imperial Valley, CA).

Forage Quality and Markets

Most California alfalfa hay is consumed by dairies. There are intense pressures on growers to produce high-quality hay (low in fiber concentration; high in protein; and free of weeds, molds, or other defects). Alfalfa forage quality, as defined by the USDA Market News, ranges from Supreme and Premium, to Good, Fair, and Utility, or very-low-quality hay. Forage quality is typically defined by the needs of dairies since the vast majority of California's alfalfa crop is consumed by this sector. The value of hay in the marketplace is often defined by total digestible nutrients (TDN), calculated from acid detergent fiber (ADF). However, neutral detergent fiber (NDF) is more commonly used by nutritionists to balance rations, and other analyses may influence price, such as crude protein (CP), digestibility, ash, and minerals (DCAD or ion balance). Price differences between high and low categories range from $25 to $80 per ton (907 kg), or as much as half of the value of the hay. A majority of the hay produced for the dairy industry is analyzed by laboratories. (see www.foragetesting.org; also see Chapter 16, "Forage Quality").

Utilization

Alfalfa can be fed fresh as pasture or green-chop, or preserved as hay, silage, or dehydrated meal, pellets, or cubes. Its main use is by live-stock. Pure alfalfa is preferred by the dairy industry, whereas grass–alfalfa mixtures (cool season forage grasses) are often favored by horse owners. Alfalfa can be successfully incor-porated into dairy, beef, goat, and horse rations, and its combination of energy, good intake, protein, and effective fiber is highly desired by animal nutritionists. Some alfalfa (as well as other hays) is exported from California and other western states, particularly Washington, to Pacific Rim countries, primarily Japan. Alfalfa has been used for human consumption in the form of "alfalfa sprouts," a very minor use of alfalfa seeds, or as health supplements made from the leaves. Industrial uses of alfalfa for production of enzymes, or fractionation of the crop to use the stems as a bioenergy source, are currently being researched (see Chapter 17, "Utilization by Livestock," and Chapter 19, "Industrial Uses").

Economics

Alfalfa must compete economically with higher-value vegetables, orchards, grapes, and tomatoes for acreage and water in California. However, it has maintained its position as the state's highest acre-age crop due to its economic value, steady demand, cash-flow characteristics, and rotational ben-efits. The value of alfalfa has, at times, exceeded $1 billion per year in California (Fig. 1.26). Unlike crops such as wheat, corn, rice, and cotton, alfalfa receives no government price support but has held its own economically in the most competitive and dynamic agricultural region in the United States. Alfalfa production entails lower investment and lower economic and biological risk of crop failure than many spe-

FIGURE 1.26

California alfalfa is frequently transported long distances.

cialty crops. It provides reliable income and profit potential and enjoys consistent demand. Alfalfa has favorable cash-flow characteristics, since it provides early income potential in spring and a steady return after each harvest over the summer, unlike annual crops which produce one income in the fall. Many growers keep alfalfa in the crop rotation mix primar-ily due to its benefits to the following crops and a steady cash flow. Cost studies have been published for alfalfa (http://alfalfa.ucdavis.edu); also see Chapter 23, "Alfalfa Marketing and Economics."

Organic Alfalfa

This sector constitutes less than about one-half percent of production but is growing due to increased conversion by some dairies to organic milk. Alfalfa is often used to transition to organic production of other crops due to its soil benefits, and is highly beneficial to organic vegetable and fruit producers. Weed and insect management and maintenance of soil fertility are key limiting issues for organic alfalfa pro-ducers (See Chapter 21, "Producing Alfalfa Hay Organically").

Seed Production

California continues to be the leading alfalfa seed producing state in the United States. Although seed acreage has diminished in recent years to less than 30,000 acres (12,000 ha), it remains important in Fresno and Imperial Counties. Alfalfa seed production is a special-ized process, requiring different irrigation and pest management skills. Growers produce seed from fields specifically designated as seed fields using wide rows on beds. Seed is also produced from hay production fields where the grow-ers produce hay during spring and allow the plant to set seed later in the summer. Irrigation must be carefully controlled to stress the plants to encourage flowering and seed production. Alfalfa is a cross-pollinated crop that requires pollinators for successful seed production, and alfalfa honey is an important by-product of seed production (see Chapter 22, "Alfalfa Seed Production").

Alfalfa and the Environment

Alfalfa is well known for its ability to improve soil conditions and to provide important wildlife habitat and environmental benefits. The deep roots of alfalfa help mitigate environmental problems by taking up nitrates from the soil, preventing contamination of groundwater. Alfalfa protects the soil from water and wind erosion with its vigorous canopy, rooting system, and lack of tillage for multiple years. Alfalfa is important for wildlife in agricultural systems. It is estimated that of 675 wildlife species inhabiting California, 25 percent of them use alfalfa for feeding, reproduction, or cover (Fig. 1.27).

FIGURE 1.27

Blue heron in alfalfa.

Potential negative effects of alfalfa on the environment include its high water use and potential effects on water quality, specifically off-site movement of organophosphate pesticides. Efforts to improve irrigation efficiency are ongoing, and methods to prevent off-site movement of pesticides have been identified.

Alfalfa's role in protecting the soil, reducing the energy costs of agriculture, N_2 fixation from biological sources, mitigating dust contamination of the air, absorbing nitrates from the soil, and providing wildlife habitat are features of interest to those interested in sustaining the agricultural landscape (see Putnam et al. 2001. Alfalfa, Wildlife and the Environment).

The Future of Alfalfa

Some have predicted the demise of alfalfa in California due to water restrictions, urbanization, and the rise in the importance of orchards, vineyards, and specialty crops. While these factors are real and important in restricting the alfalfa acreage in California, the high productivity, wide adaptation, rotation benefits, and strong demand for this crop suggest that alfalfa has an important role in the state, now and for the future.

FIGURE 1.28

Central Valley of California.

The increased demand for forage crops due to the dairy and livestock sectors has tended to counteract the trends of urban sprawl, water restrictions, and conversion to higher-value crops. Therefore, acreage has remained almost constant over the past 20 to 30 years (Fig. 1.28). This will likely continue, at least for the immediate future. The future of alfalfa in California is tied to several important factors, including water transfers, to the fate of the dairy industry, other livestock demands, and competitive crops.

Dairy Industry

Probably the most important of these is the fate of the dairy industry (Fig. 1.29). The phenomenal growth rate in dairy cow numbers in California will not continue forever. Environmental and regulatory restrictions, economics, and urbanization will eventually curtail the growth in cow numbers, but California dairying has proved to be a resilient industry, with some of the lowest costs of production in the nation. Thus, it is likely that

FIGURE 1.29

Dairies are the most important consumers of alfalfa.

California will remain the leading dairy state for the coming few decades. Although the beef cattle industry in California has been declining slowly for decades, the number of horses has steadily increased. The market for alfalfa and other forages for horses has become more important in recent years and it is anticipated that demand will continue to be high in the future.

One important trend is the replacement of alfalfa in dairy rations with corn silage, cereal forages, and cheap by-products such as distiller grains (from ethanol production), and cottonseed. The amount of alfalfa produced in the state per dairy animal has fallen from about 40 pounds per animal per day (18 kg) in the 1960s to about 20 pounds per animal per day (9 kg) today. This indicates a replacement of alfalfa in dairy rations by other ingredients. Corn silage has risen from a minor acreage crop to over 400,000 acres (162,000 ha) in 2005. The role of alfalfa in dairy rations is likely to be continually challenged in future years.

Horses

A major trend in the United States has been the increase in the number of recreational horses, which have become major consumers of both alfalfa hay and other hay products. As populations increase in the urban West, this trend is likely to intensify, creating new markets for alfalfa that are distinct from the dairy markets.

Crop Competition and Urban Sprawl

The Central Valley, where over 70 percent of California's alfalfa is produced, is one of the most rapidly urbanizing regions of the United States (Fig. 1.30). Population rates have grown from 25 to 50 percent per decade in some areas. Urban sprawl competes with agriculture for both land and water, and transfers of water are one of the primary mechanisms of urbanization. This trend in urbanization of the Central Valley is of considerable concern to those interested in sustaining agriculture for future generations. Growers will likely continue to convert acreage from crops such as alfalfa, cotton, and wheat to perennial orchards or grapes and, ultimately, to housing. This will have the effect of moving alfalfa to more marginal soils and utilizing more saline waters or wastewaters in the future.

FIGURE 1.30

Urban growth in the Central Valley.

Water and Water Transfers

Limitation of water supplies is undoubtedly the most important single issue that will impact the viability of alfalfa grown in California in the future (Fig. 1.31). In drought years, competition for water becomes especially acute, and there is little doubt that urban or environmental demands for developed water will intensify. There is also little doubt that these demands will be satisfied through transfers from agriculture, which consumes nearly 80 percent of the developed water in the state. Forage crops and annual agronomic row crops (e.g., cotton, corn) are particularly vulnerable.

California's water management policies are evolving toward a more "market-driven" water exchange system. This may enable water users to transfer water from one crop to another, or from one use to another, on a temporary basis. Alfalfa is very drought tolerant and can survive temporary droughts. Current research on deficit irritation of alfalfa may provide the basis for the feasibility of water transfers from alfalfa fields during drought periods while maintaining forage production in a water-limited future. However, it is clear that water issues will remain the most important limitation for alfalfa.

FIGURE 1.31

Water supply and quality are critical issues.

Genetic Engineering

Genetic modification of alfalfa through biotechnology, as well as traditional plant breeding, will be important in future years. The introduction of Roundup Ready alfalfa in 2005 created the first genetically modified alfalfa product. Efforts to introduce high-quality traits for more efficient fiber and protein use are ongoing and could result in significant innovation in alfalfa varieties and utilization in coming years. Genes for drought tolerance, salt tolerance, pest resistance, and yield and quality characteristics are being researched. This could result in plants that require less water and fewer pesticides, and which could be grown on poorer soils or with wastewater. However, concerns about gene transfer to organic crops or crops grown for GE-sensitive markets, and the potential for weed resistance to herbicides, may limit public market acceptance and the use of genetic engineering in alfalfa as it has in other crops.

Energy Crops and Industrial Uses

Although livestock production, particularly dairy, is likely to remain the most important use for alfalfa, industrial and energy uses for alfalfa in future years are currently under investigation. Alfalfa's productivity makes it also suitable to the production of specialty compounds, such as enzymes in the leaves, but these concepts require further research and face regulatory impediments. Alfalfa is a good candidate as an energy crop, due to its rotational benefits and its lack of need for nitrogen fertilizers, which require fossil fuels. The fractionation of alfalfa into a higher-quality leafy portion for high-quality animal feed and a lower-quality stem portion suitable for biofuels has been proposed. The development of other energy crops (e.g., corn, switchgrass) may also have profound effects on alfalfa due to competition of fermentation by-products and competition for acreage.

Environmental Services

The role of alfalfa in providing a wide range of environmental services may be increasingly recognized. Alfalfa's role in absorbing wastewater from municipalities and animal facilities is likely to become more important in future years. Forages are uniquely qualified for this role, since there are fewer risks when wastes are applied to forages, as compared with food crops. It is possible that alfalfa's role in providing a wide range of environmental benefits, from mitigation of groundwater pollution to improvement of air and water quality and provision of open spaces and wildlife habitat, may become as important as economic factors in determining acreage in the future.

It is clear from this discussion that although alfalfa has some important challenges, it has many characteristics that will enable this crop to remain a vital component of California agricultural systems in the future.

Additional Reading

Orloff, S. B., and H. Carlson, eds. 1997. Intermountain Alfalfa Management. University of California Division of Agriculture and Natural Resources, Oakland. Publication 3366. http://ucce.ucdavis.edu/files/filelibrary/2129/18336.pdf.

Putnam, D.H., M. Russelle, S. Orloff, J. Kuhn, L. Fitzhugh, L. Godfrey, A. Kiess, R. Long. 2001. Alfalfa, wildlife and the environment; The importance and benefits of alfalfa in the 21st century. California Alfalfa and Forage Association, Novato, CA. http://alfalfa.ucdavis.edu.

2

Choosing Appropriate Sites for Alfalfa Production

Steve B. Orloff
Farm Advisor, University of California Cooperative Extension, Yreka, CA

Most of the agricultural areas of the arid Southwest are well suited for alfalfa production. Because of the nearly ideal climate and soils in many southwestern areas, the alfalfa yield potential is greater than in any other geographic region in the United States. The long, warm summers and relatively mild winters make for an extended growing season. In California, the length of the frost-free period typically ranges from 314 days in the Imperial Valley to 307 days in the Sacramento Valley. Most of the soils are alluvial and are fertile and deep, which is ideal for alfalfa production.

One of the first steps before embarking on alfalfa production is selecting the proper site. This is a critical step because site conditions can limit both yield and profit potential. The characteristics of a site may also affect alfalfa quality as well as stand persistence and ability to combat weed competition. When alfalfa is grown on sites that provide adequate rooting depth, nutrition, aeration, and water and have no salinity or alkalinity problems, growers using good management practices can produce hay yields of 8–10 tons per acre (19–22 Mg/ha^{-1}) per year or higher (Fig. 2.1). Greater management skills are required for profitable alfalfa production on marginal or undesirable sites. Remember, the better the site, the higher the yield potential. Some site limitations can be overcome or reduced, but the cost may be high, affecting future profitability. If site conditions are poor, alfalfa production may be unprofitable even under optimal management.

FIGURE 2.1.

The climatic conditions in the southwestern United States are nearly ideal for producing alfalfa. Yields of at least 8 to 10 tons per acre (18 to 22 Mg ha⁻¹) are feasible on sites with adequate rooting depth, nutrition, aeration, water and proper management.

Soil and Water Factors Affecting Site Selection

Consider the physical and chemical properties of the soil, the likelihood of waterlogging, and the quantity and quality of available irrigation water when selecting a site for alfalfa (Table 2.1). For surface irrigation, the topography and associated leveling costs are also important. Also assess biological factors, such as the presence of diseases, weeds, or nematodes, as well as crop rotation plans before planting alfalfa on a site.

Examine Soil Properties

The first step to determine the suitability of a site for alfalfa is to know the soil types present. Alfalfa can be grown on a wide range of soil types, from sands to heavy clays, and there is a wide variation in soil types throughout the Central Valley and Low Desert regions of

TABLE 2.1

Physical characteristics of ideal, marginal, and undesirable sites for alfalfa production

Characteristic	Ideal	Marginal	Undesirable[1]
Soil texture	Sandy loam, silt loam, clay loam	Loamy sand, silty clay	Sand, clay
Soil depth (ft)	>6	3–6	<3
Soil chemistry[2]			
(pH)	6.3–7.5	5.8–6.3 and 7.5–8.2	<5.8 or >8.2
Salinity (EC$_{e\ in\ mmho/cm}$)	0–2	2–5	>5
Exchangeable Sodium Percentage (ESP)	<7	7–15	>15
Boron (mg/L)	0.5–2.0	2–6	>6
Frequency of water logging or high water table	Never	Only during dormant period	Sometimes during periods of active growth
Slope	Nearly level	Slightly sloping to 12% slope	>12% slope
Water quality			
pH	6.5-7.5	7.5-8.2	>8.2
EC$_w$	<1.3	1.3–3.0	>3.0
SAR	<6.0	6.0–9.0	>9.0

Note: These categories are approximate and should be modified when warranted by experience, local practices, special conditions, or irrigation method.
[1] These sites are considered unsuitable for profitable alfalfa production unless reclaimed or specialized management is employed.
[2] Values are based on saturated paste extract analysis and are adapted from Lancaster and Orloff (1997).

California. Sandy soils are common in many areas on the east side of the Central Valley, whereas heavy clay loam soils are typical along the west side. Organic soils may be found in the San Joaquin–Sacramento Delta area. A thorough knowledge of the soil type found in a field to be planted to alfalfa is important because soil type has a profound effect on crop management, including water-holding capacity, fertility and nutrient availability, and drainage.

Soil surveys, published by the USDA Natural Resources Conservation Service (NRCS), contain maps to assist growers with the identification of soil units found on the farm. Maps are available at NRCS offices or on the Web at http://websoilsurvey.nrcs.usda. gov/app/WebSoilSurvey.aspx. Additional information is included on soil texture and changes in soil texture with depth, presence of hardpans, water-holding capacity, drainage, and infiltration rate. These soil survey maps and descriptions are generalized and may not provide the level of site-specific information desired. However, soil survey information is an excellent first step to ascertain the suitability of a site for alfalfa production. If the survey indicates that the site may have promise, have the soil and water analyzed for chemical characteristics (see Chapters 6–7: "Alfalfa Fertilization Strategies" and "Irrigating Alfalfa in Arid Regions"). Do this before planting alfalfa on the site.

Understand Your Soil Texture

The term "soil texture" refers to the relative proportion of sand, silt, and clay in soil. Soil texture affects the water-holding capacity and infiltration rate, the rate at which irrigation water will enter the soil profile. Clay holds the most water and sand the least. Usually, sandy soil has the fastest water infiltration rate and clay soil the slowest, but there are some areas in the San Joaquin Valley with sandy loam soils that "seal over," severely limiting infiltration. Soil textural characteristics, as well as other factors such as quality of irrigation water, influence irrigation system design, irrigation practices, and nutrient management.

Alfalfa can be successfully produced on a wide range of soil textures, but sandy loam, silt loam, and clay loam soils are generally preferred. These soil types provide the best combination of water infiltration, water-holding capacity, and aeration for alfalfa.

More extreme soils, such as very heavy "adobe-type" clay soils or very sandy soils, make management more difficult. Sands and loamy sands have such low water-holding capacities that fields must be irrigated every few days, a task that is difficult with surface irrigation systems, but easily achieved with center pivot or linear move irrigation. In addition, uniform surface irrigation without excessive deep percolation is nearly impossible on very sandy soils.

Alfalfa production on very fine-textured clay soils can be challenging as well. Water infiltration and drainage are extremely slow in these soils. Aeration may be poor because the small pore spaces associated with fine soils limit the diffusion of oxygen to plant roots, impairing root growth. These soils may not drain adequately during winter or spring flood events. Seedling diseases and root diseases are more common on heavy clays. Drainage can be so slow that scald can occur during the summer irrigation season (see Chapter 10: "Alfalfa Diseases and Management").

Examine Soil Structure, Depth, and Profile

The soil provides the rooting medium from which the alfalfa draws water and nutrients. It consists not only of sand, silt, and clay, but of organic matter and structural layers that influence crop growth and development. The deeper the soil, the more water and nutrient storage capacity the site provides. If soil profile characteristics are not well known, use a backhoe to dig several evaluation pits at least 4 feet (1.2 m) deep in a potential field. Examine the soil profile for soil textural changes and any potential

> *Alfalfa can be successfully produced on a wide range of soil textures, but sandy loam, silt loam, and clay loam soils are generally preferred.*

impedance to root development, such as hardpans or other restrictive layers.

An ideal site has deep, uniformly textured soil with no drainage or salt problems. Under the best conditions, alfalfa roots will extend 6–12 feet (1.8–3.6 m) deep or more. Unfortunately, not all soils are that deep. A site should provide a minimum of 3 feet (0.9 m) of unrestricted rooting depth to be suitable for alfalfa production.

> *A site should provide a minimum of 3 feet of rooting depth to be suitable for alfalfa production.*

Like shallow soils, restrictive subsurface layers limit alfalfa production. The most common problems in the West are hardpans, claypans, sand, gravel lenses, and stratified or layered soils. These reduce alfalfa yields because they present a barrier to root penetration or inhibit water infiltration and drainage (Fig. 2.2).

Soil profile problems are not limited to compacted layers—changes in texture within the soil profile can have a similar effect. A clay layer within a sandy loam soil or a layer of sand within a loam or clay loam soil can restrict root penetration and soil water movement. An abrupt change in soil texture impedes the downward movement of water, even when water is moving from a clay soil into a sandy layer. Water does not move into a lower layer that has a coarser texture than the layer above it to any appreciable degree until the layer above is saturated. Consequently, a zone of poor aeration often forms at the interface between such layers and can even result in a temporarily perched water table. In general, the more abrupt the textural change, the greater the negative effects of soil layers.

Deep tillage can help reduce, but usually cannot eliminate, problems associated with hardpans, claypans, and layered soils. Deep ripping is effective to temporarily ameliorate hardpan problems. However, ripping alone is not enough to solve a claypan or layered-soil problem (Fig. 2.3). These problems are only solved by mixing soils to a depth below the restrictive layer. This is usually accomplished with a moldboard plow or slip plow. Major physical modification of soils is expensive (often in excess of $200 per acre [0.405 ha]), and alfalfa production seldom justifies the cost. When possible, select an alternative site free of restrictive subsurface layers.

Consider Waterlogging and Fluctuating Water Tables

Some areas of the Central Valley are subject to fluctuating water tables and intermittent flooding, especially sites adjacent to the Sacramento River or other major waterways. During years of above-average precipitation, the water table at some sites may be well within the root zone of alfalfa.

Alfalfa does not tolerate wet soil conditions during periods of active growth (Fig. 2.4). Prolonged saturated soil and perched or fluctuating water tables in the root zone can severely reduce yields and stand life. Oxygen depletion in the root zone and diseases of the root and crown, such as Phytophthora root rot, are usually the result of excessively wet conditions.

An intermittent or fluctuating high water table is usually more damaging than a stable high water table. With a stable high water table, the alfalfa roots are restricted to the well-aerated soil above the zone of saturation (capillary fringe) that may extend 1–3 feet above the actual depth of the water table. However, with a fluctuating water table, roots

FIGURE 2.2

Hardpans and other restrictive layers can impede alfalfa root growth and development. Note the root turns sideways at the depth of the soil impediment.

FIGURE 2.3

A dense clay hardpan, in this case at about 23 inches, can restrict root development and drainage. Claypans require mixing for a long-term solution because they will reform if only fractured by deep ripping (A). Stratified soils with an abrupt change in texture limit root development and water movement, like the layer of white sand below fine sandy loam in this photo (B).

may grow below the high water table level when conditions are favorable, only to become damaged when the water table rises. Damage that occurs from waterlogging, reduced yield and even stand loss, depends on the time of year when waterlogged conditions occur and the duration. Waterlogging is far more serious during the growing season than during the winter when the alfalfa is more dormant. Furthermore, the longer waterlogging persists and the warmer the temperature, the greater the injury to the crop.

Deep tillage can improve internal drainage in some soils. Precise field leveling, such as laser leveling, or tile drainage may also help correct waterlogging problems, but the resulting increase in alfalfa production may be insufficient to recover the costs. Whenever possible, it is best to avoid sites prone to waterlogging or a fluctuating high water table.

FIGURE 2.4

Drainage characteristics are critical aspects of site selection. Excessive standing water can harm alfalfa stands especially during periods of active growth.

Topography May Affect Success

The suitability of a field for alfalfa production can depend on its topography or slope. Most fields on the valley floor of the Central Valley and Low Desert of California are relatively level, and topography is not a concern. However, there are some locations, especially foothill areas, where slope or undulating fields may be a constraint. Nearly level fields are important for irrigation and water penetration. The relative importance of topography depends on the irrigation system. A level field with proper slope is far more important with flood irrigation than it is with sprinkler irrigation. Flood irrigation is precluded on fields with excessive fall or side fall. A typical slope for border-strip flood irrigated fields is 0.01–0.02 percent (a 1–2 foot fall per 1,000 linear feet), whereas sprinkler irrigation is feasible on fields with up to a 12–15 percent slope. Uneven or undulating fields may require extensive land leveling before producing alfalfa. This is costly and results in major cut and fill areas that often cause variable alfalfa growth.

Soil Chemical Properties Affecting Alfalfa

Soil Fertility

The parent material of a soil largely determines its mineral content and fertility. The alluvial soils of California's Central Valley are relatively fertile, and typically phosphorus is the only nutrient that may be deficient for alfalfa production. Potassium, sulfur, and boron can also be deficient in some fields, but these deficiencies are more rare. These nutrient deficiencies are easily corrected through proper diagnosis and fertilizer application (see Chapter 6: "Alfalfa Fertilization Strategies"). Inherent soil fertility, although important, does not limit site selection in this region.

Soil pH

Soil pH is the measure of acidity or alkalinity of a soil. Soil pH affects nutrient availability and can indicate problems with soil structure. Maximum nutrient availability for most crops occurs when pH values are between 6.0 and 7.0. However, higher pH values (6.3–7.5) are recommended for alfalfa production because they favor activity of nitrogen-fixing Rhizobium bacteria. Soils with pH values below 6.0 are unsuitable. Liming before planting is highly recommended for acidic (low pH) soils, particularly if pH decreases with increasing soil depth. More detail on liming acid soils is found in Chapter 6: "Alfalfa Fertilization Strategies." Soil pH values that are too high can also be a problem. Values above 8.2 are often associated with excess salinity and soil structural problems (see "Salinity and Sodicity," below). High pH sites are relatively unproductive and can have problems with water infiltration unless reclaimed (see Chapter 7: "Irrigating Alfalfa in Arid Regions"). Both high and low pH soils occur in California's Central Valley. However, pH problems in the Central Valley are usually mild enough that they can be dealt with through proper management.

> *Soil pH values 6.3–7.5 are recommended for alfalfa production because they favor activity of nitrogen-fixing Rhizobium bacteria.*

Salinity and Sodicity

Excess levels of salts (saline soils) and sodium (sodic soils) occasionally cause problems in the Central Valley and Low Desert areas (Fig. 2.5). Soils formed in enclosed basins under low-rainfall or desert conditions are prone to salinity. Much of the southwestern portion of the San Joaquin Valley, characterized by alluvial soils formed by ancient floods and erosion of the saline coastal mountains, has salt-affected soils. Although salinity and sodicity do not entirely preclude the possibility of alfalfa production, they do present challenges. Steps for reclamation may be necessary.

Alfalfa is moderately sensitive to salt. High salt levels may be toxic and can reduce water availability. Visual indicators of excess salt include slick spots, white or black crusts on the soil surface, marginal leaf burn, and the presence of salt-tolerant weeds. Laboratory analysis of soils is required to confirm visual symptoms and to determine the type and degree of salinity. When salinity is suspected, carefully sample fields at different depths throughout the root zone. Analyze samples from the different depths separately to determine the degree of the salinity problem at different depths and the depth where salts accumulate. The results can help determine the source of the problem and the best mitigation measures.

Soil salts are measured by making a watery paste of the soil and extracting the water, which contains the soluble salts. Total salinity is measured by determining the electrical conductivity (EC_e) of this soil extract. Salts conduct electricity; therefore, the higher the electrical conductivity of the soil extract, the greater the salinity of the soil. EC_e values above 2.0 millimhos per centimeter (mmho/cm) can suppress alfalfa yields, depending on the specific ions in the soil–water solution. Alfalfa suffers a 10 percent yield reduction when soil salinity levels reach approximately 3.4 mmho/cm. In general, soils

FIGURE 2.5

Excess salts can significantly reduce alfalfa production potential. Severely salt affected soils should be avoided.

> *Alfalfa is moderately sensitive to salt. High salt levels may be toxic and can reduce water availability.*

with EC_e values above 5.0 should be avoided or reclaimed before planting alfalfa. If drainage is adequate, saline soils can be reclaimed by deep leaching. To achieve deep leaching, apply water in excess of crop needs. This is most easily accomplished by reclaiming the soil before planting alfalfa, or by applying water during the dormant season when alfalfa is not growing as actively. Barley or other salt-tolerant annual crops may be grown during the process of reclamation and to assist in identification of saline "hot spots." Proper drainage is key, because leaching is not feasible if drainage is poor.

Excess sodium can also be a significant yield-limiting factor. High sodium levels cause clay particles to disperse. This degrades soil structure; the soil surface seals, and water infiltration slows. Soils with an exchangeable sodium percentage above 15 are considered sodic. This means that more than 15 percent of the exchange sites (negatively charged positions on soil particles that hold onto positively charged elements and compounds) are occupied with sodium rather than beneficial elements, such as calcium, magnesium, or potassium. To correct such a sodic condition, begin with a laboratory analysis to determine the gypsum requirement of the soil. Gypsum requirement refers to the amount of calcium required to displace sodium on the exchange sites. Sulfur can be used instead of gypsum to reclaim soils that are high in calcium carbonate. After an amendment has been applied and sodium replaced with calcium, the displaced sodium must be leached below the alfalfa root zone.

In general, it is best to avoid sites that are adversely affected with excess salts or sodium. The reclamation process usually requires several years and, in the case of sodic soils, a substantial investment in soil amendments is required. Subsurface drainage systems may also be required to effectively reclaim a site for sustainable economical alfalfa production.

Water Requirements of Alfalfa

When selecting a potential site for alfalfa production, be sure that there is an adequate supply of quality water available for season-long irrigation. Most (>99%) of the alfalfa in the arid Southwest is irrigated to supply between 70 and 100 percent of the total crop water needs. Both quantity and quality of irrigation water can limit alfalfa yields. Irrigation water must also be available at the appropriate frequency to avoid stressing the alfalfa.

Water Quantity

Irrigation water supply can limit site selection, sometimes more severely than soil limitations (Fig. 2.6). Alfalfa uses more water than many crops—primarily because of its longer growing season and the fact that it is a perennial crop and reaches full canopy cover sooner in the season. If water supplies are insufficient, yield will be reduced regardless of the effectiveness of other management practices. Water use in agricultural crops is measured as a depth of water assumed to cover the entire field area. Water use of alfalfa in the arid Southwest typically peaks in July; levels in the San Joaquin Valley average about 0.33 inches (8.4 mm) per day, and can climb to as high as 0.5 inches (12.7 mm) per day in the southern deserts (see Chapter 7, "Irrigating Alfalfa

in Arid Regions"). The water supply must be sufficient to meet daily water use accumulated since the last irrigation, plus allow for nonuniformity in the irrigation system. Generally, about 48 inches (1,220 mm) of irrigation water is needed over the season in California's Central Valley, and greater amounts are necessary under desert conditions. Three to 6 inches (76–152 mm) of water is typically applied per irrigation. The amount required depends on the climate of the area and the uniformity of water application. Failure to meet peak water needs results in reduced seasonal yields and profits. Growers should apply amounts sufficient to supply the evapotranspiration (ET) requirements, plus 10–25 percent extra for irrigation system losses, irrigation inefficiencies, and runoff. ET requirements for different zones are given in Chapter 7: "Irrigating Alfalfa in Arid Regions." Adequate water supplies are

> *About 48 inches of irrigation water is needed over the season in California's Central Valley, with greater amounts necessary under desert conditions.*

FIGURE 2.6

Ample irrigation water supply is a prerequisite for a site to be suitable for alfalfa production in the arid West.

essential; thus, if the site does not have a sufficient quantity of water, select another location for alfalfa.

Water Quality

Poor water quality is occasionally a problem in the selection of sites for alfalfa production. Water from wells may contain excess salt. Excess sodium or bicarbonates, or both, can cause infiltration problems. Excess selenium or molybdenum, or both, in the soil or water can cause feed quality problems to livestock. Some surface water sources contain excess colloidal clays, salts, or weed seeds that can present management and stand-life problems. See Table 2.1 for guidelines about water quality. Toxicities caused by foliar absorption of sodium and chlorides, most common during periods of very low humidity and high winds, can result from sprinkler irrigation but would not be a problem with flood irrigation.

Little can be done to improve irrigation water quality. In fact, soil reclamation efforts are unproductive if irrigation water quality is poor. The only cost-effective method of dealing with poor irrigation water is to find an alternative water source or blend the existing water with higher-quality water.

Biological Factors Affecting Site Selection

Most people just assess the physical attributes of the location when considering the suitability of a site for alfalfa production. However, biological factors may be equally important and can render a site undesirable for alfalfa production.

Check for Likelihood of Diseases

Alfalfa is susceptible to numerous diseases. Some rotation crops are hosts for the same diseases that plague alfalfa. Examples of disease organisms that attack alfalfa that are also problems in common rotation crops include Verticillium wilt, Sclerotinia crown and stem rot, Rhizoctonia root rot, and Phytophthora root rot (see Chapter 10, "Alfalfa Diseases and Management," for more detail on alfalfa dis-

eases and host ranges). If a disease that was present in the previous crop is also a problem for alfalfa production, it is recommended that a nonhost crop be planted before planting alfalfa. Similarly, if alfalfa is a host crop for a disease that also attacks a subsequent higher-value crop, plant another nonhost crop rather than alfalfa. Carefully check varietal tolerance to diseases, because this can vary considerably from one variety to another.

Check for Nematodes

When present in sufficient numbers, microscopic parasitic worms called nematodes are a serious alfalfa production problem (see Chapter 11, "Parasitic Nematodes in Alfalfa"). Nematodes usually do not kill alfalfa but can reduce plant vigor to such a degree that alfalfa production is unprofitable. The primary nematodes that damage alfalfa include root knot, lesion, and stem nematode. The same species that infest alfalfa may attack other plants as well—the root knot nematodes *Meloidogyne incognita* (Kofoid & White) and *M. hapla* Chitwood are most common, infecting cotton, dry beans, tomatoes, and many other agronomic crops. If nematodes are suspected, send a soil sample to a qualified laboratory that performs nematode screenings before establishing alfalfa. Avoid planting alfalfa in fields that have nematode species that attack alfalfa unless populations are so low that a problem is not anticipated or if highly resistant alfalfa cultivars are planted.

> *Nematodes usually do not kill alfalfa but can reduce plant vigor to such a degree that alfalfa production is unprofitable.*

Crop Rotation Considerations

Rotating crops, as opposed to continuous cropping, is a strongly recommended agronomic practice. Planting alfalfa after alfalfa, commonly called back-to-back alfalfa, is not advised. Residues from old alfalfa crowns can be toxic to alfalfa seedlings; such residues may reduce establishment and growth of new alfalfa if there is not a sufficient time interval between alfalfa crops (see Chapter 4, "Alfalfa Stand Establishment," for more information on autotoxicity). Crop rotation also helps to prevent the buildup of damaging pest populations, including plant pathogens, nematodes, and some insects. Rodent pest populations, especially meadow voles (*Microtus* spp.) and pocket gophers (*Thomomys* spp.), can increase dramatically in alfalfa. The tillage associated with annual cropping disrupts their burrow systems and can nearly eliminate rodent pest problems. Crop rotation is also an effective weed management strategy. Some weed species, especially perennial weeds such as Bermudagrass and dandelion, can proliferate in an alfalfa production system. Rotating to a different crop can help reduce the populations of many problematic weeds. For example, controlling many broadleaf weeds is easier and less expensive in a cereal crop than in alfalfa.

Herbicide Carryover

When selecting a site for alfalfa production, take into account the previous crop and any residual soil-active herbicides that may have been used to control weeds in that crop. Refer to the herbicide label to determine if there are any plant-back restrictions that would preclude planting alfalfa. If there is any possibility that a harmful level of herbicide residue is present, have the soil analyzed before planting alfalfa. Analyzing soil for herbicide residue can be expensive. A less expensive alternative is to perform a bioassay. Collect soil from the field and place it in a small container. If possible, also collect soil from an untreated area with the same soil type. Seed alfalfa and observe the plants for initial emergence and vigor for a few weeks. If emergence or vigor is retarded, do not plant alfalfa.

Rotational Benefit of Alfalfa to Other Crops

Just as it is beneficial to rotate other crops between alfalfa plantings, alfalfa, a deep-rooted perennial, is an exceptional rotation crop between plantings of other crops. Its extensive root system improves soil tilth and soil structure by creating channels that encourage water penetration and biological activity in the root zone. Over the life of an alfalfa stand, considerable organic matter is added to the soil through leaf litter and the decomposition of alfalfa roots. This greatly benefits the growth and yield of subsequent crops, such as corn, tomato, wheat, or specialty crops.

One key value of alfalfa in a crop rotation is its ability to fix atmospheric nitrogen (N_2). This occurs through the symbiotic relationship between alfalfa and the bacteria (*Sinorhizobium meliloti* (Dangeard), De Lajudie et al.) that live in the nodules on alfalfa roots. Estimates for N_2 fixation of alfalfa range from 120 to 540 pounds of N per acre per year (134–605 kg ha^{-1}). A portion of this nitrogen, often assumed to be 40–60 pounds of N per acre (44–67 kg ha^{-1}), is available to crops that follow alfalfa in the rotation schedule. Higher amounts have been observed in some cases.

Even though alfalfa "makes" its own nitrogen needed for plant growth, it is also efficient at recyling nutrients. In the presence of high soil nitrate levels, the extensive alfalfa root system is able to capture these and other nutrients, thereby reducing leaching. This is especially important when alfalfa follows shallow-rooted vegetables or other crops that typically receive large applications of nitrogen-containing fertilizers that may remain in the lower root zone. Because of alfalfa's many benefits in a crop rotation, the decision of which field or site on which to plant alfalfa should be influenced by the total cropping pattern, including what is planted before and after the alfalfa crop.

Additional Reading

Ayers, R. S., and D. W. Westcot. 1985. Water quality for agriculture. Irrigation and drainage. United Nations Food and Agriculture Organization, Rome. Paper 29.

Hanson, B., S. R. Grattan, and A. Fulton. 1993. Agricultural salinity and drainage. University of California Irrigation Program, Davis. Water Management Series Publication 93-01.

Lancaster, D. L., and S. B. Orloff. 1997. Site selection. Pp. 3–8. in: S. B. Orloff and H. L. Carlson, eds., Intermountain alfalfa management. University of California Division of Agriculture and Natural Resources, Oakland. Publication 3366.

Marble, V. L. 1990. Factors to optimize alfalfa production in the 1990s. Pp. 4–45 in: Proceedings, 20th California Alfalfa Symposium. December 6–7, Visalia, CA.

Orloff, S. B., and H. L. Carlson, eds. 1997. Intermountain alfalfa management. University of California Division of Agriculture and Natural Resources, Oakland. Publication 3366.

Richards, L. A., ed. 1954. Diagnosis and improvement of saline and alkali soils. U.S. Department of Agriculture, Washington, D.C. Handbook 60.

3

Alfalfa Growth and Development

Shannon C. Mueller
Farm Advisor, University of California Cooperative Extension, Fresno, CA

Larry R. Teuber
Professor, Department of Plant Sciences, University of California, Davis

All aspects of alfalfa management require a thorough understanding of the growth and development of the crop. Basic knowledge of the botanical features of alfalfa, its growth patterns, and its developmental stages are keys to better management of a healthy, productive stand. Plant growth affects yield components, while plant morphology impacts many management decisions, including scheduling of herbicide treatments and harvest. This chapter describes the processes of alfalfa growth and defines precise stages of development.

Germination and Emergence

Alfalfa seeds begin germination shortly after planting, provided soil temperatures are approximately 65°F (18°C) and adequate moisture is present. Seeds will not germinate when soil temperatures are below about 35°F (1.7°C) or above 104°F (40°C). Absorption of water by the seed is the first step in the germination process and takes place when moisture is present in sufficient quantities to penetrate the seed coat. A small portion of alfalfa seed is highly resistant to water penetration; it is referred to as "hard seed." Germination of hard seed is delayed many weeks or months after the majority of seed germinates. Seed produced in California typically has very little hard seed, whereas seed produced under different soil and climatic conditions can have up to 60 percent hard seed. Seed lots with a high percentage of hard seed (>10%) may be scarified using specialized equipment to improve germination.

Mature seeds contain tiny immature leaves (cotyledons) and stored carbohydrates (endosperm), as well as the immature primary root (radicle). The first observable evidence of germination is the belowground elongation and penetration of the radicle into the soil to produce an unbranched taproot. After radicle emergence, the area below the cotyledons (hypocotyl) straightens and elongates, and the cotyledons are pulled above the soil surface (Fig. 3.1). The first true leaf produced is a unifoliolate (single leaflet) leaf. The seedling stem (primary shoot) continues to develop into a mature plant, producing alternately arranged trifoliolate (three leaflets per leaf) or multifoli-

olate (more than three leaflets per leaf) leaves. Subsequently produced stems are referred to as secondary stems.

Contractile Growth and Crown Development

A unique feature of early alfalfa development is contractile growth, or the formation of the crown during stand establishment. Contractile growth begins as early as 1 week after emergence and is usually complete within 16 weeks. As the primary and secondary shoots grow, the hypocotyl (portion of the stem below the cotyledonary node) shortens and thickens through a process known as contractile growth. This takes place when parenchyma cells in the hypocotyl simultaneously expand laterally and shorten longitudinally. Outer tissues of the hypocotyl, which do not actively contract, are lifted in folds and wrinkles over the surface, producing the characteristic rough appearance of contracted roots and stems. As a consequence of contractile growth, both the cotyledonary node and the unifoliolate node may be pulled beneath the soil surface to form the *crown* of the mature plant (Fig. 3.2). All of these processes are influenced by soil temperature and, to a lesser extent, by photoperiod.

Importance of Crown Development

The adaptive value of contractile growth is to provide protection of growing points from desiccation, cold, or

FIGURE 3.1

Alfalfa seedling growth and development. The two leaves that first appear after emergence are called cotyledons or seed leaves. The next leaf to emerge is the first true leaf. It is unifoliolate. The second and subsequent leaves are usually trifoliolate, but may also be multifoliolate.

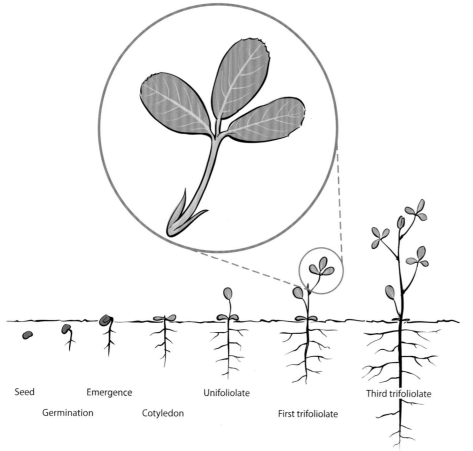

Seed   Emergence   Unifoliolate   Third trifoliolate
      Germination   Cotyledon   First trifoliolate

It is important to
allow sufficient
time for contractile
growth to take
place before field
operations begin,
especially harvest.

mechanical damage. Varieties with greater fall dormancy tend to have more pronounced contractile growth, resulting in the nodes being pulled further below the soil surface than they would be in less dormant varieties. It is important to give time for seedling crown formation to occur before beginning any farming practices that might disrupt the process, especially harvest operations. Protecting young seedlings from weed competition and insect damage is also critical to the long-term health of the developing crown. An argument in favor of fall planting is that it allows time for crown formation before the onset of cold weather. Well-developed crowns contain a large number of buds, which can lead to higher yields after cutting.

Root Development and N₂ Fixation

The radicle thickens and develops into the primary taproot. Smaller secondary roots begin to develop on the radicle as it grows deeper. Within 4 weeks after germination, root hairs on the radicle become infected with nitrogen-fixing bacteria, *Rhizobium meliloti* Dang., and begin to form nodules. It is within these nodules that nitrogen fixation occurs, converting atmospheric nitrogen into a form the plant can use. Estimates of N_2 (molecular nitrogen) fixation in alfalfa vary from about 40 to 400 pounds (18 to 181 kg) of N_2 fixed acre^{-1} year^{-1} with an average of about 175 pounds (79 kg) of N_2 fixed acre^{-1} year^{-1}. Conditions ideal for alfalfa plant growth are also ideal for nitrogen fixation: neutral soil pH and adequate moisture are two of the most important.

Populations of *Rhizobium* bacteria inhabit the soil naturally or as a result of previous alfalfa production on that site. However, it is recommended that *Rhizobium* strains specific to alfalfa be introduced at planting by the addition of inoculum to the seed.

During stand establishment, it is important to allow roots to penetrate deep into the soil, below areas where a restrictive soil compaction zone (plow pan) could potentially be created during initial harvest operations. Established alfalfa taproots have been known to extend more than 6 feet below the soil surface, provided there are no restricting layers. It is in these roots that the carbohydrates produced by photosynthesis are stored. Stored carbohydrates (root reserves) provide energy for regrowth after cutting, winter survival, and initial growth in the spring. Alfalfa plants use

FIGURE 3.2

The young alfalfa plant undergoes a growth phase known as contractile growth. This process in alfalfa involves a change in the shape of cells in the hypocotyl or seedling axis below the cotyledons and upper portion of the primary root from long and narrow to short and wide, as a result of carbohydrate or food storage. This shift pulls the lower stem nodes beneath the soil surface. Most winter-hardy alfalfa varieties have several nodes pulled well below the soil surface in the seeding year. Contractile growth greatly aids winter survival of alfalfa by providing soil insulation for the perennial overwintering crown structures.

Source: http://www.ext.nodak.edu/extpubs/plantsci/hay/r648w.htm

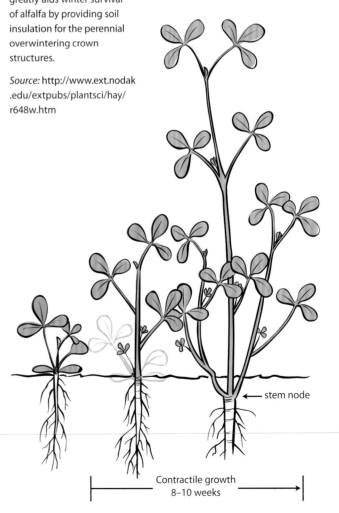

← stem node

|— Contractile growth 8–10 weeks —|

stored carbohydrates until leaf development is sufficient to provide energy for plant growth from photosynthesis. Once plants reach 8 to 12 inches in height (20 to 30 cm), enough energy is produced to maintain growth; at the same time, root reserves are replenished in preparation for the next cutting, or for winter survival.

Influence of Photoperiod and Soil Temperature on Alfalfa Seedling Development

Photoperiod (day length) and soil temperature both influence seedling development by affecting growth rate, stem initiation, and the allocation of photosynthetic products to the development of roots and stems. Not all cultivars respond equally to these environmental triggers. Seedling development of *dormant* cultivars is almost equally influenced by photoperiod and soil temperature, whereas seedling development of *nondormant* cultivars is essentially independent of photoperiod but is strongly influenced by soil temperature. Although the effect of photoperiod is less than that of temperature in cultivars grown throughout most of California, there are growth characteristics influenced by photoperiod that influence planting decisions. The importance of these considerations during stand establishment is covered in Chapter 4, "Alfalfa Stand Establishment."

Optimum temperatures for alfalfa seedling development are in the range of 68° to 72°F (20°C to 22°C), depending on the dormancy of the cultivar. During the first 4 weeks following germination, the optimum soil temperature for root growth is slightly higher, between 69° and 76°F (21°C to 24°C). Dormant cultivars generally have lower optimum temperatures during this initial growth phase than do nondormant cultivars.

A photoperiod of approximately 12 hours stimulates the formation of initial crown buds and stems from the axils of the cotyledons and the unifoliolate leaf, forming the primary crown. Photoperiods shorter than 12 hours favor allocation of photosynthate (dry matter) to the development of roots. Therefore, with fall planting, seedlings develop under cooling temperatures and shortening day lengths. Under these conditions, seedlings might be expected to rapidly develop the initial crown and form plants with a stronger crown and larger root system than seedlings developing under the warmer conditions and increasing day lengths associated with spring and summer planting.

Plant Age and Stage of Development

Alfalfa growth and development is controlled by the genetic potential of the plant interacting with the environment. It is important to make the distinction between plant *age* and *stage of development*. Alfalfa does not reach a specific stage of development at a given age. For example, if environmental conditions don't trigger changes in morphological development leading to the formation of reproductive structures, the plant will continue to grow vegetatively. On the other hand, specific environmental conditions (temperature, photoperiod, moisture status, salinity) can trigger the plant to transition into reproductive stages at a very young age. Most management decisions should be based on stage of development, not age.

Plant Maturity and Forage Quality

Forage quality changes over time as alfalfa plants grow and mature. It is well known that alfalfa yields increase as the crop matures, whereas the nutritional value of the forage declines significantly (Fig. 3.3). In young pre-bud alfalfa, the quality of the forage is high because of the high proportion of leaves to

Seedling development of dormant cultivars is influenced by both day length and soil temperature, whereas non-dormant cultivars are influenced mostly by soil temperature.

FIGURE 3.3

Forage yield relative to quality (forage digestibility) at different alfalfa growth stages.

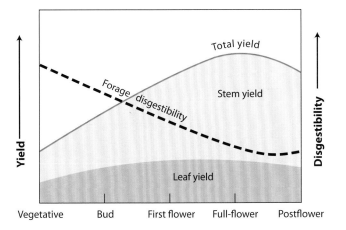

understanding of alfalfa development and the changes that impact alfalfa quality will help growers balance the yield–quality tradeoff.

Although *quality* is often defined in terms of low fiber content (acid detergent fiber [ADF] and neutral detergent fiber [NDF] concentration), which results in high total digestible nutrients (TDN) or relative feed value (RFV), growers should be aware of the penalties resulting from attempts to minimize fiber concentrations by reducing the interval between cuttings. Shorter cutting intervals do not allow sufficient time for root reserves to accumulate; thus, alfalfa vigor and the yield of subsequent cuttings are reduced and effective stand life can be severely reduced. Furthermore, harvesting alfalfa at immature stages of development, especially in cool spring weather, can result in inadequate fiber levels for ruminants, which can be critical for animals used for reproduction and lactation. Other sources of fiber must then be added to the diet.

Predicting Alfalfa Quality

Historically, the stage of alfalfa development was estimated using the reproductive status of the most mature stems in the canopy. Thus, alfalfa was said to be at a "late bud" or "early bloom" stage of growth. Alfalfa maturity was also defined in terms of the presence and length of regrowth buds. These estimates of maturity were associated with various quality parameters. In the 1980s, researchers studied more precise methods to assess maturity and used them to more accurately predict the quality of the growing alfalfa crop. More recently, predictive equations for alfalfa quality based on the height of the most mature stem show promise as a rapid and inexpensive method of estimating alfalfa fiber components, but early efforts were not as successful in predicting crude protein. Modifications to these prediction systems continue to be evaluated. Overall, forage quality predictions based on the maturity of the crop work well, because the cumulative effect of environmental factors on crop growth and quality is expressed in large part by alfalfa's morphological stage of development.

stems, but the yield is low. As the plant grows and matures, the proportion of leaves and stems changes. Stems lengthen and become more fibrous, increasing their total proportion in the forage. There is no concomitant increase in leaf percentage; thus, overall quality declines. To maximize yield, quality, and persistence, the grower must schedule management practices to maximize forage yield while achieving a level of quality to meet the nutritional requirements of the livestock that will consume it, without reducing desired stand life. The yield of high-quality forage is maximized in most cases by not harvesting until flower buds can be seen at the stem tips. During the vegetative period, before flower buds appear, yield generally increases faster than quality declines. However, during the flowering period, reduction in quality is very rapid, due primarily to increased fiber (cellulose and lignin) concentration in the stems. Within any regrowth interval, the trends in yield and quality can be modified by prevailing environmental conditions, such as changes in temperature.

The maturity of the alfalfa when it is harvested has the greatest impact on forage quality. It is also the variable most easily controlled by growers. Cutting according to the stage of development uses the plant as a harvest indicator and generally provides more consistent yield and quality among varieties and over years and locations compared to other harvest scheduling strategies. Improving the

Determining Stage of Development of Alfalfa

As alfalfa develops, changes in the plant can be observed on individual stems (Fig. 3.4). The stems progressively pass through vegetative, bud, flower, and seed pod stages. Numerous stems at various stages of development are typically found on one plant and in any given field. Precise definition of the average (mean) stage of development is the first step in many quality prediction systems. The *Mean Stage* method averages a large number of individual stems and is a precise method used to relate maturity to forage quality in a field. The *Mean Stage of*

Development is determined by examining individual stems and classifying them according to the staging system defined by Kalu and Fick (1981). A detailed protocol for collecting a sample and calculating Mean Stage of Development can be found in Fick and Mueller (1989).

Descriptions of Alfalfa Developmental Stages

Vegetative Stages

At early stages of development, reproductive structures are not visible on alfalfa stems. Leaf and stem formation characterize vegetative growth. The three vegetative stages are distinguished by stem length.

Stage 0:   Early Vegetative
Stem length ≤ 6 inches (15 cm); no visible buds, flowers or seed pods

Stage 1:   Mid-Vegetative
Stem length 6–12 inches (16–30 cm); no visible buds, flowers, or seed pods

Stage 2:   Late Vegetative
Stem length ≥ 12 inches (31 cm); no visible buds, flowers, or seed pods

Bud Stages

Flower buds first appear clustered near the tip of the stem or an axillary branch, because of the closely spaced nodes in that part of the shoot. At the transition from the vegetative stages to the bud stages, flower buds can be difficult to identify. At first, buds are small, distinctly round, and appear

FIGURE 3.4

Alfalfa stages of development as denoted on a single stem. *After illustration by Lisa Richter.*

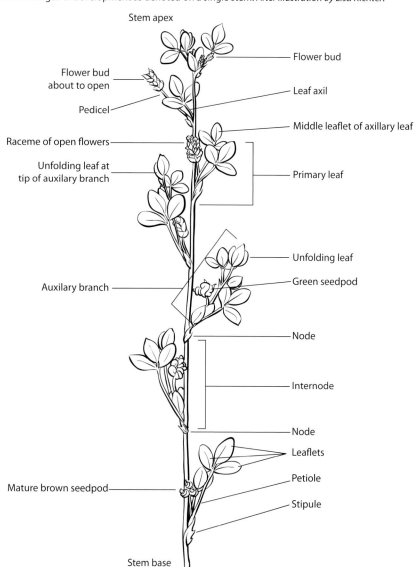

hairy or fuzzy. In contrast, new leaves are flat-tened and oblong. As the nodes elongate, it becomes easier to distinguish individual nodes for the purposes of counting.

Stage 3: Early Bud
      1–2 nodes with visible buds; no flow-ers or seed pods

Stage 4: Late Bud
      ≥ 3 nodes with visible buds; no flowers or seed pods

Flowering Stages

When environmental conditions meet specific requirements for temperature and photoperiod, flower buds develop into flowers. In fall, when there are fewer than 12 hours of daylight, buds may abort without forming flowers. Flowers may be purple, cream, yellow, white, or varie-gated combinations of those colors, depending on variety. Flowers may be open or closed. To be counted as an "open" flower, the standard petal (main large petal) of the flower must be unfolded. One or more flowers within the raceme (group of many flowers) may be open; however, the definition of stage 5 describes open flowers at only one node. Because one raceme arises from each node, the number of racemes with open flowers is actually what is counted. Flowering usually begins near the apex of the stem while buds are still develop-ing rapidly above and below the point of initial flower opening.

Stage 5: Early Flower
      One node with one open flower; no seed pods

Stage 6: Late Flower
      ≥ 2 nodes with open flowers; no seed pods

Seed Development Stages

If flowers are pollinated, they will ordinarily develop seed pods. In some environments, pol-lination is poor and only a few flowers form seed. Typically, alfalfa is harvested for forage well before the seed-bearing stages, which is when quality is lowest.

Stage 7: Early Seed Pod
      1–3 nodes with green seed pods

Stage 8: Late Seed Pod
      ≥ 4 nodes with green seed pods

Stage 9: Ripe Seed Pod
      Nodes with mostly brown, mature seed pods

Calculating the Mean Stage of Development

Two methods have been used to calculate the Mean Stage of Development for alfalfa forage. Mean Stage by Weight (MSW) is based on the dry weight of stems in each stage. Mean Stage by Count (MSC) uses the number of stems in each stage category to quantify maturity. Both procedures require a random sample of at least 40 alfalfa stems obtained from 5 to 6 places in a field, representing the natural range of growth patterns in that field. Individual stems are separated into the stages of devel-opment described above, based on their morphological characteristics. Most young samples have stems in only two or three categories. Older, more mature forage samples can have stems in each stage, from vegetative through seed pod.

> *Two methods have been used to precisely describe alfalfa growth stages: Mean Stage by Weight (MSW) and Mean Stage by Count (MSC).*

Stems from each stage should be counted to determine the mean stage by the MSC proce-dure. For MSW, stems from each stage should be dried in a forced-air oven at approximately 140°F (60°C) in individual bags, then weighed.

MSC is calculated as the average of the individual stage categories present in the sample, weighted for the number of stems in each stage. MSW is calculated similarly, except the average of the individual stages is weighted for the dry weights of stems in each stage.

Example:

If an alfalfa sample had

    4 stems in Stage 0
    5 stems in Stage 1
    5 stems in Stage 2
    10 stems in Stage 3
    15 stems in Stage 4
    2 stems in Stage 5

MSC is calculated as

$$\frac{(4 \times 0) + (5 \times 1) + (5 \times 2) + (10 \times 3) + (15 \times 4) + (2 \times 5)}{(4 + 5 + 10 + 15 + 2)}$$

which equals

$$\frac{5 + 10 + 30 + 60 + 10}{41} \quad or \quad \frac{115}{41} = 2.8$$

MSW would be calculated the same way, but instead of the *number* of stems in each stage, the *dry weight* of stems in each stage would be multiplied by the stage number, and the sum of the products would be divided by the total dry weight of all stems combined.

It is recommended that a decimal point be included with calculated mean stage values to distinguish a mean stage estimate from a rating of an individual stem.

Because stage of development and quality are closely associated in alfalfa, quality can be predicted by calculating mean stage. Predicting quality of the standing crop can help schedule when to harvest. Both MSW and MSC quantify morphological development of alfalfa. Most users prefer MSC because it is less tedious; however, only MSW is closely related to forage quality once crown buds start to elongate in an older canopy. Rapid, less complicated techniques for predicting quality have evolved from the Mean Stage system. For example, in 1998, Orloff and Putnam produced an *Alfalfa Quality Prediction Stick* with growth stages printed on three sides of the stick and corresponding percent ADF values associated with various

heights. Instructions printed on the fourth side of the stick guide growers through the process of predicting ADF using growth stage and height.

Additional Reading

Fick, G.W., and S.C. Mueller. 1989. Alfalfa quality, maturity, and mean stage of development. Department of Agronomy, College of Agriculture and Life Sciences. Cornell University, Information Bulletin 217.

Fick, G.W., D.A. Holt, and D.G. Lugg, 1988. Environmental physiology and crop growth. Pp. 163–194 in: Alfalfa and alfalfa improvement, A.A. Hanson, D.K. Barnes, and R.R. Hill, Jr., eds. American Society of Agronomy, Madison, WI. Publication 29.

Kalu, B., and G.W. Fick. 1981. Quantifying Morphological development of alfalfa for studies of herbage quality. Crop Sci. 21:267–271.

Teuber, L.R., and M.A. Brick. 1988. Morphology and Anatomy. Pp. 125–162 in: Alfalfa and alfalfa improvement, A.A. Hanson, D.K. Barnes, and R.R. Hill, Jr., eds. American Society of Agronomy, Madison, WI. Publication 29.

Teuber, L., J. Jernstedt, and K. Foord, 1988. Alfalfa growth and development. Pp. 39–44 in: Proceedings, 18th California Alfalfa Symposium. December 7–8. Modesto, CA.

4

Alfalfa Stand Establishment

Shannon C. Mueller
Farm Advisor, University of California Cooperative Extension, Fresno, CA

Carol A. Frate
Farm Advisor, University of California Cooperative Extension, Tulare, CA

Marsha Campbell Mathews
Farm Advisor, University of California Cooperative Extension, Modesto, CA

Seedling establishment is a critical phase in the life of an alfalfa stand, impacting production for many years. Time spent planning and preparing for stand establishment pays off in many ways, resulting in a dense, vigorous stand that produces high-quality, high-yielding alfalfa throughout the life of the stand. If a stand fails to establish, replanting requires additional time and expense. Furthermore, reworking the seedbed often delays planting beyond the optimum time, and options for alternative crops that may take the place of alfalfa become limited. On the other hand, accepting a marginal stand could result in lower yield potential, shorter stand life, weed pressure, and reductions in forage quality.

Optimum Environmental Conditions for Stand Establishment

Temperature and photoperiod (day length) influence alfalfa seedling development. They influence growth rate, stem initiation, and the allocation of photosynthates to the development of roots and stems. Using weather records from a given area and information regarding the response of alfalfa seedlings to temperature

Predicted optimum dates of planting for Davis, Fresno, and Indio, California, based on average monthly photoperiod and soil temperature.

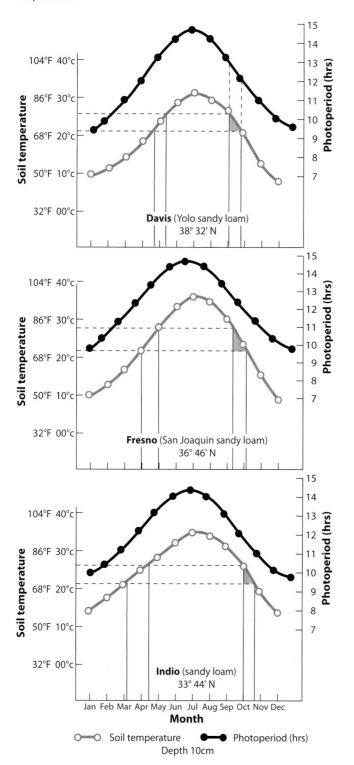

and photoperiod, the optimum time to plant alfalfa can be predicted. If the alfalfa plant is given as close to optimum conditions for development as possible, the risk of stand failure declines.

Historically, growers in Mediterranean and desert zones, such as California's Central and Imperial Valleys, have planted alfalfa in late fall through early spring to take advantage of winter and spring rainfall for germination. Although the chance for rainfall is greater during this period, the weather is often cold, slowing alfalfa seedling growth and allowing winter weeds to compete heavily with the alfalfa, reducing the chance of successful stand establishment. During prolonged periods of cool temperatures and high humidity common during this period, diseases, such as Sclerotinia stem and crown rot (*Sclerotinia* spp.), may also harm seedling stands. Planting dates are also restricted by crop rotations. Crops such as cotton, harvested in late fall, force growers to delay planting until November, December, or January, when cotton residue can be destroyed and alfalfa seedbeds prepared.

Optimum Conditions for Germination

Alfalfa seed germinates best at soil temperatures from 65° to 85°F (18°–29°C). When the soil temperature is 40°F (4°C), it takes alfalfa six days to germinate, but germination takes only two days at 65°F (18°C). Larry Teuber at UC Davis evaluated alfalfa seedling growth and development in response to variations in temperature and photoperiod (Fig. 4.1). The optimum temperature for root growth during the first month was 69°–76°F (21°–24°C), depending on dormancy class. Shoot growth is optimum at temperatures ranging from 72° to 76°F (22°–24°C). Alfalfa stops growing when the air temperature drops below 42°–34°F (6°–1°C), depending on the variety. In the Central Valley, optimum temperatures for alfalfa shoot growth occur from mid-September through early October, and from late April to early May. In California's desert regions, warm conditions extend later in the fall and begin earlier in the spring. The risks of late-fall or winter plantings are much lower in these desert areas than in the higher rainfall and cooler areas of the Central Valley.

Cultivar Interactions

Not all cultivars respond in the same way to environmental conditions. Photoperiod influences alfalfa growth and development to varying degrees, depending on the dormancy class of the cultivar. The effect of photoperiod is less than that of temperature in cultivars grown throughout California. However, there are two major growth characteristics influenced by photoperiod: (1) initiation of crown buds and stems, and (2) allocation of photosynthates to the roots. Photoperiods longer than 12 hours favor shoot development, whereas photoperiods shorter than 12 hours promote root growth. This information was combined with temperature response data to identify optimum planting dates for several locations throughout California. For arid climates similar to the Central Valley, fall planting dates from September 15 to October 31 and spring planting dates from February 1 to March 15 have the greatest potential for successful stand establishment.

Planting Dates

Several replicated field trials have confirmed the recommended planting dates for the Central Valley. In a Sacramento Valley trial conducted on cracking clay loam soils, data showed a yield advantage of almost 4 tons per acre (9.0 Mg ha⁻¹) the first season for a September planting compared to a March planting. October and November plantings, although better than the March planting, did not yield as high as the mid-September planting. The early planting yield advantage carried over into the second season (Table 4.1). In a second study (Table 4.1), the September planting emerged rapidly, resulting in an excellent stand, and yield advantages over later plantings were even more pronounced than in the previous trial. The September planting yielded almost 9 tons (8.2 Mg) in the first season, compared with only 4.1 tons (3.7 Mg) from the spring planting. In the second year after establishment, yields were equivalent for all planting dates. When

production for the two years is combined, the September planting produced 2.7 more tons per acre (6.0 Mg ha⁻¹) than the November planting, and 4.6 more tons per acre (10.2 Mg ha⁻¹) than the March planting.

A similar study was conducted in the southern Central Valley (western Fresno County, Panoche clay loam soil). There was a 1-ton (0.9-Mg) yield advantage for a September planting, compared to a November planting the first year, and a 3-ton

> *Planting in the fall (Sept.–Oct.) produces 20-30 percent higher yields the first year than spring planting.*

TABLE 4.1

First and second year yield data for planting date trials, Yolo County, Sacramento Valley, California, 1977–1978 and 1978–1979

Planting Date	Yield, Tons per Acre* (90% Dry Matter)			Total No. of Cuttings for Two Years
1977–1978	**First Year**	**Second Year**	**Total**	
14 Sept.	8.1[a†]	9.1[a]	17.2[a]	11
17 Oct.	7.3[b]	8.8[a]	16.0[b]	11
16 Nov.	6.2[c]	8.3[b]	14.5[c]	10
21 Mar.	4.4[d]	8.1[b]	12.6[d]	9
LSD (0.05)	0.57	0.43	0.88	
1978–1979	**First Year**	**Second Year**	**Total**	
22 Sept.	8.9[a]	8.3	17.2	11
24 Oct.	6.1[b]	9.9	16.0	11
27 Nov.	5.7[c]	8.8	14.5	10
14 Mar.	4.1[c]	8.5	12.6	9
LSD (0.05)	0.42	NA	NA	

†Within a column, means followed by the same letter are not significantly different at the 5 percent level of probability. Comparisons are valid only within individual years, not between years.

NA: statistical information was not provided in the reference source for the table.

*To convert tons per acre to Mg ha⁻¹, multiply by 2.24.

(2.7-Mg) yield advantage for a September planting, compared to either a December or April planting. The advantage of early fall planting continued through the second production year. Combining yields from the first two years, the September planting produced 4.5 tons per acre (10.1 Mg ha^{-1}) more than either the December or April plantings. It also yielded over 2 tons per acre (4.5 Mg ha^{-1}) more for the combined two years than the November planting date (Table 4.2).

In another trial in the southern Central Valley (Fresno County, Hanford sandy loam soil), an October planting produced 0.7 tons per acre (1.6 Mg ha^{-1}) more than a November planting and 4 tons per acre (9.0 Mg ha^{-1}) more than a February planting (Table 4.3). These data support September and early October as optimum times for establishing an alfalfa stand in the Central Valley. Planting in the fall gives 20–30 percent higher yields the first year, compared to spring planting. This response often persists into the second year as a result of increased vigor and a longer growth period before the first cutting. Planting date restrictions are less in California's Low Desert

Regions, because winter conditions are milder, but advantages are also seen with October plantings, compared to planting under mid-winter conditions.

Practical Considerations

There are challenges when planting alfalfa in September. The biggest hurdle is providing moisture to the seed at a time of year when rain is not expected. This can be achieved by pre-irrigating and planting to moisture (assuring that moisture is present at seeding depth) or by irrigating after planting using sprinklers or surface irrigation systems. In addition, September plantings result in a larger canopy in December and January, which retains moisture and humidity and favors Sclerotinia stem and crown rot disease. Egyptian alfalfa weevil, *Hypera brunneipennis* (Gyllenhal), often infests early-planted fields, resulting in the need to spray in March, which is not typical for seedling fields planted in November or later.

There are examples of stands successfully established outside the recommended planting dates; however, the risk of failure is greater. More consistent results are achieved when research-based recommendations are followed. When following cotton that is picked late, the ground is often too wet to be worked. As planting is delayed, there is a danger that frost will kill the developing seedlings, or win-

TABLE 4.2

First and second year yield data for planting date trial, West Side Research and Extension Center, Fresno County, San Joaquin Valley, California, 1979–1981

| Planting Date | Yield, Tons per Acre* (90% Dry Matter) | | |
	First Year (1980)	Second Year (1981)	Total
18 Sept.	7.4^{a†}	7.5^a	14.9
14 Nov.	6.4^b	6.5^b	12.9
13 Dec.	4.6^c	6.1^b	10.7
11 Apr.	4.5^c	6.3^b	10.8
28 May	3.0^d	6.2^b	9.2
LSD (0.05)	0.72	0.61	NA

†Within a column, means followed by the same letter are not significantly different at the 5 percent level of probability. Comparisons are valid only within individual years, not between years.

NA: statistical information was not provided in the reference source for the table.

*To convert tons per acre to Mg ha-1, multiply by 2.24.

TABLE 4.3

Alfalfa planting date study, Fresno County, southern Central Valley (Hanford sandy loam soil), California, 1988–1989

Planting Date	First Year Yield, Tons per Acre* (90% Dry Matter)	No. of Cuts
12 Oct.	13.3^{a†}	7
7 Nov.	12.6^b	7
23 Feb.	9.3^c	6
LSD (0.05)	0.63	

†Means followed by the same letter are not significantly different at the 5 percent level of probability.

*To convert tons per acre to Mg ha^{-1}, multiply by 2.24.

ter weeds will out-compete the alfalfa. Under such conditions, delaying planting until spring may be more desirable. Alternatively, planting a winter cereal after cotton followed by an early-maturing summer annual crop and delaying alfalfa planting by one year may be a better strategy than seeding under sub-optimal conditions.

Benefits of Early Fall Stand Establishment

* More rapid germination resulting from warmer temperatures.

* Increased vigor and ability of alfalfa seedlings to compete with winter weeds.

* Development of a deeper, more vigorous root system.

* Higher yields that may persist into future production years.

* Yield advantages from early fall plantings may offset the cost of renting sprinklers.

* Alfalfa seedlings from September plantings can withstand herbicide applications.

* The weather in September and October is more predictable than later fall or winter.

Seedbed Preparation

To plant during the recommended period, growers must prepare seedbeds in advance and have the ability to provide moisture to germinate seed and maintain seedling growth. This is often one of the greatest barriers to adoption of recommended early fall planting dates. Proper field preparation before planting is crucial because the stand will be intensively managed and harvested for 3 to 5 years, or longer. Planning and preparing properly for stand establishment may reduce future weed and disease problems, promote water-use efficiency, and result in higher yield and longer stand life.

Surveying the Site

Following destruction of residues from the previous crop, soil samples should be taken to determine fertility status and pH so that necessary amendments can be incorporated during seedbed preparation. Knowledge of previous weed problems is also important for determining the need for herbicides. A strategy for controlling weeds should be developed as the site is prepared. Weeds compete with alfalfa for light, water, and nutrients, and, if not controlled, reduce nutritional value of the forage. They can reduce seedling vigor and in some cases reduce alfalfa plant density to such a degree that the field has to be replanted. Preplant irrigation and cultivation can eliminate some weeds, but herbicides may also be needed. See Chapter 6, "Alfalfa Fertilization Strategies," for more detailed information on soil fertility and Chapter 8, "Weed Management," for weed management information.

Alfalfa performs best on well-drained, relatively deep soils with a minimum rooting depth of 3–4 feet (0.9–1.2 m). Limitations to rooting depth may be caused by physical or chemical factors, such as hardpans, stratified soils, or salts, that restrict productivity and

Alfalfa performs best on well-drained, relatively deep soils, with a minimum rooting depth of 3–4 feet.

lower yield. Poor drainage or high water tables may also limit root growth. Hardpans exist naturally in some soils, whereas restrictions known as plow pans are created by agricultural practices that promote compaction. These practices include working wet soils, driving equipment over moist or freshly cultivated soils, increasing equipment weight to apply more power or traction, and repeated cultivation of dry soils to make a smoother seedbed. Whether compaction becomes a limiting factor in plant growth depends on how it directly affects water percolation, aeration, and root extension, and indirectly affects nutrient uptake, plant diseases, and growth rate. The serious effects of soil compaction are usually found between the surface and 18 inches (45.7 cm) deep, but in some cases the effect can be found as deep as 24 inches (61.0 cm).

Stratified, or naturally layered, soils occur when there are textural differences within a soil profile (e.g., layers of sand within a loam or clay loam soil, or clay layers within a sandy loam soil). Restrictive layers are usually found deep within the soil profile, deeper than those created by compaction, so they are more difficult to correct by tillage. Using a backhoe to evaluate the distribution of roots in a soil profile will assist in determining whether soil layering or compaction problems exist in a field. See Chapter 2, "Choosing Appropriate Sites," for a better understanding of the limitations of different sites.

Deep Tillage

Layered or compacted soils respond to mixing by deep plowing, ripping, or other tillage operations to create a soil profile with more uniform texture (Fig. 4.2). Deep tillage breaks up compacted or dense layers in the soil. It increases infiltration rate, fractures stratified layers, mixes the soil profile, and reduces bulk density and soil strength. Rooting depth is often improved with deep tillage where there are subsurface impediments. The cost of deep tillage versus its potential benefits must be carefully evaluated because economic returns are difficult to predict. The cost of deep tillage varies, depending on the horsepower requirement and desired depth of tillage, and the results are often not easy to see. It takes a significant yield increase to recover the cost of deep tillage and it is not well understood how long the effects of deep tillage last.

Tools for deep tillage include large moldboard and disc plows, rippers, and chisels. Rippers and chisels come in a wide variety of sizes and shapes. Curved shanks require less draft than straight shanks to loosen the same amount of soil. Soil moisture content, depth, and spacing of ripper shanks influence the outcome. Rippers pull more easily through moist soils, but do a less effective job than when the operation is performed on dry soils. Ripping is most effective when shanks are spaced no more than 3 feet (0.9 m) apart. Shank spacing should be equal to or less than the depth of ripping. Ripping never breaks the soil straight across between the points of adjacent shanks. Ripping in one direction with closely spaced shanks results in more of the soil being shattered than

FIGURE 4.2

Deep tillage is frequently performed on heavy soils with subsurface impediments.

does ripping in two directions with widely spaced shanks.

Depending on soil type and crop rotation, ripping before establishment of each alfalfa stand should be adequate. Fields can be ripped in the fall prior to a spring or subsequent fall seeding of alfalfa.

Plowing and Conventional Tillage

Ripping shatters compacted layers, but does not mix the soil, so the beneficial effects of ripping may be short-lived in layered soils. Deep plowing with moldboard or disc plows is particularly effective in layered soils because plowing inverts and mixes stratified layers. Plows move all of the soil to a depth of 18–30 inches (45.7–76.2 cm) depending on the size of the equipment. Plows have the potential to loosen compaction, providing the moisture content is such that the soil will crumble rather than form into clods. If deeper mixing is desired, a slip plow can be used to reach 5 or 6 feet (1.5–1.8 m) deep. Slip plowing displaces and cracks more soil than does ripping, but requires correspondingly higher energy inputs. However, a slip plow only mixes the soil in the trench it makes, so the mixing job is not as thorough as that of moldboard or disc plows. Slip plowing followed by moldboard or disc plowing, rather than either operation alone, gives the best chance of achieving the desired results. Soils require extra time, tillage, or irrigation to firm up or settle after plowing. If possible, freshly plowed soil should not be disturbed for several weeks to avoid re-compaction.

Even if it is determined that deep tillage is not necessary, ripping to moderate depths (20–32 inches [50.8–81.3 cm]) is usually cost effective and recommended to reduce compaction from agricultural operations in preceding crops. Although less expensive to rectify, soils compacted by field equipment must be dealt with repeatedly because farming practices rather quickly re-compact soil that has been loosened by tillage.

Land Leveling

Once deep tillage and plowing operations are complete, the field should be disked and planed. Leveling fields to be planted to alfalfa is extremely important because water must flow evenly over the flat surface. With flood irrigation systems, laser leveling is usually recommended to prepare the field. Laser leveling should be a two-step process. The field is first leveled following any necessary deep tillage operation. Then, once the irrigation borders are established, the area between them should be leveled and a uniform slope achieved. The final smoothing of the field is usually achieved with a land plane to remove any minor irregularities in the soil surface (Fig. 4.3). Eliminating high and low spots in the field will improve the efficiency of the irrigation system and prevent harvest problems. Depending on the rotation, laser leveling the field may not be necessary each time an alfalfa stand is established. However, touching up the level and slope between borders is always recommended.

> *Leveling fields for alfalfa is extremely important because water must flow evenly over the flat surface.*

FIGURE 4.3

Land leveling to *eliminate high and low spots* is critical to long-term success of surface irrigation.

Checks and Borders

Levees used with border irrigation serve to guide the water as it moves down-slope through the field (Fig. 4.4). Most levees are about 2–4 feet (0.6–1.2 m) wide and 6–8 inches (15.2–20.3 cm) high. These dimensions allow for easy passage of equipment across the border and maximum use of space for alfalfa production. The tops of the levees only need to be a few inches above the water surface while irrigation takes place. Because an alfalfa planting is kept for several years, great care should be taken in constructing the levees so that a level surface the full width of the area between adjacent levees (the check) is maintained. Using cross-checkers, which strip soil from the full width of the check and deposit it along a line to make levees, is recommended. After the soil has been deposited for the levee, a shaper is used to achieve the desired uniform cross-section. The width between the levees ranges from 15 to 20 feet (4.5–6.1 m) on the narrow side, to 50–100 feet (15.2–30.5 m) or more, and should be based on soil type, slope, length of the checks, and flow rate of water available for irrigating the field. Width of harvesting equipment should be taken into consideration in determining the width of irrigation checks. For example, the width of the check should be some multiple of the width of the swather header. See Chapter 7, "Irrigating Alfalfa," for more detailed information about designing and installing an irrigation system.

FIGURE 4.4

Border-check irrigation systems are the most commonly used in California.

The Seedbed

Planting on the Flat

After levees are constructed, the checks are generally floated with a drag scraper to prepare a smooth seedbed for planting that is sufficiently firm to provide good seed-to-soil contact such that seeds absorb moisture and don't dry out. A grower might use a spring tooth harrow to fluff up the seedbed, or a ring roller or cultipacker to pack it down in preparation for seeding, or both. The final seedbed should be fine, firm, and perfectly leveled, with very small (grape-size or smaller) clods. On some silty-clay soil types, golf-ball-size clods are acceptable and melt over the seed during irrigation. Use of press wheels or rolling after seeding may help assure seed-to-soil contact on many soil types. Excessive tillage to create extremely fine seedbeds may lead to crusting after irrigation or heavy rains. Measuring the depth of a footprint left in the prepared seedbed can help a grower assess firmness. If the heel print is greater than ½ inch (1.3 cm) deep, the seedbed is too fluffy and stand establishment may be negatively affected. Sandy soils can tolerate more than ½ inch of fluffy conditions than heavier soils.

The final seedbed should be fine, firm, and perfectly leveled, with very small (grape-size or smaller) clods.

"Bedded" or "Corrugated" Alfalfa

On heavy, poorly drained soils, seed may be planted on beds or corrugations (Fig. 4.5). Although more expensive to prepare, seed planted in this way enables alfalfa production on soils that otherwise would present severe limitations. This practice is not advantageous on well-drained soils. Corrugated planting is a modification of bed planting with lower beds (shallower furrows). Corrugated or bedded alfalfa is a common practice in limited areas of the western United States. With corrugated alfalfa, the crop is furrow-irrigated rather than flooded on flat surfaces using bordered checks. Bedding improves water drainage, thus protecting the alfalfa crown and roots. Furrows move excess water out of the field, which prevents flooding. Although common in the northern Central Valley and Imperial Valley on heavy soils, this approach is rarely used in the southern Central Valley.

Many growers use a 40–60 inch (1.0–1.5 m) bed with 4–6-inch (10.2–15.2 cm) deep furrows, but beds 21 inches (about 0.5 m) wide with deeper furrows are sometimes used on heavier soils. The furrows are sometimes seeded and sometimes not, depending on depth (smaller corrugations are seeded, whereas deep furrows in the bedded fields are kept clean). With deep furrows in bedded alfalfa, equipment must be modified so that the wheels run only in the furrow. When the alfalfa beds are kept low, swathers, rakes, tractors, balers, and harrow-beds have no difficulty traversing the field. Bed width is critical. If beds are too wide, water may not move by capillary action (sub) to the center during irrigation. In soils with elevated salt levels, seedling emergence in the center of the bed may be a problem as salts move with the water front and concentrate there. If gaps between beds are too wide, the chance of having weed problems increases. Another factor influencing bed width is the duration of an irrigation set required to sub across the bed. If the time required to wet the soil to the center of the bed is too long, many of the advantages of a bedding system are lost.

Beds usually start about 20 feet (6.1 m) into the field when irrigating from a fixed head ditch. A border levee from the ditch to the beginning of the corrugation should be developed at intervals suited to the particular field. A similar area should be created at the end of the field, but borders may not be necessary. The area should allow for two swather passes at the top and bottom ends of the field. Equipment can turn in this area without crossing the furrows. The border levee at the top end will guide the water to the furrows.

An advantage to this system is that plants can be easily irrigated up during stand establishment. After planting, water is trickled down the furrows and allowed to sub across the beds

FIGURE 4.5

Bedded or corrugated alfalfa in the Sacramento Valley, California. Beds range from 24"-60", and furrows range from shallow to 8-10" deep.

from both sides. A slow irrigation of this kind can provide the moisture needed for germination and early root development during the fall and spring months. Another advantage is that hay may cure more quickly because of increased airflow beneath the windrow.

Seeding Rates

Seeding rates vary with seed characteristics, soil type, climate, seedbed condition, and method of planting. There are approximately 220,000 alfalfa seeds per pound (454 g) of raw seed. If distribution was perfectly uniform and every seed germinated and emerged, a 20 pound per acre (22.4 kg ha[-1]) seeding rate would result in 100 plants per square foot (0.09 m²), far more than is typically observed in a newly seeded stand. Numerous factors reduce the actual alfalfa emergence, including poor seedbed conditions, seeding depth control, insufficient or excessive moisture, poor seed germination, seedling diseases, and inclement weather. Therefore, a seeding rate of 20–25 pounds per acre (22–28 kg ha[-1]) broadcast or 15–20 pounds per acre (17–22 kg ha[-1]) drilled typically results in 20–50 plants per square foot (0.09 m²) one month after seeding, which is considered an adequate stand. Higher seeding rates may be justified if the seedbed is rough, the seed is planted late, the seed is broadcast rather than drilled, alkalinity and salinity are problems, or moisture conditions are marginal. Usually it is better to correct these problems rather than to increase the seeding rate to compensate for poor planting conditions.

At the end of the first season, about 40–50 percent of the plants typically remain. Higher seeding rates generally do not result in improved yield or alfalfa stand density except under the poorest of seedbed conditions. A natural thinning process takes place so that, although a stand may be thicker initially, there is no difference in plant density after the first year of production. Lower plant populations have higher survival rates, resulting in the same final plant population achieved with higher seeding rates (Table 4.4).

Seed Treatment

Seed may be coated or treated for a variety of reasons. One of the simplest reasons is to extend short seed supplies; in that case, the seed is coated with an inert material. Although the number of pounds of planting material may be the same, when using coated seed, approximately one-third fewer seeds will actually be planted because of the weight of the coating (seed coatings are typically about 33 % of the total seed weight). More often, coatings are used to provide fungicide or *Rhizobium* bacte-

ria in close proximity to the seed to enhance seedling survival and development. Potential benefits from coating seed include:

- quick sprouting and more effective establishment of seedling populations

- improved performance of *Rhizobium* bacteria

- protection of seed from insects and disease organisms

- incorporation of growth factors, fertilizers, micronutrients, and pesticides

However, positive benefits in favor of seed coatings have not been observed consistently in research trials. There is a lot of natural variation in soil populations of alfalfa seedling pathogens and in the effect of soil and environmental conditions (e.g., temperature and moisture) on their ability to cause disease. Large losses resulting from disease will occur in some fields, but not in others. Consequently, there are times when seed coated with fungicide confers a distinct advantage, and times when it does not.

In research trials conducted in the Central Valley in 1988–1989, raw and coated seed, treated with or containing a variety of inoculum types and fungicides, were compared.

TABLE 4.4

Effect of seeding rate on alfalfa plant density and yield the first and second year after seeding. West Side Research and Extension Center, Fresno County, San Joaquin Valley, California, 1979–1981.

Seeding Rate (Pounds per Acre*)	1 Month after Planting	1 Year after Planting	Percent Survival	1980 Yield	1981 Yield
	(Number of plants per ft**)			(Tons dry matter per Acre***)	
10	12.7[a†]	8.4[a]	66	5.2	6.3[b]
20	21.9[b]	9.5[ab]	44	5.2	6.5[ab]
30	30.0[c]	10.7[ab]	36	5.2	6.6[a]
40	35.4[d]	11.2[b]	32	5.1	6.6[a]
LSD (0.05)	3.21	2.68		NS	0.17

[†]Within a column, means followed by the same letter(s) are not significantly different at the 5 percent level of probability.

NS: not significant.

* To convert pounds per acre to kg ha^{-1}, multiply by 1.12.

** To convert number of plants per ft^2 to number per m^2, multiply by 9.29 x 10^{-2}.

*** To convert tons per acre to Mg ha^{-1}, multiply by 2.24.

Coated seed and raw seed were planted at a rate of 25 pounds per acre (28 kg ha⁻¹) on three planting dates. Initial and final stand counts for the October planting were not significantly different for any of the treatments. Initial stand counts ranged from 34 to 51 plants per square foot (0.09 m²). Final stand counts ranged from 9 to 15 plants per square foot (0.09 m²). For the November and late February plantings, initial stand counts were lower for coated seed compared to raw seed, because fewer coated seeds were planted per acre. Adding fungicides or *Rhizobium* inoculum to the seed coating did not provide an advantage in terms of stand establishment. However, with raw seed, Apron fungicide (metalaxyl) increased the initial stand count for the November planting. Within planting dates, by the end of the first

production year, all plant populations were comparable. Within harvests and planting dates, there were no significant effects of seed treatment on forage yield. A trial at UC Davis showed similar results.

From our research and experience, seed coatings do not appear to enhance or detract from establishing alfalfa stands. Reduction in the number of seedlings per unit area can result from the fact that fewer seeds per pound are sown with coated seed, but percent survival can be higher than with raw seed (Table 4.5). Although percent survival was higher with coated seed in some treatments, initial stand counts were lower, and there were no differences between any treatments in stand counts at the end of the first year, and no effect on yield. The value of seed treatments with Apron

TABLE 4.5

Effect of seed treatment and planting date on alfalfa seedling survival at three planting dates. Kearney Research and Extension Center, Fresno County, southern Central Valley, California, 1988–1989. All plots seeded at 25 lbs/acre (28 kg ha⁻¹)

Seed Treatment	12 Oct. 1988 Planting Dates		7 Nov. 1988 Percent Survival*		23 Feb. 1989	
	1ˢᵗ Month	Final	1ˢᵗ Month	Final	1ˢᵗ Month	Final
Raw Seed	39.0	10.8	39.4ᵃ†	12.8ᵉᶠ	56.6	14.4ᵇᶜ
Raw Seed+Apron	45.6	13.4	51.8ᵇᶜᵈ	14.8ᵈᵉᶠ	57.5	13.1ᶜ
Raw Seed+p.p. inoc.**	40.1	11.7	48.0ᵃᵇᶜ	11.5ᶠ	51.9	14.1ᵇᶜ
Raw Seed+p.p. inoc.+Apron	38.0	11.1	48.9ᵃᵇᶜ	13.9ᵈᵉᶠ	57.8	14.6ᵇᶜ
Raw Seed+granular inoculum	41.9	9.9	44.2ᵃᵇ	17.3ᶜᵈᵉ	51.8	15.7ᵇᶜ
Coated Seed	58.2	14.7	58.1ᶜᵈᵉ	22.9ᵃ	58.0	19.3ᵃᵇ
Coated Seed+Apron	50.7	14.6	60.2ᵈᵉ	17.8ᵇᶜᵈ	57.5	21.3ᵃ
Coated Seed+inoc.	45.4	13.3	47.7ᵃᵇᶜ	21.3ᵃᵇᶜ	59.7	21.4ᵃ
Coated Seed+inoc.+Apron	49.9	14.4	58.1ᶜᵈᵉ	23.9ᵃ	61.8	17.6ᵃᵇ
Coated Seed+inoc.+Apron+Rovral***	54.3	11.7	63.6ᵉ	22.3ᵃᵇ	70.5	21.6ᵃ
LSD (0.05)	NS	NS	11.22	4.86	NS	5.24
CV (%)****	31.8	21.7	14.9	18.8	14.0	20.1

† Within a column, means followed by the same letter(s) are not significantly different at the 5 percent level of probability.

NS: not significant.

* Percent Survival: number of surviving plants vs. number of seed originally planted. Final evaluation took place on Nov. 7, 1989.

** p.p. inoc.: powdered peat inoculum

*** Rovral: iprodione. This material is not registered for use on alfalfa in California. Check with your local Extension office to determine its status in your area.

**** C.V.: coefficient of variation

or similar fungicides will depend on the degree of disease pressure. Seed treatments should be viewed as a form of "risk management" that may only pay off occasionally, as in an insurance policy. Use of raw seed may be completely acceptable under optimum conditions, but inoculation with *Rhizobium* and treatment with Apron may be appropriate when seeding under suboptimum conditions.

Inoculating Seed

Nitrogen-fixing *Rhizobium meliloti* Dang. bacteria are found in alfalfa root nodules and are capable of fixing from the atmosphere almost all of the nitrogen the alfalfa crop needs. Most fields in California being considered for alfalfa production have a native population of *Rhizobium* bacteria because alfalfa or clover has been grown previously. For those fields, native populations can provide adequate nodulation and nitrogen fixation for the life of the stand. Soils without a recent history (within the past 10 years) of alfalfa may need to be inoculated with strains of alfalfa *Rhizobium* bacteria selected for their effectiveness in nitrogen fixation. Growers may purchase inoculum and apply it to the seed before planting, or as discussed previously, a seed company may have applied the *Rhizobium* bacteria to the seed directly or in a coating. When buying inoculum, be sure the word "alfalfa" is listed on the container and that the seal on the bag has not been broken. Check the expiration date on the inoculum bag and store in a cool, dry place, preferably a refrigerator. If buying pre-inoculated seed, check the date that the seed was inoculated. Seed inoculated 6 months ago or longer should be re-inoculated before planting.

Inoculum should be applied to the seed following the instructions on the package for either the powdered peat or granular types. Poor nodulation may result from low soil pH levels, use of the wrong kind of bacteria, use of inoculum in which the bacteria are dead, or improper application of the bacteria to seed.

Seeding Method

There are essentially two methods used to plant alfalfa: broadcast (by ground or air) and drill. When properly calibrated to achieve the desired seeding rate and a uniform planting depth, and when used in a well-prepared seedbed, successful stands can result from either of these methods. Each has advantages and disadvantages.

Broadcast Seeding. Several types of seeders are commonly used to broadcast seed evenly on the soil surface. A cultipacker seeder (e.g., Brillion seeder) does an excellent job of planting alfalfa because it has a roller in front to firm the soil and a roller following behind the seed drop that covers and presses the seed into the soil at an optimum depth. Air-flow ground applicators can be used to broadcast seed evenly over the soil surface, sometimes along with other operations, such as application of fertilizers. With large acreages, or when soil is too wet to support ground equipment, planting seed by air works well. Planting seed by air may be the least expensive method, but there can be disadvantages. Flying seed on to a field may require more seed, may result in more skips, and there is less control over depth of seeding. With all broadcast methods except the Brillion seeder, seed must be covered after broadcast seeding to maximize germination and emergence. A cultipacker or ring roller is an excellent tool for this purpose. Firming the soil around the seed gives it greater contact with moisture and enhances germination. A spike-toothed harrow usually incorporates seed into the top 3 inches of soil, too deep for optimum emergence, and does not provide the desired seed-to-soil contact; it is therefore not recommended.

Drill Seeding. Grain drills, which place the seed in rows at a uniform depth, can be used successfully to establish alfalfa. Seed typically drops behind a disk opener and is covered by press wheels or a corrugated roller. Better drills have good depth control, which should be carefully adjusted for seeding depth. Drills with poor depth control should not be used. Fertilizers may be placed below the seed at planting, if desired. One disadvantage of drilling versus broadcast seeding is the unplanted space between rows, which provides an open area for weed invasion. Some growers drill in two directions, perpendicular to each other, to reduce the possibility of large skips from planter problems. As with broadcast seeding, the seed must be covered and the soil must be firmed around the seed after planting. This can be accomplished using press wheels attached to the planter, by pulling a cultipacker behind the planter, or in a separate operation with rollers or cultipackers.

The most important, but often ignored, step in the seeding process is calibration of the planter. Manufacturer recommended settings are based on average values, and it is important to check the actual flow of seed through the planter before planting. Planter calibration is time well spent to prevent seeding mistakes. Relying solely on settings recommended by the manufacturer, or using the setting from the previous year, may result in significantly under- or over-applying seed to the field. Alfalfa seed size varies, especially when planting coated versus raw seed. Coated seed flows 5–28 percent faster through common seed metering units than does raw seed at the same planter setting.

Seeding Depth

Recommended seeding depth for most California conditions ranges from 0.25 to 0.50 inch (0.6–1.3 cm), depending on soil type and condition. Seed should not be planted at depths greater than 0.75 inch (1.9 cm). Only 2 percent of seeds planted 2.5 inches (6.0 cm) deep will emerge, but 70 percent will come through when planted 0.25–0.50 inch (0.6–1.3 cm) deep. Seed placement is related to the condition of the seedbed at the time of planting. If the soil surface is powdery or fluffy, seed may be placed too deep for maximum emergence. Seed planted too shallowly or with poor seed-to-soil contact can dry out before germination is complete. Planting depth can be evaluated by looking for seeds on the soil surface after the planter or cultipacker has passed by. Seed is likely to be too deep if there are no seeds visible on the soil surface.

Recommended seeding depth for most California conditions ranges from 0.25 to 0.50 inch (0.6–1.3 cm), depending on soil type and condition.

Irrigation—Providing Moisture for New Stands

There are three options to consider for providing moisture to germinate alfalfa seed: (1) plant prior to anticipated rain, (2) plant and irrigate immediately after seeding, or (3) pre-irrigate and plant to moisture. The value of each strategy will depend on tolerance of risk, soil type, reliability of rainfall, and adherence to recommended times of planting.

Pre-Irrigation

No matter which option is selected, in most situations pre-irrigation is generally a good idea. It fills the soil profile to field capacity, germinates weed seedlings that can then be removed by cultivation or contact herbicides, and settles the soil, allowing elimination of high or low areas in the seedbed before planting. With pre-irrigation, sufficient time must be allocated before planting for soil to be dry enough to support planting equipment. A concern, especially during fall and on clay soils, is that rainfall following pre-irrigation may prevent planting for an extended period. For these reasons, some growers choose not to pre-irrigate. The advantage to planting before anticipated rain is that it saves the cost of labor and water for irrigation. However, weather forecasts can be unreliable and, during the optimum planting period in the fall, moisture is not available from precipitation. The advantage to planting and irrigating immediately afterward is the ability to plant during the optimum planting period even though rain is unlikely. To be successful, it is important that seeding depth be no more than 0.5 inch (1.3 cm), and ideally 0.25 inch (0.6 cm) or less. If soil crusting occurs before seedling emergence, additional light irrigations are necessary to soften the surface.

The third alternative, pre-irrigating and planting to moisture, is not without challenges, especially if soil moisture is more than 0.5 inch (1.3 cm) from the surface at the time of planting. Moisture levels can be inconsistent, and too-shallow placement of seed results in uneven stands because some seed germinates immediately and other seed will need additional water before germination. Seed planted too deeply may result in weak seedlings that struggle to reach the soil surface from greater depths. Additionally, wheel tracks from planting equipment are often more frequent following pre-irrigation because, in the effort to conserve soil moisture, planting takes place as soon as possible following irrigation.

Early Fall Planting and Irrigation

Many growers irrigate their alfalfa to establish stands during the optimum time in the fall (Fig. 4.6). This is due to the clear advantage of early fall planting versus winter planting. Soil in the root zone must remain moist while alfalfa seed is germinating and the young seedlings are developing. Newly emerged seedlings are not as resilient as established plants, so they must not be subjected to stress from either too much or too little water. Relying on winter or spring rains to germinate seed and maintain young seedlings often results in uneven stands. Even if rainfall leads to successful germination and emergence, subsequent irrigations may be required to maintain seedlings because of a lack of deep moisture in the soil profile and the shallow rooting depth of young seedlings. Roots grow in the presence of moisture, not in search of it, and growth will stop if soil in the root zone becomes too dry. Conversely, over-irrigation may stimulate seedling diseases.

Several methods are used to provide the necessary moisture for germination and seed-

> *Relying on winter or spring rains to germinate seed and maintain young seedlings often results in uneven stands.*

FIGURE 4.6

Irrigation must be sufficient to prevent desiccation and crusting, and allow emergence of seedlings, but not allow standing water which encourages diseases.

ling growth. Sprinkler irrigation is the best method for providing small quantities of water at frequent intervals to promote germination and seedling establishment. Where sprinklers are not available, growers have successfully established stands using flood or furrow irrigation systems.

Flood Irrigating New Stands

Establishing stands with flood irrigation has been successful on both sandy and heavy soils. It is generally more challenging than using sprinklers, because both uniformity of application and crusting are more difficult to control. If this strategy is to be used, it is extremely important to carefully level the field to avoid high and low spots, since uneven germination will result when high areas don't receive sufficient moisture and seedlings may drown in low areas. This is a more critical issue when flood irrigating seedling fields than when establishing stands with sprinklers. Crusting is a major hazard when flood irrigating during establishment, and growers must have a strategy for additional quick irrigations to prevent crusting, which is not easy to do with flood systems. Another option for heavy soil is to plant alfalfa on beds or corrugations as described previously. In these cases, with good capillary action on heavy soils, water subs across the beds, enabling germination. During the first several irrigations, it is especially important that water drains off within a few hours. Preventing water from backing up into previously irrigated checks will reduce the risk of stand failure resulting from flooding in those areas. Although sprinkler irrigation for stand establishment is the preferred method, growers can flood irrigate new stands successfully by paying careful attention to initial leveling and timing irrigation with weather patterns to prevent crusting.

Sprinkler Irrigating New Stands

Most growers see the advantage of sprinkler irrigation on newly seeded alfalfa from germination through emergence (Fig. 4.7). Growers must weigh the potential yield increase with early planting and the value of current hay prices against the cost of sprinkler rentals, expenses related to labor and management requirements, and the cost of water. Historically, the increased cost for sprinklers has been justified in view of the extra production resulting from early fall planting. If sprinklers are used only during stand establishment, a hand move system or wheel lines are recommended.

Initially, sprinklers should be run long enough to completely fill the top 6 inches (15.2 cm) of the soil profile. Subsequent shorter irrigations may be necessary only to wet the top inch (2.5 cm) or so, to prevent desiccation of the germinating seeds and prevent crusting. Keeping the surface too wet may result in seedling diseases; irrigate just frequently enough to provide moisture for the young, developing seedlings. Run times will vary, depending on residual soil moisture content following the previous crop. Sets that are too long can cause puddling, and seedlings will not survive in those areas. When sprinkler irrigation is used, germination and emergence take only a few days in mid-September to early October, and it is rare not to obtain an excel-

> *The increased cost for sprinklers has been justified in view of the extra production resulting from early fall planting.*

FIGURE 4.7

Sprinklers are commonly used for stand establishment. Subsequently, growers often switch to gravity-fed surface irrigation.

lent stand. Caution is advised to make sure that sprinkler fittings do not leak, leading to washed out or flooded areas. After the crop has reached a more mature stage (e.g., 3–4 trifoliolate leaves) and at least 6 inches (15 cm) of root development, flood irrigation can be used.

Planting to Moisture

Some growers plant to moisture, which can be successful if moisture is very near the soil surface, but it is a riskier approach to stand establishment. Pre-irrigation may provide sufficient moisture for germination. However, alfalfa should only be planted to moisture if (1) sufficient moisture will remain in the root zone throughout the germination process, (2) moisture is present near enough to the soil surface to prevent planting too deep, and (3) good seed–soil contact is assured to allow seeds to take up moisture.

Alternative Practices for Stand Establishment

Companion Crops

Small grains, usually oat, have a long history of being planted as a companion crop during alfalfa establishment. Other forage legumes, like berseem clover, are more recent introductions to companion cropping systems. Companion crops may protect newly emerging alfalfa seedlings from water or wind erosion and have also been shown to suppress weeds and increase first cutting yields. Although establishing alfalfa with companion crops is common in other parts of the country, this practice is not common in California. At issue is stand reduction and lower yields resulting from early competition from the companion crop during establishment. These situations can arise when the alfalfa is planted at a low seeding rate and the companion crop is planted at a higher seeding rate. In general, alfalfa should be planted at the recommended seeding rate (20–25 pounds per acre; 22.4–28.0 kg ha^{-1}), whereas a companion crop of oat should be planted at 8–16 pounds per acre (9.0–17.9 kg ha^{-1}), or berseem clover at 6–8 pounds per acre (6.7–9.0 kg ha^{-1}).

For oat, harvest should take place when oat plants begin to head out, while the alfalfa is still developing below. Raking the field can cause the oat to shatter, creating problems with mixtures later in the season, so raking should be avoided. Short-stature, midseason oat varieties are recommended with early-fall planting because they mature more closely with the alfalfa and are less likely to lodge. In spring plantings, an early-maturing variety will achieve greater growth by the time alfalfa is ready to harvest.

For berseem clover, yield advantages can be expected for the first three to four cuts in the spring. Longer curing times are required for these high-moisture forage mixtures early in the season, so systems where early cuttings are green chopped or ensiled are better suited than hay production systems.

University of California publication 21594, *Overseeding and Companion Cropping in Alfalfa,* contains detailed information on the risks and benefits of companion cropping as well as specific recommendations to improve the chance of success.

No-Till and Reduced-Tillage Seeding

Interest in reduced-tillage systems for alfalfa is increasing; however, research and experience are limited in California. Alfalfa is commonly grown in rotation with silage crops (corn and winter forage) that require heavy equipment at harvest. The greatest concern regarding no-till or reduced-tillage systems is the ability of alfalfa to form a deep taproot without tillage to break up traffic compaction from the previous crop(s). In addition, experience with no-till planting of alfalfa into residues of other crops is limited. Furthermore, alfalfa is typically seeded at drill spacings that are narrower than the 7.5-inch (19-cm) spacing that is common on most no-till drills.

There is, however, a growing experience base for establishing crops into older, retiring alfalfa plantings using no-till and strip-till techniques. Growers in Arizona have successfully established no-till, late-planted, double-cropped cotton into alfalfa. Strip-tillage ahead of corn planting has been investigated in several San Joaquin Valley dairy forage production fields with success. Strip-till implements typically include a cutting coulter that cuts residues ahead of a sub-soiling shank that is followed by some type of clod-breaking implement.

The majority of soil compaction research has been done on tillage systems. Soil is compacted to a significantly lesser degree under established no-till systems than under standard tillage systems. Strategies have been identified for the critical and often difficult transition

> *The greatest concern regarding no-till or reduced-tillage systems with alfalfa is the inability to correct long-term soil conditions, including subsurface impediments and surface re-leveling.*

period to no-till. The objective is to maintain yields while allowing the soil to build humus and regain its structural stability so that it will reestablish pore space and be able to resist greater compaction forces over the long term. Over time, soil under no-till management tends to have higher soil organic matter in the surface layer, higher biological activity, including earthworms, and a firm but resilient soil matrix with macropores for air and water movement that better supports traffic than does tilled soil.

Research suggests that soil compaction can still be a significant problem in no-till systems. A number of preventive, as well as remediating, management strategies have been identified to assist in the transition from tillage to no-till and to prevent compaction in no-till systems. Before converting to no-till, an evaluation of the soil profile for yield-limiting compaction should be conducted using an inexpensive soil penetrometer, or by examining root growth. If root growth is restricted or flattened, there may be potential for yield loss if the situation is not corrected. Vertical tillage implements that loosen the compacted soil layer, but that also preserve residues and macropore systems in surface layers, can be used. The first principle for avoiding compaction is to limit traffic to times when the soil is dry. Other considerations for avoiding soil compaction include using dual-wheeled or track-type tractors, taking weights off tractors, and using GPS guidance systems to achieve controlled traffic farming. However, controlled-traffic, conservation-tillage, dairy-forage production systems have not been fully developed or tested in California.

Special Problems During Stand Establishment

Crusting

If a crust forms on the soil surface after irrigation or rainfall, light irrigations may be required to soften the crust and permit seedlings to emerge.

Seed Washing

When flood irrigating a stand to germinate seeds, the force of the water may wash seed from around valve or gated pipe openings. Installing baffles around valves or socks at open gates can minimize this problem.

Seedling Diseases

Seedling diseases are a major consideration during the initial period of stand establishment, especially on heavy soils and under cold conditions. Pre-emergence damping-off by soil-borne fungi such as *Fusarium* sp., *Pythium* sp., and Phytophthora and Rhizoctonia root rots appears to be the most significant seedling disease of alfalfa during stand establishment. There are fungicides available, most often included in seed coatings, that may reduce losses from some seedling diseases; however, they are rarely economical. Most growers plant at high enough seeding rates to compensate for some loss resulting from disease. Planting alfalfa in well-drained soils is the best way to reduce the incidence of these "wet-soil" diseases.

Sclerotinia stem and crown rot, also called white mold, cannot be controlled by fungicides applied to the seed or seedling. This disease can be severe in some areas if the winter is wet or foggy. Although the impact of this disease on seedling stands and future productivity has not been measured, growers in some areas are often reluctant to plant alfalfa before late January–early February because of increased risk of infection.

Insects

Another factor worth considering in newly established stands is the Egyptian alfalfa weevil (*Hypera brunneipennis* [Gyllenhal]). Typically, Egyptian Alfalfa Weevil is not a problem in seedling fields; however, early-planted alfalfa that is established and growing by November can be attractive to adult weevils. Females lay eggs during the winter, creating a larvae problem in the spring, just as with established alfalfa. Monitoring weevil populations in early fall-planted alfalfa fields is especially important. Blue alfalfa aphid (*Acyrthosiphon kondoi* Shinji), pea aphid (*Acyrthosiphon pisum* [Harris]), and cowpea aphid (*Aphis craccivora* Koch) may be a problem in the spring on fall-planted stands. Growers are urged to check fields for the presence of these aphids.

Weeds

Weeds compete with alfalfa for light, nutrients, and water (Fig. 4.8). Depending on the planting date, the environment may be more favorable for weed growth than for alfalfa growth. If weeds are not controlled, they can prevent establishment of the alfalfa and reduce overall productivity and profitability of the stand. Seedling weed control techniques are fully covered in Chapter 8, "Weed Management."

Autotoxicity

Overseeding alfalfa into depleted stands or seeding a new stand into a field where alfalfa has just been removed is usually unsuccessful. When seeding into existing stands, competition may be the major factor that limits seedling establishment, but other factors, such as high levels of pathogenic organisms in the soil and autotoxicity, may also contribute. In fields with a recent history of alfalfa, pathogens and autotoxicity are thought to be most common factors responsible for establishment problems.

Autotoxicity occurs when a plant or plant substance inhibits the growth of other plants of the same species. In research trials, alfalfa extracts significantly increased the number of days to germination, reduced percent germination, and reduced root and shoot length of alfalfa. The toxic substance produced by alfalfa is medicarpin. Autotoxicity is only a factor when alfalfa is being reseeded into an existing stand or in a field where alfalfa has recently been removed.

> *Overseeding alfalfa into depleted stands or seeding a new stand into a field where alfalfa has just been removed is usually unsuccessful.*

FIGURE 4.8

The endpoint of the stand establishment process: a weed-free stand of vigorously-growing alfalfa seedlings. See Chapter 8, "Weed Management in Alfalfa," for a thorough discussion of weed control during establishment.

The degree to which autotoxicity becomes a limiting factor in new stand establishment depends on the age and density of the previous stand. An older stand with high plant density will exhibit greater autotoxicity than either a failed new seeding or an older, sparse stand. Another factor influencing the extent of autotoxicity is the amount of residue incorporated into the soil at the time of stand removal. Medicarpin is water-soluble and is released from the decomposing crop residue. Large amounts of residue result in high concentrations of medicarpin.

A suitable interval must be observed between removal of an existing alfalfa stand and establishment of a new stand, but there is considerable debate as to how long this interval should be. The necessary interval varies with environment, soil, and management. Weather conditions influence the rate at which medicarpin breaks down. Warm, moist soil conditions enhance the breakdown of medicarpin. Some researchers report no autotoxicity problems when a 2–3 week interval exists between plowing or chemically removing the stand and seeding a new stand. In arid climates, the general recommendation is to plant an intervening crop before attempting to establish a new stand of alfalfa where an old one has just been removed. One strategy is to remove the existing stand in the fall, plant a winter forage or cereal crop in the winter, and plant alfalfa again in the spring. An even better strategy is to follow the winter crop with a summer annual, postponing establishment of a new alfalfa stand until September–October, when conditions are optimal.

Frost

Alfalfa seedlings have good frost tolerance at emergence and after the third trifoliolate leaf has developed. There is an intermediate period, during the first and second trifoliolate leaf stages, when alfalfa seedlings are more sensitive to cold temperatures. Therefore, planting early enough to allow time for development to the third trifoliolate leaf stage before the first frost is important. Alfalfa plants will generally survive freezing temperatures if a crown has developed. This allows the plant to store carbohydrates in the roots for winter survival and spring regrowth.

Evaluating Stand Establishment

A seedling stand should not be removed if there is a uniform population of at least 12 plants per square foot (0.09 m²), although 20 plants per square foot (0.09 m²) is generally a better initial population. Root size, crown size, and the number of stems per crown should increase annually, compensating for the reduced number of plants, provided the alfalfa is not stressed by short cutting intervals. It is important to reseed thin or bare areas in a newly seeded field as soon as possible to improve the chance of the new seedlings surviving.

Attempting to thicken an established stand by reseeding thin areas is rarely effective. The seeds may germinate, but seedlings seldom survive to contribute to yield in an established stand because of competition, flooding, disease problems, and autotoxicity. It is important to identify the reason the stand was lost before attempting to reseed. If plants died because of disease or flooding, for example, at the end of a check, the condition must be corrected before new seedlings would be able to survive.

Although the point at which established stands should be removed is somewhat dependent on crown size, generally when five or fewer plants per square foot (0.09 m²) remain, fields become weedy, are less productive, and should be removed. Recent research in Wisconsin suggests that the number of stems per square foot is a better means to evaluate productivity of alfalfa stands than the number of crowns. Results recommended replacing stands with fewer than 40 stems per square foot (measured at 6 inches [15.2 cm] of regrowth) and maintaining stands with 55 stems per square foot (0.09 m²) or more.

Adequate stand density for optimal production

End of Production Year	# Plants per ft² (0.09 m²)
1	10–20
2	8–12
3	6–9

First Harvest After Planting

Alfalfa plants need to be well established before taking the first harvest. Surplus carbohydrates produced during photosynthesis are stored in the alfalfa taproot, providing energy for regrowth following a cutting. Sufficient root reserves must be available or regrowth may be retarded and yield may be impacted. Growers often rely on the appearance of bloom to determine the appropriate timing for first harvest, but it is important to also evaluate root growth. Roots should be well established before initiating traffic on the stand. If it is questionable whether the stand is ready, err on the side of caution. If early cutting is necessary, allow extra time before the second cutting to ensure that root reserves have been replenished.

Additional Reading

Canevari, W.M., D.H. Putnam, W.T. Lanini, R.F. Long, S.B. Orloff, B.A. Reed, and R.V. Vargas. 2000. Overseeding and companion cropping in alfalfa. University of California Division of Agriculture and Natural Resources, Oakland. Publication 21594.

Hall, M.H., J.A. Jennings, and G.E. Shewmaker. 2004. Alfalfa establishment guide. Forage and Grazinglands Online, http://www.plantmanagementnetwork.org/pub/fg/management/2004/alfalfa/.

Marble, V.L. 1990. Factors to optimize alfalfa production in the 1990s. Pp. 4–45 in: Proceedings, 20th California Alfalfa Symposium. December 6–7. Visalia, CA.

Mathews, M.C., and C.A. Frate. 1995. Establishing excellent stands in early fall using flood or sprinkler irrigation. Pp. 17–21 in: Proceedings, 25th California Alfalfa Symposium. December 7–8. Modesto, CA.

Mueller, S.C. 1992. Stand establishment. Pp. 16–20 in: Central San Joaquin Valley Alfalfa establishment and production, S.C. Mueller, C.A. Frate, and R. Vargas, eds. University of California Cooperative Extension, Fresno County, CA.

Schmierer, J.L., S.B. Orloff, and R.W. Benton. 1995. Stand establishment. Pp. 9–19 in: Intermountain alfalfa management, S. B. Orloff and H.L. Carlson, eds. University of California Division of Agriculture and Natural Resources, Oakland, CA. Publication 3366.

Tesar, M.B., and V.L. Marble, 1988. Alfalfa establishment. Pp. 303–332 in: Alfalfa and alfalfa improvement, A.A. Hanson, D.K. Barnes, and R.R. Hill, Jr., eds. American Society of Agronomy, Madison, WI. Publication 29.

Teuber, L., J. Jernstedt, and K. Foord, 1988. Alfalfa growth and development. Pp. 39–44 in: Proceedings, 18th California Alfalfa Symposium. December 7–8. Modesto, CA.

Wildman, W. E., 1981. Effects of different tillage operations on problem soils. Pp. 27–36 in: Proceedings, 11th California Alfalfa Symposium. December 9–10. Fresno, CA.

5

Choosing an Alfalfa Variety

Daniel H. Putnam
Forage Extension Specialist, Department of Plant Sciences,
University of California, Davis

Steve B. Orloff
Farm Advisor, University of California Cooperative Extension, Yreka, CA

Larry R. Teuber
Professor, Department of Plant Sciences, University of California, Davis

Variety selection is an important decision in alfalfa production, affecting crop yield, crop quality, and pest management. Alfalfa varieties grown under the same conditions may differ up to 30 percent in yield. Returns from a simple process of variety selection can be worth hundreds of dollars per unit of land area. Some growers do not take the trouble to compare varieties and lose thousands of dollars in revenue as a result. They seldom recognize this loss, since deficiencies in varieties are difficult to see without a means of comparison. Because alfalfa is a perennial crop, growers are stuck with their choice for many years.

Selecting an alfalfa variety is a primary step in an integrated pest management (IPM) program for alfalfa. Breeders have successfully developed alfalfa lines resistant to insects, diseases, and nematodes, more so perhaps, than all other crops. Variety selection is often the *only* cost-effective measure for dealing with some insects and diseases. It is important for growers to take advantage of decades of plant breeding that has made pest-resistant, high-yielding, high-quality varieties available.

Many varieties are available, and new ones become available each year. This makes variety selection a challenge. Here, a scientific approach to variety selection that weighs the importance of yield, persistence, quality, and pest resistance is suggested.

What Is an Alfalfa Variety?

An alfalfa variety represents a population of plants consisting of genetically diverse individuals that have been selected for improved traits, such as yield, fall dormancy, forage quality, persistence, and disease and insect resistance. During the past five decades, plant breeders have made remarkable advances using conventional crossing techniques, hybridization, screening methods for specific traits, and more recently, biotechnology. Significant improvements have been made in adapting alfalfa to many environments. These improvements came from selection for fall dormancy and resistance to insects such as aphids and diseases like Phytophthora. In 2005, the first transgenic alfalfa varieties containing the Roundup Ready (RR) biotech trait were commercialized.

Certified seed of over 300 alfalfa varieties (also called cultivars) are actively marketed in the United States, and over a thousand have been produced during the past 50 years. A listing of marketed alfalfa varieties, including their fall dormancy and pest-resistance rating, is maintained by the National Alfalfa and Forage Alliance (www.alfalfa.org). A history of variety releases is maintained by the North American Alfalfa Improvement Conference (www.naaic .org).

Although alfalfa fields appear to be completely uniform from a distance, careful observation indicates considerable plant-to-plant variation. This variation is due primarily to genetic diversity that has been maintained by the inheritance and methods of breeding. Unlike varieties of some species that are composed of genetically uniform plants, alfalfa cultivars are diverse populations of plants (multiple genotypes). Alfalfa is a polyploid (alfalfa plants have four complete sets of chromosomes, whereas most crop plants have two sets), which means that the offspring of alfalfa crosses are much more diverse than most crop species. This genetic diversity has been a major asset, enabling alfalfa varieties to be well adapted over a wide range of environments, and to resist a wide range of insects, diseases, and nematodes to a greater degree than any other crop.

Modern alfalfa varieties, however, are still populations rather than uniform genetic strains. These populations have traits such as yield, fall dormancy, and pest and disease resistance that are significantly different from older, unimproved lines. But individual plants within a variety are not genetically identical. A trait is present in certain frequencies in the population of plants within a variety. This is pertinent, especially to the issue of pest resistance, since some susceptible plants remain in even highly resistant varieties, and some low-yielding plants remain in a high-yielding variety. Understanding the nature of alfalfa varieties as populations of many different types of plants is very important when evaluating variety performance with regard to adaptation, yield, fall dormancy, and pest and disease ratings.

FIGURE 5.1

Seed cost as a percentage of production costs during stand establishment (left) and production costs over 4 years of production (right).

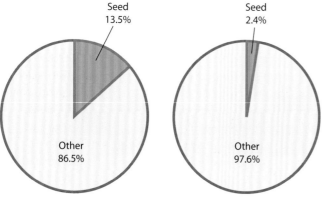

Establishment costs **4-Year production costs**

Economics of Variety Choice

Alfalfa seed cost currently varies between approximately $1.00 and $4.50 per pound ($2–$10 per kg), not including technology fees from biotech traits. However, seed cost is a relatively insignificant part of production costs, generally around 2–3 percent of total production costs over 4 years (Fig. 5.1). One-tenth of a ton (200 lb or 91 kg of hay) improvement in yield per year is all that is required to justify even a $2 per pound ($2.50 per kg) increase in the price of seed (Fig. 5.2). Differences in variety performance in forage yield trials conducted by the University of California and other universities are nearly always many times this amount (Fig. 5.2). An example from the Kearney Research and Extension Center, near Fresno, California, shows that variety choice can gen-

erate hundreds of dollars per acre returns per year compared with planting lower yielding varieties (Fig. 5.3). Although it is true that other characteristics in addition to yield are important, and many factors other than variety may affect performance on growers' fields, it is clear that variety performance, not

FIGURE 5.2

Yield difference (tons per acre per year) required to justify increases in seed price of improved varieties (left) compared with average annual differences between highest and lowest yielding varieties at UC alfalfa variety trials over the past 5–8 years (right). Assumptions: Hay price $130/ton, 20 lb/acre seeding rate, amortized over 4 years. Typically, less than 0.1 tons per acre production is necessary to justify a $2.00/lb increase in seed cost.

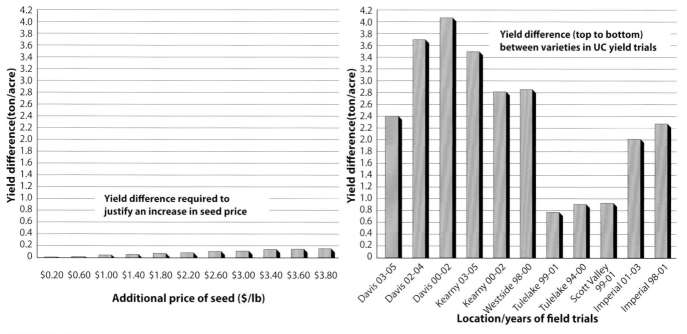

FIGURE 5.3

Potential average *additional* revenue per year resulting from variety choice based on a 3-year variety trial (03–05), Fresno, California. Assumptions: hay at $130/ton. Calculation is based on yield differences resulting from variety only.

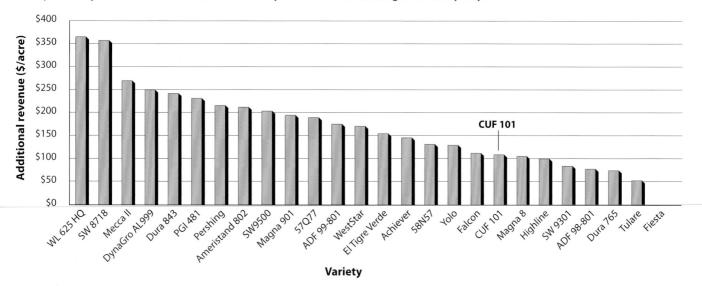

seed price, is the primary economic factor for variety selection. In terms of profitability, the price of seed should be the last criterion by which varieties are chosen.

A Scientific Process for Choosing an Alfalfa Variety

> *A common mistake is to choose a variety based solely on price, habit, or the salesmanship of the dealer.*

Many growers do not give variety selection the careful consideration it deserves. A common mistake is to choose a variety based solely on price, growth habit, or the salesmanship of the dealer. We suggest the following criteria for variety selection, based on the potential for profitability on the farm:

1. yield potential

2. fall dormancy

3. pest resistance

4. stand persistence

5. potential forage quality desired

6. added value of a specific biotech trait

7. on-farm tests of performance

8. price/availability/service

These criteria are in their approximate order of importance, but the significance of each factor will vary depending on a range of factors. These criteria obviously overlap. For example, pest resistance will impact stand persistence and yield. Fall dormancy impacts adaptation, yield potential, and forage quality, as well as stand persistence. However, each of these factors can be evaluated separately, and decisions can be made based on the overall goal of crop production. Finally, a grower should conduct on-farm strip trials to confirm the performance and value of a variety.

1. Choose a Group of High-Yielding Varieties from Yield Tests

Yield is an excellent indicator of the adaptation of a variety to an area and takes into account many other characteristics of the variety, including fall dormancy; insect, pest, and disease resistance; and stand persistence. Yield potential is typically the most important economic factor for growers and thus should be the first consideration for variety selection.

It is nearly impossible to determine the relative yield potential of different varieties without planting them side by side in replicated field trials. Tests done by universities provide unbiased measurements of relative forage yield. These trials typically compare varieties from many private and public sources. The yield of varieties planted side by side under uniform conditions is carefully measured and compared using statistically valid experimental designs. Data are published each year for many different locations in California and made available at http://alfalfa.ucdavis.edu and for other states at http://www.naaic.org/.

Should growers just choose the top line? Although it is tempting to simply select the top yielding variety, there are typically a group of varieties near the top of a trial that should be considered the high-yielding group. It is important to find unbiased data from trials conducted in areas that most nearly represent the soil and environment on your farm. Table 5.1 provides an example of a multiple-year yield summary for alfalfa varieties from trials conducted at the Kearney Research and Extension Center, Fresno County, California. Yield values followed by the same letter should be considered statistically equivalent (Table 5.1). This "high-yielding group" is often the top one-fourth to one-third of the varieties in the trial.

Seasonal trends. Some varieties yield more during the first cuttings of the year (spring), and less during the summer period, or visa versa (Fig. 5.4). Generally, the more dormant varieties tend to be relatively higher yielding in the spring than the nondormant varieties. These seasonal trends may be important to

TABLE 5.1

Example table showing yield results for released varieties from a multiyear trial conducted at Kearney Field Station, 2003–2005. This trial was planted in May, 2003, so the first-year yields are partial yields. Fall dormancy will frequently have an effect on yield, but there is a range of yields within dormancy groups as well. Generally, the top group A, B, and C should be considered the "top yielding" groups for this area. Up-to-date yield results are available from http://alfalfa.ucdavis.edu and other university Web sources.

Released Varieties	FD*	2003 Yield	2004 Yield	2005 Yield	Average		% of CUF101
		Dry t/a (rank)					
AL999	9	9.0 (1)	12.4(7)	11.9 (5)	11.1 (1)	A**	121.0
WL625HQ	9	8.3 (3)	12.8 (2)	12.3 (1)	11.1 (2)	A	120.9
Sequoia	9	8.0 (8)	12.6 (4)	12.1 (3)	10.9 (3)	A B	118.3
Magna995(DS995)	9	8.4 (2)	12.4 (9)	11.5 (7)	10.8 (5)	A B C D	117.0
Magna901	9	8.1 (6)	12.7 (3)	11.2 (13)	10.7 (6)	A B C D	115.9
CW1010(CW89064)	10	7.8 (13)	12.5 (5)	11.4 (9)	10.6 (8)	A B C D E F	114.8
Meccalll	9	78 (10)	12.4 (10)	11.3 (12)	10.5 (10)	A B C D E F G	114.1
Dura843	8	7.5 (28)	12.1 (11)	11.3 (10)	10.3 (12)	A B C D E F G H	111.9
Westan	8	7.6 (25)	12.0 (13)	10.7 (19)	10.1 (15)	B C D E F G H I	109.6
58N57	8	7.6 (24)	11.6 (17)	10.8 (17)	10.0 (17)	C D E F G H I K L	108.7
Westar	8	8.0 (9)	116 (21)	10.4 (25)	10.0 (18)	C D E F G H I K L M	108.5
Salado	9	8.2 (4)	11.6 (18)	10.1 (30)	10.0 (19)	C D E F G H I K L M	108.4
WL530HQ	8	7.7 (16)	11.2 (26)	10.9 (14)	10.0 (21)	D E F G H I K L M	108.1
CW801 (CW58073)	8	7.7 (18)	11.0 (30)	10.7 (20)	9.8 (22)	E F G H I K L M N	106.6
Magna801fq	8	7.7 (20)	10.9 (32)	10.8 (18)	9.8 (24)	E F G H I K L M N	106.3
59N49	9	7.6 (26)	11.6 (19)	10.2 (29)	9.8 (25)	E F G H I K L M N	106.2
Magna788(DS788)	8	7.6 (22)	11.1 (29)	10.6 (22)	9.8 (26)	E F G H I K L M N	106.2
Pershing	8	78 (11)	108 (35)	10.6 (23)	9.7 (27)	F G H I K L M N	105.6
SW100(SW101)	10	7.7 (21)	11.4 (23)	10.0 (33)	9.7 (28)	G H I K L M N	105.1
CW704	7	7.4 (30)	11.4 (24)	10.3 (27)	9.7 (29)	G H I K L M N	105.1
CW907	9	7.3 (32)	11.1 (28)	10.5 (24)	9.6 (30)	H I K L M N	104.6
ArtesiaSunrise	7	78 (15)	11.2 (27)	9.7 (37)	9.5 (31)	H I K L M N	103.7
FG03-01	8	7.8 (12)	10.9 (34)	9.5 (38)	9.4 (33)	I K L M N	102.0
C-241	5	7.5 (27)	10.4 (38)	10.2 (28)	9.4 (34)	I K L M N	101.8
CUF101	9	7.2 (35)	116 (20)	8.9 (39)	9.2 (36)	K L M N	100.0
Dura765	7	6.8 (40)	10.9 (33)	9.8 (36)	9.2 (37)	L M N	99.5
DelRio	6	7.0 (38)	10.5 (37)	9.9 (35)	9.1 (38)	M N	99.3
WL325HQ	3	7.2 (36)	7.6 (40)	7.9 (40)	7.6 (40)	O	82.1
Mean		7.65	11.49	10.68	9.94		
CV		7.10	10.30	5.90	7.80		
LSD (05)		0.76	1.66	0.89	0.85		

Note: Variety × year interaction is significant. Trial seeded at 25 Ib/acre viable seed on Hanford fine sandy loam soil at UC Kearney Agriculture Center, Parlier, CA.

*FD = Fall dormancy rating reported by seed companies.

**Entries followed by the same letter are not significantly different at the 5% level of probability.

FIGURE 5.4

Seasonal yield pattern (by rank) of alfalfa varieties, example from Davis trial, 2005—harvest is April through October. Some varieties start off strong but yields decline in late summer (variety with final rank of 35), whereas other varieties may start off moderately and develop higher yields later (varieties ranked 1 and 2). Variety ranked 27 produces poorly in the spring, but is high ranking in the fall harvests. Other varieties are more consistent throughout the season (variety rank 22).

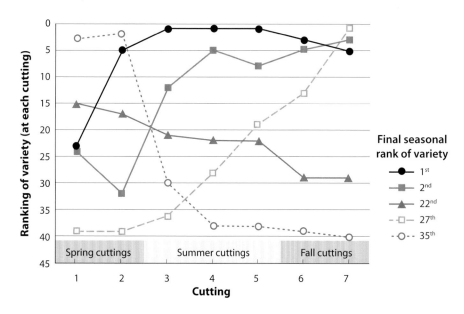

FIGURE 5.5

Over-the-years yield pattern of alfalfa varieties, data from West Side Field Station, Fresno County, California. Some varieties are consistently high or low yielding (varieties with rank 1 and 55, respectively). Others show trends over the years (varieties ranked 14 and 37). Therefore, do not use single-year observations to select alfalfa varieties.

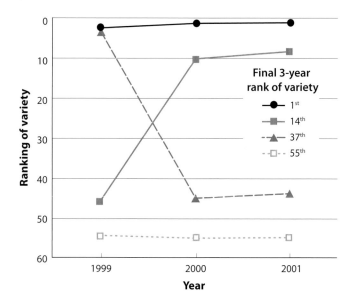

growers who seek high yields during spring when quality tends to be higher, or during summer when hay curing is easier. However, for most growers, high average season-long yields are likely to be more important than seasonal trends.

Importance of multiple-year trials. Because alfalfa is a perennial, it is important to take into consideration data from a number of years to assess yield potential. Never rely solely on the first year of data from a newly planted trial. Some varieties have only moderate yields in the first year but perform much better in the second and subsequent production years to become top-yielding lines (Fig. 5.5). Other varieties may be very high yielding the first year, but fail miserably by the third year of production. Therefore, yield performance over the entire desired stand life is the most important criterion, not just yield for a single season. Generally, we have found that yield trends from a 3-year trial in Mediterranean and desert climates are likely to be good indicators for subsequent years of production.

2. Select an Appropriate Fall Dormancy Rating

Fall dormancy (FD) is one of the most important traits of an alfalfa variety, affecting adaptation, yield, persistence, and quality. Fall dormancy is described and quantified as the degree of growth (plant height) during the fall. Fall dormancy is under genetic control and is a manifestation of the plant's physiological response to cool temperatures and reduced day length. Varieties are rated for fall dormancy by seed companies and independent tests, such as those conducted by UC Davis scientists.

Varieties with fall dormancy ratings (FD) from 1 to 4 are considered dormant, 5 to 7 semi-dormant, and 8 to 11 nondormant. New varieties are compared with standard check varieties to determine their ratings (Fig. 5.6). Nondormant varieties are dramatically taller in the fall and exhibit greater fall and winter growth than dormant varieties grown in a Mediterranean climate (Fig. 5.7). Nondormant varieties may exhibit height differences during other parts of the year as well, but not as pronounced.

FIGURE 5.6

Fall Dormancy of standard check varieties used to rate fall dormancy of alfalfa varieties. In this example, a new variety is measured to be closest in natural plant height under fall conditions to the check variety "Pierce" and thus receives a rating of 8.0.

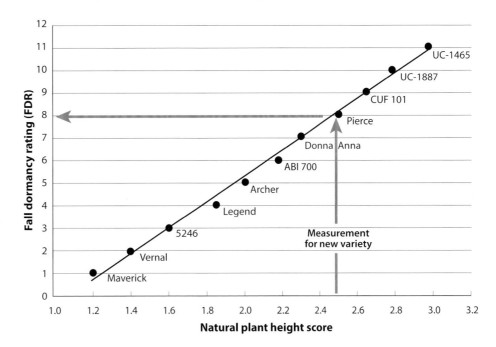

Environment, experience, and the objectives of the grower determine the optimum FD choice. Varieties with higher FD tend to be higher yielding, but this is not always the case. One approach is to choose the highest FD that can survive in a region because those varieties with higher FD tend to be higher yielding. However, quality and long-term stand persistence are also important considerations. Varieties with a higher FD tend to be higher yielding in Mediterranean and desert zones, but may be lower quality and less persistent. Generally, in the northern part of the San Joaquin and Sacramento Valleys (6–7 cut system) semi-dormant and nondormant varieties with FDs of 6–8 are higher yielding, but growers frequently plant FD 3–4 varieties because of their better persistence on heavy soils and higher quality. Varieties with FDs of 7–9 tend to top yield trials in the lower San Joaquin Valley, whereas in the low deserts of the Imperial Valley and Palo Verde Valley, FDs of 8–11 are most commonly grown.

In contrast, dormant or semi-dormant varieties (FD 2–5) are most appropriate for areas with cold winter conditions, such as

FIGURE 5.7

Differences in fall dormancy (FD) in December, Davis, California. The fall dormancy trait of alfalfa is best expressed in fall and winter, but differences in height and regrowth rate can also be seen during spring and summer months.

Intermountain valleys. In these areas, consideration of winter survival characteristics is important (see University of Wisconsin Web site: http://www.uwex.edu/ces/crops/uwforage/alfalfa.htm for uniform trials; and from Tulelake: http://alfalfa.ucdavis.edu). Stand loss in Mediterranean and arid zones is most common in summer and does not seem to be related to winter hardiness.

Fall dormancy is also strongly associated with forage quality. In some regions, growers elect to plant lower FD varieties than those that would produce the highest yield, with the objective of achieving higher-quality forage. This is covered in more detail below.

3. Choose a Variety with the Best Insect and Disease Resistance

Alfalfa has benefited from decades of plant breeding, improving both yield and pest resistance. The first success was the incorporation of bacterial wilt resistance in the 1940s, followed in the 1950s through 1970s with multiple pest resistance to major insects and other diseases, a process that continues today. Recently, varieties with resistance to potato leaf hopper and silverleaf whitefly have been developed, adding these traits to those of resistance to aphids, nematodes, and root diseases developed over the past 40 years. Detailed pest resistance ratings of current varieties are given at the National Alfalfa and Forage Alliance Web site (http://www.alfalfa.org).

It is important to determine the most significant diseases, nematodes, and insect pests in your region to decide what is needed as a pest-resistance package. Recommendations developed from experience over a long period are provided in Table 5.2 to aid in judging the importance of different pests for your region.

It is important to determine the most significant diseases, nematodes, and insect pests in your region to decide the best pest-resistance package.

Different pests are important for different regions and for different soil types. For example, verticillium wilt is more important in the Central and Northern Coastal Regions, High Desert, and Intermountain area, but is not seen in the Low Desert. Phytophthora resistance is especially important on heavy soils or in high-rainfall areas. Resistance to pea aphid, blue alfalfa aphid, and spotted alfalfa aphid is critical for the Low Desert and San Joaquin Valley Regions (Table 5.2).

The importance of pest resistance of alfalfa varieties to an integrated pest management program (IPM) cannot be overemphasized. Diseases or nematodes are seldom controlled effectively by chemical sprays, and variety selection is often the *only* cost-effective method available. Figure 5.8 illustrates the value of variety resistance for pea aphid and for Phytophthora root rot.

Resistance to pests is not absolute. Due to the nature of alfalfa varieties as populations, some plants will remain susceptible even within a highly resistant line. An alfalfa variety that is classified as highly resistant (HR) to a given insect or disease has by definition greater than 50 percent of the plants exhibiting resistance, resistant varieties (R) are those with 35–50 percent of the plants exhibiting resistance, and so on (see below). In some cases, the level of resistance can be influenced by climatic conditions. Temperatures less than 60°F (15°C) reduce the resistance to pea aphid, blue alfalfa aphid, and spotted alfalfa aphid. This is especially important with pea and blue alfalfa aphids, which are cool-weather aphids. Cooler than normal spring temperatures may result in a breakdown of resistance and an increase in

Pest resistance ratings:		% of Plants resistant
HR	Highly resistant	>50
R	Resistant	35–50
MR	Moderately resistant	20–35
LR	Little resistance	5–20
S	Susceptible	<5

NOTE: Pest resistance is determined independently in greenhouse seedling tests. See http://www.naaic.org/ for description of tests.

TABLE 5.2

Suggested fall dormancy ratings and minimum pest resistance ratings for different California climatic zones

Zone	FD	BW	VW	FW	PRR	SAA	PA	BAA	SN	SRKN	NRKN
Intermountain	2-4	R	R	HR	R	S	R	MR	R	R	R
Sacramento Valley	4-8	MR	R	HR	HR	R	HR	HR	HR	R	R
San Joaquin Valley	7-9	MR	R	HR	HR	HR	HR	HR	HR	HR	HR
Coastal	4-8	MR	HR	HR	HR	MR	HR	HR	HR	HR	HR
High Desert	4-8	MR	HR	HR	HR	R	R	R	R	HR	HR
Low Desert	8-11	S	S	HR	HR	HR	HR	HR	HR	HR	HR

FD = fall dormancy; BW = bacterial wilt; VW = verticillium wilt; FW = fusarium wilt; PRR = phytophthora root rot; SAA = spotted alfalfa aphid;
PA = pea aphid; BAA = blue alfalfa aphid; SN = stem nematode; SRKN = southern root knot nematode; NRKN = northern root knot nematode.
HR = highly resistant; R = resistant; MR = moderately resistant; S = susceptible

FIGURE 5.8

Crop vigor and stand can be affected by disease and insect resistance. Photo A shows varieties resistant to (left) and susceptible to (right) pea aphid. Photo B shows varieties resistant to (left) and susceptible to (right) Phytophthora root rot (photo courtesy, Oklahoma State University). Photo C shows selection for Silverleaf Whitefly resistance (UC Impalo WF) in the Imperial Valley of California.

aphid populations, even in so-called resistant varieties.

Resistance to pests should be considered an insurance policy that is an important benefit of improved varieties. Even if a pest is not present each year, resistance may become valuable over the life span of an alfalfa stand. For example, growers in the Sacramento Valley had neglected to select varieties resistant to stem nematode since it hadn't been a problem for years. In 2002–2003, many fields were suddenly infested with stem nematode, leaving many growers wishing they had selected resistant varieties, which is our only cost-effective measure for this pest.

4. Consider Stand Persistence

Most growers in the Central Valley and Imperial Valley of California keep their stands in for 3–4 years before rotating to another crop. Stand loss in these regions is exacerbated by frequent harvests, traffic, summer heat, scald, winter flooding, cold winter temperatures, soil compaction, and soil-borne diseases. Stand loss provides incentives for growers to rotate quickly to another crop rather than keeping stands for longer periods. Although keeping an alfalfa stand in for longer than 4 years may be economically beneficial in some cases, this is not the case if yields are significantly lower in the third, fourth, and subsequent years. This is frequently the case with nondormant varieties.

Generally, more dormant varieties tend to have better stand persistence than do non-dormant varieties, if within their areas of adaptation. However, these varieties also tend to have lower yields in the Mediterranean and desert zones. In the northern Central Valley, varieties with FDs of 8–11 frequently have poor persistence, whereas varieties with FDs of 5–7 last longer. Further south, the yield penalty of the lower FD varieties becomes much higher, and thus these varieties are not recommended. The objectives of the individual grower, whether yield, persistence, or quality, is more important, should be considered to determine which fall dormancy is best. Soils prone to flooding may require more dormant lines, which may tolerate flooded conditions better than nondormant lines.

Diseases, particularly Phytophthora root rot, can be very destructive to alfalfa stands, limiting stand life. Choice of varieties with high resistance (HR) to Phytophthora root rot and to nematodes is an important method for improving stand life.

5. Choosing Varieties to Achieve High Quality

Many agronomic factors affect forage quality—one of which is variety selection. Although varieties may differ in forage quality, agronomic practices, such as cutting schedule and weed control, influence quality to a greater degree than does variety.

The potential forage quality of an alfalfa variety should not be considered without considering yield. In our trials, higher-quality varieties have almost always been lower yielding. There is a yield–quality tradeoff with varieties, just as there is with cutting schedules (see Chapter 13, "Harvest Strategies for Alfalfa"). Therefore, we recommend that growers balance yield and quality factors and consider the importance of both.

Although varieties may differ in forage quality, agronomic practices, such as cutting schedule and weed control, influence quality to a greater degree than does variety.

Fall dormancy has a profound effect on forage quality. At UC Davis, it was found that each unit decrease in FD caused an average of 0.6 percentage unit decrease in ADF, a similar decrease in NDF values, and a 0.6 percent increase in crude protein, averaged across 3 years and three cutting schedules, all harvests (Fig. 5.9). However, the yields of the more dormant varieties were much lower, an average of 0.66 tons/acre (1.5 Mg/ha) reduction per unit of FD, than the nondormant varieties (Fig. 5.9).

Economics of the yield–quality tradeoff.
To choose a variety for quality, one must be prepared to accept the yield loss that typically results from such a choice. Although it is tempting to think that variety selection is a magic bullet to deliver a higher-quality product, it is more often a compromise between yield, quality, and stand persistence. This can be managed to some degree by comparing the yield differences between varieties with their probable increased value from higher quality (Table 5.3). For example, if two varieties differ by 2 tons per acre per year (4.48 Mg/ha), it would be necessary to improve the price per ton of the lower yielding variety by 33 percent at an 8 ton (7.25 Mg) yield level (Table 5.3). If there are forage quality data to give a grower confidence that this will occur, choose the higher-quality (but lower-yielding) variety. If not, select the higher-yielding variety. Examples of yield–quality tradeoff result-

FIGURE 5.9

Fall dormancy effects on ADF and yield of alfalfa varieties, Davis, California (average of 3 years, three cutting schedules, and three replications, all harvests each year).

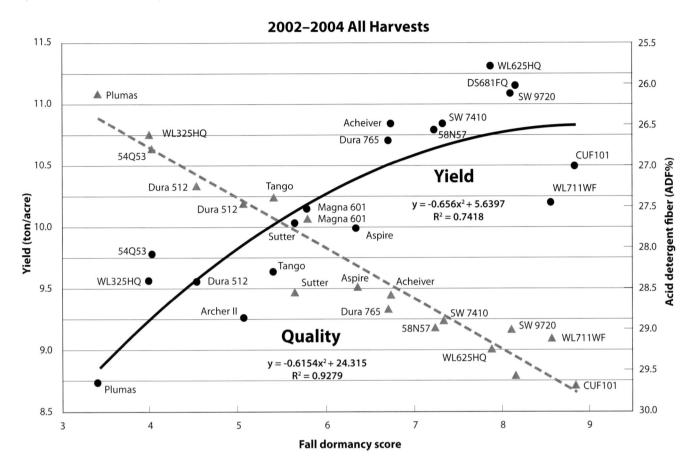

6. Consider Biotech Traits

ing from the FD of a variety are illustrated in Figure 5.9.

In 2005, the first biotech trait in alfalfa was commercialized—Roundup Ready (RR) alfalfa. Several other biotech traits will likely be introduced in the future, traits that may contribute to improved feeding value, pest resistance, or other attributes. The introduction of biotech traits into alfalfa expands the scope of variety selection beyond the factors of yield, quality, persistence, and pest resistance. However, those factors are still of primary importance for variety selection.

Selection of RR alfalfa varieties is fundamentally no different than selection of conventional alfalfa varieties, with the exception of the additional dimensions of weed management and market acceptance of a genetically engineered (GE) crop. RR varieties should be chosen for their yield potential, pest resistance, stand persistence, and quality—just like conventional varieties. Under most circumstances, it is not usually cost-effective to choose a lower-yielding RR variety just to obtain the Roundup resistance trait—this may result in significantly lower returns because of lower yields.

The value and advantages of the RR (or other biotech) trait must be compared economically with the additional costs (or other negative features) of that trait. Purchase of RR alfalfa is a purchase of a weed-control system, not just a variety, and should be thought of in relationship to that system.

TABLE. 5.3

Minimum percentage price improvement required to justify a yield decline due to variety choice or cutting schedule on an annual or a per-cutting basis

Starting Yield t/a	Reduction in Yield (Per Cutting Basis, t/a)									
	0.1	0.2	0.3	0.4	0.5	0.6	0.7	0.8	0.9	1.0
	Minimum Price Improvement Required									
0.4	33.3%	100.0%	300.0%							
0.6	20.0%	50.0%	100.0%	200.0%	500.0%					
0.8	14.3%	33.3%	60.0%	100.0%	166.7%	300.0%	700.0%			
1	11.1%	25.0%	42.9%	66.7%	100.0%	150.0%	233.3%	400.0%	900.0%	
1.2	9.1%	20.0%	33.3%	50.0%	71.4%	100.0%	140.0%	200.0%	300.0%	500.0%
1.4	7.7%	16.7%	27.3%	40.0%	55.6%	75.0%	100.0%	133.3%	180.0%	250.0%
1.6	6.7%	14.3%	23.1%	33.3%	45.5%	60.0%	77.8%	100.0%	128.6%	166.7%
1.8	5.9%	12.5%	20.0%	28.6%	38.5%	50.0%	63.6%	80.0%	100.0%	125.0%
2	5.3%	11.1%	17.6%	25.0%	33.3%	42.9%	53.8%	66.7%	81.8%	100.0%
2.2	4.8%	10.0%	15.8%	22.2%	29.4%	37.5%	46.7%	57.1%	69.2%	83.3%
2.4	4.3%	9.1%	14.3%	20.0%	26.3%	33.3%	41.2%	50.0%	60.0%	71.4%
2.6	4.0%	8.3%	13.0%	18.2%	23.8%	30.0%	36.8%	44.4%	52.9%	62.5%
2.8	3.7%	7.7%	12.0%	16.7%	21.7%	27.3%	33.3%	40.0%	47.4%	55.6%
3	3.4%	7.1%	11.1%	15.4%	20.0%	25.0%	30.4%	36.4%	42.9%	50.0%

Starting Yield t/a	Reduction in Yield (Annual Basis, t/a)									
	0.2	0.4	0.6	0.8	1.0	1.5	2.0	2.5	3.0	3.5
	Minimum Price Improvement Required									
4	5.3%	11.1%	17.6%	25.0%	33.3%	60.0%	100.0%	166.7%	300.0%	700.0%
5	4.2%	8.7%	13.6%	19.0%	25.0%	42.9%	66.7%	100.0%	150.0%	233.3%
6	3.4%	7.1%	11.1%	15.4%	20.0%	33.3%	50.0%	71.4%	100.0%	140.0%
7	2.9%	6.1%	9.4%	12.9%	16.7%	27.3%	40.0%	55.6%	75.0%	100.0%
8	2.6%	5.3%	8.1%	11.1%	14.3%	23.1%	33.3%	45.5%	60.0%	77.8%
9	2.3%	4.7%	7.1%	9.8%	12.5%	20.0%	28.6%	38.5%	50.0%	63.6%
10	2.0%	4.2%	6.4%	8.7%	11.1%	17.6%	25.0%	33.3%	42.9%	53.8%
11	1.9%	3.8%	5.8%	7.8%	10.0%	15.8%	22.2%	29.4%	37.5%	46.7%
12	1.7%	3.4%	5.3%	7.1%	9.1%	14.3%	20.0%	26.3%	33.3%	41.2%
13	1.6%	3.2%	4.8%	6.6%	8.3%	13.0%	18.2%	23.8%	30.0%	36.8%
14	1.4%	2.9%	4.5%	6.1%	7.7%	12.0%	16.7%	21.7%	27.3%	33.3%

How to use this table: This table can be used to estimate short-term and long-term tradeoffs between yield and quality. For example if a "Late" cutting schedule would normally yield 1.4 tons/acre, and a grower wants to cut early for quality, he should require a minimum of 27.3% improvement in price (top part of table) if his yield is reduced by 0.3 t/a by that earlier cutting strategy. If a higher yielding variety has an 8 ton/acre yield potential, a variety that yields 1.5 tons/acre less should return a minimum of 23.1% greater price through improved quality to justify choosing that variety.

In addition to cost issues, growers should consider the degree of success of their current weed-control strategies and market considerations. Most experts believe that the majority of alfalfa markets will not be sensitive to the RR trait. However, there are some markets that will not accept RR alfalfa or varieties with other biotech traits. Certification for organic alfalfa requires that no biotech traits (and no herbicides) be used, which disallows use of RR alfalfa varieties. Exporters have generally required that alfalfa for export be non-biotech. A full discussion of the RR trait and the methods to assure coexistence of biotech and nonbiotech traits is provided elsewhere (see Van Dynze et al., 2004, and Putnam 2006).

7. Conduct On-Farm Strip Trials

On-farm strip trials are valuable to confirm small plot experimental data and to make sure a particular variety will perform well on your farm. With the many soil types and microclimates in California, it is impossible to conduct university or company trials under all the possible conditions. You may want to consult with your Cooperative Extension Farm Advisor before conducting strip trials. It is important to replicate strips over your field (not plant separate fields or split fields in half) because varieties must be observed on the same soil type and under the same management. Plots should be replicated and randomized, if possible. For example, if you wanted to test four varieties, plant randomized checks or strips of each variety. Three replications (each variety planted in three separate strips) should normally be sufficient. Sometimes differences between varieties can be detected by counting bales, but bale weight and moisture are often too variable for precise estimates of yield using this method. Small-plot trials tend to be more accurate, especially if the expected differences are small. Seed companies are also usually very helpful in setting up strip trials on farms. In addition to yield, on-farm strip trials are very useful to assess differences in stand persistence, pest resistance, and traffic resistance.

8. Compare Service, Availability, and Price

The last (and probably least important) aspect of variety selection is price of seed, along with aspects such as service by the seed company. Availability is also an obvious limitation—seed companies change varieties frequently, which is frustrating to growers who wish to have longer-term tests. Service by the seed company is important, since seed salesmen and consultants can provide other advice in addition to variety selection. Do not purchase seed based on habit or what the local seed dealers happen to have on hand. The economics of alfalfa production show that performance, not price, is the key economic factor for variety choice (see Figs. 5.2–5.3), and gains (or losses) of hundreds of dollars per acre (or hectare) may ride on the choice of variety. This becomes more critical as biotech traits are introduced, increasing the importance of performance vs. the price of the seed.

Summary

Growers have benefited from decades of plant breeding that have produced hundreds of alfalfa varieties from which to choose. Variety choice can be quite important economically, returning hundreds of dollars per acre (or hectare) with a small investment in time and attention. Performance is much more important economically than seed cost, as improved seed can provide economic returns manyfold times the additional cost. A systematic approach to variety selection, which takes into account yield potential, fall dormancy, pest resistance, stand persistence, forage quality, and biotech traits will enable growers to find the best possible varieties for their ranch.

Additional Reading

American Alfalfa and Forage Alliance. Variety Leaflet. Current listing of varieties marketed in the U.S., with fall dormancy ratings and pest resistance ratings. http://www.alfalfa.org/.

North American Alfalfa Improvement Council. Listing of variety releases, nationwide variety testing sites, and standardized evaluation methods. http://www.naaic.org/.

Putnam, D.H. 2006. Methods to enable co-existence of diverse production systems involving genetically-engineered alfalfa. University of California Division of Agriculture and Natural Resources, Oakland. http://alfalfa.ucdavis.edu.

Putnam, D.H., S.B. Orloff, and L.R. Teuber. 2005. Varieties and cutting schedules affect the yield quality tradeoff. Proceedings, California Alfalfa and Forage Symposium, December 12–15. UC Cooperative Extension. http://alfalfa.ucdavis.edu.

University of California Alfalfa Workgroup Web site Variety Trial Reports. Includes current data, and a searchable database of more than 30 years of UC variety trials. http://alfalfa.ucdavis.edu/+producing/variety.html.

Van Dynze, A., D.H. Putnam, S. Orloff, T. Lanini, M. Canevari, R. Vargas, K. Hembree, S. Mueller, L. Teuber. 2004. Roundup Ready alfalfa: an emerging technology. University of California Division of Agriculture and Natural Resources, Oakland. http://anrcatalog.ucdavis.edu.

6

Alfalfa Fertilization Strategies

Roland D. Meyer
Cooperative Extension Specialist Emeritus, Department of Land, Air, and Water Resources, University of California, Davis

Daniel B. Marcum
Farm Advisor, University of California Cooperative Extension, McArthur, CA

Steve B. Orloff
Farm Advisor, University of California Cooperative Extension, Yreka, CA

Jerry L. Schmierer
Farm Advisor, University of California Cooperative Extension, Colusa, CA

P roviding an adequate supply of nutrients is important for alfalfa production and is essential for maintaining high and profitable yields. However, supplying proper plant nutrition requires complex and often difficult management decisions. The process includes an analysis of which nutrients are needed, selection of the proper fertilizer, application rate, timing and placement, economics, record keeping, and environmental considerations. This chapter serves as a guide to alfalfa fertilization in the arid and semi-arid alfalfa production regions of the world, which include the Sacramento, San Joaquin, and Imperial Valleys of California, and coastal valley regions of the state. Information on appropriate methods of sampling alfalfa and interpreting soil and tissue tests are included.

Before applying fertilizer to alfalfa, consider other factors that may limit yield. It makes little sense to apply fertilizers when another factor is more limiting to plant growth. For example, an application of phosphorus, even when phosphorus is deficient, may not increase yields if water is not sufficient to allow plants to grow in response to the applied fertilizer.

Since historical trends help with management decisions, thorough, well-organized records of plant tissue and soil-test information are important. Records should include information about date of sampling; crop yield and fertilizer application history; and, most importantly, the location of the samples. The advent of GPS (global positioning system) technology provides for accurate location of where samples are taken, allowing the sampler to return to the same location for future sampling.

TABLE 6.1

Common nutritional and fertilizer requirements of alfalfa in arid and semi-arid regions

Element Needed	Symbol	Fertilizer Required[a]
Nitrogen	N	Seldom
Phosphorus	P	Frequently
Potassium	K	Less frequently
Calcium[b]	Ca	Never
Magnesium	Mg	Less frequently
Sulfur[c]	S	Less frequently
Iron	Fe	Never
Manganese	Mn	Never
Chlorine	Cl	Never
Boron	B	Seldom
Zinc	Zn	Never
Copper	Cu	Never
Molybdenum[d]	Mo	Less frequently
Nickel	Ni	Never
Cobalt[e]	Co	Never

a. Frequently: 25% or more of the acreage shows need for fertilization with this nutrient. Less frequently: Less than 25% of the acreage shows need for fertilization.

   Seldom: Less than 1% of the acreage shows need for fertilization.

   Never: A deficiency has never been reported or observed.

b. Liming materials containing calcium are used for pH amendment of acid soils.

c. Various forms of sulfur are used for soil salinity management.

d. Needed in Sacramento Valley but may be in excess in San Joaquin and Imperial Valleys and coastal valleys.

e. Necessary for nitrogen fixation only.

Essential Plant Nutrients

Seventeen elements are needed, in varying amounts, for plant growth (see Table 6.1). Carbon, hydrogen, and oxygen come from water and from carbon dioxide in the air. The other 14 elements are obtained from either the soil or fixation of atmospheric nitrogen by bacteria in root nodules. Another nutrient, cobalt, is essential to legumes for nitrogen fixation. Growth slows or stops when a plant is unable to obtain one or more of the essential elements. Thus, all nutrients must be available to the plant in adequate quantities throughout the production season. The nutrients that are most commonly in short supply for alfalfa production are phosphorus, followed by potassium, sulfur, molybdenum, and boron (Table 6.1).

Diagnosis of Nutrient Deficiencies

A key aspect of designing a fertilization program is evaluating the nutritional status of the alfalfa crop. Nutritional status can be evaluated by visual observation, soil analysis, or plant tissue testing. Using all three in combination provides the best results.

Visual Observation

Nutrient deficiencies may be expressed as visual plant symptoms, such as obvious plant stunting or yellowing. Table 6.2 summarizes visual symptoms of common deficiencies (also see Color Plates 6.1 through 6.7 at the end of this chapter). Unfortunately, visual symptoms are seldom definitive and can be easily confused or mistaken for symptoms caused by other factors, such as insect injury, diseases, excess water, salt or water stress, restricted root growth, or rodent damage. Additionally, significant yield losses may have already occurred by the time the symptoms appear. Thus, visual diagnosis should always be confirmed with laboratory analysis or test strips with selected fertilizers.

Soil and Tissue Testing

Both soil and plant tissue test results are used to detect plant nutrient deficiencies. These two tests differ in their ability to reliably diagnose nutrition problems in alfalfa (Table 6.3). To fully understand and correct problems, test both soil and tissue.

Soil Testing

Soil tests provide an estimate of nutrient availability for uptake by plants and are most useful for assessing the fertility of fields prior to planting. Soil sampling methods are critical, since soil samples must adequately reflect the nutrient status of a field. Although a single representative sample of an entire field provides an average value, it is not the best way to develop recommendations for parts of the field that are less productive. The best technique is to divide each field into two or three areas, representing good, medium, and poor alfalfa growth areas. Studying soil maps of a field may be helpful, but delineating these production areas based on variations in plant growth is more effective. Within each area, establish permanent benchmark locations measuring approximately 50 × 50 feet (15 × 15 m) (Fig. 6.1). To ensure that you will be able to find each benchmark area again, describe it in relation to measured distances to specific landmarks on the edge of the field or with the help of global positioning systems. By using this method to collect soil and plant tissue samples, a grower will be able to compare areas of the field with different production levels, develop appropriate management responses, and track changes over the years.

The best time to sample soil is soon after irrigation or rainfall, when the probe can easily penetrate the moist soil. Before taking a soil sample, remove debris or residual plant material from the soil surface. The sample can be taken with a shovel, but a hollow, open-faced

TABLE 6.2

Nutrient deficiency symptoms observed in alfalfa

Deficiency	Symptoms
Nitrogen	Generally yellow, stunted plants
Phosphorus	Stunted plants with small leaves; sometimes leaves are dark blue-green
Potassium	Pinhead-size yellow or white spots on margins of upper leaves; on more mature leaves, yellow turning to brown leaf tips and edges
Sulfur	Generally yellow, stunted plants
Boron	Leaves on the upper part of plant are yellow on top and reddish purple on the underside; internodes are short
Molybdenum	Generally yellow, stunted plants

TABLE 6.3

Relative reliability of soil and plant tissue testing for nutrient deficiency

Nutrient	Soil Testing	Tissue Testing
Phosphorus	Good	Excellent
Potassium	Good	Excellent
Sulfur	Very poor	Excellent
Boron	Poor	Excellent
Molybdenum	Not recommended	Excellent

FIGURE 6.1

Recommended soil and plant tissue sampling procedures involve establishing permanent benchmark sampling locations (50 × 50 feet or 5 × 5 m) within areas of the field that support good, medium, and poor alfalfa growth. Define these benchmark areas in relation to measured distances to specific landmarks on the edge of the field or use global positioning systems.

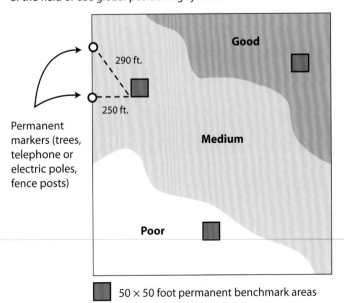

■ 50 × 50 foot permanent benchmark areas

tube, such as an Oakfield soil probe, is preferred. Sample the top 6–8 inches (15–20 cm) of soil unless a salt problem or an acidic soil is suspected. If this is likely, then the second foot (12–24 inches [30–60 cm]) and even the third foot (24–36 inches [60–90 cm]) should also be sampled. Take 15 to 20 cores at random from each benchmark area and mix them thoroughly in a plastic bucket to produce a single 1-pint (0.47 L) composite sample for each benchmark area. Since there is usually less variability, only 8 to 12 cores need to be composited for the second- and third-foot samples. Place each sample in a separate double-thick paper bag and air dry the soil at room temperature before mailing to the laboratory. To get a complete assessment of the nutrition status of an alfalfa field, perform all the soil and tissue tests cited in Table 6.4. A list of laboratories is found in University of California Special Publication 3024, *California Commercial Laboratories Providing Agricultural Testing.*

Taking soil samples every year may not be necessary once historical trends have been established. Sampling benchmark areas every time alfalfa is planted is usually sufficient to establish trends. If poor alfalfa growth is observed in other parts of the field, take samples from both good and poor growth areas so the fertility level of the two areas can be compared. Table 6.5 lists guidelines for interpreting soil test results with values given for deficient, marginal, adequate, and high levels. An economic yield response to fertilizer application is very likely for values below the deficient level, somewhat likely for values in the marginal level, and unlikely for values over the adequate level (Table 6.5).

> *Plant tissue testing…by far the most precise method of determining the nutrient needs of alfalfa.*

TABLE 6.4

Suggested tests for a complete examination of soil and alfalfa tissue

Soil	Plant Tissue
pH[a]	Phosphorus (PO_4–P)
Phosphorus	Potassium
Potassium	Sulfur (SO_4–S)
EC_e[a]	Boron
Calcium, Magnesium, Sodium[a]	Molybdenum
SAR[a]	Copper

a. These tests evaluate factors that affect the availability of nutrients and the presence of undesirable salt levels. EC_e = electrical conductivity of saturated paste extract (dS/m or mmho/cm); SAR = sodium adsorption ratio.

TABLE 6.5

Interpretation of soil test results for alfalfa production

Nutrient	Extract[b]	Soil Value (ppm)[a]			
		Deficient	Marginal	Adequate	High
Phosphorus	Bicarbonate	<5	5–10	10–20	>20
Potassium	Ammonium acetate	<40	40–80	80–125	>125
Boron	Saturated paste	0.1[c]	0.1–0.2	0.2–0.4	>0.4[d]

a. An economic yield response to fertilizer application is very likely for values below the deficient level, somewhat likely for values in the marginal range, and unlikely for values over the adequate level.

b. Soil test values are based on use of the cited extract; values for other extracts are different.

c. Soil testing is not a suitable method to diagnose a deficiency. Use a plant tissue test.

d. Possible toxicity to sensitive crops, such as cereals.

Plant Tissue Testing

The most precise method of determining the nutrient needs of alfalfa is plant tissue testing. Although soil tests are helpful, plant tissue tests are the best reflection of what the plant has taken up and are far more accurate than soil tests, particularly for sulfur, boron, and molybdenum. Plant tissue tests are useful in monitoring nutritional status and evaluating the effectiveness of current fertilization practices.

The best time to take a tissue sample is when the crop is at the one-tenth bloom growth stage or when regrowth length measures ¼–½ inch (0.6–1.3 cm). Since alfalfa is often cut before one-tenth bloom (e.g., bud stage) to attain high-quality forage, preliminary research results indicate that phosphorus concentration should be 1,200 ppm PO_4–P at mid-bud and even higher, 1,600 ppm, at very early bud stage. Other nutrient concentrations should be approximately 10 percent higher than when sampled at the one-tenth bloom growth stage. Samples can be collected at any cutting, but collection at first cutting is preferred because it is the best time to detect a sulfur deficiency. Collect 40 to 60 stems from at least 30 plants in each of the same benchmark areas from which the soil samples are collected.

Different plant parts are analyzed for different nutrients (Fig. 6.2). Cut each sample into three sections of equal length. Discard the bottom one-third; place the top one-third in one paper bag and the middle one-third in another. Dry the samples in a warm room or oven. After drying, separate leaves from stems in the middle one-third sample by rubbing the sample between your hands. Put leaves and stems into separate bags. Figure 6.2 and Table 6.6 list the analyses that should be performed on the samples. Table 6.6 gives guidelines for interpreting plant tissue-test results. The top 6 inches (15 cm) or one-third of the plant, or even whole plant samples collected from baled hay, can give an approximate concentration of phosphorus, potassium, sulfur, molybdenum,

or boron for nutrient evaluation. Table A in the Appendix (at the end of this chapter) is useful for interpreting these analytical results.

Tissue tests can determine only the single most limiting nutrient affecting plant growth—the concentration of other nutrients may actually increase due to reduced growth. Therefore, correct the most severe deficiency first. After it is corrected, take new plant tissue samples to determine if other nutrients are deficient. Also, low concentrations of a nutrient in plant tissue may not always indicate a deficiency in the soil. Remember that plant analysis reflects nutrient uptake by the plant; a problem affecting roots, such as nematodes, can affect nutrient uptake as well.

Correction of Nutrient Deficiencies

Apply fertilizer to correct nutrient deficiencies after careful consideration of the amount of nutrients removed by alfalfa, the yield potential of the field, current soil and plant tissue-test levels, and historic responses to fertilization. Table 6.7 indicates the amounts of nutrients removed by 6-, 8-, 10-, and 12-ton per acre (13.4-, 17.9-, 22.4-, and 26.9-Mg/ha) alfalfa crops.

FIGURE 6.2

Plant tissue sampling and testing: (A) Collect 40 to 60 stems, including leaves from at least 30 plants. (B) Cut stems into three sections of equal length. (C) Discard the bottom third. Place the top third in one paper bag and the middle third in another. Dry the samples. Separate leaves from stems in middle third by rubbing between hands. Put leaves in one bag and stems in another bag. Analyze top-third sample for boron, molybdenum, and copper. Analyze leaves from the middle third for sulfur (SO_4–S) and the stems from middle third for phosphorus (PO_4–P) and potassium. See Table 6.6 for interpretation of data.

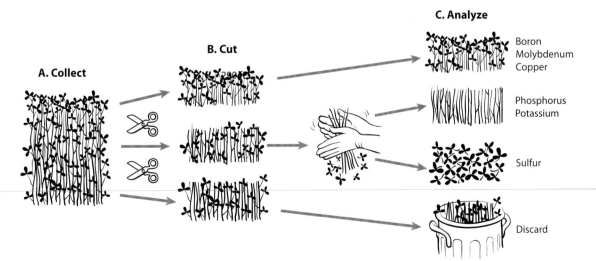

TABLE 6.6

Interpretation of test results for alfalfa plant tissue samples taken at one-tenth bloom

Nutrient	Plant Part	Unit	Plant Tissue Value[a]			
			Deficient[b]	Marginal	Adequate	High
Phosphorus (PO$_4$–P)	Middle third, stems	ppm	300–500	500–800	800–1,500	Over 1,500
Potassium	Middle third, stems	%	0.40–0.65	0.65–0.80	0.80–1.5	Over 1.5[c]
Sulfur (SO$_4$–S)	Middle third, leaves	ppm	0–400	400–800	800–1,000	Over 1,000[d]
Boron	Top third	ppm	Under 15	15–20	20–40	Over 200[e]
Molybdenum	Top third	ppm	Under 0.3	0.3–1.0	1–5	5–10[f]

a. Phosphorus concentration should be higher if alfalfa is cut at bud stage, 1,200 ppm at mid-bud, and even higher, 1,600 ppm, if cut at very early bud stage. Other nutrient concentrations should be approximately 10% higher than when sampled at the one-tenth bloom growth stage (multiply tabular values by 1.10), (ppm = mg/kg).

b. An economic yield response to fertilizer applications is very likely for values below the deficient level, somewhat likely for values in the marginal level, and unlikely for values over the adequate level.

c. Alfalfa having greater than 3% potassium may cause animal health problems, particularly if the magnesium concentration is not greater than 0.25%.

d. Alfalfa having greater than 3,000 ppm SO$_4$–S may intensify molybdenosis in ruminants.

e. A concentration over 200 may cause reduced growth and vigor.

f. A concentration over 10 may cause molybdenosis in ruminants. Copper concentrations should be twice as high as molybdenum concentrations.

TABLE 6.7

Nutrients removed in 6, 8, 10, and 12 tons/acre of alfalfa hay

Nutrient	Symbol	Alfalfa Crop Yield[a]			
		6 ton/acre	8 ton/acre	10 ton/acre	12 ton/acre
		Nutrient Removal, lb/acre			
Nitrogen	N	360	480	600	720
Phosphorus	P (P$_2$O$_5$)	31 (71)	42 (95)	52 (119)	62 (143)
Potassium	K (K$_2$O)	240 (288)	320 (384)	400 (480)	480 (576)
Calcium	Ca	192	256	320	384
Magnesium	Mg	40	53	66	79
Sulfur	S	24	32	40	48
Iron	Fe	2.3	3.0	3.8	4.6
Manganese	Mn	1.5	2.0	2.5	3.0
Chlorine	Cl	1.5	2.0	2.5	3.0
Boron	B	0.4	0.5	0.6	0.7
Zinc	Zn	0.3	0.4	0.5	0.6
Copper	Cu	0.12	0.16	0.20	0.24
Molybdenum	Mo	0.024	0.032	0.04	0.048

a. Nutrient quantities are given on a 100% dry matter basis, (ton/acre × 2.24 = Mg/ha, and lb/acre × 1.12 = kg/ha).

Nitrogen

Applying nitrogen fertilizer to alfalfa is seldom beneficial or profitable. Adequate nitrogen is almost always provided by the symbiotic nitrogen-fixing bacteria (*Rhizobium meliloti* Dang.) that live in nodules on alfalfa roots (Fig. 6.3). *Symbiotic* means that both the plants and bacteria benefit. The alfalfa plants benefit from the nitrogen provided by rhizobia, and the bacteria benefit from the food source (carbohydrates) provided by the alfalfa plants. Because of this relationship, applying nitrogen to alfalfa seldom results in an economic yield response. In those rare cases where nitrogen fertilizer does result in a yield increase, the problem is probably ineffective inoculation or conditions that inhibit or retard the development of the rhizobia (e.g., low soil pH, waterlogged soils, cold conditions, compacted soil, or extremely shallow root zone). Molybdenum and cobalt deficiencies are other possibilities.

Symptoms of nitrogen deficiency include stunted growth and a light green or yellow color. A nitrogen deficiency is suspected when the newly planted field contains stunted or small, yellow plants along with scattered tall, dark-green, inoculated plants (Color Plates 6.2 and 6.3). An examination of the roots usually shows no nodules on the stunted, yellow plants and several nodules on the green, healthy plants. Poor nodulation is often associated with fields having no history of alfalfa production; a low soil pH (<6.3); use of outdated inoculant; or hot, dry seedbed conditions.

The most common cause of nitrogen deficiency is poor inoculation and nodule formation after planting. Proper inoculation is necessary to ensure that alfalfa has an adequate supply of nitrogen. Most alfalfa seed currently purchased has been inoculated; however, if the field being seeded has not had a recent history of alfalfa, it would be desirable to inoculate the seed. For effective nodulation, inoculate seed with fresh inoculant, and do not expose it to hot, dry conditions prior to germination. Inoculants should be kept in cool areas and are preferably refrigerated before use. Inoculation is particularly critical in fields planted to a first crop of alfalfa. Fields with a history of alfalfa plantings seldom have inoculation problems as a result of high residual *Rhizobium* populations from previous crops. Planting pre-inoculated seed in these situations should be adequate to establish good inoculation.

If poor nodulation occurs in a young stand of alfalfa, inoculate seed at two to five times the normal rate, and drill it into the stand at 3–5 pounds seed per acre (3.4–5.6 kg/ha). Follow with a light irrigation. If it is discovered after the alfalfa has been planted that the soil pH is below 6.3, then surface-applied lime at approximately 1 ton per acre (2.24 Mg/ha) may establish inoculation of the alfalfa. Also, it is desirable to apply 40–50 pounds nitrogen per acre (45–56 kg/ha) per cutting to retain stand density until the plants become inoculated. Usually, after the alfalfa has overwintered, all plants in the field will be inoculated.

Light green or yellow plants may also indicate a sulfur or molybdenum deficiency. Use a plant tissue test to identify the specific deficiency. Nitrogen deficiency may also result from a molybdenum deficiency, since molybdenum has a role in nitrogen fixation. Sulfur and molybdenum deficiencies will be discussed later in this chapter.

> *Applying nitrogen fertilizer to alfalfa is seldom beneficial or profitable. Adequate nitrogen is provided by the symbiotic nitrogen-fixing bacteria (*Rhizobium meliloti* Dang.) that live in nodules on alfalfa roots.*

FIGURE 6.3

Nitrogen-fixing nodules are pinkish and easily dislodge from the root.

Phosphorus

Phosphorus is the most commonly deficient nutrient in alfalfa in the Sacramento, San Joaquin, and Imperial Valleys, in coastal California valleys, and in many other alfalfa producing environments in Mediterranean and desert zones. Before planting, use a soil test to assess the phosphorus and potassium needs, as soil tests are fairly reliable for determining the status of these nutrients in the soil (this is not the case for sulfur, boron, or molybdenum). As indicated in Table 6.5, soil with a phosphorus level of less than 5 parts per million (ppm or mg/kg) is considered deficient; soil with 5–10 ppm phosphorus is marginal; and soil with 10 ppm or greater phosphorus is initially adequate. A plant tissue test for phosphorus is preferred over soil testing after alfalfa is established. Phosphorus deficiency is very difficult to identify visually (Color Plate 6.1) because it looks like moisture stress or several other stresses that cause stunted plants with dark leaves.

To correct a phosphorus deficiency, a high-analysis phosphorus fertilizer, such as 0-45-0, 11-52-0, or liquid 10-34-0, is usually the most economical. In alfalfa, these three common phosphorus sources result in the same yield response per pound of P_2O_5 applied. Liquid or granular phosphorus fertilizers with water solubility values greater that 55 percent are nearly equal in terms of plant availability. Rock phosphate, however, is not recommended because of low phosphate availability, particularly when applied to anything other than very acid soils (those with a pH less than 5.5). When higher nitrogen-containing fertilizers, such as 16-20-0 or 18-46-0, are applied prior to or at planting, take care to control weeds because the supplemental nitrogen will stimulate their growth.

Before planting, use soil tests to determine the amount of phosphorus needed (Table 6.8). Incorporate no more than a 2-year supply of fertilizer into the top 2–4 inches (5–10 cm) of soil. Use a double disk to incorporate and mix the fertilizer with the soil. Avoid deep plowing after spreading the fertilizer because this decreases the efficient uptake of phosphorus by the plant. Even if high rates of phosphorus are applied (>200 lb P_2O_5 per acre, [224 kg/ha]), it may be economical to reapply after 2 years. Use plant tissue analysis to determine the need for phosphorus after the seedling year. Applying phosphorus fertilizers on the soil surface in an established stand has been very effective. Apply fertilizer any time, but applications made from October through February are preferred because alfalfa responses to phosphorus fertilizer are not usually observed until 60 to 90 days after application.

Table 6.8 gives a range of application rates because some soils and growing conditions require larger amounts to meet nutritional requirements and maintain high alfalfa yields. Various combinations of phosphorus amounts and application timing can be used to achieve the rates recommended. Recent UC Davis

TABLE 6.8

Recommended phosphorus and potassium application rates based on results of soil or plant tissue tests

Nutrient	Yield Level (ton/acre)	Soil or Plant Tissue Test Result		
		Deficient[a]	Marginal	Adequate
		Application Rate, lb/acre		
Phosphorus (P_2O_5)	8	120–180	60–90	0–45
	12	180–270	90–130	0–60
Potassium (K_2O)	8	300–400	150–200	0–100
	12	400–600	200–300	0–150

a. An economic yield response to fertilizer applications is very likely for values below the deficient level, somewhat likely for values in the marginal level, and unlikely for values over the adequate level (ton/acre × 2.24 = Mg/ha; lb/acre × 1.12 = kg/ha).

research has indicated that fewer applications (at least every 2 years) of higher rates can be applied more economically than lower rates (less than 50 lb P_2O_5 per acre [56 kg/ha]) applied each year. For more efficient use of phosphorus fertilizers, single application rates should not exceed 100–150 pounds P_2O_5 per acre (112–168 kg/ha) and should be applied during late fall or winter prior to alfalfa growth. If higher rates of phosphorus are needed, then apply half in late fall or winter prior to alfalfa growth and the second half after the second or third cutting. Mid-season applications of phosphorus can be injected into the irrigation water provided there is good water distribution and no tailwater leaves the ranch. It can also be applied on the soil surface as either dry granular or a liquid fertilizer before the initiation of much regrowth. Take plant tissue samples 60–90 days after a fertilizer application to re-evaluate the fertility status.

Potassium

Potassium deficiency is less frequent in the Imperial Valley and coastal valleys of California but is often observed on the east side of the Sacramento and northern San Joaquin Valleys, where soils tend to be low in potassium. Like a lack of phosphorus, a potassium deficiency can be diagnosed by either a soil or plant tissue test. The visual symptoms of potassium deficiency are pinhead-size white or yellow spots on new leaves (see Color Plate 6.6). Unlike the symptoms of other nutrient shortages, those of potassium deficiency are distinctive and fairly reliable. Note, however, that genetic differences between alfalfa plants affect symptom development; not all potassium-deficient plants show deficiency symptoms.

The visual symptoms of potassium deficiency are pinhead-size white or yellow spots on new leaves. Unlike the symptoms of other nutrient shortages, those of potassium deficiency are distinctive and fairly reliable.

Also, some insects, such as blue alfalfa aphid, and diseases cause symptoms similar to those of potassium deficiency.

The most economical fertilizer for correcting this deficiency is muriate of potash (0-0-60). Sometimes potassium sulfate (0-0-52, 18% sulfur) is used when sulfur is also deficient. However, compared to muriate of potash, potassium sulfate and other mixed fertilizers are usually more expensive per pound of potassium. Table 6.8 lists recommended potassium rates for both preplant-incorporated and surface applications. Applications on the soil surface are very effective and can be made at any time. For the most efficient use of the potassium fertilizers, single application rates should not exceed 200–300 pounds K_2O per acre (224–336 kg/ha) and should be applied during late fall or winter prior to alfalfa growth, and again if needed after the second or third cutting. Like phosphorus, the growth response to applied potassium may not be observed until 60–90 days after fertilizer application.

Sulfur

Historically, sulfur has only been deficient in alfalfa in the Sacramento Valley and perhaps the east side of the northern San Joaquin Valley. Visual deficiency symptoms include stunting and a light green or yellow color—symptoms that may also indicate nitrogen or molybdenum deficiency (see Color Plates 6.2 and 6.4). Only tissue testing can confirm a sulfur deficiency; soil tests do not provide reliable results. It is important to have an adequate level of available sulfate–sulfur in the soil at the time of planting. Two principle forms of fertilizer sulfur exist: (1) long-term, slowly available elemental sulfur, and (2) short-term, rapidly available sulfate. The most economical practice is to apply and incorporate 200–300 pounds of elemental sulfur per acre (224–336 kg/ha) before planting. Elemental sulfur is gradually converted to the sulfate form and should last 3 to 5 years or longer.

To ensure a multiple-year supply of available sulfur, the particle size of elemental sulfur must range from large to small. Small particles are rapidly converted to the sulfate form; the large particles will continue to release sulfate over several years. Ideally, 10 percent of elemental sulfur should pass through a 100-mesh screen; 30 percent through a 50-mesh screen; and the remaining 60 percent through a 6-mesh screen. Very fine grades of sulfur are readily available but do not persist long enough to provide a multiple-year supply. Fertilizers used to supply the sulfate form of sulfur include gypsum (15–17% sulfur), ammonium sulfate 21-0-0 (24% sulfur), and 16-20-0 (14–15% sulfur).

Gypsum, as well as elemental sulfur and other materials, are often used to aid in water penetration of "low-salt" content irrigation water and reclamation of "high-salt" content soils. Growers may apply from 500 to 1,000 pounds of gypsum per acre (560–1,120 kg/ha) every year or two to accomplish these objectives.

Iron

On rare occasions, growers have observed symptoms of iron deficiency in alfalfa, but only tissue tests have been helpful in confirming the problem. The deficiency produces nearly white or canary-yellow plants in areas where drainage is poor. Iron deficiency in alfalfa is associated with high pH or poorly drained soils high in lime. If the soil pH is greater than 8.0 and free lime is present, begin to correct the iron deficiency by lowering the soil pH using high rates of elemental sulfur (at least 1,000 lb per acre [1,120 kg/ha]). Also, it is important to improve drainage in low areas of the field.

Boron

Although deficiency symptoms are easily identified (Color Plate 6.7), boron deficiency is more effectively confirmed with a plant tissue test. Early stages of boron deficiency are often associated with drought conditions and, in a few cases, potassium deficiencies. Adequate supplies of boron are more important for production of alfalfa seed than for production of alfalfa hay. When tissue tests indicate boron

is deficient and boron-sensitive crops, such as cereals, are likely to be planted in the field within 12 months, broadcast 1–3 pounds of boron per acre (1.12–3.36 kg/ha) on the soil surface. Use higher rates of 3.5–7 pounds per acre (3.9–7.8 kg/ha) if boron-tolerant crops, such as alfalfa, sugarbeets, or onions, will be grown for the next 24 months. Use the lower rates on sandy soils; the higher rates are suggested for fine-textured soils. Higher rates of boron will often provide an adequate supply for 5–7 years. The most common boron fertilizers are 45–48 percent borate (14.3–14.9% boron) and 65–68 percent borate (20.4–21.1% boron). Boron is usually applied as a granular product, either by air or through the small seed box in a grain drill. Some forms can be applied as a liquid along with herbicide applications; make sure the boron and herbicide are compatible before mixing them.

> *Adequate supplies of boron are more important for production of alfalfa seed than for production of alfalfa hay.*

Molybdenum

Molybdenum deficiency is infrequent in the Central Valley, but has been found on the west side of the Sacramento Valley. Generally toxicities of molybdenum are more likely to occur in the San Joaquin and Imperial Valleys and some of the coastal valleys. Symptoms of molybdenum deficiency are like those of nitrogen and sulfur deficiency: light green or yellow, stunted plants (Color Plates 6.2 and 6.5). A positive response to ammonium sulfate fertilizer could mean a nitrogen, sulfur, or molybdenum deficiency. A positive response to urea rules out a sulfur deficiency but could indicate a shortage of nitrogen or molybdenum. Plant tissue testing or applying sulfur and molybdenum fertilizers to separate trial strips are the only means of confirming a molybdenum deficiency.

The most common molybdenum fertilizer is sodium molybdate (40% molybdenum), but ammonium molybdate can be used as well. Apply 0.4 pound per acre of molybdenum (1 pound per acre or 1.12 kg/ha sodium molybdate) during winter or before regrowth has resumed after cutting. Broadcast on the soil surface only and avoid application to any plant foliage. A single application of 0.4 pound per acre molybdenum should last from 5 to 15 years. Thorough records of molybdenum application times and amounts along with repeated tissue testing are essential to determine when to apply or reapply the nutrient.

Do not apply excessive molybdenum (that is, double or triple coverage)—the concentration of the element in alfalfa may become so high that the forage becomes toxic to livestock. For the same reason, do not apply molybdenum directly on foliage. Analyzing the top one-third of the plant for both copper and molybdenum can detect deficiencies and suboptimum ratios of these elements. Consult an animal nutrition specialist if you suspect molybdenum problems.

Record Keeping

Clear and complete records are essential to a successful alfalfa fertilization program. Keep a record for each field and include the location of permanent benchmark sampling areas, dates of sampling, soil and plant tissue test results, fertilizer application dates, fertilizers applied and the rate of application, and crop yields. This information can help you evaluate both the need for and the response to applied fertilizer and allow you to develop an economical, long-term fertilization program.

Additional Reading

DANR Analytical Laboratory. 1991. California commercial laboratories providing agricultural testing. University of California Division of Agriculture and Natural Resources, Oakland. Special Publication 3024.

Kelling, K.A., and J.E. Matocha. 1990. Plant analysis as an aid in fertilizing forage crops. Pp. 603–643 in: R.L. Westerman, ed., Soil testing and plant analysis, 3rd ed. Soil Science Society of America, Madison, WI.

Martin, W.E., and J.E. Matocha. 1973. Plant analysis as an aid in the fertilization of forage crops. Pp. 393–426 in: L.M. Walsh and J.D. Beaton, eds., Soil testing and plant analysis, revised edition. Soil Science Society of America, Madison, WI.

Meyer, R.D., and W.E. Martin. 1983. Plant analysis as a guide for fertilization of alfalfa. Pp. 32–33 in: H.M. Reisenauer, ed., Soil and plant tissue testing in California. University of California Division of Agriculture and Natural Resources, Oakland. Bulletin 1879.

Phillips, R.L., and R.D. Meyer. 1993. Molybdenum concentration of alfalfa in Kern County, California: 1950 versus 1985. Commun. Soil Sci. Plant Anal. 24(19–20): 2725–2731.

Reisenauer, H.M., J. Quick, R.E. Voss, and A.L. Brown. 1983. Chemical soil tests for soil fertility evaluation. Pp. 39–41 in: H.M. Reisenauer, ed., Soil and plant tissue testing in California. University of California Division of Agriculture and Natural Resources, Oakland. Bulletin 1879.

Soil Improvement Committee, California Fertilizer Association. 2003. Western Fertilizer Handbook, 9th ed. Interstate Printers and Publishers, Danville, IL.

Appendix

TABLE A

Interpretation of test results for alfalfa plant tissue samples taken at one-tenth bloom for top 6 inches or one-third of plant samples or whole plant samples collected from baled hay

Nutrient	Unit	Plant Tissue Value[a]			
		Deficient[b]	Marginal	Adequate	High
Top 6 inches or one-third of plant sample					
Phosphorus	%	<0.20	0.21–0.25	0.26–0.70	>0.70
Potassium	%	<1.75	1.76–2.00	2.01–3.50	>3.5[c]
Sulfur	%	<0.20	0.20–0.25	0.26–0.50	>0.50[d]
Boron	ppm	<15	16–20	21–40	>200[e]
Molybdenum	ppm	<0.3	0.4–1.0	1–5	5–10[f]
Whole plant samples collected from baled hay					
Phosphorus	%	<0.20	0.21–0.22	0.23–0.30	>0.30
Potassium	%	<0.80	0.81–1.09	1.10–1.40	1.40–3.00[c]
Sulfur	%	<0.20	0.20–0.22	0.23–0.30	>0.40[d]
Boron	ppm	<15	16–20	21–80	>200[e]
Molybdenum	ppm	<0.3	0.4–1.0	1–5	5–10[f]

a. Phosphorus concentration should be higher if alfalfa is cut at bud stage, 0.26% at mid-bud and even higher, 0.28%, if cut at very early bud stage. Other nutrient concentrations should be approximately 10% higher than when sampled at the one-tenth bloom growth stage (multiply tabular values by 1.10), (ppm = mg/kg).

b. An economic yield response to fertilizer applications is very likely for values below the deficient level, somewhat likely for values in the marginal level, and unlikely for values over the adequate level.

c. Alfalfa having greater than 3% potassium may cause animal health problems, particularly if the magnesium concentration is not greater than 0.25%.

d. Alfalfa having greater than 3,000 ppm SO_4–S, or approximately 0.4% sulfur, may intensify molybdenosis in ruminants.

e. A concentration over 200 may cause reduced growth and vigor.

f. A concentration over 10 may cause molybdenosis in ruminants. Copper concentrations should be twice as high as molybdenum concentrations.

Color Plates

PLATE 6.1

Phosphorus deficiency, although characterized by stunted plants with small leaves, is difficult—if not impossible—to identify visually, because many other problems cause similar symptoms. Contrast the phosphorus-deficient plants (left) with those that received phosphorus fertilizer (right).

PLATES 6.2

Nitrogen, sulfur, and molybdenum deficiencies all cause yellowing and stunting. (A,B,C) These photos illustrate the progressive development of the deficiency and chlorotic leaf symptoms (left) versus healthy leaves (right).

PLATE 6.3

Nitrogen deficiency is evident soon after planting, when seedlings reach 4 to 8 inches (10 to 20 cm) in height, In a field with nitrogen-deficient alfalfa, stunted yellow plants are scattered among taller dark green plants. The yellow plants result from poor inoculation by Rhizobia bacteria; the dark green plants have been adequately inoculated.

PLATE 6.4

Sulfur deficiency can occur at any time or growth stage, but it is most common in spring, when alfalfa starts growing and soils are cold or wet. Contrast the yellow sulfur-deficient plants with the green normal growth where sulfur was applied.

PLATE 6.5

Molybdenum deficiency generally occurs after the first or perhaps second cutting. Regrowth of molybdenum-deficient alfalfa, like that of alfalfa deficient in sulfur, may be extremely yellow and stunted. This photo shows a strip of yellow plants between green plants; the green plants received an application of molybdenum.

PLATES 6.6

(A) The upper portion of this alfalfa stem exhibits potassium-deficiency symptoms. (B) The first symptoms to appear are yellow or white spots, each about the size of a pinhead, near the margins of upper leaves. (C and D) As the plant becomes more deficient, leaf tips and margins become more chlorotic. When leaves mature, the yellow tissue dies and turns brown.

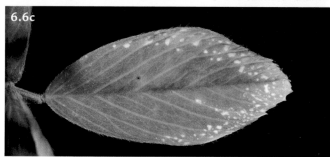

PLATES 6.7

(A) The yellow and reddish chlorotic leaf tips and margins associated with boron deficiency are somewhat similar to potassium-deficiency symptoms. (B) Leaves of boron-deficient alfalfa are reddish purple on the underside, and sometimes on the top. (C) After an irrigation, or when regrowth occurs, a new stem may initiate at the base of the third or fourth leaf from the top of the plant. The new stem appears normal at first, but the internodes (stem segments between leaves) become increasingly shorter. Later, the leaves of the new stem also exhibit boron-deficiency symptoms—yellow on top and reddish purple on the underside.

7

Irrigating Alfalfa in Arid Regions

Blaine R. Hanson
*Irrigation Specialist, Department of Land, Air, and Water Resources,
University of California, Davis*

Khaled M. Bali
*Farm Advisor, University of California Cooperative Extension,
Holtville, CA*

Blake L. Sanden
*Farm Advisor, University of California Cooperative Extension,
Bakersfield, CA*

In Mediterranean and desert regions such as the U.S. Southwest, alfalfa must be irrigated to maximize farm profit. Although there is some dryland alfalfa, more than 90 percent of alfalfa grown in the 11 western U.S. states is irrigated. Good irrigation management is critical to successful alfalfa production, and it requires an understanding of the relationship between crop yield and water and the limitations of different irrigation systems. Properly managing an irrigation system requires knowledge of irrigation scheduling: determining *when* to irrigate, *how much* water to apply, and applying the water with *high irrigation efficiency*. This chapter focuses on methods for managing irrigation water to realize alfalfa yields that maximize farm income.

Evapotranspiration, Applied Water, and Yield

Evapotranspiration

In arid and semiarid environments, alfalfa yield and revenue are related to the amount of water used by the crop. The technical term for crop water use is crop evapotranspiration (ET), water that is evaporated into the atmosphere as a result of producing a crop. It consists of two components, transpiration and evaporation. Transpiration is water taken up by plants that evaporates directly from plant leaves, whereas evaporation is water evaporated directly from the soil. ET is affected by climate, plant type and stage of growth, health of the plant, salinity, and soil moisture content. Climate factors include solar radiation, air temperature, wind, and humidity, with solar radiation by far the most important factor because it provides most

of the energy to evaporate water. ET will be small for a small plant canopy (e.g., just after harvest) and will consist mostly of evaporation because much of the soil is exposed to the sun's rays. As the canopy cover increases, ET becomes primarily transpiration because the mature plant canopy covers most of the soil, slowing evaporation. However, insufficient soil moisture will decrease ET and yield.

The ET of alfalfa depends on time of year and time after harvest (Fig. 7.1). Early in the year, ET is small due to the cool climatic conditions in the spring. ET then increases until midsummer, after which ET decreases with time. There can be considerable variability in ET from day to day due to climate variability, particularly temperature, wind, and solar radiation. Regardless of the time of year, ET decreases just after a harvest (see arrows in Fig. 7.1), then rapidly increases to a maximum level just before the next harvest.

ET can be measured as a depth of water, such as inches, feet, millimeters, or centimeters. Using the depth of water standardizes ET values, regardless of field size. The depth of water is the ratio of the volume of water applied to a field to the area of the field. Depth can be easily converted to volume. The volume of water is normally expressed as acre-inches, acre-feet, or hectare-meters, hectare-centimeters, liters, or megaliters. Thus, 1 inch (25.4 mm) of water is 1 acre-inch of water applied over 1 acre of land (0.405 ha), or 1 acre-inch per acre. One acre-inch of water equals 27,158 gallons (102.8 m³); 1 acre-foot equals 325,900 gallons (1,234 m³). Multiply by 12.33 to convert acre-foot (acre-ft) units into hectare-centimeters (ha-cm).

FIGURE 7.1

Daily evapotranspiration rates of a flood-irrigated alfalfa field, San Joaquin Valley of California. ET of alfalfa is affected by season, but also by harvest and regrowth (harvest dates shown).

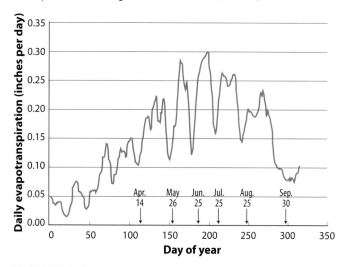

FIGURE 7.2

Effect of seasonal evapotranspiration on alfalfa yield for the San Joaquin Valley of California (Grimes et al. 1992).

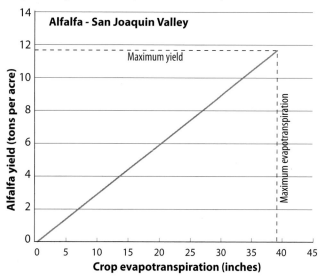

Effect of Evapotranspiration and Applied Water on Crop Yield

Seasonal alfalfa yield is directly related to seasonal ET (Fig. 7.2). Alfalfa yield increases as ET increases, with maximum yield occurring at maximum seasonal ET (determined by climatic conditions). Insufficient soil moisture, the result of insufficient applied water, is usually the reason that ET is less than maximum, which results in reduced yield.

The relationship between applied water and yield may differ from the ET-yield relationship. The effect of applied water on yield can differ throughout the year. Little yield response to applied water may occur for the first harvest simply because stored soil moisture from winter and spring precipitation may be sufficient for crop growth and to satisfy the ET of the crop (Fig. 7.3A). For later cuttings, stored moisture from winter/spring may be depleted; thus, yield increases as applied water increases (Fig. 7.3B,C). However, water applications that exceed the maximum ET or the water-holding capacity of the soil will have no effect on yield, as seen for water applications exceeding 5 inches (127 mm) for the second harvest (Fig. 7.3B).

Seasonal Alfalfa Evapotranspiration

The seasonal ET of alfalfa varies with location. The average historical seasonal ET for various locations in California is 48–49 inches (1219–1247 mm) for the Central Valley, 33 inches (840 mm) for the northeastern mountain areas, and 76 inches (1930 mm) for the southern desert areas (Hanson et al. 1999).

Irrigation Scheduling

Irrigation scheduling involves determining "When should irrigation occur?" and "How much water should be applied?" The answers to these questions are critical for properly managing irrigation water for alfalfa production.

When Should Irrigation Occur?

Irrigate before the yield is reduced by insufficient soil moisture. This requires irrigating frequently enough to prevent excessive soil moisture depletion. A standard approach to irrigation scheduling (called the water balance or checkbook method) is to determine how much soil moisture can be depleted between irrigations without reducing crop yield, then irrigate when total alfalfa ET between irrigations equals that depletion. An allowable soil moisture depletion commonly used for alfalfa

is 50 percent, meaning 50 percent of the available soil moisture can be depleted between irrigations without reducing yield. The interval between irrigations is the number of days required for the total ET to equal that depletion.

FIGURE 7.3

Effect of applied water on alfalfa yield for the first, second, and third harvests. To convert inches to mm, multiply × 25.4.

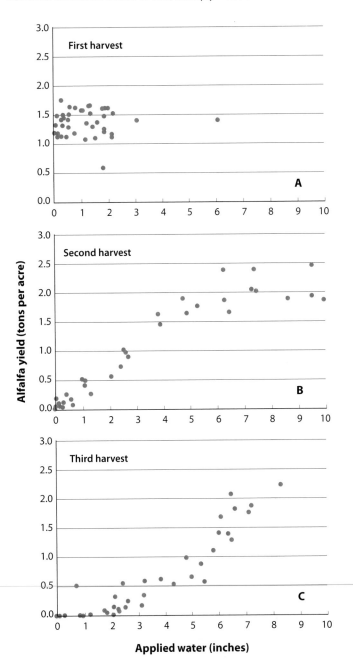

How Much Water Has Been Depleted?

Soil moisture is normally described as inches of water per foot of soil or millimeters of water per meter of soil. The available soil moisture is the total amount of moisture that can be extracted from the soil by a plant root system and depends on soil type and structure and rooting depth. The upper limit for the available soil moisture is the field capacity. This is the maximum soil moisture storage capacity of the soil and is defined as the soil moisture content at which deep percolation ceases after irrigation. The lower limit of available soil moisture is the permanent wilting point (soil moisture content at which permanent plant wilt occurs). Table 7.1 lists available soil moisture for different soil types.

Allowing a plant to use all of the available soil moisture will cause permanent wilting, so only 50 percent of the available soil moisture should be used before irrigation to avoid alfalfa crop stress due to insufficient soil moisture. At the time of 50 percent depletion, calculations of the amount of water that has been used must be made. This amount is the allowable depletion, defined as the amount of soil moisture that can be used without decreasing yield. The total amount of available soil moisture also depends on root depth. The total available soil moisture is determined by multiplying the values in Table 7.1 by the root depth. Thus, for example, from Table 7.1, on a sandy clay soil with a rooting depth of 4 feet, the available soil moisture would be 1.6 inches/foot × 4 feet = 6.4 inches (16.4 cm) available water, and the allowable depletion would be 3.2 inches (8.2 cm) of water in that rooting depth.

Estimating Crop Water Use (ET)

It is important to estimate how much water has been used within a defined period of time (the crop ET) to determine irrigation scheduling (amount and timing). Alfalfa ET can be estimated using Equation 1:

$$ET = K_c \times ET_o \ [\text{Eq. 1}]$$

where ET is crop evapotranspiration, K_c is a crop coefficient, and ET_o is the evapotranspiration of a reference crop, defined as the ET of a well-watered grass. ET_o in California varies from region to region, and is available from the California Irrigation Management Information System (CIMIS) (www.cimis.water.ca.gov).

Although the CIMIS program provides ET_o values on an actual time basis, historical or long-term averages of ET_o can be used for the Central Valley of California with minimal error in ET estimates. Historical values are more convenient to use and allow one to develop an irrigation schedule at the start of irrigation in spring for the entire growing season. Table 7.2 lists historical daily values of ET_o for selected locations in California.

The K_c depends on the alfalfa stage of growth. The K_c is smallest just after a harvest, about 0.4 to 0.5, and reaches a maximum just prior to harvest, about 1.1 to 1.2. However, it is more practical to use average alfalfa K_c values over the season for irrigation scheduling (Table 7.3) because of the difficulty in adjusting the actual coefficient for alfalfa growth due to rapidly changing K_c as the alfalfa grows between harvests. Table 7.3 also contains K_c values for grass hay, clover, and pasture.

Determining the historical alfalfa ET is simplified by using the values listed in Table 7.4 for different areas of California. These values were determined using Equation 1, the ET_o

TABLE 7.1

Available soil moisture for various soil textures. Fine-textured soils (clays, silty soils) hold substantially more water than sandy soils.

Soil Texture	Available Soil Moisture (in/ft*)
Sand	0.7
Loamy sand	1.1
Sandy loam	1.4
Loam	1.8
Silt loam	1.8
Sandy clay loam	1.3
Sandy clay	1.6
Clay loam	1.7
Silty clay loam	1.9
Silty clay	2.4
Clay	2.2

*To convert inches to millimeters, multiply by 25.4. To convert feet to meters, multiply by 0.304.

values in Table 7.2, and the alfalfa crop coefficients in Table 7.3. For irrigators of grass hay, clover, and pasture, ET will need to be calculated using the procedure described in the following section.

Irrigation Scheduling—Determining Timing and Quantity

The procedure for determining when to irrigate based on an allowable depletion is as follows:

Step 1: Determine the total allowable soil moisture depletion by multiplying the available soil moisture in Table 7.1 by the root depth, then multiplying by 0.5 (which is the allowable depletion expressed as a decimal fraction).

Step 2: Determine the daily ET_o for a given time period and location (Table 7.2).

Step 3: Determine the K_c (Table 7.3).

TABLE 7.2

Historical reference crop evapotranspiration (inches* per day) for various alfalfa-growing regions in California

		Low Desert	San Joaquin Valley			Sacramento Valley			Intermountain
		Brawley	Shafter	Five Points	Parlier	Davis	Nicolaus	Durham	McArthur
					(Inches/day)				
Jan	1–15	0.07	0.03	0.04	0.03	0.03	0.03	0.03	0.02
	16–31	0.09	0.05	0.05	0.04	0.05	0.04	0.05	0.03
Feb	1–15	0.10	0.07	0.06	0.06	0.06	0.06	0.06	0.04
	16–29	0.13	0.09	0.09	0.08	0.09	0.09	0.09	0.07
Mar	1–15	0.16	0.11	0.11	0.10	0.09	0.09	0.09	0.08
	16–31	0.19	0.14	0.15	0.13	0.14	0.12	0.12	0.11
Apr	1–15	0.22	0.19	0.20	0.17	0.18	0.15	0.16	0.14
	16–30	0.25	0.20	0.22	0.19	0.20	0.18	0.17	0.14
May	1–15	0.28	0.24	0.26	0.22	0.23	0.21	0.21	0.18
	16–31	0.29	0.26	0.27	0.24	0.24	0.21	0.22	0.19
Jun	1–15	0.31	0.27	0.29	0.26	0.28	0.24	0.25	0.22
	16–30	0.32	0.28	0.30	0.27	0.29	0.26	0.26	0.25
Jul	1–15	0.31	0.28	0.30	0.27	0.29	0.26	0.27	0.27
	16–31	0.29	0.26	0.28	0.25	0.27	0.25	0.25	0.25
Aug	1–15	0.29	0.25	0.28	0.24	0.26	0.24	0.24	0.25
	16–31	0.28	0.23	0.25	0.22	0.24	0.21	0.21	0.22
Sep	1–15	0.26	0.21	0.23	0.19	0.21	0.19	0.19	0.18
	16–30	0.22	0.18	0.20	0.15	0.18	0.16	0.16	0.14
Oct	1–15	0.19	0.16	0.17	0.13	0.16	0.13	0.14	0.12
	16–31	0.15	0.12	0.13	0.09	0.12	0.09	0.10	0.08
Nov	1–15	0.12	0.08	0.10	0.07	0.09	0.07	0.07	0.05
	16–30	0.10	0.06	0.07	0.04	0.06	0.05	0.05	0.03
Dec	1–15	0.07	0.05	0.05	0.03	0.05	0.03	0.04	0.02
	16–31	0.07	0.03	0.03	0.02	0.04	0.04	0.03	0.02

*To convert inches to millimeters, multiply by 25.4.

Step 4: Calculate the daily ET using Equation 1, or use the values in Table 7.4 for alfalfa.

Step 5: Determine the interval between irrigations by dividing the total allowable soil moisture depletion by the daily crop ET.

Scheduling Example

Determine the interval between irrigations for alfalfa from June 16 through June 30 for a field in the Fresno area. The soil type is silt loam, and root depth is 5 feet (1.52 m).

Step 1: The available soil moisture for silt loam is 1.8 inches (46 mm) per foot (0.305 m) (Table 7.1). The total allowable soil moisture depletion is 1.8 inches (46 mm) per foot × 5 feet (1.52 m) (rooting depth) × 0.5 = 4.5 inches (114 mm). The allowable depletion is 50 percent of the total available soil moisture, or 0.5 expressed as a decimal fraction.

Step 2: The ET_o for June 16–30 is 0.27 inches (6.8 mm) per day (Table 7.2, Parlier location).

Step 3: The K_c is 0.95 for a dry location with moderate wind (Table 7.3).

Step 4: The ET is 0.95 × 0.27 inches (6.9 mm) per day = 0.26 inches (6.6 mm) per day. The daily ET of 0.26 inches (6.6 mm) per day can also be found in Table 7.4, thus eliminating Steps 2 and 3 for alfalfa.

Step 5: The desired interval between irrigations can be calculated as: 4.5 inches ÷ 0.26 inches per day (114 mm ÷ 6.6 mm per day) = 17 days.

This method is inappropriate for shallow groundwater conditions. This method assumes that the soil moisture depletion between irrigations equals the ET. Under shallow groundwater conditions, this assumption is invalid because some of the crop's water can come from the groundwater; thus, the soil moisture depletion between irrigations will be smaller than the ET.

This procedure also assumes that infiltration of the furrow or border (flood) irrigation water is sufficient to replace all ET that was depleted since the last irrigation. This is not always the case. Many semiarid soil types "seal up" over the season, which limits the recharge of soil moisture. This is particularly a problem where sandy loam soils are irrigated with very low-salt water. With cracking clay loam soils, infiltration is primarily controlled by water flow into the cracks. Once the cracks seal shut, little infiltration may occur.

Influence of Cutting Schedule

Scheduling irrigations of alfalfa is complicated by the harvest schedule, which occurs about every 28 to 30 days in most areas. The first irrigation after harvest cannot occur until the alfalfa bales are removed. The final irrigation between harvests will need to occur at a time that provides sufficient soil drying before the harvest. Thus, irrigation scheduling of alfalfa is often controlled by the harvest schedule, not by allowable soil moisture depletion.

Growers are limited to the choice of irrigating once, twice, or sometimes three times between harvests, depending upon soil type and time of year. One irrigation between harvests may result in excessive soil moisture depletion between harvests, whereas with two

TABLE 7.3

Average crop coefficients for forage crops. *Source:* Doorenbos and Pruitt, 1977

Climatic Condition		Crop Coefficients (Kc)			
		Alfalfa	Grass Hay	Clover	Pasture
Humid, with light to moderate wind	average	0.85	0.80	1.00	0.95
	peak	1.05	1.05	1.05	1.05
	low	0.50	0.60	0.55	0.55
Dry with light to moderate wind	average	0.95	0.90	1.05	1.00
	peak	1.15	1.10	1.15	1.10
	low	0.40	0.55	0.55	0.50
Strong wind	average	1.05	1.00	1.10	1.05
	peak	1.25	1.15	1.20	1.15
	low	0.30	0.50	0.55	0.50

or three irrigations between harvests, irrigations will occur before the allowable depletion occurs. For these situations, efficient irrigation requires relatively small applications of water.

The constraints resulting from soil problems and harvest schedules may mean that irrigation should occur before the allowable depletion occurs, the determination of which was discussed earlier. Thus, a management allowable depletion (MAD) should be used, which takes these constraints into account. Usually, the MAD will be smaller than the calculated allowable depletion based on a 50 percent allowable depletion. The MAD will need to be determined from field experience and soil moisture measurements. Smaller water applications may be required to achieve MAD.

Managing Flood Irrigation

Flood or border irrigation systems are difficult to manage efficiently, since large quantities of water are required to move water down the checks, and it takes considerable time for water to advance or flow across the field. Additionally, a large quantity of water may pond on the soil surface during the irrigation event, especially at the tail ends of fields (discussed later). As a result, small water applications may not be feasible unless very

TABLE 7.4

Historical evapotranspiration of alfalfa (inches* per day) for various locations in California

		Shafter	Five Points	Parlier	Davis	Nicolaus	Durham	McArthur	Brawley
Jan	1–15	0.03	0.04	0.03	0.03	0.03	0.03	0.02	0.07
	16–31	0.05	0.05	0.04	0.05	0.04	0.05	0.03	0.09
Feb	1–15	0.07	0.06	0.06	0.06	0.06	0.06	0.04	0.11
	16–29	0.09	0.09	0.08	0.09	0.09	0.09	0.07	0.14
Mar	1–15	0.12	0.12	0.10	0.09	0.09	0.09	0.08	0.17
	16–31	0.15	0.16	0.12	0.13	0.11	0.11	0.10	0.20
Apr	1–15	0.20	0.21	0.16	0.17	0.14	0.15	0.13	0.23
	16–30	0.21	0.23	0.18	0.19	0.17	0.16	0.13	0.26
May	1–15	0.25	0.27	0.21	0.22	0.20	0.20	0.17	0.29
	16–31	0.27	0.28	0.23	0.23	0.20	0.21	0.18	0.30
Jun	1–15	0.28	0.30	0.25	0.27	0.23	0.24	0.21	0.33
	16–30	0.29	0.32	0.26	0.28	0.25	0.25	0.24	0.34
Jul	1–15	0.29	0.32	0.26	0.28	0.25	0.26	0.26	0.33
	16–31	0.27	0.29	0.24	0.26	0.24	0.24	0.24	0.30
Aug	1–15	0.26	0.29	0.23	0.25	0.23	0.23	0.24	0.30
	16–31	0.24	0.26	0.21	0.23	0.20	0.20	0.21	0.29
Sep	1–15	0.22	0.24	0.18	0.20	0.18	0.18	0.17	0.27
	16–30	0.19	0.21	0.14	0.17	0.15	0.15	0.13	0.23
Oct	1–15	0.17	0.18	0.12	0.15	0.12	0.13	0.11	0.20
	16–31	0.13	0.14	0.09	0.11	0.09	0.10	0.08	0.16
Nov	1–15	0.08	0.11	0.07	0.09	0.07	0.07	0.05	0.13
	16–30	0.06	0.07	0.04	0.06	0.05	0.05	0.03	0.11
Dec	1–15	0.05	0.05	0.03	0.05	0.03	0.04	0.02	0.07
	16–31	0.03	0.03	0.02	0.04	0.04	0.03	0.02	0.07

*To convert inches to millimeters, multiply by 25.4.

short check lengths are used. Multiple irrigations between harvests will probably result in infiltrated amounts exceeding the soil moisture depletion for the field lengths normally used for flood irrigation. These amounts may move beyond the root zone, depending on soil type.

A trial-and-error approach will be needed to determine the irrigation set time for flood irrigation. The irrigation set time should equal the time for the water to flow to about 70 to 90 percent of the check length, depending on site-specific conditions. These conditions include infiltration rate, surface roughness, field length, check width, inflow rate, and slope. At that time, the water should be stopped or cut off. However, if the set time is too short, water may not reach the end of the field. If the set time is too long, runoff and infiltration may be excessive.

Managing Sprinkler Irrigation

Small applications of water are possible with sprinkler irrigation. Managing the irrigation water will consist of matching the ET between irrigations with the amount of water applied with the sprinkler irrigation system. The amount of water to be applied by sprinkler irrigation can be determined with the following steps:

Step 1: Determine the daily ET_o (Table 7.2).

Step 2: Determine the K_c (Table 7.3).

Step 3: Determine the daily alfalfa ET using Equation 1 or using Table 7.4. Use of Table 7.4 eliminates Steps 1 and 2.

Step 4: Determine the total ET between irrigations by multiplying the daily ET (Step 3) by the days since the last irrigation.

Step 5: Determine the amount to be applied by dividing the total ET by the irrigation efficiency, expressed as a decimal fraction. Irrigation efficiency values of 0.7 to 0.75 are recommended for hand-move and wheel-line sprinklers, and 0.85 for center-pivot sprinkler machines.

Sprinkler Timing
The amount of water applied should equal the alfalfa ET or soil moisture depletion between

irrigations and an additional amount to account for the irrigation efficiency. The irrigation set time needed for sprinkler irrigation can be determined using either of the two following methods:

- Calculate the required irrigation set time using Equation 2 (below). The flow rate into the field is required for this approach.

$$T = 449 \times A \times D \div Q \text{ [Eq. 2]}$$

where T is the irrigation time per set (hours per set), A is the acres (ha) irrigated per set, D is the desired inches (mm) of water to be applied, and Q is the field flow rate in gallons (l) per minute, or cubic meters per hour. D is equal to the ET divided by the irrigation efficiency (IE). Use an IE value of 0.75 for wheel-line and hand-move sprinkler systems and 0.85 for center pivot systems. This method is appropriate for all sprinkler systems. The constant 449 is the conversion factor for English units; use 165 for metric units.

- Determine the application rate (AR) of the sprinkler. This method is appropriate for wheel-line and hand-move sprinkler systems. The irrigation set time is calculated from Equation 3:

$$T = D \div AR \text{ [Eq. 3]}$$

where T equals the irrigation set time (hours) and AR is the application rate (inches [mm] per hour). The application rate depends on the discharge rate of an individual sprinkler and the overlapped sprinkler spacing, and can be determined from Equation 4:

$$AR = (96.3 \times q) \div (S_l \times S_m) \text{ [Eq. 4]}$$

where q is the individual sprinkler discharge rate in gallons (or liters) per minute, S_l is the sprinkler spacing along the lateral line in feet (m), and S_m is the lateral spacing along the main line in feet (m). The constant 96.3 is used for English units; use 59.8 for metric units. The sprinkler discharge rate can be measured by inserting a garden hose over the nozzle and measuring the time to fill a container of a known volume with water. This measurement may be needed for older sprinkler systems that may have worn nozzles. The sprinkler discharge rate can also be estimated from Table 7.5 by measuring the nozzle pressure with a pitot gauge (available from irrigation supply stores) and the nozzle size.

Since so many variables are involved (soil peculiarities, temporary weather patterns, crop growth differences, etc.), ET-based irrigation management methods should be used in combination with soil monitoring to reflect real-world conditions.

Soil Moisture Monitoring

Soil moisture monitoring should be used in combination with the water balance or ET method, as a method of "ground truthing" the effectiveness of an irrigation strategy. Soil moisture monitoring can provide the following information to help evaluate the irrigation water management of alfalfa:

- Did sufficient water infiltrate the soil to an adequate depth?

- Has too much water been applied?

- What is the water uptake pattern of the roots?

- When should irrigation occur?

- How long does it take for water to infiltrate the soil?

Knowledge of soil wetting and drying patterns can assist managers to determine whether the ET approach should be modified for individual field conditions.

Many soil moisture sensors are available for measuring either soil moisture or soil-moisture tension. Soil-moisture tension is the tenacity with which water is retained by the soil: the higher the tension, the drier the soil. The sensors should be installed at about one-fourth to one-third of the root zone depth for irrigation scheduling purposes and at the bottom of the root zone to ensure adequacy of irrigation.

Although many sensors are available, only a few are practical for monitoring soil moisture in alfalfa fields. One type of sensor that is well-suited for alfalfa fields is the Watermark electrical resistance block (Irrometer, Inc., Riverside, CA) (Fig. 7.4). This instrument is inexpensive, easy to install and read, requires no maintenance, and is not susceptible to damage from harvesting equipment. It provides readings in centibars of soil-moisture tension, which can be compared with appropriate guidelines (Table 7.6) to determine when to irrigate. Sidebar 1 describes a procedure for installing and using this instrument, which is also covered in detail in Orloff et al. 2001. This

TABLE 7.5

Application rates for various pressures and nozzle sizes for a 40 × 60 foot (12 × 18 m) spacing

Pressure (psi)	Nozzle Size (inches*)			
	5/32	11/64	3/16	13/64
	inches per hour			
30	0.15	0.18	0.22	0.26
35	0.16	0.20	0.24	0.28
40	0.18	0.21	0.25	0.30
45	0.19	0.22	0.26	0.33
50	0.20	0.24	0.28	0.34
55	0.21	0.25	0.29	0.36
60	0.22	0.26	0.31	0.37

*To convert inches to millimeters, multiply by 25.4.

FIGURE 7.4

One type of sensor that is well-suited for alfalfa fields is the Watermark electrical resistance block.

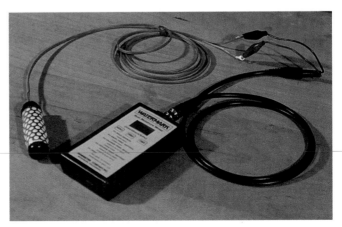

publication and a downloadable Excel spreadsheet are available at http://alfalfa,ucdavis.edu.

The use of these electrical resistance blocks is illustrated by soil-moisture tension readings made in 2003 and 2004 in the same flood-irrigated field (Figs. 7.6–7.7). Soil type was clay loam. In 2003, one irrigation occurred between harvests. Soil-moisture tensions at about 1 foot (30 cm) deep just before harvests in June and July ranged from approximately 100 centibars to more than 200 centibars, suggesting soil moisture depletions between harvests exceeded the allowable depletion, particularly in July, and that more frequent irrigation was needed (Fig. 7.6). In 2004, two irrigations occurred between harvests to

---

Sidebar 1:

Installing Watermark Electrical Resistance Blocks

Step 1: Soak blocks in water for a few minutes to saturate them.

Step 2: Check the block readings before installing to ensure that they are working.

Step 3: Make a small-diameter hole with a soil probe or a small-diameter auger to a depth slightly deeper than that desired.

Step 4: Make a slurry of water mixed with a small amount of soil, and, if possible, gypsum, and pour down the hole to provide good contact between soil and block. This contact is vital because water must flow in and out of the block for the block to respond to changes in soil-moisture tension.

Step 5: Push the block into the slurry in the bottom of the hole with a length of PVC pipe (1/2 in. [12.7 mm], Schedule 80). Cut a notch in the bottom of the pipe for the wire lead of the block to prevent the wire from being damaged during installation.

Step 6: Remove the pipe and backfill the hole with soil removed from the hole. Do not damage the wire leads during the backfilling. As the hole is filled, pack the backfilled soil in the hole with the PVC pipe. Be sure to identify each block with a tag or knots in the wire to indicate its depth of installation.

Step 7: Allow the blocks to equilibrate with the soil moisture for about 24 hours before making readings of soil-moisture tension.

Step 8: Compare the block readings with the threshold values in Table 7.6 to determine when to irrigate.

At a minimum, install one block at approximately one-fourth to one-third of the root zone to schedule irrigations, and a block at the bottom of the root zone to monitor depth of wetting. Blocks installed at different depths, however, provide better information on depth of wetting and soil-moisture uptake patterns. One approach is to install blocks at depths of 12, 24, and 48 inches (0.3, 0.6, and 1.2 m). Little change in block readings at the lower depths or increasing values of tension during the irrigation season indicate insufficient water applications.

Install at least two sites of blocks for every 40 acres (16 ha). This might consist of one site about 200 feet (61 m) from the head end of the field and a second site 200 to 300 feet (61–91 m) from the tail

TABLE 7.6

Threshold values of soil-moisture tension at which irrigation should occur for alfalfa for different soil types (Orloff et al. 2001). Values are based on a 50 percent depletion of available soil moisture for different soil types.

Soil Type	Threshold Soil-Moisture Tension (centibars)
Sand or loamy sand	40–50
Sandy loam	50–70
Loam	60–90
Clay loam or clay	90–120

Installing Watermark Sensors (continued)

end of the same check. More sites may be needed, depending on soil texture variability and cropping patterns in a field. Separate stations for problem areas or for areas having different soil conditions or crops are recommended.

Periodic measurements of soil moisture normally are made once or twice per week. However, research has shown that continuous measurements of soil moisture better describe the trends in soil moisture over time. Continuous measurements require that the sensors be connected to a data logger. The data logger can be installed in the field near the sensors (which makes it susceptible to damage from harvesting equipment) or on the side of the field, which requires wires to connect the logger to the sensors (Fig. 7.5). A procedure for installing a wire is to shank a four- to seven-lead sprinkler or phone wire under the field surface with a fertilizer

knife out to the end of the field and attaching a data logger. This cable is then attached to the buried blocks (use waterproof connectors), leaving no wires or equipment in the field that interfere with equipment and can be hard to find. If a data logger is not used, it still may be desirable to install a buried wire for the hand-read meter.

In very sandy soils, electrical resistance blocks and tensiometers may not work very well. This is because in unsaturated sandy soils, water flow through the soil is extremely slow; thus water flow into and out of the block also will be very slow and will not reflect the actual changes in soil-moisture tension.

FIGURE 7.5

A recommended installation layout for soil moisture sensors in an alfalfa field.

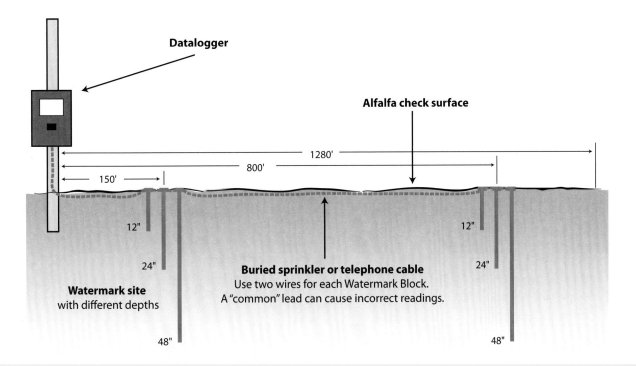

FIGURE 7.6

Soil-moisture tension for a flood-irrigated field irrigated once per harvest.

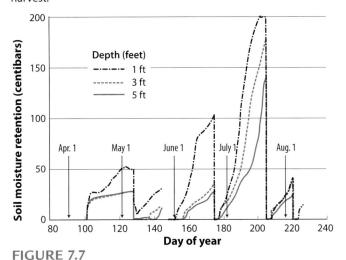

FIGURE 7.7

Soil-moisture tension for a flood-irrigated field irrigated two times between harvests.

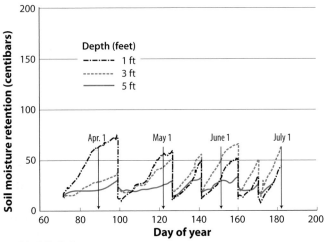

FIGURE 7.8

Soil-moisture tension for a sprinkler-irrigated field irrigated too frequently.

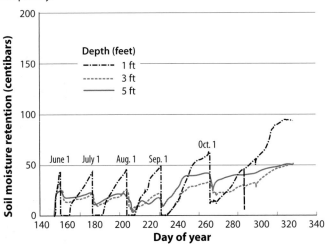

reduce or eliminate crop stress due to insufficient soil moisture. Soil-moisture tensions just before harvest ranged from 50 to 70 centibars at 1 foot (30 cm) deep (Fig. 7.7). However, these soil-moisture tension values indicate that these irrigations probably occurred at soil moisture depletions smaller than the allowable depletion, a situation that is unavoidable because of the harvest schedule.

Watermark blocks have also been used to evaluate the irrigation water management of sprinkler irrigation systems. In one case, relatively small soil-moisture tension values occurred at all depths throughout the irrigation season with values at the 1-foot (30 cm) depth never exceeding 50 centibars until near the end of the irrigation season (Fig. 7.8). At the deeper depths, tension values were less than 30 centibars. These data suggest that a longer interval between irrigations should be used. Contributions by shallow groundwater to the ET may be responsible for this result.

Soil moisture sensors can also be used to determine if the infiltration time is sufficient. Data from Watermark block measurements (not shown) showed that only about 2 to 3 hours were needed to infiltrate water to about 5 feet (1.5 m) deep in cracked soils. This indicates that in these cracked soils, only 2 to 3 hours of ponding are needed along the lower part of the field to infiltrate water. Note: ponding during flood irrigation events should be limited during times of high temperatures, due to the risk of scald.

Uniformity and Efficiency of Irrigation Systems

Uniformity and efficiency describe the performance of irrigation systems. Uniformity refers to the evenness at which water is applied or infiltrated throughout the field and depends on system design and maintenance. Efficiency refers to the ability of an irrigation system to match the water needed for crop production with applied irrigation water and depends on system design, maintenance, and management. Higher irrigation uniformity results in a greater potential irrigation efficiency of a properly managed irrigation system.

If all parts of a field received exactly the same amount of water, the uniformity would be 100 percent. However, regardless of the irrigation method, some areas of a field will receive more or less water than other areas, providing uniformities of less than 100 percent. If the least-watered areas of the field receive an amount equal to the soil moisture depletion, excess amounts of water will be applied to other areas, resulting in water percolating below the root zone, commonly called deep percolation. This water is not effectively used by crops, is considered lost water, and lowers irrigation efficiency. Lower distribution uniformities result in greater differences in applied or infiltrated water throughout the field and more drainage below the root zone.

An index commonly used to assess the uniformity of infiltrated water is the distribution uniformity (DU), calculated as follows:

$$DU = \frac{100\ \overline{X}_{LQ}}{\overline{X}},$$

where $\overline{X}$ is the average amount of infiltrated or applied water for the entire field, and $\overline{X}_{LQ}$ is the average of the lowest one-fourth of the measurements of applied or infiltrated water, commonly called the low quarter (usually the lower end of the field for flood irrigation). $\overline{X}_{LQ}$ is referred to as the minimum amount of infiltrated or applied water.

Irrigation efficiency is the ratio of the amount of water beneficially used for crop production to the amount of water applied to the field. Evapotranspiration (ET) is the largest single beneficial use of irrigation water in crop production. Leaching for salinity control is also a beneficial use.

Losses affecting the irrigation efficiency are percolation below the root zone, surface runoff, and evaporation from sprinklers before water reaches the soil. Percolation occurs when the amount of infiltrated water exceeds the soil moisture storage capacity of the soil. Surface runoff occurs when the application rate of the irrigation water exceeds the infiltration rate and is difficult to avoid for flood irrigation systems. This loss can be eliminated by recovering the surface runoff and using it elsewhere or recirculating the runoff back to the "head" of the field during irrigation. Evaporative losses

from sprinklers can be important and are dependent on nozzle and sprinkler characteristics and climate, but generally do not exceed 10 percent of the applied water.

The DU of a properly irrigated field is approximately equal to its potential irrigation efficiency, assuming surface runoff is beneficially used. Table 7.7 lists potential practical irrigation efficiencies developed from irrigation system evaluation data.

Flood or Border Irrigation Systems

Border or check flood irrigation systems, which cause a sheet of water to flow across the field, are the dominant systems used for alfalfa in California. The advantages of this method are that it is almost completely gravity powered, and it is inexpensive, both in terms of system costs and energy costs. Disadvantages are that its performance depends strongly on soil properties, such as the infiltration rate, slope, surface roughness, and border design. It is the most difficult irrigation method to manage efficiently because of these factors; thus, a trial-and-error approach is normally used to manage these systems.

Border or check flood irrigation systems used in California usually have slopes from 0.1 percent to 0.2 percent and use small "border checks" (or small levees) about 6 inches (15 cm) high to confine water to a check width of 10 to 100 feet (3.05–30.5 m) wide so that water moves down the field. Laser-monitored earth-scraping equipment is normally used for

TABLE 7.7

Practical potential irrigation efficiencies (Hanson 1995)

Irrigation Method	Irrigation Efficiency (%)
Sprinkler	
Continuous-move	80–90
Periodic-move	70–80
Portable solid-set	70–80
Microirrigation	80–90
Furrow	70–85
Border check	70–85

field leveling and smoothing, a critical aspect of its success. Field length in the direction of flow varies, but a 1,200- to 1,300-foot (366–400 m) check length is common. Sometimes flood systems are combined with "corrugated" or "bedded" systems that facilitate water movement and drainage on finer-textured soil.

Design variables for flood irrigation include slope, border length, border inflow rate, surface roughness, and infiltration rate. Recommended field lengths and flow rates for various soil types are shown in Table 7.8.

A description of the behavior of flood irrigation is as follows:

- At the start of the irrigation, the water starts flowing or advancing down the check.

- At the same time, water ponds on the soil surface. During the irrigation, the amount of ponded or stored water is substantial and may be 3 to 4 inches (76–102 mm) deep. (Note: In contrast, stored water during furrow irrigation is insignificant relative to the amount applied.)

- The ponded water infiltrates the soil as water flows across the field.

- At cutoff, the irrigation water is stopped. The ponded water, however, continues to flow down the field and infiltrate into the soil after cutoff. It may supply all of the soil

moisture replenishment along the lower part of the field. (Note: In contrast, infiltration after cutoff is insignificant for furrow irrigation.)

- The stored water also causes surface runoff at the end of the field. The longer the irrigation set time, the more the potential runoff from the stored water.

The flow of water across the field is characterized by the advance curve, which shows the time at which water arrives at any given distance along the field length (Fig. 7.9). The recession curve shows the time at which water no longer ponds on the soil surface at any given distance along the field length (Fig. 7.9). The difference between advance time and recession time at any distance along the check length is the time during which water infiltrates the soil or the infiltration time. These infiltration times vary along the field length, resulting in more water infiltrating in some parts of the field compared to other areas, lowering DU.

Improving Flood Irrigation Systems

Flood irrigation system efficiency can be improved by reducing deep percolation below the root zone and reducing surface runoff. However, measures that reduce deep percolation can increase surface runoff and vice versa.

TABLE 7.8

Recommended unit flow rates and border lengths for field slopes of 0.1 to 0.2 percent

Soil Type	Check Length (feet[1])	Unit Flow Rate (gpm/foot* of width)
Clay	1,300	7 to 10
Clay loam	1,300	10 to 15
Loam	1,300	25 to 35
Loam	600	15 to 20
Sandy loam	600	25 to 30
Sandy	600	30 to 40

*Multiply units per foot by 0.304 to determine check length in meters. Multiply gallons per minute (gpm) by 0.227 to obtain cubic meters per hour (cu m/hr).

FIGURE 7.9

Advance and recession curves for a flood-irrigated field.

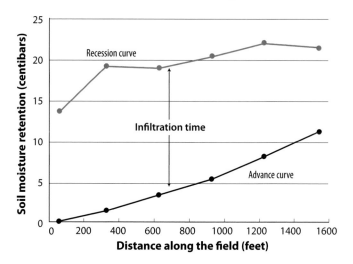

Some measures commonly recommended include:

Increase the check flow rate. This commonly-recommended measure reduces the advance time to the end of the field, thus decreasing variability in infiltration times along the field length. Yet, field evaluations showed only a minor improvement in the performance of flood irrigation under higher flow rates compared with lower flow rates (Howe and Heerman 1970; Schwankl 1990; B. Hanson, unpubl. data). The higher flow rates can potentially increase surface runoff.

Reduce the field length. This is the most effective measure for improving uniformity and for reducing percolation below the root zone. Studies have shown that shortening the field length by half can reduce percolation by at least 50 percent. The distribution DU of infiltrated water will be increased by 10 to 15 percentage points compared with the normal field length. Using the original flow rate into the check, the new advance time to the end of the shortened field generally will be 30–40 percent of the advance time to the end of the original field length. Thus, the irrigation set time must be reduced to account for the new advance time. Failure to reduce the set time will greatly increase both deep percolation and surface runoff. A major problem with this measure is the potential for increased surface runoff, which could be two to four times more runoff for the reduced length compared with the original field length (Hanson 1989).

Select an appropriate cutoff time. The amount of surface runoff or tailwater can be greatly reduced by decreasing the cutoff time of the irrigation water. This is the most effective measure for reducing surface runoff. The cutoff time for a given field may need to be determined on a trial-and-error basis. The cutoff time should occur before the water reaches the end of the field, except for sandy soils with high infiltration rates. However, the cutoff time should allow sufficient water to infiltrate the end of the field. Research in the Imperial

TABLE 7.9

Effect of cutoff time on applied water, surface runoff, and distribution uniformity (DU)

Cutoff Time (minutes)	Applied Water (inches*)	Surface Runoff (inches*)	DU (%)
800	12.8	2.8	89
700	12.1	1.6	87
600	11.2	0.5	82
550	10.7	0.06	78
500	9.8	0	62

*To convert inches to millimeters, multiply by 25.4.

Valley showed runoff to be about 2 percent of the infiltrated volume, for a cutoff time equal to the time for water to travel or advance to about 70 percent of the field length in cracked clay soil (Grismer and Bali 2001; Bali et al. 2001). A procedure for estimating the cutoff time for cracked clay soil is shown in Sidebar 2.

The effect of reducing the cutoff time on surface runoff is shown in Table 7.9, using data from evaluations of flood irrigation systems. The advance time to the end of this field was 670 minutes. A cutoff time of 800 minutes (grower's cutoff time) resulted in substantial surface runoff. Reducing the cutoff time to 600 minutes decreased the surface runoff by 82 percent, yet the infiltration time at the end of the field was adequate. However, a cutoff time of 500 minutes resulted in incomplete advance to the end of the field; thus, no infiltration occurred at the end of the field. The effect of the decreasing cutoff times on the uniformity of infiltrated water was slight until cutoff times were much less than the advance time.

Recover surface runoff. Recirculation systems (commonly called tailwater-return systems), or storage-reuse systems, can dramatically improve efficiency of flood irrigation systems. Recirculation systems involve collecting the surface runoff in a small reservoir at the lower end of the field and then recirculating the water back to the "head" of the field during irrigation, using a low lift pump and a buried or portable pipeline. The recirculated water should be used

Sidebar 2:

Management of Flood-Irrigation in Heavy Soils

Selecting an appropriate cutoff time can prevent excessive surface runoff. A relatively simple technique that predicts the cutoff time necessary to minimize runoff and to improve water use efficiency has been developed for heavy, cracked clay soil (Grismer and Tod 1994). In these soils, water flow into the cracks accounts for most of the infiltration. Little infiltration occurs after the cracks swell shut. Although the method is applicable for all soils, it works best with heavy clay soils. The main objective is to fill the soil cracks with water with little or no runoff. Based on experience in heavy clay soils in the Imperial Valley, the cutoff distance for most 0.25-mile (0.4-km) run borders is from 850 to 1,050 feet (259–320 m) for a wide range of flow rates and field conditions.

The following information is needed to estimate the cutoff time necessary to minimize or eliminate runoff:

- Border or check width and length (feet [meters]).

- Average check flow rate in cubic feet per second (cfs)[1].

- The times for the advancing water to reach 300 feet and 400 feet (91 m and 122 m) down the field.

This method requires the following setup in the field:

- Measure the flow rate.

- Place one stake at 300 ft (91 m) from the water inlet.

- Place a second stake at 400 ft (122 m) from the inlet.

The procedure for estimating the cutoff distance is:

Step 1: Determine the flow rate into a check.

Step 2. Determine the time difference of the water advance between the first and second stakes by subtracting the 400-foot (122-m) time (second stake) from the 300-foot (91-m) time (first stake).

Step 3: Use Table 7.10 to determine the cutoff distance for the check flow rate and the time difference.

Example

Determine the cutoff distance for a 1,200-foot-(366-m) long field with 65-foot (20-m) check widths. Four checks or borders are irrigated during each set using a flow rate of 9 cfs[1].

Step 1: The average flow rate per check is 9 cfs[1] ÷ 4 = 2.25 cfs/border.

Step 2: The time required for water to advance from the first stake to the second stake = 26 minutes.

Step 3: From Table 7.10, the cutoff distance for 2.2 cfs[1] and a time of 26 minutes is about 970 feet (296 m) down the field length.

[1]Note: 1 cfs = 449 gallons (2,041 l) per minute.

TABLE 7.10

Irrigation cutoff distance for border-irrigated alfalfa field

(Border width 65 ft [20 m], border length 1,200 ft [366 m], slope 0.1%)

Time (min)/100 ft [30 m] of advance	Flow rate (cfs)[1]				
	2.0	2.2	2.4	2.6	2.8
	Estimated cutoff distance (ft)[2]				
16				845	855
18	850	865	875	885	895
20	890	890	910	920	925
22	915	925	935	945	950
24	940	950	955	965	970
26	960	970	975	985	990
28	975	985	990	1,000	1,005
30	990	1,000	1,005	1,010	
32	1,000	1,010	1,020		

[1]1 cubic foot per second (cfs) = 449 gallons per minute
[2]To convert feet to meters, multiply by 0.304.

to irrigate an additional area of the field. Simply recirculating the runoff back to the same irrigation set that generated the runoff results only in temporarily storing the water on the field and will increase the amount of runoff.

Similarly, a storage/reuse system involves storing all of the surface runoff from a field, then using that water to irrigate another field at the appropriate time. This approach requires a farm with multiple adjacent fields, a relatively large reservoir, and distribution systems to convey surface runoff to the storage reservoir and to convey the stored water to the desired fields.

Care should be taken that water quality is not degraded from storage-reuse systems. Pesticides have been found to infiltrate groundwater on some soil types, primarily from catchment basins, originating from field runoff. In these cases, steps to seal basins from subsurface infiltration may be effective at preventing contamination.

Sprinkler Irrigation Systems

Sprinkler irrigation systems used for alfalfa production are wheel-line or side-roll systems, hand-move systems, and center-pivot and linear-move sprinkler machines. Wheel-line and hand-move sprinklers are classified as periodic-move systems, whereas center-pivots and linear-moves are classified as continuous-move systems.

Wheel-line/Hand-move Sprinkler Systems

Wheel-line sprinkler systems consist of aluminum lateral pipes rigidly coupled together and mounted on large aluminum wheels. The lateral pipe is the axle of the system, with the wheel spacing equal to the sprinkler spacing and the sprinklers located midway between wheels. The sprinkler lateral is moved with an engine mounted at the center of the line that twists the pipe and causes the lateral to roll sideways, hence the common name of side-roll sprinklers. Wheel-line systems are best suited for fields that are rectangular with relatively

uniform topography. Frequently, one wheel-line lateral is used for each 40 acres (15 ha). A common sprinkler spacing for both wheel-lines and hand-moves is 40 × 60 feet (12 × 18 m).

The move distance depends on the wheel diameter and the number of wheel revolutions. Normally, lateral moves of 60 feet (18 m) are common; these require four revolutions of a 4.8-foot (1.5-m) diameter wheel (circumference equals 15 feet [4.6 m]). Before moving the lateral, the pipe must be drained using quick drains installed at each sprinkler location.

Wheel-line and hand-move laterals frequently are about 1,300 feet (396 m) long. A 4-inch (102-mm) diameter pipe is commonly used; however, 5-inch (127-mm) pipe is also used, which results in less pressure loss along the lateral length. A sprinkler spacing of 40 feet (12 m) is normally used along the lateral, whereas a 60-foot (18-cm) lateral spacing along the mainline is frequently used. However, sometimes a 30-foot (9-m) sprinkler spacing and a 50-foot (15-m) lateral spacing are used.

Sprinkler nozzles normally used for wheel-line and hand-move systems are 5/32 inch (3.96 mm), 11/64 inch (4.34 mm), 3/16 inch (4.75 mm), and 13/64 inch (5.16 mm). In some cases, a small nozzle, called a spreader nozzle, is also used along with the larger nozzle. Self levelers are recommended for wheel-line systems to ensure that the sprinkler remains upright after a move.

Factors Affecting Performance

Primary factors affecting the uniformity of sprinkler systems are pressure losses in the mainline, submains, and laterals, and the areal distribution of water between sprinklers.

Pressure Losses. Pressure losses are caused by friction between the flowing water and the pipe wall and by elevation differences throughout the field. Factors affecting friction losses are the flow rate of water, length and diameter of the pipeline, and pipe material. Pressure losses are very sensitive to pipe diameter. For a given flow rate, pressure losses along a 4-inch (102-mm) diameter lateral are nearly three times those of a 5-inch (127-mm) diameter lateral. Pressure decreases rapidly with distance along the lateral for the first one-third of the lateral length and thereafter decreases slowly with distance due to a progressively decreasing flow rate with distance along the lateral. A change in elevation of 2.31 feet (0.704 m) causes a pressure change of 1 psi (6.9 x 10³).

Sprinkler Uniformity. Sprinkler uniformity can be measured by performing catch-can tests that measure actual applied water across a given area. Catch-can uniformity describes the real distribution of water between sprinklers.

It depends on sprinkler pressure, wind speed, sprinkler and lateral spacings, sprinkler head and nozzle type, and system maintenance.

Contour plots of the water application pattern of a single sprinkler are shown in Figure 7.10. These plots were developed by first measuring the applied water at many locations around the sprinkler with catch cans. Both applied water and can location were entered into graphics software (Surfer, Golden Software, Golden, CO), which drew lines of equal water applications and then assigned colors to the water applications. Blue represents a high application; red indicates a very small application.

The water application pattern of a single sprinkler operating at an acceptable pressure shows a circular pattern, with high applications near the sprinkler (dark blue to light blue) and decreasing with distance from the sprinkler (Fig. 7.10A). Near the edge of the pattern (yellow, red), water applications decreased rapidly with distance. Insufficient pressure results in a donut-shaped pattern due to inadequate spray breakup, with large applications near the sprinkler and near the edge of the pattern (blue to green) (Fig. 7.10B). Wind distorts the pattern of a single sprinkler by blowing most of the water downwind of the sprinkler (Fig. 7.10C).

Relatively high uniformity of applied water is achieved by overlapping the water application patterns of a single sprinkler. Uniformity is highly dependent on the sprinkler spacing along the lateral, the lateral spacing along the mainline, and wind speed. The overlapped pattern of a 40 × 60 foot (12 × 18 m) spacing shows relatively small differences in applied water throughout the wetted area under low wind conditions (2 mph), resulting in a DU equal to 85 percent (Fig. 7.11A). Under high wind conditions (18 mph), large differences in applied

FIGURE 7.10

Water distribution pattern of (A) a single sprinkler operating at an acceptable pressure (low wind conditions); (B) a single nozzle operating at a low pressure (low wind conditions); and (C) a single nozzle operating at an acceptable pressure under high wind conditions. The black dots show the locations of the sprinkler for each pattern. The arrow shows the wind direction.

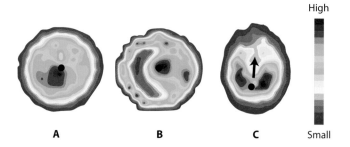

FIGURE 7.11

Contour plots of the applied water for overlapped sprinklers (40 ft × 60 ft [12 m × 18 m]) for (A) a low wind condition (11/64 in. [3.96 mm], 55 psi, 2 mph, DU = 85%), (B) a high wind condition with the lateral perpendicular to the wind direction (11/64 in. [3.96 mm], 40 psi, 18 mph, DU = 35%), and (C) a high wind condition with the lateral parallel to the wind direction (11/64 in. [3.96 mm], 40 psi, 18 mph, DU = 25%). The black dots show the locations of the sprinklers. The arrows indicate the wind direction.

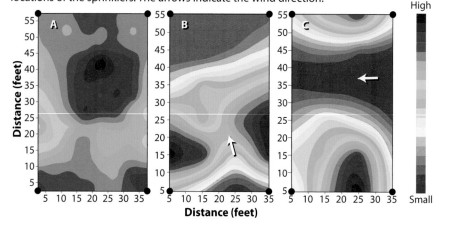

water occurred throughout the wetted area, as indicated by the colors ranging from dark blue to red. The DU was 34 percent for a wind direction perpendicular to the sprinkler lateral (Fig. 7.11B) and 25 percent for a wind direction parallel to the sprinkler lateral (Fig. 7.11C).

The contour plots in Figure 7.12 show the effect of sprinkler spacings on the DU. The DU decreased slightly as the sprinkler spacing increased for low wind conditions (2 mph) (Fig. 7.12A). Relatively low DUs occurred only for very large spacings. High wind conditions (10 mph) resulted in large decreases in DU as sprinkler spacing increased (Fig. 7.12B). High DUs occurred only for relatively small spacings. The DU decreases in a straight line manner as wind speed increases (Fig. 7.13).

Improvement Measures. Methods for improving the uniformity of existing wheel-line or hand-move systems include the following:

- Install flow-control nozzles where the pressure variation is excessive.

- Use appropriate sprinkler spacings.

- Maintain adequate sprinkler pressure.

- Offset laterals (beneficial for high wind conditions).

- Maintain system. Avoid mixing nozzle sizes; repair malfunctioning sprinklers and leaks; replace rubber orifice in nozzles periodically; and maintain risers in a vertical position.

Flow-control nozzles that contain a flexible orifice that changes diameter as pressure changes can be installed; thus, less variation occurs in sprinkler discharge rate with pressure compared to standard nozzles. Note: the

FIGURE 7.12

Distribution uniformity for a 11/64-in. [3.96-mm] diameter nozzle at 55 psi for different sprinkler spacings for (A) wind speeds of 2 mph and (B) 20 mph (mph × 1.6 = km/hr; ft × 0.304 = m).

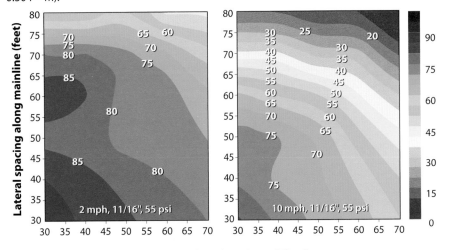

FIGURE 7.13

Effect of wind speed on distribution uniformity (mph × 1.6 = km/hr).

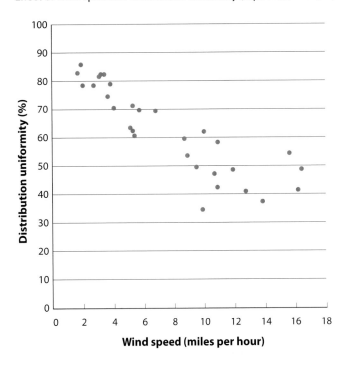

rubber orifice in these nozzles will eventually harden, resulting in much higher and nonuniform nozzle discharge rates. They should be periodically checked and replaced every 2 to 3 years.

Center-pivot/Linear-move Sprinkler Irrigation

Center pivot machines consist of a lateral pipeline mounted on top of self-propelled towers. The lateral is suspended about 10 feet (3 m) above the ground. Distance between towers or span length can range from 90 to 250 feet (27–76 m). A flexible joint connects the spans together. A typical lateral length is about 1,300 feet (396 m), which can irrigate about 130 acres (52.6 ha), for a complete circle. The common lateral diameter is 6 5/8 (6.625) inches (168 mm), but diameters up to 10 inches (254 mm) also are available. The lateral rotates around a fixed pivot point, with the rate of rotation controlled by the outermost tower.

High-pressure center pivots use impact sprinklers mounted on top of the lateral. Low-pressure systems use spray nozzles, spinners, or rotator nozzles installed at the end of drop tubes. The drop tube is suspended just above the plant canopy. The drop-tube approach is less susceptible to wind effects compared with impact sprinklers.

Because the center-pivot machines rotate about a fixed point, more and more area is irrigated per unit length of lateral as the distance along the lateral from the pivot point increases. Thus, application rates must increase with distance from the pivot point to maintain high field-wide uniformity. Application rates are increased by using progressively larger nozzles, progressively smaller sprinkler spacings, or some combination of both. Application rates may exceed several inches (mm) per hour near the end of the lateral, whereas application rates are a fraction of this near the center of the pivot.

Center-pivot systems are best suited for soils with high infiltration rates, relatively uniform topography, and no aboveground obstructions. The high application rates of center-pivot systems have restricted their use in many areas of California because infiltration rates of many California soils, particularly in the Central Valley, are too low to be suitable for this irrigation method.

Linear-move sprinkler machines use the same technology as center-pivots, but they travel in a straight line. A water supply ditch or pipeline that parallels the travel direction is required. A guidance system is used to keep the machine traveling in a straight line. An engine-driven pump is mounted on the tower adjacent to the ditch to supply water and electrical power to the lateral. These systems are best suited for rectangular fields with no obstructions and a relatively uniform topography. An uneven topography can cause problems with the guidance system. In contrast to center-pivot systems, the application rate along the lateral length is relatively constant since all towers travel at the same speed. This system can be used on soils with low infiltration rates.

Distribution uniformities of center-pivot and linear-move sprinkler machines normally are higher than those of hand-move and wheel-line sprinklers. The more-or-less continuous movement of these machines maintains a better precipitation pattern even as the wind speed increases. Potential distribution uniformities of these machines are 80 to 90 percent.

Drip Irrigation

Drip irrigation precisely applies water throughout a field, in terms of both amount and location. Potential advantages of drip irrigation include increased crop yield, reduced water and energy costs, and reduced fertilizer costs. Potential disadvantages include the high capital cost of drip irrigation systems, possible increased energy costs compared with those of flood or border irrigation, and maintenance costs to prevent clogging and repair leaks. One advantage of drip irrigation of alfalfa is that irrigations could continue during the harvest period as long as no wetting of the soil surface occurs. However, drip irrigation is not widely used in alfalfa, and important practical limitations must be considered.

> *One advantage of drip irrigation of alfalfa is that irrigations could continue during the harvest period as long as no wetting of the soil surface occurs.*

Drip irrigation systems discharge small amounts of water through emitters periodically installed at set distances along drip lines. Emitter discharge rates can range from 0.13 gallons (0.59 l) per hour to 2 gallons (9.1 l) per hour, depending on the type of material and size of hose used for drip laterals.

Components of a drip system include pump, filters (primary and secondary), injection equipment for fertigation and chemical treatment for clogging, flow meter, mainline and submains, manifolds, drip lines and emitters, pressure regulators, and flushing valves/manifolds. More detail about drip irrigation systems is found in Hanson et al. (1997).

Normally, drip irrigation of row crops uses a flexible drip tape that inflates upon pressurization. The drip tape may be either installed on the ground surface (surface drip system) or buried (subsurface drip systems). Depending on the grower's preferences for cultivation equipment and crop rotation, drip lines are usually installed at depths of 9 to 18 inches (229–457 mm). Because of harvesting and other traffic considerations, surface drip is not practical for alfalfa. Subsurface drip lines may need to be installed as deep as 18 to 24 inches (457 to 610 mm) to prevent wetting of the soil surface during irrigation, which could cause problems for the harvesting equipment. A drip tape wall thickness of 15 mil provides sufficiently heavy walls to prevent damage by wireworms and other subterranean insects with scraping mouthparts that can cause pinhole leaks in the tape. However, a 10-mil wall thickness is the most common compromise between cost and this type of possible damage, usually providing adequate performance.

For deeper installations, heavy-walled drip tubing with inline emitters is recommended. Drip tubing is a flexible hard hose that retains its roundness when empty. Drip tubing may be needed for alfalfa drip irrigation systems because the drip lines may need to be installed at depths deeper than 15 inches (38 cm) to prevent surface wetting of the soil, which can cause problems with the harvesting equipment.

Drip emitters are highly susceptible to clogging. Suspended materials in the irrigation water, such as algae, sand, silt, and clay, can block the flow passage in the emitters.

Precipitation of chemicals such as calcium carbonate and iron oxide, biological growths, and root intrusion can also reduce or block flow. Thus, proper filtration must be used to remove suspended materials from the irrigation water, and chemical treatment of the water may be needed to prevent or correct clogging problems caused by precipitation or biological growths. These matters are addressed in Schwankl et al. (2008). Fields to be used for drip irrigation of alfalfa should be free of burrowing rodents before installing a drip system. Irrigation setups that allow occasional flood irrigations for alfalfa may assist in controlling burrowing rodents, which have been found to have increased populations in drip systems.

Does drip irrigation of alfalfa pay? Factors that determine the answer to this question include the capital and maintenance costs of the drip systems, the effect of drip irrigation on energy costs, yield, and water and fertilizer use. Crop price will also play a major role. If the combination of yield increase and crop price increases profits under drip irrigation compared to other irrigation methods, then drip irrigation pays. However, low crop prices may prevent drip irrigation from being more profitable compared to other irrigation methods, even though drip irrigation results in higher yields. The answer is very site specific and cannot be predicted with any degree of confidence without first experimenting with drip irrigation of alfalfa.

The potential for yield improvements (and therefore improvements in water-use efficiency) are potential positive features of drip irrigation for alfalfa, but there are important cost and practical limitations.

Does drip irrigation save water? Because proper irrigation scheduling with a drip system reduces stress in alfalfa, the crop can potentially use more water than with other irrigation systems. From the production function shown in Figure 7.1, increased yield means that the crop is using more water. So, unless surface runoff from the field is substantial and not reused, or the soil is very sandy with lots of deep percolation lost below the root zone, water savings may not result from using drip irrigation. Hutmacher et al. (2001) found little savings of water with drip compared with surface irrigation systems, and some practical problems with some drip configurations, but significant yield improvements with buried drip compared with surface systems. The potential for yield improvements (and therefore improvements in water-use efficiency) are potential positive features of drip irrigation for alfalfa, but there are important cost and practical limitations.

Summary

Irrigation management is one of the most critical aspects of successful alfalfa production. Water levels (deficit or excess) limit alfalfa production to a greater degree than any other factor in western states. Key management factors include (1) irrigation system design for maximum uniformity and efficiency, (2) irrigation scheduling to determine when to apply irrigation water and how much to apply, using data on evaporative demand and soil characteristics, and (3) soil moisture monitoring to determine accuracy of irrigation application, presence of soil moisture, and to monitor moisture over the season.

Additional Reading

Bali, K.M., M.E. Grismer, and I.C. Todd. 2001. Reduced-runoff irrigation of alfalfa in Imperial Valley, California. Journal of Irrigation and Drainage Engineering 127(3):123–130.

Doorenbos, J., and W.O. Pruitt. 1975. Guidelines for predicting crop water requirements. FAO Irrigation and Drainage Paper 24. United Nations. Rome, Italy.

———. 1977. Guidelines for predicting crop water requirements. FAO Irrigation and Drainage Paper 24. United Nations. Rome, Italy.

Grimes, D.W., P.L. Wiley, and W.R. Sheesley. 1992. Alfalfa yield and plant water relations with variable irrigation. Crop Science 32:1381–1387.

Grismer, M.E., and K.M. Bali. 2001. Reduced-runoff irrigation of sudangrass hay, Imperial Valley, California. Journal of Irrigation and Drainage Engineering 127(5):319–323.

Grismer, M.E., and I.C. Todd. 1994. Field evaluation helps calculate irrigation time for cracking clay soils. California Agriculture 48(4):33–36.

Hanson, B.R. 1989. Drainage reduction potential of furrow irrigation. California Agriculture 43(1): 6–8.

———. 1995. Practical potential irrigation efficiencies. Proceedings, International Conference on Water Resources Engineering. Aug. 14–18. San Antonio, TX.

Hanson, B.R., D.B. Marcum, and R.W. Benton. 1989. Irrigating alfalfa for maximum profit. ASAE Paper 89-2091. Presented at the 1989 International Summer Meeting of the ASAE and CSAE, Quebec, Ontario.

Hanson, B., L. Schwankl, and A. Fulton. 1999. Scheduling irrigations: When and how much water to apply. University of California Division of Agriculture and Natural Resources, Oakland. Publication 3396.

Hutmacher, R.B., C.J. Phene, R.M. Mead, P. Shouse, D. Clark, S.S. Vail, R. Swain, M.S. Peters, C.A. Hawk, D. Kershaw, T. Donovan, J. Jobes, and J. Fargerlund. 2001. Subsurface drip and furrow irrigation comparison with alfalfa in the Imperial Valley. In: 31st California Alfalfa & Forage Symposium. December 11–13. Modesto, CA. Department of Agronomy and Range Science Extension, University of California, Davis.

Orloff, S., B. Hanson, and D. Putnam. 2001. Soil-moisture monitoring. University of California Cooperative Extension, Siskiyou County, Yreka, CA.

Schwankl, L., B. Hanson, T. Prichard. 2008. Maintaining microirrigation systems. University of California Division of Agriculture and Natural Resources, Oakland. Publication 21637.

8

Weed Management in Alfalfa

Mick Canevari
Farm Advisor, University of California Cooperative Extension, Stockton, CA

Ron N. Vargas
Farm Advisor Emeritus, University of California Cooperative Extension, Madera, CA

Steve B. Orloff
Farm Advisor, University of California Cooperative Extension, Yreka, CA

Weeds are serious economic pests of alfalfa. A variety of different weed species, including annuals and perennials, warm and cool season grasses and broadleaf plants, and parasitic and poisonous plants, infest alfalfa hay grown throughout the arid alfalfa production regions of the West. Weeds in alfalfa directly compete for the same resources required for alfalfa growth and development: water, nutrients, light, and space. If weeds are left uncontrolled, they will reduce alfalfa yield and weaken or even destroy the stand, particularly if left unchecked during the seeding period (Table 8.1). Weeds have a large effect on forage quality. Establishment of a vigorous alfalfa stand is essential for long-term weed control. In older alfalfa fields, weeds are quick to fill in open spaces when stands decline. It is nearly impossible to control weeds in a thin or weak alfalfa stand.

Weeds affect alfalfa during two distinct periods: stand establishment and in established fields. Yield is sometimes reduced, but more often yield is the same or actually higher when weeds are not controlled. However, the feeding value of the hay is usually drastically reduced. For example, in one study, protein content was as low as 9 percent in hay that contained 80 percent weeds. When weeds were controlled with herbicides, the protein content rose to over 20 percent. Thus, an effective weed control program can more than double the nutritive value of the hay.

Weeds affect quality because most weeds are less palatable and less nutritious than alfalfa. Although some weeds make high quality forage, they are too mature at the time alfalfa is harvested. The loss of feeding value from weed infestation can be due to physical, chemical, or toxic factors. Many weeds are much lower in protein and higher in fiber than alfalfa. Additionally, when certain weeds, such as foxtail or pigeongrass (*Setaria* spp.) or wild barley (*Hordeum* spp.), are present in hay, livestock may develop serious mouth and throat ulcerations. This is due to physical factors, such as prickly or spiney texture. Other weeds, including wild celery (*Apium leptophyllum* [Pers.] Muell.), Mexican tea (*Chenopodium ambrosioides* L.), creeping swinecress (*Coronopus didymus* [L.] Smith), and mustards (*Brassica* spp.), can contribute off flavors in milk. Weeds such as coast fiddleneck (*Amsinckia intermedia* [Fischer & C. Meyer] Ganders) and common groundsel (*Senecio vulgaris* L.) contain alkaloids that are toxic to livestock, especially horses. Weeds that contain higher moisture than alfalfa at baling can cause mold and off-color hay (tobacco hay) and lead to haystack and barn fires.

Understand the Biology of Your Weeds

An understanding of the life cycle, germination, flowering, and seed formation of weeds and their method of propagation is necessary for effective weed management. Weeds are classified into three groups according to their life cycle: annual, biennial, and perennial, and can be broadleaf or grassy weeds. Table 8.2 lists common weeds present in alfalfa in California and their life cycles.

Annual Weeds

These are plants that emerge from seed, grow vegetatively, flower, and produce seed all within a year. Annual weeds are classified into winter or summer, depending on their season of growth. Winter annuals germinate in the fall and winter with the cool temperatures and high rainfall. Summer annual weeds germinate as soil temperatures increase in the spring and early summer. Grasses are the most common summer annual weed problem in alfalfa. Yellow and green foxtail (*Setaria* spp.) and watergrass or barnyardgrass (*Echinochloa crus-galli* [L.] P. Beauv.) are usually the most problematic. They begin germinating in early February and continue through July. Plants are vegeta-

TABLE 8.1

Lack of effective weed control during stand establishment can dramatically reduce alfalfa yield, and result in poor stands, regardless of seeding rate

	Alfalfa Seeding Rates	Alfalfa 1st Season Yield	Weed 1st Season Yield	Alfalfa Stand End of Year 1
	Pounds per acre	Tons per acre	Tons per acre	Plants per ft^2
Fiddleneck	15	0.5	12.7	0.9
	30	0.1	12.2	0.8
Common Groundsel	15	6.1	1.8	9.9
	30	6.3	1.7	11.6
Annual Bluegrass	15	6.9	1.5	10.7
	30	7.5	1.3	11.7
Hand Weeded	15	8.3	0.16	11.9
	30	8.1	0.13	11.8

Conversions: To obtain kg per ha, multiply pounds per acre by 1.12. To obtain megagrams per hectare, multiply tons per acre by 2.24. To obtain plants per meter^2, multiply plants per ft^2 by 9.29 x 10^{-2}.

tive through June when seedheads develop and appear above the alfalfa canopy. New seed heads are continually produced during each cutting cycle (typically on a 28- to 30-day interval).

Biennial Weeds

These plants take up to 2 years to complete their life cycle. Vegetative growth occurs dur-

TABLE 8.2

Weeds commonly found in alfalfa and their life cycles

ANNUALS	
annual bluegrass (w)	California burclover (w)
volunteer cereals (w)	roughseed buttercup (w)
common chickweed (w)	cheeseweed (*malva* sp.) (w)
coast fiddleneck (w)	cocklebur (s)
common groundsel (w)	fillarees (w)
miner's lettuce (w)	henbit (w)
mustards (w)	prickly lettuce (w)
London rocket (w)	blessed milk thistle (w)
Italian ryegrass (w)	shepherd's purse (w)
wild celery (s)	bristly oxtongue (w)
annual sowthistle (w)	common purslane (w)
yellow starthistle (w)	toad rush (w)
barnyardgrass (s)	Persian speedwell (w)
dodder (s)	creeping swinecress (w)
foxtail, yellow and green (s)	common lambsquarters (s)
prostrate knotweed (s)	
nightshades (s)	

BIENNIALS	
buckhorn plantain (s)	Mexican tea (s)

PERENNIALS	
Bermudagrass (s)	dandelion (s)
Johnsongrass (s)	curly dock (s)
nutsedge (s)	dallisgrass (s)
field bindweed (s)	goosegrass (s)

s = spring and summer germination w = fall and winter germination.

ing the first year, and seed production often does not occur until the second year. The few biennials that are problems in alfalfa are mostly broadleaves, including buckhorn plantain (*Plantago lanceolata* [L.]), blessed milk thistle (*Silybum marianum* [L.] Gaertn.), and Mexican tea.

Perennial Weeds

Perennial weeds live 2 years or longer. Vegetative growth and reproductive parts develop during the first year and subsequent years of the life cycle. Reproduction occurs by seed or by vegetative structures, including rhizomes, stolons, and tubers. Problem perennial weeds include yellow and purple nutsedge (*Cyperus* spp.), Johnsongrass (*Sorghum halepense* [L.] Pers.), Bermudagrass (*Cynodon dactylon* [L.] Pers.), field bindweed (*Convolvulus arvensis* L.), curly dock (*Rumex crispus* L.), and dandelion (*Taraxacum officinale* Wigg.). Some perennials, such as dallisgrass (*Paspalum dilatatum* Poiret), only reproduce from seed. Johnsongrass reproduces by seed and rhizomes. Nutsedge, even though it develops seed, only reproduces by tubers. Bermudagrass reproduces by seed or stolons (aboveground roots).

Weed Control During Stand Establishment

The importance of weed control during stand establishment cannot be overemphasized. Weed competition in new alfalfa plantings can cause irreversible damage to the productivity of the stand. Weed competition in seedling alfalfa impedes root development, lowers forage quality and alfalfa yield, and thins the alfalfa stand. Competitive effects of weeds during early growth can extend well into the first year, the second year, and often throughout the life of the stand. The presence of poisonous weeds such as common groundsel, coast fiddleneck, and poison hemlock (*Conium maculatum* L.) can make the hay completely unmarketable.

The first step toward an effective weed-control program in alfalfa is to use farming practices that promote a healthy, vigorous stand that will compete effectively with weeds. Weed control during stand establishment involves integrating many factors, including cultural practices and use of herbicides.

Controlling Weeds through Crop Rotation

It is advisable to rotate out of alfalfa for 2 or 3 years to reduce disease pressure and disrupt weed and insect life cycles. Occasionally alfalfa is replanted within 1 year. However, this practice is not recommended and usually results in greater expense and shorter stand life, and it requires more inputs to manage pests.

Know the weed history of a field prior to planting. Fields infested with perennial weeds are not well suited for alfalfa. Use crop rotations with annual crops such as wheat and corn that compete more aggressively with perennial weeds and allow the use of registered herbicides that control bindweed, nutsedge, and Johnsongrass effectively. An integrated approach that includes crop rotation is the key to management of perennial weeds. Nutsedge, an important perennial weed problem in alfalfa, can be managed by rotating with cotton, corn, or beans and with the use of herbicides and continuous cultivation. Control of yellow nutsedge through crop rotation was demonstrated in a study comparing four cropping systems in California. A 2-year rotation of alfalfa with applications of EPTC, 2 years of barley double-cropped with corn and using a thiocarbamate herbicide, and 2 years of barley followed by fallow with glyphosate applications all reduced the viable nutsedge tubers by 96 to 98 percent when compared to continuously grown cotton. Field bindweed is more easily controlled in fields of small grains with the use of 2,4-D herbicide or glyphosate after crop harvest.

> *It is advisable to rotate out of alfalfa for 2 or 3 years to reduce disease pressure and disrupt weed and insect life cycles.*

Seedbed Preparation

Proper land leveling and laser finishing promote the uniform distribution of irrigation water and improve drainage, and is also an important first step for effective weed management. If fields are not properly leveled, water collects in low spots, drowning out the alfalfa, leading to weed infestations. Non-uniform water distribution adversely affects alfalfa growth, reducing its ability to compete with weeds. A well-prepared seedbed promotes uniform germination and rapid growth of alfalfa seedlings. Good seedbed preparation often involves ripping or chiseling and the use of finishing discs, harrows, and ring rollers to produce a firm, trash-free seedbed.

Fertilization

Healthy alfalfa is an excellent competitor with weeds. Proper soil fertility is important to maximize the competitiveness of alfalfa. Soil analysis is advised to determine the nutritional status of the soil before applying preplant fertilizer. Fertility requirements can be met with commercial fertilizers or manures. If manures are used, they should be composted to kill existing weed seeds. Fertilizers containing high amounts of nitrogen promote weeds and are not recommended in pure stands of alfalfa (see Chapter 6, "Alfalfa Fertilization Strategies").

Pre-irrigation

Weed problems are reduced by pre-irrigating to promote weed germination before planting. After emergence, weed seedlings are controlled through cultivation. This does not completely eliminate all weeds, but it reduces the viable seed population and makes other control measures more effective. Pre-irrigation also enhances final seedbed preparation, promotes uniform planting depth, and aids in the incorporation of pre-plant herbicides by minimizing the large clods in the soil.

Variety Selection

Selecting a well-adapted alfalfa variety is important to minimize weed infestations (see Chapter 5, "Choosing an Alfalfa Variety"). Fall dormancy influences the ability of alfalfa to compete with weeds. Dormant varieties often grow too slowly in the San Joaquin Valley and Low Desert, giving weeds a competitive advantage. Selecting varieties with the appropriate insect, nematode, and disease resistance will prevent many problems and increase the chances of a vigorous and persistent stand. Plant certified seed that is free of noxious weed seed. Use alfalfa seed inoculated with nitrogen-fixing *Rhizobium* bacteria when seeding a field without a recent history of alfalfa.

Planting Dates

One of the most important cultural practices for controlling weeds is to plant at an optimum time for the alfalfa seedling growth, and when weed populations and growing conditions do not favor the weeds. The range of soil temperature suitable for alfalfa planting and germination is from 65° to 85°F (18° to 29°C), which is typically in the early fall (Sept.–Oct.) in California's deserts and Central Valley. Time of planting can have a large effect on weed problems. Alfalfa planted too late in the fall will germinate and grow very slowly. Winter annual weeds germinate in late fall and winter and are better adapted to cold temperatures than is alfalfa, and they will grow more rapidly and compete vigorously with the alfalfa (Fig. 8.1). In contrast, summer planting in very hot conditions can also slow alfalfa establishment and result in infestations of summer weeds and grasses that flourish under these conditions. Refer to Chapter 4, "Alfalfa Stand

Establishment," for optimal planting dates for different regions.

Seeding Depth and Rate

Alfalfa seeding depth and rate are critical for successful establishment. Seeding rates vary, depending on seedbed conditions and planting method. A seeding rate of 15–20 pounds (17–22 kg/ha) drilled, or 20–25 pounds per acre (22–28 kg/ha) broadcast planted, will usually result in a competitive alfalfa stand. Seeding alfalfa at higher rates than these will further improve the ability of the alfalfa to compete with weeds, but the additional seed cost is usually not justified.

Companion Crops or Nurse Crops

Companion crops (also referred to as "nurse crops") consist of a second species planted along with the alfalfa during the establishment phase. Small grains (e.g., oat, wheat, and barley) are commonly used as companion crops, oat being the most common. The purpose is to prevent soil erosion and suppress weeds while the alfalfa is becoming established. Most companion crops germinate and grow faster than alfalfa and provide additional competition against rapidly growing weeds. Companion crops can reduce weed populations and, in

FIGURE 8.1

Monthly high and low average temperatures used as a planting guide for weed germination for the San Joaquin and Sacramento Valleys of California. Alfalfa Planting Guide.

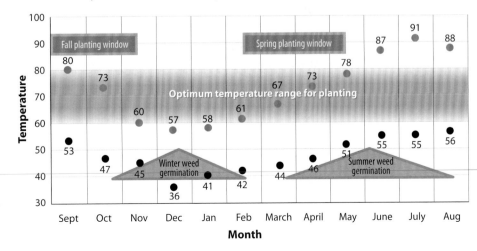

some cases, eliminate the need for herbicides during the establishment period.

By replacing most weeds with a desired plant species, first-harvest forage quality and yield may be improved. However, companion crops have several drawbacks. If seeded at too high a rate, companion crops can negatively impact the seedling alfalfa in the same manner as weeds and can lower alfalfa vigor and stand density. Forage quality of alfalfa is reduced by most companion crops compared with stands of pure alfalfa.

Irrigation

Irrigation practices significantly impact weed infestation levels. Overwatering, especially when it results in standing water being present for several hours, creates anaerobic conditions and provides an environment conducive to diseases or scald. Alfalfa mortality may result, allowing weed encroachment. Water-loving weeds, such as nutsedge, curly dock, watergrass and foxtail, invade the field where standing water has killed the alfalfa. Harvesting too soon after irrigation when soils are moist may cause permanent ruts and soil compaction, which leads to standing water and ultimately to weed growth. Excessive soil moisture at harvest and frequent watering promote the growth of shallow-rooted summer annual weeds, particularly grasses, over the deeper-rooted alfalfa.

> *Excessive soil moisture at harvest and frequent watering promote the growth of shallow-rooted summer annual weeds.*

Cutting Management

Early mowing or clipping can inhibit weed growth and be an effective way to rescue a new alfalfa planting that is heavily infested. Mowing tall weeds that shade the small seedling alfalfa improves sunlight penetration into the canopy, allowing alfalfa to grow and compete more successfully during the next regrowth. Annual grassy weeds, if cut too early, will recover after mowing and contaminate subsequent cuttings. Mowing immature alfalfa is not a preferred practice because it slows alfalfa development and depletes carbohydrate root reserves. However, early harvest to remove weeds may be a practical way to rescue a heavily weed-infested, newly seeded alfalfa field. It may be the best (or only) option if the weeds have grown beyond the optimum treatment timing for herbicides.

Cutting intervals have a profound impact on the weed infestation level in established stands. Short cutting intervals (such as 20–25 days) do not allow the alfalfa plants enough time to build up sufficient stored carbohydrates in their roots to initiate vigorous growth after cutting. This gives weeds a competitive advantage. Extending the time interval between harvests can reduce weed problems in established stands but lowers the nutritional quality of the alfalfa.

Herbicide Controls During Establishment

Chemical weed control is used on probably 80 percent of the alfalfa acreage in California for seedling weed control. Herbicides are considered an integral component of a total weed-management system, and when coupled with cultural practices, weeds can be efficiently and effectively controlled. Herbicides used in the establishment phase can be grouped into categories, based on their application timing relative to newly planted alfalfa (see "UC IPM Pest Management Guidelines: Alfalfa" [www.ipm.ucdavis.edu]) for more details on herbicide use and selectivity.

Pre-plant herbicides are applied and mixed into the soil before planting and control weeds at germination or through root uptake. Post-plant, pre-emergence herbicides are applied after planting the crop but before the weeds or the crop have emerged. Post-emergence herbicides are applied after weed and/or crop emergence.

Pre-plant Herbicides

Pre-plant herbicides are applied to soil and thoroughly incorporated before planting alfalfa. EPTC (Eptam) and benefin (Balan) are two pre-plant herbicides used primarily for stand establishment. They are selective, soil-active herbicides that control a wide range of leaf and grassy weeds before they emerge. Pre-plant-incorporated herbicides perform best when thoroughly mixed into soil in a seedbed free of large clods.

Benefin and EPTC effectively control small-seeded broadleaf plants and grasses. Benefin generally controls weeds for 3 months and EPTC for 6 weeks. Benefin is effective for spring plantings because it controls many summer annual weeds, such as pigweed (*Amaranthus* spp.), common lambsquarters (*Chenopodium album* L.), and barnyardgrass. It is less effective for fall plantings because it does not adequately control many of the winter annual weeds that infest fall plantings, such as mustard species and common groundsel.

EPTC belongs to the thiocarbamate chemical family, which is very volatile and therefore requires immediate incorporation into the soil. EPTC controls many of the same grasses and broadleaf weeds as benefin, and it also suppresses the perennial problem weed nutsedge. EPTC is effective for pre-emergence control of volunteer cereals. EPTC and benefin can be combined at reduced rates of each to expand the spectrum of weeds controlled. EPTC injury symptoms of alfalfa include cupping and crinkling of leaves (Color Plate 8.6 at the end of this chapter).

Post-plant, Pre-emergence Herbicides

Herbicides classified for this use are applied after the alfalfa is planted but before it emerges. Although this is not a common practice in the West, there are circumstances when soil conditions and timing favor this decision. EPTC can also be used at this timing and applied after planting. No-till or minimum-till systems often rely on post-plant, pre-emergence applications of herbicides as an effective weed-management tool. Glyphosate and paraquat kill existing vegetation after planting but before alfalfa emerges.

Post-emergence Herbicides

Post-emergence herbicides are applied to the crop after weeds and alfalfa emerge. These herbicides are more commonly used than pre-emergence herbicides because they are generally more effective and provide more flexibility. A major advantage of post-emergence herbicides is that herbicide selection is made after weed emergence, after the weeds have been properly identified. Thus, the most effective herbicide can be selected.

Proper timing depends on the post-emergence herbicide and its safety. For example, post-emergence *selective* herbicides that cause minimal injury (e.g., clethodim) can be applied at a smaller alfalfa growth stage than *nonselective* herbicides (e.g., paraquat) (Table 8.3). Some herbicides are applied when one trifoliolate leaf is visible, and others require that three or more trifoliolate leaves are fully developed. It is critical to identify the appropriate alfalfa growth stage for the herbicide chosen.

TABLE 8.3

Rate and timing for herbicides registered for use on newly planted alfalfa

Herbicide	Stage of Alfalfa Growth Before Treatment	Rate lbs. a.i./A
Gramoxone Inteon	3 trifoliolate leaves 6 trifoliolate leaves 9 trifoliolate leaves	0.126 0.25 0.25–0.46
Buctril	2–4 trifoliolate leaves	0.25–0.375
Velpar	6-inch root growth/ multiple stems	0.25–0.375
Poast	2–4 trifoliolate leaves	0.1–0.46
Prism	2–4 trifoliolate leaves	0.095–0.176
2,4-DB	1–4 trifoliolate leaves	0.375–0.46
Pursuit	2–4 trifoliolate leaves	0.047–0.094
Raptor	2–4 trifoliolate leaves	0.03–0.046
Glyphosate: (Roundup Ready Alfalfa)	flexible	22–44 oz

Conversion: To convert pounds/acre to kg/ha, multiple by 1.12.

As a rule, making an application at the earliest stage when weeds are small will provide the most consistent and effective weed control. More weed control failures in seedling alfalfa occur from treating the crop too late than from any other factor. Less-selective herbicides are generally applied at a more advanced growth stage, when alfalfa can withstand a higher amount of leaf burn. When applied at a later timing, usually beyond the three- or four-leaf stage (Fig. 8.2), the alfalfa will usually grow out of the injury symptoms, lowering yields only for the first cutting, if at all. Nonselective herbicides are specifically used when weeds are large or not controlled by other herbicides. The safety of nonselective herbicides to alfalfa seedlings is marginal and requires special attention when selecting the rate in relation to seedling size.

Bromoxynil (Buctril). This is a selective contact herbicide for broadleaf weed control. It is applied when the alfalfa plants have two or

FIGURE 8.2

The number of trifoliolate leaves indicate whether plants are old enough for herbicide treatments.

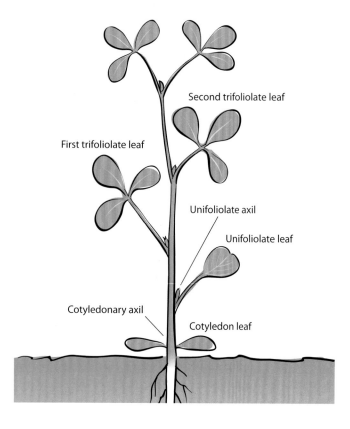

more trifoliolate leaves. It is especially effective on coast fiddleneck, mustards, common groundsel, and annual sowthistle (*Sonchus oleraceus* L.). With a diverse weed spectrum, including numerous grass and broadleaf weeds, Buctril is often tank-mixed with other herbicides to provide broad-spectrum control with a single application. Avoid spraying when temperatures are expected to exceed 80°F (27°C) for 3 days after application. The best results are achieved when weeds are small, from 1 to 3 inches (2.5 to 7.6 cm) tall. Since it is a contact herbicide, thorough spray coverage is very important; this is accomplished using higher spray volumes of 20–30 gallons per acre (185-280 liters per ha). Bromoxynil injury symptoms of alfalfa include leaf burning and necrotic tissue (Color Plate 8.7).

2,4-DB (Butyrac, Butoxone). This is a broadleaf-selective herbicide that translocates from the leaves to the rest of the plant. It is used for broadleaf weeds such as prickly lettuce (*Lactuca serriola* L.), annual sowthistle, and mustards and is also effective on perennial curly dock. It is applied when alfalfa reaches the two-trifoliolate leaf stage. The effectiveness of 2,4-DB is enhanced in warm temperatures. Erratic control occurs when conditions are cold and foggy. To broaden the spectrum of control, 2,4-DB is often tank-mixed with other herbicides. Injury symptoms to alfalfa from 2,4-DB can include slight twisting and narrow, cupped leaves (Color Plate 8.8).

Sethoxydim/clethodim (Poast/Prism). These are selective grass herbicides that control both annuals and perennials. They have no toxic effect on alfalfa or broadleaf weeds, including sedges. These herbicides work best on immature grasses up to the tillering stage (before heading) that are vigorously growing and not drought stressed. Poast or Prism can be used between alfalfa cuttings to control summer grasses, including yellow and green foxtail, barnyardgrass, and perennials: Bermudagrass, Johnsongrass, and goosegrass (*Eleusine indica* [L.] Gaertn.). Well-established perennial grasses usually require multiple or sequential applications. Both herbicides can be tank-mixed with many broadleaf herbicides.

Paraquat (Gramoxone Inteon). This is a non-selective contact herbicide that controls a wide range of broadleaf and grassy weeds. Paraquat is injurious to alfalfa seedlings when applied before the three-trifoliate leaf stage or when an excessive rate is used. The rate is based on the size of the alfalfa plants, rather than weed size, to maintain crop safety. Higher rates can be applied to larger alfalfa plants. Paraquat is not tank-mixed with other post-emergence herbicides because it controls a broad spectrum of grasses and broadleaf weeds, and its mode of action can inhibit the effectiveness of systemic herbicides. Paraquat is commonly used when weeds become too large for other herbicides. It is not the first herbicide of choice but is often considered a rescue treatment to reduce the volume of weed canopy overtopping young alfalfa seedlings. Paraquat injury symptoms of alfalfa include burning and necrotic leaves (Color Plate 8.9).

Imazethapyr (Pursuit). This is a selective systemic herbicide that controls most broadleaf weeds and some grasses. Apply Pursuit to small weeds that are not moisture stressed after alfalfa has developed two trifoliolate leaves. Pursuit is very effective at controlling winter annuals such as mustards, shepherd's purse (*Capsella bursa-pastoris* L.), creeping swinecress, chickweed (*Cerastium* spp.), and many more. It is in the ALS (acetolactate synthesis) inhibitor herbicide family, and continual use beyond stand establishment or 2 years should be avoided to minimize the potential for herbicide resistance. There are restrictions on when other crops can be planted after applications of Pursuit (called plant-back intervals). Plant-back intervals range from 6 to 40 months, which reduces long-term use of this herbicide in older established stands. Imazethapyr injury symptoms of alfalfa include yellow, stunted growth.

Imazamox (Raptor). This is a selective, translocated herbicide that controls broadleaf and grass weeds. The weed spectrum controlled is similar to those controlled by Pursuit, except that it is far more effective on grasses, especially winter annual grasses. Raptor is applied to alfalfa with two or more trifoliolate leaves. It is in the same chemical family (ALS inhibitor)

as Pursuit; therefore, it is not recommended to alternate Raptor and Pursuit applications. Combining Raptor with other broadleaf herbicides can broaden the spectrum of weeds controlled, especially for weeds not adequately controlled with Raptor, such as prickly lettuce, annual sowthistle, redmaids (*Calandrinia ciliata*), and coast fiddleneck. Performance is best when weeds are small, 1–3 inches (2.5–7.6 cm) in height and growing vigorously. The addition of a nitrogen fertilizer with a surfactant (as per label recommendations) greatly enhances control of marginally sensitive weeds. Crop rotation guidelines are half of those for Pursuit, and the pre-harvest interval is 20 days, which allows for applications between cuttings. Imazamox injury symptoms of alfalfa include yellow, stunted growth.

Weed Control in Established Alfalfa Stands

In most alfalfa growing regions, weeds can plague alfalfa production during the fall and winter dormant period, as well as during the summer growing season. Weed problems in established alfalfa stands can be divided into winter annuals, summer annuals, perennial weeds, and parasitic weeds, each of which may require a different control strategy.

Control of Winter Annuals in Established Alfalfa

Winter annual weeds consist of broadleaf and grassy weeds that germinate and grow vigorously during the late fall and winter and compete with the established alfalfa crop when the crop is dormant. The most common annual weeds in established alfalfa during this period in California's Mediterranean and desert zones are numerous and depend largely on the field history and crop rotation. For a comprehensive list of weeds that infest alfalfa fields, refer to Table 8.2.

Cultural Methods

Certain cultural practices during winter months, such as light cultivation, grazing, and flaming, can reduce winter weed populations.

Cultivation. Dormant established alfalfa can be lightly cultivated with a spring-tooth harrow during winter if soil moisture is low enough to prevent compaction. Small weed seedlings will be uprooted, but injury to alfalfa crowns may also occur. Crown injury can delay the first cutting, reduce yields, and predispose the alfalfa to crown disease. Normally, cultivation is only partially effective; some weeds re-root, weeds may emerge after cultivation, and perennials are not controlled. Timing and skill are critical as cultivation must take place after weed emergence but before the alfalfa has much growth. Techniques should minimize injury to the alfalfa.

Grazing. "Sheeping" or grazing-off alfalfa and weed growth during late fall and winter can reduce weed growth significantly if soil conditions allow. Some weeds are quite palatable and nutritious to grazing animals, and grazing can reduce winter weed competition (Color Plate 8.10). Grazing can be coupled with chemical methods, thereby improving chemical weed control. Spray coverage is increased by exposing the soil and young weeds so that herbicides can then be uniformly applied after grazing. Soil compaction and damage to crowns is a major risk of grazing for weed control. A large number of animals should graze the field rapidly because prolonged intensive grazing can deplete root reserves, reduce vigor, and lead to a thin, weedy stand (see Chapter 18, "Alfalfa Grazing Management"). Risk of nitrate poisoning to grazing livestock should be considered with some types of weeds (especially lambsquarters, pigweed, and grasses). Some weeds, such as common groundsel, can be poisonous to livestock.

> *Grazing can be coupled with chemical methods, thereby improving chemical weed control.*

Flaming. Flame throwers can be used as effective weed control measures. This generally has a similar effect as "burn back" herbicides such as Gramoxone (paraquat), killing weeds, but also killing some of the alfalfa foliage. Flaming large areas can be expensive, but flaming is often appropriate for smaller weed-infested areas, and has been used for control of dodder.

Herbicide Controls for Winter Annuals

Herbicides are normally required for complete winter annual weed control in alfalfa. Diuron (Karmex and Direx), hexazinone (Velpar), norflurazon (Solicam), pronamide (Kerb), paraquat (Gramoxone Extra), imazethapyr (Pursuit), imazamox (Raptor) and metribuzin (Sencor in selected regions) are registered for winter annual weed control in established alfalfa. Apply soil-active, pre-emergence (pre-emergence for the weed) herbicides in fall, winter, or spring before new alfalfa growth begins and before weeds germinate. Pre-emergence herbicides must be incorporated by winter rainfall or sprinkler irrigation (consult the label). Certain soil-active herbicides can cause yellowing of foliage and delay the first cutting when used on alfalfa that has already resumed growth. Many of the soil-active herbicides have a 1- to 2-year plant-back restriction, limiting their use in the last years of the alfalfa stand's life. Consider the weeds present, soil texture and organic matter content, rainfall patterns, and the remaining stand life before selecting the appropriate herbicide. These soil-residual herbicides are often tank-mixed to broaden the weed-control spectrum (see the UC IPM Pest Management Guidelines: Alfalfa [www.ipm.ucdavis.edu] for more details on herbicide use and selectivity).

Diuron (Karmex and Direx) controls many broadleaf weeds and some grasses but usually does not adequately control common groundsel, speedwell (*Veronica officinalis* L.), and wild oat (*Avena fatua*). Apply before alfalfa growth begins and before weeds are well established, generally no later than January. Only stands 1 year or older can be treated, and because diuron persists in the soil, it cannot be used on fields in their last year of production. Treated fields may be replanted to any crop after 1 year from the last application if the rate does not exceed 2 pounds per acre (2.24 kg/ha). Diuron injury symptoms of alfalfa include leaf yellowing and interveinal chlorosis (Color Plate 8.11).

Hexazinone (Velpar) controls a range of broadleaf weeds and some grass weeds, including common groundsel, chickweed, miner's lettuce (*Claytonia perfoliata* Willd. spp. *perfoliata*), and annual bluegrass (*Poa annua* L). It also suppresses some biennials and perennials, such as dandelion, buckhorn plantain, and speedwell. Many crops cannot be planted for 18 months following treatment without yield damage. Hexazinone injury symptoms of alfalfa include leaf yellowing and interveinal chlorosis.

Norflurazon (Solicam) controls many broadleaf and grassy weeds and suppresses nutsedge, a difficult perennial weed that escapes most herbicides. Applications can be made to both dormant and actively growing alfalfa, but if used during the growing season, norflurazon cannot be applied within 28 days of harvest. Norflurazon will not control emerged weeds. If emerged weeds are present at the time of application, norflurazon must be tank-mixed with an herbicide with foliar activity, such as paraquat. Twenty-four months is the rotational interval after the last application of norflurazon. Norflurazon alfalfa injury includes bleached (white) leaves.

Paraquat (Gramoxone Inteon) is used as a "burn-down" herbicide and is the herbicide of choice when weed populations have germinated and are 2–4 inches (5–10 cm) tall. Apply Gramoxone alone or in combination with soil-active herbicides diuron, hexazinone, or norflurazon for extended residual control. Rates depend on weed size. Leaf burn will occur if alfalfa regrowth has resumed. Alfalfa cannot be harvested or grazed within 60 days of application. Gramoxone does not adequately control larger weeds or perennials. It is especially important that weeds are thoroughly covered with the spray solution since gramoxone does not translocate through the plant. Gramoxone is often used during the last year of an alfalfa stand.

Imazethapyr (Pursuit) can be applied post-emergence to established alfalfa but because of its soil activity should not be used during the last year of production because of plant-back restrictions, which range from 4 to 40 months, depending on cropping type. Sugarbeets are especially sensitive to residual Pursuit and cannot be planted for 40 months after application. Pursuit is rarely used on established alfalfa because herbicide activity is slow in winter months and is less effective on large weeds and grasses than other herbicides used in dormant alfalfa. Therefore, Pusuit has limited potential as a soil pre-emergence herbicide. It may be useful for late applications where other herbicides are restricted and would cause excessive injury.

Imazamox (Raptor) is in the same chemical family as Pursuit (an ALS inhibitor) but has a shorter soil life. Raptor has the advantage that harvest can take place immediately after application. This makes it a useful product for use during the growing season since it can be applied between cuttings to control a variety of broadleaf weeds and some grassy weeds.

Control of Summer Annuals in Established Alfalfa

Summer annual weed problems include, but are not limited to, grasses such as yellow and green foxtail (*Setaria* spp.), crabgrass (*Digitaria* spp.), barnyardgrass or watergrass, and southwestern cupgrass (*Eriochloa gracilis* [Fourn.] A. S. Hitchc.). These weeds germinate in early to late spring and can severely contaminate alfalfa fields, especially those that have poor stands or exhibit poor growth due to soil compaction, poor fertility, or frequent cuttings.

Cultural Methods

To reduce the spread of these weeds, keep the alfalfa growing vigorously through proper irrigation management and soil fertility, and with cutting schedules that allow sufficient time between harvests to maintain crop vigor. As detailed in Chapter 13, " Harvest Strategies for Alfalfa", a "staggered" cutting schedule (alternating long and short intervals) enables plants to recover from defoliation to more vigorously compete with weeds. A dense, vigorous alfalfa stand reduces the amount of light reaching the soil surface, preventing weeds from germinating and becoming established. Residual soil-applied herbicides applied during winter for control of winter annual broadleaf weeds can sometimes increase summer grass problems. For example, Karmex and Velpar are effective for most winter annuals, but they only control foxtail for a short time. With the winter annuals eliminated, the later germinating grasses flourish, having little competition, and fill in the empty spaces. It is important to anticipate and address the problem of grass invasions during the summer.

Herbicide Controls for Summer Annuals

Trifluralin (Treflan/TR-10). Summer grasses in established alfalfa are most commonly controlled with trifluralin granules (Treflan TR-10). Apply in winter or early spring before grasses germinate. January to mid-February is the best time to apply trifluralin in the San Joaquin Valley because the summer annual foxtails germinate as early as mid-February. At least 0.5 inches (1.3 cm) of rainfall or sprinkler irrigation is needed within 3 days after application to incorporate the herbicide. Trifluralin injury symptoms (stunted growth) are generally observed in established alfalfa.

Pendimethalin (Prowl). This herbicide controls a similar weed spectrum to trifluralin TR 10. Prowl differs from TR-10 in that, as a liquid formulation, it can be applied by itself or tank mixed with other post or pre-emergent herbicides in the same application. It is especially effective for control of most summer grasses including seteria species, yellow and green foxtail; and some broadleaf weeds provided it is applied before they germinate and emerge. When Prowl is applied in late winter or in the spring after first cutting, effective weed control can be achieved for several months into the summer. The actual length of control depends on the rate used. It can also be used in newly

planted seedling stands after the alfalfa crop has emerged as a pre-emergent tool for later germinating weeds. Prowl has relatively low volatility loss on the soil surface, however, it still must be moved into the soil by rainfall or an irrigation within 7–10 days after an application for best results.

EPTC (Eptam) liquid applied in irrigation water or applied as a broadcast granular just ahead of irrigation can also control summer grasses. This herbicide must be uniformly metered into the water during irrigation. Best results are obtained when fields are properly leveled, allowing irrigation water to be uniformly applied. As with trifluralin, EPTC must be applied before grasses emerge in mid-February. One application controls grasses for 30 to 45 days, so repeated applications are necessary for season-long control. EPTC injury symptoms of alfalfa can include cupping and crinkling leaves and shortened internodes.

Sethoxydim (Poast) or **Clethodim** (Prism, select) are also used as post-emergence treatments in fields where summer grasses have already emerged or escaped an earlier trifluralin application. Apply the herbicide after the first or second cutting before grasses become too large and well tillered. The best timing is after bale removal and within 2 to 4 days after the field has been irrigated as these herbicides do not perform well on moisture-stressed weeds. Injury symptoms have not been observed in alfalfa.

Dodder

The parasitic weed dodder (*Cuscuta* spp.) is one of the most serious weed problems in alfalfa and presents unique challenges to the producer. Dodder is a rootless, yellow-orange, threadlike parasitic weed that penetrates into alfalfa stems and forms a dense tangled mat, sometimes several feet in diameter (Color Plate 8.12). Dodder can reduce yield of newly planted and established alfalfa stands and shorten stand life. Dodder seeds survive in soil for many years; therefore it is difficult to manage solely through fallowing or crop rotations. Because dodder is especially difficult to control after it attaches to alfalfa, prevention and pre-emergence control are the best strategies. A dense, vigorously growing stand of alfalfa slows dodder development, as it requires sunlight to thrive, but a dense stand alone is not sufficient. Prevention of seed production is critical for long-term dodder management.

Trifluralin (Treflan TR-10) granular herbicide application before dodder germination is the most effective program to manage dodder in conventional cultivars. Dodder typically germinates in late February in the San Joaquin Valley. Two pounds of trifluralin active ingredient (20 pounds of 10% trifluralin granular per acre) (22 kg/ha) controls dodder for 3 months; an additional 20-pound application after the first cutting is needed for large populations and extended control. Once dodder has attached and imbedded its haustoria (sucker-like tissues) into the alfalfa stem, control becomes more difficult.

Pendimethalin (Prowl) liquid herbicide is an effective herbicide for dodder control in alfalfa. Herbicide timing is very important and similar to Trifluralin TR-10. Application must be made before dodder germinates and attaches to the alfalfa plant. In the Central Valley, dodder germination begins in February and is continuous throughout the warm periods. Research has shown that split applications of herbicide made 60 days apart provide longer and more effective control than one single high rate. As is the case for all pre-emergent herbicides, a timely rain or irrigation is needed for incorporation for the best results.

Attached dodder is controlled by flaming with a propane-fueled burner (may be restricted in certain air pollution control districts) and flail mowing. For effective control by flaming, the alfalfa stems and foliage must be burned below the point of dodder attachment. Repeat treatments may be necessary after each cutting because dodder continues to germinate from seed through most of the growing season.

Flail mowed alfalfa is cut near the ground surface to remove attached dodder. Alfalfa

regrowth can be slow after flail mowing, especially if cut too short. This may extend the number of days between cuttings required to achieve a normal yield, but flail mowing is generally less injurious to yield and stand life than is flaming.

The use of glyphosate in Roundup Ready alfalfa is effective when applied at the early attachment period, before the dodder colonies become too large. Multiple applications may be needed throughout the season.

Few post-emergence herbicides are available for dodder control. However, Pursuit has been successful in controlling dodder at germination and early attachment to alfalfa. As is the case with many post-emergence herbicides, coverage of the entire weed is essential. The best success has been in seedling alfalfa when both alfalfa and dodder plants are thoroughly covered with the herbicide solution. Pursuit will not translocate through the alfalfa plant to dodder or by soil uptake since dodder is rootless.

Control of Perennials in Established Alfalfa

Several perennial weeds, such as dandelion, nutsedge, Bermudagrass, Johnsongrass, and short-lived perennials such as curly dock and buckhorn plantain, commonly infest alfalfa. Once established, perennials are difficult to remove in established alfalfa, so site selection and prevention are key components of perennial weed-control strategy. Control options for established perennial weeds are limited to a few herbicides that only provide marginal control at best and only when an alfalfa stand is healthy.

Yellow and purple nutsedge can cause serious problems in alfalfa. When other weeds are controlled with residual and/or selective grass

Perennials are difficult to remove in established alfalfa, so site selection and prevention are key components of perennial weed-control strategy.

herbicides, nutsedge populations can increase due to the lack of competition. Excessive irrigations also cause nutsedge to flourish.

EPTC (Eptam) or **norflurazon** (Solicam) beginning in February, before or just as plants emerge, can suppress nutsedge. With both herbicides, it is important to make the initial application before nutsedge emergence and sequential applications for season-long suppression.

Johnsongrass growth from rhizomes and Bermudagrass growth from stolons are not controlled with any of the residual herbicides used in established alfalfa. **Sethoxydim** (Poast) and **clethodim** (Prism) will provide acceptable control if applied when the grass is 12–18 inches (30–46 cm) tall, but usually two to three treatments are necessary.

Timely applications of **2,4-DB** (Butoxone, Butyrac) can suppress some broadleaf perennials, such as curly dock and field bindweed. Curly dock, also referred to as sour dock, can be a problem in established alfalfa, especially in low areas of the field or at ends of the field that tend to collect water and stay moist for extended periods. Control is achieved with a fall application of 2,4-DB made before a freeze or drought conditions stress the plant. However, once curly dock becomes well established, soil-residual herbicides have no effect.

Roundup Ready Alfalfa System

Glyphosate (Roundup), using Roundup Ready (RR) Alfalfa varieties. Commercial alfalfa varieties genetically engineered for resistance to glyphosate herbicide were released in 2005. This technology, combining herbicides with a variety genetically engineered to be tolerant of the herbicide, enables Roundup to be applied post-emergence both during stand establishment and in established stands. This technology provides the advantages of wide-spectrum weed control and very low risk of crop injury. It enables considerable flexibility in timing of application compared with many other seedling weed-control strategies.

Most broad-spectrum herbicides injure the alfalfa crop to some degree. Crop injury has been demonstrated to be dramatically reduced or eliminated with RR Alfalfa. Furthermore, there are few effective weed-control programs for some of the most difficult-to-control perennial weeds in alfalfa (Bermudagrass, nutsedge, Johnsongrass, and dandelion) that could be improved with the RR strategy. Adequate control of these tough perennials could add years to stand life.

A disadvantage of this strategy is the lack of residual control, since glyphosate kills only emerged weeds. Therefore, it is important to spray Roundup after most of the weeds have emerged or when there is enough crop canopy to outcompete late-emerging weeds. On the other hand, do not delay application so long that weeds become large and are difficult to control. Generally, the best time to treat seedling alfalfa is when the alfalfa is between the three- and six-trifoliolate leaf stages. There is usually bare soil with earlier applications, allowing subsequent weed emergence. With later applications, weeds may be too large for adequate control and with heavy weed infestations, alfalfa stand density or vigor may be affected before the herbicide is applied. Sometimes it may be necessary to make two applications of glyphosate during alfalfa stand establishment.

Preventing the development of glyphosate resistance in weeds is a major concern with the overuse of Roundup in alfalfa. Continuous use of glyphosate in an RR Alfalfa system can lead to weed species shifts or weeds developing resistance to glyphosate. We recommend diverse systems which incorporate cultural methods as well as rotations or tank mixes of herbicides to prevent weed resistance or weed shifts (Figure 8.3). Additionally, growers should be assured that their buyers of the hay or animal product are not sensitive to the presence of a genetically engineered (GE) crop. The RR technology is reviewed in detail in Van Dynze et al. 2004 "Roundup Ready Alfalfa: An Emerging Technology."

FIGURE 8.3

Example weed management strategies for glyphosate-resistant alfalfa with continuous glyphosate applications compared with an herbicide strategy that includes herbicide rotations during a 4-year alfalfa stand. A combination of soil residual herbicides and different modes of action is recommended to prevent weed shifts and herbicide resistance. Note: these are examples only—appropriate strategies should be modified for different regions and weed pressures.

Year	Objective	Season	Continuous Glyphosate Strategy	Rotational Herbicide Strategy
Seedling	Control weeds that compete during stand establishment	Fall	Glyphosate	Glyphosate
1	Control late-emerging weeds during establishment	Winter (late)	Glyphosate	Glyphosate*
1	Summer annual weed control may not be needed first year	Spring		
1	Summer annual weed control may not be needed first year	Summer		
1	Summer annual weed control may not be needed first year	Fall		
2	Control winter annual weeds and/or pre-emergence control of summer weeds	Winter	Glyphosate	Soil residual herbicide or tank mix* of soil residual herbicide with Glyphosate**
2	Summer annual weed control/Dodder	Spring		
2	Summer annual weed control/Dodder	Summer	Glyphosate	
2	Summer annual weed control/Dodder	Fall		
3	Control winter annual weeds and/or pre-emergence control of summer weeds	Winter	Glyphosate	Soil residual herbicide or tank mix* of soil residual with Glyphosate**
3	Control summer annual grassy weeds/ Dodder	Spring	Glyphosate	
3	Control summer annual grassy weeds/ Dodder	Summer (mid)	Glyphosate	
3	Control summer annual grassy weeds/ Dodder	Fall		
4	Control winter annual weeds	Winter	Glyphosate	Glyphosate
4	Control summer annual grassy weeds/ Dodder	Spring	Glyphosate	
4	Control summer annual grassy weeds/ Dodder	Summer (mid)	Glyphosate	Glyphosate
4	(Stand take-out)	Fall (late)	Tillage and/or 2,4-D + dicamba as necessary	Tillage and/or 2,4-D + dicamba as necessary
(4 years)	**Total Number of Glyphosate Applications**		10	4–6

* Tank mixing with another herbicide is advised if significant populations of glyphosate tolerant weeds such as burning nettle are present.

**Soil residual herbicide (depending on location and weed spectrum, use hexazinone, diuron, or metribuzin) for pre-emergence control of winter annual weeds. An application of a dinitroaniline herbicide (pendimethalin or trifluralin) applied at this time will control summer annual grassy weeds.

Summary

An integrated approach to weed management assures an effective and cost-efficient system over the life of the alfalfa stand. A key aspect of an integrated weed control program is careful attention to the stand establishment period. Using sound production practices that promote longer alfalfa life and higher yields generally provides weed-free fields and better performance from herbicides. Relying only on a chemical approach for weed management will generally fail over time if recommended cultural practices aren't used in a total management system.

A successful weed-management program integrates a total cultural system that includes the following practices:

- monitoring and controlling problem weeds, especially perennials prior to planting

- land leveling to enhance efficient irrigation applications and tailwater drainage

- seedbed preparation and planting time that promote fast germination and emergence

- selecting pest-resistant varieties best suited for your area and market

- maintaining nutritional balance and soil chemistry that promote vigorous alfalfa growth

- cutting alfalfa on longer cycles to keep alfalfa vigorous and competitive with weeds

- timely controlling of insects to maintain a healthier stand with more foliage to shade weeds

- managing irrigation to prevent damage to the plant from excess water and disease

- choosing the right herbicide and applying when weeds are small

Additional Reading

Canevari, M., R. Vargas, S. Orloff, and R. Norris. 1990. Alfalfa weed control in California. University of California Division of Agriculture and Natural Resources, Oakland. Publication 2143.

Canevari, W.M. 2006. Weeds in seedling alfalfa. UC IPM Pest Management Guidelines: Alfalfa. University of California Division of Agriculture and Natural Resources, Oakland. Publication 3430. http://www.ipm.ucdavis.edu/PMG/r1701111.html.

Canevari, W.M., D. Colbert, W.T. Lanini, and J.P. Orr. 2002. Post-emergence weed control in seedling alfalfa and phytotoxicity symptoms. University of California Division of Agriculture and Natural Resources, Oakland. Publication 21615.

Canevari, W.M., S.B. Orloff, W.T. Lanini, and R.G. Wilson, UC Cooperative Extension, and R.N. Vargas. 2006. Weeds in established alfalfa. UC IPM Pest Management Guidelines: Alfalfa. University of California Division of Agriculture and Natural Resources, Oakland. Publication 3430. http://www.ipm.ucdavis.edu/PMG/r1700111.html.

DiTomaso, J., and E. Healy. 2007. Weeds of California and other western states. University of California Division of Agriculture and Natural Resources, Oakland. Publication 3488.

Orloff, S., and W.L. Mitich. 2002. Principals of weed control: Alfalfa. California Weed Science Society, 3rd ed.

Shewmaker, G.E. 2005. Idaho forage handbook, 3rd ed. University of Idaho Extension, Moscow, ID. Bulletin 547.

Van Deynze, A., D. Putnam, S. Orloff, T. Lanini, M. Canevari, R. Vargas, K. Hembre, S. Mueller, and L. Teuber. 2004. Roundup Ready alfalfa: An emerging technology. University of California Division of Agriculture and Natural Resources, Oakland. Publication 8153.

Color Plates

PLATE 8.1

Weedy alfalfa field.

PLATE 8.2

Perennial weeds, yellow nutsedge.

PLATE 8.3

Poisonous weeds, coast fiddleneck.

PLATE 8.4

Clean alfalfa field.

PLATE 8.5

Companion planting of oats.

PLATE 8.6

EPTC injury symptoms include cupping and crinkling of leaves.

PLATE 8.7

Bromoxynil injury symptoms include burning and necrotic leaf tissue.

PLATE 8.8

2,4-DB symptoms can include slight twisting and narrow cupped leaves.

PLATE 8.9

Paraquat injury symptoms include burning and necrotic leaves.

PLATE 8.10

Sheep grazing alfalfa assists in controlling winter weeds.

PLATE 8.11

Hexazinone and Diuron injury symptoms include leaf yellowing and interveinal chlorosis.

PLATE 8.12

Dodder in alfalfa.

9

Managing Insects in Alfalfa

Charles G. Summers
Entomologist, University of California
Kearney Agricultural Center, Parlier, CA

Larry D. Godfrey
Extension Entomologist, Department of Entomology,
University of California, Davis

Eric T. Natwick
Entomology Farm Advisor, University of California
Cooperative Extension, Holtville, CA

Over 1,000 species of arthropods have been observed in alfalfa fields. Of these, fewer than 20 cause injury, and fewer still are serious pests. The number of phytophagous (plant-eating) species is far exceeded by the number of non-plant feeders, and many of the latter are predators or parasites. Alfalfa has been called "the insectary of the Central Valley" since it is home to many predators and parasites that move among crops and provide biological control of pests in diverse cropping systems, as well as in alfalfa.

Although only a few pest species infest alfalfa, they can cause substantial yield and quality losses if present in high numbers. Some pests, such as the Egyptian alfalfa weevil (*Hypera brunneipennis* Boheman), routinely cause damage annually in established alfalfa. Most pests, however, tend to be more sporadic, causing yield losses on a less frequent basis. An effective pest management program can significantly reduce the losses caused by these pests. To implement an Integrated Pest Management (IPM) strategy to optimize economic returns in alfalfa, the following principles must be observed:

- correct identification of pest and natural enemy species

- use of economic threshold values, including natural enemy activity

- careful monitoring and sampling of pest and natural enemy populations

- implementation of control strategies that minimize effects to natural enemies and other nontarget species

Insect Identification

Proper identification of pest and natural enemy species cannot be overemphasized. Many insect species, particularly in the immature stages, are similar in appearance and may easily be mistaken for each other. For example, lygus bug (*Lygus* spp.) nymphs, which feed in alfalfa, may be confused with big-eyed bug (*Geocoris* spp.) nymphs, a natural enemy that helps control insect pests. Pea aphids (*Acyrthosiphon pisum* Harris) and blue alfalfa aphids (*A. kondoi* Shinji) are similar in appearance and can easily be misidentified. Since their economic thresholds differ, improper identification can lead to improper management decisions. Failure to properly identify natural enemy species may lead to unnecessary pesticide applications if predator or parasite populations are sufficient to maintain pest numbers below economic thresholds. A series of color photos of pests and natural enemies can be found at the end of this chapter (Color Plates 9.1–9.24).

Economic Thresholds

The economic threshold is defined as the pest population at which control measures should be initiated to prevent yield or quality losses. Economic damage has been most often defined in terms of yield reduction, but forage quality must also be considered. Because many insects, such as alfalfa weevils and caterpillars, are leaf feeders, and forage quality is highest in leaves, reduction in quality may be as important as yield reduction. Aphids and leafhoppers deposit large quantities of honeydew on the

leaves, resulting in the growth of sooty molds that may make the hay unmarketable or unpalatable to livestock. Some economic threshold levels, such as those for alfalfa caterpillars and some aphid species, take parasite abundance into account and thus require information on natural enemy populations as well as pest populations before informed decisions can be made.

Monitoring and Sampling

Pest population levels can increase rapidly, from a few individuals to numbers exceeding the economic threshold in a short time. Sampling for pests and natural enemies is critical for implementing an IPM program. Insect populations vary from year to year and from field to field. Some general trends can be derived based on field histories, but examination of the insect population in each field is the only reliable way to accurately assess population levels. Keep records of pest and natural enemy numbers, along with information on weather conditions and other crop production practices used in each field. Fields should be monitored weekly during periods of pest activity (Fig. 9.1) and more often as pest numbers approach economic threshold levels.

Standard Sweep-net Techniques

Sampling for specific insect pests is discussed in the description of each species. However, since the use of a sweep net is so universal in sampling alfalfa, both for pest and natural enemy species, this section is devoted to the proper use of this tool.

A 15-inch- (38-cm-) diameter sweep net (diameter of the hoop) with a 26-inch (66-cm) handle is the standard sampling tool used in alfalfa. The net should be swung in a 180° arc such that the net rim strikes the top 6 inches (15 cm) of alfalfa growth. The net should be held slightly at an angle, so that the bottom edge strikes the alfalfa before the top edge passes through. This facilitates gathering insects into the net. Each 180° arc is considered one sweep. Take a sweep right to left, walk a step, and take a second sweep, left to right, and so on (Fig. 9.2).

After taking the desired number of sweeps, quickly pull the net up through the air to force insects into the bottom of the net bag and grasp the net bag at about the midpoint. The net bag can then be slowly inverted while releasing the grasp on the bag to allow the insects, such as leafhoppers, to slowly escape and be counted. If large numbers are netted, or if they are slow moving, such as caterpillar larvae, the net contents can be dumped into a white enamel pan, and counts can then be made. If insect numbers are very high, place the net contents

in a paper bag and return it to the laboratory or office. The sample should be chilled to slow down the movement of highly active insects. Pest management decisions, however, are generally made before such high numbers build up. Samples should be collected from all portions of the field. Nonrepresentative parts of the field, such as field edges, should be avoided. A common practice is to trace an "X" or "W" pattern within the field to be certain that a representative sample is taken. A minimum of four locations in each field should be sampled. Then, average the counts taken from all areas to determine the overall average number per sweep.

FIGURE 9.1

Seasonal occurrence of the major alfalfa pests in the Imperial Valley and the Central Valley of California.

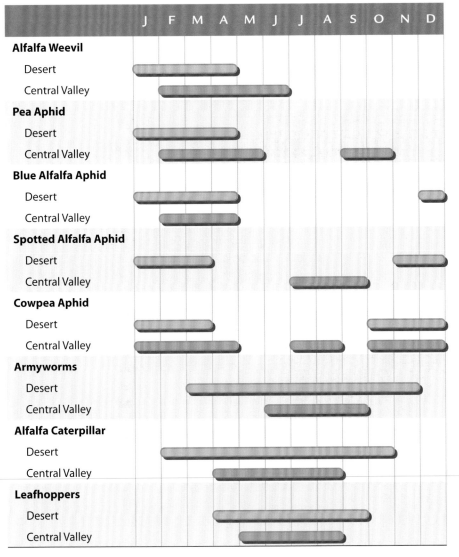

FIGURE 9.2

A single sweep is one 180° arc taken as you walk through the alfalfa.

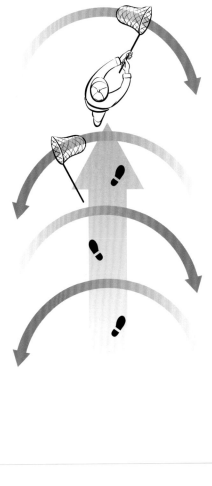

Integrated Pest Management Strategies

Integrated pest management involves the use of all available strategies to properly manage pests. These strategies include selection of pest-resistant varieties, manipulation of cutting schedules (accelerated or delayed), habitat modification by the use of strip-border cutting, grazing, use of biological controls, and judicious use of pesticides, when required. These strategies are discussed for each pest later in this chapter.

Resistant Varieties

Selection of pest resistant varieties is a key element in the management of several alfalfa pests. Varietal resistance is not absolute and means only that a certain percentage of the plants in the population are resistant, not all of them. For example "highly resistant" (HR) means that a minimum of 50 percent of the plants are resistant. Therefore, if pest populations are particularly high, severe damage can still result, even in highly resistant varieties. See Chapter 5 ("Choosing an Alfalfa Variety") for a complete discussion of pest resistance. Resistance is also discussed in sections on individual pests. A list of alfalfa varieties and the pests they are resistant to, including insects, diseases, and nematodes, is available from the National Alfalfa and Forage Alliance and can be accessed at http://www.alfalfa.org.

> *Selection of pest resistant varieties is a key element in the management of several alfalfa pests.*

Border-strip Harvesting

Border-strip harvesting involves leaving uncut strips of alfalfa at various intervals across the field. These border strips serve as a refuge for natural enemies and to retain lygus bugs in the alfalfa where they do little harm, and keeps them out of neighboring crops, such as cotton or beans, where they can cause significant damage. Uncut strips, 10–14 feet (3–4 m) wide, are left adjacent to every second irrigation border (or levee). An actual levee is not needed; strips can be left at approximately 150–200-foot (45–61-m) intervals across the field. At the next harvest, these strips are cut with one-half of the alfalfa strip going into one windrow, together with half the swather width containing new alfalfa (right side of the swather), and the other one-half going into a second windrow (left side of the swather). This blending of old and new alfalfa minimizes quality problems that might arise from the older hay. At this cutting, new uncut strips are then left adjacent to the alternate irrigation borders.

Chemical Controls

Insecticides may be needed when pests reach economic threshold levels, despite the use of alternative, nonchemical control strategies. When using pesticides, it is important that the proper chemical, rate, timing, and application method be used. The selected chemical should be easy on natural enemies while maximizing control of the pest. Selection of an insecticide depends on several factors, including proper registration, effect on the pest to be controlled, pre-harvest interval, reentry interval, cost, desired length of residual control, and selectivity to natural enemies.

Since chemicals and their registrations change frequently, we will not present insecticide recommendations here. Please refer to the "UC IPM Pest Management Guidelines for Alfalfa Hay," available at http://www.ipm .ucdavis.edu/PMG/selectnewpest.alfalfa-hay .html or from your local University of California Cooperative Extension Office. These guidelines contain the latest update of chemicals recommended for pest control in alfalfa in California. In other states, consult your county extension office. The most important thing to do when applying insecticides is to read and follow the label instructions.

Although they are important tools, insecticides have some drawbacks, which include:

Secondary outbreaks of pests can occur when an insecticide is applied to control a pest but inadvertently kills natural enemies. These natural enemies may have been important for controlling another insect pest, and without this natural control, the second pest builds to high enough levels to become damaging. This new pest is called a secondary pest and its rise to pest status resulted from the insecticide application.

Pest resurgence is another drawback from insecticide applications. Similar to a secondary outbreak, this results from the effects of non-selective insecticides on natural enemies. The insecticide initially controls the target pest but also destroys populations of natural enemies. Pest resurgence results when pest populations rebound but the natural enemy populations are delayed or develop more slowly than the pest.

Hazards to honeybees can be a problem with insecticides used in alfalfa. A hay crop is normally harvested before the alfalfa plants are in bloom and attractive to bees, but blooming weeds can sometimes entice bees into alfalfa fields. This is particularly true before the first cutting when blooming weeds are most common. Many tree fruits are in bloom at that time and require bees for pollination.

Phytotoxicity (chemical injury, foliage burn) to alfalfa plants under certain conditions can result from insecticide sprays. Environmental conditions can influence insecticide properties and the hardiness of the alfalfa plant and its susceptibility to phytotoxicity from insecticides.

Off-site movement of insecticides has become an increasing concern in recent years. This movement can result from aerial drift or movement through surface water and ground-

water. Alfalfa has been implicated in movement of some organophosphate and, to a lesser extent, pyrethroid insecticides into surface waters. Volatile organic compounds (VOCs) are of concern as pollutants from insecticides and adjuvants. Refer to the UC IPM Web site http://ipm.ucdavis.edu/PMG/selectnewpest.alfalfa-hay.html for more information on water quality protection.

Safety to pesticide applicators, handlers, field scouts, and others associated with alfalfa culture is of concern. Likewise, effects on birds, mammals, and invertebrates after insecticide application represent an important consideration regarding the selection of pesticides for use in alfalfa.

Insecticide resistance is a concern in all crops. Insecticide resistance takes place when some insect pests survive an insecticide treatment. The survivors then pass the genes for resistance on to the next generation. The more frequent the insecticide application, the more rapidly a population develops resistance. Eventually, insecticides are rendered ineffective through this phenomenon. Resistance management is the process used to maintain susceptibility, and therefore insecticide efficacy, within a pest population. It is important for growers to reduce the number of insecticide applications to reduce the potential for resistance. Alternating insecticides with different modes of actions is another method used to maintain susceptibility. Fortunately, problems with insecticide resistance in insects attacking alfalfa hay are rare.

> *It is important for growers to reduce the number of insecticide applications to reduce the potential for resistance.*

The remainder of this chapter discusses the insect pests found in alfalfa with a brief description of the insect, its biology, and its damage. We also discuss economic thresholds and techniques for monitoring and sampling, and provide management guidelines.

Important Insect Pests— Alfalfa Weevil

Alfalfa weevil (*Hypera postica* Gyllenhal) and Egyptian alfalfa weevil (*H. brunneipennis* Boheman) are the most important insect pests of alfalfa in California (Color Plate 9.1). The two species are very similar; the appearance of the adults and larvae is identical. Separate introductions of these pests from foreign sources have resulted in the separate species designations. Research indicates, however, that the two are likely biotypes of the same species.

There are some important biological differences between the alfalfa weevil and Egyptian alfalfa weevil, the most significant being that the former dominates in cooler climates of the Intermountain Region and the Coast, while the latter flourishes in the Central and Imperial Valleys and the High Desert. Egyptian alfalfa weevil larvae encapsulate eggs of the parasite *Bathyplectes curculionis* (Thomson), whereas larvae of the alfalfa weevil do not. The management of these two pests is identical and they will be considered together.

The larval form of these weevils inflicts the majority of the damage to alfalfa (Color Plate 9.2). Early instars feed in the terminals, and larger larvae feed on the leaflets. Under severe pressure, the plants can be completely defoliated. Damage begins in spring (Fig. 9.1) and accumulates over a 4–6-week period. The larvae are legless and about 0.25 inch (0.6 cm) long when fully grown. They are pale green, a thin white line runs down the center of the back, and the head is black. They pupate in a loosely woven cocoon, either on the soil surface or attached to foliage. After 2–3 weeks of pupation, the new adult emerges. Adult weevils are dark gray and about 0.20 inch (0.5 cm) long. Adults feed on alfalfa stems for a short time, rasping the epidermis along the length of the stem. They then leave the field, seeking sites in which to spend the summer in a state of estivation (summer hibernation). These sites include areas under the loose bark of trees, especially eucalyptus, or in any place they can wedge their bodies, such as in rough-barked trees (walnut), cracks in almost any surface, or under shake shingles on homes.

In recent years, Egyptian alfalfa weevil has evolved from a univoltine (one generation per year) into a multivoltine (several generations per year) insect. Rather than leaving the field as noted above, some adults remain in the alfalfa, mate, and continue to lay eggs. These eggs soon hatch, giving rise to a second, and sometimes third, generation of weevil larvae that continue to cause damage to subsequent cuttings. After the first cutting, fields should continue to be monitored either using a sweep net or visual observation if the alfalfa is too short to sweep to be certain that no additional weevil larvae are present.

In late fall or early winter, adults that have spent the summer in aestivation emerge and return to alfalfa fields. The adults mate, and the females begin inserting their lemon-yellow eggs into alfalfa stems. Eggs usually hatch in late winter–early spring. The key period for management of alfalfa weevil and Egyptian alfalfa weevil is typically before the first cutting, although later cutting, as noted above, can also be damaged.

Monitoring and Management Guidelines for Alfalfa Weevil

Alfalfa weevil larvae are sampled using a standard 15-inch- (38-cm-) diameter sweep net. Sampling should be conducted in at least four areas of the field and by taking five 180° sweeps per area. The economic threshold for initiating chemical control is 15–20 larvae per sweep. Control options include insecticides and early harvest. With the early harvest option, alfalfa regrowth for the second cutting should be closely monitored for feeding damage.

Biological control with generalist predators is not effective because the complex of natural enemies has not yet developed during this late winter–early spring period. Specific weevil parasites have been introduced into California but have been largely ineffective against both alfalfa weevil biotypes. An alfalfa weevil-specific fungus, in many alfalfa-growing regions of California, aids in biological control. In years of heavy rainfall, the fungus *Zoophthora phytonomi* (Arthur) infects the larvae, causing their death. Look for brown or discolored larvae on the underside of leaves at the top of the plant. In some regions, the fungus maintains weevil populations below the economic threshold level and may help minimize the need for chemical intervention.

Although some success has been achieved in developing resistant varieties, these are mainly restricted to dormant cultivars that are not well adapted to California's Mediterranean climate. Sources of resistance in nondormant cultivars have been identified but have not yet been incorporated into commercial varieties.

Grazing sheep in January and February in the Low Desert consume weevil eggs and larvae. Lambs cropping the forage down to ground level improve hay yields and quality at the first harvest. Care should be taken to ensure that sheep do not graze fields that are waterlogged from winter rains. See Chapter 17 on "Alfalfa Utilization by Livestock" for more information.

Important Insect Pests— Aphids

Pea aphid (*Acyrthosiphon pisum* [Harris]), blue alfalfa aphid (*Acyrthosiphon kondoi* Shinji), spotted alfalfa aphid (*Therioaphis maculate* Buckton), and cowpea aphid (*Aphis craccivora* Koch) are the principal aphids associated with alfalfa (Color Plates 9.3 – 9.7). They suck large quantities of sap from the plants and inject a toxin into the plant as part of the normal feeding process. This results in stunted plants with shortened internodes and yellow, distorted, and misshapen leaves. In addition, aphids secrete large amounts of honeydew, a sugary byproduct of digestion, on which a number of sooty molds grow. These sooty molds reduce photosynthesis and render the leaves and stems unpalatable to livestock.

Aphids reproduce by giving birth to live young. These young, while still inside their mother, also have young developing within them, a phenomenon called "telescoping of generations." This is why aphid populations can build so rapidly. Under proper temperature conditions, an aphid may go from newly born to producing offspring in 5–7 days.

Pea Aphid and Blue Alfalfa Aphid

Pea aphid and blue alfalfa aphid are large, green aphids with long legs, antennae, cornicles, and cauda (Fig. 9.3). They generally occur together in alfalfa. Pea aphid (Color Plate 9.3) and blue alfalfa aphid (Color Plate 9.4) are similar in appearance but can be distinguished from each other by the antennae. The pea aphid has dark bands at the joints between the antennal segments, whereas the antennae of the blue alfalfa aphid are uniformly dark (Color Plate 9.5).

It is important to distinguish between these two aphids because the blue alfalfa aphid causes more damage than does the pea aphid; they have different economic thresholds. Recently, a pink biotype of the pea aphid has been observed in California's Central Valley. This biotype looks identical to the green pea aphid except its body is a light pink. It still retains the banding on the antennae typical of the pea aphid. It is not known if the pink biotype causes more or less damage than the green biotype, but there is some evidence that the pink biotype is less susceptible to parasites than is the green biotype. For the time being, however, they should be treated the same. Both pea aphid and blue alfalfa aphid prefer cool temperatures and commonly reach damaging levels in the spring. Pea aphid may also reappear in the fall (Fig. 9.1). Blue alfalfa aphid is

FIGURE 9.3

Morphological features of an aphid useful in identification.

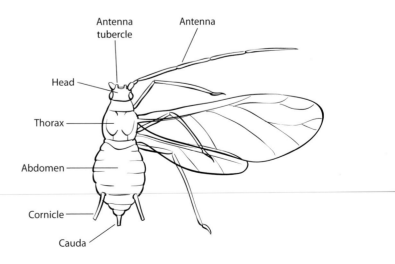

more tolerant of cool temperatures than is pea aphid and therefore may be seen earlier in the spring.

Both species may be present in the field at the same time as the alfalfa weevil. Damage is more severe on short hay than on taller alfalfa. Both species inject a toxin into the alfalfa while feeding, but the toxin injected by the blue alfalfa aphid is more potent than that injected by the pea aphid. The blue alfalfa aphid prefers the plant terminals, whereas pea aphid is more widely distributed over the plant. Both species prefer stem tissue over leaf tissue.

Monitoring and Management Guidelines for Pea and Blue Aphids

Stem samples are used to determine pea and blue alfalfa aphid densities. A minimum of five stems should be taken at random from each of four areas in the field, for a total of 20 stems. Care should be taken not to dislodge the aphids during removal of the stem. The stems may be shaken into a sweep net bag or beaten into a white pan or on a large sheet of white paper to dislodge the aphids for counting.

Resistant alfalfa varieties are available for the management of both pea aphid and blue alfalfa aphid and should be planted wherever these aphids are a problem. However, prolonged periods of below-normal temperatures may decrease the level of blue alfalfa aphid resistance in alfalfa, thereby resulting in injury

to otherwise resistant varieties. Thus, additional sampling may be needed during such periods. New varieties with improved resistance and forage characteristics are constantly being developed. Contact your local Farm Advisor or the National Alfalfa and Forage Alliance (www.alfalfa.org), for a list of the currently recommended varieties for your area.

Pea aphid and blue alfalfa aphid are attacked by a number of predators, parasites, and diseases. The most significant predator is the ladybird beetle (Color Plate 9.21A–B), and treatment thresholds for pea aphid are based on the number of ladybird beetle adults and larvae present (Table 9.1). Other predators include green lacewing larvae (*Chrysoperla* spp.), big-eyed bugs (*Geocoris* sp.), damsel bugs (*Nabis* spp.), and syrphid fly larvae. The parasitic wasp (*Aphidius smithi* Sharama and Subba Rao), attacks pea aphid, and *A. ervi* Haliday attacks both species. The wasp lays an egg inside the aphid and, after hatching, the parasite larva kills the aphid by consuming its internal organs. Parasitized aphids, called mummies, are light tan and appear bloated. A circular hole cut into the back of the aphid indicates that the adult parasite has emerged (Color Plate 9.24).

Both aphid species are also attacked by a fungal disease (*Erynia neoaphidis* Remaudière and Hennebert). This fungus is particularly effective during periods of warm, wet weather in the spring. Aphids killed by the fungus are pink to tan and appear to be flattened against the leaf. Close inspection often reveals the presence of fungal mycelia growing on the aphid body. The parasites and fungal disease can quickly reduce the aphid population, sometimes in a matter of a few days. Growers and Pest Control Advisors (PCAs) should look for signs of parasites or disease when checking fields, and, if present, continue to check the field every 2 to 3 days to see if the aphid population declines. If it does, insecticides may not be necessary. If natural enemies fail to keep the aphid populations in check, an insecticide treatment may be needed. Economic thresholds for both pea aphid and blue alfalfa aphid are shown in Table 9.1. If both aphids are present, use blue alfalfa aphid treatment thresholds.

TABLE 9.1

Treatment thresholds for pea aphid and blue alfalfa aphid in the Central and Imperial Valleys of California

Plant Height	Pea Aphid	Blue Alfalfa Aphid
Under 10 inches (25 cm)	40–50 per stem*	10–12 per stem
Over 10 inches (25 cm)	70–80 per stem*	40–50 per stem
Over 20 inches (50 cm)	100 + per stem*	40–50 per stem

*Do not treat if the ratio of ladybird beetles to pea aphids is equal to or exceeds the following: On standing alfalfa, one or more adults to 5–10 aphids per stem or three or more larvae to 40 aphids per stem. On stubble, one or more larvae to 50 aphids per stem.

Spotted Alfalfa Aphid

The spotted alfalfa aphid is pale yellow and has five or six rows of dark spots running lengthwise down the back of the abdomen (Color Plate 9.6). Spotted alfalfa aphids prefer warm weather and are generally found during the summer months (Fig 9.1). In the Imperial Valley, high populations may continue into the fall and winter (Fig. 9.1). The toxin injected by the spotted alfalfa aphid is extremely potent, and if large populations are present, they may kill the plant. Spotted alfalfa aphid secretes large quantities of honeydew, and plants become very sticky and covered with sooty molds at relatively low aphid densities.

Monitoring and Management Guidelines for Spotted Alfalfa Aphid

As with pea aphid and blue alfalfa aphid, it is important to sample frequently during periods of maximum aphid activity (Fig. 9.1). Follow the guidelines listed above for sampling pea and blue alfalfa aphids to determine levels of spotted alfalfa aphid infestations. Unlike pea and blue alfalfa aphids, spotted alfalfa aphids frequently colonize the leaves, so also count aphids that may remain on the leaves. In addition, take several sweep samples in at least four areas of the field to determine the population density of ladybird beetles.

Most alfalfa varieties grown in California are resistant to spotted alfalfa aphid. These resistant varieties constitute the most important control strategy for spotted alfalfa aphid. However, biotypes of spotted alfalfa aphid capable of infesting previously resistant varieties are constantly evolving. Fields, even those planted to resistant varieties, should be checked periodically. When selecting a variety, make sure that you have the most recent information available on variety resistance (www.alfalfa.org).

Spotted alfalfa aphid is preyed on by the same predator complex that attacks pea aphid and blue alfalfa aphid. Additionally, two parasitic wasps, *Trioxys* sp. and *Praon* sp., help to keep spotted alfalfa aphid populations under control. Parasitized aphids are similar in appearance to those previously described for pea and blue alfalfa aphids. Spotted alfalfa aphids are also attacked by a fungal disease, and appear similar to diseased pea and blue alfalfa aphids, as described above.

In the event that host plant resistance fails and natural enemies do not maintain spotted alfalfa aphid numbers below economic threshold levels, insecticide intervention may become necessary. Action thresholds for spotted alfalfa aphid are shown in Table 9.2. Note that these threshold values are adjusted for the presence of ladybird beetles in the field, so ladybird beetle numbers should be determined by taking sweep net samples.

Cowpea Aphid

Cowpea aphid is the newest aphid pest of alfalfa in California but is common in other alfalfa growing regions, especially Argentina, China, and the Middle East. It is easily distinguished from other alfalfa aphids since it is the only black aphid found in alfalfa (Color Plate 9.7). Individuals may be shiny black or a dull slate-black. They have white legs with dark bands at the joints. Although cowpea aphid has historically been present in alfalfa in very low numbers, it rarely, if ever, reached population levels that caused damage or yield loss. However, during the winter and spring of 1998, elevated populations of cowpea aphid were common in alfalfa in the Low Desert and were also found in higher that normal numbers in the High Desert. During the following two

TABLE 9.2

Treatment thresholds for spotted alfalfa aphid in the Central and Imperial Valleys

Time of Occurrence	No. of Aphids per Stem
Spring months	40 aphids per stem*
Summer months	20 aphids per stem*
After last cutting in the fall	50–70 aphids per stem
Newly seeded alfalfa in lower desert	20 aphids per stem

*Do not treat if the ratio of ladybird beetles to aphids is equal to or exceeds the following: On standing alfalfa, one or more adults to 5–10 aphids, three or more larvae to 40 aphids. On stubble, one or more larvae to 50 aphids.

years, it spread throughout the Central Valley from Kern to Glenn Counties and into the Intermountain counties. Historically, cowpea aphid appears during the hot summer months, then disappears as temperatures cool in the fall. However, the cowpea aphid currently infesting alfalfa appears to thrive in cool as well as hot temperatures. In the Central Valley, populations generally reach highest numbers from February through April, and in the desert, numbers peak from October through January. In the San Joaquin Valley, populations have also reached treatable levels in August and September (Fig. 9.1). Like the spotted alfalfa aphid, cowpea aphid injects a powerful toxin into the plant during feeding, and under severe aphid pressure, cowpea aphids can kill alfalfa plants. Cowpea aphid is a prolific honeydew producer, and the alfalfa becomes sticky and covered with sooty molds at relatively low aphid densities.

Monitoring and Management Guidelines for Cowpea Aphid

Cowpea aphid is attacked by two common aphid parasites, *Lysiphlebus* sp. and *Diaeretiella* sp. These parasitic wasps have been collected throughout the state wherever cowpea aphid occurs. Parasitized aphids appear bloated, as described for pea aphid and blue alfalfa aphid. In the Low Desert, the seven-spotted ladybird beetle (*Coccinella septempunctata* L.) is an important predator of cowpea aphid. There are currently no commercially available alfalfa varieties resistant to cowpea aphid. Sample for cowpea aphid as described in monitoring and management guidelines for pea aphid and blue alfalfa aphid. Currently, no economic thresholds have been developed for cowpea aphids, and we recommend that the economic threshold values developed for blue alfalfa aphid be used until specific threshold values for cowpea aphid have been established.

Important Insect Pests— Caterpillars

The larval forms (caterpillars) of several species of Lepidoptera (butterflies, moths, and skippers) are important pests of alfalfa. The larvae feed on foliage, and often several species may be present at one time. Damage generally occurs during the summer months (Fig. 9.1).

Armyworms

Beet armyworm (*Spodoptera exigua* [Hübner]) and western yellowstriped armyworm (*S. praefica* [Grote]) are common pests in the Central Valley and desert valleys from June through September (Fig. 9.1). They may occasionally damage alfalfa as early as April or May in the Low Desert valleys of Southern California (Fig. 9.1). Egg masses of both species are deposited on the upper side of leaves. White cottony scales cover beet armyworm egg masses (Color Plate 9.8), and western yellowstriped armyworm egg masses are covered with gray cottony scales (Color Plate 9.11). These help protect the eggs from predators and parasites. Eggs hatch in a few days, and larvae reach full size in 2–3 weeks. The larvae pupate on or just under the soil surface.

Adults of both species are brown, nocturnal moths with a 1.25-inch (3-cm) wingspan. Because they are nocturnal, the adults are seldom seen, but they may fly up as you walk through the field, landing again a short distance away. There are four to five generations of beet armyworm and western yellowstriped armyworm per year in the Low Desert and four generations in the Central Valley. The final generations of each species overwinter as pupae in the soil.

Beet armyworm larvae are smooth skinned and are usually olive green (Color Plate 9.9), but the color varies from bright green to purplish green. They have very fine dark stripes on their backs and pale yellow stripes on each side. Western yellowstriped armyworm larvae appear smooth, are usually black, and two prominent orange-yellow stripes and many narrow stripes line each side of the body (Color Plate 9.12). The beet armyworm possesses a dark spot on the lateral surface of the second thoracic segment (second segment with legs), whereas the western yellowstriped armyworm has a spot on the lateral surface of the first abdominal segment (first segment behind the thorax and lacking legs). First instar larvae of both species are gregarious, remaining together near where the egg mass was deposited. They web the alfalfa terminal leaves together and skeletonize the leaves by consuming the interveinal tissue but leave the leaf veins intact (Color Plate 9.10). As they skeletonize the leaves around where they hatched, the terminals turn whitish and are referred to as "whitecaps." The larvae later disperse throughout the surrounding alfalfa where they continue to consume leaf tissue.

Monitoring and Management Guidelines for Armyworms

Monitor fields weekly by making a minimum of five 180° sweeps at each of four locations per field using a standard sweep net. Check fields weekly, then two to three times per week if populations approach the economic threshold. If the alfalfa is only a few days away from cutting, early harvest will minimize armyworm damage. The worms begin to leave the field almost immediately after cutting. If susceptible crops, such as cotton or sugar beets, are planted adjacent to the alfalfa, it may be necessary to protect them from armyworm invasion by leaving a strip of uncut alfalfa adjacent to the crop, or treating the first few rows of the adjoining crop.

Spiders and various species of predacious bugs (see Table 9.3, p. 148) prey on the larvae of both armyworm species and help to maintain populations at an acceptable level. A wasp, *Hyposoter exiguae* (Viereck), preys on both armyworm species by depositing an egg inside the larva. The developing parasite larva consumes the internal organs of the armyworm, which results in its death. Parasitism can be observed by pulling the heads from 0.5 inch (1.3 cm) or longer armyworms and squeezing the body contents out toward the head end. The *Hyposoter* larva, which is a light translucent green, will be pushed out of the parasitized armyworm (Color Plate 9.23). Checking for parasitism is important because the economic threshold levels are designed to take parasite activity into account. Armyworm larvae are also attacked by a nuclear polyhedrosis virus. This virus kills the larvae within a few days. Diseased caterpillars first appear yellowish and limp and after death hang from the plants as shapeless, dark tubes oozing the disintegrated body contents. The virus may completely control an armyworm infestation within a few days. If chemical controls are required, treat with an insecticide when there are 15 or more nonparasitized 0.5-inch- (1.3-cm-) long armyworms of either species per sweep. Select a chemical such as *Bacillus thuringiensis* Berliner that is harmless to the armyworm's natural enemies.

Alfalfa Caterpillar

The alfalfa caterpillar (*Colias eurytheme* Boisduval) is the larval form of one of the most noticeable pests of alfalfa; the bright yellow butterflies are commonly seen in the vicinity of alfalfa fields throughout the summer (Color Plate 9.13). Adults migrating between fields may be so numerous that they cause a potential driving hazard by covering the windshields of vehicles. They are common in the Central Valley from June through September and from May through October in the Imperial Valley (Fig. 9.1).

The adult female deposits single, yellow, football-shaped eggs on the upper surface of alfalfa leaves (Color Plate 9.14). Oviposition takes place on new growth alfalfa (<6 inches [15.2 cm] tall). These eggs hatch in 3–7 days, and the larvae consume the alfalfa leaves. The velvety green larvae have a white stripe along each side of the body and develop into 1.5-inch- (3.8-cm-) long individuals in 14–17 days (Color Plate 9.15). When mature, the larvae pupate, forming a yellowish chrysalis that is attached to an alfalfa stem. They produce four

Spiders and various species of predacious bugs prey on the larvae of both armyworm species and help to maintain populations at an acceptable level.

to five generations per year, and each generation is closely synchronized with the hay cutting cycle; thus they pupate before the hay is cut.

Alfalfa caterpillar larvae consume the entire leaf, including the veins, as opposed to armyworm larvae that consume the interveinal tissue but leave the veins intact. The alfalfa caterpillar is parasitized by a wasp, *Cotesia medicaginis* (Cresson). Parasitized larvae are easily distinguished by pulling the head of a caterpillar larva off and gently "rolling" the white, translucent parasite larva out (Color Plate 9.22). It is important to determine the amount of parasitism because the economic threshold levels take the amount of parasitism into account. These parasitized alfalfa caterpillar larvae perish in about 5 days, although they stop feeding soon after parasitism begins. The parasite larva spins a fuzzy, yellowish cocoon that is attached to the upper surface of the leaflet. Alfalfa caterpillars may also be attacked by naturally occurring *B. thuringiensis*. When infected, the larvae turn brown and appear to disintegrate.

Monitoring and Management Guidelines for Alfalfa Caterpillar

Monitor alfalfa caterpillar populations by taking a minimum of five 180° sweeps in four locations throughout the field. If cutting is only a few days away, the alfalfa caterpillar can be controlled by harvesting. Border-strip cutting can also be used to manage alfalfa caterpillar populations. This technique serves to retain parasite larvae in the alfalfa fields, thus resulting in improved biological control. Microbial insecticides, such as *B. thuringiensis,* can be applied in worst-case situations. *Bacillus thuringiensis* protects the parasites that will aid in controlling future generations. An average of 10 nonparasitized larvae per sweep indicates that an insecticide treatment is needed.

Leafhoppers

Leafhoppers are very important pests in Midwestern alfalfa production systems, but less important in the Mediterranean and desert zones of California. Of the several species of leafhoppers that inhabit alfalfa stands in California, three are important pests: potato leafhopper (*Empoasca fabae* [Harris]), garden leafhopper (*E. solana* DeLong) and Mexican leafhopper (*E. mexara* Ross and Moore). They are collectively known as "*Empoasca* leafhoppers." They all have the same general overall appearance and can only be distinguished from each other by examining the genitalia. They all cause identical damage. Adults are small (0.125-inch- [0.3-cm-] long), bright green, wedge-shaped insects (Color Plate 9.16). Nymphs (immatures) also have green, wedge-shaped bodies and run rapidly when disturbed. They may run forward, backward, or from side to side. Their curious movement, plus their shape, serves to distinguish them from lygus bug nymphs and slower-moving aphids. Other green leafhoppers (sharpshooters) may occasionally be present in alfalfa, but they are much larger and prefer to feed on grassy weeds, particularly bermudagrass, rather than alfalfa. Other small leafhoppers found in alfalfa are brown or gray and do no apparent damage.

The most common damage symptom caused by *Empoasca* leafhoppers is a yellow, wedged-shaped discoloration at the tip of each leaflet (Color Plate 9.17). Frequently, the leaf margin and tissue surrounding this area turns red. This symptom may occasionally be confused with boron deficiency but can easily be distinguished from the latter by the presence of the insect. Plants may become stunted and have very short internodes. Although *Empoasca* leafhoppers may be found throughout the year, damage in the Central Valley generally occurs during July, August, and occasionally into September. In the Imperial Valley, damage may begin as early as June and continue through September (Fig. 9.1).

Monitoring and Management Guidelines for Leafhoppers

At the first sign of injury, sample the field with a standard sweep net. Although we recommend that field margins be excluded when sampling for most insects, leafhopper sampling is the exception because infestations frequently begin on the field margin. Be sure to include field edges in your samples, and keep the results separate from the rest of the field. Often, leafhopper infestations are confined to the first 50–100 feet (15-30 m) of the field margin. If this is the case, treat only the field edges if leafhopper counts exceed the economic threshold but are not found farther into the field.

A minimum of four areas over the entire field should be sampled by taking 10 sweeps in each area and counting the number of adults and nymphs. If economic thresholds are reached (see below) and alfalfa is within a few days of harvest, cutting will control *Empoasca* leafhoppers. If alfalfa is 2 or more weeks away from harvest, treatments should be applied if counts reach five leafhoppers (adults and nymphs combined) per sweep. Alfalfa scheduled for harvesting in 10 days to 2 weeks should be treated if counts reach 10 individuals per sweep.

Although some alfalfa varieties with resistance to potato leafhopper have been developed, there are none available that are adapted to the arid West. Resistant varieties are available for areas of the Midwest and Northeast. These are generally dormant varieties that are not grown in our area.

Occasional Alfalfa Pests

Cutworms

Granulate cutworm (*Agrotis subterranea* [F.]) and variegated cutworm (*Peridroma sausia* Hübner) are occasional pests of High Desert and Central Valley alfalfa, but are frequent pests in the Low Desert when alfalfa is planted on beds. The white or greenish eggs are laid in irregular masses on alfalfa leaves or stems, often near the base of the plant. Larvae can grow to 2 inches (5 cm) in length. The heavy-bodied larvae appear as smooth-skinned caterpillars of various colors and patterns. Larvae roll into a "C" shape when disturbed (Color Plate 9.18). Cutworm larvae hide under loose soil, in soil cracks, or under duff during the day and move to the plants at night to feed.

In the Central Valley, variegated cutworm populations may develop in weedy areas and migrate into seedling stands or occasionally to mature stands. Seedling alfalfa stands can be severely damaged by cutworms, which cut the seedlings off at or just below the soil surface. Established fields are damaged when cutworms cut off new growth or feed on alfalfa foliage.

Granulate cutworm is a devastating pest in bed-planted alfalfa but can also be a pest of alfalfa planted on flat ground. Low Desert alfalfa fields are attacked by granulate cutworm

> *Granulate and variegated cutworms are occasional pests of the High Desert, but are frequent pests in the Low Desert when alfalfa is planted on beds.*

from May through October, but the pest is resident in fields throughout the year. Established alfalfa fields can be severely injured when cutworms cut off new shoots at or below ground level following harvest. The pest often goes undetected after cutting and hay removal. The problem becomes apparent when the field is watered and there is little or no regrowth as a result of cutworms feeding.

Monitoring and Management Guidelines for Cutworms

Cultural practices can help with management of cutworms. Cutworms are most injurious in fields with high plant residue. Preplant tillage and abatement of weedy refuge areas around fields help prevent cutworm infestations. Flood irrigation will drown many cutworm larvae. Flood irrigation during daylight hours will attract egrets, ibises, gulls, and other birds that prey on the cutworm as the advancing water forces the larvae from hiding. Monitoring and treatment guidelines have not been established for cutworms. Cutworms can be detected by looking under duff and carefully digging to a depth of 1 inch (2.5 cm) in loose soil near alfalfa crowns. When cutworm numbers exceed one or two per foot of row, or if severe damage is apparent, treatment is usually warranted. If chemical controls become necessary, it is recommended that fields be sprayed near sundown when cutworms are becoming active.

Alfalfa Webworm

Several species of webworms may occasionally damage alfalfa, but the alfalfa webworm (*Loxostege cerealis* [Zeller]) is the most common. Webworms are caterpillars that feed primarily on leaves in areas protected by webs. Larvae are green to yellow with a broad light-colored stripe down the middle of the back, and they vary from 0.5 to 1.5 inches (1.2 to 3.8 cm) in length. Webworms overwinter as larvae in the soil. Females lay eggs when the adults emerge in early spring. Larvae feed for 3 to 5 weeks. Early feeding takes place beneath webbing on the undersides of the leaves. If numbers are high, this webbing will be clearly visible and will cover extensive areas of foliage. As the webworms grow larger, they venture out from the webbing but will rapidly retreat into it when disturbed. Management actions are seldom warranted and no treatment thresholds exist.

FIGURE 9.4

Clover root curculio larvae can be distinguished from ground mealy bug by its brown head capsule and lack of waxy filaments.

Alfalfa Looper

Alfalfa looper (*Autographa californica* [Speyer]) larvae are about 0.75 inch (1.9 cm) long. This greenish caterpillar tapers from back to front and has a single white stripe on either side of the abdomen. It walks with a characteristic looping motion. Larvae feed on leaves, causing ragged-edged holes in the leaf and on the leaf margins. Damage is most evident in spring. Control of alfalfa loopers is seldom needed.

Clover Root Curculio

The clover root curculio (*Sitona hispidulus* F.), is a recognized alfalfa pest in the eastern half of the United States but is generally not a problem in California. Clover root curculio is more common in the sandy soils of the San Joaquin Valley than in the heavier soils of the Sacramento Valley. The adults are slightly smaller than alfalfa weevil adults and are a mottled gray-brown. The damage is done by the legless, white grub-like larvae (Fig. 9.4) that feed on alfalfa roots, leaving gouges in the taproot. This damage has been detrimental to alfalfa yield and stand longevity in the eastern United States and also facilitates root rot diseases by providing entry points for fungi. In California, damage is usually limited, and there are no thresholds or control measures available.

Ground Mealybug

Most mealybugs are foliage feeders, but there is a group of mealybugs that feed exclusively on roots. The ground mealybug, *Rhizoecus kondonis* Kuwana, feeds on alfalfa roots and can cause severe damage to alfalfa. Ground mealybug is restricted to the heavier soils of the Sacramento Valley and is not found in the San Joaquin or Imperial Valleys. Feeding interacts with stressful environmental conditions, resulting in greatly reduced plant growth that is particularly evident during the summer. There are three ground mealybug generations per year; populations peak in early winter, spring, and midsummer. All life stages live in the soil. Ground mealybug is a small, (1-2 mm) whitish insect. The ground mealybug has slender, waxy filaments that form a sort of netting over some individuals (Fig. 9.5). The ground mealybug also secretes a small amount of wax, which can give the soil a somewhat bluish appearance when the mealybugs are abundant.

Infestations in alfalfa fields generally occur in circular patches and spread slowly. There are no thresholds or control measures for this pest. Crop rotation may help, but this pest appears to survive on several crop plant and weed species. There is differential survival across host species, so rotation to a less-preferred host may aid in management. In a greenhouse study, greatest survival was on potato, tomato, safflower, and alfalfa, followed by cotton, cantaloupe, dry land rice, sugar beets, and wheat. There was only slight survival on field corn and kidney beans. However, there were no plant species without some level of survival.

Spider Mites

Spider mites (*Tetranychus* spp.) are pests in alfalfa grown for seed, and only infrequently inhabit alfalfa grown for hay. Serious damage in hay fields is generally associated with water stress. Spider mite infestations are usually confined to the lower leaves, but in severe infestations, the terminals may be webbed together. Infested leaves are covered with webbing and turn yellow. Spider mites are small pests, with adults about the size of a small pinhead, variable in color (green or yellow) with dark pigmented spots. Adult spider mites have eight legs and are oblong to spherical in shape. The damaged leaves may become desiccated and fall from the plants. Spider mites have become more common in alfalfa grown for hay in the Low Desert in recent years. Definitive monitoring and treatment guidelines have not been developed because spider mites are a sporadic problem in alfalfa grown for hay. A timely irrigation usually reduces the impact of spider mites within a few days.

FIGURE 9.5

The ground mealybug has slender, waxy filaments that form a sort of netting over some individuals.

Silverleaf Whitefly

Silverleaf whitefly (*Bemisia argentifolii* Bellows and Perring), causes serious damage to over 200 crops including alfalfa. Alfalfa has been subject to significant yield and quality loss in the Imperial Valley in some years. Although this pest can also be found in the southern San Joaquin Valley (south of Merced County) during late summer, it has never reached levels capable of causing serious injury to alfalfa. Silverleaf whitefly adults are tiny (0.06 inch [0.15 cm] long), yellowish insects with white wings. Their wings are held roof-like over the body and generally do not meet over the back but have a small space separating them. Eggs are tiny, cigar-shaped, and creamy-white and are laid randomly on the undersides of leaves. Nymphs are found on the underside of the leaves, appear scale-like, and are clear to translucent yellow. Dense populations of silverleaf whitefly reduce hay quality by contaminating alfalfa with honeydew and sooty molds that grow on the honeydew. As noted in the discussion of

Silverleaf whitefly has caused significant yield and quality loss to alfalfa in the Imperial Valley.

aphids, sooty molds may reduce photosynthesis and the palatability of alfalfa to livestock.

Definitive monitoring and treatment guidelines have not been developed for whitefly control in alfalfa. Whitefly-resistant cultivars are available and should be planted in areas with a history of silverleaf whitefly damage to alfalfa.

Grasshoppers and Mormon Crickets

Grasshoppers (*Melanoplus* spp., *Trimerotropis* spp.) are normally of little concern in desert alfalfa. However, populations may build up in the foothills around the Central Valley after a wet spring, and later migrate to nearby alfalfa fields. Damage is usually limited to a few weeks after weeds dry up in the foothills. Grasshoppers may complete one to three generations per year, depending on the species and geographic location.

Control can sometimes be achieved by spraying an insecticide around field margins adjacent to the source of migration or by broadcasting insecticide bait over a vegetation-free buffer strip in advance of the migrating grasshoppers.

Mormon crickets (*Anabrus simplex* Haldeman) are not true crickets but are more closely related to katydids. The heavy-bodied, tan adults are about 1–2 inches (2.5–5 cm) long. The wings are small and useless; these insects do not fly. The antennae are as long as the body, and the female has a sword-shaped ovipositor as long as the body. When they are half grown, they begin migrating from their rangeland breeding grounds. The migrations occur at air temperatures of 65°–95°F (18–35°C).

Mormon crickets become pests only once or twice in a decade. Management centers on preventing invasions of fields with barriers or insecticide baits. Because these insects cannot fly, linear barriers of 10-inch (25 cm) strips of 28- to 30-gauge galvanized iron, held on edge with stakes, may stop swarms. Soil pits or water traps may be made at intervals to catch crickets halted by the barrier. Bait treatments on the border of the field may be effective at limiting an invasion.

Threecornered Alfalfa Hopper

The threecornered alfalfa hopper (*Spissistilus festinus* [Say]) is commonly found in desert alfalfa but is not a problem in the Central Valley, although numbers in the San Joaquin Valley have increased substantially in recent years. Adults are light green, thick-bodied, triangular insects about 0.25 inch (0.6 cm) long and readily fly when disturbed (Color Plate 9.19). Nymphs are grayish-white, soft bodied, and have saw-toothed spines on their backs. Nymphs are confined to the lower portions of the plant and may not be picked up in a sweep net. Populations build up in spring and persist into fall. They feed by sucking juices from the plant. Adult female treehoppers girdle stems by depositing eggs, causing the stem and leaves to turn red, purple, or yellow above the girdle. Definitive monitoring and treatment guidelines have not been developed.

Blister Beetles

Blister beetles (*Epicauta* spp., *Lytta* spp., *Tegrodera* spp.) are narrow and elongate, and the covering over the wings is soft and flexible. They may be solid colored (black or gray) or striped (usually orange, or yellow and black) and are among the largest beetles likely to be swept from alfalfa (Color Plate 9.20). Blister beetles contain a chemical, cantharidin, which is toxic to livestock. A few ingested insects are enough to kill a horse. Cantharidin is contained in the hemolymph (blood) of the beetles and may contaminate forage directly by beetles killed during harvest and incorporated into baled hay or indirectly by transfer of the hemolymph from crushed beetles onto forage. As the name implies, handling these insects may result in blisters, similar to burns, on the hands or fingers. Blister beetles have been a serious problem in alfalfa in the northern, midwestern, and southern United States for many years but, until recently, have not been a problem in California. In recent years, alfalfa contaminated with blister beetles in the southern Owens Valley has been linked to the death of several dairy cows. It is not known if blister beetles may become more widespread in California. Growers and PCAs are advised to be on the lookout for blister beetles and to contact their Farm Advisor if these insects are found. Although most likely encountered in spring, they may be found any time during the growing season. To reduce the incidence of blister beetles in alfalfa, hay should be cut before bloom. If beetles are found, remove the conditioner wheels from the swather to prevent crushing the beetles. Also, these beetles congregate on field edges or in groups within the field. Such areas should be skipped when cutting or the bales picked up separately and isolated from bales picked up from the rest of the field.

Thrips

Thrips are minute, slender-bodied insects usually possessing two pairs of long, narrow wings, the margins of which are fringed with long hairs. Thrips are commonly found in alfalfa throughout the year. Western flower thrips (*Frankliniella* spp.) are distributed statewide. They feed mainly on pollen but will also feed on leaves by rasping the leaf surface. Under unusually high population levels, they may cause leaf crinkling, puckering, and distortion. This is often interpreted as economic injury. There is no evidence, however, that western flower thrips are causing economic damage, despite the leaf distortion. Insecticide control is not recommended because the damage done to natural enemy populations typically greatly outweighs any benefits derived from controlling the thrips.

> *There is no evidence that western flower thrips are causing economic damage, despite the leaf distortion they cause.*

One thrips species, *Caliothrips phaseoli* (Hood), is emerging as a possible pest, particularly in the Imperial Valley. This thrips is similar to the bean thrips (*C. fasciatus* [Pergande]), but can cause damage to seedling alfalfa. During fall 2001 and all of 2002, *C. phaseoli* caused stand loss in Imperial Valley seedling alfalfa fields. These thrips cause leaf spotting and leaf drop in established alfalfa stands. Monitoring and treatment guidelines have not been developed. However, insecticide applications may be required if seedlings are being killed by this pest.

Beneficial Insects— Natural Enemies of Pests

Alfalfa is an important reservoir for natural enemies of insect pests (Table 9.3). It is important for growers to identify these insects (Color Plates 9.21–9.24) and to monitor their populations. These natural enemies have been discussed together with the individual pest species. Do not treat alfalfa with insecticides until the economic treatment level for a specific pest has been reached and the predator and parasite populations have been assessed for their potential roll in controlling the pest. Insecticides often destroy beneficial insects, leading to severe secondary pest outbreaks. Alfalfa produces many beneficial insects that move into other cropping systems and provide biological control of pests there.

Birds are important predators of insect pests in desert alfalfa. Egrets, ibis and gulls feed on crickets, cutworms, and other insects forced to move at the leading edge of flood irrigation water. Blackbirds in the Imperial and Central Valleys eat alfalfa weevil larvae, aphids on alfalfa stems, cutworms, and other insect pests.

TABLE 9.3

Natural enemy species and the species they prey on that are commonly found in alfalfa

Common name	Scientific name	Predator	Parasite	Prey
	Bathyplectes curculionis		■	Alfalfa weevil
	B. anurus		■	Egyptian alfalfa weevil
	Aphidius spp.		■	Aphids
	Lysiphlebus spp.		■	Aphids
	Diaeretiella spp.		■	Aphids
	Cotesia (Apenteles) medicaginis		■	Alfalfa caterpillar
	Hyposoter exiguae		■	*Spodoptera* spp. caterpillars
	Anaphes sp.		■	Lygus egg
	Trichogramma spp.		■	Caterpillar eggs
Collops beetles	*Collops* spp.	■		Various small insects
Convergent ladybird beetle	*Hippodamia convergens*	■		Aphids and whiteflies
Seven-spotted ladybird beetle	*Coccinella septempunctata* *Coccinella* spp.	■		Aphids and whiteflies
Bigeyed bugs	*Geocoris* spp.	■		Aphids and small caterpillars
Minute pirate bugs	*Orius* spp.	■		Aphids and small caterpillars
Damsel bugs	*Nabis* spp.	■		Caterpillars and other insects
Assassin bugs	*Zelus* spp. *Sinea* spp.	■		Caterpillars and other insects
Lacewings	*Chrysoperla* sp. *Chrysopa* sp. and others	■		Aphids and small caterpillars
Spiders	Various species	■		Caterpillars and other insects
Six-spotted thrips	*Scolothrips sexmaculatus*	■		Various small insects, eggs, and mites

Additional Reading

Summers, C.G. 1998. Integrated pest management in forage alfalfa. Integrated Pest Management Reviews 3(3): 127–154.

Summers, C.G., and L.D. Godfrey. 2001. Insects and mites in: UC IPM Pest Management Guidelines for Alfalfa Hay. http://www.ipm.ucdavis.edu/PMG/selectnewpest.alfalfahay.html.

Summers, C.G., D.G. Gilchrist, and R.F. Norris, eds. 1981. Integrated pest management for alfalfa hay. University of California Division of Agriculture and Natural Resources, Oakland. Publication 4104. University Of California Integrated Pest Management Guidelines. http://www.ipm.ucdavis.edu/pmg/selectnewpest.alfalfa-hay.html

Color Plates

Important Insect Pests

PLATE 9.1

Adult alfalfa weevils are gray-brown beetles with a pronounced snout.

PLATE 9.2

Alfalfa weevil larvae are bright green in color with a black head and a prominent white stripe down the back.

PLATE 9.3

Pea aphids are large aphids with long legs, antennae, and cornicles. They are bright green in color and both winged and wingless forms may be found feeding on the stems.

PLATE 9.4

Blue alfalfa aphids are also large green aphids with an appearance very similar to that of the pea aphid. They tend to be a bit darker in color, hence the name "blue alfalfa aphid."

PLATE 9.5

Pea and blue alfalfa aphids can be distinguished by examining the antennae. The antennae of the pea aphid, shown here, has a dark band at each joint while the antennae of the blue alfalfa aphid are a uniform brown color.

PLATE 9.6

Spotted alfalfa aphids are easily distinguished by the several rows of dark spots down their backs.

PLATE 9.7

Cowpea aphids are dull or shiny black in color with white legs. They can be found any time of the year. They are the only black aphid to be found in alfalfa.

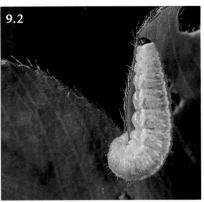

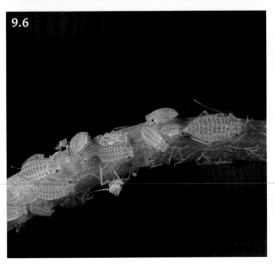

PLATE 9.8

Beet armyworms lay their eggs in clusters on the upper surface of the leaf. The female removes scales from her body and packs them around the egg mass as protection from predators and parasites. In the beet armyworm, the scales are white in color.

PLATE 9.9

The beet armyworm is a large, smooth skin caterpillar. They are usually olive green in color, but may vary from bright green to almost black. They have a prominent light strip down the side.

PLATE 9.10

Both beet armyworm and western yellow striped armyworm feed on the leaves. They consume leaf material from between the veins leaving the veins intact.

PLATE 9.11

Western yellow striped armyworm also lays its eggs in clusters on the upper surface of the leaf. The eggs are surrounded by gray scales as protection from predators and parasites.

PLATE 9.12

Western yellow striped armyworm larvae are smooth skin caterpillars. The are usually dark in color, but may occasionally be green. They have orange or yellow stripes down the side.

PLATE 9.13

Alfalfa caterpillar adults are light to dark yellow in color. When huge numbers of these butterflies can be seen flying into alfalfa fields, it is a sign of an upcoming problem.

PLATE 9.14

Alfalfa caterpillar eggs are laid singly on the upper leaf surface. They are whitish in color and resemble a football on a kicking tee.

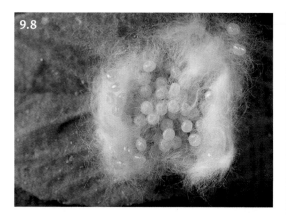

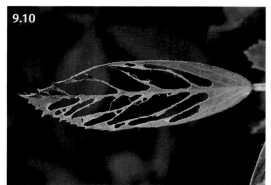

PLATE 9.15

Alfalfa caterpillar larvae are bright green with a white stripe along the side. The body is covered with small hairs which give the larvae a "velvety" appearance. When feeding, alfalfa caterpillar larvae consume the entire leaf.

PLATE 9.16

Empoasca leafhoppers are small, wedge shaped insects that are bright green in color.

PLATE 9.17

Empoasca leafhopper feeding results in reddening and yellowing of the foliage. The wedge shaped discoloration shown here is classic leafhopper damage.

PLATE 9.18

Cutworm larvae frequently curl up into a "C" shape when disturbed.

PLATE 9.19

The three cornered alfalfa hopper is increasing in number in both the Central Valley and the southern deserts.

PLATE 9.20

The soldier blister beetle, also known as the iron cross blister beetle, has been found in small numbers in the High Desert of California.

Natural Enemies of Pests

PLATES 9.21

(A) Ladybug adults and (B) larvae are aphid predators and consume large numbers of these pests.

PLATES 9.22

Alfalfa Caterpillar Parasite. (A) The alfalfa caterpillar is attacked by a parasitic wasp. (B) The parasite larva can easily be expressed from the living caterpillar to check for parasitism. (C) The "fuzzy" yellow pupa is found on the upper surface of the leaf.

PLATES 9.23

Hyposoter. (A) Armyworms are parasitized by a large wasp. (B) The parasite larva is greenish in color and can easily be expressed from the caterpillar. (C) The pupa can be found on the upper surface of the leaf and are mottled black and white.

PLATE 9.24

Aphid Parasite. Aphids are attacked by several parasitic wasps, which develop inside of the aphid's body. The parasitized aphid appears bloated and is usually light tan in color. The round hole indicates that the parasite has emerged.

10

Alfalfa Diseases and Management

Carol A. Frate
Farm Advisor, University of California Cooperative Extension, Tulare, CA

R. Michael Davis
Extension Specialist, Department of Plant Pathology,
University of California, Davis

Diseases can cause major yield reduction in alfalfa and reduce the feeding value of the forage. Leaves, stems, roots, and crown can be affected (Table 10.1). Often the influence of diseases goes unrecognized, particularly root diseases, as symptoms can be subtle or mistaken for something other than disease, and pathogens can be hard to detect. Pathogens that cause alfalfa diseases include fungi, bacteria, viruses, and nematodes. Abiotic diseases, which are not caused by infectious pathogens but instead by environmental factors such as extreme temperatures or mineral deficiencies, are mentioned at the end of this chapter. Nematodes are discussed in detail in Chapter 11, "Parasitic Nematodes in Alfalfa." Refer to the UC IPM Guidelines online (http://ipm.ucdavis.edu) for the latest information on disease control for alfalfa.

For a plant disease to develop, the variety must be susceptible to the pathogen, the pathogen must be present, and environmental conditions must favor disease development. Temperature and moisture are the environmental factors that most frequently determine if a disease will occur once the susceptible host and the pathogen are present.

TABLE 10.1

Common diseases of alfalfa

Symptom	Disease	Pathogen	Environmental Conditions Favoring Disease	Comments
Seedlings fail to emerge, die after emergence, or are very weak	Pre- or post-emergence damping-off	Several species of fungi, including species of *Pythium, Rhizoctonia,* and *Phytophthora*	Cold temperatures that slow down seedling growth; excess soil moisture	Fungicide seed treatments reduce risk
Brown leaf spots	common leaf spot	*Pseudopeziza medicaginis*	Moderate temperatures (60°–75°F [15°–24°C]); dew or rain	Look for apothecia in leaf spot
Mottled yellow blotches on leaf	downy mildew	*Peronospora trifoliorum*	Humidity at or near 100%; temperatures in the 60s°F, 15–21°C	Look for fungal growth on the underside of leaves in the morning
Small black to brown spots on stems, petioles, and leaves	spring blackstem	*Phoma medicaginis*	Favored by moderate temperatures (mid 60s–70s°F, 15–21°C) and moisture	
Leaf spot with diffuse brown border	Stagonospora leaf spot	*Stagonospora meliloti*	Cool and moist; fall–spring	Look for pycnidia in the center of the leaf spot; can also infect crowns and roots
Leaf spot with definite dark border and tan center	Stemphylium leaf spot	*Stemphylium botryosum*	Cool temperatures (60°–70°F [15°–21°C]) and moisture	
Reddish brown leaf spots	rust	*Uromyces striatus* var. *medicaginis*	Cool and moist; spring	Uncommon; leaf spots filled with reddish brown spores
Scattered dead, light-colored stems	Anthracnose	*Colletotrichum trifolii*	Warm	Mostly found in late spring and summer; can also infect crowns and roots
Plants wilting; tan to black lesions where lateral roots emerge; main tap root rotted	Phytophthora root and crown rot	*Phytophthora megasperma*	Saturated soil; more common under moderate temperatures but occasionally under high temperatures	Can be confused with scald when occurs with high temperatures
Plants wilting; white mycelium at base of plant	Sclerotinia stem and crown rot	*Sclerotinia* spp.	High humidity; foggy; cool	Look for sclerotia
Low vigor or dying plants; cracked bark on crowns or roots; red flecks in diseased tissue	Stagonospora crown and root rot	*Stagonospora meliloti*	Can be found year-round	Red flecking in diseased tissue is characteristic
Tan elliptical lesions in tap root where lateral roots emerge	Rhizoctonia root canker, crown and stem rot	*Rhizoctonia solani*	High soil temperatures; high soil moisture	Found mainly in Palo Verde, Coachella, and Imperial Valleys; in winter the root lesions are black and inactive
Yellow-green foliage; stunted growth	bacterial wilt	*Clavibacter michiganensis* subsp. *insidiosum*		Uncommon due to resistant varieties; cross section of infected root has yellowish tan center; brown pockets inside bark are sometimes evident
Wilting shoots; bleached color leaves and stems	Fusarium wilt	*Fusarium oxysporum* (f.) sp. *medicaginis*	High soil temperatures	Reddish streaks in inner portion of root
Yellow leaf tips, often in V-shaped pattern; stem with petioles but leaves have fallen, stem remains stiff and green until all leaves dead	Verticillium wilt	*Verticillium albo-atrum*		Has been found in Mojave Desert and a few coastal areas; use resistant varieties in areas where disease occurs
Low vigor, dying plants, crown with dry rot and dark black internally at the base of stems	Anthracnose crown rot	*Colletotrichum trifolii*	Warm weather and moisture by rain or irrigation	Also infects stems resulting in dead bleached stems in the crop canopy

Control of Alfalfa Diseases

Few fungicides are registered on alfalfa in the United States. The economics of pesticide registration and alfalfa production has not been conducive to the use of pesticides for disease control in alfalfa, with the exception of seed treatments. Variety tolerance or resistance is the primary tool for managing many alfalfa diseases, making variety selection a very important component for successful alfalfa production. The National Alfalfa Alliance produces an annual publication that is available under "Variety Leaflet" online at http://www.alfalfa.org. It lists commercial varieties and their resistance level for bacterial, Fusarium, and Verticillium wilts; anthracnose; and Phytophthora root rot. For many "minor" diseases, differences in varietal susceptibility exist, but they are not well documented and the information is not readily available. For a discussion on alfalfa resistance to pests, refer to Chapter 5, "Choosing an Alfalfa Variety."

In addition to variety selection, the integration of other strategies, such as irrigation management, planting methods, promotion of crop vigor, manipulation of cutting schedules, canopy management, and crop rotation, also plays an important role in disease management. Each of these techniques will be discussed in relationship to specific diseases.

Seedling Diseases or Damping-off

Causal Organisms and Symptoms

Seedling death, before or soon after emergence, is referred to as damping-off. Several soilborne fungi, including *Pythium* spp., *Rhizoctonia* spp., and *Phytophthora* spp., cause damping-off of alfalfa wherever alfalfa is grown. Excessive soil moisture, compacted or poorly drained soils, and temperatures unfavorable for seedling growth favor damping-off. The end result is a poor stand of plants that are low in vigor. Damping-off can be devastating to the long-term productivity of a new alfalfa seeding.

Seeds destroyed before germination are discolored and soft. After germination, symptoms include brown necrotic lesions along any point on the young seedling, including lesions that girdle the root or stem, leading to plant death (Color Plate 10.1 at the end of this chapter). Some infected plants escape death but are nevertheless weakened as a result of being partially girdled or having a reduced root system. These plants may be stunted and chlorotic to varying degrees. As seedlings grow older, pathogenic fungi can destroy only the outer layer of cells around the stem. A dark, constricted area near the soil surface identifies this type of injury. The magnitude of the discolored area is dependent upon the age of the seedling, as well as the duration of environmental conditions favorable for disease development. As alfalfa seedlings continue to grow, root-tip necrosis may continue to develop, but the risk of plant death from post-emergence damping-off decreases rapidly.

Pythium ultimum (Trow) and *P. irregulare* (Buisman) cause both pre- and post-emergence damping-off of alfalfa in California. *Pythium violae* (Chester & Hickman) incites root-tip necrosis and inhibition of lateral root formation. *Rhizoctonia solani* (Kuhn) may kill seedlings prior to emergence but usually causes post-emergence necrosis of the stem at or near the soil surface, with a distinct margin between infected and healthy tissue. *Phytophthora megasperma* (f.) sp. *medicaginis* (Kuan & Erwin), another common soilborne pathogen, can be particularly devastating in poorly drained soils (see "Phytophthora Root and Crown Rot").

Pythium spp. survive in soil as sporangia, hyphal swellings, and thick-walled oospores (see "Glossary" for definition of plant pathology terms). These structures are stimulated to germinate by nutrients that occur in seed and root exudates. In some species, secondary infections may occur from zoospores released from sporangia. Zoospores are motile and swim short distances in water films in soil or move greater distances in surface water. Damping-off caused by *Pythium* spp. usually occurs in fields with poor drainage under cool soil temperatures; however, *P. aphanerdamatum* ([Edson] Fitzp.)

is more likely to infect plants under warm soil conditions.

Rhizoctonia solani survives between crops as sclerotia in soil and as mycelia in infested plant debris. It infects host cells directly or through natural openings and wounds. Damage by *R. solani* is often related to the amount of organic matter that remains in the soil from the previous crop, with damage increasing as the level of organic matter increases.

Managing Seedling Diseases

Pythium spp. and *Rhizoctonia* spp. are common in agricultural soils. Both are transported by water, contaminated soil on equipment, and movement of infected plant materials. Both have wide host ranges.

Seedlings are most susceptible to damping-off following seed germination and shortly after emergence. Therefore, disease is more likely when this extremely susceptible period is extended, which may be the result of unfa-vorable temperatures, excessive moisture, low light, incorrect planting depth, or improper fertilization.

Cultural and chemical measures are generally effective means of controlling damping-off. Planting high-quality seed under environmental conditions favoring rapid germination and seedling growth reduces the chance of infection. Excessive irrigation, compaction, and poor drainage of soils should be avoided. Fungicide seed treatments that are effective against *Rhizoctonia* and *Pythium* are available. Although crop rotations do not eliminate these pathogens because of their wide host ranges, rotations with crops like small grains may help to reduce inoculum levels.

Foliar Diseases

Diseases that cause foliar symptoms can reduce yield and quality by reducing photosynthesis and defoliating plants. Defoliation decreases both yield and quality. Most foliar diseases are favored by leaf wetness and therefore are less of a problem in the relatively dry climates of Mediterranean and desert areas than in climates with high summer humidity and rainfall (Fig. 10.1). However, even in these drier climates, leaf spots occur in spring, winter, and fall following rain, long periods of dew formation, or foggy weather. Irrigation, either by flood or sprinkler, may also favor diseases if not managed properly. Usually only one cutting, or two at most, are affected, but a few leaf spot-causing fungi are capable of invading and killing crowns, resulting in stand loss over time.

FIGURE 10.1

Generalized disease cycle for most leaf spot diseases.

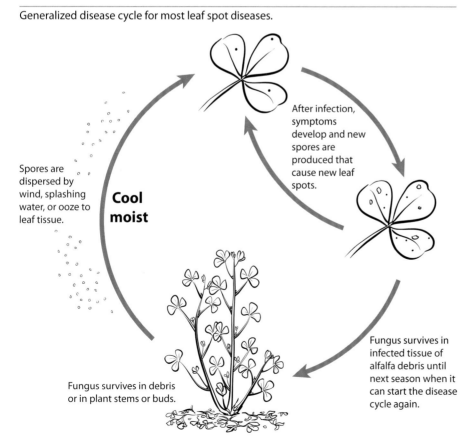

Spores are dispersed by wind, splashing water, or ooze to leaf tissue.

Cool moist

After infection, symptoms develop and new spores are produced that cause new leaf spots.

Fungus survives in infected tissue of alfalfa debris until next season when it can start the disease cycle again.

Fungus survives in debris or in plant stems or buds.

Common Leaf Spot

Common leaf spot, caused by the fungus *Pseudopeziza medicaginis* ([Lib.] Sacc.), usually occurs from winter through early spring.

> *In irrigated fields in California, common leaf spot can cause more leaf loss during curing, raking, and baling than before cutting.*

Symptoms include small (1/8 in. [0.3 cm] in diameter), circular, brown to black spots on the upper surface of leaves (Color Plate 10.2). Margins of spots are characteristically toothed or uneven. As the disease progresses, infected leaves turn yellow and drop. In cool, moist weather, the fungus produces circular, raised, brown fruiting bodies, called "apothecia," within the spots. These structures are visible through a hand lens. During cool, moist periods, spores are forcibly discharged into the air from apothecia. Spores that land on alfalfa leaves initiate infection if favorable environmental conditions are present. The fungus survives in undecomposed leaves and leaf debris on the soil surface.

Infected alfalfa should be cut in a timely manner because the severity of the disease increases as the plant continues to grow. Although the disease does not kill plants, defoliation reduces vigor, hay quality, and yield. In irrigated fields in California, common leaf spot can cause more leaf loss during curing, raking, and baling than before cutting. Most growers just live with this disease because information on which varieties are less susceptible is not widely available.

Downy Mildew

Downy mildew, caused by the pathogen *Peronospora trifoliorum* (de Bary), occurs when temperatures are cool and humidity is near 100 percent. Because this fungus requires moisture to form spores and for spores to germinate, this disease occurs only during extended wet periods in California. Little disease occurs when temperatures exceed 65°F (18°C) and humidity is low. The upper surface of infected leaves turns light green, in some cases almost a mottled yellow (Color Plate 10.3a). On the underside of the affected area, bluish gray areas of mycelia, spores (sporangia), and branched, spore-bearing structures (sporangiophores) can be seen through a hand lens (Color Plate 10.3b). These are more often found in the morning when humidity in the canopy is high. Sometimes entire buds and leaves become infected, resulting in systemic infection causing distortion and general yellowing of leaves (Color Plate 10.3c). Spring-planted fields are most likely to be affected because plants are in the seedling stage when weather tends to be most favorable for the disease. Infected leaves may drop from the plant, reducing yield and quality. Mycellium in systemically infected crown buds and shoots and resistant resting spores (oospores) in debris is how the fungus survives summer conditions. This disease rarely results in plant death, and stand survival is usually not affected.

Spring Blackstem

Spring blackstem is caused by the fungus *Phoma medicaginis* (Malbr. & Roum.). Symptoms include small, black to dark brown spots on lower leaves, petioles, and stems that range from irregular to triangular in shape (Color Plate 10.4). As they increase in size, lesions coalesce and become light brown. Affected leaves turn yellow and often wither before falling. Lesions on stems and petioles enlarge and may girdle and blacken large areas near the base of the plant. Young shoots are often killed. Most damage occurs before the first cutting. The fungus also causes crown and root rot.

The pathogen produces brown to black fruiting bodies (pycnidia) on overwintered stem lesions and on fallen leaves. In early spring, spores released from pycnidia are splashed onto foliage and stems by rain or overhead irrigation. In addition, new shoots are infected as they grow through infested crop residue or stubble. The fungus also may be seed-borne.

Control measures include early cutting to reduce leaf loss and planting pathogen-free seed.

Stagonospora Leaf Spot

Spots on leaves and stems caused by the fungus *Stagonospora meliloti* ([Lasch] Petr.) are most commonly found in spring when conditions are moist and cool. Spots are characterized by a brown, diffuse border with a light tan center (Color Plate 10.5). Small, dark fruiting bodies (pycnidia) that appear as black dots develop in the center of the lesion. Leaves with multiple infections often defoliate after pycnidia form. Spores from pycnidia moved by rain or irrigation water germinate and can infect leaves, stems, or crowns. The crown and root rot phase of the disease is discussed under "Root, Stem, and Crown Diseases" in this chapter.

Stemphylium Leaf Spot

A tan center and a dark border around an irregularly shaped lesion (Color Plates 10.6) distinguish this leaf spot disease caused by the fungus *Stemphylium botryosum* (Wallr.). Once the border is formed, the spot does not increase in size. Spores form in the center of the lesion. Cool temperatures (60°–70°F [15.5°–21°C]) and moist weather favor infection and spread. The disease is usually found in first and second cuttings. Because defoliation occurs only under heavy disease pressure, Stemphylium leaf spot is not considered as serious as some other leaf-spot diseases.

A different strain of the fungus that is more active under warm temperatures exists in the midwestern and eastern United States. Spots will not have a dark border and will continue expanding, affecting large portions of leaves.

There are no known control measures available. Early cutting may reduce the incidence of the disease and forestall significant leaf loss in years when the disease is particularly severe. Although there may be some resistant varieties, this is not commonly tested or reported by seed companies.

Rust

Rust, caused by *Uromyces striatus* (Schröt. var. *medicaginis* [Pass.] Arth.), is easily distinguished from other foliar diseases by the masses of reddish brown spores produced from pustules located on both sides of leaves, and on petioles and stems. Heavily infected leaves drop prematurely, reducing yield and quality. The disease is rather rare in Mediterranean and desert climates, and no control measures are used.

Root, Stem, and Crown Diseases

Diseases affecting crowns and roots may lead to plant death, resulting in stand and yield reductions, and therefore in the long run can be more important than leaf diseases, although at times less obvious.

Anthracnose

Anthracnose (also called southern anthracnose), caused by the fungus *Colletotrichum trifolii* (Bain. & Essary), is a common problem in older alfalfa stands. The disease affects leaves, stems, and crowns, but crown rot is the most important phase of the disease. The most obvious symptom of anthracnose in the crown is a dry, bluish black, V-shaped rot (Color Plate 10.7). As the decay spreads down into the root, the color turns tan to brick red. Dead stems associated with such crowns are sometimes bleached white. Because stems die suddenly, dead leaves remain attached to the stem (Color Plate 10.8).

On stems, Anthracnose is identified by small, irregularly shaped blackened areas that become large, oval or diamond-shaped, straw-colored lesions with black borders (Color Plate 10.9). Tiny fruiting bodies (acervuli) containing salmon-colored spores develop in the lesions. As lesions enlarge, they may coalesce, girdling and killing affected stems. In summer and fall, dead, white shoots are scattered throughout the field. The tip of the affected stem is often curled over like a shepherd's crook.

The fungus persists in alfalfa debris and crowns. The disease reaches maximum severity during late summer and early fall, coincident with warm, humid weather. During the growing season, spores on stem lesions are a source of inoculum. Splashing rain and irrigation water disperse spores onto growing stems and petioles. Spores may also be spread by seed contaminated during the threshing process.

Control of anthracnose primarily involves the use of resistant cultivars. In infested fields, alfalfa can be harvested before losses become too severe. Rotation with crops other than clover and alfalfa for 2 years will eliminate sources of inoculum in the field.

Phytophthora Root and Crown Rot

This is one of the most common diseases in alfalfa. Phytophthora root and crown rot commonly occurs in poorly drained or overwatered soils throughout alfalfa growing regions. Primary symptoms include tan to brown lesions on taproots, especially where a lateral root emerges (Color Plate 10.10). Lesions eventually turn black, while the center of the root turns yellow. In the root interior, orange to reddish streaks spread several centimeters from the rotted ends of the roots toward the crown. Occasionally, the disease may spread to the crown from the taproot. If the crown becomes infected, the plant will probably die. Often the lower part of the taproot is completely rotted, and lateral roots become larger than normal. Although these plants may survive, the lateral roots will never grow very deep, limiting the plant's ability to take up water from lower in the soil profile. If infection is limited, the plant may continue growing at a reduced rate but will be more susceptible to other pests and diseases. Root and crown rot can be injurious to seedling stands but is more common in established fields.

Phytophthora root and crown rot is favored by waterlogged soil conditions and is associated with poorly drained fields or parts of fields. The disease commonly occurs at the tail end of flood-irrigated fields where water collects. This disease is typically associated with moderate temperatures (75°–81°F [24°–27°C] for optimum growth), but a high temperature isolate has been reported in the Low Desert production areas of California that has a temperature optimum of 81°–91°F (27°–33°C).

The causal organism *P. megasperma* (f.) sp. *medicaginis* survives in soil as thick-walled oospores or as mycelia in infected plant tissue. It produces thin-walled sporangia that release motile zoospores in the presence of free water. Pre-plant land preparation is critical in controlling this disease—any soil preparation that enables good drainage and prevents standing water will reduce disease occurrence. Appropriate slope and deep tillage to minimize soil compaction will reduce the likelihood that Phytophthora root and crown rot will occur. Reducing the length of flood irrigation runs, shortening irrigation time, leveling land, installing a tailwater ditch to remove excess water, and planting on beds will further reduce the chances of disease occurrence. Installation and maintenance of tile drains may be necessary in some cases. Return water should be used with caution because spores of the pathogen can be carried in recirculated irrigation water.

Fortunately, there are many cultivars resistant to Phytophthora root rot. They are listed in the National Alfalfa Alliance publication or on their Web site: (http://www.alfalfa.org). Resistant varieties should be used along with sound cultural practices in fields known to have problems with Phytophthora.

> *Appropriate slope and deep tillage to minimize soil compaction will reduce the likelihood that Phytophthora root and crown rot will occur.*

Rhizoctonia Root Canker, Crown and Stem Rot

Rhizoctonia root canker and crown rot occur during periods of high temperatures and high soil moisture. The causal fungus, *R. solani*, occurs worldwide. It can cause serious seedling damping-off; however, in California, most new stands are planted when temperatures are less than ideal for its development. Only certain strains of the fungus can cause the root canker form of the disease. In California, the disease is found mainly in the Palo Verde, Imperial, and Coachella Valleys. Tan, elliptical lesions on the taproot in the areas where lateral roots emerge are distinctive symptoms. In winter, when the fungus is inactive, these sunken lesions will turn black and at that stage appear to be inactive (Color Plate 10.11). If roots are girdled during summer, the plant will die. If disease severity is low to moderate, new roots emerge when temperatures are too cool for the fungus to be active. New infections occur the following summer when conditions are once again favorable. The fungus can also infect the crown at the location where new buds emerge and move into the crown, killing tissue. During cool weather the infection stops, but if significant portions of the crown have been killed, fewer stems will emerge.

No control measures are known. There are currently no resistant varieties for Rhizoctonia root and crown disease of alfalfa.

Sclerotinia Stem and Crown Rot

Sclerotinia stem and crown rot, caused by *Sclerotinia trifoliorum* (Eriks.) or *S. sclerotiorum* ([Lib.] de Bary), can cause substantial damage to alfalfa under wet, cool conditions that are common during foggy Central Valley winters. It is not common during dry winters or in desert regions.

This disease is characterized by the presence of white, cottony fungal strands (mycelia) on crowns or stems and by the presence of

FIGURE 10.2

Disease cycle for *Sclerotinia* on alfalfa.

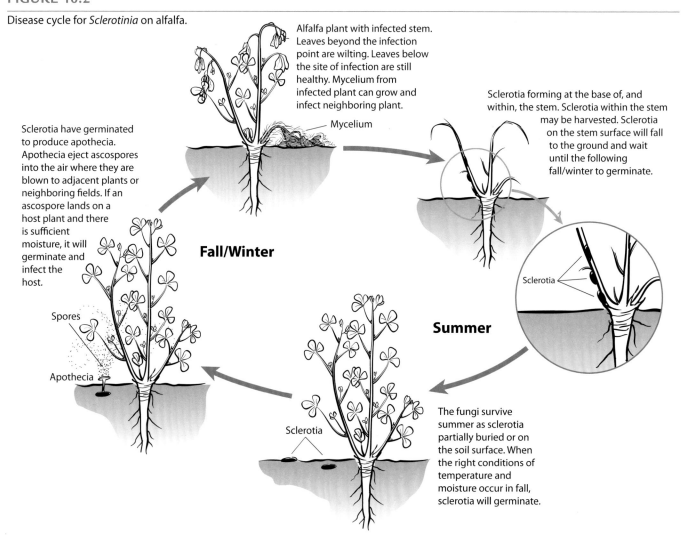

Alfalfa plant with infected stem. Leaves beyond the infection point are wilting. Leaves below the site of infection are still healthy. Mycelium from infected plant can grow and infect neighboring plant.

Mycelium

Sclerotia forming at the base of, and within, the stem. Sclerotia within the stem may be harvested. Sclerotia on the stem surface will fall to the ground and wait until the following fall/winter to germinate.

Sclerotia have germinated to produce apothecia. Apothecia eject ascospores into the air where they are blown to adjacent plants or neighboring fields. If an ascospore lands on a host plant and there is sufficient moisture, it will germinate and infect the host.

Fall/Winter

Sclerotia

Spores

Summer

Apothecia

Sclerotia

The fungi survive summer as sclerotia partially buried or on the soil surface. When the right conditions of temperature and moisture occur in fall, sclerotia will germinate.

black, hard structures (sclerotia) at the base of crowns and stems, or inside the stems. Sclerotia are round or irregularly shaped (0.1–0.3 in. [2–8 mm] in diameter) (Color Plate 10.12a). When broken open, the interior is white. The disease cycle of both fungal species that cause Sclerotinia stem and root rot of alfalfa is similar (Fig. 10.2). The fungi survive summer as sclerotia partially buried or on the soil surface. In late fall or early winter, once temperatures cool and soils become wet from rain or irrigation, sclerotia germinate and form small (0.25 inch [5 mm] in diameter or less), orange, yellow, or tan mushroom-like structures (apothecia) on the soil surface (Color Plate 10.12b). Apothecia produce millions of spores that are carried by air currents to surrounding plants or fields (Fig 10.3). If conditions are wet and temperatures are low (50°–68°F [10°–20° C]), spores that fall on susceptible alfalfa tissue germinate and infect the plant. If conditions continue to be favorable for disease development, white, cottony mycelial growth will form on stems and around the crown and spread to nearby plants (Color Plate 10.12c).

This disease causes stem death and, if the crown is infected, the plant might die. If plants are young, weakened by other factors, or if conditions are extremely favorable for disease development over a prolonged period, substantial stand loss may occur. However, in established, healthy alfalfa, plants often survive even when all stems of a plant are killed. Healthy stems will be produced the following spring.

There is no effective genetic-based resistance incorporated into nondormant commercial varieties at this time. For established fields, the best strategy is to remove as much foliage before winter as possible by mowing or grazing. This, along with good weed control, opens the canopy, allowing air movement and sunshine around the bases of plants, thereby reducing the humidity and moisture required by the fungus to initiate and maintain infections.

In wet or foggy winters, this disease can be serious on seedling stands planted the previous September or October. By December, there is dense growth that promotes humidity in and around plants. Weeds such as chickweed

FIGURE 10.3

Ascospores being discharged from apothecia of Sclerotinia sclerotiorum.

(*Stellaria media* [L.] Vill.) further increase the chances of disease development by adding to the humidity within the canopy.

Research has shown that burning back seedling growth with herbicides, especially once the disease has started, is not very effective in reducing Sclerotinia disease. Deep plowing of fields before planting will prevent germination of most sclerotia that may be present in the field. However, neighboring alfalfa fields or weed hosts can be the source of new infections. Fungicide trials show promising results, but no fungicides have been registered for use on alfalfa in California.

Although plantings in early February in the San Joaquin Valley are likely to escape this disease, there are other disadvantages of planting at that time of the year, such as increased risk of damping-off, slow early growth, and reduced yields in the first year. Growers who plant in September and October find that the benefit of early planting usually outweighs the risk of Sclerotinia and they continue that practice despite potential damage to seedling fields from this disease.

Stagonospora Crown and Root Rot

Crown and root rot caused by the fungus *S. meliloti* is widespread in the Mediterranean and desert zones of California and is one of the primary reasons for early stand decline. Plant vigor decreases because of the slow death of the crown tissue that is caused by this disease. Symptoms include rough and cracked bark tissue on infected roots and crowns. The presence of red flecks in diseased root tissue is a distinctive diagnostic symptom (Color Plate 10.13). Fine, red streaks also occur in the xylem (the water-conducting tissue) in the center of the root, below rotted portions of the crown. Affected crown tissue is generally firm and dry, unless secondary organisms invade the tissue. Foliar symptoms caused by this pathogen when it infects stems and leaves are discussed under "Foliar Diseases."

Spores of *S. meliloti* form in very small, dark brown, round or pear-shaped structures (pycnidia) and are spread by water that splashes from infected leaves, stems, or plant debris. The fungus enters the crown through stems and grows slowly downward into the taproot. Although infection can take 6 months to 2 years to kill a plant, and aboveground symptoms may be overlooked, the disease reduces plant vigor and yield. Crown infections can occur throughout the year but the disease is most damaging when alfalfa is not actively growing.

To minimize the effects of Stagonospora crown and root rot, it is important to provide optimum growing conditions for the alfalfa crop. Rotating out of alfalfa for 2 years eliminates sources of inoculum within a field.

> *To minimize the effects of Stagonospora crown and root rot, it is important to provide optimum growing conditions for the alfalfa crop.*

Wilt Diseases

Wilt diseases are characterized by the pathogen invading the vascular system (water- and sugar-conducting tissues) of plants, leading to the plant wilting and usually dying. Often, the surface of the root displays no obvious disease symptoms.

Bacterial Wilt

Bacterial wilt, caused by the bacterium *Clavibacter michiganensis* subsp. *insidiosus* ([McCulloch] Davis et al.), occurs in most areas of California but is rarely seen today due to the development of wilt-resistant cultivars. Bacterial wilt was the first disease for which resistant cultivars were developed, and few alfalfa varieties are released today without at least some level of bacterial wilt resistance.

Disease symptoms rarely appear before the second or third year of a stand, which may be another reason why this disease is not considered to be that serious in the southern San Joaquin Valley and desert valleys, where stands usually are removed after 3 to 4 years. Aboveground symptoms include yellow-green foliage and stunted growth (Color Plate 10.14). Leaflets may be mottled and slightly cupped or curled upward. Stems on affected plants may be thin and weak. Disease symptoms are most evident in regrowth after harvest. A cross section of an infected taproot reveals a yellowish tan color in the center. Brown pockets on the inside of bark tissue are sometimes evident. Once infected, plants do not usually recover. Within 5 to 8 months after showing symptoms, plants frequently die. Infected plants are prone to winter kill if a freeze occurs.

The bacterium survives in plant residue in soil and enters plants through wounds in the roots and crown or through the cut ends of freshly mowed stems. Disease severity and incidence increase when root-knot nematodes are present in soil (see Chapter 11, "Parasitic Nematodes in Alfalfa"). The bacterium can survive in dry plant tissue or seed for up to 10 years and can be disseminated over long distances in seed and dry hay. However, the population of the organism in soil declines quickly when infected plant residue decomposes. The bacterium can be spread by surface water, tillage, and harvesting equipment. The greatest incidence of the disease occurs in poorly drained areas of fields, and large areas can be infected during periods of continuously wet weather.

Resistant cultivars generally keep this disease under control. If bacterial wilt is discovered in a field, that field should be mowed last to prevent the spread of inoculum by the mower to younger stands. Within a field, infested areas should be mowed last and never mowed when the foliage is wet.

Fusarium Wilt

Wilting shoots are the first obvious symptom of Fusarium wilt, caused by the fungus *Fusarium oxysporum* (Schlechtend.:Fr. [f.] sp. *medicaginis* [Weimer] W. C. Snyder & H. N. Hans.). Bleaching of leaf and stem tissues follows, and there may be a reddish tint to the foliage. On roots, dark reddish brown streaks occur internally (Color Plate 10.15). In advanced stages, the entire inner portion of the stem may be discolored. This dark discoloration is in contrast to the yellow-brown discoloration caused by bacterial wilt. Fusarium wilt is favored by high soil temperatures, and while significant in the past, this disease occurs infrequently due to the development of resistant cultivars.

Verticillium Wilt

Verticillium wilt of alfalfa, caused by the fungus *Verticillium albo-atrum* (Reinke and Berth), can be a serious disease in susceptible varieties. Yields have been reduced up to 50 percent by the second year of production. This disease has been found in California's Mojave Desert and in Riverside and San Bernardino Counties in southern California, and in a few coastal areas. It is not known to occur in the Central Valley or the Imperial, Palo Verde, or Coachella Valleys of California. It is much more common in the Intermountain regions of the West, and in the Pacific Northwest and eastern U.S. regions. Symptoms include yellowing of leaf

tips, sometimes in a V-shaped pattern. This yellowing should not be confused with that caused by *Empoasca* spp. leafhopper feeding (see Chapter 9, "Managing Insects in Alfalfa"). The edges of some apical leaflets will roll upward. As symptoms progress, leaves become desiccated (Color Plate 10.16) and sometimes develop a reddish hue. The leaves may drop, leaving behind a stiff petiole. The infected stem does not wilt and remains green until all leaves are dead. Xylem tissue in roots turns brown.

Verticillium albo-atrum can be carried internally and externally on alfalfa seed. The fungus also survives in alfalfa hay and in animal manure. It penetrates alfalfa roots directly or through wounds. Spreading within an alfalfa field can also occur through infection of cut stems when swathing. The fungus has been detected on sheep that are trucked from one region to another to graze fields in winter months.

The most practical control measure is to plant resistant varieties. In areas where the disease does not occur, care to prevent importation of infected seed or plant materials is recommended. Verticillium is not considered a serious problem in the Mediterranean or desert regions of California.

Diseases of Limited or Minor Importance

Phymatotrichum Root Rot

Phymatotrichum root rot, also called Phymatotrichopsis root rot, cotton root rot, and Texas root rot, is limited to certain areas in the deserts of Southern California (the Palo Verde Valley, and to a lesser extent, the Imperial and Coachella Valleys) and Texas and Arizona. The causal fungus, *Phymatotrichopsis omnivora* (Duggar) Hennebert (= *Phymatotrichum omnivorum* [Duggar]), has a host range of more than 1,800 plant species.

Extensive research in Arizona and Texas has shown that *P. omnivora* infestation is limited to certain soil types and that the infestation most likely was originally associated with natural desert flora before the introduction of agriculture.

The disease develops late in spring as soil temperatures rise. The first symptom on alfalfa is a rot of the outer surfaces of the roots, followed by bronzing of leaves and sudden wilting. Plants die quickly when taproots are girdled. A sheath of soil clings to the roots with white to tan mycelial strands on the root surface. The disease appears as somewhat circular spots (fairy rings) within the field (Color Plate 10.17).

The fungus survives many years in soil as sclerotia, as deep as 6 feet (2 m) or more. Sclerotia produce mycelial strands that grow through soil and eventually contact a root. The growth of the fungus is favored by moist soil conditions. The soil temperature range for growth is from 59° to 95°F (15° to 35°C), with an optimum of 82°F (28°C). The fungus is more prevalent in alkaline soils than in acidic soils; calcareous soils with high clay content are particularly favorable for this disease.

> *Because the causal fungus of Phymatotrichum Root Rot is virtually impossible to eradicate and could affect the value of the land, the disease diagnosis should be confirmed by an expert diagnostician.*

Because the causal fungus is virtually impossible to eradicate and could affect the value of the land, the disease diagnosis should be confirmed by an expert diagnostician. Crop rotation with nonsusceptible crops such as corn, sorghum, or onion can help prevent the increase in size of infested areas within a field, but it will not eliminate the infestation. No resistant cultivars are available.

Summer Black Stem and Leaf Spot

Cercospora medicaginis (Ell. & Ev.) is the causal agent of summer blackstem, which has been observed in the Imperial Valley. Defoliation from the base of the stem to the top is the most obvious symptom, but leaf spots usually appear first. Leaf spots are brown at first and surrounded by a wavy margin. As spores on the surface of the spot are produced, the spot appears gray or silvery. A diffuse yellow margin often surrounds the spot, and brown lesions may form on stems. High humidity and temperatures ranging from 75° to 82°F (24° to 28°C) favor disease development. Symptoms usually appear after the alfalfa has grown a dense canopy. Early harvest before extensive defoliation will minimize losses. There are no resistant cultivars.

Crown Wart and Crown Gall

Both crown wart and crown gall, two rare diseases on alfalfa in California, are caused by pathogens that produce galls or swellings on crowns and stems of alfalfa (Color Plate 10.18). Crown wart is caused by the fungus *Physoderma alfalfae* (Pat. & Lagerh.), and alfalfa is the only host. It is usually confined to fields with excessive soil moisture during early spring months. It is rare, but when it occurs it can cause damage. The fungus survives as resting spores that release zoospores under favorable conditions. Zoospores infect crown buds, causing cells to divide and enlarge, forming galls that reach full development in early summer. Resting spores of *P. alfalfae* can be easily seen by examination of tissue with a compound microscope. This differentiates it from bacteria-caused crown gall because bacteria are difficult to see with a compound microscope. Good drainage and avoiding excessive irrigation are the major control measures of crown wart. Alfalfa should not be planted after alfalfa on infested land.

Crown gall is caused by the bacterium *Agrobacterium tumefaciens* (Smith & Townsend), which is pathogenic on many plant species. It rarely occurs in alfalfa but has been found in the low desert climate of the Imperial Valley. The bacteria enter through fresh wounds less than 24 hours old. In reaction to infection, plant cells enlarge and divide to form irregularly shaped galls on crown branches at or just below the soil line. The potential for yield loss is not fully known because the disease has occurred so rarely.

Alfalfa Dwarf

Alfalfa dwarf was first recognized as an alfalfa disease in Southern California in the 1920s. Infected plants are stunted and exhibit small, bluish green leaves and fine stems (Color Plate 10.19). The size of the taproot is normal, but when sliced the taproot tissue is abnormally yellowish with dark streaks of dead tissue scattered throughout. In newly infected plants, the yellowing is mostly in a ring beginning under the bark. Unlike bacterial wilt, there are no pockets of infection beneath the bark. Eventually, infected plants die.

Dwarf is not recognized as an economic disease of alfalfa. However, the bacterium that causes alfalfa dwarf, *Xylella fastidiosa* (Wells et al.), is the same pathogen that causes Pierce's Disease of grapes, a very important grape disease in California. The role that alfalfa plays in the epidemiology of Pierce's Disease can be important. Increased levels of Pierce's Disease in grapes located adjacent to alfalfa fields containing infected plants have been documented in the San Joaquin Valley. Before the introduction of the glassy-winged sharpshooter (*Homalodisca coagulata* [Say]), the primary vectors of Pierce's Disease in California were several species of sharpshooter leafhoppers. These sharpshooters are primarily grass feeders, found commonly in grassy weeds infesting alfalfa. It is believed that alfalfa in such fields becomes infected almost by accident, when these insects would occasionally probe the alfalfa while searching for hosts. Although glassy-winged sharpshooter is known to feed on alfalfa, it appears that when other hosts are available, alfalfa is not a favored host of this vector. Thus, it is not expected that glassy-winged sharpshooter in alfalfa will play a key role in the epidemiology of alfalfa dwarf or Pierce's Disease.

Viruses

There are no viruses in California known to be of economic importance in alfalfa production. Two viruses, Alfalfa Mosaic Virus (AMV) and Cucumber Mosaic Virus (CMV), are the most common viruses detected in this crop. Symptoms of AMV, consisting of yellow mottling or streaking on leaves (Color Plate 10.20), can be seen at times, but at other times the symptoms are masked and leaves appear normal. CMV shows no symptoms in alfalfa. These and other viruses may be transmitted by aphids that feed on alfalfa and then move to other fields. Thus, alfalfa can serve as a reservoir for viruses important in other crops. For example, AMV can cause problems in tomatoes, peppers, and potatoes. CMV is one of several viruses that cause plant death in garbanzo beans grown in the San Joaquin Valley. It is also an important pathogen of cucurbits such as squash, melons, and pumpkins. Currently, however, there is no information documenting how significant a role alfalfa plays in the epidemiology of these viruses in other crops.

Abiotic Disease-like Symptoms

Frost and Freeze Injury

In general, alfalfa tolerates the cold weather usually associated with Central Valley and desert area winters in California. However, occasional frosts can turn exposed leaves, especially those at the top of plants, brown. Some varieties are more affected than others, and tall, uncut alfalfa tends to be affected more than short alfalfa. There can be injury if newly planted alfalfa is just emerging and only a few unifoliolate (single) leaves have developed during a cold spell (less than 26°F [-3°C]). Injury results in discolored, weak plants, and death usually results. Once plants have a few trifoliolate leaves, they are more capable of tolerating low temperatures experienced in the Central Valley and desert valleys.

Scald or High Temperature Flooding Injury

Scald is a hazard in hot regions of Mediterranean and desert zones, especially when alfalfa is grown on heavy soils. It is an abiotic malady caused by the combination of high soil temperatures and water-saturated soil over an extended length of time. Death is due to lack of oxygen to roots. Scald is usually limited to hot desert valleys (Imperial and Palo Verde Valleys) when soil is saturated for long periods after irrigation or rainfall. However, scald has been observed in the San Joaquin and Sacramento Valleys during hot weather. Affected plants may die within 3 to 4 days after irrigation.

Symptoms include off-color (whitish or tan) foliage and wilting, even though the soil is wet (Color Plate 10.21). Roots may rot and have a putrid odor when removed from the soil. The water-conducting tissue (xylem) of affected roots becomes brown and necrotic. Fields that have been recently mowed are much more susceptible to scald than fields closer to harvest.

When air temperatures exceed 104°–113°F (40°–45°C), alfalfa is extremely susceptible to flooding injury. Lack of sufficient soil aeration at high temperatures is probably the main factor, with poor tailwater management being a key trigger on heavy soils.

The primary control measure is proper water management. Irrigating for relatively short periods (e.g., 4 hrs) or at night during periods of high daytime temperatures reduces the likelihood of scald. Some soils, however, remain saturated long after irrigation because of heavy clay soil, poor drainage, slope of the land, and length of the irrigation run. Irrigations should be avoided when temperatures are excessively high, over 109°F (43°C). Newly mowed plants should not be irrigated until enough regrowth occurs to prevent submersion of entire plants;

Irrigating for relatively short periods (e.g., 4 hrs) or at night during periods of high daytime temperatures reduces the likelihood of scald.

thus a 3–6 day delay after cutting may be recommended.

Scald is often confused with Phytophthora root rot because both require saturated soil conditions. If temperatures (at the soil surface) have not exceeded 100°F (38°C), it is probably not scald.

Air Pollution

Air pollutants cause crop injury, such as reduced photosynthetic rates and early senescence, which adversely affect crop yield and quality. Many air pollutants (e.g., ammonia, chlorine, hydrogen chloride, hydrogen fluoride, or sulfur dioxide) are capable of causing plant damage, but only the photochemical oxidants (ozone and peroxyacetyl nitrate [PAN]) are of major concern. Both are formed by the reactions of oxygen, oxides of nitrogen, and organic molecules in the presence of sunlight. The primary source of these precursor molecules is automobile exhaust, but industrial processes and other forms of combustion contribute to air pollution.

High levels of ozone cause a bleached stippling on upper leaf surfaces and isolated necrotic spots distributed between the veins of injured leaves (Color Plate 10.22). Symptoms usually appear on middle-aged and older leaves. Affected leaves may senesce and fall. High concentrations of ozone are associated with low wind velocities and bright sunlight.

PAN injury begins with the absorption of gas through the plant stomates (pores in the leaves) and the collapse of adjacent mesophyll cells. The collapsed tissues produce air pockets between the lower epidermis and the palisade cells. Refraction of light through these air pockets is apparently responsible for the silvery or glazed appearance on the undersurface of the leaf. Symptoms on alfalfa leaves resemble those described for ozone injuries, but the lesions may be larger. In addition, a silver or copper sheen is frequently apparent on affected leaves. PAN injury is generally limited to certain urban areas where the combination of dense vehicular traffic and steep topography traps the pollutants.

Nutrient Deficiencies and Herbicide Injury

Symptoms of nutrient deficiencies, herbicide injuries, and insect feeding can sometimes be confused with diseases. General stunting, yellowing, and leaf distortion can be due to disease, nutrient deficiency (e.g., low levels of phosphorus), herbicide injury or insects. Nutrient deficiencies are described in Chapter 6, "Alfalfa Fertilization Strategies," herbicide injuries are described in Chapter 8, "Weed Management in Alfalfa," and insect feeding symptoms are discussed in Chapter 9, "Managing Insects in Alfalfa."

Additional Reading

Erwin, D.C., and A.B. Howell. 1998. Verticillium survives heat in Mojave Desert alfalfa. California Agriculture 53(4): 24–27.

Flint, M.L. (author), and C.G. Summers, D.G. Gilchrist, and R.F. Norris (technical coordinators). 1985. Integrated pest management for alfalfa hay. UC Statewide IPM Project, University of California Division of Agriculture and Natural Resources, Oakland. Publication 3312

Frate, C.A. 1997. Sclerotinia stem and crown rot of alfalfa in the central San Joaquin Valley. P. 93–101 in: Proceedings, 27th California Alfalfa Symposium, Dec 10–11, Visalia, CA.

Leath, K.T., D.C. Erwin, and G.D. Griffin. 1988. Diseases and nematodes. In: Alfalfa and alfalfa improvement. Agron. Monograph No. 29. ASA-CSSA-SSSA, Madison, WI.

National Alfalfa Alliance. Fall dormancy and pest resistance ratings for alfalfa varieties. Kennewick, WA.

Stuteville, D.L., and D.C. Erwin, eds. Compendium of alfalfa diseases, 2nd ed. 1990. American Phytopathological Society. St, Paul, MN.

Teuber, L.R., K.L. Taggard, and L. Gibbs. 1996. Alfalfa cultivars: Pest resistance levels and what they mean. Pages 219–230 in: Proceedings, 27th National Alfalfa Symposium, Dec 9–10, San Diego.

Glossary of Plant Pathology Terms

Abiotic: not living, a disease that is caused by something that is not living and not infectious.

Acervulus (*pl.* acervuli): a fruiting body produced by some species of fungi and that is usually at least partially embedded in plant tissue.

Apothecium (*pl.* apothecia): a fruiting body of one group of fungi (Ascomycetes) that generally contains spores that are ejected.

Fruiting body: in fungi, a structure in which or on which spores are produced. Examples are apothecia and pycnidia.

Hypha (*pl.* hyphae): microscopic, threadlike vegetative growth of fungi.

Inoculum: the pathogen or part of the pathogen that infects a plant. For most fungus-caused diseases, spores are the inoculum.

Mycelium (*pl.* mycelia): refers to numerous hypae growing close together, usually visible to the unaided eye.

Oospore (*pl.* oospores): a thick-walled, microscopic, resting/survival spore produced by the Oomycete group of organisms.

Pycnidium (*pl.* pycnidia): a type of dark, fungal fruiting body that is embedded in leaves or stems and which can also act as a survival structure. Spores from pycnidia usually need free water to allow for them to ooze out of the fruiting body.

Sclerotium (*pl.* sclerotia): a resting or survival structure produced by some fungi species that is usually dark and often visible with the unaided eye.

Sporangium (*pl.* sporangia): microscopic spores that may germinate directly or contain more spores within them, produced by some fungus species.

Survival structure: a form of a pathogen that can withstand environmental conditions that are unfavorable for the pathogen's survival. They can be composed of special vegetative structures, fruiting bodies, or spores, depending on the species of fungus. Examples are sclerotia, pycnidia, and oospores.

Zoospore (*pl.* zoospores): a type of spore produced by some fungus species that has one or more flagella and therefore can actively move through water. Mostly found in Oomycetes, such as some *Pythium* and *Phythophthora* species.

Color Plates

PLATE 10.1

Damping-off. The seedling on the far left is healthy while those in the center show various stages of damping-off. Note lesions on roots of the seedling second from the left and the pruned root system of the seedling third from the left. The seedling on the far right has recovered from root pruning caused by damping-off organisms.

PLATE 10.2

Common leaf spot. Infected leaves with small circular black or brown spots of common leaf spot. Note the raised fruiting bodies in the center of the lesions. Severely infected leaves usually fall from the plant.

PLATES 10.3

Downy mildew. (A) Leaves infected with downy mildew show a blotchy yellow pattern on the upper surface. (B) On the lower surface the fungus appears as a gray, furry mass. (C) Systemic infection by the downy mildew fungus results in distortion of all leaves from the infected growing point.

PLATE 10.4

Spring blackstem. Black lesions on leaf and petiole due to spring black stem. Note that there are no raised fruiting bodies in the center of these lesions unlike those associated with common leaf spot.

PLATE 10.5

Stagonospora leaf lesions. Leaf lesions of Stagonospora leaf spot are easily visible symptoms of this disease. The lesions are generally associated with the leaf margin and are irregular in shape.

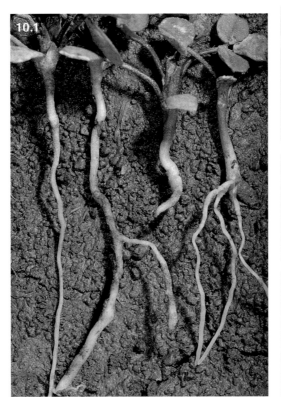

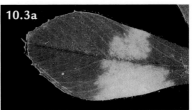

PLATES 10.6

Stemphylium leaf spot. (A) Leaves infected with Stemphylium leaf spot exhibit irregular shaped brown or tan spots on the upper surface of the leaves. (B) Upon close inspection, mature lesions are tan in color with a dark border. They can be distinguished from common leaf spot by their irregular shape and lack of fruiting bodies and from spring black stem by their color and shape.

PLATE 10.7

Anthracnose crown rot. Alfalfa crown with Anthracnose crown rot showing the dark v-shaped rotted area.

PLATE 10.8

Anthracnose crown and stem rot. Flagged stem due to infection with anthracnose caused by *Colletotrichum trifolii*.

PLATE 10.9

Anthracnose stem lesion. Anthracnose lesion on stem with dark border. Fresh lesions contain spores in a salmon-colored matrix.

PLATE 10.10

Phytophthora root rot. Lesions of Phytophthora root rot on alfalfa roots. Note the dark discolorations and the large lateral roots which are compensating for the lost taproot.

PLATE 10.11

Rhizoctonia root rot. Rhizoctonia root lesions are yellow to tan during the growing season but turn black in winter.

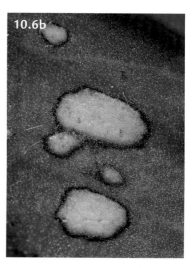
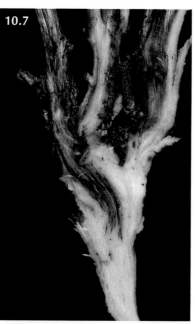

PLATES 10.12

Sclerotinia stem and crown rot. (A) Black, pebble-like sclerotium which formed inside an infected stem. Sclerotia also form externally at the base of infected stems. (B) Apothecium of *Sclerotinia* sp., growing from buried sclerotium, usually found after soil temperatures have cooled and rain or irrigation have occurred. (C) Mycelium of Sclerotinia.

PLATE 10.13

Stagonospora crown rot. Red and orange speckles scattered through a longitudinal section of the crown are the most distinctive symptom of Stagonospora crown and root rot.

PLATE 10.14

Bacterial wilt. The small, yellowish plant on the right is infected with bacterial wilt. This disease is seldom seen today thanks to resistant varieties.

PLATE 10.15

Fusarium wilt. A root infected with Fusarium wilt shows a brownish to reddish discoloration in the center.

PLATE 10.16

Verticillium wilt. Foliar symptoms of verticillium wilt are similar to those caused by gopher feeding. However, the stems of plants infected with the disease do not wilt and usually retain their green color. Near the top of shoots, the stems between the leaves (internodes) are short, and the plant cannot be pulled out of the ground easily.

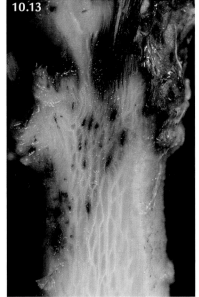

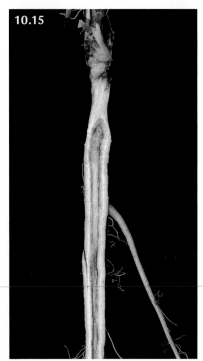

PLATE 10.17

Phymatotrichum root rot. This disease, which is limited to certain desert soil types of the southwestern U.S., usually starts as somewhat circular spots in which plants have suddenly wilted and died. Diagnosis should be confirmed by an expert.

PLATE 10.18

Crown wart. Distinctive symptom of crown wart is growth of galls on crown.

PLATE 10.19

Alfalfa dwarf. The small, stunted plant on the right is infected with alfalfa dwarf caused by the bacterium, *Xylella fastidiosa*, which is transmitted by sharp-shooter leafhoppers.

PLATE 10.20

Alfalfa mosaic. Alfalfa mosaic virus shows a bright yellow mottling on the leaves and is transmitted by several species of aphids.

PLATE 10.21

Scald and flooding injury. Alfalfa in the foreground has been killed by a combination of high temperatures and water logged soil due to flooding. Note that plants on the levees, above the flooding, have survived.

PLATE 10.22

Ozone injury. Alfalfa leaves damaged by ozone show bleached areas between the veins. PAN damage is similar.

11

Parasitic Nematodes in Alfalfa

Becky B. Westerdahl
Extension Nematologist, Department of Nematology
University of California, Davis

Carol A. Frate
Farm Advisor, University of California Cooperative Extension, Tulare, CA

Plant-parasitic nematodes are microscopic, unsegmented roundworms that frequently inhabit alfalfa fields. They can cause considerable economic losses and are often unrecognized by growers as a chronic and sometimes severe yield-reducing factor.

The nematodes that parasitize and damage alfalfa are less than one-tenth of an inch long and are found in soil, within roots, or within the crowns, stems, and leaves of plants. In the soil, nematodes live and move within the film of water that lines soil pore spaces. They are small enough to move between individual soil particles (Fig. 11.1). It is not uncommon for a single teaspoon of soil from an alfalfa field to contain 50 nematodes, or for a single inch of alfalfa stem or feeder root to contain 200.

Description

Nematodes have a relatively simple body structure (Fig. 11.2). The external covering or cuticle is transparent, permitting the major internal organs and systems, such as the digestive tract and reproductive system, to be visible when viewed through a microscope. Nematodes possess a spear or stylet that is used to pierce and feed on plant tissues (Fig. 11.3). The nematode life cycle consists of an egg stage, four gradually enlarging juvenile stages, and an adult stage (Fig. 11.4). Between each juvenile stage, nematodes

FIGURE 11.1

Soil-dwelling plant-parasitic nematodes feed on plant roots and can move within the film of water that lines soil pores.

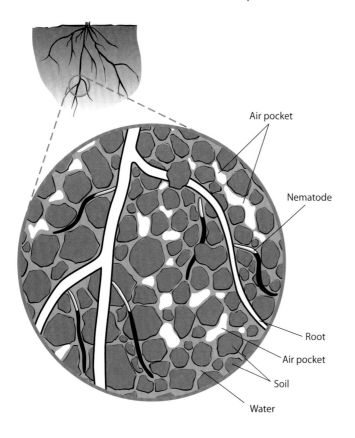

Air pocket

Nematode

Root

Air pocket

Soil

Water

FIGURE 11.2

Body structure of a typical plant-parasitic nematode.

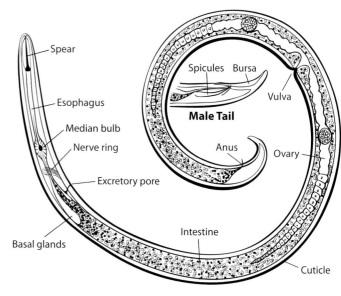

Spear

Esophagus

Median bulb

Nerve ring

Excretory pore

Basal glands

Spicules   Bursa

Vulva

Male Tail

Anus

Ovary

Intestine

Cuticle

FIGURE 11.3

Nematodes use a spear (also called a stylet) to feed on plant tissue.

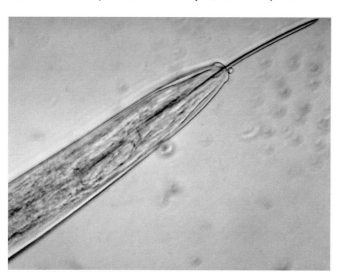

FIGURE 11.4

Life cycle of a typical plant-parasitic nematode.

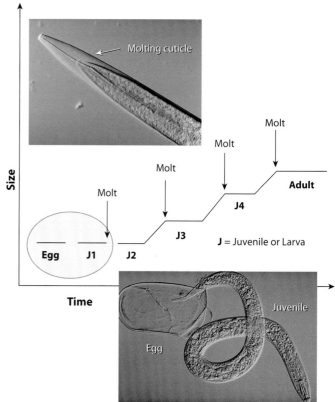

Molting cuticle

Molt

Molt

Molt

Adult

Molt

J4

J3

J = Juvenile or Larva

Egg   **J1**   **J2**

Size

Time

Egg

Juvenile

molt or shed their cuticle. The length of a single generation can vary from a few days to a full year, depending on the species, the soil temperature, and other factors. Nematodes feeding on alfalfa can pass through several generations each year. Adult female nematodes can lay several hundred to one thousand eggs.

To conduct a nematode pest-management program, it is important to understand nematode biology, symptoms and signs of nematode damage, how nematodes injure plants, how to sample for nematodes, and the principles underlying various management techniques. Strategies for managing nematodes in alfalfa include site selection, the use of certified seed, using clean equipment and irrigation water, weed management, and the use of resistant varieties, crop rotation, fallow, organic amendments, and chemical nematicides.

Types of Nematodes

As many as 15 different plant-parasitic nematodes have been found in alfalfa fields in California (Table 11.1). Each species has a scientific and a common name and both are regularly used by nematologists. The common name is derived from a morphological characteristic of the nematode, from plant damage symptoms, or from the typical location of the nematode within a host.

Life-history Patterns

Nematodes commonly found in alfalfa fields exhibit several different life-history patterns (Fig. 11.5). Stubby-root, dagger, needle, ring, spiral, and stunt nematodes reside primarily outside the root and are considered ectoparasites. They use stylets to feed on roots; however, all stages of their life cycle are passed outside of roots in the soil. Stem nematodes and lesion nematodes reside primarily within the plant and are considered migratory endoparasites (living primarily inside the root). Life-cycle stages for these nematodes take place within the plant (stems, leaves, and crown for stem nematodes; roots for lesion nematodes) as well as in adjacent soil. Root-knot nematodes are sedentary (immobile) endoparasites. The second stage juvenile enters a root, takes up a permanent feeding site and then develops into an immobile adult female within the root.

TABLE 11.1

Nematodes found in California alfalfa fields

Common Name	Scientific Name
Nematodes Commonly Causing Injury	
Stem nematode*	*Ditylenchus dipsaci* (Kuhn and Filipjev)
Northern root-knot nematode*	*Meloidogyne hapla* Chitwood
Javanese root-knot nematode	*M. javanica* (Treub, Chitwood)
Southern root-knot nematode*	*M. incognita* (Kofoid and White) Chitwood
Peanut root-knot nematode	*M. arenaria* (Neal) Chitwood
Columbia root-knot nematode	*M. chitwoodi* Golden, O'Bannon, Santo, Finley
Other Nematodes Found	
Lesion nematode*	*Pratylenchus penetrans* (Cobb) Filipjev and Schuurmans-Stekhoven
Dagger nematode	*Xiphinema americanum* Cobb
Needle nematode	*Longidorus africanus* (Micol.) Meyl
Ring nematode*	*Mesocriconema curvatus* (Raski) Loof and DeGrisse
Stunt nematode*	*Merlinius brevidens* (Allen) Siddiqi
Stunt nematode	*Tylenchorhynchus* sp. Cobb
Spiral nematode	*Helicotylenchus* sp. Steiner
Stubby-root nematode*	*Trichodorus* sp. Cobb
Stubby-root nematode	*Paratrichodorus* sp. Siddiqi

*These nematodes have been shown to reduce yields in alfalfa.

Ectoparasite (e.g., dagger nematode)

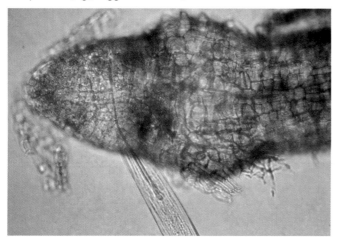

Migratory Endoparasite (e.g., stem nematode)

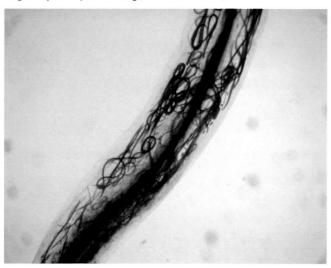

FIGURE 11.5

Examples of nematode life-history patterns. All stages of ectoparasites are found outside the root in the soil. Migratory endoparasites can be either in the root or in the soil. The juveniles of sedentary endoparasites are motile stages moving through the soil to find host roots. Once they enter a root and start to feed and become adults, they enlarge and can no longer move.

Sedentary Endoparasite (e.g., root-knot nematode)

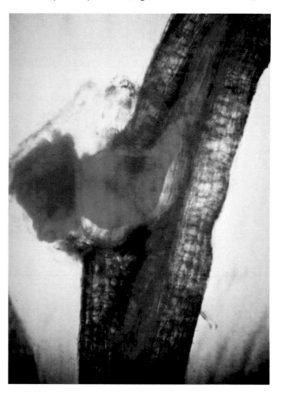

The root cells around her head enlarge to form a gall or knot.

Knowledge of these life-history patterns can be helpful when making management decisions. For example, some nematicides, parasites, or soil amendments can be expected to be active only in the soil and so would be more effective against ectoparasites than against endoparasites. Other nematicidal agents might move systemically through the plant and would be effective against endoparasites. Beneficial parasites might be able to penetrate roots and actively seek out nematodes and would then be effective against endoparasitic nematodes.

Injury to Plant

Nematodes do not typically kill plants. They are plant stressors and act in conjunction with other stress factors in the field to reduce growth and yield. Penetration and movement by nematodes through plant tissues result in mechanical injury to cells and subsequent cell death and necrosis. Mechanical injury interrupts the uptake and flow of water and nutrients from roots and the flow of food from leaves to roots. In addition, nematodes create openings in roots through which other microorganisms can enter. For example, southern root-knot nematode (*Meloidogyne incognita* [Kofoid and White] Chitwood) can increase the severity of Fusarium wilt in alfalfa. Northern root-knot nematode (*M. hapla* Chitwood) can increase the incidence of bacterial wilt in both resistant and susceptible alfalfa cultivars. All of the above factors increase the susceptibility of plants to environmental stresses, such as moisture, freezing, or heat stress.

Because of the complex interactions that occur in the field, it is difficult to say that observed problems are specifically caused by nematodes. A number of experiments have been conducted with various nematodes on alfalfa in either greenhouse plots or microplots where conditions can be easily controlled. In these tests, the following nematodes have been shown to cause significant growth reductions: stem nematode (*Ditylenchus dipsaci* [Kuhn] Filipjev 1936); northern root-knot nematode; southern root-knot nematode; stubby-root nematode (*Trichodorus* sp. Cobb); stunt nematode (*Tylenchorhynchus clarus* Allen); lesion nematode (*Pratylenchus penetrans* [Cobb] Filipjev and Schuurmans-Stekhoven); and ring nematode (*Mesocriconema curvatus* [Raski] Loof and DeGrisse).

Only a few of the nematode species identified above are consistently associated with damage to alfalfa in the Mediterranean and desert production zones of California. The most important of those that will be covered in this chapter are stem nematode and root-knot nematode. However, if any of the nematodes mentioned above are present in a field at the time of planting, they could cause stunting of seedling alfalfa.

Root-knot Nematodes

Roots infested with root-knot nematodes may exhibit knots or galls and may branch excessively. Compared to galls formed on many other plants, root-knot galls on alfalfa are typically much smaller. Root-knot galls can be distinguished from nitrogen-fixing bacteria nodules by rubbing the roots between your fingers. Galls, unlike nodules, are not easily dislodged. Also, nodules reveal a pink coloration when rubbed between the fingers (Fig. 11.6). This pink is not apparent in galls. Symptoms above ground level include stunting,

slower growth than expected, or unexplained dieback and chlorosis.

Five species of root-knot nematodes are associated with alfalfa in California. These species have wide and variable host ranges, different temperature optimums, and different degrees of pathogenicity. For example, in the San Joaquin Valley, damage from northern root-knot nematode has been more significant than damage from other species. Because of their

FIGURE 11.6

It is important to distinguish between the beneficial nodules (A) from bacteria that fix nitrogen for the plant, and those of root-knot galls (B) that result from parasitic root-knot nematodes on alfalfa.

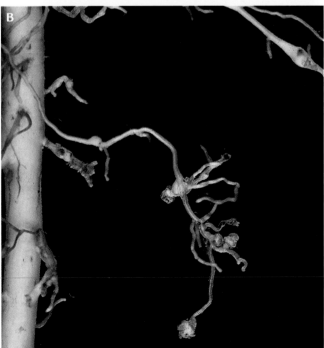

wide host ranges, root-knot nematodes create problems for many susceptible crops that might be grown in rotation with alfalfa. In the San Joaquin Valley, perennial crops, such as trees and vines, are not susceptible to the root-knot species that infest alfalfa. Some vegetable and field crops may show damage if planted in a field following infested alfalfa or may increase root-knot nematode populations that might affect a subsequent alfalfa planting if a susceptible variety is planted.

The range of temperatures for development of southern root-knot, peanut root-knot (*M. arenaria* [Neal] Chitwood), and Javanese root-knot (*M. javanica* [Treub] Chitwood) nematodes is approximately 65–75°F (18–24°C), whereas the range for northern root-knot and Columbia root-knot (*M. chitwoodi* Golden, O'Bannon, Santo, and Finley, 1980) is approximately 41–77°F (5–25°C). Under these conditions, root-knot nematodes can complete a generation in 4–6 weeks and produce multiple generations per year. The pathogenic situation for Columbia root-knot nematode is further complicated by its having at least two morphologically indistinguishable races, only one of which is known to reproduce on alfalfa. The alfalfa race does not appear to be widely distributed in California.

Variety Resistance

Most varieties of dormancy classes 7–9 are resistant or highly resistant to the southern root-knot nematode. Fewer varieties are resistant to northern root-knot nematode. It is difficult to distinguish between these two species of root-knot nematode because they are very similar morphologically. If laboratory samples indicate the presence of root-knot nematodes but the species is not identified, choose a variety that has some resistance to both southern and northern root-knot nematodes. As a general rule, when planting on sandy ground, select a variety that has a high or at least moderately high level of resistance to root-knot nematodes.

> *As a general rule, when planting on sandy ground, select a variety that has a high or at least moderately high level of resistance to root-knot nematodes.*

Stem Nematode

Stem nematode is known to attack over 450 plant species. However, there are at least 20 stem nematode biological races, some of which have a limited host range. This nematode was first identified in Germany in 1881 and was first reported in the United States in 1923. This species is believed to have been spread by debris in seed. When viewed under a microscope, these different races appear to be morphologically identical. They can only be distinguished by their host range (e.g., a race for alfalfa and a race for garlic and onions).

Infected plants will have shortened, stunted, and chlorotic stems (see Color Plates 11.1a and 11.1b). The nodes swell, and the internodes are short. These symptoms are associated with the release of digestive enzymes by the nematode and a resulting physiological imbalance of growth hormones produced by the plant.

This nematode is unusual because it spends none of its active life in the soil, but rather lives in the aboveground portion of the plant. The first larval stage remains in the egg, but subsequent larval stages and adults are able to infect developing alfalfa bud tissue. Optimum temperatures for invasion and reproduction in alfalfa are 59–68°F (15–20°C). Root nematodes reproduce in temperatures from 41–86°F (5–30°C). A life cycle can be completed in 19–23 days in susceptible cultivars; thus, multiple generations are possible in a single growing season.

Stem nematode is very sensitive to environmental conditions. Damage is most severe during moist, cool weather in cooler, sprinkler-irrigated inland valleys and foggy coastal areas. This species ranges as far south in the Central Valley as Madera County. Typically, damage is seen in the first and second cuttings. Hot, dry conditions later in the growing season reduce its activity. When environmental conditions are unfavorable for development, the fourth stage larva can serve as a desiccation-resistant survival stage in which the nematode's metabolism slows to an almost undetectable level. During such conditions, large numbers may survive in the crowns. When cool, moist conditions return, metabolic activity increases and development resumes. Typically, only small numbers of this nematode are found in the soil. Under favorable conditions, they will move in a film of water from the soil to crowns where young leaves and shoots are developing. They have been observed entering plants through stomata (minute openings in the epidermis of a plant through which gaseous interchange takes place).

Planting resistant varieties is the most effective control measure. Reduce the possibility of introducing this nematode into fields by planting certified seed and by cleaning equipment used for harvesting. If some fields are already infected, harvest them after harvesting healthy fields. Clean harvesting equipment between fields when you know a field is infested.

Management Techniques

There are few cost-effective treatments for existing infestations of nematodes in alfalfa. The key approaches to management include site selection, crop rotation, variety selection, and other management techniques that prevent nematodes from spreading. Determination of species and presence of nematodes is a key first step.

Sampling Techniques

Because there are few distinctive nematode diagnostic symptoms or signs, soil, root, and aboveground plant tissue samples should be taken and sent to a diagnostic laboratory when plant vigor seems limited without an apparent cause. To begin the procedure, visually divide the field into sampling areas that represent differences in soil texture, drainage patterns, or cropping history. Take a separate sample from each area so that each can be managed separately. Because nematodes are usually not uniformly distributed within a field, it is necessary to take a series of subsamples from throughout the area to accurately determine if nematodes are present. In a fallow field, samples should be collected randomly from the sample area. In an established field, collect separate subsamples from areas that show symptoms and from adjacent healthy areas.

It is usually better to sample at the edge rather than the middle of an unhealthy area because roots in the center of the area may be too decayed to support a good nematode population, compared to more healthy areas around the edge. Samples should include feeder roots, when possible, and be taken when soil is moist. Because most nematode species feed on roots, they are more prevalent in the rooting zone of the current or previous crop, and this is the area from which subsamples should be taken. Mix the subsamples together and place 1 quart of the mixed soil and roots in a plastic bag. Seal the bag, and place a label on the outside of the bag. Keep samples cool, but do not freeze, and transport as soon as possible to a diagnostic laboratory. Be certain that the laboratory knows that alfalfa is the current or planned crop for the field so that they will use appropriate extraction techniques.

> *It is usually better to sample at the edge rather than the middle of an unhealthy area because roots in the center of the area may be too decayed to support a good nematode population...*

Treatment Thresholds

During recent years, increasing emphasis has been placed on the development and use of damage thresholds for making management decisions for pests. For many reasons, it is difficult to establish damage thresholds for nematodes. These include difficulties in obtaining representative samples, variability in extraction methods, efficiencies of different laboratories, and the many biotic and abiotic factors that influence populations. However, sampling periodically to determine if plant-parasitic nematodes are present can be very helpful in establishing the need for a nematode management program. If the nematodes discussed above as pathogens inhabit a field with below-normal growth and yield and no other explanation for the problem can be found, it is likely that nematodes are contributing to the problem. To determine if the nematode population is increasing or is remaining stable, a grower should sample an infested field at least once a year and at the same time each year.

Selection of Planting Site

Whenever possible, alfalfa should be planted in an area that is not infested with nematodes known to be pathogenic on alfalfa. Crop rotation can minimize populations if care is taken in the selection of crops planted between alfalfa crops. This is why proper identification of the nematode species present is so important.

Chemical Nematicides

Four chemicals are currently registered for preplant use on alfalfa in California: (1) 1,3-Dichloropropene (Telone II, 1,3-D), (2) chloropicrin, (3) metam-sodium (Vapam, Metam, Soil Prep, Sectagon, etc.), and (4) methyl bromide. However, because of their expense, fumigants are not likely to be a cost-effective control measure for plant-parasitic nematodes on alfalfa. There are no nematicides registered for postplant use on alfalfa in California.

Choice of Variety

A number of factors in addition to nematodes should be considered when choosing a variety (see Chapter 5, "Choosing an Alfalfa Variety"). From the standpoint of nematode management alone, varieties are available that are resistant to stem, northern root-knot, or to southern root-knot nematodes individually, but not to

both pest species. The fact that multiple nematode resistance is not widely available means that it is important to determine the species of nematodes present in a field before choosing a variety. Confusion exists over the terminology used for defining nematode resistance in varieties of alfalfa and in processing tomatoes. Root-knot nematode resistant alfalfa tolerates the presence of root-knot nematodes but allows them to reproduce so that populations that could be damaging to a following crop will be present at crop termination. Root-knot resistant tomatoes, on the other hand, do not allow reproduction by southern, Javanese, and peanut root-knot nematodes, resulting in lower population levels at crop termination than at planting.

> *It is important to determine the species of nematodes present in a field before choosing a variety.*

Certified Seed

It is important to buy only certified seed with a high level of resistance to minimize the chance of contaminating previously uninfested land. Until the importance of seed as a source of transmission of stem nematode was understood, as many as 17,000 nematodes were found per pound of alfalfa seed.

Clean Equipment

To minimize transfer of plant-parasitic nematodes, water should be used to remove soil and plant debris from farm equipment before moving equipment between fields.

Irrigation Water

Although growers might not have a choice of sources for irrigation water, they should be aware that surface irrigation water has been shown to be a potential source of nematode contamination. Whether there is a serious potential for contaminating alfalfa fields from irrigation water has not been determined. However, it is clear that runoff water from a known nematode-infested field should not be used to irrigate an uncontaminated field. In studies conducted in the state of Washington, more than a dozen different genera of plant-parasitic nematodes were found free floating in water samples taken from irrigation canals. Irrigating susceptible plants in a greenhouse with water from these infested samples resulted in nematode infestation. If a serious contamination problem is suspected, settling ponds can be used to reduce inoculum because most plant-parasitic nematodes will settle out within a short period, and nematode-free water can be pumped from the top of the pond.

Weed Management

Burning weeds within infested fields in the fall has been shown to decrease problems from stem nematodes the following spring. Conversely, for unknown reasons, experimental spring burning of weeds appears to make the nematode infestation problem worse.

Move Equipment on Dry Soils

Delaying cutting until the top 2–3 inches of soil is dry will minimize spread and reinfestation of stem nematode.

Crop Rotation

California crops, which have worked well in rotations for the race of stem nematode typically found on alfalfa, include small grain (wheat, oats, barley, triticale), beans, cotton, corn, sorghum, lettuce, melons, carrots, and tomatoes. A 3–4 year rotation is usually recommended. Care should be taken to destroy all volunteer alfalfa from previous crops. Otherwise, they will serve as a source of reinfestation after the rotation is completed.

Because of the wide host ranges of the species of root-knot nematode found in alfalfa in

California, crop rotation is not usually a feasible method of managing this nematode.

Fallow

The length of time that many nematodes can survive in weed-free fallow soil is not known. For the stem nematode, survival in the absence of hosts depends on environmental conditions. It can be as short as 2 years in rotation to grain in areas of high rainfall or irrigation, or as long as 20 years in the dormant stage in fallow soil in areas with little rain.

Root-knot nematode populations are likely to decrease 80–90 percent within a year in fallow soil. However, until host roots or crowns and stems from a previous crop have rotted, they could continue to support nematodes.

> *Root-knot nematode populations are likely to decrease 80–90 percent within a year in fallow soil. However, until host roots or crowns and stems from a previous crop have rotted, they could continue to support nematodes.*

Biological Control

Many soils contain predators that attack nematodes, such as soil-dwelling mites and tardigrades, and even other nematodes. Also within soils are various types of parasitic fungi that may result in some level of natural biological control. It is estimated that naturally present predators and parasites may consume up to 95 percent of plant-parasitic nematodes inhabiting an environment, but those that are left are still enough to cause problems. There are no registered microbial nematicides.

Amendments

The addition of amendments to soil, such as green manures, chitin, sesame chaff, animal manure, humic acid, organic fertilizer, compost, and/or proprietary mixtures of beneficial microbials, is generally proclaimed to be beneficial to plant growth. With respect to nematode management, such benefits may include: (1) stimulation of the growth of nematophagous fungi (organisms capable of killing the nematodes); (2) improvements in soil structure, in water retention, and in plant nutrition that would reduce stress on nematode-infested plants; and (3) production of nematicidal (nematode-killing) breakdown products (e.g., high-glucosinolate rapeseed or broccoli residues, which decompose to produce compounds similar to the nematicide metam sodium). Because of the complex nature of the possible interactions, interpretation of results following addition of soil amendments is difficult. Sufficient data are not available to predict with any certainty the nematode mortality that might result with these materials. In some cases, the addition of amendments has resulted in phytotoxicity in some crops, thus a product should first be tested in a small area of the field. Also, it is possible that nematode populations could increase following application of an amendment that results in an improved root system. If the amendment results in reduced stress on the crop and the development of a healthier root system, this root system could support a larger nematode population. Leaving untreated areas for comparison to amended areas is a good method for judging the success or failure of soil amendments. Evaluation should include both nematode samples and plant yield.

An Integrated Approach

In general, a combination of management techniques provides the best nematode control. For example, a management program for stem nematode might involve the use of crop rotation, certified seed, use of a nematode resistant variety, fall burning of weeds, and washing equipment before and after use in each field. For root-infecting nematodes, yearly soil sampling can help growers interpret stress symptoms in a crop. A proper nutrition and irrigation program can help to reduce stress caused by nematodes. The use of soil amendments in portions of fields that can be compared to unamended areas might provide growers with additional management tools for their particular growing conditions. The best results can be expected when alfalfa is not suffering from other biotic and abiotic problems in addition to nematodes.

Additional Reading

Griffin, G.D. 1984. Nematode parasites of alfalfa, cereals, and grasses. Pp. 243–321 in: Plant and insect nematodes, W.R. Nickle, ed. New York.

Stuteville, D.L., and D.C. Erwin, eds. 1990. Compendium of alfalfa diseases, 2nd ed. American Phytopathological Society, St. Paul. 84 pp.

Color Plates

11.1a

PLATES 11.1

(A) Stem-nematode damage. Note stunted plants and shortened internodes (middle/right) compared to normal plant (left). (B) Stem nematode injury in the field. Note stunted plants.

11.1b

12

Integrated Management of Vertebrate Pests in Alfalfa

Desley A. Whisson
Lecturer in Wildlife and Conservation Biology School of Life and
Environmental Sciences, Faculty of Science and Technology
Deakin University, Burwood, Victoria, Australia

Terrell P. Salmon
Wildlife Specialist, University of California Cooperative Extension
San Diego, CA

Alfalfa is an attractive habitat and food source to a wide variety of vertebrates. Significant reductions in yield can result from vertebrates feeding on the leaves, stems, and roots of alfalfa plants. In addition, the burrows and soil mounds created by some of these pests may cause problems with irrigation (primarily in flood-irrigated fields) and result in damage to harvest equipment and disruptions to harvest. Pocket gophers (*Thomomys* sp.), meadow voles (*Microtus californicus* Peale), and ground squirrels (*Spermophilus beecheyi* Richardson) are the most serious of the pest species in California alfalfa fields. However, black-tailed jackrabbits (*Lepus californicus* Gray), cottontail rabbits (*Sylvilagus audubonii* [Baird]), deer (*Odocoileus hemionus* Rafinesque), and occasionally migrating waterfowl can also cause serious damage in certain areas.

The potential for damage due to vertebrate pests varies between fields and can be dependent on such factors as cultural practices (e.g., irrigation, field rotation), soil type, field location, and the surrounding habitats. Fields near rangeland, forested areas, and other uncultivated weedy areas are generally at higher risk and are more quickly invaded than fields bordered by frequently cultivated land.

Vertebrate Management Strategies

The most successful management strategy requires knowledge of the biology and behavior of vertebrate pests and regular monitoring for them in and around fields. Historical records of pest population levels and control measures implemented, and analysis of the economics of control procedures and their potential effectiveness, can help determine the best management approach. Consideration also must be given to the presence of nonpest species. In many areas, the presence of endangered species may limit your choice of control measures.

Control options vary with the pest, and for that reason it is very important to correctly identify the species that is causing the damage before implementing a management program. This can be achieved by observing the location and type of damage within the field, the pest species present, and their signs, such as feces, tracks, burrows, and mounds. For most vertebrate pests, more than one method is available to manage their populations. Table 12.1 lists control options that may be used for vertebrate pests in alfalfa. Each of these options is discussed in more detail for each species.

Biological Control

Vertebrate populations are affected most by availability of food and cover; diseases and predators play a relatively minor role. A number of predators, including hawks, owls, foxes, coyotes, and snakes, feed on some of the rodent species that are pests in alfalfa. Installing owl boxes and predator perches may help attract predators and be part of an integrated pest management program. However, predators seldom keep rodent pests from reaching damaging levels. The high reproductive rate of small rodents allows their populations to compensate for losses due to predation. Additionally, predators often modify their diets according to the relative abundance of prey species.

Development of New Control Tools

Research into development of new control methods and studies to satisfy EPA's data requirements to maintain current pesticide registrations for vertebrate pests in alfalfa are supported by the rodenticide bait surcharge program of the California Department of Food and Agriculture. Research undertaken since 1995 has investigated the efficacy and nontarget hazards of zinc phosphide for the control of meadow voles, the use of chlorophacinone for the control of pocket gophers, baiting strategies

TABLE 12.1

Control options for vertebrate pests in alfalfa

Pest	Habitat modification	Trap	Fence	Frighten	Shoot	Bait	Burrow fumigation
Pocket gopher (*Thomomys* sp.)	■	■				■	■
Meadow vole (*Microtus californicus*)	■					■	
California ground squirrel (*Spermophilus beecheyi*)	■	■			■	■	■
Black-tailed jackrabbit (*Lepus californicus*)	■	■	■		■	■	
Cottontail rabbit (*Sylvilagus audubonii*)	■	■	■		■	■	
Deer (*Odocoileus hemionus*)			■	■	■		

for California ground squirrels, and management strategies for black-tailed jackrabbits.

Many innovative control methods have been proposed as being more environmentally friendly than some of the traditional approaches. When considering alternative approaches, you should remember that testimonials aren't necessarily proof of effectiveness. Check with your local farm advisor's office to determine if the technique has proven to be successful in controlled scientific tests. As an example, burrow exploding devices (e.g., Rodentorch, Rodex 4000) have gained popularity in California. These devices deliver and ignite a mixture of propane and oxygen into a burrow system. Burrowing rodents supposedly die as a result of concussion. Research has shown that these devices, at best, reduce burrowing rodent populations by about 50 percent. Because of the rapid rate at which pests can repopulate an area, 50 percent control is not sufficient to provide an economic benefit. Additionally, these devices are labor intensive to use and should not be used where there is a potential for fire.

Legal Aspects of Vertebrate Pest Management

Under the California Fish and Game Code, pocket gophers, meadow voles, California ground squirrels, black-tailed jackrabbits, and cottontails may be lethally removed at any time by the owner or tenant of a property, if they are causing, or about to cause, a crop depredation. Deer may only be lethally removed by legal hunting or under a depredation permit obtained from the California Department of Fish and Game.

Only pesticides that are registered with California's Department of Pesticide Regulation (DPR) can be used for vertebrate pest control. Registered materials are listed in DPR's database that is available online at http://www.cdpr.ca.gov/. You may also contact your County Agricultural Commissioner for information on registered materials.

In some areas, the presence of federally and state protected endangered species in and around alfalfa fields may restrict management options. Species most likely to be of concern include the San Joaquin kit fox (*Vulpes macrotus* Merriam), kangaroo rats (*Dipodomys* sp.), and the blunt-nosed leopard lizard (*Gambelia silus* Stejneger). Where these species occur, special guidelines apply to the use of toxic baits and fumigants for vertebrate control. Detailed maps that show the ranges of endangered species and that give information on restrictions on pest control activities are available from the local County Agricultural Commissioner or the University of California Cooperative Extension. Additional information may also be obtained from the DPR Web site (http://www.cdpr.ca.gov/docs/es/intro.htm).

Live traps are sometimes used for managing vertebrate pests. Under the California Fish and Game Code, it is illegal to trap and relocate an animal. Live-trapped pest animals should be humanely euthanized. Methods currently approved by the American Veterinary Medical Association (AVMA) include shooting or gassing with carbon dioxide. Drowning is not a humane method of euthanasia.

A range of strategies for managing specific vertebrate pests are discussed below in relationship to specific species.

Pocket Gophers

Pocket gophers (*Thomomys* spp.) are the most common and most destructive vertebrate pests of alfalfa in Mediterranean and desert zones of California. Because breeding is regulated by the availability of green forage, in alfalfa fields pocket gophers may breed year-round, resulting in high population densities. Pocket gophers feed primarily on the taproot of alfalfa plants, thereby weakening or killing plants, resulting in significant yield reduction. Their burrowing can cause serious problems with irrigation as well as harvesting equipment. In addition, soil mounds may kill the alfalfa plants they cover and create weed seed beds. The damage incurred by gophers to an alfalfa field causes general stand decline and is permanent. Even after gophers have been controlled, the effect of previous gopher feeding continues to reduce yields.

Pocket gophers are burrowing rodents whose name is derived from the pair of large, external, fur-lined cheek pouches in which they can carry food and nesting material. Pocket gophers are 6–8 inches (15–20 cm) long and have bodies well adapted to an underground existence (Fig. 12.1). They are powerfully built in the forequarters, are equipped with large claws for digging, and have a short neck and a fairly small and flattened head. Gophers have small external ears, small eyes, and lips that close behind their large incisors, thereby enabling them to keep soil out of the mouth while burrowing. Gophers use their short whiskers and tails to help navigate tunnels. They seldom travel aboveground; however, they may sometimes be seen feeding or pushing dirt out of their burrow system. They are generally more active excavating soil in the spring and fall than during the heat of summer. In uncultivated and nonirrigated areas the female normally produces one litter per year during the rainy season, when green forage is plentiful. In irrigated alfalfa fields at low elevations, pocket gophers may breed year-round. Average litter size is five or six. Pocket gophers have a maximum life span of about 5 years.

Pocket gophers are very territorial and antisocial. As soon as the young are weaned, they leave their mother's burrow and establish their own territory. The burrow system can cover an area from a few hundred square feet (10–20 m²) up to more than 1,000 square feet (93 m²). Territories are generally smaller for younger individuals or in areas with abun-

dant food, such as alfalfa fields. Tunnels are 2–3 inches (5–8 cm) in diameter, and most are from 8–12 inches (20–30 cm) below the ground. The nests and food storage chambers are somewhat deeper.

Tunnels are usually deeper in sandy soils than in clay soils. One gopher may create several mounds in a day (Fig. 12.2). Crescent shaped mounds of fresh soil indicate their presence. These are formed as the animals push soil out of their burrows through lateral tunnels up to the surface. They plug the burrow soon after digging it to preserve fairly constant temperatures and humidity within the burrow system. Gophers may dig secondary tunnels off the main burrow for occasional aboveground grazing. In these cases, no distinctive mounds are formed. Fresh mounds of loose, finely textured soil indicate an active pocket gopher system. Because gophers also backfill old tunnels, the number of fresh mounds is not an indication of the number of gophers in an area.

Pocket gophers generally feed inside the burrow, several inches (centimeters) to a foot (30 cm) below the soil surface. Their feeding most often damages the roots, although they also eat the crowns and stems of alfalfa plants. The animals often pull the whole plants underground into their burrows. Aboveground feeding is restricted to a small area around burrow entrances.

FIGURE 12.1

Pocket gophers seldom travel aboveground; however, they may sometimes be seen feeding or pushing dirt out of their burrow system.

FIGURE 12.2

One gopher may create several mounds in a day. Crescent-shaped mounds of fresh soil indicate their presence.

Management Guidelines

Although a healthy stand of alfalfa can tolerate some gopher feeding, large populations of pocket gophers cause serious economic damage. Where forage is available year-round in irrigated fields, gopher populations may grow significantly throughout the year. A successful pocket gopher control program depends on early detection and control measures appropriate to the location and situation. Since individual burrow systems must be treated to control gophers, the cost of control increases in proportion to the number of gophers present. Additionally, the presence of burrow systems makes it easier for other gophers to invade a field. Limiting the number of burrow systems by controlling gophers as they appear may reduce treatment costs in the long term. Because mounds are difficult to detect when alfalfa is tall, the best way to monitor a pocket gopher population in alfalfa is to check for new mounds in a field shortly after harvesting.

Most alfalfa growers rely on poison baits for gopher control. Where populations are low or in alfalfa being produced organically, traps can be used. Control efforts should be concentrated in late winter to early spring when the alfalfa is breaking dormancy and before the gophers have given birth. Pocket gophers should be controlled around the perimeters as well as within the fields to reduce the potential for population increase by invasion. Flood irrigation may reduce gopher populations, but it does not eliminate the problem. Rotation to row crops or other field crops, such as barley, wheat, oats, or rye, will greatly reduce gopher population levels.

Baits

A number of rodenticides are currently registered for pocket gopher control. Of these, the best and most widely used is strychnine, an acute poison presented on grain. Anticoagulant baits are also available but are generally less cost effective because the gopher must ingest multiple doses over time. The bait is placed in the pocket gophers' main burrow runways. Depending on the level of infestation and the area to be treated, baits may be applied either by hand or mechanically using a burrow builder.

Hand-baiting is time-consuming and is generally only undertaken when the level of infestation is low or only a small area needs to be treated. Bait is placed by using either a special hand-operated bait dispenser probe or by making an opening to the burrow system with a probe and then placing the bait. The key to the success of these methods is accurately locating the gopher's main burrow. The main burrow is generally found 8–12 inches (20–30 cm) away from the plug on fresh, fan-shaped mounds. Once this is located, a rounded tablespoon (≈15 ml) of the bait is placed in the burrow and the hole closed with a rock, clod, or some other material to exclude light and prevent soil from falling on the bait. Two or three different places in the burrow system should be treated. If gopher activity continues for more than 2 days after treatment, the burrow should be treated again. Read and follow label instructions for recommended amounts and application rates.

When the level of pocket gopher infestation is high, mechanical burrow builders (Fig. 12.3) provide the most economical method of control. The burrow builder is a tractor-drawn device that constructs an artificial burrow and deposits poison bait at preset intervals and quantities. These artificial burrows are made at depths similar to burrows created by pocket gophers and in parallel rows

FIGURE 12.3

Mechanical burrow builder for large-scale application of strychnine bait for control of pocket gophers.

spaced at 20–25-foot (6–7-m) intervals so that they may intercept many natural pocket gopher runways. The pocket gophers readily explore these artificial tunnels and consume the poisoned bait. In some situations, 0.5-percent strychnine bait will give effective pocket gopher control when applied using a burrow builder. However, where it is not giving good control, a 1.8-percent strychnine bait may give superior results. The 1.8-percent bait is not registered for hand-baiting applications.

Successful control using burrow builders depends largely on soil moisture. If the soil is too wet, the tunnel may not close and may allow sunlight to penetrate the burrow. If the soil is too dry, the burrow may collapse. Burrow builders should only be used in areas where gophers are present, not as a preventive measure. As gophers seek areas with low resistance to digging, building a burrow where gophers are not present may actually facilitate the spread of those not poisoned by the treatment.

Traps

Trapping can provide economical and satisfactory control over small areas, or remove those animals remaining after a chemical control program. It is generally more effective in spring and fall when pocket gophers are most active. Several types and brands of gopher traps are available, the more common being the two-pronged pincer trap (Macabee) and the box-type trap (Fig. 12.4). Two traps facing opposite directions are placed in the main tunnel. This placement will intercept a pocket gopher coming from either direction. The traps are wired to a stake to prevent loss of the trap. The hole made to set the traps is then covered to exclude light from the burrow system. Traps should be inspected at least twice a day and moved to a different location if 3 days elapse without catching a gopher.

Other methods

Pocket gophers can easily withstand normal irrigation, but flooding sometimes forces them out of their burrows where they become vulnerable to predation. Fumigation with smoke or gas cartridges is not effective because gophers quickly seal off their burrows when they detect smoke or gas. However, aluminum phosphide fumigation (a restricted-use material) can be effective if applied when there is ample soil moisture to retain toxic gas. Follow label instructions and all of the safety precautions. To use aluminum phosphide, first probe to find the main burrow as with hand application of bait, then insert the number of tablets prescribed by the label into the burrow and seal the probe hole. As with other control methods, you need to keep monitoring for signs of renewed gopher activity. Retreat the area if you find new mounds after 24 to 48 hours. As pocket gophers feed on the taproot of alfalfa, varieties with several large roots rather than a single taproot usually suffer less when pocket gophers feed on them. Crop rotation can also help minimize problems with pocket gophers. Grain crops provide habitat that is less

FIGURE 12.4

Box (A) and Macabee (B) traps used for trapping pocket gophers.

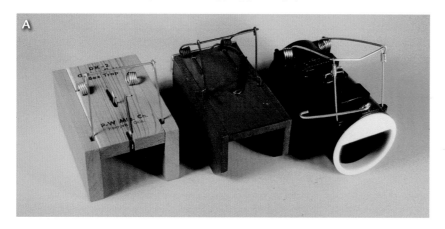
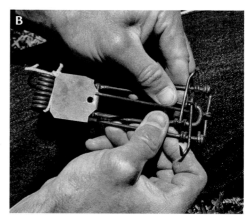

suitable for pocket gophers because they do not establish root systems with large underground storage structures and therefore do not provide a good source of food for pocket gophers year-round. Deep tillage when an alfalfa field is taken out of production may reduce the potential for pocket gopher problems by disrupting burrow systems.

Ground Squirrels

Ground squirrels (*Spermophilus beecheyi*) inhabit most of the Mediterranean and desert regions of California where alfalfa is grown. The California ground squirrel is a large ground squirrel with gray-brown fur mottled by light flecks, and a semi-bushy tail (Fig. 12.5). In native habitats, a squirrel consumes green foliage in spring and seeds later in the season when green foliage is no longer available. In alfalfa, however, squirrels will continue to feed on the crop throughout the year. Ground squirrels damage alfalfa by injuring stem buds and crowns as they feed on the plants, resulting in reduced growth and vigor. Because the California ground squirrel prefers to live on field edges or along fence rows or roadsides, damage due to this species is most common on field perimeters.

Unlike pocket gophers, ground squirrels are frequently visible, spending much of their time sunning, feeding, or socializing in and around fields. Burrows provide protection as well as a place to sleep and rest, rear young, and store food. The systems are not as extensive as those of pocket gophers but can be as deep as 6 feet. Ground squirrel burrows are much larger in diameter than pocket gopher burrows, and the burrow entrances are always unplugged (Fig. 12.6).

Ground squirrels are social animals and live in groups. Females have one litter per year in the spring, averaging seven to eight young. About 6 weeks after birth, the young ground squirrels emerge from the burrows and begin to graze on forage. During the hottest and driest part of the summer, many adult squirrels go into a resting state (estivation) until temperatures become more favorable in the fall. Most squirrels, especially the adults, hibernate in the winter. Because of these periods of inactivity,

FIGURE 12.5

The California ground squirrel is a large ground squirrel with gray-brown fur mottled by light flecks, and a semi-bushy tail.

FIGURE 12.6

Ground squirrels usually burrow outside alfalfa fields but can inhabit them if the irrigation is fairly light.

ground squirrel numbers may often appear to be much greater in spring and early fall than at other times of the year.

Management Guidelines

Poison baits, burrow fumigants, and trapping represent the three major control options available for ground squirrels. The success of these in controlling ground squirrels varies and is largely dependent on correct timing.

Baits

Poison baits are the most commonly used control tool. The acute rodenticide zinc phosphide, and the anticoagulants diphacinone and chlorophacinone are currently registered for ground squirrel control in California. Because the baits consist of treated grains (the seeds of cereal grasses and other food plants), they are most effective in the late spring and fall when seeds are the preferred food of the ground squirrel. Grain baits are not registered for broadcast application on alfalfa fields, but may be broadcast around the field edge or provided in bait stations that are designed to contain enough bait for the required multiple feedings and to reduce the risks to nontarget wildlife.

Fumigation

Burrow fumigation can be extremely effective in controlling ground squirrels. It is most successful in the spring or after irrigating when soil moisture is high because moist soil closes up surface cracks and helps retain a high toxic level of gas in the burrow. Fumigation is not as effective during summer and winter when most ground squirrels are inactive. At these times, the squirrels plug their burrow systems behind them and aren't exposed to the gas. A number of fumigants are registered for ground squirrel control. Acrolein (Magnacide) is a restricted-use material that is injected into burrows via a dispensing rod, with nitrogen gas as the propellant. Gas cartridges (smoke bombs) and aluminum phosphide tablets (Phostoxin and Fumitoxin) are easy and relatively safe fumigants to use. Cartridges are placed in burrows that show evidence of recent squirrel activity. After the cartridge fuse has been ignited, it is pushed deep into the burrow with a shovel or stick, then the burrow entrance is plugged quickly with soil to seal in the toxic gas. Aluminum phosphide tablets, also a restricted use material, react with the atmospheric and soil moisture to produce phosphine gas. These tablets are also placed deep into the opening of each burrow, then the entrance is sealed with a wad of newspaper and tamped soil.

Traps

Trapping ground squirrels sometimes provides satisfactory control of small numbers of squirrels. A number of kill traps (e.g., Conibear trap, modified pocket gopher trap) are available.

Other methods

Shooting may also be useful in some situations, such as where population levels are low or to control survivors of other control operations. It is seldom effective when dealing with large ground squirrel populations.

Meadow Voles

Meadow voles (*Microtus* sp.), sometimes called field mice, have a mature body length of 4–6 inches (10–15 cm); heavy bodies; short legs and tail; small eyes; and small, partially hidden ears (Fig. 12.7). Their soft, dense fur is blackish to grayish brown. Meadow voles are active year-round in a variety of crops. Alfalfa provides excellent food and habitat for this pest. Meadow voles feed on all parts of the

FIGURE 12.7

Meadow voles are common but usually hide from sight.

FIGURE 12.8

Meadow vole burrows are usually open and connected by trails.

plant, foraging on stems, leaves, and seeds in the spring, summer, and fall and concentrating on a diet of roots and crowns in the winter.

Meadow voles dig short, shallow burrows and make underground nests of grass, stems, and leaves. A good indication that significant numbers of meadow voles are in the field is the presence of well-worn trails 2 inches (5 cm) wide, leading to unplugged, small entrance holes in areas of the field where foraging is evident (Fig. 12.8). These trails are most evident in late winter before the alfalfa resumes growth. Meadow voles reproduce very rapidly, and populations fluctuate considerably. A female can produce from two to five litters per year; each litter averages four or five young. Spring is the peak breeding period; a second shorter breeding period occurs in fall. A heavily infested alfalfa field may support a peak population of 1,000 to 3,000 animals per acre (405 to 1,215 per hectare).

Management Guidelines

Cultural practices that reduce vole habitat within the field as well as surrounding areas can be effective in reducing the potential for serious problems. These practices include controlling weeds; cultivating fencerows, roadsides, and ditch banks; and reducing ground cover in adjacent orchards. These areas often provide a habitat from which the meadow voles can invade an alfalfa field. The easiest time to detect populations is after harvest and raking of the field. This is also the best time to apply controls because the voles begin their spring breeding cycle shortly before or just after the alfalfa begins to grow.

Baits

Where meadow vole problems are serious, applying bait is the only effective control measure. Zinc phosphide is the only bait registered for control of meadow voles in alfalfa. It may be applied by hand to burrows and runways, or broadcast to heavily infested areas. Adjacent noncrop areas that provide habitat to meadow voles should also be treated. To minimize the potential for bait shyness and reduction in bait efficacy developing, it should not be used in the same field more than once in a 6-month period. Zinc phosphide is a restricted use mate-

rial and may therefore only be applied under permit from the local County Agricultural Commissioner; local restrictions may apply.

Anticoagulant baits may not be used in alfalfa but can be applied by hand or broadcast at any time along fencerows and in surrounding noncrop areas to reduce the source of meadow voles. To be effective, anticoagulant bait must be available for meadow voles to consume over a period of several days. Bait stations are generally ineffective due to meadow vole range and behavior.

Hares and Rabbits

The black-tailed jackrabbit, actually a hare (*Lepus* sp.), is the most common rabbit-like pest in California alfalfa fields. The black-tailed jackrabbit has very long ears, short front legs, and long hind legs. The cottontail rabbit, a true rabbit, can be a pest in local areas. Cottontails (*Sylvilagus* sp.) are smaller than jackrabbits and have much shorter ears (Fig. 12.9). Rabbits and hares are classified as game mammals and can be taken by legal sport hunting methods during hunting seasons. Owners and tenants of agricultural lands may take hares or rabbits that cause agricultural damage at any time without a depredation permit.

Management Guidelines

Rabbits and hares are most active at night, feeding mostly at dusk and dawn. Alfalfa is

FIGURE 12.9

Cottontail rabbits (A) are smaller than jackrabbits (B) and have much shorter ears.

a favored food, and damage to plants can be significant in areas where there are large populations. A combination of methods, including exclusion and baits, may be helpful in controlling populations.

Exclusion

Fences, although expensive, are often the only effective means of minimizing damage caused by rabbits. Rabbit fences should be made out of 1-inch (2.5-cm) woven wire mesh and be at least 36 inches (90 cm) high and supported by posts. The bottom 6 inches (15 cm) of fence should be bent at a right angle away from the alfalfa field and buried 6 inches (15 cm) under the soil.

Baits

Anticoagulant baits (diphacinone and chlorophacinone) are registered for use in bait stations against rabbits and hares. Because they will not enter enclosed stations, the bait should be presented in a feeder in areas frequented by rabbits, such as runways and resting or feeding areas. Prebaiting with untreated bait may allow rabbits and hares to become accustomed to feeding from the station. Once they feed on the untreated bait (usually after 3 to 5 days) and begin to consume all untreated bait in a single night, this bait can be replaced with poison baits. Bait should be provided until all evidence of feeding has ceased. Bait stations are frequently covered during most daylight hours to exclude nontarget animals from the bait.

Shooting

Shooting may be useful in some situations for hares and rabbits, although it is quite labor intensive.

Deer

Deer may occasionally cause significant damage to alfalfa fields in areas where nearby habitats, especially wooded or brushy areas, provide cover (Fig. 12.10). Because deer are night feeders and may not be observed in fields, footprints, scat, and damage are often the first evidence of their activities.

It is illegal to use traps or poisons to control deer. Noise-making devices and lights sometimes discourage deer, but results are erratic and long-term effectiveness is unlikely. Although deer are classified as game animals, depredation permits to shoot deer out of season may be issued by local game wardens. A variety of regulations must be followed to comply with permit requirements. Deer numbers may also be reduced during the regular deer sport-hunting season, and hunting should be encouraged where deer are an ongoing problem. Deer-proof fences are costly but provide the only effective control in many situations.

Additional Reading

California Department of Food and Agriculture. 1994. Vertebrate pest control handbook. J.P. Clark, ed. CDFA, Sacramento.

Orloff, S.B., T.P. Salmon, and W.P. Gorenzel. 1995. Vertebrate pests. Pp. 8593 in: S.B. Orloff, H.L. Carlson, and L.R. Teuber, eds. Intermountain alfalfa management. University of California Division of Agriculture and Natural Resources, Oakland. Publication 3366.

Salmon, T.P., and R. Marsh. 1981. Vertebrate pests. Pp. 32–41 in: M.J. Haley. and L. Baker, eds. Integrated pest management for alfalfa hay. University of California Division of Agriculture and Natural Resources, Oakland. Publication 4104.

FIGURE 12.10

Deer can move into an alfalfa field at night and do significant damage.

13

Harvest Strategies for Alfalfa

Steve B. Orloff
Farm Advisor, University of California Cooperative Extension, Yreka, CA

Daniel H. Putnam
*Forage Extension Specialist, Department of Plant Sciences,
University of California, Davis*

H arvest management decisions are critical to the profitability of an alfalfa crop. The timing of alfalfa harvests is
the primary method by which growers can influence the
nutritional quality of alfalfa hay. Additionally, harvest timing
has a profound influence on forage yield and stand life as well as
pest management, particularly weed infestation. It is difficult to
overemphasize the importance of cutting schedules to alfalfa performance and overall profitability.

The Yield–Quality–Persistence Tradeoff

Deciding when to cut alfalfa is a difficult management decision.
There are several tradeoffs involved, and no single cutting schedule fits all situations. Alfalfa yield and forage quality are almost
always inversely related within a growth cycle. Alfalfa harvested
at an immature growth stage (short interval between cuttings)
results in relatively low yield but high forage quality. Conversely,
cutting alfalfa at a mature growth stage (long interval between
cuttings) results in high yield but low forage quality. This relationship of alfalfa growth and development is often termed
the yield–quality tradeoff (Fig. 13.1), and is fundamental to

understanding the influence of cutting schedules on alfalfa performance.

In addition to the yield–quality tradeoff within a growth period, cutting schedules influence the number of harvests possible in a year, thereby influencing seasonal yield and costs. Additionally, cutting alfalfa at immature growth stages shortens stand life and increases weed invasion due to the deterioration in plant health from frequent cuttings.

Alfalfa Growth and Root Reserves

To better understand the effects of time of cutting, it is helpful to review some principles of alfalfa growth and development (see Chapter 3, "Alfalfa Growth and Development"). Plant leaves use energy from the sun, through the process of photosynthesis, to transform carbon dioxide and water into carbohydrates. These carbohydrates (primarily sugars and starches) are translocated to the roots during the latter portion of the growth cycle (Fig. 13.2). These are commonly called "root reserves," and they provide the energy for initial growth in spring and regrowth after cutting. Protein and minerals are also stored in the root and crown of alfalfa plants in a similar fashion.

When active growth resumes in spring or following a cutting, the alfalfa plant relies on carbohydrates from the roots to support this growth until new leaves can photosynthesize sufficient carbohydrates to satisfy the needs of the growing plant. When growing nondormant alfalfa varieties in Mediterranean climates, this takes about 2 weeks after cutting, or until the alfalfa attains a height of 6–8 inches (15–20 cm). From approximately this point on, there is a net increase in carbohydrates, and the plant begins replenishing its root reserves. Carbohydrate reserves in roots and crowns increase with plant maturity, until full flowering of the alfalfa. Cutting alfalfa at excessively immature growth stages, which occurs when cutting intervals are very short, does not allow enough time for the alfalfa to replenish root reserves (Fig. 13.3), and the vigor of subsequent new growth is affected. Stand life may also

FIGURE 13.2

Plants use energy from the sun during growth to transform carbon dioxide and water to carbohydrates. Carbohydrates for alfalfa regrowth are translocated to the roots. Plants harvested at an immature stage accumulate fewer "root reserves" for subsequent regrowth.

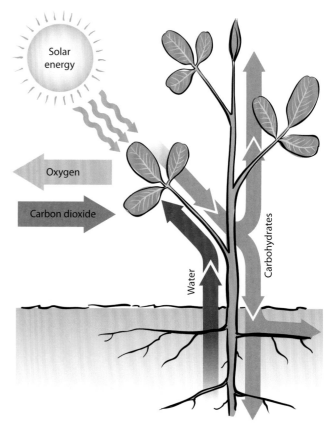

FIGURE 13.1

The yield–quality tradeoff for alfalfa hay. Over a growth period, yields increase while forage digestibility declines. This dataset is from Yolo County, CA, 2 years, spring, summer, and fall cuttings, which accounts for the "scatter" of the data, but the fundamental relationship can be seen.

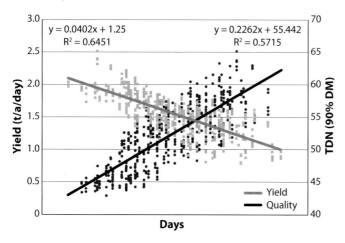

be reduced if alfalfa is repeatedly cut before root reserves are restored. Repeatedly cutting immature alfalfa plants in attempts to obtain high-quality hay, in combination with other stresses such as water stress, scalding, pest stress, and equipment traffic, are the most common reasons for stand loss in Mediterranean and desert regions.

The Effects of Plant Maturity on Yield

Alfalfa yield per cutting increases as plants mature during a growth period and the interval between cuttings increases. Yield can double as alfalfa goes from the pre-bud to full-bloom stage. In theory, maximum yield occurs when alfalfa reaches full bloom (Fig. 13.1). However, as a result of leaf senescence and loss from lower portions of mature alfalfa plants, maximum alfalfa yield is often reached at around 50-percent bloom and may level off after this point. Most California growers harvest during early to late-bud stage, and well before the alfalfa exceeds 50-percent bloom. Stages of alfalfa growth are provided in Tables 13.1 and 13.2.

In Mediterranean and arid environments, increases in yield are mostly linear, from early vegetative to early bloom stages, with each day bringing a steady increase in the dry matter accumulation of the crop. The actual rate of yield increase varies, depending on environmental conditions (such as weather, soil fertility, soil moisture levels) as well as alfalfa variety and other management factors. In research trials conducted in the Central Valley (Yolo and Fresno Counties), yield increased from 65–221 pounds (29–100 kg) of dry matter per acre (33–112 kg/ha) per day as alfalfa matured from the vegetative pre-bud stage to full bloom (Fig. 13.4).

FIGURE 13.3

Cutting at different growth stages affects the carbohydrate content of alfalfa roots.

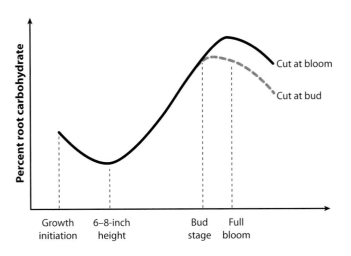

TABLE 13.1

Relationship between stage of maturity and crown bud development

Stage of Maturity	Crown Bud Development
Flower bud stage	50% of the crown with buds ¼ in. or less
10% bloom	60% of the crowns with regrowth ½ in.
50% bloom	90–100% of the crowns with regrowth 1 to 2 in.
Full bloom	100% of the crowns with bud regrowth in excess of 2 in.

TABLE 13.2

Definition of alfalfa developmental stages for individual alfalfa stems

Stage Number	Stage	Stage Definition
0	Early vegetative	Stem length ≤ 5 inches (13 cm); no buds, flowers, or seed pods
1	Mid vegetative	Stem length 6–12 inches (15–30 cm); no buds, flowers, or seed pods
2	Late vegetative	Stem length > 12 inches (30 cm); no buds, flowers, or seed pods
3	Early bud	1–2 nodes with buds; no flowers or seed pods
4	Late bud	≥ 3 nodes with buds; no flowers or seed pods
5	Early flower	One node with one open flower; no seed pods
6	Late flower	≥ 2 nodes with open flowers, no seed pods
7	Early seed pod	1–3 nodes with green seed pods
8	Late seed pod	≥ 4 nodes with green seed pods
9	Ripe seed pod	Nodes with mostly brown mature seed pods

FIGURE 13.4

Average daily increase in yield (bottom graph), and decline in quality (increase in ADF, NDF, decrease in CP, top three graphs), as alfalfa matures from pre-bud to full bloom at Yolo County, Fresno County, and Siskiyou County, CA, during different seasons (Ackerly 2001).

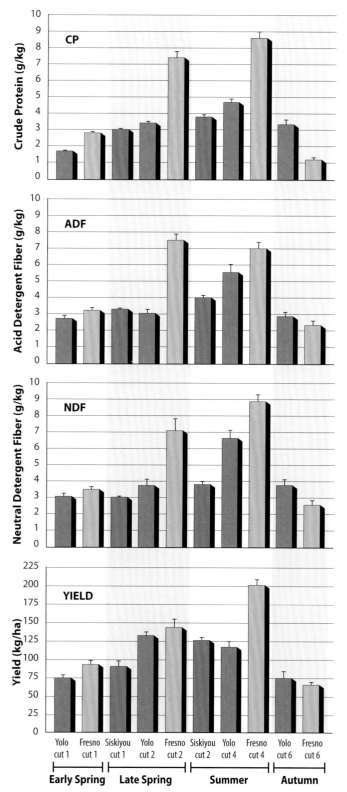

The Effects of Plant Maturity on Forage Quality

In contrast to yield, forage quality and digestibility decline dramatically with advancing alfalfa maturity (Fig. 13.1), (also see Chapter 16, "Forage Quality and Testing"). There are two primary reasons for this decline. First, as alfalfa plants grow, the proportion of stems to leaves (as a percentage of the dry matter yield) increases rapidly. During the vegetative stages, the weight of leaves may be up to 70 percent of the total yield. However, as the plant ages, the stems continue to grow, whereas the leaf biomass remains relatively constant, so the leaf percentage declines to 40–45 percent of the crop by mid bloom (Fig. 13.5). Because leaves are much higher in forage quality than stems, forage quality declines. In addition, the quality of the stem material itself declines rapidly as the plant grows and matures (Fig. 13.6). The forage quality of the leaf portion changes little with increased maturity, but the stems rapidly become much more fibrous, especially the highly indigestible lignin component.

The combined effect of declining leaf percentage and increased fiber in the stems dramatically affects forage quality as the alfalfa plant matures. These morphological changes cause reliable and powerful negative effects on forage quality during the growth period and

FIGURE 13.5

Effect of plant maturity on leaf percentage, first cutting, Davis, CA, (Ackerly 2001). Leaf percentage has a powerful effect on forage quality, and ranges from about 65% to 40% over a growth period.

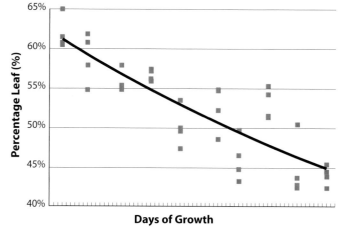

understanding these changes is important for making cutting schedule decisions.

Seasonal and Environmental Effects on Cutting Schedule Decisions

The optimum cutting strategy may be impacted by location, time of year, and even time of day. Changes in acid detergent fiber (ADF), neutral detergent fiber (NDF), and crude protein (CP) are much more rapid during summer months than during spring and fall (Fig. 13.4). In studies in the Sacramento Valley, ADF and NDF increase about 0.3 percentage points per day during spring, but about 0.6–0.7 percentage points per day during summer. Similarly, CP decreases much more rapidly during summer months, compared to spring or fall. Thus, losses in quality are much more rapid during hot summer months than during spring or fall. Consequently, a 28-day harvest schedule, for example, will result in higher quality in spring and fall versus summer.

Seasonal effects are primarily due to changes in temperature, solar radiation, and photoperiod (day length). Of these, temperature appears to exert the greatest influence. Within a season, quality declines much more rapidly at warmer locations. For example, in our studies, loss in quality was much greater in Fresno County (which has hotter days and nights) compared with Yolo County (Fig. 13.4). The final cutting of the season in all Mediterranean and desert regions typically yields less but has much higher quality than previous cuttings because the growth rate slows in response to cooler nighttime temperatures and shorter day lengths.

Alfalfa producers frequently complain about the difficulty in producing high-quality alfalfa in midsummer. Even when cut at the same growth stage, alfalfa harvested in spring and fall will usually have higher digestibility than alfalfa cut in midsummer. The decline in forage quality with advancing maturity is much slower in early spring and fall than in summer (Fig. 13.4). Poor forage quality in summer months is caused by rapid rates of fiber and

FIGURE 13.6

Effect of plant maturity on TDN content (calculated from ADF) on the stem, leaf, and whole-plant components of alfalfa, first cut, Davis, CA (Ackerly, 2001).

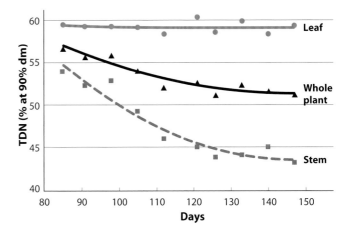

lignin accumulation and lower leaf-to-stem ratios.

Although obtaining high quality on every cutting during summer months may be nearly impossible, especially in the hot desert and Mediterranean regions, growers may want to consider "staggered" cuttings that allow some harvests to be high yield but low quality, and cut alternating harvests early for higher quality. This approach provides a "rest" period after a short cutting interval to give the plant more time to replenish root reserves. This concept is discussed more later in this chapter.

Time of Day Influences

There is some evidence that harvesting during afternoon periods (e.g., noon through 8 p.m.) may result in higher-energy, lower-fiber hay. In the afternoon, sugars and starches may temporarily accumulate in plant tissue due to the rapid rate of photosynthesis. At night, these compounds are respired and used by the plant, slightly increasing the fiber level. Accumulation of sugars (and other soluble components) in the cells may lower the fiber and the crude protein concentration due to dilution with cell solutes. Cell solutes (mostly sugars) contribute to the energy value of the forage and may improve palatability.

If alfalfa is cut in the afternoon, and respiration in windrows is minimal, the higher concentration of soluble carbohydrates may contribute 1 to 1.5 percent of the total digestible nutrients (TDN) of the forage. Although TDNs are higher in afternoon harvests, lower CP levels are often observed, due to dilution of the protein with soluble carbohydrates. All other factors being equal, we recommend afternoon cutting (compared to early morning), if feasible, to help "tip the balance" toward higher quality.

It is likely that the advantage of afternoon harvest would be greatest under mild, sunny conditions, not under cloudy growing condi-

tions or excessive heat. Diurnal changes in quality may only be preserved where the forage is properly conditioned and curing conditions after cutting favor minimal respiration in the windrow.

How Many Harvests Over the Year?

The principles discussed earlier in regard to the yield–quality tradeoff hold true for the selection of a cutting schedule for the season as well. More cuttings per year do not equate to higher total production per year. In fact, the opposite can be the case. Within reason, a long cutting interval (fewer harvests) will generally result in higher total seasonal production (Table 13.3, Fig. 13.7). Cutting five to six times in the Central Valley of California at full bloom (harvest interval of 37 days) resulted in an average yield over 3 years of 11.6 tons per acre (25.9 Mg per ha) per year. In contrast, harvesting at pre-bud, every 21 days for a total of nine to ten cuttings per year, resulted in a 3-year average yield of 7.5 tons per acre (16.8 Mg per ha) per year (Table 13.3). A separate study conducted during 2002-2004 showed a clear advantage of

FIGURE 13.7

Effect of cutting schedules (Early, 23 days; Mid, 28 days; Late, 34 days) on yield of alfalfa, average 2002–2004, Davis, CA. Data averaged across 18 varieties, all cuts. The darker portions of the bar graph represent higher quality yields from each cutting schedule, averaged over 3 years.

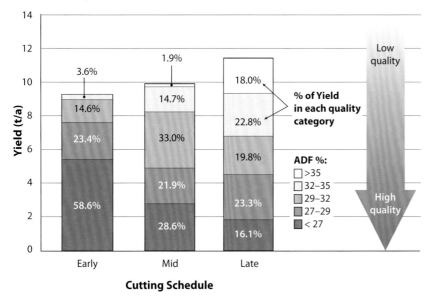

TABLE 13.3

Effects of different alfalfa cutting frequencies on 3-year average yield and quality, weeds, and stand at the end of the third year at Davis, CA (*Source:* V. Marble, 1974)

Maturity at harvest	Harvest interval (days)	Harvests per year	Yield tons/A	TDN*	Crude protein	Leaves	Weeds	Stand
Pre-bud	21	9–10	7.5	56.3	29.1	58	48	29
Mid-bud	25	8–9	8.8	54.2	25.2	56	54	38
10% bloom	29	7	9.9	52.4	21.3	53	8	45
50% bloom	33	6–7	11.4	52.0	18.0	50	0	56
100% bloom	37	5–6	11.6	50.1	16.9	47	0	50

*Percent total digestible nutrients (TDN) expressed on a 90-percent dry-matter basis calculated from modified crude fiber (MCF)

late cutting schedules (typically 5-6 cuts) for yield, but a large component of these harvests were low quality (Fig. 13.7). Similarly, short cutting schedules (23 days) resulted in high quality but lower yields (Fig. 13.7).

Frequent cutting also reduces alfalfa stand life and vigor. In the Central Valley, plots harvested at 50 or 100 percent bloom (five harvests per year) had no weeds, whereas plots cut at pre-bud or mid-bud (eight to nine times per year) had approximately 50 percent weed cover after 3 years (Table 13.3). This is due to stand loss in the treatments where the alfalfa was cut more frequently.

Identifying the Best Cutting Schedule Strategy

Selection of the best cutting schedule is not an easy task, since so many factors are involved. It requires the integration of all the topics mentioned above into a season-long harvest management plan, which includes market considerations as well as agronomic factors. The timing of an individual cutting should not be considered alone, but in relation to its effect on the entire production season, with consideration of stand life and economics over time. Several factors are important: the quality of the hay desired, time of year, weather conditions, desired stand life, and practical considerations, such as the irrigation schedule, harvests costs, whether the grower uses a custom harvester, and market conditions.

The growth stage at which alfalfa is cut should reflect the intended use of the hay. Alfalfa intended for use as a feed for beef cows or for recreational horses can be of much lower quality than that sold to dairies for high-producing milking cows. Alfalfa hay

intended for the dairy market must be cut early (late-bud stage at the latest) for the necessary quality to be achieved, at least for most dairy buyers. Conversely, hay intended for beef cattle or horses can be cut later, at 10- to 30-percent bloom, to maximize yields with acceptable quality for these classes of livestock. See Chapter 17 which cover utilization of alfalfa by various classes of livestock.

Weather conditions alter the growth rate and forage quality of alfalfa. Therefore, a cutting schedule should account for changes in weather. In addition, rain or extremely poor curing conditions can reduce the forage quality of alfalfa hay after harvest. If preserving alfalfa as hay, it is best to avoid cutting when very poor curing conditions or rain are anticipated.

Economic Considerations

Deciding when to harvest is largely an economic decision. Given the existence of the yield–quality tradeoff, the decision is not easy. Early harvest results in low yield but high forage quality and price, whereas delayed harvest results in increased yield but forage quality and price decline. The optimal time to cut alfalfa depends on the cutting schedule that generates the highest revenue (Fig. 13.8).

FIGURE 13.8

Gross returns as affected by alfalfa cutting schedules. Although there are several possible outcomes, a typical curve shows that early growth produces high quality but insufficient yields, followed by an optimum combination of yield and quality, and subsequently a decline in gross returns due to loss in quality. Under some market conditions, very high yields at long cutting schedules may result in a recovery of gross returns.

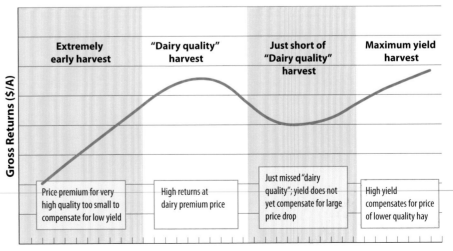

Consider the difference in price between premium dairy quality and less-digestible hay (typically hay used for beef cows or nonlactating dairy cows). This price difference varies significantly over the season and from year to year. The average differences due to quality have been approximately $7.00 per unit ADF in California markets over eight seasons, but range from $4.00 to $9.00, depending on year and location. This averages about $45.00 from top to bottom market categories. To determine the most profitable approach, take into account the rate of change in yield and quality for that season and the current price differential between the different quality market classes for alfalfa hay.

Pest management decisions may also impact cutting schedules. The decision to harvest early to control an insect pest without resorting to spraying is an option for weevil control in spring and worm control in summer. Additionally, allowing longer growth periods at least a few times during the year may enable an alfalfa crop to compete more vigorously with weeds.

Common Cutting Schedule Strategies

Calendar Dates

Alfalfa fields are frequently harvested on a calendar basis, using a predetermined fixed interval and fixed number of cuttings per season. The advantage of this method is that it facilitates planning. It allows advance scheduling of irrigation, cutting of other fields, and bale pickup. Cutting fields on a calendar basis is common when a custom harvester is employed to harvest fields. Custom harvesters often harvest fields on a predetermined interval, typically every 26–28 days, to schedule the harvest of other clients' fields.

The problem with harvesting alfalfa on a calendar basis is that it does not account for variable weather conditions, different rates of growth due to dormancy of the variety, temperature, season, or differences in growth between fields. For example, 28-day alfalfa during a

hot August period will likely be very different than 28-day alfalfa during a cool May. Weather in most Mediterranean and arid climates is relatively constant during the summer months but can still fluctuate enough even during the summer to affect yield and quality at a constant cutting interval. Spring and fall weather is more variable than summer, and there should be enough flexibility in the cutting schedule to allow for adjusting to weather changes. The dormancy of a variety also influences its rate of development (Chapter 5, "Choosing an Alfalfa Variety"). In general, a less dormant variety will be more mature on a given date than a more dormant variety. Scheduling harvests using the calendar fails to account for the stage of growth of the crop at each harvest.

Harvesting by Growth Stage

Another method of scheduling alfalfa harvests uses the growth stage of alfalfa to indicate the appropriate time to cut and thus the number of cuttings per season. The grower selects a specific alfalfa growth stage (such as pre-bud, bud, 10-percent bloom) at which harvest will begin. This method takes into account the effects of environmental and varietal differences and results in more consistent, predictable forage yield and quality than when harvesting on a calendar basis. Generally, the alfalfa growth stage at harvest is based on the appearance of bud or bloom; however, regrowth from crown buds is also used to indicate the proper time to cut (Tables 13.1 and 13.2).

Harvesting by growth stage results in more consistent, predictable forage yield and quality than when harvesting on a calendar basis.

The primary drawback to cutting based on stage of development rather than a calendar basis is that it is more management intensive and requires the ability to make labor and schedule adjustments. Additionally, the "stage" of development often does not always correspond to known values of quality and yield across environments. For example, a "full-bloom" alfalfa in the deserts of California may be higher in quality than a full-bloom alfalfa in a cooler environment. That is because flowering under desert conditions often occurs very early (sometimes within 10 days) and actually produces a higher-quality plant (lower stem percentage) than a full-bloom alfalfa growing in a cooler environment (higher stem percentage).

Growth Models

Growing-degree day models have been developed for some areas of the country to predict alfalfa growth and quality. These models have not been consistently accurate across cuttings, years, or environments. The problem may be that although temperature is a major factor, it is not the only factor affecting alfalfa growth and development. Most growing-degree day models developed for the Midwest for predicting forage quality are limited to the first cutting. The usefulness of this approach for Mediterranean regions is questionable, as winters are mild and the alfalfa often never goes truly dormant, making it difficult to apply a growing-degree day model.

Numerical Staging

Methods have been developed to quantitatively assess the maturity of alfalfa. One such method is a 10 stage numerical system (Table 13.2) in which alfalfa growth stages are described based on stem length or the presence of reproductive structures (see Chapter 3, "Alfalfa Growth and Development"). Alfalfa stems are visually evaluated and categorized. Only the first seven stages are used for hay production. These numerical categories can then be used to predict the forage quality of a standing alfalfa crop by determining a weighted average for a sample. Either the weight of the stems (mean stage by weight [MSW]) or the number of stems (mean stage by count [MSC]) that falls into each category is multiplied by the number corresponding to that stage. This number is then divided by the total weight or count for the MSW or MSC method, respectively (see Chapter 3, "Alfalfa Growth and Development" for examples of these calcula-

tions). Correlations between the mean stage value and the forage quality are used as a harvest decision tool.

PEAQ

A variation of this system, which is easier to use, was developed to predict the forage quality of alfalfa. The system is called Predictive Equations for Alfalfa Quality (PEAQ). This method uses the numeric growth stages, as determined by the scoring system described in Chapter 3. The PEAQ method involves evaluating only the most mature stem in a sample and the height of the single tallest stem to predict the forage quality of a standing alfalfa crop. PEAQ has worked well to predict forage quality in short-season production regions where dormant alfalfa varieties are produced. This technique may not be as accurate for Mediterranean regions where semidormant and nondormant varieties are produced and there is not as much variation in plant height over the season as there is in short-growing-season areas.

> *PEAQ has worked well to predict forage quality in short-season production regions where dormant alfalfa varieties are produced.*

Staggered Cutting Schedules

To achieve dairy-quality hay in midsummer, alfalfa must be cut at an extremely immature growth stage. However, this may not be worthwhile. The yield sacrifice associated with such early cutting is significant. Additionally, continued frequent harvests are harmful to root reserves, regrowth potential, and ultimately stand life. A "rest period" in midsummer would allow more time for the alfalfa to store root reserves. Therefore, it may be best to delay harvest and produce beef or horse hay in midsummer, targeting early spring and fall harvests for the dairy market. "Staggering" longer cutting intervals with shorter intervals may be beneficial in a single field, but practical considerations (scheduling of water, labor, machines) may limit this approach.

Although scheduling harvests by the calendar is most convenient, this strategy may result in harvests that "just miss" high quality, yet don't maximize yield (Fig. 13.8). The most common cutting schedule in the Low Desert and Mediterranean regions of California is 28 days, and many growers harvest as often as 21–24 days to achieve high quality. Even with frequent cutting, growers often fail to achieve high quality due to high summer temperatures (see Chapter 16, "Forage Quality and Testing"). Repeatedly harvesting at such short intervals in an attempt to achieve high quality may cause severe stand loss, weed intrusion, and low yields, and is not recommended.

> *Although scheduling harvests by the calendar is most convenient, this strategy may result in harvests that "just miss" high quality, yet don't maximize yield.*

A more complex strategy that involves staggering short and long cutting intervals may be beneficial to account for the need for high-quality hay while maintaining high yield and increased stand life. This approach entails planning a "short–long" cutting cycle, or a "cut for yield then cut for quality" strategy. This may be accomplished by changing the order of fields harvested from the first to the last field, so that the order is different in the second cutting compared with the first, and different in the third compared with the second. This allows a "recovery period" after a short cutting cycle during which the plant has an opportunity to recover its root reserves before subsequent cuttings. Growers may schedule an additional irrigation during this period to maximize yield and plant recovery.

This approach incorporates the agronomic advantages of long cutting cycles, while still producing high-quality forage to satisfy the quality demands of dairy markets at other harvests. From a marketing perspective, this strategy allows a continual stream of both high-

and medium-quality harvests for different market uses. Compared with continual early harvests, this strategy should improve alfalfa vigor and stand longevity and help prevent weed invasion.

Although this approach introduces greater complexity and requires a higher level of management, a "staggered" strategy which allows at least one to three "recovery" periods during the season is likely to contribute to long-term profitability.

Cutting Height

Occasionally, questions arise regarding the appropriate cutting height for alfalfa. The bottom of the stem is the least nutritious part of the alfalfa plant. Perhaps raising the cutting height could improve the nutritional quality of the alfalfa. Studies from the central and northern United States have shown that average annual yields of dry matter, protein, and digestible dry matter decrease as cutting height increases from 3 to 9 inches (8 to 23 cm). Wisconsin data shows that cutting above 2 inches (5 cm) results in a yield reduction of 0.5 tons per acre per year (1.12 Mg per ha^{-1}) per inch of additional cutting height. Raising the cutting height did increase forage quality, but it resulted in a significant decrease in yield. Therefore, leaving a stubble height of no more than 2–4 inches (5–10 cm) is recommended when cutting alfalfa.

Fall and Winter Harvest Management

The timing of the last harvest in the fall is an important consideration. Weather conditions may dictate when to make the last hay harvest. However, greenchop, silage, or grazing with sheep may be feasible later in the season when a hay harvest is not possible. Weather conditions are not the only factors to consider. Keep in mind the effect of fall harvest management on stand life and vigor. The timing of the last harvest in fall is very important in cold areas of the country where winter conditions are harsher than in Mediterranean regions. The importance of fall harvest management is not as obvious in Mediterranean and arid climates where nondormant alfalfa varieties are produced.

Late fall or winter harvesting can affect yield the following year, as well as stand life, weediness, and the degree of damage by the Egyptian alfalfa weevil and aphids. Just as too frequent a cutting interval during the normal production season can excessively deplete root reserves, so can harvesting too many times during late fall or winter. Research in the Central Valley of California indicated that it is possible to harvest alfalfa once in November or December without harming yield the next season, seriously damaging stand and vigor, or increasing weed contamination. However, additional harvests before the following spring can have detrimental long-term effects on alfalfa.

Research in the Imperial Valley showed no reduction in yield, vigor, or stand density with one or two late fall to winter harvests, provided there was a rest period of at least 45 days between harvests made from December through mid-February. Winter grazing of alfalfa in these desert environments may be advantageous, since haymaking is difficult. A sufficient rest period is also advised before grazing, because grazing, like cutting, can excessively deplete root reserves. Caution should be used to avoid animal traffic damage to crowns if the soil is wet.

Additional Reading

Ackerly, T. 2001. Characterizing and predicting the yield/quality tradeoff in alfalfa. Masters thesis. Department of Agronomy and Range Science, University of California, Davis. 104 pp.

Marble, V.L. 1990. Factors to optimize alfalfa production in the 1990s. Pp. 4–45 in: Proceedings, 20th California Alfalfa Symposium. December 6–7, Visalia, CA.

Marble, V.L., G. Peterson, and C.A. Schoner, Jr. 1988. Effect of fall/winter cutting on alfalfa (*Medicago sativa* L.) yield, pest management, and stand life. Pp. 45–58 in: Proceedings, 18th California Alfalfa Symposium. December 7–8, Modesto, CA.

Orloff, S.B., and V.L. Marble. 1997. Harvest management. Pp. 103–107 in: S.B. Orloff and H.L. Carlson eds., Intermountain alfalfa management. University of California Division of Agriculture and Natural Resources, Oakland. Publication 3366.

Sheaffer, C.C., G.D. Lacefield, and V.L. Marble. 1988. Cutting schedules and stands. Pp. 412–437 in: A.A. Hanson, D.K. Barnes, and R.R. Hill, Jr. eds., Alfalfa and alfalfa improvement. American Society of Agronomy, Crop Science Society of America, and Soil Science Society of America. Madison, WI. Number 29.

Undersander, D., N. Martin, D. Cosgrove, K. Kelling, M. Schmitt, J. Wedberg, R. Becker, C. Grau, and J. Doll. 1991. Alfalfa management guide. American Society of Agronomy, Crop Science Society of America, and Soil Science Society of America, Madison, WI.

14

Harvesting, Curing, and Preservation of Alfalfa

Steve B. Orloff
Farm Advisor, University of California Cooperative Extension, Yreka, CA

Shannon C. Mueller
Farm Advisor, University of California Cooperative Extension, Fresno, CA

S ignificant yield and quality losses result when alfalfa is not properly cured, preserved, and stored. Growers invest considerable time, inputs and money into producing a high yielding, high quality alfalfa crop. The goals of harvesting are to cut alfalfa at the growth stage that provides the optimum combination of yield and quality and to maintain quality and minimize losses through proper preservation. All of the efforts that go into producing high-quality alfalfa can be nullified if the crop is not harvested and stored properly.

Harvesting and Processing Strategies

Alfalfa offers tremendous flexibility in providing feed for animal consumption. The majority of the alfalfa produced in the western United States is harvested and baled as hay. However, growers may opt to cut and feed the alfalfa directly to dairy cows (green-chop), or ensile the alfalfa in large plastic bags, covered piles, or pits. Packaging alfalfa into cubes and pellets has also been practiced but is not common today.

The main difference between the alfalfa products is moisture content. Moisture content is the critical aspect of success for hay and ensilage success (Fig. 14.1). Greenchop has the highest moisture content, followed by silage, and lastly hay and cubes. Each harvest strategy has advantages and disadvantages, since each harvest and storage option has potential risks of dry matter and quality losses (Table 14.1). The alfalfa preservation strategy of choice depends on several factors: whether the alfalfa is sold or fed on-farm, distance to market, weather conditions, equipment available, and market demand for different alfalfa products. A description of the different alfalfa products and methods involved in their production is provided in this chapter.

Greenchop Alfalfa

Greenchopping is a harvest technique that involves cutting and chopping alfalfa into a feed wagon. The fresh forage is then delivered directly to the animals. Greenchopping alfalfa is common practice for the first cutting in the spring and late cuttings in the fall when making hay is risky due to weather conditions, and

when fields are in close proximity to animals. However, there are operators that greenchop some of their alfalfa throughout the year.

Advantages

If all cuttings in a growing season are greenchopped for direct feeding or silage, an overall yield increase of 10–12 percent is expected. Several factors contribute to the yield increase. Handling the forage when it has a high moisture content avoids leaf loss that occurs when raking or baling for hay production. This also contributes to higher quality. Traffic in the field from tractors and equipment used in raking, baling, hauling, and stacking is reduced in a greenchop system because the forage is harvested and removed in a single pass.

There are two distinct advantages to reducing traffic in the field, which lead to improved yield and stand longevity. Greenchop methods avoid heavy traffic, which can result in soil compaction problems that limit production. Traffic also damages the crowns and injures newly emerging shoots. This may contribute to disease problems and delayed regrowth. Traffic has a much greater effect on regrowing stems several days after harvest (during raking and baling), and a negligible effect during cutting. Removing the forage from the field immediately or soon after cutting has many advantages. Irrigation can follow shortly after harvest, resulting in less stress to the alfalfa. Reducing traffic damage and preventing stress from delayed irrigation allow for the crop to come back more quickly following harvest, often allowing for an additional cutting each growing season.

The ability of greenchop systems to avoid quality damage due to rainy weather is also an important advantage, compared to making hay. This is especially true in the spring and fall, when field drying times are much longer and weather more unpredictable in Mediterranean climates.

Disadvantages

Greenchopping is only practical when the field and the animals to

FIGURE 14.1

Moisture ranges for proper preservation of alfalfa as silage or hay.

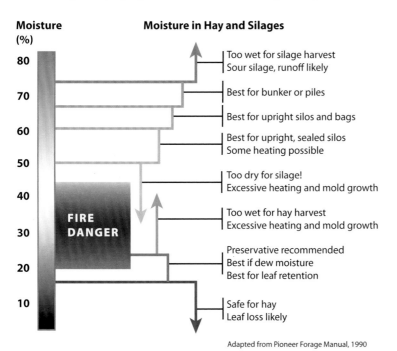

Adapted from Pioneer Forage Manual, 1990

be fed are in close proximity. Greenchop is a high-moisture feed (75–80% water), and hauling that amount of water long distances is not economical. A disadvantage to greenchop from the dairy perspective is the day-to-day variability of the feed. The forage must be fed quickly, so the grower only cuts as much feed as can be used that day. The alfalfa remaining in the field declines in quality as plants continue to mature. Variability is even greater if more than one field is being greenchopped to supply the fresh forage. Another disadvantage is that equipment must be taken to the field on a daily basis to harvest a supply of forage.

Exercise caution when greenchop is first fed, or when it is fed at the end of the season when moisture content is higher, because bloat can be a factor. The potential for bloat also exists if the alfalfa is very immature when greenchopped. Additionally, greenchop systems can cause excessive looseness in the stool when fed at high rates. In some cases, nutritionists would recommend feeding dry feeds in combination with greenchop, or feeding greenchop incorporated with a total mixed ration (TMR).

Alfalfa Silage (Haylage)

Alfalfa can be stored for a long period by ensiling it. Silage is a preserved feed that retains its nutrient value when handled properly. Table 14.2 lists proper silage-making processes that prevent losses and retain quality. To make alfalfa silage (haylage), the alfalfa is cut and left in the field to wilt until it reaches 60–70 percent moisture content. Depending on the weather, the alfalfa may remain in the windrow from a half day to a full day to reach the desired moisture content. Uniformity in

TABLE 14.1

Estimation of typical dry matter (DM) yield losses and quality changes during the major processes used in alfalfa harvest and storage (adapted from Rotz and Muck, 1994; Rotz, 2005)

Process	Loss in Yield (DM) Range (%)	Loss in Yield (DM) Average (%)	Change in Forage Quality (DM basis) CP (%)	Change in Forage Quality (DM basis) NDF (%)	Change in Forage Quality (DM basis) DDM* (%)
Post-Harvest Field Losses					
Respiration losses**	-1 to -7	-4	+0.9	+1.7	-1.7
Rain damage**, 0.2 inch	-3 to -7	-5	-0.4	+1.4	-1.5
1.0 inch	-7 to -27	-17	-1.7	+6.0	-7.0
2.0 inch	-12 to -50	-30	-3.5	+14.0	-14.0
Harvest Effects					
Mowing/conditioning	-1 to -4	-2	-0.7	+1.2	-1.4
Tedding	-2 to -8	-3	-0.5	+0.9	-1.2
Swath inversion	-1 to -3	-1	0.0	0.0	0.0
Raking	-1 to -20	-5	-0.5	+1.0	-1.2
Baling, small bale	-2 to -6	-4	-0.9	+1.5	-2.0
round bale	-3 to -9	-6	-1.7	+3.0	-4.0
large rectangular bale	-1 to -4	-3	-0.7	+1.0	-1.5
Chopping	-1 to -8	-3	0.0	0.0	0.0
Storage Effects					
Hay storage, covered	-3 to -9	-5	-0.7	2.0	-2.0
outside	-6 to -30	-15	0.0	5.0	-7.0
Silo storage, sealed	-6 to -14	-8	1.4	0.7	-3.7
stave	-7 to -17	-10	1.8	1.7	-4.7
bunker	-10 to -16	-12	2.3	2.7	-5.6

* Decrease in digestible dry matter or total digestible nutrients (TDN). This also reflects the loss of energy available to the animal.

** Respiration loss includes plant and microbial respiration for crops cured without rain damage. Rain damage includes leaf loss, nutrient leaching, and respiration resulting from rewetting.

moisture content is important. Moisture should be tested throughout the harvest to keep it within the desired range. If too much moisture remains in the forage at the time of ensiling, nutrients are leached from the pile or pit and run off. Fermentation may also be negatively affected. On the other hand, if the forage is too dry (< 50% moisture content), it is difficult to pack tightly in the pile, pit, or bag. As a result, proper preservation may not be achieved. Heat damage or mold formation may result when forage is too dry. Quality and digestibility are both reduced by browning reactions associated with heating.

Once the alfalfa has reached the target moisture content, windrows are raked together. A forage harvester chops the forage from the windrow and blows it into a silage truck. Alfalfa should be chopped to a theoretical length of cut (TLC) from 0.75 to 1 inch (1.9 to 2.5 cm). If the chop is longer than this, the forage is difficult to pack tightly, especially if it is on the dry side of the recommended range. If the chop is too short, feeding the forage may lead to metabolic problems in the animals consuming the haylage. Silage trucks transport the chopped forage to its final destination and dump it into a pile or pit, or pack it into a bag. Upright silos are rarely used for haylage in this area. Working quickly to tightly pack the forage and covering it to eliminate and exclude oxygen are critically important to the silage-making process. A polyethylene sheet or tarp is placed over the pile and weighted down with discarded tires or other weights. If silage is left uncovered, losses of 51 percent in the top 4 feet can be expected; overall losses of 32 percent or more have been recorded. Inspect covers or bags routinely for punctures or tears. Preventing oxygen from leaking into the system can greatly reduce storage losses.

The Fermentation Process

The main objective in silage preservation is to exclude oxygen as quickly as possible from the silage mass and reduce pH rapidly through bacterial fermentation. There are four phases to the fermentation process (Fig. 14.2): aerobic, lag, fermentation, and stable.

In the *aerobic* phase, plant respiration and aerobic microorganisms consume oxygen trapped in air spaces in the silage mass. Once oxygen is depleted, the system becomes anaerobic. The transition from an aerobic to an anaerobic environment happens quickly, within a few hours under optimum conditions.

TABLE 14.2

Proper silage making practices

Practice	Reason	Benefits
Minimize drying time.	Reduce respiration.	Reduced nutrient and energy losses. More sugar for fermentation. Lower silage pH.
Chop at correct TLC.[1] Fill silo quickly. Enhance compaction. Seal silo carefully.	Minimize exposure to oxygen.	Reduced nutrient and energy losses. More sugar for fermentation. Reduced silo temperatures. Less heat damage (browning). Faster pH decline. More extensive pH decline. Better aerobic stability. Less chance of *listeria*. Less protein solubilization.
Ensile at 30%–50% DM content.	Optimize fermentation.	Reduced nutrient and energy losses. Proper silo temperatures. Less heat damage (browning). Control *clostridia*. Prevent effluent flow.
Leave silo sealed for at least 14 days.	Allow complete fermentation.	Lower silage pH. More fermentation acids. Better aerobic stability. Less chance of *listeria*.
Unload 2–6 in./day. Keep smooth surface.	Stay ahead of spoilage.	Limit aerobic deterioration.
Discard deteriorated silage.	Avoid animal health problems.	Prevent toxic poisoning, myocotic infections. Prevent listeriosis, clostridial toxins.

Source: Pitt (1990).

[1]TLC is theoretical length of cut.

Once the system becomes anaerobic, the *lag* phase begins. During this phase, cell membranes break down and anaerobic bacteria begin to grow and multiply rapidly, using the plant sugars as a substrate.

During the *fermentation* phase, bacteria convert sugars to acetic and lactic acids, resulting in a low pH and high concentration of lactic acid (at least 70%) in the ensiled forage. Lactic acid is the most efficient fermentation acid and will quickly drop the pH of the silage. The faster fermentation is completed, the more nutrients will be retained in the silage. Well-fermented alfalfa silage should have a pH from 4 to 5. At this pH range, the bacteria die out and the silage enters the *stable* phase, where it remains until feeding begins. The anaerobic (oxygen-free) environment also prevents mold and yeast growth. An online Interactive Module to understand silage-making processes is available (Hall and Wilson 2004).

Inoculating Silage Crops

Alfalfa can be difficult to ensile because of low sugar content and high buffering capacity, as compared to corn or other grasses. Some growers apply silage additives (inoculants) to the forage to aid in the fermentation and preservation process. Most silage additives are designed to improve fermentation by providing bacteria and enzymes. Additives add to the population or enhance the growth of lactic acid bacteria, increasing their production of organic acids that reduce pH. Other types of additives, categorized as inhibitors, slow down various processes in silage preservation and are either aerobic or anaerobic. They include materials like propionates (aerobic inhibitors) or lactic acid (anaerobic inhibitor). Silage additives may improve recovery of silage dry matter by reducing the loss of dry matter during the ensiling process and/or at feeding. Finally, they may improve digestibility, intake, and animal performance.

Composition and application rate should be considered in order to predict the success of an additive. Comparisons between products should be based on the amount of active ingredient supplied per unit (pound) of forage. A common unit is the number of colony-forming

FIGURE 14.2

Sequence of phases during the ensiling process. *Source:* Pitt, 1990.

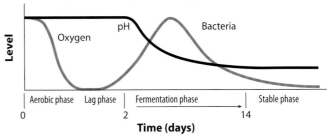

units added per gram of fresh forage (cfu/gram forage). In general, the more cfu's per gram of forage added by an inoculant, the more likely it is to be effective. At a minimum, an additive should provide 10^5 cfu/g. The intention is that the added microorganisms should dominate the fermentation; produce lactic acid as the sole end product; be able to grow over a wide range of pH, temperature, and moisture conditions; and ferment a wide range of plant sugars. Uniform distribution of the inoculant in the forage is critical for promoting bacterial access to plant sugar. The recommended point of application is during chopping, and liquid materials are preferred over granular.

It is best to wait at least 3–4 weeks to allow for maximum fermentation before the alfalfa haylage is fed. This will result in better aerobic stability. The rate at which the silage is fed must be sufficient to prevent the exposed silage from heating and spoiling. Good management of the feeding face of an open silage pit is critical to prevent spoilage. An average rate of 6 inches silage removal from the face per day is a common recommendation, taking care to remove silage from the entire exposed face. It is important to limit the disturbance of the packed silage to avoid piles of loose haylage. Estimates of storage losses in haylage range from 2 to 12 percent from surface spoilage and fermentation. Losses are often greater in a pile or pit than in bags, where there is less surface exposed at any one time.

Advantages of Silage

The yield and quality advantages listed earlier for greenchop apply to an alfalfa silage (haylage) system as well. There are more nutrients preserved per acre because of reduced

> *The wetter ration is more palatable and digestible, and is preferred by cows, especially during the hot summer months.*

leaf losses, and weather damage is much easier to avoid, compared with haymaking. Although the forage is allowed to wilt in the field, it typically requires only 2–6 hours mid-season, and from 15 to 20 hours during spring and fall, to achieve the proper moisture content for haylage. It is still a high-moisture feed, and traffic is reduced, compared to a haymaking system. There are benefits associated with feeding haylage to cows. The wetter ration is more palatable and digestible, and is preferred by cows, especially during the hot summer months. It is better suited as an ingredient in total mixed rations (TMRs).

Disadvantages of Silage

Although field losses are minimal with silage systems, dry matter losses during fermentation can be much higher than in stored hay, often equaling or exceeding the potential field losses observed in haymaking (Fig. 14.3). Additionally there is frequently a loss in digestibility in alfalfa silage compared with fresh or preserved hay (Table 14.1). Since silage is higher in moisture than hay, silage production is limited to those areas in close proximity to the location where the silage will be utilized. Competition for a limited number of custom operators (e.g., baggers) can be an issue. When using bags, a large space to store the product is required because silage bags are typically 10 feet wide and 250 feet long, and they can't be stacked. The bags need to be on a firm surface that allows for access during winter. Bags can be easily punctured or torn, so vigilance is required on the part of dairy personnel to monitor the condition of the bags and make necessary repairs. Once the feed is used, disposal of the plastic bags can be a problem. When haylage is stored in piles or pits, the space requirement is also significant, but not as large as that required for bagged haylage.

When silage is exposed to air, yeast and mold growth cause deterioration resulting from changes in chemical composition, pH, and temperature. Deteriorated forage is usually white due to mold growth, but can be various other colors, depending on mold species. Mold may contain toxins, which are poisonous at certain levels of intake. Aerobic spoilage occurs to some degree in virtually all sealed silos until fermentation is complete and once the silage is disturbed. With poor management, storage and/or losses during feeding can be very high.

A major disadvantage of ensiling alfalfa is protein availability. Through the ensiling process, much of the protein of alfalfa is converted into non-protein nitrogen (NPN). This may be a problem because this protein is made available too rapidly in the rumen, and often is simply excreted as urea. Alfalfa protein from hay is more slowly metabolized by rumen microbes, and thereby is more available to the animal.

FIGURE 14.3

Effect of moisture content on silage losses during harvest and storage.

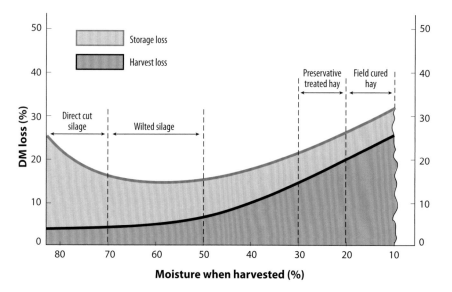

Determining the Value of Standing Alfalfa for Greenchop or Silage

There are several considerations when estimating the value of alfalfa for greenchop or silage. Both the grower and buyer can gain some advantages by greenchopping alfalfa for either direct feeding or ensiling, as compared to making hay. From the grower's perspective, greenchopping reduces yield and quality losses, as described above. The buyer will gain because protein and total digestible nutrients (TDN) of the haylage will be greater than those of hay. Sorting and refusal in the feed bunk will also be less with haylage than with hay, especially in lower-quality or weedy hay. Some losses do occur in the ensiling process, however. Yield losses (including shrinkage) of 3–7 percent can be expected in bags, and 10–30 percent in a pit-storage system. Such losses would not occur with greenchop.

With any alfalfa forage, price usually depends on factors such as quality, availability, and cost of production. Moisture content is the single largest factor in pricing greenchop or haylage. Because baled hay has significantly lower moisture content than direct-cut alfalfa, the buyer is less concerned with how much is being paid for the "water" in the forage. For

Calculating the Value of Alfalfa at Different Moisture Levels

Using moisture information, you can adjust the selling price of a typical forage to reflect the difference in moisture content (MC) between two forages. The formula for making this adjustment is:

$$\text{Value of Typical Forage (\$/Ton)} \times \frac{\text{\% DM of Forage to be Priced}}{\text{\% DM of Typical Forage}} = \text{Adjusted Value (\$/Ton)}$$

Dry matter (DM) and moisture content (MC) relate to each other such that,

% MC + % DM = 100%

Determining Forage Moisture Content Using a Microwave Oven

1. Chop fresh forage into 1–2 inch lengths for ease of handling.

2. Weigh out approximately 100 grams (3.5 ounces) of chopped forage.

3. Spread forage thinly on a microwave-safe dish and place in the microwave.

4. Heat for 2 minutes and reweigh.

   a. If forage is not completely dry, reheat for 30 seconds and reweigh. (Microwaves vary considerably in drying capacity. It is better to dry for short intervals and reweigh until the last two weights are constant, than to overdry and run the risk of burning and damage to the oven.) Continue this process until back-to-back weights are the same or charring occurs.

   b. If charring occurs, use the previous weight.

5. Calculate moisture content using the following equation:

   $$\% \text{ moisture content} = \frac{[(W1 - W2) \times 100]}{W1}$$

   W1 = weight of forage before heating
   W2 = weight of forage after heating

6. Dry matter (DM) equals 100% minus % moisture content

   Example: If moisture content = 14%
   DM = 100 − 14 = 86%

   To protect the oven, it is recommend that you place a small cup of water in the back of the microwave before beginning this procedure.

greenchop or haylage, however, moisture content varies considerably, and a change of just a few percentage points greatly influences the amount of dry matter (DM) in the load. What is important is the DM being purchased or sold. Always sample the forage as it comes from the field and run a DM analysis. A laboratory analysis will cost about $5–10 per sample, and results are usually available in 24 hours. Dry matter can also be determined on-farm, using a microwave technique (see sidebar). A simple and inexpensive moisture-content measurement ensures that both seller and buyer get a fair price.

When marketing alfalfa for greenchop or silage, the price should be based on the current price for hay in the area (assumed to be at 10–12% moisture) and on actual moisture content of the product. Make purchasing decisions at equivalent moisture contents to accurately determine the price per ton of dry matter. Moisture content should be measured and the product sold on an adjusted DM basis. Harvest costs and labor savings are also important and may be factored into the final price. Although it is often not factored into price negotiations, potential yield increases from greenchopped fields (12%/season) or the fact that a grower is often able to harvest an additional cutting for greenchop when haymaking is not possible, are economic advantages.

Greenchop Example:

A dairy farmer would like to buy greenchop from a neighboring alfalfa grower. The dairy farmer will harvest the greenchop. Moisture content of the greenchop at the time of harvest and feeding is estimated to be 80 percent (DM = 100% − 80% = 20%). Hay is currently selling for $140 per ton (88% DM). The grower's cost for swathing, raking, baling, and roadsiding the hay is $25 per ton. How much is the greenchop worth per ton at 20 percent DM?

To answer this question, it is first necessary to subtract hay harvesting costs from the current hay price. This must be done to account for the fact that the dairy farmer will be harvesting the greenchop. Therefore the standing crop, greenchop equivalent of the baled hay price is $140 − $25 = $115 per ton, unadjusted for moisture differences. An adjust-

ment for moisture can be made using the previous equation to determine the value of the greenchop at 20 percent DM.

$$\$115/\text{Ton} \times (20\% \ / \ 88\%) = \$26.14/\text{Ton}$$

Silage Example:

A dairy farmer would like to buy alfalfa for haylage from a nearby grower who will deliver it to him/her. They agreed to price the haylage on the basis of alfalfa hay. The dairy farmer can buy alfalfa hay delivered to the farm for $140 per ton (88% DM). It is expected that the haylage will have about 45 percent dry matter upon delivery, and will shrink by 15 percent during storage. What price should the haylage receive?

Two adjustments are needed for haylage that has just been harvested and placed in storage. The first adjustment should account for shrinkage during the storage period, and the second should adjust for moisture differences between hay and haylage.

Sample Calculation to Estimate the Value of Wilted Alfalfa Intended for Haylage Compared with the Price of Dry Hay

1. Current market price per ton for alfalfa hay — $200

2. Typical % DM of hay (as a decimal) — 0.90

3. Divide line 1 by line 2 to get the value of 100% dry matter hay in the market — $200 ÷ 0.90 = $222.22

4. Enter % DM of wilted alfalfa (as a decimal, in this case, 45% DM)* — 0.45

5. Multiply line 4 by line 3 to get the value of wilted alfalfa per ton — 0.45 × $222.22 = $100.00

*The dairyman preserving the alfalfa as silage should be aware that further shrinkage occurs during the ensiling process in addition to the moisture loss. Typical shrinkage (% weight loss between wilted forage and "as fed" haylage after fermentation) is 15%.

The Alfalfa Haymaking Process

Haymaking is a four-step process. (1) It begins with cutting, which is usually done with a 12-, 14-, or 16-foot (3.6-, 4.3-, or 4.9 m) swather. (2) After a few days, the partially cured hay is raked to turn the windrow, and usually two windrows are combined or laid side by side. This procedure hastens the curing process and improves the efficiency of the baling operation. This is sometimes repeated when curing conditions are poor or when it rains. (3) After the hay has dried sufficiently, it is baled. (4) Finally, it is hauled to the edge of the field (roadsided) and stored until it is transported, sold, or fed. One of the most critical aspects of harvesting is drying the cut alfalfa to a point where it can be safely baled. The drying process and factors that influence drying rate are discussed below.

Hay Curing

Even though the West is blessed with generally good curing conditions, there are times when weather conditions make haymaking a challenge. Rapid, uniform curing is important to minimize quality losses caused by bleaching, respiration, leaf loss, and rain damage. It also improves subsequent yields by reducing the effect of windrow shading, lessening traffic damage to regrowth, and allowing timely irrigation after cutting.

The moisture content of alfalfa growing in the field is generally from 75 to 83 percent. The drying rate of cut alfalfa depends on environmental variables, including solar radiation, temperature, relative humidity, soil moisture, and wind velocity. Research in Michigan and California indicates that solar radiation is by far the most significant environmental factor influencing drying rate.

The objective of the hay producer is to use management practices that accelerate the drying rate, considering weather and other factors. To determine which management practices would be most effective, it is helpful to understand the alfalfa drying process, which takes place in two phases. The drying rate during each phase is governed by the resistance to water loss from the plant (Fig. 14.4 explains various resistances to moisture loss). The first phase, or rapid-drying phase, accounts for approximately 75 percent of the moisture that is lost during the curing process and requires only 20 percent of the total drying time. The stomata (leaf pores) are wide open, and moisture is lost from leaves through these openings and from water transfer from the stems through the leaves. Some water also departs through the cut ends of stems and through bruised tissue. The main limiting factor to drying during the first phase is boundary-layer resistance, the resistance offered by the layer of still, moist air around the plant. Wind moving over and through the windrow can accelerate drying by replacing the moist air in the boundary layer with drier air. The first phase is usually complete before the end of the first day after cutting. The second phase, the slow-drying phase, commences at about 40 percent moisture content when the stomata close. Stomatal resistance increases immensely and drying rate depends on cuticular resistance. Compared to moisture loss in the rapid-drying phase, moisture loss is extremely slow in the slow-drying phase. In fact, the drying rate in this phase is 1/100 of the initial drying rate. There are large differences between leaf and stem tissue in rates of drying, with stems being much slower.

Mechanical Conditioning

To accelerate curing, many growers mechanically condition or crimp the alfalfa as they cut it. Mechanical conditioning has become a widely accepted practice. Most conditioners

FIGURE 14.4

Resistances to water loss from alfalfa.

Boundary-layer resistance: resistance related to the layer of still, moist air close to the plant surface

Cuticular resistance: the resistance of the plant surface to water movement

Stomatal resistance: resistance that is controlled by the pores on leaf and stem surfaces

lightly crush the forage between intermeshing rollers located behind the header of the swather. A number of designs are used, depending on the swather manufacturer. The intermeshing rollers are made of rubber or steel and crush or break the stems. The aggressiveness of crimping and the frequency of the crushing along the stem depend on the crimper design. The primary rationale for crimping is to facilitate water loss from the stems, bringing the drying rate of stems more in line with that of leaves. In theory, more aggressive crimping will have a greater benefit, but if the mechanical conditioning is too severe, shredded leaves may be lost, and the drying rate can slow if air movement is restricted in a dense mat of forage.

> *Mechanical conditioning affects both phases of the drying process. It accelerates the rapid phase by crushing stems, and it accelerates the slower phase by breaking the cuticle.*

Mechanical conditioning affects both phases of the drying process. It accelerates the rapid phase by crushing stems, and it accelerates the slower phase by breaking the cuticle. Sometimes growers question the effectiveness of mechanical conditioning and wonder if the cutting operation could be simplified if the conditioning rollers were removed. Research has shown that mechanical conditioning hastens the drying process by as much as 30 percent. Drying time saved by mechanical conditioning can vary considerably, however, depending on weather and alfalfa yield. Conditioners should be set so that stems are cracked and crushed but not cut or shredded. Consult the swather owner's manual for proper conditioner adjustment.

Maceration

The term "maceration" refers to severe mechanical conditioning that takes place at the time of cutting. The maceration process splits and shreds stems and abrades the waxy cuticle coating on plants. Stems are actually broken and split into numerous pieces, while the leaves and upper stem segments are crushed and pureed.

As a result, there is a significant increase in the surface area of the plant exposed to the environment and a large reduction in curing time. After the alfalfa is macerated, it is pressed into a cohesive mat that remains intact and suspended on the alfalfa stubble. This way, leaves and stem segments don't fall through the stubble onto the ground. Using this system, curing time has been reduced to as little as 5 hours in studies conducted in the Midwest. The improvement in curing time is greatest under favorable curing conditions—warm, dry, sunny days. However, the difference in drying rate between macerated and nonmacerated forage is progressively reduced when drying conditions become less favorable. Under poor conditions, there may be little difference.

In addition to the more rapid curing rate of macerated forage, maceration also improves digestibility. Feeding trials have demonstrated an increase in digestibility of 10 percent or more for macerated forage. This means that even at the same fiber level, macerated alfalfa would be more digestible than conventionally harvested alfalfa. The improvement in digestibility is believed to be due to the actual rupturing of plant cells during maceration. The surface area of the forage is increased, and rumen microbes have greater access to the interior of cells, accelerating the digestion process.

Severe maceration, including the formation of a cohesive mat, is needed to achieve the benefits described above. There are different degrees of maceration. Some commercial macerators intensively condition the forage, but they do not macerate it to the same degree as the prototypes used in the initial research. Therefore, use caution when considering the purchase of a macerator-type harvester—drying rate and digestibility may not be improved to the same degree as was documented in initial research. In addition, macerated forage is not as visually appealing, due to the cut stems and off color, when compared with conventionally harvested alfalfa. This may impact marketing ability, especially when selling hay for retail or export markets. If severe macerating equipment were developed (like the original prototypes evaluated), special handling could be required, rather than just the use of a conventional baler.

Chemical Conditioning

Chemical conditioning involves the use of a drying agent, usually potassium carbonate or a mixture of potassium and sodium carbonate. A drying agent is applied to the alfalfa during swathing by mounting a spray boom to the swather header. The chemical hastens the drying process by allowing water to pass more freely through the waxy cuticle on the plant surface. Thus, drying agents affect the second, or slow, phase of the drying process. These drying agents are most effective when the weather is warm and sunny. Unfortunately, under poor curing conditions, when enhanced drying is needed most (e.g., early spring or late fall), drying agents present little to no advantage. Furthermore, drying agents can present a problem when rain falls on treated hay, since treated hay reabsorbs water more readily than untreated hay. For these reasons and others (e.g., cost of the drying agents, the need to haul large volumes of water to and through the field for applications, and the relatively good curing conditions most of the year), drying agents are not believed to be cost effective and have not been widely adopted in the arid West.

Swath Management

Wide windrows dry more rapidly than narrow windrows. This has been demonstrated in several California trials and in numerous trials throughout the United States. The extent of the advantage that wide windrows offer depends on the geographic area, time of year, and yield level. In general, wide windrows are most beneficial in late spring or early summer, when yields are high and day length is long (solar radiation is greater than in late summer or fall). Wide windrows often dry one day faster than narrow windrows because the forage is spread out and more of the alfalfa is exposed to radiant solar energy. Also, boundary-layer resistance is less with wide windrows, so they do not inhibit moisture movement to the degree narrow ones do. Wide windrows improve the uniformity of drying, which affects how soon after cutting alfalfa can be raked and baled. When a grower can safely rake and bale is determined not by the average windrow moisture content, but by the moisture content of the wettest portion of the windrow. Therefore, since the moisture content of wide windrows is relatively uniform, they can be raked and baled earlier. If wide windrows are not raked earlier, their advantage is lost.

Some growers are reluctant to switch to wide windrows; they fear that, because wide windrows expose more surface area to the elements, extensive color loss from bleaching will result. Color, while not an important characteristic of the nutritional value of the hay, is important for some marketing channels, such as the export or horse market. Researchers have not observed a significant color difference, provided that the wide windrows are raked at least a day earlier than conventional windrows. Although wide windrows do expose more alfalfa, they usually can be raked and baled sooner, so exposure time is reduced. Also, wide windrows remain wide only until they have dried sufficiently to rake. Raking is usually done after the first drying phase. Little bleaching takes place during the initial phase because the waxy cuticle of the plant is largely intact. During the final curing phase, when most bleaching occurs, wide windrows have been raked and combined, so they are no wider than raked conventional windrows.

Many growers have not switched to wide windrows because of equipment limitations. The width of conditioning rollers and windrow baffles determines windrow width. New swather designs have conditioners nearly as wide as the swather header, and growers can alter windrow width with a simple adjustment of a lever. Inexpensive windrow conditioner shields have also been developed that modify traditional swathers so they can spread windrows.

Because of their width, wide windrows must be raked before baling, and the alfalfa generally cannot be baled directly out of the swath. Obviously, this is not a problem

> *Although wide windrows do expose more alfalfa, they usually can be raked and baled sooner, so exposure time is reduced.*

in areas where windrows are always raked. Also, windrow width should not be greater than that which can be easily managed with available rakes. There must be sufficient area between the windrows so that a tractor can pass through without running over the edge of either window, and the windrows should not be so wide that the rake cannot spread far enough to combine the two windrows. In addition, the windrow should not be so wide that it becomes too thin and patchy because this can cause excessive leaf loss during raking.

Raking

The purpose of raking is to expedite the drying process by transferring the alfalfa to drier soil and inverting the windrow. Inversion exposes high-moisture alfalfa from the bottom of the windrow to better drying conditions, increased solar radiation, and the effects of wind. Also, raking usually combines two windrows into one, improving the efficiency of baling and roadsiding. Raking is very effective in improving the drying rate, but it must be done at the proper moisture content; otherwise, excessive yield and quality losses will result (Fig. 14.5). Many growers rake alfalfa when it is too dry, leading to excessive leaf loss.

The optimum moisture content for raking is 35–40 percent. At this moisture content, a significant increase in drying rate is achieved, while severe leaf loss is avoided. Raking at too high a moisture content may twist rather than invert the hay and can actually slow the drying rate by restricting air movement within the windrow. Leaf loss associated with raking hay when it is too dry can be significant. In one study, when hay was raked at 20 percent moisture content, 21 percent of the leaves were lost; when raked at 50 percent moisture content, only 5 percent were lost (Table 14.3).

Hay raked on the same day as baling is too dry. The greatest loss is in the leaf fraction. Such loss significantly reduces the quality of the hay, since leaves are the most nutritious component of alfalfa. Research has shown that raking alfalfa hay that was too dry was more detrimental to hay quality than baling when too dry. In one study, late raking resulted in a 25 percent loss in yield and a 2- to 4-percentage-unit reduction in TDN. Baling when too dry resulted in a 5 percent yield loss. If alfalfa was both raked *and* baled too dry, the

FIGURE 14.5

The effect of moisture content and swath thickness on dry-matter losses during raking. *Source:* C. A. Rotz, Michigan State University.

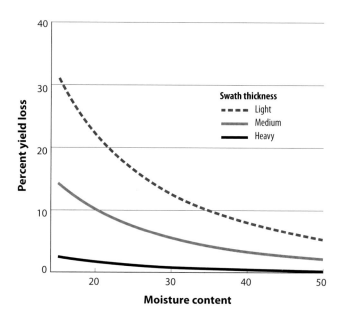

TABLE 14.3

Moisture effects on yield and leaf loss during harvest operations.

Operation	Yield Loss[1] (%)	Leaf Loss (%)
Mowing and conditioning	2	3
Raking		
At 60% moisture	2	3
At 50% moisture	3	5
At 33% moisture	7	12
At 20% moisture	12	21
Baling, pickup, and chamber		
At 25% moisture	3	4
At 20% moisture	4	6
At 12% moisture	6	8

Source: Pitt (1990).

[1] Reported on a 100% dry-matter basis.

yield loss increased 10 percent over the raking loss.

Baling and Storage

Alfalfa must be baled within a relatively narrow range of moisture content to avoid losses in yield and quality. Whenever possible, refrain from baling hay that is below 12 percent moisture because leaf shatter (leaf material that is detached from the stem yet captured in the bale) and leaf loss (lost to the ground) will be excessive. Hay baled at too high a moisture content is subject to problems with mold, discoloration, and even spontaneous combustion (see Moisture Content for Safe Storage later in the chapter). The maximum moisture content for baling depends on bale size and density. In general, bale small two-tie bales at less than 20 percent moisture, larger and denser three-tie bales at less than 17 percent, and large bales at less than 14 percent.

The source of moisture within the bale affects the upper moisture limit for safe baling. Hay can be baled at a higher moisture content when the moisture source is free moisture (dew) than when it is moisture trapped inside the stem (stem moisture). Free moisture is more readily dissipated than is stem moisture. How the hay is stacked after harvest also influences the moisture content at which alfalfa can be safely baled. A slightly higher moisture content at baling is sometimes safe, provided the alfalfa is stacked with an air gap between loads.

The air gap facilitates more rapid dissipation of moisture from the bale. This is especially important for large bales, which weigh 0.5 to 1 ton (0.45 to 0.91 Mg).

Moisture Content Estimates

A simple and practical method to determine if alfalfa hay can be safely baled is to grab a handful of alfalfa with both hands and twist it by rotating your wrists in opposite directions. If the stems crack and break, the hay is usually dry enough to bale. This practice is not very precise, and it takes experience to develop proficiency.

The thumbnail test is a better method. Scrape an alfalfa stem with your thumbnail. If the epidermis, or outside layer, cannot be peeled back, the hay has dried sufficiently (Fig 14.6).

A moisture meter is also a valuable tool to evaluate the moisture content of hay. Resistance-type moisture meters are used as hand probes or mounted in the baler chamber for on-the-go moisture monitoring. Meters often indicate a moisture content that is slightly higher than the actual content, and should be used to predict general trends, not precise moisture. They measure stem moisture less accurately than they measure dew moisture. Although moisture meters do not provide a precise assessment of the true moisture content of

FIGURE 14.6

Three field methods for evaluating the moisture content of alfalfa hay. (A) *The twist method*: Grab a handful of alfalfa with both hands and twist it by rotating your wrists in opposite directions. If the stems crack and break, the hay is dry enough to bale. (B) *The thumbnail test*: Scrape an alfalfa stem with your thumbnail. If the epidermis, or outside layer, cannot be peeled back, the hay has dried sufficiently. (C) *Resistance moisture meters*: Probe the bale several times and read the meter to learn the moisture content. Units are also available to monitor hay moisture in the bale chamber from the cab of a tractor.

hay, with enough experience, moisture meters are very useful tools for assessing whether it is safe to bale hay.

Moisture meters are ordinarily only used to assess the moisture content of baled hay. However, knowing the moisture content of alfalfa in the windrow before it is baled would help the grower determine whether the alfalfa is dry enough to bale. An improved method was developed by the University of Idaho: alfalfa from the windrow is packed into a section of PVC pipe and compacted to simulate a bale. The standard moisture meter probe is then inserted into the forage inside the pipe. This simple and practical technique improves the accuracy of windrow moisture testing.

A microwave oven is sometimes used to determine the moisture content of alfalfa hay. The technique is outlined in the silage section of this chapter. Although this method is accurate, it is more tedious than field assessments of forage moisture content and may not be practical when the grower needs to assess moisture at several locations in a field.

Using Dew to Improve Baling Conditions

After alfalfa is fully cured, dew or high relative humidity is needed to soften the leaves. Otherwise, there will be excessive leaf loss (shatter) during baling. For example, there is usually ample dew in the Central Valley of California. However, sometimes (mostly in midsummer) dew or humidity is insufficient. Delaying the baling operation to wait for dew is undesirable; yield declines and leaf loss increases the longer hay is left in the windrow. In addition, waiting for dew postpones other necessary operations, such as irrigation, that are critical after cutting. Additionally, when baling is delayed, the amount of alfalfa regrowth increases, and the degree of traffic damage to regrowth increases accordingly.

Windrows can be sprayed with water to compensate for a lack of dew on days when humidity is insufficient to permit baling. Water sprayed on the windrow (approximately 40–50 gallons per acre [375–468 L ha⁻¹]) can improve baling conditions, reducing leaf loss.

Depending on weather conditions, allow 10–30 minutes between water application and baling; this time allows the water to penetrate and soften the leaves. This practice is often an acceptable substitute for natural dew, or it can be used to extend the baling period on days with marginal humidity. However, applying water to windrows does not make midday baling possible. The high evaporation rate at this time negates the effectiveness of spraying.

> *Windrows can be sprayed with water to compensate for a lack of dew on days when humidity is insufficient to permit baling.*

Moisture Content for Safe Storage

The maximum moisture content for safe hay storage is influenced by the uniformity of moisture within bales, climatic conditions during storage, and ventilation at the storage site. The moisture content of bales can be reduced somewhat by allowing high-moisture bales to remain in the field until late afternoon to reduce their moisture content; then roadside them. Another way to reduce moisture content is to position balewagon loads outside, with a gap between the stacks before storing the bales in a barn. Unfortunately, these methods are only partially effective; neither method can rapidly dissipate moisture deep within the bales.

Significant yield and quality losses can occur during storage. Studies have indicated dry matter losses of one percentage point for each percentage of moisture above 10 percent. Quality losses can take several forms. Molds may develop in hay stored at a moisture content greater than 20 percent. Molds can produce toxins that reduce palatability and are hazardous to livestock. Mold respiration causes heating, and, when hay temperatures exceed 100°F (38°C), browning reactions begin. Reactions that occur during browning, coupled with heating from mold growth, can cause temperatures to increase further. Heating may reduce the protein and energy available to the animal that consumes the hay (Table 14.4). When bale temperatures exceed 150°F (66°C), spontaneous combustion can result. This is most likely in hay with a moisture content over 30 percent and most often occurs with large (0.5–1 ton [0.45–.91 Mg]) bales.

Heating during the first month actually helps to dry hay (often termed the "sweat"). After the first month, hay has usually dried to a moisture content where it is stable and can be stored safely. Therefore, any problems that result from storing hay with excessive moisture are most likely to occur during the first month of storage. Although the majority of dry matter losses during storage take place in the first month, researchers in the Midwest found that losses continue at a rate of about 0.5 percent per month for the remainder of the storage period.

Hay Preservatives

Preservatives are intended to allow storage of alfalfa hay baled at moisture contents higher than would ordinarily be considered safe. They are used on hay baled from 18 to 30 percent moisture. The advantages of baling at higher moisture contents are reduced leaf loss and reduced field curing time, which may help avoid rain damage.

Hay preservatives are usually applied at baling. Organic acids, primarily propionic acid or propionic–acetic acid blends, are the most common preservatives. They prevent mold growth and heating losses by lowering alfalfa pH and retarding the growth of microorganisms that cause hay spoilage. One disadvantage of preservative use is cost. What is more, preservatives are seldom 100 percent effective. The causes of erratic effectiveness are uneven application and areas of excessively high moisture content within a bale (often called a "slug"). In addition, propionic acid is hazardous to skin and eyes and corrosive to farm equipment.

Buffered propionic acids are available to avoid corrosion problems. Alternatives to propionic acid include microbial inoculants and enzymatic products, but their results have been unsatisfactory in most university tests.

Most researchers conclude that using a preservative to allow high-moisture baling to reduce leaf loss is not usually cost effective. Preservative use may be justified if the product can be used selectively—only when rain is imminent or just for high-moisture areas of the field. As everyone knows, predicting rain can be very difficult, so it may not be practical to only use a preservative to avoid rain damage. However, equipment is now available that does enable the producer to only use the preservative in areas of the field where the alfalfa moisture warrants it. Moisture sensors in the bale chamber electronically control whether the preservative is applied and the rate of application. Using a preservative in this fashion may be economical for fields where moisture content varies widely.

Cubing of Alfalfa

Alfalfa hay can also be processed into cubes. Cubes have never been as popular as baled hay in California and, over time, their popularity has dwindled. Except for the actual baling operation itself, most of the processes

TABLE 14.4

Problems associated with hay heating

Temperature	Problem
115°–125°F (46°–52°C)	When coupled with high moisture, molds and odors develop and decrease palatability.
>120°F (>49°C)	Heating reduces digestibility of protein, fiber, and carbohydrate compounds.
130°–140°F (54°–60°C)	Hay is brown and very palatable because of the carmelization of sugars; unfortunately, nutritional value is reduced.
>150°F (>66°C)	Hay may turn black, and spontaneous combustion is possible.

Source: V. L. Marble

and procedures described above for baled hay also apply to cubes. The alfalfa crop is still cut with a swather and raked to turn and combine windrows. The hay can be cubed in the field or cubed with a stationary cuber. Field cubers process the hay directly out of the windrow in the field, but they are no longer manufactured. With stationary cubers, the alfalfa windrows are dry chopped and transported off the field to be processed.

The coarsely chopped alfalfa is compressed through mechanical dies with approximately 1.25 inches square (3.18 cm²) dimension, with varied lengths. Thus, though called "cubes", most cubes are more rectangular in shape. One main advantage of cubing is that proper humidity for leaf retention is not important like it is for baling—dry conditions are preferred. Therefore, cubing works well in some desert environments where there is insufficient dew for baling. Water is added during the actual cubing process. Therefore, there is often less dust with cubes than with baled hay. A dust-free product can be especially important for horses. Care must be taken not to cube alfalfa contaminated with toxic weeds. Animals consume the whole cube and are unable to segregate the toxic weeds like they sometimes will with hay. The primary market for cubes is the horse industry or for export to foreign countries.

Conclusion

Considerable effort is involved in producing a high-quality high-yielding alfalfa crop. While harvesting, curing, and preservation are the last steps in the production process, they can have a significant impact on the ultimate feeding value of the forage. Whether preserving alfalfa as silage or hay, the production practices outlined in this chapter should be followed to avoid significant losses. Key silage-making practices include excluding as much oxygen as possible by proper packing and sealing to minimize spoilage and making sure the forage is at the proper moisture content for ensiling. Key hay-making practices include vigorous conditioning, proper swath management (i.e., conditioning and windrow width) to promote rapid curing, raking at the proper moisture content to accelerate homogeneous drying of the windrow with minimal leaf loss, and baling the alfalfa at the optimum moisture content—high enough moisture for leaf retention while still low enough so that the hay can be safely stored with little risk of mold or heating problems. Employing these practices helps retain the potential feeding quality of the alfalfa while minimizing losses.

Additional Reading

Hall, M.H., and J.R. Wilson, 2004. Understanding silage fermentation learning module. Crop Management doi:10.1094/CM-2004-0429-01-BR. http://www.plantmanagementnetwork.org/pub/cm/brief/2004/silage/

Harrison, J.H. 1995. The art and science of ensiling alfalfa. Pp. 55–62 in: Proceedings, 25th California Alfalfa Symposium. Dec. 7–8. Modesto, CA.

Meyer, J.H., and L.G. Jones. 1962. Controlling alfalfa quality. California Agricultural Experiment Station, Bulletin 784. Division of Agricultural Sciences. University of California.

Mueller, S. Determining the value of alfalfa hay, silage, or greenchop. Fresno County Cooperative Extension, Fresno, CA.

Munier, D.J. 1989. Alfalfa's response to baling versus bagging. Pp. 33–34 in: Proceedings, 19th California Alfalfa Symposium. Dec. 6–7. Visalia, CA.

Orloff, S.B. 1997. Hay curing, baling, and storage. Pp. 109–112 in: S.B. Orloff and H.L. Carlson, eds. Intermountain alfalfa management. University of California Division of Agriculture and Natural Resources, Oakland. Publication 3366.

Orloff, S.B., D. Putnam, and T. Kraus. 1997. Maceration: What is its potential for California alfalfa growers? Pp. 24–30 in: Proceedings, 27th California Alfalfa Symposium. Dec. 10–11. Visalia, CA.

Pitt, R.E. 1990. Silage and hay preservation. Northeast Regional Agricultural Engineering Service, Cornell University Cooperative Extension, Ithaca, NY. Publication NRAES-5.

Rotz, C.A. 2005. Postharvest changes in alfalfa quality. Pp. 253–262 in: Proceedings, 35th California Alfalfa Symposium. December 12–14, Visalia, CA.

Rotz, C.A., and R.E. Muck. 1994. Changes in forage quality during harvest and storage. Pp. 828–868 in: G.C. Fahey, Jr., ed. Forage quality, evaluation, and utilization. American Society of Agronomy, Crop Science Society of America, and Soil Science Society of America, Madison, WI.

15

Managing Depleted Alfalfa Stands: Overseeding and Other Options

Mick Canevari
Farm Advisor, University of California Cooperative Extension, Stockton, CA

Daniel H. Putnam
Forage Extension Specialist, Department of Plant Sciences, University of California, Davis

The productivity of alfalfa fields typically declines over time due to loss of plants and weakening of crowns from disease or other factors. These factors include traffic injury, nematodes, insect damage, weed competition, winter injury, compaction of soils, saturated soil, drought and heat stress, and rodents. As stands decline, weeds invade open areas and become more difficult to control. Eventually, yield and forage quality decline to a point where a difficult decision must be made as to whether to keep or remove an alfalfa stand.

Compelling economics may encourage some growers to remove old alfalfa stands to plant crops of higher value. Alternatively, lack of rotation opportunities may encourage others to look for ways to extend the life of their alfalfa stands, including overseeding grasses or legumes to improve productivity. Continuing to harvest a depleted stand may not be economical, especially when yields fall significantly, such that the costs of production exceed potential returns.

There are three basic options for dealing with depleted alfalfa stands:

*   Continue to harvest a marginal stand.

*   Remove the stand and rotate to another crop.

*   Attempt to increase yield and extend the stand longevity by overseeding or other measures.

This chapter provides a framework for this decision.

Analyze the Economics of Stand Removal

The relative economic value of each of these choices is the primary consideration for managing depleted alfalfa stands. An economic analysis should include an analysis of the returns for maintaining the old stand without renovation, the value of a potential rotational crop, and the costs associated with overseeding the stand and its potential market value. The anticipated yield, quality, and price of alfalfa produced from a new, renovated field or overseeded forage crop must be compared with continuing to harvest a marginal stand.

Unfortunately, the economics of stand removal are difficult to assess due to the many factors involved (see sidebar). Weed or pest pressures, excessive soil compaction from wheel traffic, or irrigation problems may dictate that depleted stands be removed. Crop rotation opportunities may encourage growers to remove old alfalfa stands and plant crops of higher value. Alternatively, production of alfalfa mixes may provide a significant market opportunity for the horse market, causing growers to consider overseeding old stands with grasses or legumes. In each of these cases, the relative costs and potential returns of each option must be considered. The agronomic advantages of crop rotations that break disease cycles and assist in managing weeds and the opportunity for soil renovation should not be forgotten in an economic analysis.

Continue Harvesting Depleted Stands?

An obvious (and the easiest) choice is to continue to harvest a depleted stand. However, this may be the least desirable choice from an economic perspective, because yields may decline 20, 30, or even 50 percent less than normal in older or damaged stands. A decision to continue harvesting may raise the cost of production per ton, since most costs (irrigation, harvesting, land) are fixed. Additionally, quality is usually very low in depleted stands because of weed intrusion, further reducing the potential value of the crop. Once yields have fallen 25 percent below normal and weeds become a factor, an evaluation of the field should be made.

Sometimes, lower yields are due to fertility or irrigation problems. If alfalfa stands are good, the roots are healthy, and weeds can be controlled, analysis of the soil and plants to correct fertility problems may enable growers to improve productivity of older stands. If root systems are disease-free and absent of soil com-

---

Factors to consider when deciding whether to replace, extend, or overseed an alfalfa stand

*   Plant population of existing stand

*   Vigor of remaining plants

*   Projected yield and quality of old versus new stand

*   Rotational crop opportunities

*   Weed intrusion in the old stand

*   Chronic traffic damage of existing stands

*   Degree of soil compaction

*   Irrigation problems necessitating soil tillage or leveling

*   Fertility status of the field

*   Market opportunities for mixed alfalfa–grass or overseeded crop

paction and nematodes, sometimes older fields can be brought back through fertilization (if nutrients are limiting), careful irrigation practices, and lengthening the cutting schedules. However, reclaiming an old stand with cultural practices is usually unsuccessful.

More often, older stands that are compromised by diseased and weakened plants, low plant populations, or weeds are candidates for either crop rotation or overseeding (Fig. 15.1). Although stand persistence is a desirable quality in alfalfa, growers should take a hard economic look at depleted stands and rotate to other crops or overseed to renovate older stands, rather than to continue harvesting suboptimum fields.

When Do Alfalfa Stands Become Questionable?

Stand viability is often evaluated by measuring the number of plants or stems per unit area. Under most conditions, when alfalfa stands fall below four to six plants per square foot, yields begin to decline. However, numbers of plants are not the only factor. The health, size, and regrowth potential of individual plants are also important to determine the viability and regrowth potential of alfalfa stands.

Table 15.1 shows common plant densities for alfalfa in the seedling stage and subsequent production years, as well as those for older stands. The number of stems per unit area is usually more important than plant density because the number of stems determines crop yield and also affects competition with weeds through canopy cover. Stem densities above about 55 stems per square foot have been found to adequately maintain yields whereas some yield reduction is expected from 40 to 55 stems per square foot. Growers should consider some type of renovation when stem densities fall below approximately 39 stems per square foot (Table 15.2). If stem counts are generally above this level and weeds are kept in check, continuing to harvest the crop may be the best strategy.

It is also important to examine the health of existing plants to identify problems that would shorten regrowth potential of the stand. Dig up 15–20 plants over a representative

area of the field. Roots from plants with considerable root disease (e.g., Phytophthora or Rhizoctonia root rot as discussed in the alfalfa disease chapter, Chapter 10) should be compared with healthy, white roots. The size of the

FIGURE 15.1

When stands fall below an acceptable level, crop rotation or overseeding are the most viable options.

TABLE 15.1

Common stand densities for alfalfa in various years of production. Stands are considered suboptimum when they fall below 3–6 plants/ft^2, but numbers of stems per unit area (see Table 15.2) is more important than numbers of plants

Production year[1]	Stand density (plants/ft2)
Seedling stand	> 25 (range 25–80)
End of year 1	15–25
End of year 2	10–15
End of year 3	6–12
Old or weakened depleted stands	< 4–6, consider replacing stand or overseeding with another forage.

TABLE 15.2

The impact of stem density on the yield potential of alfalfa*

Stand density (stems/ft^2)	Effect
> 55	Stem density does not limit yield.
40–55	Some yield reduction is expected.
< 39	Consider replacing stand or overseeding with another forage.

*Adapted from University of Wisconsin recommendations (Undersander et al., UW Extension Bulletin A3620).

root and crown and the number of vigorous buds on the crown are also good indicators of plant health and regrowth potential. Although some disease is typically present in older fields, stands with more than 50 percent moderately or severely diseased plants will likely have continued plant losses and yield reduction.

The Advantages of Crop Rotation

When the costs of producing alfalfa hay negate net returns, rotation to another crop has a number of advantages and is generally the recommended practice. Crop rotation after 4–5 years of alfalfa production has a range of benefits to the succeeding crop. First, crops following alfalfa receive a "free" source of residual nitrogen from the nitrogen-fixing nodules in the alfalfa roots. Disease problems for alfalfa or for other crops (e.g., corn, cotton, wheat)

are also reduced by crop rotation. Improved soil tilth (the crumbliness or structure of the soil) is additionally benefited by years of alfalfa production. Growers of tomatoes or specialty crops frequently try to follow alfalfa because of the soil tilth or rotational benefits to the succeeding crop. If a grower plans to plant alfalfa in the same field again, rotation of 1 or 2 years with another crop is recommended to reduce potential pest and disease problems.

Overseeding to Extend Stand Life

In years when the hay market is strong and rotational crops are not profitable, it may be desirable to overseed a depleted alfalfa stand to increase yields and extend stand life. Overseeding another forage species into a depleted alfalfa stand can significantly improve the yield and marketability of older or damaged alfalfa stands. However, the overseeded species and the harvest schedule must match the needs of the market, whether dairy, dry cow, or horse market, and be compatible with available harvesting equipment. Potential overseeded forage species include annual and perennial grasses and legumes (Fig. 15.2).

Establishing Overseeded Crops

All recommendations for successful stand establishment of forage crops apply equally or perhaps to a greater degree to the planting of overseeded crops into alfalfa (see Chapter 4, "Alfalfa Stand Establishment"). This includes good seedbed preparation, optimum planting date, selection of appropriate varieties, and good irrigation management.

Seedbed preparation, or evaluation of seedbed conditions, is very important for successful establishment of any crop overseeded into existing alfalfa stands. Usually, a minimum amount of tillage is required, but no-till seeding can be used under some conditions. The objective is to break up the soil surface in the top 1–3 inches with just enough tillage to kill weeds but with minimal damage to alfalfa crowns. Normally, one pass with a spring tooth

FIGURE 15.2

Oats overseeded into alfalfa is a short-term (one cut) option for older alfalfa stands.

harrow or a light disking is all that is needed. If weed pressure is high or if the ground is hard, two passes may be needed. Before tillage, excessive weed growth can also be removed with herbicides (see Chapter 8, "Weed Management in Alfalfa"), but caution is advised because new seedlings may be affected by the herbicides (consult label for plant-back restrictions).

After seedbed preparation, planting can be accomplished by broadcasting or using a drill or no-till seeder, depending on seed size. The field may need to be rolled (using a ring-roller or other device) after broadcast planting to firm the seedbed, break clods, optimize soil–seed contact, and enhance germination. Overseeding can also be performed using a conventional grain drill without tillage, if the soil is sufficiently soft to allow penetration by the drill and to cover the seed, and if weed infestations are minimal.

Irrigation of overseeded forages is usually beneficial for promoting early germination, which leads to a uniform plant population and vigorous seedling stand. Failures of overseeded species are often due to insufficient water in the root zone of shallow-rooted seedlings and competition for water and light. Selection of seeding rates and planting times depends on location, circumstances, and the species being planted. Seeding rates and timings are provided in Table 15.3. Early fall irrigation of cool-season overseeded species helps the seedlings to become established and compete against winter weeds and diseases. Time of seeding has a potentially large effect on success of overseeding because different species have different optimum conditions for seedling development.

TABLE 15.3

Seeding dates and rates for crops overseeded into alfalfa

Crop	Sacramento–San Joaquin Valleys	Seeding rate lb/acre	Seeding rate kg/ha
Cereals (oat, barley, wheat, triticale)	Oct–Jan	40–60	45–67
Annual ryegrass	Oct–Dec	4–8	4.5–9
Berseem clover	Oct–Dec	6–12	6.7–13.4
Bromegrass	Sept–Nov	20–30	22–33
"Kemal" festulolium	Sept–Nov	4–8	4.5–9
Orchardgrass	Sept–Nov	4–8	4.5–9
Perennial ryegrass	Sept–Dec	4–8	4.5–9
Red clover	Oct–Dec	8–12	9–13.4
Sudangrass	May–Jun	40–100	45–67
Tall fescue	Sept–Dec	4–8	4.5–9
Teff	May–June	4–8	4.5-9
Timothy	Not practiced	4	4.5–6.7

Selecting the Right Species for Overseeding

The species selected for overseeding depends on how long growers want to keep their alfalfa stands. The species selected can affect yield, forage quality, and the suitability of the forage for the end market (see sidebar). Perennials are appropriate to increase the stand life for more than a year, whereas annuals would be used to extend the stand life for only 1 year or less. Legumes are high-quality forages that are suitable for the dairy market, whereas grasses are primarily appropriate for the horse hay or dry cow market. Overseeded forages may also increase the drying time of early spring harvests, especially those species that increase biomass. In addition, grasses overseeded into alfalfa will require nitrogen applications to maintain high yields, which may be costly. Although alfalfa fixes its own nitrogen, it does not generally produce enough to maximize grass yields in the mixture.

Overseeding grasses into alfalfa creates a forage mix that generally has lower nutritional value than alfalfa hay. However, grass–alfalfa mixtures generally provide sufficient energy and protein for most pleasure horses, and demand for these mixtures by the horse market has been strong in recent years. These grass–alfalfa forages are also highly acceptable for dry cows, beef cattle, and other livestock. Typically, grass–alfalfa mixtures, especially mixtures with cereals, produce higher yields than legume–alfalfa mixtures.

Overseeding legumes into declining alfalfa stands creates a different forage product than does overseeding grasses. Most clovers are comparable to alfalfa in nutritional value and therefore may be better suited for lactating dairy animals. Tests have shown the crude protein and fiber content of several clovers are similar to dairy-quality alfalfa hay when cut at an appropriate stage. Clovers are not affected by the Egyptian alfalfa weevil and can withstand poorly drained, saturated soil conditions that are detrimental to alfalfa.

Factors to consider when selecting the most appropriate species and cultivar for overseeding in alfalfa

- **Length of time.** Determine how long the field will be in production (annuals vs. perennials).

- **Market.** Consider forage quality and appearance for the dairy, horse, or other livestock market.

- **Yield.** Use variety trial results or local experience to determine the yield potential of the different species.

- **Quality.** Alfalfa and grasses differ significantly in quality, and there are differences between warm-season and cool-season grasses in quality.

- **Disease management.** Select species and cultivars that are known to withstand diseases.

- **Harvest compatibility.** Some forages (e.g., berseem or ryegrass) may need to be grazed or green-chopped in the early spring due to lengthened drying time.

Overseeding Annual Grasses

Cool-season annual grasses make the greatest yield contributions to forage mixtures early in the growing season and decline by midsummer. For this reason, using an annual grass is an appropriate choice if the alfalfa is to be removed after one or two cuttings in the late spring. Annual cool-season grass species used for overseeding include cereals such as wheat, barley, oat, triticale, and annual ryegrass. Sudangrass and teff are warm-season annual grasses to consider for seeding in spring and summer.

> *Using an annual grass is an appropriate choice if the alfalfa is to be removed after one or two cuttings in the late spring.*

Cereals: Wheat (*Triticum aestivum* L. ssp. *aestivum*), barley (*Hordeum vulgare* L.), oat (*Avena sativa* L.), and triticale (*Triticum aestivum* × *Secale cereale*) grow best under cool temperatures and provide a single high-yielding spring forage cut, or, if harvested early, in one or two harvests. Oat is the most common cereal crop used for overseeding and has a well-established demand for horse or dry cow hay. Hooded (or beardless) barley, wheat, and triticale are also seeded into alfalfa, making excellent forage quality if harvested at the right time. Overseeded cereal forages are a high-yield, short-term option and appropriate for green-chop, haylage, and haying situations, and fit well with dairy and municipal waste applications. However, cereals can be very aggressive and often outcompete the remaining alfalfa, so stands are generally finished and renovated after the harvest is complete.

Annual Ryegrass (*Lolium multiflorum* Lam.).
Annual ryegrass (or Italian ryegrass) is a cool-season grass that is popular because of its high yield potential, high palatability, and ability to withstand wet, saturated soils and accept quantities of dairy wastewater. Alfalfa–ryegrass mixtures have gained popularity for the horse and dairy industries. Like cereal grains, annual ryegrass is also planted in the fall but provides multiple harvests in the spring through early summer, depending on the weather. Yields decline in midsummer. Ryegrass is often more palatable to grazing livestock than other grasses. Ryegrasses consist of both diploid and tetraploid annual ryegrass, and Italian-type varieties. These differ in yield potential, heading dates, and forage quality; the tetraploid types are generally higher yielding, and the Italian types somewhat higher in quality.

Sudangrass (*Sorghum bicolor* [L.] Moench).
Sudangrass and sorghum–sudangrass crosses are warm-season, high-yielding grasses that can be overseeded into alfalfa in late spring or summer. These grasses thrive under high temperatures and do poorly under cool conditions. Sudangrass has been seeded into alfalfa stands late in the spring when alfalfa has been damaged from winter flooding and it is too late to plant cool-season species. Sudangrass hay is typically not favored by the horse or dairy markets, so markets should be carefully investigated before planting sudangrass. Sorghum–sudangrass crosses and sorghum (milo) types can be overseeded, but are more appropriate for silage harvests than hay.

Teff (*Eragrostis tef*). Teff (also spelled tef), an old-world crop and staple grain of Ethiopia, is currently being investigated as a fine-stemmed annual grass forage that would be planted in late spring or early summer. For situations where stands have been damaged by winter flooding or other hazards, teff may be overseeded in May or June, with an expected two to three harvests before fall. Teff produces fine-stemmed grass forage that may be suitable for dry cows or horses.

Overseeding Perennial Grasses

Perennial grasses are desirable for overseeding into alfalfa when the goal is to extend the life of the alfalfa stand for more than 1 year. Alfalfa–perennial grass mixtures are usually quite appropriate for the horse hay market (Fig. 15.3).

Compared with annuals, perennial grasses are slow to establish, and one season is usually required before the full yield potential is reached. However, once established, they survive for several years and predominate in weak areas of the alfalfa stand. The relative proportion of grass to alfalfa usually increases as the stand ages because grasses are typically more competitive than the alfalfa. Perennial grasses will also dominate open areas and provide significant competition with undesirable summer weeds.

Several perennial grass species have been evaluated for overseeding into alfalfa

Perennial grasses are desirable for overseeding into alfalfa when the goal is to extend the life of the alfalfa stand for more than 1 year.

FIGURE 15.3

Perennial grasses such as orchardgrass overseeded into alfalfa create a desirable mix for the horse market.

in California. These include bromegrass, orchardgrass, perennial ryegrass, and "Kemal" festulolium (tall fescue + ryegrass cross), tall fescue, and timothy. These are all classified as cool-season grasses and produce best in spring and fall. Fall seedings are almost always much more successful than spring seedings, and summer seedings should not be attempted. No single perennial grass is best suited for all field and climatic conditions, markets, and locations.

Bromegrass (*Bromus* spp. [the species of *Bromus* used for forages are various]) as an overseeded forage has generally been much less competitive with alfalfa than have other grasses; it can be difficult to establish, and yields are usually lower than for other perennial grasses. Bromegrasses are more common in pasture mixes and for grazing than for haying situations.

Orchardgrass (*Dactylis glomerata* L.) is highly valued by the horse hay market. This forage is best suited for overseeding in cooler regions of California, such as the Intermountain area and the northern San Joaquin and Sacramento Valleys. However, orchardgrass is not heat tolerant, so production will decline during summer.

Perennial ryegrass (*Lolium perenne* L.) and "Kemal" *festulolium* (a ryegrass + fescue cross) perform well during the first and last parts of the harvest season in the Central Valley of California. Perennial ryegrass does not perform as well in cooler regions and has not persisted well in some colder-climate areas because of winter injury. The market is fair for horses if endophyte-free varieties are planted ("endophytes" are fungi that live inside plants).

Tall fescue (*Festuca arundinacea* Schreb.) is easy to establish, and it has been the highest-yielding perennial grass in several tests in different areas of California. Recently, higher-quality tall fescue varieties have been developed that may improve marketability for the horse and dairy markets. Some fescue varieties are known to harbor endophytes, so be sure to plant only *endophyte-free* or novel-endophyte tall fescue varieties. Endophytes in fescue varieties produce anti-nutritional compounds that may negatively affect the health of some classes of livestock, including horses. The tall fescue endophyte-free variety is likely one of our best heat-tolerant options. If an alfalfa–grass mixture is desired for only 1 or 2 years, tall fescue may be a good choice because of its rapid establishment and high yield potential, but be sure to know your market and find a buyer who would be interested in fescue forages.

Timothy (*Phleum pratense* L.) hay is highly valued by the horse market and has high market acceptability for exports. Because timothy is adapted only to environments where cool summer weather and moist soil conditions prevail, it is only successful in cooler growing regions of our state. Timothy generally is not suited for California's hot Central Valley and desert climates. Stand establishment of timothy can be extremely slow and difficult in overseeding situations. Even under favorable growing conditions, timothy does not yield as well as many other perennial grasses when overseeded into alfalfa.

Need for Nitrogen Management

To maintain good yields, growers should fertilize their mixed alfalfa–grass stands to supply sufficient nitrogen for optimum yields. Although alfalfa fields contain residual nitrogen after several years of production, this residual nitrogen is often depleted by the first growth of a high-yielding overseeded grass crop. Growers should calculate supplying from 40 to 60 pounds of nitrogen per ton of forage yield (from soil residual and fertilizer sources) to satisfy the nitrogen requirements of most grasses. Nitrogen applications also improve the crude protein content of alfalfa–grass mixtures. Nitrogen can be supplied by manures or commercial fertilizers.

Overseeding Annual Legumes

Overseeding legumes into declining alfalfa stands offers some advantages compared with overseeding grasses. Legumes have higher crude protein and lower fiber than grasses, making them suitable for the dairy market.

Clover–alfalfa mixed hays also make excellent feed for beef cattle and sheep and a highly acceptable feed for horses. Clovers tolerate wet soils, thus they generally perform better than alfalfa on heavier-textured soils prone to flooding. In addition, clovers are not affected by alfalfa weevils or alfalfa caterpillars, reducing the need for chemical control in legume-overseeded stands.

> *Clover–alfalfa mixed hays also make excellent feed for beef cattle and sheep and a highly acceptable feed for horses.*

A disadvantage of clovers is their inability to remain a bright green color in the bale. High moisture environments or rain during curing will cause a browning of the foliage, an undesirable appearance that limits sales in certain markets where color is important. However, forage quality is not often affected; the quality of these clovers often rivals that of alfalfa, and they are very palatable.

There are a number of annual legumes that can be sown into existing alfalfa fields, including arrowleaf clover (*Trifolium vesiculosum* Savi), crimson clover (*T. incarnatum* L.), various annual medics (*Medicago* spp.), Persian clover (*T. resupinatum* L.), and common vetch (*Vicia sativa* L.). However, for California, the highest-yielding and most immediately adaptable annual legume for overseeding appears to be berseem clover (*T. alexandrinum* L.).

Berseem clover (*Trifolium alexandrinum* L.) is a vigorous, upright annual clover that closely resembles alfalfa (Fig. 15.4). When overseeded into alfalfa, berseem clover can significantly increase yield for the first three to four harvests. Berseem–alfalfa forage is of excellent quality, is bloat resistant, and is received favor-ably by the horse and dairy markets. Berseem also tolerates wet soil conditions. Yields of sole-cropped berseem have averaged about 6.8 tons per acre in UC Davis trials and up to 8.5 tons per acre in the Imperial Valley of California. Timing the first harvest of berseem clover to achieve high quality and to avoid rain damage has been more difficult in the northern San Joaquin Valley than in the south. Later harvests are not a problem when the climate warms and drying conditions improve, but yields are reduced during midsummer regrowths. Long-term trials have shown berseem to be slightly lower in crude protein but lower in fiber (higher in total digestible nutrients) than alfalfa at the same cutting schedule.

Overseeding Perennial Legumes

Overseeding perennial clovers may extend the life of a depleted alfalfa stand for 2, 3, or more years. Although several clover species may be grown, we have found red clover to be the most productive high-quality perennial clover for overseeding into alfalfa for hay production in Mediterranean zones.

Red Clover (*Trifolium pratense* L.) is higher yielding than many of the other clovers and has an upright growth habit suitable for haymaking, unlike many other forage clovers. Because

FIGURE 15.4

Berseem clover overseeded into old alfalfa fields provides several cuts of high-quality legume forage.

it is known for its tolerance of poorly drained soils, it may perform better than alfalfa in areas of poor drainage, such as field ends or areas compacted by harvest equipment. However, red clover hay also cures more slowly than alfalfa and turns a more brownish color compared to alfalfa. This is sometimes a negative for marketing, even though the quality of red clover and alfalfa by analysis is often quite similar. Red clover is considered a cool-season legume and is not likely to be appropriate for Low Desert Regions; berseem clover (an annual), however, is very well adapted to desert conditions.

Overseeding Alfalfa into Alfalfa

When an alfalfa stand falls below the minimum population for optimal production, it is often tempting to think that overseeding alfalfa into the existing stand may "thicken" and improve productivity. To the contrary, the majority of attempts at overseeding alfalfa into older alfalfa stands have resulted in a failure for seedlings to establish or weak seedlings, resulting in no yield benefit at the year's end. There have been situations where this practice has been successful, such as in young seedling fields, but the limitations of this practice typically outweigh the benefits. Overseeding alfalfa into established alfalfa has been a common practice in the Low Desert Region (Imperial Valley) of California and Yuma, Arizona, where it has been more successful than elsewhere in the United States.

> The majority of attempts at overseeding alfalfa into older alfalfa stands have resulted in a failure for seedlings to establish or weak seedlings, resulting in no yield benefit at the year's end.

Allelopathy, Autotoxicity, and Competition

Alfalfa secretes chemicals that may inhibit the germination and growth of alfalfa seedlings, a biological process known as allelopathy. Allelopathy is the effect of plant exudates (chemicals released from existing plants) on the germination and growth of young seedlings. Alfalfa allelochemicals can affect the germination of many species, including alfalfa itself. When alfalfa is planted into an existing alfalfa stand, the inhibition of the growth of the seedlings is known as autotoxicity.

In practice, autotoxicity cannot be separated from competition for light, nutrients, and water from the older plants or the diseases present in older stands. Some researchers have recommended that overseeding never be attempted because of autotoxicity. However, in our experience, autotoxicity may not be as important as other factors, particularly suboptimum seedbeds, irrigation problems, and competition from existing alfalfa plants and weeds in reducing success of stand establishment into existing alfalfa stands. Competition may be especially important because existing plants are thousands of times greater in size than young seedlings and easily shade out young plants or rob moisture from the soil surface. Under optimum conditions for seeding, such as the late fall planting in the Imperial Valley, seedling germination and growth is often successful in existing stands, when competition and growth of the existing stands are minimized. However, these new stands may still ultimately fail, owing to several factors that should be carefully considered.

Overseeding Alfalfa into Older Alfalfa Stands

There are many reasons why planting alfalfa into alfalfa is problematic, especially in older stands. When considering overseeding alfalfa into alfalfa, it is important to determine the original cause for the stand loss. This will improve our ability to predict the likelihood of success. When did plant losses begin? Were losses caused by temporary conditions or by long-term problems? Factors that will affect stand losses include poor soil drainage, flooding, salt toxicity, aggressive cutting schedules, irrigation mismanagement, equipment traffic damage, rodents, diseases, or an impermeable subsurface soil layer. In new stands, failure may be due to poor seed quality or seed placement that is too deep or too shallow, poor seedbed preparation, disease, weeds, insect problems, or flooding.

If the cause of stand loss is temporary and can be corrected, overseeding alfalfa has a higher chance of success. However, if the problem causing the original stand loss is recurring, the probability of success will be much lower. A careful analysis of these issues may prevent the wasting of seed and money on a reseeding project. The most frequent outcome of overseeding alfalfa into existing older alfalfa is that young seedlings are ultimately killed by the same factor (typically poor drainage, traffic, or irrigation problems) that initially killed the stand.

Replanting into a Young Alfalfa Stand

The problems of reseeding into a new stand or older alfalfa stands differ. Seedling stands with a population that falls below 10 plants per square foot during the first few weeks after emergence may be a good choice for overseeding. Early stand failure may be a temporary and correctable issue if the failure is caused by poor seed quality, seed placement that is too deep or too shallow, poor seedbed preparation, disease, weeds, insect problems, bad weather, or temporary flooding (Fig. 15.5).

Growers are often faced with the question of whether newly seeded fields can be improved by overseeding. When overseeding is timed so that existing alfalfa plants are still small—less than 6 inches tall—and adequate soil moisture is available for new seed germination, the success rate is usually high.

Successful overseeding practices include the use of a disc-type grain drill (or no-till drill) without tillage to place seed 0.50–0.75 inches deep, with minimal disturbance of existing plants. If broadcast seeding methods (by ground or air) are used, the seed should be pressed into the soil with a smooth or ring-type roller. Use of a spring or spike-tooth harrow is not recommended because it will remove or damage young, tender plants.

Overseed when the existing plants are small because large alfalfa plants create greater competition with the emerging seedlings. Although there is some competition and autotoxicity from the existing young alfalfa plants, this is not as great in young, thin stands compared with older, more mature, and fully established plants.

Common overseeding rates of alfalfa range from 10 to 20 pounds per acre. It is important to have adequate soil moisture when overseeding alfalfa to ensure rapid and uniform germination, similar to the requirements for a newly seeded alfalfa field. The most frequent error in reseeding projects is to fail to irrigate the crop for the young developing seedlings, not the established stands. This moisture can be from rainfall, sprinklers, or flood irrigation. Competition from existing plants can be severe if the crop is not well watered.

> *Seedling stands with a population that falls below 10 plants per square foot during the first few weeks after emergence may be a good choice for overseeding.*

FIGURE 15.5

Reseeded alfalfa in a young seedling field damaged by winter rains.

Compatibility with and crop safety of herbicide treatments for overseeding alfalfa should be checked. If the existing crop has been sprayed, some alfalfa herbicides will damage the germinating seedlings. Review the herbicide history of the field and read the pesticide label before overseeding. Recently, growers have discovered that overseeding of Roundup Ready alfalfa varieties has been successful, utilizing glyphosate (Roundup) to clear up weeds during the overseeding establishment process. This technology may provide flexibility for overseeding because glyphosate is less restrictive than other herbicides with regard to timing of application, crop or weed stage, and soil residual issues.

Planting Alfalfa After Alfalfa

When alfalfa stands are removed, growers may be tempted to follow alfalfa with another alfalfa planting, or "back-to-back" alfalfa. Crop rotation has many benefits (as cited above) and is one of the most important principles of crop production; thus, planting alfalfa after alfalfa is not recommended. However, in some regions where few crop rotation opportunities exist, the back-to-back alfalfa option becomes especially attractive, and, although not recommended, establishment can be successful, depending on a range of factors, including soil preparation, the presence of disease, and allelopathy.

> *Back-to-back alfalfa should not be attempted if good rotation options are available.*

The above discussion of autotoxicity and allelopathy is relevant here, since allelo-chemicals can remain in the soils after several years of alfalfa production. These may be more prevalent if the foliage (versus the root) is plowed under. However, in a study at UC Davis, alfalfa was planted immediately, 1 week, 2 weeks, and 4 weeks after plowing and tilling a 3-year-old existing stand in the fall. Stand density was reduced when alfalfa was planted immediately and at 1 week, but not affected at 2 weeks or 4 weeks, compared with fallow controls. Yields the following spring were not affected at any of the replanting times. Similar results were seen in an earlier Michigan study, whereas other studies have found more long-term negative effects of the previous alfalfa crop on the germinating seedlings. Thus, the need for crop rotation may differ, depending on climate and soil type.

Although it is always recommended to practice crop rotation as the first choice, here are the factors that might make back-to-back alfalfa more successful:

- Do not plow down foliage—only roots.

- Allow enough time from plowdown to planting (minimum of 2 weeks, but a longer time is desirable).

- Pre-irrigate soils after tillage during warm periods to encourage rapid breakdown of plant material and allelochemicals before planting.

- Correct soil problems (e.g., deep tillage, land leveling) that may impact subsequent stands.

- Prepare a good seedbed, suitable for optimum germination.

- Plant at an optimum time for the region (typically September–October in most San Joaquin, Sacramento, and desert regions, but earlier in higher-elevation regions) to allow development of healthy plants before winter conditions prevail. Optimizing time of planting is very important.

Back-to-back alfalfa should *not* be attempted if good rotation options are available, or under conditions where fields are known to have had severe disease or nematode infestations, or where soil conditions cannot be corrected during the reestablishment period. Growers should also consider the multiple benefits of crop rotations, including weed control, disease and nematode suppression, and other factors that collectively are called the "rotation effect."

Summary

Managing older or weakened alfalfa stands is one of the most challenging aspects of alfalfa production. It is difficult to assess the benefits versus the costs of maintaining or removing the stand, and growers can lose considerable income by continuing to harvest depleted stands. Stands below four to six plants per square foot, and stems below approximately 39 stems per square foot, are candidates for crop rotation or overseeding. Crop rotation is often the best decision if yields and value of the alfalfa have been greatly reduced and if other crops of equal or higher value are available for planting.

Overseeding with perennial or annual grasses or legumes to extend stand life has proved to be economically viable for growers who have developed horse or dry cow markets for their hay. Overseeding alfalfa into existing alfalfa stands can succeed in young stands but is usually unsuccessful in older stands. Growers should determine whether the cause for the original stand loss can be corrected or overcome. Planting back-to-back alfalfa is not usually recommended but can succeed if growers use management practices that mitigate the negative effects of previous stands on germination and growth.

Additional Reading

Canevari, M., D.H. Putnam, W.T. Lanini, R.F. Long, S.B. Orloff, B.A. Reed, and R.N. Vargas. Overseeding and companion cropping in alfalfa. University of California Division of Agriculture and Natural Resources, Oakland. Publication 21594.

16

Forage Quality and Testing

Daniel H. Putnam
Forage Extension Specialist, Department of Plant Sciences,
University of California, Davis

Peter Robinson
Extension Nutritionist, Department of Animal Science,
University of California, Davis

Ed DePeters
Professor of Ruminant Nutrition, Department of Animal Science,
University of California, Davis

A major challenge faced by alfalfa growers during the past 30 years has been the increased emphasis on forage quality. The need to produce high-quality hay affects marketing and price, as well as yield and stand life. Demands for high-quality alfalfa by the marketplace have been relentless. Although crop yield is still the primary economic factor determining forage crop value per unit of land area, forage quality has become a close second.

Milk production per dairy cow has more than doubled in 50 years, and increased more than 80 percent since the 1970s (Fig. 16.1). Such highly productive animals require forages with high digestibility, good palatability, high intake potential, and high protein levels, thus increasing the demand for alfalfa and other high-quality feeds. Growers have responded by producing higher-quality alfalfa; the average quality of hay tested by labs has increased dramatically since the 1970s (Fig. 16.2). The demand for high-quality forage is likely to intensify further, as dairy managers and nutritionists judge the value of alfalfa in comparison to the many other feedstuffs in a ration. Here, we examine the influence of forage quality on crop value, definitions of quality, the influences of agronomic practices on forage quality, and issues associated with forage sampling and testing.

Alfalfa Quality in the Marketplace

Dairying in the western United States is characterized by separation between the alfalfa hay producer and dairy farmer. It is estimated that >95 percent of the alfalfa grown in this region enters commerce as a hay product, unlike many other regions where alfalfa is primarily fed on-farm and only valued through the sale of milk or meat. Thus, in this region, the requirement for high-quality alfalfa hay is largely reflected in the market value of the alfalfa crop itself, and quality is frequently measured by laboratories.

Although hay prices vary considerably from year to year due to supply and demand factors, forage quality affects price every year (Table 16.1). High-quality hay prices averaged $46 per ton (907 kg) or 51 percent greater in economic value than the lowest quality in California's dairy markets over an 11-year period (Table 16.1). Quality differences tend to

be greater in a low priced year compared with a high priced year.

Hay Quality Guidelines

The USDA–Hay Market News Service has developed guidelines for reporting hay as Supreme, Premium, Good, Fair, or Utility (Table 16.2). These are based partly on lab tests and partly on subjective evaluation of hay quality indicators by buyers and sellers, such

FIGURE 16.1

Change in productivity in California dairy cows over a 50-year period (USDA data).

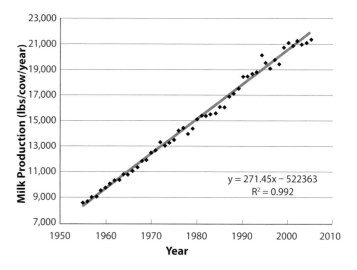

$y = 271.45x - 522363$
$R^2 = 0.992$

FIGURE 16.2

Change in hay test values over time (data from Petaluma Hay Testing Lab, Petaluma, CA).

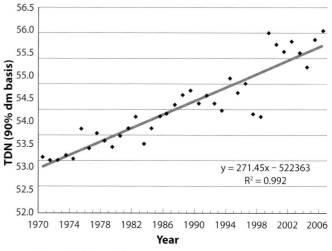

$y = 271.45x - 522363$
$R^2 = 0.992$

TDN = total digestible nutrients

Terminology

CP	=	Crude Protein
ADF	=	Acid Detergent Fiber
NDF	=	Neutral Detergent Fiber
NDFd	=	NDF digestibility
IVDDM	=	In Vitro Digestible Dry Matter
EE	=	Ether Extract
ADIN	=	Acid Detergent Insoluble Nitrogen
DE	=	Digestible Energy
ME	=	Metabolizable Energy
NE	=	Net Energy
NEl	=	Net Energy of Lactation
NEg	=	Net Energy of Gain
TDN	=	Total Digestible Nutrients
DCAD	=	Dietary Cation-Anion Difference

TABLE 16.1

Average price of alfalfa hay, as influenced by quality, across all California markets, 1996–2006. The "Supreme" category was instituted in 1999

| Year | Marketing Category | | | | Difference* | Percentage Difference (top-bottom) |
	Supreme $/ton	Premium	Good	Fair	$/ton	%
1996		129	114	100	29	29.3
1997		151	131	116	35	30.2
1998		140	122	93	47	50.3
1999	129	114	91	69	60	88.8
2000	127	111	93	77	50	65.0
2001	147	137	124	111	36	32.4
2002	142	125	107	89	53	59.6
2003	130	116	97	78	52	68.4
2004	148	135	119	101	47	46.7
2005	179	166	146	125	54	43.1
2006	166	151	132	106	60	56.9
Average	**$146**	**$134**	**$116**	**$97**	**$48**	**51.9%**

*Highest price/lowest price due to quality

TABLE 16.2

USDA quality guidelines for reporting economic data of alfalfa hay (not more than 10% grass) adapted in 2002 (2006 USDA Livestock, Hay and Grain Market News, Moses Lake, WA). Guidelines are used along with visual appearance to determine quality. All figures are expressed on 100% DM, except as noted.

Physical Descriptions of Hay Quality to be used in combination with lab tests for alfalfa hay quality categories (USDA–Market News):

Supreme: Very early maturity, pre-bloom, soft, fine stemmed, extra leafy. Factors are indicative of very high nutritive content. Hay is excellent color and free of damage.

Premium : Early maturity (i.e., pre-bloom in legumes and pre head-in grass hays), extra leafy, and fine stemmed-factors indicative of a high nutritive content. Hay is green and free of damage.

Good: Early to average maturity (i.e., early to mid-bloom in legumes and early head-in grass hays), leafy, fine to medium stemmed, free of damage other than slight discoloration.

Fair: Late maturity (i.e., mid- to late-bloom in legumes, head-in grass hays), moderate or below leaf content, and generally coarse stemmed. Hay may show light damage.

Utility: Hay in very late maturity (such as mature seed pods in legumes or mature head-in grass hays), coarse stemmed. This category could include hay discounted due to excessive damage and heavy weed content or mold. Defects will be identified in market reports when using this category.

| Category | ADF | NDF | RFV[1] | TDN[2] | TDN (90% DM)[3] | CP |
			%			
Supreme	<27	<34	>185	>62	>55.9	>22
Premium	27–29	34–36	170–185	60.5–62	54.5–55.9	20–22
Good	29–32	36–40	150–170	58–60	52.5–54.5	18–20
Fair	32–35	40–44	130–150	56–58	50.5–52.5	16–18
Utility	>35	>44	<100	<56	<50.5	<16

[1]RFV is calculated from ADF and NDF: RFV = [88.9 – (.779x % ADF)] × [(120/ %NDF)/1.29]

[2]TDN = (82.38 – [0.7515 × ADF]) according to Bath and Marble, 1989.

[3]TDN (90% DM) = TDN × 0.9.

ADF = acid detergent fiber; CP = crude protein; DM = dry matter; NDF = neutral detergent fiber; RFV = relative feed value; TDN = total digestible nutrients.

as presence of extraneous materials, including weeds and molds. However, these are guidelines, not standards, and buyers and sellers freely define and redefine quality based on a range of factors, including class of animal and personal preference. Furthermore, marketing guidelines are likely to change as forage quality concepts change over time.

Historically, several lab tests have been used for marketing. These analyses are typically a subset of a wider range of analyses used to predict animal performance in rations. A "standard" hay test in the United States currently consists of the analysis of acid detergent fiber (ADF), neutral detergent fiber (NDF), crude protein (CP), and dry matter (DM) (see "Terminology" sidebar on p. 242). Total digestible nutrients (TDN) and relative feed value (RFV) are calculated from the fiber values of ADF and/or NDF, and are commonly used for marketing. TDN, as commonly used in California, is a function only of ADF, while RFV is a function of both ADF and NDF (see "What Is Calculated" on p. 252). Other predictions, such as ME, NE$_l$, and RFQ, can also be calculated.

Although these two common methods for identifying quality in alfalfa markets (RFV and TDN) superficially appear to be different, they are actually quite similar since they are both

based on a measurement of fiber concentration. These are "fiber-based" marketing systems, and generally rank alfalfa hays similarly, since ADF and NDF are highly correlated in pure alfalfa hays. In California markets, the average change in hay price has been calculated to be approximately $7.00 per unit of ADF, using the hay marketing categories reported by USDA–Market News (Fig. 16.3). Crude protein (CP) is used less frequently in marketing alfalfa hay.

However, in recent years, dairy nutritionists are utilizing "summative equations" to predict the quality of alfalfa hay; these equations incorporate NDF, NDFd, CP, ash, and several other measurements. The use of ADF–TDN equations is largely being abandoned in favor of this approach.

Subjective Quality Factors

Subjectively-determined quality factors remain important for predicting hay quality, since not all quality attributes can be predicted from laboratory analysis. Although observation methods are poor at predicting fiber concentration, fiber digestibility, energy, or protein, hay must be examined visually to assess the importance of weeds (particularly poisonous or noxious weeds), molds or anti-palatability factors such as poor texture (hard stems or coarseness, or the presence of sooty molds, both of which affect palatability), evidence of heating, or unpleasant odor (Table 16.3). Several of these factors can have significant effects on nutritional value and animal health, and are not determined by common laboratory tests. Thus, a combination of visual and laboratory methods is recommended to fully assess the forage quality of alfalfa hay.

FIGURE 16.3

Average effect of hay quality measurements (ADF or NDF) on price in California; average of all markets, 1996–2006 (Data from USDA–Market News Reports).

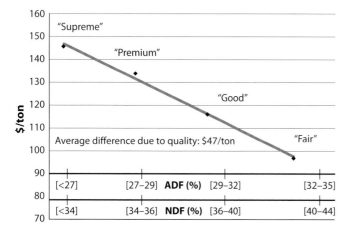

ADF = acid detergent fiber; TDN = total digestible nutrients

What Is Forage Quality?

Forage quality is defined as the potential to produce a desired animal response from a given intake of forage. Animal response could be measured in the form of milk production, animal growth, meat or wool production, or general health. However, forage quality is not an intrinsic characteristic of a plant. The definition and optimization of forage quality depends on both species and class of animal, stage of life, and the mix of feeds in the ration. Thus, optimal forage quality is a function of both animal and plant factors.

Forage Quality Is Multifaceted

Although it is often tempting to reduce the concept forage quality to one or two measurements (for example CP or ME, TDN or RFV), this usually belies a more complicated story. Forage quality is always a complex mix of nutritional traits. For example, CP is important, but many nutritionists are also interested in the availability (extent and rate of digestion) of the protein as it is degraded in the rumen since some plant protein might be too rapidly degraded and the nitrogen poorly utilized by rumen microorganisms. In "tobaccoed" (hay that has turned dark brown through heating) or moldy hay, the CP is often heat-damaged protein, essentially not degradable by ruminants, and thus of little nutritional value.

The total potential biological energy value of the forage crop (often expressed as TDN, ME, or NE) is one of the most important attributes of forages, but sources of energy include rapidly degraded soluble sugars, starches, protein, or slowly degraded fiber, each of which has particular nutritional characteristics. Some energy is released rapidly in the rumen, while other energy is only slowly released after the cellulose and hemicellulose is broken down by rumen microflora.

There are also physical aspects that affect quality (e.g., grind, fiber length, moisture), olfactory issues (e.g., odor, dustiness, chemical attractants that encourage uptake), and contaminants (e.g., toxic weeds, dirt, molds, toxic insects) that affect palatability, intake,

TABLE 16.3

Relative effectiveness of visual and laboratory methods of judging forage quality factors. Some quality factors are best evaluated visually, whereas other factors require a lab test

Quality Factor	Visual Examination	Lab Test
Leaf:Stem Ratio (Leaf %)	Good	Fair
Leaf–Stem Attachment	Excellent	Poor
Mold/Dustiness	Excellent	Poor
Texture (coarse, soft)	Excellent	Poor
Weed Content	Excellent	Fair
Noxious Weeds	Excellent	Poor
Odor	Excellent	Poor
Fiber Concentration	Poor	Excellent
Fiber Digestibility	Poor	Excellent
Protein Concentration	Poor	Excellent
Protein Degradability	Poor	Excellent
Mineral Content	Poor	Excellent

and thus overall quality. Forage quality should always be considered a multifaceted attribute of alfalfa, with several key features or important concepts. What are these principal features of forages?

What Do Animals Require From Forages?

In a discussion with animal nutritionists, several principles or concepts emerge as important requirements from forages. The principal nutritional features of forages are digestible energy content, intake potential, protein, ruminally effective fiber, and minerals or ash. Although each of these factors is important to all classes of livestock, the importance and relative rank will likely change by animal type, stage of life, and feed ration formulation. In our region, forage quality of alfalfa is most often defined in terms of milk production of high-producing dairy cows, which generally drives the discussion of forage quality, since a large percentage of the California alfalfa crop is used by the dairy sector. However, these factors are relevant in varying degrees to all classes of animals.

1. Digestible Energy (DE)

In most cases, the primary consideration for forage quality is the potential digestible energy per dry matter weight unit (lb, kg, or Mg) of forage. The supply of energy in feeds is a function of digestion and absorption of energy-containing compounds in the plant. This is usually the most important forage quality factor, since biological energy drives the animal functions of maintenance, growth, and milk production. Unfortunately, the total potential biological energy in feeds cannot be easily measured directly in routine analyses, since it is a function of both the forage and the animal, but is predicted with equations derived from several laboratory analyses.

In plants, digestible energy comes from both rapidly available and slowly available sources. The rapidly available forms include sugars, starches, and pectins, which are released quickly in the rumen and contribute energy to the animal, primarily as volatile fatty acids such as acetate, propionate, and butyrate that are absorbed through the rumen wall. However, considerable energy in forages is contained in the cell wall portion (cellulose, hemicellulose), which is made available only through enzymatic breakdown by rumen microorganisms. These are also subsequently converted into volatile fatty acids and absorbed by the animal. Although starches, sugars, and pectins are essentially 100 percent digestible, the fibrous energy component in the alfalfa cell wall is typically in the range of 30 to 60 percent digestibility. Protein also contributes to energy since it contains carbon skeletons. Lipids (oils or fats) contain considerable energy (2.2 times that of carbohydrates), but small quantities are typically contained in alfalfa forages, although lipids are more important in corn silage and other forages that contain grain.

Energy (TDN, NE, NE_l, or ME) can be predicted from a linear relationship to a fiber measurement (ADF or NDF) in alfalfa (Fig. 16.4), or by summative equations. Although there are many calculations for TDN, the most common TDN currently used for marketing in California is given in Figure 16.4. Energy is more accurately calculated from summative equations that use NDF, NDFd, ash, EE, CP, and other factors to predict energy. It is important to determine the method of calculation when comparing the energy values among and between forages. From a nutritional viewpoint, estimation of digestible energy is typically the most important factor for predicting quality of forages, although intake is often a close second.

2. Intake Potential

Some forages are digested very rapidly in the rumen, while other feeds require extended periods for complete digestion. Additionally, there are factors that cause animals to consume more or less of a forage, often termed "palatability," that are affected by species, taste, condition of the hay, odor, weed content, stem quality, and plant maturity. Palatability is the animal behavior response to the consumption of forage. Intake is a function of both palatability and rate of digestion in the rumen, and rate of passage from the rumen. Lower intake levels result in lower energy availability per unit of time, reducing animal performance and lowering the forage quality. High-fiber alfalfa often has both high fiber content and slow fiber digestibility—therefore animals can become

FIGURE 16.4

For marketing purposes, TDN has been historically calculated directly from ADF value in California and other western states. TDN is calculated on a 100% DM basis, but is sometimes expressed on a 90% DM basis, since western hay equilibrates to approximately 90% DM. This is changing since nutritionists now largely use summative equations based on NDF.

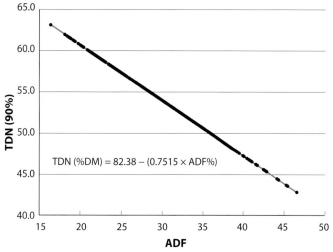

TDN (%DM) = 82.38 − (0.7515 × ADF%)

ADF = acid detergent fiber; TDN = total digestible nutrients

"filled" and stop eating. This rumen fill limits intake, which ultimately reduces energy intake and animal performance. When feed or energy intake is below requirements, milk production generally declines. Thus, potential feed intake of a forage is especially important for high-producing dairy cows. However, too-rapid rates of degradation result in poor rumen function and negatively affect animal health, causing acidosis and other health problems. Several subjective factors (e.g., visual inspection, touch, smell) may assist in predicting animal acceptance, but palatability may be less important in total mixed rations (TMRs), since other feeds and additives impact voluntary intake by ruminants.

However, the rate of ruminant degradation of the fiber fraction (NDF) is an important indicator of intake. There are several approaches to measuring, or predicting, rumen digestibility, including *in vitro digestible dry matter* (IVDDM), gas production estimates, and *in vitro* NDF digestibility (NDFd), all of which are bioassays involving digestion of a sample in rumen fluid. These methods provide information on the rate and extent of DM and NDF digestion, which can be used in predictive equations. Intake potential is one of the most important quality factors for lactating dairy cows.

3. Protein

Since amino acids from proteins are building blocks for muscle, milk, and animal enzymes, they are important nutritional attributes of forages. Although the concentration of protein (estimated by CP) is important, many nutritionists may also be interested in the amount of alfalfa protein that is degraded in the rumen or passes undegraded from the rumen and is digested in the small intestine. Rumen degraded protein (RDP) provides an estimate of CP availability in the rumen. Acid detergent insoluble CP (ADICP) estimates the undigestible (typically lignified and heat-damaged) CP. While heat damaged and undegraded protein is a negative factor, excessive degradation of CP in the rumen is also a negative quality factor if the rumen microbes do not fully utilize the ammonia nitrogen (N) for microbial protein.

This excess ammonia N is absorbed through the rumen wall, and much of the ammonia is converted to urea via an energy-dependent process, and the urea is excreted in the urine.

High rumen degradable protein can be a problem with very leafy immature alfalfa. Since inexpensive high-CP concentrate feeds are generally available, CP in alfalfa forages is often discounted compared with its energy content in alfalfa hay markets. However, as the cost of CP supplements rises, the economic value of protein in forages will become greater, particularly "rumen escape protein," absorbed in the lower intestine that is often most effectively utilized by ruminants.

> *Since amino acids from proteins are building blocks for muscle, milk, and animal enzymes, they are important nutritional attributes of forages.*

4. Ruminally Effective Fiber

The provision of ruminally effective fiber with a high level of digestibility is a major attribute provided by alfalfa hay in ruminant rations. Forage growers are faced with a quandary with this issue: As indicated above, digestible energy and intake potential are considered to be the most important quality factors. Energy and intake are inversely related to fiber concentration (ADF, NDF) in the hay. Thus, generally, as the percentage of ADF or NDF goes up, digestible energy and intake go down. As a result, dairy managers frequently demand low-NDF or low-ADF alfalfa hay.

However, reduction of fiber to very low levels can create problems in rumen function since dietary fiber stimulates rumination, chewing, and saliva production; the latter helps to stabilize rumen pH. High-producing ruminants can suffer physical problems with rumen health when "effective fiber" is too low in their diet. Thus, the fiber in alfalfa provides positive physical and chemical attributes to ruminant rations. However, if the digestibility of the fiber is too low, both DE and intake are negatively affected, thus the quandary for forage growers.

It is clear that both the concentration of the NDF and the rates of digestion of the fiber fraction are important attributes of forage quality, but the value of effective-fiber (vs. low-fiber, high-energy) hay varies, depending on the levels in the diet and class of animals to which it is being fed.

5. Ash and Minerals

Ash is an estimate of total mineral content in a forage, which could originate from normal mineral uptake by the plant, for example, phosphorus (P), potassium (K), sulfur (S), calcium (Ca), magnesium (Mg), chlorine (Cl), and sodium (Na) from excessive salt accumulation, or contamination with soil. In general, as ash increases, the level of digestible energy declines, since minerals do not contain energy. Thus, ash is considered to be a negative factor in predictions of energy for ruminants, and lower-ash alfalfa should generally contain higher energy.

> *Ash is an estimate of total mineral content in a forage, which could originate from normal mineral uptake by the plant or from excessive salt or contamination by soil.*

However, alfalfa provides several essential minerals contained in the ash fraction. Although minerals may be supplemented in the diet, the balance (or type) of mineral ions, such as Ca, P, and K in alfalfa may be important nutritionally. For example, high K is a negative attribute for dairy animals just before and just after calving (often termed the "close-up" or "transition" period), since excessive K contributes to an increased incidence of milk fever. Additionally, excessive concentrations of micronutrients (such as selenium [Se] or molybdenum [Mo]) can be toxic when present in high amounts in the diet. Conversely, hays can provide necessary micronutrients that otherwise might be limiting in diets. Nutritionists frequently are interested in the balance of mineral nutrients in forages (e.g., Dietary Cation–Anion Difference [DCAD], see below).

6. Other Factors

There are other, less-well-defined attributes of quality, such as secondary plant compounds, aromas or odor, dust, and molds, that affect sensory preference by animals, but these may be important primarily as they affect intake (factor 2) and general animal health. Toxic weeds or insects (e.g., blister beetle) can be important anti-nutritional or toxic factors, and important quality factors in hay. Each year, many animals are sickened or die from poisonous weeds, excess nitrate (from weeds), or excess micronutrient concentrations in hay (see Puschner 2006). These are all attributes under the umbrella of "forage quality."

It should be clear from the above discussions that forage quality is a complex trait that includes a range of factors.

What's in a Forage Plant?

Alfalfa plants, when considered as a feed, have several botanical, morphological, and physiological characteristics that impact the factors cited above. Nutrients are not uniformly distributed throughout the plant or the harvested crop. They are influenced by both macro- and micro-level morphological differences in plant structure and changes in plant composition (Fig. 16.5).

Moisture

A fresh standing alfalfa crop contains from about 70 to 80 percent water, which is rapidly reduced to 12–18 percent moisture at baling. Hay equilibrates to about 10 percent moisture in hay stacks under ambient western conditions. Moisture is typically 60–65 percent for haylage.

Moisture is frequently confused on hay test reports. Although some dry matter components are soluble, all quality features of alfalfa are contained in the DM component, not the water component of forage. Thus, the "as-received" percentage of moisture (or percent DM) should only be used to adjust *yield* levels, not forage quality. To understand quality, quality measurements should always be compared on a

100-percent DM basis since moisture can be added or reduced, depending on conditions. Although moisture in hay is not an important nutritional factor by itself, it can indicate excessively wet hay (indicating potential mold problems, and thereby lower quality), or excessively dry hay (indicating potentially harmful prickly stems or leaf drop).

Botanical Level— Leaves and Stems

Although an alfalfa field may appear as a uniform mass of green, the harvested crop is made up of stems, leaves, flowers, and petioles, and each part differs in nutritional value. The most important of these by weight are stems and leaves. Leaves are much more digestible and lower in fiber than stems, and can have 2–3 times more CP than stems (Fig. 16.5). Leaf tissue does not accumulate fiber and lignin to the same extent as stem tissue as the plant

grows and develops. Thus, the relative weight of leaves and stems is probably the most important determinant of quality for alfalfa. If no analysis is available, a subjective evaluation of leaf percentage is a valuable indicator of potential feeding value (Table 16.3). Leaf percentage ranges from about 55 to 65 percent in very-high-quality alfalfa to 35 to 45 percent in lower-quality alfalfa.

Microscopic Level—Cell Walls

On a microscopic level, each plant consists of millions of cells. Each cell consists of distinct components that differ in their nutritional characteristics, most prominently those compounds that are free or easily digested in the vacuoles or cytoplasm (cell solubles), and the cell wall material itself. A universal characteristic of higher plants is the presence of a cell wall (Fig. 16.5). This is the most fibrous component of the plant and provides structure

FIGURE 16.5

Alfalfa forage consists of structural components that differ dramatically in forage quality. Leaves are much lower in fiber and can have two to three times more protein than stems. Within the cell, the cell solubles or nonfiber carbohydrates (sugars and starches) are 100 percent digestible, whereas the cell wall or fiber portion are only partially digestible. NDF approximates total cell wall, and ADF approximates the most difficultly digested portions of the cell: cellulose and lignin.

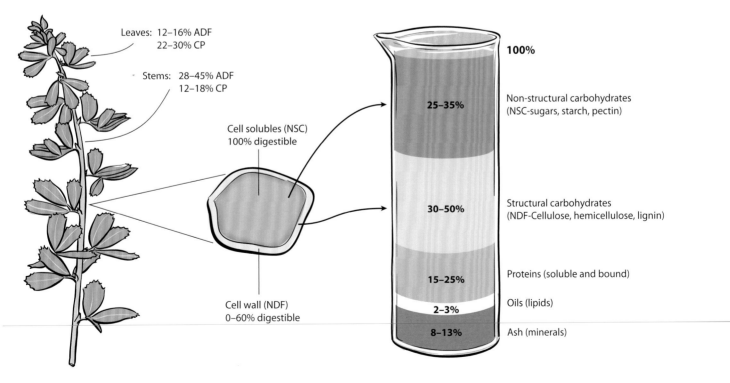

to stand up and grow, and allows movement of water through the xylem. The cell wall may be as much as 60 percent of the DM of the cell (ranging from 30 to 50 percent in alfalfa).

From an animal nutrition viewpoint, cell wall material has a large influence on forage quality, since it is typically the least digested, and thus the focus of most lab measurements. As the plant matures, cell wall content generally increases, which reduces overall plant digestibility and therefore decreases forage quality.

Cell Solubles and Nonfiber Carbohydrates

Nonfiber carbohydrates (NFC), sometimes called "cell solubles," contribute 100 percent to the energy content of the forage (with the exception of soluble minerals), and are rapidly digested, thus contributing to high intake.

Cell solubles may range from 20 to 35 percent of DM. Young plant cells are quite high in soluble carbohydrates, such as sugars and starches, and high in protein, but low in fiber. As these cells develop and mature, the secondary cell wall becomes more important, and cellulose, hemicellulose and lignin increase and proportionally reduce the cell soluble concentration.

> *Non-fiber carbohydrates (NFC), sometimes called "cell solubles" contribute 100 percent to the energy content of the forage.*

Lignification of cells creates complex cell wall structures that are more resistant to enzymatic breakdown by rumen microbes. Secondary cell wall development occurs primarily in stems, and is an important determinant of forage quality since plant maturity both increases the cell wall fraction and makes it much more difficult to digest.

Protein

Typically, alfalfa plants range from 17 to 26 percent CP; thus alfalfa is an important source of protein for animals. However, the quantity of protein degraded in the rumen from alfalfa is frequently considered to be too high in alfalfa. This may be a problem due to excess excretion of urinary urea N from ruminant feeding systems, which can be an environmental concern.

Fat

The fat content of alfalfa plants is primarily in the cell membrane portion of the cell and is typically fairly insignificant, averaging about 1.5 percent ether extract (EE) for alfalfa hay.

Minerals

Mineral content of alfalfa is approximated by the ash measurement and can be significant, ranging from 6 to 15 percent of the DM of the plant tissue.

What Is Measured?

Since forage quality has chemical, biological, and dynamic properties, both measured and calculated methods must be used to predict alfalfa forage quality. The first subject of interest to nutritionists is often the measurement of the plant cell wall component, since cell walls are present in large quantities in the plant and are the most difficult component to digest. Measurements of cell wall are often accompanied by measurements of cell wall digestibility, CP, ash, and fat, which are followed by calculations of nonfiber carbohydrate and other relative quality and energy estimates. Standard hay assays include:

Dry Matter (DM): DM is the percentage of a sample that is not water. All other forage quality components are typically expressed and compared on a 100-percent DM basis. Dry matter is measured using oven drying for 3 hours at 105°F (41°C). See NFTA Web site (www.foragetesting.com) for this and other standard methods. There are minor errors associated with oven drying since there can be a loss of volatile compounds that are not water, overestimating the moisture content. These small errors are more important in silages.

Neutral Detergent Fiber (NDF): NDF approximately measures the cellulose, hemicellulose, lignin, and some ash portion of the cell wall fraction (the slowly digestible, and indigestible, components) and is often equated with an estimate of the total plant cell wall fraction (minus the pectin). NDF is defined as the residue that remains after 1 hour of boiling in neutral detergent fiber solution. NDF is called aNDF if amylase and sulfite are used in the analysis, which is the recommended method. NDF commonly ranges from 30 to 50 percent in alfalfa hay.

Acid Detergent Fiber (ADF): ADF is a subset of NDF, and approximately measures the cellulose, lignin, and cutin component, or the least-digestible components of the cell wall. ADF is defined as the fibrous component of the plant that remains after 1 hour of boiling with an acid detergent solution. Since ADF is a component of NDF, the ADF concentration is always lower, ranging from 22 to 37 percent in alfalfa hay.

Neutral Detergent Fiber Digestibility (NDFD): *In vitro* NDF digestibility is a measurement of the digestibility of the NDF fraction in a ruminant system for a specified incubation length of time. NDFD quantifies the amount of NDF remaining after a defined number of hours of incubation in rumen fluid (typically, 24, 30, 48, or 72 hours) in a controlled lab test, and is expressed as a percentage of NDF. NDFD may also be measured using *in vivo* (within the animal itself) methods in feeding studies or using *in situ* methods (bags in rumen). Digestibility of NDF in western alfalfa hays may range from 30 to 55 percent.

Digestible Neutral Detergent Fiber (dNDF): The dNDF level is measured in the same way that NDFD is measured but is expressed as a percentage of dry matter, not as a percentage of NDF.

Crude Protein (CP): Protein in alfalfa is most commonly expressed as CP, which is calculated as the percentage of nitrogen (N) × 6.25 (reflecting the average nitrogen content of alfalfa amino acids). The correction factor of 6.25 assumes that the amino acids in alfalfa protein contains 16 percent N (the actual amount may be closer to 15.8 percent N, but 6.25 is used as a standard). Crude protein alone is seldom sufficient to predict animal performance. Measurement of amino acids may occasionally be helpful, and measurements of CP degradability in the rumen are considered very helpful. Crude protein ranges from 16 to 26 percent of DM in alfalfa hay.

Ash: Ash is a measure of total inorganic minerals in the forage as well as soil contamination. To obtain the ash percentage, samples are burned at high temperatures (932–1112°F, 500–600°C), and the remainder is weighed. Ash can contain minerals from organic compounds, for example P from phytic acid, plus some volatile minerals can be lost during the combustion process. Ash contains no energy. Specific minerals, such as P, K, S, Mg, Ca, S, Se, and manganese (Mn), are often measured separately to indicate the value of the forage in supplying those nutrients, or in identifying high levels of concern, particularly for the micronutrients Mo, Se, and Mn.

Although the above measurements are most frequently used, several other measurements may also be seen on laboratory reports and are used by nutritionists.

Lignin: Lignin is a part of NDF and ADF and is essentially undigestible. However, lignin often "shields" or blocks digestion of hemicelluloses and celluloses to which it is chemically linked. Lignin may be from 5 to 15 percent of the DM of alfalfa hay. Lignin measurements tend to be less repeatable than ADF or NDF.

Lipids or Fats (EE): The fat in alfalfa is primarily in cell membrane material and is measured as ether extract (EE). Ether extract is seldom measured in alfalfa hay because there is little triglyceride present, and the organic solvent (e.g., petroleum ether or diethyl ether) also extracts chlorophyll, waxes, volatile oils, and resins, which are not energy-containing triglycerides.

Total Nonstructural Carbohydrate (TNC) or Nonstructural Carbohydrates (NSC): TNC (or NSC) is a measure of the starch and sugar contained in forages. This has a lower value than NFC since NFC contains compounds other than starch and sugars.

***In-Vitro* Dry Matter Digestibility (IVDMD):** IVDMD is the quantity of DM digested when a known amount of alfalfa is anaerobically incubated with buffered rumen fluid typically in a test tube after a defined length of time (typically 24–72 hr). This method provides an estimate of the extent of DM digestion. It is seldom measured and used as a routine method for estimating forage quality.

***In-Vitro* Gas Production:** This is the quantity of gas produced when a known amount of ground sample is anaerobically incubated with buffered rumen fluid over a defined length of time (e.g., from 0 to 48 or 72 hr). A continuous curve with multiple readings is possible. The multiple measurements allow estimation of the extent of digestion and also the rate of digestion. Gas quantities can be used to predict Digestible Energy (DE) or Metabolized Energy (ME) content.

Ruminant *In-Situ* Measurements: Digestibility of forages can be measured with nylon bags inserted directly into the rumen of fistulated cows. Bags can be withdrawn from the rumen after different lengths of incubation time. *In situ* (also called *in sacco*) methods are often used to estimate disappearance of DM, CP, and NDF. If samples are collected over a range of incubation times, both the extent and rate of disappearance can be estimated.

Acid Detergent Insoluble Nitrogen (ADIN) and Acid Detergent Insoluble Crude Protein (ADICP): ADIN and ADICP are measured as the insoluble N remaining after a known amount of sample is boiled in acid detergent solution. The N remaining in the ADF residue is assumed to be unavailable to the animal. It is a good estimator of indigestible CP, mostly lignified and heat damaged protein, and is generally expressed as a percentage of the CP content

of the forage. Formation of ADICP can occur during "heating" in moist hay (i.e., browning). This can be expressed either as ADIN or as ADICP (which is the insoluble N × 6.25).

Rumen Undegraded Protein (RUP): RUP measures the quantity of CP that is not degraded by microbes in the rumen. Often called "rumen escape protein," it is typically measured with in situ bag methods—the protein which does not disappear from the ruminant nylon bag is considered rumen undegraded protein.

What Is Calculated?

Not all forage quality characteristics can be measured; some very important quality factors must be predicted from laboratory measurements since they are so difficult to measure routinely. These are primarily the energy and intake potential of the forage, which may be predicted using several approaches. It is very important to understand the source of the calculated numbers on laboratory reports to allow correct interpretation, since these can sometimes be calculated differently.

Non-Fiber Carbohydrates (NFCs): NFCs are those energy-containing compounds (primarily sugars, starches, and pectins) that are highly soluble and nearly 100 percent digestible by ruminants. Non-fiber carbohydrates are calculated as the difference between the total DM and the NDF, CP, ash, and EE concentrations of the forage. This is similar (but not precisely the same) as NSC (see above), which can be measured directly. The NFCs may range from 20 to 35 percent in alfalfa forage and is a major contributor to the digestible energy contained in forages.

Digestible Energy (DE): DE is the quantity of total intake energy in a forage that is not lost in feces.

Metabolizable Energy (ME): ME is the quantity of energy in a forage that is not lost in feces, urine, or rumen gasses, and is available to the animal for use.

Net Energy for Maintenance (NE$_m$): NE$_m$ is a prediction of the quantity of energy in a forage required to maintain a stable weight.

Net Energy for Gain (NE$_g$): NE$_g$ is a prediction of the quantity of energy in a forage available for body weight gain above that of maintenance.

Net Energy for Lactation (NE$_l$): NE$_l$ is a prediction of the quantity of energy in a forage available for maintenance plus milk production during lactation, and for maintenance plus the last two months of gestation for dry, pregnant cows.

Dietary Cation–Anion Difference (DCAD): DCAD in the 2001 NRC recommendations is calculated as the difference of concentrations of cations and anions as milliequivalents: meq (Na + K + 0.15 Ca + 0.15 Mg) − (Cl + 0.605 S + 0.5 P)/100 g of dietary DM.

Total Digestible Nutrients (TDN): TDN conceptually is the sum of DE contained in nonstructural carbohydrates (cell solubles), digestible NDF, crude protein, and fat. However, in practice, TDN is predicted from ADF or NDF alone (Fig. 16.4), but formulas for TDN vary widely. The "western states" equation, as published by Bath and Marble (1989), is TDN (% of DM) = 82.38 − (0.7515 × ADF%). Currently, TDN is more frequently predicted using summative equations by nutritionists.

Relative Feed Value (RFV): RFV is a marketing index for ranking cool-season grass and legumes and is calculated from ADF and NDF. The RFV is conceptually based on both digestibility and intake potential, but is mathematically highly correlated to NDF. See the NFTA Web site (www.foragetesting.org) for calculation.

Relative Forage Quality (RFQ): RFQ is an index for marketing forages, similar to RFV, but includes a component related to intake potential. The RFQ is calculated from NDF, NDFD, CP, EE, and NFC and is an index for marketing forages proposed as an improvement over RFV since it emphasizes intake potential. The RFQ is calculated from NDF, NDFD, CP, EE, and NFC. See NFTA Web site (www.foragetesting.org) for calculation.

The Hay Testing Process

Standardization of Hay Quality Measurements

A key issue impacting dairy nutritionists and hay growers, as well as buyers and sellers, is the standardization of hay testing. The process of hay testing begins with accurate sampling methods, followed by the standardization of laboratory methods and use of empirical formulas to estimate forage quality based on laboratory measurements (Fig. 16.6). Obtaining differing results from various laboratories creates confusion in the marketplace.

FIGURE 16.6

The hay testing process. Growers and marketers are responsible for sampling methods, laboratories are responsible for good lab methods, and nutritionists are responsible for providing prediction equations and interpretation of data.

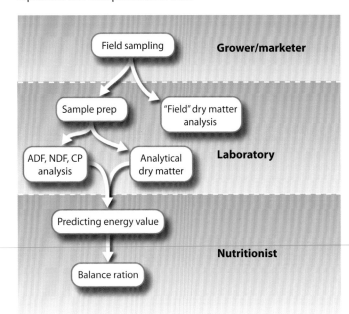

The Importance of Sampling

It is impossible to overemphasize the importance of sampling for hay quality analysis. Obtaining a representative sample of a given "lot" of hay is critical. Remember, a laboratory test is only as good as the sample provided to the lab. *Here's the dilemma:* Tons of highly variable plant material must be represented in a single, tiny, thumbnail-sized sample (Fig. 16.7). For many analyses, the sample actually analyzed by the laboratory is only 0.5 grams (0.018 oz)! This sample must represent not only the proper leaf–stem ratio and the legume/grass mix, but must also reflect the variable presence of weeds and soil variation.

Sampling variation is a major problem in hay evaluation and causes millions of dollars in lost revenue each year by either buyer or seller, and also contributes to reduced animal performance. In practice, hay sampling causes more variation in results than does laboratory variation. However, if sampling protocols are carefully followed, sampling variation can be reduced to an acceptable level, and the potential forage quality successfully predicted.

The following steps are widely considered to be the key elements of an effective standardized sampling protocol (*further details are available at* www.foragetesting.org).

Standardized Hay Sampling Protocol to Assure a Representative Sample of Hay

The principle of a good sampling protocol is to obtain an approximately 0.5-pound (227-g) sample that correctly represents the leaf–stem ratio, mixture of weeds, and field variation in a defined lot of hay.

1. **Identify a single lot of hay.** A hay lot should represent a single cutting, a single field and variety, and generally be less than 200 tons (181 Mg).

2. **Sample at the right time.** Sample as close to point of sale, or as close to feeding, as possible since dry matter and other measurements are subject to change after harvest and during storage.

3. **Always use a sharp, well-designed coring device.** Use a coring device 0.375 to 0.750 inches (0.95 to 1.9 cm) in diameter with a sharp tip at 90 degrees to the shaft, not angled. *Never* send in flakes or grab samples. The probe length should allow probing to a depth of 12–24 inches (30–61 cm). Hay probes should (1) easily penetrate the bale, (2) fairly represent the leaf–stem ratio, (3) be easy to sharpen, and (4) produce approximately 0.5 pounds (227 g) of sample in about 20 cores to a depth of 12–24 inches (30–61 cm). Some probes (e.g., the 0.75-inch [1.9-cm] Penn State probe) result in excessive samples in 20 cores. See a listing of acceptable probes at www.foragetesting.org (NFTA Web site).

FIGURE 16.7

Hay sampling protocols are critical to provide accurate quality measurements. Sampling methods must correctly represent the leaf–stem component, percentage of weeds, as well as variation due to soil type over a field in hay lots. Units for sampling should not exceed 200 tons, and should be from a single field/single cutting. See http://alfalfa.ucdavis.edu for hay sampling protocols.

4. **Sample systematically, choosing random bales.** The sampler should walk around the stack as much as possible and sample bales in a systematic fashion; for example, every fourth bale on both sides of the stack. This should prevent inadvertent choosing of bales and provide a random sample. Sample as much of the stack as possible. Don't avoid or choose bales because they look especially bad or good. If 20 cores are taken, they won't make much difference anyway.

5. **Take enough cores.** We recommend *a minimum of 20 cores* for a composite sample to represent a hay lot. This is the same for large (e.g., 1 ton [907 kg] bales), or small two-tie or three-tie bales. A larger number of core samples is useful for more variable hay lots.

6. **Use proper technique.** The probe should be inserted at a 90-degree angle, 12–18 inches (30–46 cm) deep, to sample butt ends of each hay bale, between strings or wires, not near the edge. With round bales, sample toward middle of bale on an angle directly toward the center of the bale.

7. **Sample amount: "not too big, not too small."** Sampling should be done so that about 0.5 pounds (227 g) of sample is produced. If the sample is too small, it is likely to be less representative. If the sample is too large, labs may not grind the whole sample. For example, the Penn State sampler tends to provide too large a sample, since it is in 0.75 inch (1.9 cm) diameters. If the wrong amount of sample is produced with 20 cores, a different hay sampler should be used.

8. **Handle samples correctly.** Seal the composite 20-core sample in a well-sealed plastic bag, protect from heat, and do not allow samples to be exposed to the sun.

9. **Certify your hay sample.** An online exam is available at www.foragetesting.org to allow individuals to certify their hay samples. This may be particularly important for situations where two parties are interested in the results of the sampling. The quiz allows the sampler to "self-certify" that the sample was taken using this protocol.

Choosing a Qualified NFTA Laboratory

Once a good sample is obtained, a qualified laboratory must be chosen. The first criterion for choosing a high-quality laboratory is membership in and certification by the National Forage Testing Association (NFTA). Laboratory performance is not regulated in the United States by any government agency—laboratories voluntarily submit to the NFTA performance testing program and are sent samples to test their performance. The NFTA board is made up of volunteer laboratories, university and USDA scientists, and hay growers and marketers. A laboratory must match the reference value within a certain range of variation (determined by the NFTA board) to obtain certification.

Additionally, a customer can ask for the actual NFTA grades from the laboratory's certification report and discuss issues such as laboratory practices, and ask the laboratory for their quality assurance standards. In addition, customers may conduct their own split-sample test of laboratories. To test two laboratories, either grind and carefully split the sample with an appropriate device, or better yet, ask for your ground sample back to split and send to another laboratory (never split unground samples to test laboratory performance). Don't work with a laboratory that is unwilling to assist you in testing their performance.

> *The first criterion for choosing a high-quality laboratory is membership in and certification by the National Forage Testing Association (NFTA).*

FIGURE 16.8

Changes in alfalfa leaf–stem dry matter percentage, acid detergent fiber (ADF), neutral detergent fiber (NDF), and crude protein concentrations of the first growth period, Yolo Co., CA. Marketing categories are shown as a function of ADF (USDA–Market News). Data from T. Ackerly (M.S. Thesis, UC Davis, 2000).

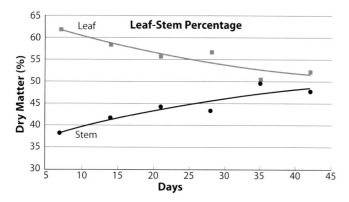

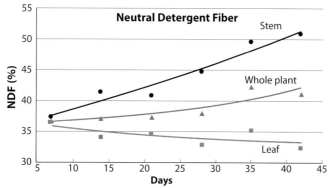

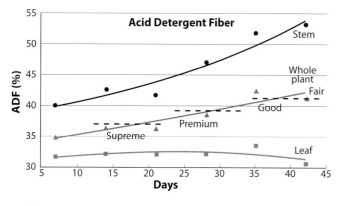

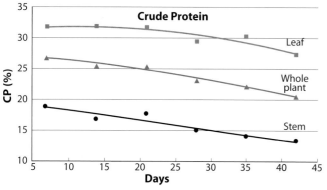

Agronomic Factors that Influence Forage Quality

The major agronomic factors that affect alfalfa quality are cutting schedules (plant maturity at harvest), weed and pest management, harvest effects, and seasonal or weather patterns. Less important effects are variety, time of day of harvest, fertilizers, and irrigation. Sometimes these factors interact in complex ways. But these factors typically affect quality via a few fundamental mechanisms, including plant maturity at harvest, leaf percentage, mixtures with weeds, and environmental effects.

Plant Maturity at Harvest

It is a universal axiom of alfalfa forage production that as a plant grows and develops, forage quality declines. Therefore, the stage at which the plant is harvested is usually the most critical factor determining forage quality. This is such an important issue that we have dedicated a whole chapter in this series to cutting schedules (see "Harvest Strategies for Alfalfa," Chapter 13), and thus it will be given only cursory treatment here.

The change in forage quality due to plant maturity is the result of two major and powerful mechanisms: First, the leaf percentage declines as the plant grows, as a percentage of the plant biomass (Fig. 16.8). This is due primarily to the increase in stem weight that occurs during growth—since the plant produces mostly stems after about 12 to 15 days (Fig. 16.8). Second, the quality of the stem fraction declines precipitously as the plant continues to grow. The ADF and NDF concentrations go up, whereas CP goes down, particularly in the stem component (Fig. 16.8). This is due to what is happening at the cellular level; the young, tender primary cell wall is strengthened by the highly lignified secondary cell wall in the stem. The rate of growth of the stem (weight increase per day), and the rate of lignification of the stem (increase in lignin percentage or NDF/ADF percentage), is also highly influenced by time of year, temperature, and other factors, such as variety.

Staging growth of the plant according to vegetative and reproductive development is an important way to identify high-quality alfalfa. Stages include vegetative, early bud, late bud, early flower, late flower, and seed production (see further details in Chapter 3 "Alfalfa Growth and Development"). The profound effect of cutting schedule and maturity on quality and yield can be seen in Table 16.4. Plant height is also closely related to forage quality. Measuring sticks, such as the UC Intermountain Alfalfa Quality Stick (see http://alfalfa.ucdavis.edu), have been developed to help predict quality from height, but these have not proven to be robust across Mediterranean and arid environments.

Leaf Percentage

The leaf percentage of hay is a major determinant of quality. Leaves may have two to three times the CP content of stems and sometimes half the fiber concentration. In some forages, leaves consist of two-thirds of the feeding value, although they may be less than 50 percent of the DM. The decline in forage quality is mainly due to stems, which decline about 0.5 percentage points in digestibility (IVDDM) per day, and increase dramatically in NDF and ADF, whereas leaves decline only very slightly over time (Table 16.4).

Although plant maturity has a dramatic effect, there are also many other factors that influence leaf percentage. These include insect and disease damage, variety, irrigation, harvest and curing effects, as well as environment. Thus, any agronomic practice that impacts leaf–stem ratio or plant maturity at harvest will affect forage quality.

Yield–Quality–Persistence Tradeoff

Although forage quality is dramatically improved by short cutting schedules (e.g., 21-day intervals), yield is also dramatically

Factors and Principles that Influence Alfalfa Quality

Primary Mechanisms

- Plant maturity at harvest
- Leaf percentage
- Mixture with weeds
- Environmental effects

Agronomic Factors

- Cutting schedules
- Rain damage
- Time of day for harvest
- Harvesting effects
- Variety
- Stand density
- Soil type and fertility
- Irrigation
- Pest interactions

reduced, as is stand life, allowing for increases in weed infestation (Table 16.4—note that the forage quality data in this table does not reflect the weed component of the mix). The tradeoff between yield, quality, weeds, and stand life is a major and complex issue for forage producers and is of tremendous economic importance. The optimum profitability point as determined by cutting schedule is rarely the point where maximum quality is obtained, nor at the point

TABLE 16.4

Effect of maturity at harvest and harvest interval on alfalfa yield, quality, leaf percentage, weeds, and stand life

Maturity at Harvest	Harvest Interval (days)	Yield (T/acre)	ADF	CP	Leaf	Weeds	Stand Percentage*
					(%)		
Pre-Bud	21	7.5	26.3	29.1	58	48	29
Mid-Bud	25	8.8	29.5	25.2	56	54	38
10% Bloom	29	9.9	32.2	21.3	53	8	45
50% Bloom	33	11.4	32.7	18.0	50	0	56
100% Bloom	37	11.6	35.5	16.9	47	0	50

Source: Marble (1974). Proceedings, 4th California Alfalfa Symposium, Dec. 4–5. UC Cooperative Extension.
*Percentage of alfalfa stand after three harvest years.
ADF = acid detergent fiber; CP = crude protein.

where maximum yield is obtained. See Chapter 13, "Harvest Strategies," for a full discussion of this issue.

Cutting Schedule

Cutting schedule is, overwhelmingly, the most powerful method under a grower's control to manipulate forage quality, since both maturity and leaf percentage are impacted. Growers have generally gravitated toward early- to late-bud harvests to attain high forage quality, but at great expense of yield and persistence (Table 16.4). If yield, stand persistence, and weeds were not important, the earliest cutting dates would typically provide the highest quality forage (Table 16.4), but these dates would rarely provide optimum economic returns. The vigorous cutting schedules commonly practiced to attain high quality may ultimately work against high-quality production since stands may thin and weeds may invade (Table 16.4). Clearly, a more integrated approach balancing yield, quality, persistence, and economics is required.

FIGURE 16.9

Seasonal influences on crude protein (top) and acid detergent fiber (bottom) values. Data average of ten nondormant varieties, 1994–1996, Kearney Ag. Center, Fresno Co., CA.

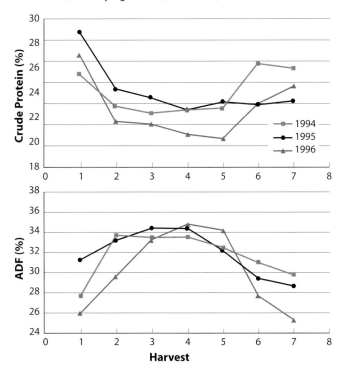

Environment and Temperature

Alfalfa forage quality is generally highest in spring (i.e., first and second cuttings) and late fall, and lowest in summer, but forage quality also changes due to temporary weather patterns. Data collected over 3 years using eight to ten mostly nondormant varieties in Fresno County, California, show large differences over the season and among years (Fig. 16.9). Seasonal and environmental differences were far greater than the differences among varieties. Seasonal and yearly variations have their effect primarily through temperature, but day length and light intensity are also important. The high temperatures of summer increase growth rate (primarily stem growth), hasten plant maturity, and increase lignification of the cell wall. High temperatures also hasten respiration rates, which in turn reduce the quantity of soluble carbohydrates in the stems and leaves. Respiration turns sugars and starches into carbon dioxide and produces energy to produce other compounds in the plant, such as cell wall material or protein. Thus, high rates of respiration have the dual effect of lowering the highly digestible "sugar pools" in the plant and hastening growth and maturity.

Weeds and Species Mixtures

Although weeds can theoretically have neutral, positive, or negative effects on alfalfa forage quality, the overwhelming effect is negative. Most weeds, especially grassy weeds, increase the NDF concentration (fiber) and lower intake, protein, and digestibility. Ironically, many weeds can increase yields of sparse alfalfa stands, since they "fill in" bare areas, but this yield increase rarely compensates for the lower quality of the forage.

The primary characteristics of weeds that influence quality are the species of weed and maturity at harvest. Some weeds, such as pigweed (*Amaranthus retroflexus* L.), lambsquarters (*Chenopodium album* L.), and volunteer cool-season grasses, may provide good forage quality if harvested early but can also contain high nitrate levels, contributing a significant risk to animal health. Some weeds, like common groundsel (*Senecio vulgaris* L.) and fiddleneck (*Amsinckia menziesii* [Lehm.] Nelson & J. F. Macbr.), are toxic to animals and thus substantially lower the feeding value, even if the energy or protein are not affected. Green and yellow foxtail (*Setaria viridis* [L.] Beauv. and *Setaria pumila* [Poiret] Roemer & Schultes), foxtail barley (*Hordeum jubatum* L.), yellow starthistle (*Centaurea solstitialis* L.), and Russian thistle (*Salsola tragus* L.) can all contribute to lowered palatability and lower animal acceptance, sometimes causing pain and injuring the mouths of the animals. Even in cases where weeds do not reduce the chemically analyzed feeding value, they may reduce the marketability of the hay due to the perception of the buyer. In practice, inability to control weeds is one of the most common causes of low forage quality of alfalfa.

Harvest Effects

The process of drying, raking, handling, and baling hay has long been known to affect forage quality. Alfalfa leaves dry much faster than stems. Since growers must wait until stem moisture is sufficiently low for baling, hay is often harvested at a point where leaves are too dry for handling. Leaf shatter is a significant hazard in western states and can reduce forage quality by reducing leaf–stem ratio. Any method, be it mechanical or chemical conditioning, wider swath width, or skillful raking that speeds the drying process of stems, may improve forage quality.

The greatest risk for leaf shatter is during raking process and baling, although any field operation may increase leaf shatter, depending on conditions. Field operations (such as intensive conditioning or wide windrows) that hasten drying of stems help preserve forage quality. Some hay preservatives may enable growers to bale under more moist conditions, thereby conserving leaf material. However, they are generally not believed to be cost-effective under most California conditions. Where extremely dry baling conditions prevail, re-wetting windrows to soften leaves just before baling can be beneficial. Dew can provide much-needed softness and leaf retention, and therefore many growers bale at night or in early morning during summer months to maximize leaf retention. Applying good harvesting skills to maintain forage quality remains a major challenge to growers.

Switching to greenchop or haylage can improve leaf retention, approaching 100 percent, since the forage is wilted, not dried, before handling. A major advantage of haylage is the ability to get the crop off the field rapidly in the spring when rains threaten, and in some cases, an additional harvest is possible. However, production of haylage may entail DM and quality losses during ensiling that may be equal to, or greater than, those losses resulting from baling. Losses of quality are least with greenchop, but dry matter intake can be lowered due to high moisture content of fresh forage.

> *Switching to greenchop or haylage can improve leaf retention, approaching 100 percent, since the forage is wilted, not dried, before handling.*

Conditioning and Particle Size or Maceration Effects

Traditional conditioners, if well adjusted, can have a significant effect on quality since they hasten stem drying. This allows growers to more closely match the drying rate of leaves and stems and to retain leaf material. Conditioning also slows respiration of carbohydrates, reducing quality loss.

Maceration, which is a "shredding" or very intensive conditioning, may have dramatic effects on forage quality. Maceration ruptures the forage cells, rather than just crushing or conditioning the stems. In experimental studies, drying rates are reduced to as little as a day, and a "mat" is produced that can then be picked up and baled, cubed, or ensiled. Maceration changes microparticle size, making cells more available for rumen fermentation. The immediate availability of the soluble fraction of forage, as well as the rate of fermentation of the NDF fraction, have been shown to be dramatically affected by maceration in studies at the USDA Dairy Forage Research Center in Madison, Wisconsin, and at the University of California at Davis (UC Davis). If commercialized, this technology may have a major effect on forage production and quality. See

Orloff et al. 1997, (www.alfalfa.ucdavis.edu) for details.

Note: if blister beetles are present, hay should not be conditioned or crushed to lessen the chances of toxicity in the hay (see "Managing Insects in Alfalfa," Chapter 9).

Time of Day

Observations from the 1940s have shown changes in soluble carbohydrate levels in alfalfa due to time of day. More recent data from Idaho, California, Utah, and other states have pointed to the advantage of harvesting alfalfa in the late afternoon, which takes advantage of the temporary accumulation of soluble carbohydrates associated with photosynthesis during the day. Accumulation of sugars (and other soluble components) in the cells may lower the apparent fiber and the crude protein concentration due simply to the greater quantity of accumulated cell solubles. As the alfalfa plant rapidly photosynthesizes in the late morning, sugars and starches may accumulate in plant tissue. At night, these compounds are respired and utilized by the plant, increasing the fiber concentration.

> *Data from Idaho, California, Utah, and other states have pointed to the advantage of harvesting alfalfa in the late afternoon.*

If hay is cut in the afternoon, and respiration in windrows is minimal, then the higher concentration of soluble carbohydrates may contribute up to 1 to 1.5 percent to the energy (ME, DE, or TDN) of the forage. There is evidence that animals prefer afternoon-harvested hay in either grazed forage or hay. The advantages of afternoon harvest would likely be greatest under cool, bright-sunshine conditions, and under conditions where the forage is highly conditioned to increase drying rates and minimize respiration in the windrow after harvest. Afternoon harvests are not necessarily appropriate in circumstances where rain damage is the more important concern, and every hour of drying time is important.

Rain Damage During Harvest

Rain reduces the level of available carbohydrates or available energy by leaching soluble components from the plant. It also decreases forage quality by increasing leaf shatter. Since soluble components are typically 100 percent digestible, leaching decreases the energy value significantly, as well as protein content and dry matter. The extent of leaching is influence by stage of maturity, forage moisture at the time of the rain, amount and intensity of rain, and condition of the hay during the rain event. Rain can increase dry matter losses caused by leaching and leaf shatter from 10 to over 50 percent, depending on the amount of rainfall.

Variety

Research from a number of locations has shown differences in quality between some, but not all, varieties under the same cutting schedule. Varieties differ primarily due to changes in leaf percentage, or because of slower growth rates, which are often a function of fall dormancy, or due to more subtle changes in cell wall structure, such as lower lignin or higher rates of cell wall degradation in the rumen. Multifoliolate varieties (varieties that produce more than three leaflets per leaf) can, in some cases, result in higher quality forage, but this is not always so. The key issue is leaf percentage and stem quality, not number of leaves. Stem quality and leaf percentage may be equal or greater with some trifoliolate leaf type varieties compared to so-called multi-leaf or multifoliolate varieties. Some trifoliolate varieties have also been developed to have a superior forage quality.

Fall dormancy has a powerful effect on quality of varieties in a Mediterranean environment. In a three-year study at UC Davis, nondormant varieties were significantly lower in quality than dormant varieties (Fig. 16.10). There was an approximately 0.6 percent increase in either ADF or NDF or a 0.6 percent decrease in CP per unit fall dormancy (FD) from FD rating 3 through 9 (the higher the number, the more nondormant the variety). Growers have found that planting of more dormant cultivars has become an important strategy for improving quality. However, the growth rates of more dormant varieties may be significantly below those of other adapted varieties in a region. Under most circumstances, growers must be prepared to accept lower yields with these varieties (see "Choosing an Alfalfa Variety," Chapter 5), particularly under longer-seasoned, warmer conditions (e.g., Southern California). Yield is still the predominant economic factor for alfalfa growers, but under some economic conditions, such as low price years, growers have been willing to sacrifice some yield for higher forage quality.

Stand Density

Leaf percentage, CP, ADF, and lignin are not largely affected by stand density per se. Evidence from studies in Wisconsin, Idaho, Oregon, and Wyoming have shown that leaf percentage, CP, ADF, and lignin were not affected by initial seeding rates. This is because at higher plant densities, the numbers of stems per crown is greatly reduced; thus the number of stems per unit area does not differ significantly between very high and moderately low densities. However, stem thickness may be slightly greater under low densities. Counteracting this effect, however, is the possibility that light penetration into the lower sections of the alfalfa canopy may improve leaf retention compared with thick stands.

A more important factor is the effect of stand density on weeds. When stand densities fall below a certain number (between four and six plants per square foot [0.929 m^2], depending on the age of the stand), open spaces become available for the growth of weeds. The weeds, in turn, can have a substantial impact upon forage quality. This is likely the most important consideration of alfalfa stand density in relationship to forage quality. Maintaining a high stand density is desirable for high yields, weed management, and high quality.

FIGURE 16.10

Effect of fall dormancy ratings on forage quality (ADF, NDF, and CP) of 18 varieties grown at Davis, California. Data points represent an average of 3 years, three cutting schedules, all harvests, about seven harvests/year (2002–2004). Lower fall dormancy of alfalfa varieties reduces ADF and NDF, and increases protein on the average, but this should be evaluated against the generally inferior yields of these varieties under Mediterranean and desert conditions.

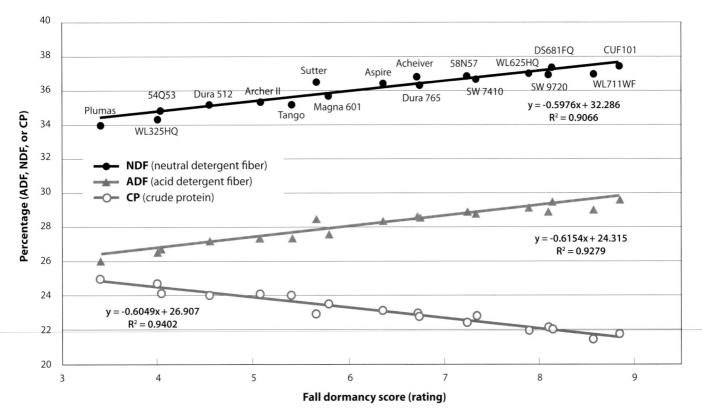

Soil Type

It has long been known that alfalfa produced on certain soils, primarily heavy clay or salty soils, produces higher quality alfalfa than that produced on sandy or loamy soils. This has been attributed to greater plant stress on those soil types, and slower growth rates, perhaps due to lack of oxygen in the root zone or salt effects. Because stress often reduces growth rates, this primarily reduces stem growth, not leaf growth. The stress seems to produce a shorter, finer-stemmed, leafier alfalfa than alfalfa harvested at the same harvest interval on sandy or loamy soil. It should be noted, however, that climatic influence might be a more important factor than soil type in comparing regions.

Fertilizers

As a rule, fertilizers are likely to have either no effect, or decrease the quality of alfalfa.

> *As a rule, fertilizers are likely to have either no effect, or decrease the quality of alfalfa.*

Most fertilizers improve yields of alfalfa when the elements contained in the fertilizer are in short supply in the soil (see "Alfalfa Fertilization Strategies," Chapter 6). Thus, if P, K, S, or micronutrients are low in soil or tissue tests, yields of alfalfa will improve with application of those fertilizers. In most cases, however, the improvement in yield that results from application of fertilizers will result in more rapid growth rates, which is more likely to decrease, not increase, forage quality as a result of increased stem growth and more rapid lignfication of the stem.

Research in California, Wisconsin, and Oregon has clearly shown that there is either no difference, or a decline in alfalfa quality, when K fertilizers were used on K-deficient sites. These results are not surprising, considering the importance of K in improving alfalfa growth and yield. Similar results have been seen with P and S. These studies indicate the importance of fertilizing for maximum yield. Additionally, a well-fertilized crop will be better able to sustain the short cutting schedules necessary for producing high-quality forage.

However, fertilizers generally do not improve quality.

Another important factor is the potential negative effect of plant nutrients on quality. It's important not to over-apply fertilizers. Dairy nutritionists emphasize the importance of minimizing the amount of K contained in hay fed to close-up cows (pregnant cows nearing birth), to prevent problems with calcium nutrition and milk fever. With excess K in the soil, "luxury consumption" occurs. Alfalfa is well known for luxury consumption of K, where the K concentration of the forage increases without an increase in yield. This is clearly not desirable, either from the grower's point of view (waste of fertilizer with no return), or from the nutritionist's point of view, due to the danger of excess K in the forage. This is a serious problem near dairies, where excess soil K cannot be controlled. This problem has been increasingly recognized, and a niche market for low-K hay has emerged—some dairies will pay $5 to $10 more per ton (907 kg) for such "low-potassium" hay.

Some growers feel that nitrogen (N) fertilizers may improve the quality of alfalfa. However, there is little evidence to support this practice for either yield or quality. Nitrogen fertilizers are unlikely to improve ME, NE, or TDN, or reduce fiber. There are some instances of N fertilizers causing slight improvements in CP concentration, but an equal or greater number of field trials show no effect of N fertilizers on CP. Nitrogen fertilizers are likely to contribute to the nonprotein N fraction in the plant, which is mostly metabolized and excreted by the animal. This has a metabolic cost and may contribute to environmental problems caused by the increased N in the animal waste. Additionally, N fertilizers encourage grassy weeds more than alfalfa, which may lower quality. Although applications of N fertilizers may make the plants look greener, it is not recommended to apply N fertilizers to alfalfa in attempts to improve forage quality or yield.

Irrigation Management

Irrigation management is probably the most important yield-limiting factor in western states. Over-applications of water, too little water, or lack of drainage are major problems with alfalfa production. However, water stress often *improves* forage quality, since the leaf–stem ratio can be improved due to lack of growth of the stem component. However, yields are linearly related to water availability and are dramatically reduced by water stress. The loss in alfalfa yield is too great to justify allowing water stress as a means of improving quality.

Insects and Diseases

Insect and disease pests can have a positive or a negative effect on forage quality, but the effect is typically negative since their feeding habits include consuming leaves, thereby decreasing the leaf percentage. Sucking insects, such as aphids, may reduce soluble carbohydrates, therefore reducing forage quality. Insects that intensively suck plant sap, such as the silverleaf whitefly (*Bemisia argentifolii* Bellows & Perring) in the Imperial Valley and cowpea aphid (*Aphis craccivora* Koch) in the Central Valley, cause widespread stickiness on the plant surface; this in turn encourages fungi (sooty molds) to develop, which lowers palatability and consumer acceptance. Generally, insects must be controlled to maintain high-quality alfalfa and prevent leaf loss (see "Managing Insects in Alfalfa," Chapter 9).

Summary

Attaining high-quality alfalfa forage is a critical aspect of profitability for alfalfa and animal productivity. Attributes of quality include digestible energy, voluntary intake, protein, ruminally effective fiber, and minerals. Forage quality has many attributes and should be evaluated through both laboratory measurements and subjective observations (odor, mold, weed content, etc.).

Measurements of plant cell wall (NDF) and its degradability (NDFD), crude protein (CP), and ash may be the most useful measurements for routine analysis, with additional analyses required for specific purposes. Interpreting the laboratory analyses themselves, as well as calculated values such as ME, DE, NE_l, TDN, and RFQ, is important for understanding laboratory tests. Cutting schedules, weed management, and harvest management are the most powerful methods for improving quality under the control of growers, but seasonal effects (spring, summer, fall) can be major determinants of forage quality. Variety, time of day of harvest, insect management, and water stress can influence quality but are usually less important than cutting schedules, harvest management, time of year, or climate. Fertilizers generally do not improve quality, but quality can differ somewhat by soil type.

Alfalfa growers who invest the time in understanding quality factors for animal performance benefit by their improved ability to successfully market their hay.

Additional Reading

Ball, D., M. Collins, G. Lacefield, N. Martin, D. Mertens, K. Olson, D. Putnam, D. Undersander, and M. Wolf. 2001. Understanding forage quality. American Farm Bureau Federation, Park Ridge, IL. Pub. 1-01. http://alfalfa.ucdavis.edu.

Bath, D.L., and V.L. Marble. 1989. Testing alfalfa for its feeding value. University of California Cooperative Extension, Oakland, CA. Leaflet 21457. WREP 109. http://alfalfa.ucdavis.edu.

Marten, G.C., D.R. Buxton, and R.F. Barnes. 1988. Feeding value (forage quality). In: Alfalfa and Alfalfa Improvement. American Society of Agronomy, Madison, WI. Monograph No. 29. http://alfalfa.ucdavis.edu.

Orloff, S., D. Putnam, and T. Kraus. 1997. Maceration: What is its potential for California growers? In: 27th California Alfalfa Symposium, December 10-11, Visalia, CA. Department of Agronomy and Range Science Extension, University of California, Davis, CA.

Puschner, B., A. Peters, and L. Woods. 2006. Toxic weeds and their impact on animals. In: 2006 Western Alfalfa Symposium, December, 11–13. Reno, NV. University of California Cooperative Extension. http://alfalfa.ucdavis.edu

Putnam, D.H., and D. Undersander. 2006. The future of forage testing for hay markets. In: Proceedings, 2006 Western Alfalfa Symposium, December, 11–13. Reno, NV. University of California Cooperative Extension. http://alfalfa.ucdavis.edu.

17

Alfalfa Utilization by Livestock

Gerald E. Higginbotham
Farm Advisor, University of California Cooperative Extension, Fresno, CA

Carolyn L. Stull
Extension Specialist, University of California School of Veterinary Medicine, Davis

Nyles G. Peterson
Farm Advisor, University of California Cooperative Extension, Riverside, CA

Anne V. Rodiek
Professor, California State University, Fresno

Barbara A. Reed
Farm Advisor, University of California Cooperative Extension, Orland, CA

Juan N. Guerrero
Farm Advisor, University of California Cooperative Extension, El Centro, CA

Alfalfa may be fed safely to a wide range of livestock, primarily ruminants (cows, sheep, and goats), but also non-ruminants (principally horses). Alfalfa is utilized as hay, silage, greenchop, as pelleted or cubed products, or grazed. In this chapter we provide an overview of the utilization patterns by the major classes of livestock and alfalfa's role for these animals. Specific feeding recommendations can be obtained from other University of California resources, and further information on forage quality is including in Chapter 16, "Forage Quality."

The major value of feeding alfalfa to livestock is its high nutritive value, especially its high-digestibility energy and protein content compared to other common forage crops. Dietary carbohydrates (both rapidly available and slowly available) provide energy, and are quantitatively the most important nutrient in the diet of livestock. Protein in the diet of livestock is necessary for growth, maintenance, lactation, and reproduction. Forage legumes are also rich in mineral content compared to grasses, and are good sources of calcium, phosphorus, and magnesium, which are critical for the formation and maintenance of the skeleton and teeth, for muscle contraction, and are a major component in milk.

Livestock Digestive Systems

The digestive systems of various types of livestock differ significantly. Humans, swine, horses, and other animals have a simple, single compartment or "true" stomach and are referred to as monogastric animals. In comparison, cattle (dairy and beef), sheep, and goats have a complex four-compartment stomach and are known as ruminants.

Ruminants

The digestive system of the ruminant is shown in Figure 17.1. The ruminant has four compartments of the digestive system: the rumen, reticulum, omasum, and abomasum. Compared to non-ruminants, ruminants have the ability to digest fiber and to utilize forage crops. Although the ruminants themselves do not digest fiber, the microbes in the rumen ferment the cellulose, hemicellulose, and other portions of the feed to high-energy products absorbed by the cow as nutrients. The very large capacity of the rumen allows extensive digestion of the fiber in forages over hours or days.

Initially, feed enters the large rumen (80% capacity of the four compartments) and mixes with the contents of the reticulum, since it is separated by an incomplete partition. The partially digested feed passes from the rumen and reticulum to the omasum for further absorption of nutrients and water. The digesta then moves into the abomasum, or true stomach, for continued degradation of and absorption of nutrients, especially protein, by the animal's own enzymes. The continued movement of digesta from the abomasum, through the small and large intestine and into the rectum, and the digestion that takes place in these compartments is similar to that of monogastric animals. The small intestine is the location where further breakdown of digesta by enzymes and absorption of nutrients occurs, which is aided by the secretion of enzymes, pancreatic juice, and bile. The large intestine has the capacity for limited fermentation and further digests and absorbs water, minerals, and vitamins. Excreted feces are the product of undigested feed products, microbial cells, and other waste products.

Non-ruminants

The digestive system of the non-ruminant is shown in Figure 17.2. Horses are the primary monogastric animals that utilize alfalfa.

Monogastrics (non-ruminants) have a digestive system vastly different from ruminants. Horses have diets composed largely of roughages. The stomach is relatively small, holding only 2–4 gallons (8–15 L), with minimal digestion occurring in the stomach. Liquid and dry matter ingesta pass through the stomach quickly, usually exiting within 15 minutes, and the stomach is empty 12 hours after ingestion. Thus, it is usually recommended that the horse be fed two or more times per day, rather than one large meal.

The small intestine of the horse contains the enzymes to digest non-fiber carbohydrates (sugars, starch)

FIGURE 17.1

The digestive system of the ruminant. *Adapted from:* J.G. Linn, M.F. Hutjens, R. Shaver, D.E. Otterby, W.T. Howard, and L.H. Kilmer, *Feeding the Dairy Herd.* University of Minnesota Extension. 2002.

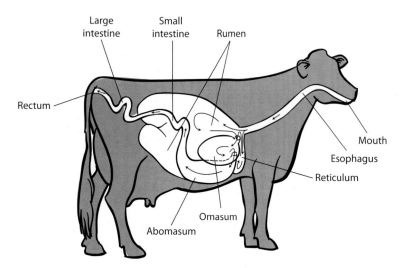

and protein, and is the site of absorption for most minerals and vitamins. The small intestine is 50–70 feet (15–21 m) long, and has the capacity to hold 10–12 gallons (38–45 L) of ingesta. Since the horse does not have a gall bladder, lipid salts are constantly secreted into the small intestine to promote emulsification of lipids. At the junction of the small and large intestine is the caecum. The relatively large caecum (7–8 gallons [26–30 L]) of the horse contains the necessary bacterial population for fiber digestion, along with some digestion of carbohydrates and bacterial protein. The active bacterial and protozoal populations in the equine caecum and bovine rumen are generally similar. The colon provides the greatest capacity of the gastrointestinal tract, with 40–50 percent of the digesta, and the slowest rate of passage, usually occurring over a period of 36–72 hours. The dry matter (DM) content of the digesta increases as it travels from the caecum to the rectum. Approximately 95 percent of the feed passes through the entire digestive tract in 65–75 hours after ingestion.

Alfalfa Utilization by Dairy Cattle

By far the most important hay crop fed to dairy cattle in the United States is alfalfa (Fig. 17.3). Alfalfa combines the virtues of high dry matter yield, high protein and mineral content, and excellent palatability. Dairy cattle nutritionists favor alfalfa hay for its high energy content, its ability to digest rapidly in the rumen, and its high protein level, which supports the protein needs of the dairy cow. Dairy utilization may account for 75–80 percent of the utilization of alfalfa in the major dairy states, such as California, Wisconsin, New York, Idaho, and New Mexico.

Nutrient Requirements

The nutrient requirements of dairy animals depend on rate of growth, body size, reproductive status, and level of milk production. Certain qualities of alfalfa forage are best suited for the different classes of dairy animals. The most efficient use of alfalfa is to be included at the appropriate amounts in balanced rations to meet animal nutritional requirements. A summary of the minimum quality of alfalfa needed

FIGURE 17.2

The digestive system of the non-ruminant (horse). *Adapted from: M.E. Ensminger and C.G. Olentine, Feeds & Nutrition, 1st Edition. 2002.*

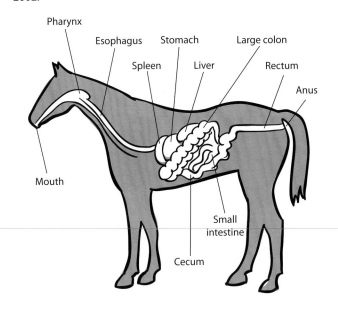

FIGURE 17.3

Total mixed rations, which include alfalfa hay, are typically fed to dairy cows.

by various classes of dairy cows is shown in Table 17.1.

Calves from 2 weeks to 3 months old benefit from high-quality forage. Calves can begin to consume small quantities of alfalfa within 2 weeks of birth. Alfalfa consumption will increase until it comprises a significant amount of the calves' diet at over 8 weeks of age. Calves 8 to 12 weeks old do not have a fully developed rumen; because of this limited rumen capacity, fiber should be limited. However, alfalfa is a particularly good source of protein, minerals, and carbohydrates, as well as sugars and easily fermented fiber. It is recommended that alfalfa provided to these animals be greater than 18 percent crude protein and less than 42 percent neutral detergent fiber (NDF). Alfalfa for dairy calves can be preserved either as hay or low-moisture silage (less than 55% moisture). High-moisture silage should be avoided because the high moisture content may limit intake and protein quality.

Heifers 3–12 months old have sufficient rumen function and capacity to utilize fiber to meet some of their requirements. Protein requirements decline and alfalfa higher in NDF and lower in protein content can be utilized, compared with younger animals. Feeding alfalfa that contains 16–18 percent crude protein and 41–46 percent NDF (33–38% acid detergent fiber [ADF]) will provide optimal growth with minimum concentrate supplementation. Heifers 12–18 months old have larger digestive tract capacities than younger heifers and can utilize more forage in their diet. Heifers at 500–1,000 pounds (227–454 kg) should be able to meet all of their nutritional needs from good-quality alfalfa containing 14–16 percent crude protein and 45–48 percent NDF. Heifers 18–24 months of age and dry cows are able to utilize alfalfa of lower quality than other classes of dairy animals. Forage that is 12–14 percent crude protein and 48–52 percent NDF is adequate. Feeding large quantities of very-high-quality alfalfa near the end of gestation may lead to milk fever in adult cows at calving because of the high potassium content. Calcium, phosphorus, magnesium, and potassium levels in dry cow diets can affect animal health post-calving. The alfalfa and other feeds should be analyzed so that the entire diet stays within mineral feeding recommendations.

Lactating cows during the first 100 days after calving have rapidly increasing nutrient requirements. The high protein and mineral content combined with low fiber concentrations make alfalfa ideal forage for early lactation cows. Alfalfa containing 19–24 percent crude protein and 38–42 percent NDF is well suited for these animals. Alfalfa lower in crude protein (CP) and higher in NDF will require the feeding of additional amounts of concentrates or high-quality forages to achieve a given level of milk production. Alfalfa with lower NDF concentrations may not provide enough fiber to maintain proper rumen function. Lactating cows during the last 200 days of lactation have reduced energy and protein demands as milk production declines. Therefore, lower quality forage can be fed at that time than during the first 100 days of lac-

TABLE 17.1

Minimum quality of alfalfa required for various classes of dairy cows

Class of dairy animal	Nutrient Parameter (DM basis)		
	TDN	NDF	CP
		%	
Calf	59.0[1]	42.0	20.0
Heifer	59.0	42.0	20.0
Bull	55.0	50.0	17.0
Dry Cow	55.0	50.0	17.0
Milking Cow			
Transition: 0–21 days in milk	62.0	36.0	23.0
90 lb (41 kg) milk/day	62.0	36.0	23.0
75 lb (34 kg) milk/day	59.0	42.0	20.0
50 lb (23 kg) milk/day	59.0	42.0	20.0

Source: National Research Council. Nutrient Requirements of Dairy Cattle, 7th rev. ed. 2001. National Academy Press, Washington, DC.

[1]TDN as expressed on a 100% DM basis, calculated from ADF or NDF. TDN is often expressed on a 90% DM basis by multiplying this number by 0.9.

Abbreviations: ADF = acid detergent fiber

CP = crude protein

DM = dry matter

NDF = neutral detergent fiber

TDN = total digestible nutrients

tation. As a general guideline, lactating dairy cows will typically consume 14–16 pounds of alfalfa hay per day. When feeding greenchop, 20–25 pounds is usually fed to lactating cows per day. Haylage is usually fed at a rate of 15–25 pounds per day. All of these amounts are on an as-fed basis.

Alfalfa for Beef Cattle

Although dairy production is the most important market for western-grown alfalfa, beef producers fulfill some component of their forage needs from alfalfa, depending upon price and availability. The grazing of alfalfa by beef cattle in California is not a common occurrence, and most of the utilization of alfalfa hay is the consumption of low- or medium-quality alfalfa hay.

Beef Grazing

Stocker steers, from 400–600 pounds (181–272 kg) may experience from 1.75–2 pounds (0.8–0.9 kg) per day of live weight gain, and even as high as 3 pounds per day (1.4 kg/d) on alfalfa pasture. Rotational grazing is the key to successfully grazing alfalfa by beef cattle (Fig. 17.4). The need for mineral supplementation for livestock will be necessary, depending on local soil conditions, particularly trace elements. It is recommended that forage samples be tested for mineral (macro and micro) levels. Contact you local livestock advisor regarding specific mineral supplementation recommendations for your local area. Ionophores, which improve animal nutrient utilization, are often incorporated into the salt mixtures of grazing cattle and can reduce the incidence of bloat and increase animal health.

A complete discussion of grazing for dairy or beef purposes can be found in Chapter 18 of this series, "Alfalfa Grazing Management."

Not all alfalfa fields are appropriate for rotational grazing. Rectangular, square, or round shaped fields are conducive to rotational grazing because the electric fence required for rotational grazing is easily adapted to these shaped fields. On square or rectangular shaped fields, temporary electric fences often coincide with irrigation borders. On fields that are irrigated with a center pivot, it is convenient to place the drinker (water supply) at the center and separate the grazing subsections in a bicycle spoke fashion.

Great care must be taken not to graze wet fields. Soil compaction caused by cattle will diminish future hay yields. Cattle should be removed from alfalfa fields during rainfall events. After irrigation, cattle should not be moved onto the field as long as the field is wet. To reduce soil compaction after a rainfall or irrigation event, the top 1 inch (2.5 cm) of soil (for loams or heavier soils) should be dry before moving cattle onto the field. Grazing cattle tend to naturally congregate around water. If possible, every cattle move onto new field subsections should be accompanied by a corresponding move of the cattle's water supply, to prevent soil compaction around the drinker.

Bloat is a risk that must be carefully considered by practitioners when grazing alfalfa. A thorough discussion of bloat can be found in Chapter 18, "Alfalfa Grazing Management."

FIGURE 17.4

Rotational grazing enables large numbers of animals to graze on small areas for a short period of time.

Alfalfa Hay for Beef Animals

Under most situations, beef cattle will not compete with dairy cattle for Supreme, Premium, or even Good alfalfa hay. Good-quality grass hays typically provide sufficient energy and protein sources for overwintering beef cows, although grass hay standards are not generally fully defined. It is a common practice to incorporate low-quality, grassy summer hay into feedlot diets in Southern California. Because of the hot summer growing conditions in Southern California deserts, summer hay is often harvested at the full-bloom stage of growth and is low in crude protein and high in fiber. Desert, summer alfalfa hays, low in quality and price, are commonly used in beef feedlot diets. These low-quality alfalfa hays are used in feedlot diets for their fiber contribution to the diet, and constitute only 10–20 percent of the diet.

> *Under most situations, beef cattle will not compete with dairy cattle for Supreme, Premium, or even Good quality alfalfa hay.*

Under certain circumstances, beef cattle grazing of alfalfa might be advantageous. The grazing of alfalfa by beef cattle requires specific management techniques to protect the alfalfa stand. The use of alfalfa hay for beef cattle is not common in California; beef cattle cannot compete with dairy cattle for premium alfalfa hays. Feedlot cattle or beef cows are good ways to market poor-quality or year-old alfalfa hay.

Alfalfa Utilization by Sheep

The United States had sheep populations exceeding 11 million in 1990; today 6.7 million sheep remain in the United States—Texas and California having the largest U.S. sheep populations (almost one-half the total). Per capita consumption of beef, although it has declined in the recent past, is still 65 pounds (29.5 kg,) in the United States, while lamb consumption is 1 pound (0.45 kg). Despite a reduced sheep population, sheep remain significant users of forage resources in the western United States.

Sheep Grazing

Although cattle and sheep may have similar digestive systems, it is incorrect to think of sheep as merely small cattle. Sheep have different nutritional requirements and different grazing characteristics than cattle. Cattle graze coarser and taller forage species because they graze to fill their much larger rumens, whereas sheep focus on more nutritious forbs, grass regrowth, and on browse.

Although there are many factors that affect forage consumption, in general grass consumption for sheep, cattle, and goats is 50, 70, and 30 percent; forb consumption is 30, 15, and 10 percent; and browse consumption is 20, 15, and 60 percent, respectively. Sheep have cleft upper lips, permitting them to graze much closer to the soil surface than cattle, which have to grab forage with their tongues, lower teeth, and upper dental pad. Sheep are selective grazers, not necessarily consuming plants in the same proportion as available plants. For example, in a field of weedy seedling alfalfa, we have recorded that grazing lambs first consumed broadleaf weeds and winter annual grasses before they consumed the seedling alfalfa. On seedling alfalfa in the irrigated Sonoran Desert, we have documented that broadleaf weeds often had higher dietary CP levels and lower NDF levels did than the alfalfa forage.

Due to the protein structure of wool and the higher propensity for multiple births, sheep have a higher crude protein requirement than cattle. Mature ewes require about 9.5 percent dietary CP, lactating ewes require about

15 percent dietary CP, and feeder lambs require 14.5 percent dietary CP. Excluding immature grasses, grasses rarely have these levels of crude protein, partially explaining the reason why sheep have such a high preference for forbs and browse.

Cattle and sheep complement each other in grazing situations since they have only moderate dietary overlaps. Much research has been published regarding the grazing of these two species, either alone or grazing together. When sheep graze with cattle, sheep have about 30 percent higher weight gains than with sheep-only grazing. At moderate stocking rates, total pounds of live weight gain per acre was greater when sheep and cattle grazed together than when each species grazed alone. Because of the dietary differences of cattle and sheep, when both species graze together the carrying capacity of a particular paddock may be increased by 10–20 percent than by single-species grazing. Cattle prefer flat, mesic sites, whereas sheep can graze on steeper or drier rangelands. On hilly or mountainous rangelands, cattle with relatively large hooves often create visible trails on flatter ground, whereas sheep with smaller hooves may graze the steeper slopes.

Sheep in Sustainable Agriculture

In many situations, sheep grazing is used to "clean up" pastures of possibly toxic plants that cattle cannot use. In the irrigated Sonoran Desert of southeastern California and southwestern Arizona, we compared the use of grazing lambs with herbicides for weed control in seedling alfalfa and concluded that grazing lambs were just as effective, or in some cases more effective, than herbicides for weed control in seedling alfalfa (Fig. 17.5).

Grazing lambs may also be used as a biological insect control measure. In one study, grazing lambs were more efficient than insecticides for control of Egyptian alfalfa weevil (*Hypera brunneipennis* Boh.) in established winter alfalfa. Plots grazed during the winter grazing season produced more hay at the first spring alfalfa harvest than insecticide-treated plots.

Sheep Grazing Methods

Every winter (December through March), from 300,000 to 400,000 lambs graze nondormant alfalfa in the irrigated Sonoran Desert along the lower Colorado River. During this period, there is sufficient high-quality forage production, yet conditions are not conducive to hay making. Lamb gains on winter-grown alfalfa are from 10–12 pounds (4.5–5.4 kg) per month. The most common grazing method is to confine about 1,600 lambs on 40-acre (16.2-ha) fields for about 10–12 days or until the alfalfa resource is totally exhausted. Grazing lambs gain equally well on weedy fields as on weed-free alfalfa. Portable water troughs should be placed at the perimeters of alfalfa fields and should be moved at least every 5 days to avoid excessive hoof traffic in any one area of the field. In California, copper (Cu) and selenium (Se) supplementation may be necessary for grazing sheep, depending on local soil deficiencies (<7 ppm of dietary DM for Cu and <0.1 ppm of dietary DM for Se).

FIGURE 17.5

Sheep grazing has been shown to control weeds and insects in alfalfa and result in excellent gains.

Utilization by Goats

Goats differ from other domestic livestock in that they are primarily browsers and will feed on shrubs, trees, and forbs in preference to grazing other forages. As browsers, goats are highly selective in their feeding habits and have agile lips. However, goats are also quite adaptive, and in confinement they will eat diets similar in composition to those of other ruminants, such as cattle and sheep. If goats are offered coarse, stemmy hay, nothing but a pile of stems will be left in the feed bunk when they are finished. The incorporation of good-quality alfalfa into the goat diet is an excellent forage choice and can be quite cost effective.

Goats can consume approximately 3–4 percent of their body weight daily, depending on age, stage of lactation, and other production demands (e.g., pregnancy, lactation). As a general rule, approximately 50 percent or more of the diet should be composed of forages. This is essential for maintaining proper functioning of the rumen and preventing acidosis.

The hay chosen for lactating feeding goats should be Extra Premium Supreme or Premium quality as described in Chapter 16, "Forage Quality and Testing." Extra Premium or Supreme hay contains less than 27 percent ADF or <34 percent NDF (100% DM basis) and is high in crude protein. This hay is completely

FIGURE 17.6

Roughages such as alfalfa hay furnish most of the energy required by goats.

free of grasses and weeds, is soft textured and highly palatable, and is typically harvested in the vegetative to early bud stages of maturity. Premium-quality hay is slightly higher in fiber content than Extra Premium hay, but this hay is still of excellent feeding value. The ADF content ranges from 27–29 percent and NDF from 34–36 percent (100% DM basis). Since some grasses and weeds can be of excellent feeding value, some weeds may be acceptable, provided they are low in fiber and high in crude protein concentration. However, noxious weeds and weeds with anti-nutritional factors or poor palatability should be avoided. Most hays in these categories are prebud, bud, or early-bloom hays.

Ration Formulation for Goats

Goats should be offered a balanced ration that meets the nutrient requirements outlined by the National Research Council's "Nutrient Requirements for Small Ruminants." These nutrients include energy, protein, fiber, vitamins, and minerals. Diets should be formulated to meet the metabolic demands such as growth, pregnancy, fiber production, or lactation.

Kids and Growing Goats

Goat kids should be started on solid foods early, to be ready for weaning at about 8 weeks of age. A grain mix for kids (kid starter) and good-quality hay can be offered free choice when the kid is a few days old. Extra Premium or Premium alfalfa hay or high-quality pasture are the best forage choices for kids, and should meet the requirements described above. Diets should allow for body weight gains from 0.3–0.5 pounds (0.1–0.2 kg) per day, depending upon the breed. Kid starter should contain 16–18 percent crude protein. Cottonseed products should be omitted from kid starter diets. Kids may be weaned as early as 8 weeks of age, when they are consuming approximately 1.5 pounds (0.7 kg) of grain per day. After weaning, high-quality forage feeding should continue as described above, but kids may gradually (4–6 weeks following weaning) switch to a 14 percent protein grain mix (no cottonseed products), similar to the diet of milking does. This feeding program can continue until breeding. Does are considered of breeding size and age when they weigh about 75 pounds (34 kg).

Nonlactating and Growing Yearling Does

Between breeding and kidding, does should be on a high-forage diet. Adequate protein, energy, mineral, and other nutrient levels must be maintained for their age and growth requirements. A few weeks prior to kidding, the does may be gradually introduced to grain feeding. The amount of grain fed depends on the body condition of the doe and the quality of the forage being fed.

Goat Pregnancy and Lactation

Rapid changes in diet during pregnancy and kidding should be avoided. If the doe is fed a total mixed ration, supplementing with long-stem alfalfa hay of premium quality or better will help stimulate feed intake. Digestive disorders can be prevented by limiting concentrates to a maximum of 60–65 percent of the diet. Although most does will lose body condition in early lactation, it is important to minimize large changes in body condition and not allow does to become overly fat or thin. Either condition will predispose them to metabolic and reproductive problems. Feeding should be adjusted throughout lactation to compensate for changes in milk production and body condition.

Dry Does, Fiber Goats, and Bucks

At the end of lactation, does should be changed to an all-forage diet, which will provide the necessary nutrients for maintenance and fetal growth. The resulting reduction in both nutrient quality and quantity will help stop milk production. For adult dairy, meat, and fiber (wool-producing) goats, maintaining body condition and health are the primary goals of a feeding program. Again, diets provided should meet the National Research Council's nutrient requirements for goats, appropriate for

metabolic demands such as growth and fiber or milk production.

If goats are grazing alfalfa, the area should be inspected first to be sure there are no toxic plants that will be a threat to the goats or humans via transmission of toxins in the milk. The alfalfa should be sampled and analyzed to determine its nutritional value. Again, diet supplements may be necessary to meet the goat's minimum nutrient requirements, depending on the quality and quantity of the pasture available.

Urinary Stones

Bucks require a balanced diet similar to that of the nonlactating doe. However, they are at risk of urinary tract obstruction (urolithiasis) under dietary conditions that may promote the formation of urinary tract stones (calculi) or a decreased water intake. The type of stone formed varies by diet and mineral status of a region. A nutritionist should be consulted to recommend a diet balanced in calcium and phosphorous.

Bucks fed entirely alfalfa hay or excessive concentrates (grain) are at higher risk of urolithiasis. Salt intake should be maximized to prevent the formation of urinary calculi. Free-choice, loose salt should be provided at all times; salt intake will be higher when salt is offered loose as opposed to in blocks. Commercial diets may be available that provide urinary acidifiers. A nutritionist should be consulted to select the best diet for bucks in a given region and for different management conditions.

Moldy hay may considerably reduce milk production and growth or weight gains, and may depress resistance to metabolic and infectious diseases.

Bloat, Mold, Insects, Weeds

Bloat, as described in detail in Chapter 18, "Alfalfa Grazing Management," can be a serious problem for ruminants, including goats. Mold can develop in baled alfalfa hay under conditions where alfalfa is baled with higher than recommended moisture levels. Moldy hay may considerably reduce milk production and growth or weight gains, and may depress resistance to metabolic and infectious diseases. The feeding of moldy alfalfa hay to any class of animals should be avoided.

The presence of weeds in alfalfa hay detracts from the quality of the hay, lowers the potential selling price, and may be hazardous to the animal consuming the hay. The predominant poisonous weeds that may be found in alfalfa hay are fiddleneck (*Amsinckia menziesii* Lemm. Nelson & J.F. Macbr.) and common groundsel (*Senecio vulgaris* L.) Because many of these poisonous plants are principally spring plants, most problems with weeds are associated with first cutting.

Weeds in alfalfa hay may also cause off-flavors in milk. The off-flavor from some weeds such as swine cress (*Coronopus didymus*) appears principally in the milk fat, whereas that from others such as bitterweed is associated with the skim milk (non-fat) portion. The

off-flavor in milk from weeds may be more pronounced with young plants such as with cocklebur (*Xanthium*) or with older plants or their seeds such as penny cress (*Noccaea fendleri ssp. californicum*). Flavors from some weeds persist for longer than 12 hours after they are eaten; therefore such weeds must be kept out of the ration. Flavors caused by some can be controlled if the weeds are withheld from the doe 5 hours before milking. These feeding recommendations are impractical for most dairy farm operations, so hay should be obtained with a very small contamination from weeds.

Blister beetles (*Epicauta* sp.) have recently been observed in the High Desert areas of California. Consumption of these beetles or alfalfa hay contaminated with blister beetles can cause death. See Chapter 9, "Managing Insects in Alfalfa," for more details. See also "Blister Beetles" in the following section on horses.

Utilization of Alfalfa by Horses

Tradition has played a large role in the selection of feeds for horses. Timothy hay and oat hay have been the favorite feed of horses for many years, but alfalfa is also widely used. Controversy exists over the use of alfalfa in horse rations (Fig. 17.7). Alfalfa hay may not be the best feed for all horses in all situations, but it contains important nutrients for many classes of horses.

Alfalfa hay is an excellent source of energy, protein, calcium, and some other nutrients for horses. Its concentration of protein and calcium often meets the nutrient needs of horses in high levels of production, such as growth and lactation, but exceeds the nutrient requirements of horses in other life stages. Grass hays are popular for horses because of the lower energy, protein, and calcium concentrations that most closely meet the nutrient requirements of the largest percentage of horses: the idle horse. The incorporation of alfalfa hay into equine diets as the sole roughage or in combination with other grass or cereal hays has been increasing over

FIGURE 17.7

Alfalfa is an excellent source of energy, protein, and calcium for horses and is very palatable, but feeding should be moderated depending upon animal activity.

the last 30 years. The palatability of alfalfa is generally better than most grass hays.

Nutritional Requirements for Horses

Some basic feeding management concepts apply to horses in all stages of production, growth, and work levels. The average horse will eat about 2 percent of its body weight daily. Diets are forage based, with at least 1 percent of the body weight being consumed as forage each day. However, it is desirable that forage make up more than 50 percent of the diet. Thus, a 1,100 pound horse will consume from 11 to 22 pounds of hay per day. Adequate forage intake is important for proper gastrointestinal fill, which is essential in maintaining the proper pH of the digestive tract and the health of the microbes in the large intestine, along with acting as a reservoir of water in the body.

Horses cannot tolerate large amounts of soluble carbohydrates, for example, from grains in their diets. The majority of soluble carbohydrates are digested and absorbed in the small intestine. When horses are fed large, infrequent meals of carbohydrates, some of the soluble carbohydrates may not be absorbed in the small intestine but pass into the large intestine. If significant amounts of soluble carbohydrate reach the large intestine, rapid fermentation by microbes produces excessive lactic acid production, causing a decrease in pH, microbial death, toxin production, and possible endotoxemia, colic, and laminitis. Many of the nutrient requirements of working, lactating, and growing horses may be met by feeding good-quality forage, such as alfalfa, and less supplementation will be necessary.

Ration Formulation for Horses

The National Research Council's "Nutrient Requirements of Horses" provides estimates of nutrient requirements of horses at different physiologic stages (Table 17.2) and also the nutrient content of various feeds commonly fed to horses. Feeding management of horses may be grouped into several categories, including diets for maintenance, pregnancy,

TABLE 17.2

Recommended nutrient intake in total diets for the horses of different production stages or work levels (dry matter [DM] basis)

	Digestible Energy Mcal/lb	Crude Protein %	Calcium %	Phosphorous %
Maintenance	0.90	8.0	0.24	0.17
Pregnancy (9–11 months)	1.00–1.10	10.0–10.6	0.43–0.45	0.32–0.34
Lactation	1.15 to 1.20	11–13.2	0.36–0.52	0.22–0.34
Growing				
Weanling	1.4	14.5	0.56–0.68	0.31–0.38
Yearling	1.3	11.3–12.6	0.34–0.45	0.19–0.25
2-year-old	1.2	10.4–11.3	0.31–0.34	0.17–0.20
Work	1.15–1.30	9.8–11.4	0.30–0.35	0.22–0.25

Source: National Research Council. 1989. Nutrient Requirements of Horses, 5th rev. edn. National Academy Press, Washington, DC.

TABLE 17.3

Nutrient content of alfalfa and grass hays (dry matter [DM] basis)

	Digestible Energy Mcal/lb	Crude Protein %	Calcium %	Phosphorous %
Alfalfa				
Early bloom	1.05	19.3	1.41	0.21
Mid bloom	1.03	18.7	1.37	0.24
Full bloom	0.98	17.0	1.19	0.24
Grass Hay				
Timothy	0.82–0.94	7.8–10.8	0.38–0.51	0.15–0.29
Oat hay	0.87	9.5	0.32	0.25
Orchardgrass	0.87–0.99	8.4–12.8	0.26–0.27	0.30–0.34

Source: National Research Council. 1989. Nutrient Requirements of Horses, 5th rev. edn. National Academy Press, Washington, DC.

lactation, growth, and work. Only alfalfa that is free of dust, weeds, toxins, and mold should be fed to horses. The protein content in quality alfalfa hay available to horse owners may range from 15 to over 20 percent crude protein, but acceptable-quality alfalfa for horses contains approximately 17 to 19 percent crude protein and 0.95–1.1 Mcal/lb (2.1–2.4 Mcal/kg) of digestible energy (Table 17.3). These feeds normally consist of weed-free alfalfa hay or alfalfa–grass mixtures in the Fair-to-Good categories in the California marketplace. Exceeding the recommended crude protein level for horses of different physiologic states may not be beneficial to their dietary needs. Choice of alfalfa protein and energy characteristics depends highly upon the stage of growth of the animal.

Maintenance of Horses

A mature idle horse requires a maintenance diet, which is relatively low in nutrient requirements compared to other diets but still requires a need for bulk in the diet. For these horses, acceptable quality alfalfa (17–19% crude protein and 0.95–1.1 Mcal/lb [2.1–2.4 Mcal/kg]) will meet the nutrient requirements (energy, protein, etc.) long before the gastrointestinal fill requirement is met. Grass hay (9–12% crude protein and 0.85–0.95 Mcal/lb [1.9–2.1 Mcal/kg]), alone or in combination with alfalfa, will meet their nutrient requirements and provide enough bulk in the diet for gastrointestinal fill. Digestive disturbances may occur without adequate roughage to maintain the microbial population in the large intestine. Additionally, abnormal behaviors may develop, such as cribbing, stall weaving, or chewing the manes and tails of other herd members.

Nutrient needs of horses during pregnancy are not greater than maintenance until the last 3 months of pregnancy.

Pregnancy and Lactation for Mares

Nutrient needs during pregnancy are not greater than maintenance until the last 3 months of pregnancy. A diet of acceptable-quality alfalfa (17–19% crude protein and 0.95–1.1 Mcal/lb [2.1–2.4 Mcal/kg]) fed to 100 percent of the energy need in the last trimester also provides 179 percent of the protein requirement, 290 percent of the calcium requirement, but only 78 percent of the phosphorous needs. General nutrition rules hold that the calcium to phosphorous ratio (Ca:P) should be in the range of 1:1 to 2:1. The Ca:P of alfalfa hay is always greater than 2:1, sometimes as high as 6:1 or 8:1. There is no clear consensus within the horse industry on whether phosphorous supplementation should be implemented to bring this ratio closer to 2:1 or if the high Ca:P can be tolerated once the phosphorous requirement is met.

Alfalfa hay is a good source of lysine, the first limiting amino acid in horse diets. During lactation, especially early lactation, the nutrient requirements are high. Alfalfa fed up to 2.5 percent of body weight cannot alone meet the energy requirement. Thus, concentrate, usually in the form of cereal grains such as oats or corn, must be added to the diet as an energy source. Other supplements may be required to meet any deficiencies such as of trace minerals or vitamins.

Growing Horses

Nutrients such as energy, crude protein and essential amino acids, and calcium and phosphorus are important in rations for growing horses. Alfalfa, when balanced with oats, provides or exceeds these nutrient requirements. However, protein availability and associated amino acids may be marginal in meeting the nutrient requirements. Digestion of protein in the small intestine allows amino acids to be absorbed into the bloodstream and then utilized for growth. Much of the protein in alfalfa will bypass digestion in the small intestine. Protein that reaches the large intestine can be utilized for microbial growth rather than growth of the horse. Feeds with a higher level of small intestine digested protein, such as soybean meal, should be considered for growing horses to ensure adequacy of absorbable protein and lysine. Additional supplementation may be required to correct for deficiencies or imbalances in nutrients of the diets of growing horses to promote optimal growth and skeletal development.

Working Horses

The primary nutrient needed for work is energy, and the energy requirements are proportional to the amount of work performed. At low levels of work, energy and other nutrient requirements may be met by simply feeding more of the maintenance diet. Diets for working horses would be similar to those fed to weanlings or mares in late gestation, but not as nutrient dense as diets for horses in early lactation or long yearlings (18 months). The higher energy content of alfalfa as compared to grass hay would be advantageous, with concentrates balancing the diet. Horses undergoing intense work (racehorses) may require additional energy in their diet, along with increases in protein, calcium, and phosphorous.

Special Considerations

Starved Horses

Horses neglected without feed over a long period may require a nutritional rehabilitation program to successfully reintroduce feed. Small, frequent (six times per day) meals of alfalfa have been shown to be physiologically supportive during refeeding. Large electrolyte shifts during initial refeeding may be fatal to a starved horse. The high density of nutrients provided by alfalfa, especially of magnesium and phosphorus, assists in minimizing these electrolyte deficiencies.

Excessive Protein

Alfalfa hay may contain excessive protein over the protein requirement for a particular horse. This excess protein is converted to energy in the horse along with the by-product of nitrogen. Nitrogen is subsequently eliminated from the horse in the form of urea in the urine. Thus, feeding alfalfa hay, especially compared to grass hay, increases the amount of ammonia in the urine, and a strong odor may be present in the stable. Lung irritation from the ammonia may result in stables without adequate ventilation and/or proper stall cleaning.

Enteroliths (Stones)

Enteroliths are intestinal stones that form in the large intestine of some horses. These may migrate in the large intestine and sometimes into the small intestine, and may become lodged or cause total blockage leading to colic and possible death. Reports have shown that a large majority of horses treated for enteroliths were fed a diet that contained at least 50 percent alfalfa. Enteroliths are formed over time, usually years, by the building of concentric rings around a foreign object, such as a small pebble or piece of baling wire. The rings are formed from a crystalline combination of magnesium, ammonia, and phosphorous that is readily available in alfalfa and some water sources. Enteroliths have been found in all breeds of horses, but Arabians and quarter horses are the most commonly affected. Enteroliths occur in horses worldwide, but the highest prevalence has been monitored in California. Over 900 horses were diagnosed with conditions involving enteroliths at the Veterinary Medical Teaching Hospital at the University of California, Davis, from 1973 through 1996.

> *Reports have shown that a large majority of horses treated for enteroliths were fed a diet that contained at least 50 percent alfalfa.*

Blister Beetles

Horses are very sensitive to blister beetle toxicosis, which usually occurs from consuming blister beetles in alfalfa hay cut after midsummer. The hay is usually cut, crimped, and swathed in one operation, which captures the crushed beetle (see Chapter 9, "Managing Insects in Alfalfa"). Clinical signs depend on the number of beetles ingested, but can range from a mild fever, colic, and even death. It is estimated that the ingestion of 125 beetles would provide a lethal dose of the toxin cantharidin. Often more than one horse in a stable during the same period will be affected. There is no specific antidote for cantharidin, but early supportive therapy is often helpful. Recovery or death usually occurs within 1 to 3 days. The potential for blister beetle toxicosis exists throughout the United States, but most cases are located in the southwest. It has been reported that in a 26-month period in Texas, 53 cases of blister beetle toxicosis were diagnosed. Peak incidence occurs in the late summer and early fall.

> *The usual cause of botulism in hay is decaying small animal carcasses that are inadvertently baled into the hay.*

Botulism

The bacteria causing botulism (*Clostridium botulinum*) produce several different neurotoxins that cause a progressive paralysis, often initially recognized by feed and water spilling from the mouth due to the inability of the horse to swallow. Veterinary care should be sought immediately. Horses may die suddenly. The usual cause in adult horses is from decaying small animal carcasses that are inadvertently baled into the hay. The hay also may appear moldy, usually indicated by the presence of white mold on the edges or within the bale; this is often accompanied by dust. Botulism is uncommon, but acute outbreaks may occur involving a number of horses ingesting contaminated feeds such as hay cubes or pellets.

Developmental Orthopedic Disease in Horses

Developmental Orthopedic Disease (DOD) is a multi-factorial syndrome that involves the abnormal development of the long bones during periods of fast growth in horses. It can manifest in many ways, including angular and flexural limb deformities, cysts and ulcerations of articular cartilage, and bone malformations in both the long bones of the limbs and cervical bones of the neck. Genetics are thought to play a role, but the exact mechanism is unknown.

Among nutritional contributors, excessive energy, protein, and/or a high Ca:P may predispose a horse to DOD. Thus, high nutrient feeds, such as alfalfa, fed in abundance may contribute to DOD in some horses.

Buying Hay for Horses

Several facts about horse owners may shed light on how to meet their needs for buying alfalfa. Only 20 percent of the horses in the United States are kept for profit-motivated activities such as racing and breeding, whereas 80 percent are involved in nonprofit activities such as recreation or companionship. Ninety percent of the horse-owning public has some college education, and 80 percent are women. Since the majority of horse owners do not own horses for a business, many horse operations run on a hand-to-mouth financial cycle. Owners of only one or two horses will likely buy hay at the feed store one bale at a time, so the appearance of the bale is important. Hay must be free of mold and dust, along with being uniform from bale to bale. Many female horse owners appreciate lighter-weight bales. Hay must be palatable; if the horse isn't enthusiastic about eating its hay, the owner won't want to purchase it. It is not uncommon for a horse owner to return a partial bale of unsatisfactory hay and ask for a refund.

Alfalfa suppliers may sell their services as well as their products to horse owners. Many stables don't have enough room or shelter from weather for large purchases of hay, and the storage and care of stacked hay is problematic. Horse owners may be willing to pay for the delivery of small loads of hay in a timely manner or the stacking, crowning, and securing of tarps on larger loads of hay delivered to the stable. Additionally, large purchases of hay stored at the seller's facility with delivery of smaller amounts throughout the year may be beneficial to some stables. Horse owners generally discover hay suppliers by word of mouth. Networking with feed-store owners, veterinarians, farriers, or others in equine business may increase sales.

Many horse owners are concerned about buying a quality hay to meet their horses' nutritional needs. Traditionally, buyers of large purchases of hay for horses have not requested to review the results of an objective hay test or analysis, which scientifically determines the nutrient composition. Visual appraisal of hay does not always reflect the actual nutrient composition of the hay, but the report from a hay test will indicate the protein and energy levels of the hay, along with the concentration of some selected trace minerals and vitamins. This information may be beneficial in recommending a particular supply of hay and to develop appropriate feeding programs to balance nutrients. If a hay supplier can talk knowledgeably about the individual horses' nutrient requirements, but not necessarily in great detail, this can build a trusting relationship between the horse owner and hay supplier. The extra efforts to network with horse owners, supply quality hay in a timely manner, deliver small loads, provide other convenience services, and educate horse owners on different aspects of buying, storing, and feeding of alfalfa contribute to the profitability of marketing alfalfa hay to the horse community.

Additional Reading

Bell, C.E., J.N. Guerrero, and E.Y. Granados. 1996. A comparison of sheep grazing with herbicides for weed control in seedling alfalfa in the irrigated Sonoran Desert. J. Prod. Agric. 9:123–129.

Collar, C., L. Foley, J. Glenn, P. Hullinger, B. Reed, J. Rowe, and C. Stull. 2000. Goat care practices, 1st ed. University of California Cooperative Extension, University of California, Davis. http://www.vetmed.ucdavis.edu/vetext/INF-GO_CarePrax2000.pdf

Guerrero, J.N., M.I. Lopez, and C.E. Bell. 1997. Lamb performance on seedling alfalfa with predetermined alfalfa/weed biomass differences in the irrigated Sonoran Desert. Sheep and Goat Res. J. 13(2): 71–77.

Guerrero, J.N., E.T. Natwick, M.I. Lopez, and A.R. dos Santos. 2002. Grazing lambs control insects in alfalfa. Proc. West. Sect. Am. Soc. Anim. Sci. 53:377–380.

Lewis, Lon D. 1995. Equine clinical nutrition: feeding and care. Williams and Wilkins, Media, PA.

Mitchell, A.R., J.N. Guerrero, and V.L. Marble. 1991. Winter sheep grazing in the irrigated Sonoran Desert: II. Soil properties and alfalfa regrowth. J. Prod. Agric. 4:422–426.

Morley, F.H.W., ed. 1981. Grazing animals. Elsevier, NY.

National Research Council. 1989. Nutrient requirements of horses, 5th ed. Washington, DC.

———. 2001. Nutrient requirements of dairy cattle, 7th ed. Washington, DC.

———. 2007. Nutrient requirements of small ruminants: Sheep, goats, cervids and New World camelids. Washington, DC.

18

Alfalfa Grazing Management

Carlos A. Cangiano
Research Scientist, INTA EEA Balcarce, Provincia de Buenos Aires, Argentina

Alejandro R. Castillo
Farm Advisor, University of California Cooperative Extension, Merced, CA

Juan N. Guerrero
Farm Advisor, University of California Cooperative Extension, El Centro, CA

Daniel H. Putnam
Forage Extension Specialist, Department of Plant Sciences, University of California, Davis

Grazing alfalfa with dairy or beef animals is not a common practice in California or even in the United States. Although a limited number of alfalfa acres are grazed in the humid Midwest and East, it is rare in the West, and the ruminant alfalfa forage systems throughout the United States consist of hay- and haylage-based harvest methods. However, there is increased interest in grazing in North America due to harvest cost issues, environmental benefits, and interest in organic, natural, or grass-fed products in the market, and animal welfare. Since some component of grazing is required for organic certification, grazing of alfalfa has received increased interest.

Grazing alfalfa is a more common practice in Australia, New Zealand, and Argentina. Argentina grazes more alfalfa than any country. Milk and meat production systems are based primarily on grazing alfalfa, especially in the rainfed regions of the Pampas. Producers in the Pampas use more than 5 million hectares (12 million acres) of alfalfa for grazing. Alfalfa varieties and growing conditions in the Pampas are remarkably similar to California. Here we discuss important concepts of alfalfa grazing management for efficient milk and meat production, based primarily on the Argentine experience, especially as they may relate to California conditions.

Principal Benefits and Limitations of Grazing Alfalfa

Some comparative economic studies on dairy farms indicate that intensive grazing systems may be a viable management tool for improving dairy profitability compared to a confinement system. A recent study indicates that using rotational grazing decreases animal production costs compared with harvested forage systems. There are a range of potential benefits,

chiefly lower investment and production costs, but also lower culling rates, improved herd health, and environmental benefits from better recycling of wastes and reduced nutrient concentration at a single location. Stocker steers from 400 to 600 pounds (181 to 272 kg) may gain from 1.75 to 2 pounds (0.8 to 0.9 kg) per day and even as high as 3.0 pounds (1.4 kg) per day on alfalfa pasture. Animals generally have fewer hoof and leg problems or mastitis problems on pasture compared with cramped cement feedlots. Alfalfa pasture returns more nutrients to the soil than hay crops. Nutrient cycling is accomplished by the animals themselves in grazing systems, but distribution for plant uptake and control of wastes in grazing systems may not be optimal. There are likely to be public acceptance and animal welfare benefits of grazing systems as well, compared with feed-lot type dairies, as consumers become more interested in the origin of their food. There are lower fossil fuel energy requirements, since use of harvest machinery is minimal in grazing systems.

In general, compared to intensive, free-stall feeding systems, the main limitation of grazing systems is lower milk production per cow. Grazers have less control of forage yield and quality over the season. This creates challenges for ration balancing to optimize milk production. There is an energy cost to the animal walking to and from pastures that results in lower production. Weeds and compaction from animals' hooves can be significant problems that result from grazing under suboptimum conditions. Labor requirements for management of fences and animals are higher, and there is a logistical limit to farm size in grazing units. These disadvantages may be mitigated by integration of intensive grazing management with feeding practices that include silages and hay forage products to adjust quality and intake of feeds to improve milk production.

In the most productive Argentine systems, approximately half of the diet is typically composed of silages, grains, and by-products that supplement grazing. Potential milk yield of high-stocking-rate alfalfa grazing systems could be 25 to 30 kilograms (55 to 66 lb) of milk per cow per day, or 8,000 to 9,000 kilograms (18,000 to 20,000 lb) of milk per cow

Advantages and Disadvantages of Grazing vs. Feedlot Forage Systems

Advantages

- Low cost
- Low fossil fuel requirement
- Animal health
- Animal welfare
- Reduced waste issues—dispersed nutrient cycling
- Consumer preference in some markets
- Sustainability of agricultural systems

Disadvantages/Challenges

- Lower per-animal productivity
- Bloat risk
- Variable yield over season
- Lack of control over quality
- Labor requirements
- Compaction of soil, plant damage
- Need for higher level of management
- Weed intrusion
- Difficulty in balancing rations
- Control of manures from pastures

annually. Under these conditions, dietary balance through supplementation integrated with careful grazing management plays a critical role.

Practical Concepts and Principles for Managing Alfalfa Pastures

Growth and Defoliation of Alfalfa

As alfalfa grows and develops, a range of morphological changes affects forage quality, yield, and therefore milk production, as well as stand persistence (see Chapter 3, "Alfalfa Growth and Development," and Chapter 16, "Forage Quality and Testing," for details). An alfalfa pasture is made up of a population of stems of varying ages; some more mature, and some less mature, and this population changes over time as the crop transitions from high to low quality as it matures. Defoliation results in the need for regeneration of alfalfa shoots, which requires root reserves of carbohydrates and protein; frequent and early harvests improve quality but deplete stand vigor (See Chapter 13, "Harvest Strategies").

In addition, weeds and/or other forage species (e.g., grasses) that compete with alfalfa may be present. There is competition for light, nutrients, and water between species and individuals within species. Grazing affects these competitive relationships as well as subsequent regrowth from crowns. Over time, these competitive relationships produce changes in botanical composition, resulting in changes in forage mass, quality, seasonal production, and, consequently, animal production. For that reason, grazing managers should consider the morphogenic characteristics of the alfalfa over the season and over years, as well as grazing impacts on other forage species and/or weeds.

Plants have two mechanisms to survive defoliation under grazing conditions: (a) chemical or physical defenses, or (b) tolerance of its consequences. Some plants have evolved chemical defenses, such as alkaloids or tannins, or physical barriers to grazing, such as spines or needles, that reduce plant palatability. Alfalfa is a plant which lacks these defense mechanisms (which is why it is such an important forage) but has evolved the grazing tolerance mechanisms of rapid foliage regrowth after defoliation and abundant root reserves to allow regrowth. These allow the plant to survive multiple harvests (within limits) over the season, and over many years. In the case of alfalfa, the leaves, stems, buds, and apical meristems are always susceptible to defoliation by grazing, but very frequent defoliation results in depletion of plant root reserves. Subsequent regrowth after cutting or grazing originates primarily in the crown buds (at the top of the root) or in the basal part of the remaining stems.

During each growth period, alfalfa foliage produces energy (sugars and starches) and protein reserves that are exported to the roots to enable further root development. Root storage reserves are important to subsequent regrowth. It is estimated that alfalfa begins the process of translocating reserves to the roots only after about 15–18 days of growth; thus early, frequent, and intensive grazing may have significant negative effects on subsequent regrowth and stand persistence due to depletion of root reserves.

Forage Accumulation Patterns

After defoliation, alfalfa regenerates both leaf and stem material. As the crop becomes more mature, the stem portion increases significantly, but the leaf material remains constant, and toward the end of the growth period, dead material accumulates (Fig. 18.1). After about 42 days of regrowth, the amount of new leaf production may be similar to the amount of accumulated dead plant material. The forage accumulation rate depends on the season and the length of the accumulation period. Generally, maximum forage accumulation rates (mass per unit area per day) are highest in early summer (until high temperatures become limiting), somewhat slower in spring, slower yet in fall, and very slow in winter (Fig. 18.2). Additionally, alfalfa variety (particularly fall dormancy rating), fertility, irrigation, and other factors affect growth rates. Pasture management systems need to be continually adjusted

FIGURE 18.1

Alfalfa dry matter accumulation patterns during spring regrowth.

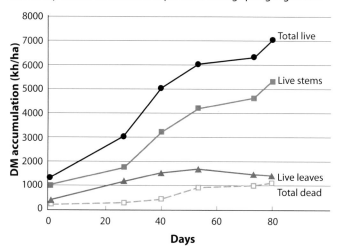

FIGURE 18.2

Seasonal changes in alfalfa dry matter accumulation rates under irrigation.

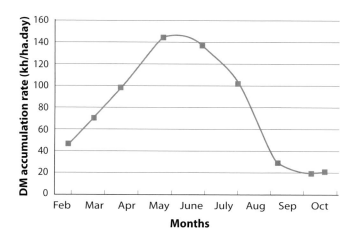

for growth patterns, depending on crop status and time of year.

Defoliation Management Under Grazing

Grazing of alfalfa involves three important factors: (1) *frequency*, or the time between two consecutive defoliations; (2) *intensity*, measured as the quantity of forage mass removed. This is also referred to as the efficiency of pasture utilization, or as the percentage harvested. Since animals are selective for both species (weed, grass, or alfalfa crop) and plant parts (leaves vs. stems), intensity influences both yield and quality; and (3) *timing*, related to the phenological stage of the plants at harvest.

Generally, alfalfa should be grazed at the beginning of flowering or when the first new regrowth appears in the crown (this may occur before flowering in some environments). Nevertheless, to simplify management practices, growers often graze at specific intervals. Similar to hay cutting schedules, grazing frequency should maintain a good level of root reserves after defoliation through providing an adequate "rest regrowth period," which leads to high dry matter production, quality, and stand persistence through time.

Grazing intensity may be estimated from the stubble height remaining after defoliation. After defoliation, the crown buds and basal shoots from the crown are the main

growing points from which regrowth is generated. Shoots originated from axilar buds in the remaining stubble are less important. It is suggested that a stubble height of 5–7 centimeters (2–3 in.) is enough to sustain a high rate of regrowth and to strike a proper balance between high rates of regrowth and pasture utilization. However, stubble height (intensity of grazing) has a profound effect on forage quality.

Rest Periods, Rotations, and Schedules

Research has demonstrated that recommendations for managing alfalfa under grazing conditions should be similar to those for hay production (see Chapter 13, "Harvest Strategies for Alfalfa," for cutting schedule recommendations). Increasing grazing frequency (less time between defoliation) by using short rotation frequency decreases forage yield and persistence of the plants significantly, but forage quality is better. Continuous stocking at high stocking rates without rotation is an extreme case that causes severe stand loss and is not recommended (Fig. 18.3). Rotational grazing management with rest periods of at least 35 days allows recovery of the alfalfa before subsequent defoliation.

This rest period should be adjusted according to seasonal effects and factors such as drought, variety, and fertility. The objective is to maintain a high forage value and avoid grazing the new regrowth coming from the crown.

Rotational grazing entails division of a field into paddocks of appropriate size and control of animals, often by use of temporary fencing or the use of existing fields in a system of pastures. The basic principle is managing livestock for defoliation at specific plant maturity, followed by a rest period before subsequent defoliation. A grazing cycle consists of a grazing period that is followed by a rest period, which can be of various time sequences (Table 18.1). Both the rest period and the grazing time are important to crop productivity and animal performance.

Long, intensive grazing periods where plants are grazed close to the ground increase harvest efficiency but may reduce plant survival and result in harvests of lower quality. Short grazing periods are used for dairies; the electrical fences are moved each day (for

example, one paddock per day) or even each half day. These systems are more labor intensive and when moderately stocked, result in lower harvest efficiency but higher milk production. In a rotational stocking program, a grazing period of 7 to 10 days with at least 35 days of rest is considered safe for the alfalfa pasture and adequate for animal production. There is a range of combinations for grazing and rest periods that achieves a grazing cycle of 40 days (Table 18.1). Generally, no more than six to eight paddocks or fields should be included in the rotational grazing system. Adjustments can be made for each farm, based on season, alfalfa variety, level of supplements in the diet, field shape, availability of drinking water, and labor force availability.

Watering, Rainfall, and Compaction

Watering cattle on pasture is often a challenge for grazing systems since foot traffic can create problems due to mud, trails, and compaction. Feasibility of watering infrastructure may be a limiting factor in a grazing system. On fields that are irrigated with a center pivot, it is advisable to place the waterer at the center and separate the grazing subsections in a bicycle-spoke fashion.

Care must be taken not to graze wet fields. Soil compaction caused by cattle will diminish future yields and reduce stand persistence. Animals should be removed from alfalfa fields during rainfall events or irrigation; cattle should not be moved onto the field as long as the field is wet. However, the effect of foot traffic is highly dependent on soil type and amount of moisture. To reduce soil compaction after a rainfall event or an irrigation, the top 1 inch (2.5 cm) of soil (for loams or heavier soils) should be dry before moving cattle onto the field. Grazing cattle tend to naturally congregate around water. If possible, every cattle move onto new field subsections should be accompanied by a corresponding move of the cattle's water supply,

FIGURE 18.3

Alfalfa stand percentage (as a function of the initial number of plants) is affected more by continuous grazing compared with rotational grazing (7 days grazing followed by 35 days resting).

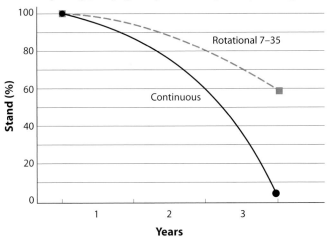

TABLE 18.1

Relationship between the numbers of subdivisions (paddocks), and grazing and resting days, for a grazing cycle of 40 days

Number of subdivisions (paddocks)	2	4	6	8	10	12	14	16
Grazing period (days)	20	10	6.7	5	4	3.3	2.9	2.5
Resting period (days)	20	30	33.3	35	36	36.7	37.1	37.5

to prevent soil compaction around the water basin. Concrete aprons around water supplies are advisable.

Determining Stocking Rates and Grazing Strategies

The grazing process may entail division of a field into paddocks of appropriate size, facilitated by use of temporary or permanent fences to control animals. Alternatively, several fields may be used together as a grazing unit or system for management purposes. Animals are moved to paddocks each day, frequently twice per day. In a grazing period (½, 1, 3, or more days long), once a field is grazed a rest period

---

Determining Alfalfa Pasture Requirements for a Group of Animals (example)

Dietary needs of animal:

= 20 kg (44 lb) DM/cow/day
50% to be obtained from pasture:
= 10 kg (22 lb) /cow/day

Available forage (measured or from experience):

= 0.224 kg/m² (e.g., about 1 ton/acre dry matter)

Grazing intensity: 60%

= 0.135 kg/m² harvested

Area needed for one animal:

= 74 m² per cow per day (10 kg divided by 0.135 kg/m²)

Area needed for 100 animals:

= 7,400 m² (0.74 ha or 1.66 acres) per day (74 m² × 100)

Remember:

• Adjust for moisture content.

• Consider number of harvests/year (calculate on a DM basis).

• Consider additional acreage needed for stored forages.

---

follows. A second harvest or grazing may follow the same pattern in sequence so that the same rest period (usually about 35 days) is followed for all paddocks. Grazers may further subdivide a paddock during a grazing period to intensify grazing in one section (e.g., half of the grazing on one side), followed by another section a few hours later, depending on labor availability.

Grazers may choose paddock size and stocking rate by trial and error but may also use a formula. The first step in using a formula is to estimate the dry matter intake needs of the animal. Secondly, it is important to estimate the total dry matter available in the field at the time of grazing. The third step is to know the percentage of the pasture to be utilized. Lastly, it is useful to know the quantity and quality of available supplements, as well as the quality of the forage available for grazing. The latter information may be useful only for a more sophisticated nutritional approach to grazing, requiring a higher level of management and ration balancing.

To estimate stocking rates, paddock sizes, and grazing duration, an assessment of alfalfa grazing resources would be helpful. A "grazing management unit" (the aggregate collection of fields and/or paddocks) should be selected. This is the grazing land area that will be used to support a group of animals for an entire grazing season, considering pasture allowance, the grazing and resting periods, and the number of cattle. Then, the stocking rate (or the number of animals/day/area of land) can be calculated, as follows:

1. **Determining an animal's requirements.** The diets should be balanced according to animal requirements and feed availability (including stored forages, concentrates, and pasture). For example, according to nutritional recommendations, it may be estimated that the animals will require a total dry matter intake (DMI) of 20 kilograms (44.1 lb) per cow, per day and 50 percent of the diet (10 kg [22.1 lb] DMI) is projected to be provided by the alfalfa pasture.

2. Forage mass and pasture utilization. There are several methods to assess the yield (standing forage) of the pasture, such as cutting and weighing small portions, disc meter, eye calibration, and so on. A detailed description of yield estimation techniques is out of the scope of this chapter. Experience may be the best guide. Plant height has a good relationship to yield, but this can be misleading as well. Use cutting samples from small quadrats, and a microwave oven to adjust for dry matter. This method may be useful to calculate dry matter yields until enough experience is gathered to determine yield for a field from visual estimates. After yield per unit area and total area is estimated, the pasture utilization (which is almost always less than 100%) should be estimated. Pasture utilization efficiency is often estimated at 60 percent or less (e.g., 45%–60%) for dairy animals, greater for beef cows, dry cows, sheep, or heifers. These estimates should be checked by verifying actual pasture offered versus pasture refused, by measuring stubble clippings over the season. Adjust for moisture content (e.g., all calculations on a dry-matter basis).

3. Daily paddock estimations (see sidebar on previous page). If a grower can produce about 1 ton per acre (100% DM basis) forage per harvest (equivalent to 2.24 Mg/ha), then 0.224 kilograms (4.9 lb) per M² alfalfa is determined to be available for grazing. With 60 percent utilization, 0.134 kg per M² will be harvested per animal, per day by grazing. To satisfy the 10 kilograms (22.1 lb) per day animal requirement, we will need about 74 M² (800 ft²) per animal, per day. For a group of 100 dairy cows, it will then be necessary to provide grazing from 7,400 M² (0.74 ha [1.8] acres per day) of alfalfa forage.

These calculations provide a rough estimate of dry matter intake needs for cows but do not take into account forage quality and forage intake differences across the season, and other factors, such as quality of the supplements.

These estimates must be adjusted to accommodate seasonal changes in productivity and quality, for specific classes and breeds of animals, and by experience with specific fields.

Variety and Grazing Intensity Interactions

Defoliation frequency is one of the most important variables for maintaining high pasture yields and persistence. The defoliation frequency (by cutting and/or grazing) may have different effects, depending on the fall dormancy class of the variety. Nondormant varieties generally demonstrate higher productivity with low defoliation frequencies (30 days or more; Fig. 18.4). However, defoliation frequencies of 25 days or less significantly decrease the performance of nondormant alfalfa varieties (class 8–10), which are usually less persistent.

Nondormant varieties have also been more sensitive than intermediate dormancy varieties to frequent defoliation in autumn due to higher growth. The high defoliation frequency in autumn–winter of nondormant varieties negatively affects and delays the regrowth in the following spring. Nondormant varieties are likely to be much more sensitive to intensive grazing conditions when compared to dormant varieties. The causes of these variety

FIGURE 18.4

Relative forage yield of alfalfa affected by varieties with different fall dormancy ratings and frequency of defoliation. H = high frequency (21-25 days), HI = high - intermediate (28-29 days), LI = low – intermediate (33-35 days), L = low (37-42 days).

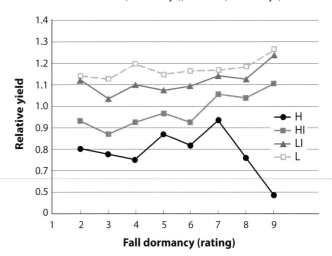

differences under grazing conditions are not clear but could include diseases, root nitrogen or carbohydrate reserves, or crown bud metabolism. These results are likely to be applicable to most regions within the Central Valley and deserts of California, but no research has been done on alfalfa variety–grazing interactions in California.

Managing Alfalfa—Perennial Grass Mixtures

Alfalfa for grazing is frequently mixed with grasses, like perennial ryegrass, orchardgrass, fescue, bromegrass, and timothy. Some advantages for these mixes are: (1) higher production and pasture distribution throughout the year;

FIGURE 18.5

Vertical distribution of leaves and stems in alfalfa plants close to flowering. The alfalfa canopy has a significantly greater leaf percentage on the upper portion than on the lower portions of the canopy. Each curve represents about 100% of leaves and stems yield added at different heights.

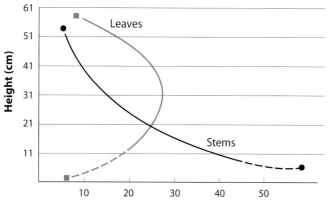

Dry matter yield of leaves and stems (% of total)

TABLE 18.2

In-vitro dry matter digestibility (IVDMD) and crude protein (CP) contents of leaves and stems at different vertical layers in a spring alfalfa pasture

Layer (cm [in.] above ground)	Leaves		Stems	
	IVDMD (%)	CP (%)	IVDMD (%)	CP (%)
> 30 [12]	74.3 ± 0.9[a]	26.4 ± 0.7[a]	66.8 ± 0.6[a]	13.8 ± 1.0[a]
20–30 [8–12]	69.3 ± 0.5[b]	27.4 ± 1.1[a]	58.2 ± 0.4[b]	9.0 ± 1.4[b]
10–20 [4–8]	68.8 ± 0.7[b]	28.0 ± 0.5[a]	53.9 ± 0.3[b]	9.0 ± 0.2[b]
< 10 [4]	68.4 ± 1.8[b]	28.3 ± 0.6[a]	40.7 ± 1.8[c]	8.1 ± 0.1[b]

[a–c] Means within columns followed by different letters are significantly different (P < 0.05).

(2) lower variation between years; (3) better dietary balance or energy–protein ratio; (4) reduction in weeds; and (5) lower risk of bloat. The most appropriate grass will depend on location and expectation of animal performance.

The main disadvantages of mixing alfalfa and perennial grasses are: (1) increased complexity of grazing (animal selection, diet impacts); (2) maintaining the competitive balance between the pasture's components; (3) differential nutritional changes based on phenology stage and the relative contribution of species; and (4) difficulty in obtaining high-quality forage reserves (hay, silage) and, consequently, lower animal responses.

Canopy Structure: How Do Animals Harvest Alfalfa Pasture?

Before flowering (during vegetative stages), plants have a higher concentration of leaves on the top layers. Close to flowering, leaves are concentrated on the medium to upper layers, and the stem proportions dominate at the lower layers (Fig. 18.5). Leaves do not change much in quality within the canopy, whereas stems decrease significantly in dry matter digestibility and crude protein from the top to the bottom of the canopy (Table 18.2). This indicates that the quality of the whole plant is mainly affected by stem quality, which is dramatically affected by plant maturity over time.

The changes from the top to bottom layers are important for grazing and may affect diet selection by animals, daily intake, and efficiency of pasture utilization. Stem digestibility varies a great deal not only within years, but also between years. During hot summers, the digestibility of stems could be low—less than 40 percent digestible.

Grazing animals do not uniformly

harvest alfalfa. They do not quickly graze to the ground like mechanical harvests, but instead harvest sections of the canopy. The amount (weight) of these sections (or "bites") can be estimated using the proportion (percentage) of the area covered, the forage height, and its density (kg/ha per centimeter [t/a per inch] of height) (Fig. 18.6). The bite essentially determines harvested yield, animal intake, and forage quality. Animals usually consume alfalfa forage by horizons, according to the depth of each bite. During a first grazing, bovines consume about 50 percent of the available forage by volume from the top of the canopy (Fig. 18.6), independent of the cattle's body weight. In subsequent grazings, animals consume about 50 percent of the available remaining forage. For example, animals may consume a first horizon (H_1) of 15.6 centimeters (6 in.), leaving 2,625 kilograms (2.9 tons) dry matter per hectare with 14.4 centimeters (5.7 in.) of height (Fig. 18.7). This second horizon (H_2) will have a bite with 7.6 centimeters (3 in.), and so on (Fig. 18.7). Forage quality will also reduce significantly from top to bottom of the canopy (Fig. 18.8), as animals select the best parts of the plants first, and then the stemmy, fibrous portions of the plant at the bottom. Thus, during a grazing event, animals will consume less when they graze the lower layers of the pasture, and this forage is progressively lower in quality. This sequential grazing process has major implications on grazing management.

Intake Under Alfalfa Grazing

Dry matter intake of forages is a critical aspect of forage quality and animal performance (see Chapter 16, "Forage Quality and Testing"). Dry matter intake may be an important limitation when grazing high-moisture pastures. At

FIGURE 18.6

Bite dimensions and bite mass of a grazing bovine. Generally, in a first grazing, animals will consume 50% of the available forage by weight or volume.

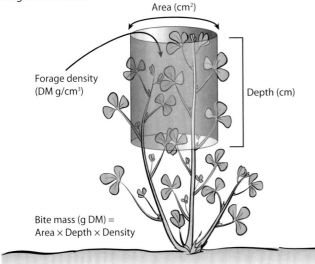

FIGURE 18.7

After the first grazing, herds will graze another approximately 50% of the available forage in the second grazing, and in a third grazing, again about 50%.

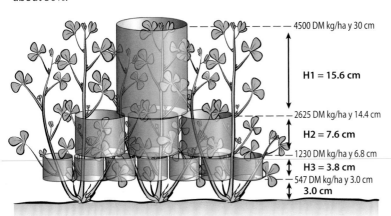

FIGURE 18.8

Digestibility of alfalfa pastures varies significantly by location in the canopy, with the highest quality at the top, lowest at the bottom.

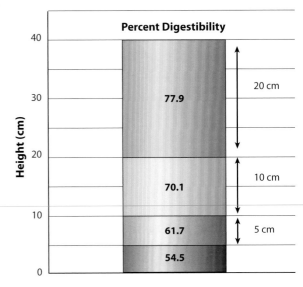

identical dry matter digestibility, the animal's intake and animal production from alfalfa is nearly always higher than from grasses. This is due to the higher rumen rates of degradation of alfalfa (rumen breakdown) and grazing selection preference for alfalfa leaves versus stems. These factors enable grazed alfalfa to maintain its quality even in the advanced maturity stages of the plants. However, maintenance of quality is dependent on grazing pressure.

Trade-off Between Forage Quality, Animal Performance, and Forage Utilization Efficiency

With dairy grazing systems, there is a clear trade-off between maintaining high milk production through grazing high-quality forages and more intensive grazing to maximize harvest efficiency. A third (and important) factor is maintaining stand life or persistence over time, which is affected by grazing intensity.

The highest pasture utilization is achieved through the most intensive grazing pressure (grazing plants completely to the ground), but

does not necessarily result in the highest animal performance. Intensive grazing maximizes forage yield and efficiency (percentage of the crop harvested). However, grazing alfalfa when the pasture has mostly low-quality stems at the bottom of the canopy forces the animals to consume a diet with significantly lower quality. This decreases total daily intake, affecting body weight gain or milk yield per animal.

There is a trade-off between complete forage utilization (yield and harvest efficiency) through intensive grazing and the animal´s performance, daily gain, or milk production (Fig. 18.9). Frequently, less intensive, shorter grazing periods will benefit milk production or daily gain, but of course, complete forage utilization is compromised and increased labor is required. As forage allowance (the amount of forage available per grazing animal, per day) increases, energy intake and animal daily gain increases from less than 0.3 kilogram (0.7 lb) to more than 1.2 kilograms (2.6 lb) of daily liveweight gain, but pasture utilization efficiency decreases constantly (Fig. 18.9).

From this general relationship we could conclude that to get 1 kilogram (2.2 lb) of daily liveweight gain, the efficiency of pasture utilization has to be low (about 30%) and the forage allowance high, near 60 grams (0.13 lb) of dry matter per kilogram of liveweight. This relationship is far from being universal. In spring, high pasture utilization (more than 70%) or a low daily forage allowance (30 g [0.07 lb] of dry matter per kilogram liveweight) is compatible with liveweight daily gain of more than 1 kilogram (2.2 lb). At the end of summer or autumn this same utilization rate may provide less than 0.5 kilogram (1.1 lb)/day of daily gain.

It is not possible to define a forage allowance that applies to all pasture conditions and animal requirements. In Fig. 18.10, two simulations are presented to evaluate the animal's daily intake in a 7-day rotational grazing system. The forage allowance was the constant, and the forage mass and digestibility were variables. In Fig. 18.10a, steers were decreasing the rate of intake (grams of dry matter per minute) but maintained the estimated potential intake. Figure 18.10b indicates that after 4 days steers decreased both intake rate and digestible dry matter intake, and could not maintain

FIGURE 18.9

Forage allowance, daily gain of steers, and efficiency of utilization of pure and mixed alfalfa pastures.

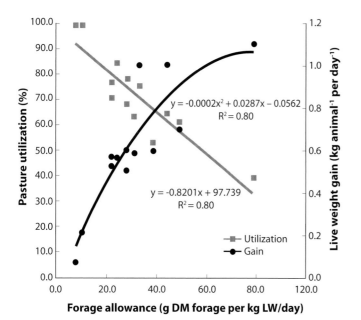

the potential intake, even though they grazed a higher digestibility pasture. The same factors are important for milk production as for daily gain.

Therefore, grazing duration will need to be adjusted, depending on both the available forage mass and its estimated quality. Seasonal variation in forage yield and quality is one of the greatest challenges for producing milk under grazing conditions.

Balancing Diets Under Alfalfa Grazing

Successful grazing management systems usually incorporate some component of supplementation to improve animal health and performance. Pasture supplementation provides additional nutrients to satisfy the animal's requirements for energy, protein, minerals, and improved intake, and enables production during seasonal reductions of forage from pastures. The main advantages of supplementation are: (1) increased animal performance (health, reproduction, milk yield and composition, or liveweight gain); (2) greater stocking rate and efficiency of pasture utilization; (3) compensation for seasonal lack of forage and (4) increased farm profitability.

When supplementing alfalfa pasture, serious consideration should be give to balancing diets with several nutrients. First, alfalfa is generally high in crude protein concentration (17–26%) but also high in rumen degradable protein. The rate of rumen degradation of the fresh alfalfa protein is often too rapid and exceeds the requirements of rumen microbes for ammonia. Consequently, there is excess ammonia generated in the rumen, and this is usually excreted as urea through the urine and to a lesser extent through elevated milk urea

levels. Second, high-quality alfalfa pasture is low in effective fiber. Effective fiber (estimated as a neutral detergent fiber requirement) often increases rumen residence time, which improves the ability of the diet to stimulate chewing and healthy rumen conditions. Third, pastures may be unbalanced for minerals (e.g., have excessive potassium or deficiencies of sodium, zinc, selenium, or copper).

Partial Mixed Rations

Nutritionists must provide a supplementation strategy to balance diets based on dietary needs of the animal for maintenance, growth, or milk

FIGURE 18.10

Rate of intake and daily intake of grazing steers in rotational stocking in two alfalfa pastures with: a) high forage mass–low digestibility; b) low forage mass–high digestibility. In both cases live weights and forage allowances were constant.

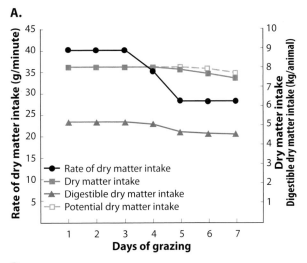

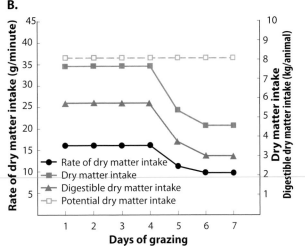

production. In grazing systems, other feed ingredients (silages, hays, byproducts, and concentrated feeds) are provided as partial mixed rations (PMR). This is similar to the total mixed rations (TMR) concept, where the total diet is integrated into one ration. Partial mixed rations are a blend of forage, grain, meals, minerals, vitamins or other supplements which are provided to the animal, not including the pasture contribution.

Protein Degradation

Under some grazing conditions, the degradation of alfalfa protein in ruminants is too rapid, and supplementation with an energy source may be necessary. The problem of rapid protein degradation in the rumen (and excretion of this nitrogen as urea) may occur with hay and particularly with alfalfa silage, but is especially a problem under grazing conditions. This problem is exacerbated by environmental conditions. Alfalfa protein often degrades much more rapidly in spring than under late summer grazing conditions (Table 18.3).

When animals graze for several hours on pasture with a high soluble nitrogen fraction and high rumen rates of degradation, amonnia levels can exceed levels that can be effectively used by rumen microbes, given the amount of energy available to them. This excess nitrogen can be wasted as urea. Energy availability and protein utilization are closely related during rumen fermentation. For that reason, some researchers suggest that supplementation with several carbohydrate sources, like soluble sugars, pectin, and starches, with different rates of rumen degradation and energy availabilities in the rumen should be more efficient than those supplements based on fewer ingredients.

For dairy cattle, PMRs should be provided to the animals after the morning milking or before animals are moved to grazing paddocks. This practice would supply dietary energy before grazing to enable rumen bacteria to consume more ammonia nitrogen

from the alfalfa. Pastures tend to be more balanced (between protein and sugar content) in the afternoon, and animals are not so hungry, reducing possible bloat problems. In summertime, to minimize heat stress, grazing should occur late in the afternoon or at night; animals may recognize electrical fences and graze as efficiently as during daylight hours.

Supplementing with rumen bypass protein or undegradable protein may improve the apparent low efficiency of nitrogen utilization when grazing high-quality pasture. However, recent studies have concluded that merely increasing the supply of undegradable protein in dairy diets does not consistently improve milk production. Positive responses were obtained using undegradable proteins when feeding alfalfa silage for lactating animals, but not when supplementing grazed alfalfa. It was concluded that grazed forages are a much more effective source of protein than ensiled forages. Ensiling alfalfa tends to significantly increase the percentage of nonprotein nitrogen and enhances the degradability of the protein, making protein utilization less efficient. Balancing protein fractions according to animal requirements for energy (which allows for better utilization by microbes) is much more effective than supplying undegradable proteins. Improving protein nitrogen absorption is important from an environmental point of view, because fewer gases and nutrients are excreted.

TABLE 18.3

Rumen degradability of protein nitrogen (N) fractions in fresh alfalfa. Alfalfa protein frequently degrades too rapidly, especially in lush spring pastures

	CP %	N Fractions (% CP)			Kd[4] % per h
		A[1]	B[2]	C[3]	
Late Summer	22.7	17.2	79.0	3.8	20.0
Spring	24.1	30.5	67.1	2.4	24.2

A[1] = Nitrogen fraction, which is very rapidly available in the rumen, and is composed of nonprotein nitrogen (peptides, free amino acids, nitrates); B[2] = True protein fraction, which is the potentially degradable fraction, degrading at the rate of Kd in the rumen; C[3] = the undegradable protein fraction that is not degraded; Kd[4] = rumen rate of degradation of "B" fraction by microorganisms in the rumen.

Supplementing Individual Feeds

Managers may also choose to supplement pasture with individual feeds, such as concentrate (grains) or forages (hays or silages), as opposed to a PMR mixed ration. These may substitute for the dry matter intake from pasture (kilograms or pounds reduction in herbage intake per kilograms or pounds of supplement). In studies under alfalfa grazing supplemented with corn grain (from 0 to 6.3 kg [13.9 lb] of corn per cow, per day), a lineal reduction of 0.66 kilograms [1.46 lb] of grazed alfalfa per kilogram of corn grain was estimated, both expressed as dry matter (Fig. 18.11). Corn grain supplementation significantly increased total daily intake and especially milk yield.

Research on production responses (kilograms of milk or meat per kilograms of supplementation with grains or forages) have been conducted worldwide to determine animals' responses under grazing conditions. A recent review of this research concluded that with high-quality pastures, milk production increases linearly as the amount of concen-

trated feeds increases from 1.2 to 10 kilograms (2.6 to 22 lb) per cow, per day (dry matter basis), with an overall response of 1 kilogram (2.2 lb) of milk per kilogram/pound of concentrate. Generally, milk protein content was increased, but milk fat concentrations reduced. These lower concentrations of milk fat could be related to lower dietary intake of effective fiber. For this reason, some long hay (1–2 kg [2.2–4.4] per cow, per day) or ruminal buffers in the diet are recommended when grazing high-quality pastures supplemented with concentrated feeds, especially at the higher rates. When other forages (hays or silages) are used as supplements, milk or meat responses are variable and depend on the supplement quality and dietary balance. In general, when the supplemented forages have lower quality compared to alfalfa pasture, responses are nonexistent or negative. High-quality forage supplements, with top-quality alfalfa hay or high-quality corn silage, did not affect production when substitution rates were high (about 1:1).

Some final suggestions about supplementation: (1) make a plan with your nutritionist to balance rations for each group of animals; (2) carefully analyze the daily movement, behavior, and health of animals according to PMR, grazing, and milking routines; (3) analyze the feed quality from pasture, feeds, and drinking water for animals; (4) estimate pasture offered (allowances) and refusal; and (5) to improve efficiency of protein utilization, use mixtures of different energy sources, grains, and energy byproducts.

Grouping Animals and Logistics

The movement of animals in grazing systems is an important issue that requires planning for effective supplementation strategy and logistical groupings. The main limitations for grouping animals (e.g., fresh cows, or high and low milking strings) are farm facilities and labor and management availability. The distances and movements of animals from pastures to milking parlors require special attention, as long walking distances, hilly pastures, dust, and mud significantly increase

FIGURE 18.11

Effect of corn grain supplementation on total dry matter intake and milk yield of dairy cows grazing alfalfa.

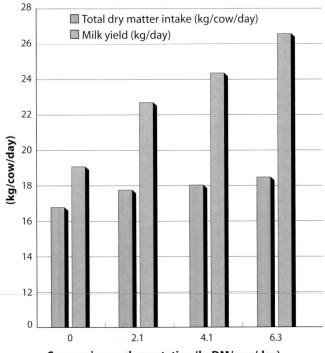

energy requirements. Some ration-balancing computer programs can account for this energy demand from walking and grazing.

There appears to be no problem with small groups of cows, but for group sizes larger than 400 cows, there is a need to reevaluate productivity, feeding, and other behaviors. Overcrowded animals in free stalls can exhibit reduced reproduction and feeding activity, and altered resting behavior. These effects have not been observed as much under grazing conditions.

Preventing Bloat

Frothy bloat is probably the greatest single fear that livestock producers have about grazing alfalfa. In spite of the great potential of animal production from grazed alfalfa, the problem of pasture bloat continues to limit the widespread adoption of alfalfa for grazing. Although bloat is a management concern for grazing alfalfa (killing animals in some cases), there are measures that can significantly reduce the risk. Millions of animals safely graze alfalfa pastures each year, and farmers and researchers have developed management tools to lessen the likelihood of bloat.

Fresh alfalfa has a higher initial rate of rumen degradation compared to most grasses. The rapid microbial colonization and digestion of alfalfa reduces particle size and increases rate of passage through the rumen, enabling animals to consume greater quantities of forage. Whereas this rapid digestion and particle size reduction is responsible for the high productivity of cattle on alfalfa pasture, it is also the characteristic of alfalfa that is responsible for bloat.

A primary plant factor contributing to bloat is the production of stable foam, which is not easily dissipated in the rumen. This is followed by obstruction of the cardia or esophagus, reducing the elimination of fermentation gases via eructation (belching). Consequently, relatively large amounts of gases are trapped in the rumen. An adult cow may produce about 400 liters (88 gal) of gas per day, and during a bloating episode most of the gas is trapped in protein-rich foam. As gas accumulates, the expanding rumen exerts pressure on the diaphragm, heart, and lungs, impairing respiration, and ultimately may result in death.

Symptoms

Bloat levels range from mild to severe. A mild bloat episode consists of a smooth left external distention of the rumen wall, and animals do not show apparent behavioral symptoms (Fig. 18.12a).

A moderate bloat causes a more prominent left external distention of the rumen wall (Fig. 18.12b); pinching the distended skin by hand can indicate moderate bloat, if the skin is taut. During moderate bloat, animals may present symptoms of pain, anxiety, and nervousness. Sometimes animals try to step with the front legs on higher parts of the ground to help liberate the gas. This position also alleviates the pressure of rumen content on the respiratory and circulatory systems. Animals normally stop eating until the rumen returns to normal size.

During severe bloat, both sides of the animal are distended, particularly the left side (Fig. 18.12c). The skin on the left side is tense, and it is not possible to pinch it. The animal looks tired; the mouth is open and may present asphyxia symptoms. The

FIGURE 18.12

Degrees of bloat can be estimated visually: (a) mild, (b) moderate, (c) severe.

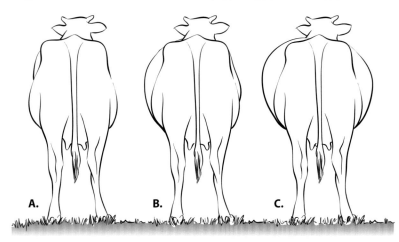

animal breathes and walks with difficulty, and may stagger. In these extreme cases of severe bloat, an emergency rumenotomy (physically puncturing the rumen and inserting a tube) may be necessary, which is accompanied by an explosive release of rumen contents and marked relief for the animal.

Economic losses produced by bloat range from depressed milk production in cases of mild bloat to animal death in severe cases. Estimated annual death rates recorded for grazed alfalfa pastures can be 1 percent or less in well-managed systems.

Management Steps to Preventing Bloat

Management strategies for reduced levels of bloat can be divided into three main groups: (1) pasture and animal management; (2) use of bloat preventive products; and (3) use of non-bloating alfalfa varieties.

Bloat is primarily a problem when hungry animals are first released into a lush, high-quality alfalfa pasture without acclimatizing or pre-feeding to reduce hunger or using anti-bloat measures. A range of strategies can be used to mitigate the effects of bloat in grazing beef or dairy systems utilizing alfalfa. Successful managers use a combination of these techniques.

- **Graze mature alfalfa.** Bloat risk is highest when alfalfa is at vegetative to early bloom stages. As alfalfa enters into the full-bloom or post-bloom stages, soluble protein levels decrease, plant cell walls thicken, lignin content increases, and the rate of digestion of alfalfa in the rumen decreases. Many experienced producers do not allow their cattle to graze alfalfa until it is in full bloom. However, during early spring or late summer grazing, even mature alfalfa pastures can result in bloat, especially at low stocking rates. Grazing at full bloom results in an obvious penalty for milk production, however, and mature alfalfa is not recommended for high-producing dairy animals.

- **Mix grasses or non-bloating legumes.** Although pure alfalfa stands can be successfully grazed, bloat problems decrease when pastures combine grasses and alfalfa, or include other non-bloating legumes, like sainfoin (*Onobrychis viciifolia* Scop.) or birdsfoot trefoil (*Lotus corniculatus* L). However, these practices may reduce animal performance, lower hay quality, and require economic evaluation.

- **Pre-feed before grazing.** Do not allow hungry animals to graze lush alfalfa pastures. Feed other forage (silage, hay, or mixed supplements) before grazing so cattle are not hungry. In some circumstances, high levels of rich starch supplements (such as ground corn, barley, or wheat) may increase the bloat problem. Short grazing intervals (3–6 hr) on new, lush pastures are more likely to result in bloat compared to cattle left on pastures. Thus, animals can "acclimatize" to bloat-prone pasture conditions.

- **Movement of animals.** Allow animals to enter a new paddock in rotational grazing at the beginning of the afternoon, when the soluble carbohydrate content of the pasture is higher. Initiating grazing in the afternoon will also increase the likelihood of slower intake due to higher air temperatures.

- **Wilting alfalfa forage.** Pre-wilting alfalfa for about 24 hours, or reducing dry matter content to 50 percent, may reduce bloat. The pasture can be mowed with a mower-conditioner, after which the animals are allowed to graze the cut alfalfa. This management strategy increases the efficiency of pasture utilization, and there is no need for a later cut to clean remaining stubble (a common practice). The disadvantage is that animals are obligated to consume all of the cut material, including stems, and don't select the high-quality material as they do when grazing fresh plants. In this case, it may be advisable to graze alfalfa before significant flowering (bud stage) to offer high-quality forage.

- **Intensify grazing, avoiding selectivity.** More intensive grazing will force animals to graze more stem material versus leaves.

However, it is difficult to manage animal selectivity, and since bloat can be produced in the first 30 minutes of grazing, intensive grazing may not be effective in preventing bloat. Additionally, increasing stocking rates affects forage intake and animal performance. It is recommended that animals be observed at the beginning of each grazing period.

• **Identify susceptible animals.** It has been suggested that the tendency to bloat is an inherited trait in animal populations. If a group of susceptible animals can be identified, they should be used as testers for bloat at the beginning of each grazing period. Conversely, culling of animals that tend to bloat has been effective in reducing herd bloating problems.

• **Observe weather patterns.** Bloat might be related to some weather conditions. For example, never graze fresh-frozen alfalfa plants; wait for 3 to 4 days after the frozen top growth is dry. Bloat might also be more of a problem under cool, wet conditions, which reduce plant fiber development and result in high-protein, high-carbohydrate leafy forage.

Use of Preventive Supplemental Products to Reduce Bloat

Several products can be used to control alfalfa bloat, such as feed additives, supplements, or pasture blocks.

• **Nonionic surfactants.** Agents that reduce foam production, like vegetable fats and minerals oils, can be mixed with feeds, in water troughs, and pasture blocks. Also, spraying these agents onto the alfalfa pasture is equally effective. This method is effective on highly controlled strip grazing when animals are not receiving supplements or other feeds. Animals should have access to paddocks that are treated daily.

• **Synthetic antifoaming agents or tension-active agents.** Several synthetic products that reduce surface tension may be used to prevent bloat. An example includes poloxalene, a synthetic polymer

nonionic surfactant, which is effective at treating legume bloat and can be supplied daily, mixed with other feeds or pasture blocks.

• **Ionophore antibiotics.** Ionophore antibiotics can inhibit the growth of most gram-positive bacteria in the rumen, reducing the severity of alfalfa bloat. These compounds can be mixed with other feeds, or supplied as controlled-release rumen capsules or as pasture blocks.

Use of Nonbloating Alfalfa Cultivars

Plant breeders have recently developed alfalfa varieties with a reduced risk of bloat. These have mainly been selected for a lower rate of initial rumen degradation. Some varieties have been released in Canada and Argentina and have been evaluated in comparison to traditional alfalfa varieties. The results of field trials indicate a reduction of bloat problems. However, it is not certain whether these varieties are available in the United States in fall dormancy groups appropriate for Mediterranean and desert zones.

Another strategy to reduce bloat is to insert genes that express tannins into alfalfa. Tannins (condensed or hydrolyzable) have the potential to bind proteins in the rumen, slowing rumen protein breakdown. This research is continuing at centers in Canada, the United States, and Australia.

However, despite decades of conventional plant breeding and advances in biotechnology, researchers have not completely resolved alfalfa bloat problems. The specific factors responsible for stable foam production in the rumen are not fully understood. The key management tools are keen observation during early grazing periods on fresh, high quality forage and taking quick preventative steps. Most scientists are optimistic that genetic advancements may eventually assist in significantly reducing this risk. Currently, dairy and meat producers must use good herd and forage management practices to minimize risk and economic losses as a consequence of bloat under alfalfa grazing.

Herd Health and Environmental Effects of Grazing

Most animal scientists and herd managers have observed reduced disease exposure under grazing systems compared with feedlot-style dairies. Mastitis (a common udder infection) is generally much lower under grazing, since infected bedding is minimized. Foot and leg problems (common on cement pads in feedlots) are much lower under grazing conditions.

Environmentally, grazing greatly reduces the amount of manures in holding pens or lagoons, reducing the necessity to mechanically recycle these waste products to crops. The concentration of livestock wastes (salts, nitrogen, minerals) at feedlot-style dairy and beef operations has proved to be a significant environmental concern in California and other regions. It is a significant challenge to recycle these concentrated nutrients effectively. Grazing animals recycle nutrients to pastures directly, reducing (but not eliminating) the need for manure-management infrastructure. Distribution of recycled wastes under grazing is not always uniform, and grazed paddocks can themselves become environmental hazards. However, uniformity can be improved through controlled grazing and management.

Additionally, the fossil-fuel use in live-stock-forage systems is significantly lower in grazing systems compared with feedlot-style livestock systems, due to reduction (or elimination) of machine harvesting.

On the negative side, pasture-deposited manures can contaminate surface waters through runoff if pastures are not managed to prevent runoff. Simple management practices, however, can prevent this. It is not clear whether grazing systems are necessarily better than feedlot systems in terms of air pollution (there is little research to indicate results either way). Pollutants present in grazed pastures are reduced at the source with reduced lagoon and solid manure storage systems, and with fewer processed stored feeds such as silage. Some waste gases may be readily absorbed in situ directly by the pasture, reducing those emissions.

Summary

Grazing of alfalfa, while not a common practice in California or the United States, has the potential to be viable for milk or meat production. Grazers in many parts of the world have demonstrated the productivity and viability of grazing alfalfa as a low-input milk or meat production system, which can be optimized with careful forage management strategies and the judicious use of supplements to balance animal nutritional requirements. Grazing systems, when well managed, are more complex than feedlot-type systems and require a high level of understanding of both animal and plant biology. The principle disadvantages of intensive grazing systems are fluctuations and uncertainties in forage quality and production, lower yield efficiency, generally lower milk yields, and higher labor requirements for movement of cows and fence maintenance. The principle advantages are lower costs of production, protection from severe fluctuations in feed commodity prices, lower fossil fuel requirements, improved animal health, public acceptance, and environmental benefits.

19

Alfalfa for Industrial and Other Uses

Shannon C. Mueller
Farm Advisor, University of California Cooperative Extension, Fresno, CA

Dan J. Undersander
Extension and Research Forage Agronomist, Department of Agronomy, University of Wisconsin, Madison

Daniel H. Putnam
Forage Extension Specialist, Department of Plant Sciences, University of California, Davis

Alfalfa growers throughout the world appreciate the high yielding, high quality characteristics of their crop and its value to the farm enterprise. Alfalfa is recognized as a high quality feed with tremendous versatility. It can be harvested and fed as greenchop, hay, cubes, haylage, or silage, or it can be grazed. It is also used for human consumption and as a nutritional supplement. The potential exists for alfalfa to be used for industrial purposes, providing farmers with new high-value products and adding to their profit margin. Exploitation of these potential food, feed, and industrial products will expand markets for alfalfa. To accomplish this goal, there is a need to develop new technologies to convert alfalfa into important value-added goods such as biodegradable plastics, high-quality animal feeds, improved textiles, pharmaceutical ingredients, and enzymes.

Although biotechnology will provide many of the new products for industrial utilization, there are opportunities for utilization of conventional alfalfa to produce value-added goods. Alfalfa has many advantages over other agronomic crops as a source of new value-added products. With its long growing season and 3- to 5-year stand life, it has great production potential. Its nitrogen-fixing capabilities make alfalfa superior to other crops in that it does not require supplemental nitrogen fertilizer.

This is an advantage because it reduces the need for increased utilization of fossil fuels to supply fertilizer to produce biomass. In addition, varieties are adapted to production areas throughout the world, and host plant resistance affords significant pest control, limiting the need for pesticides. Combined, these characteristics make alfalfa a highly sustainable and desirable crop for industrial and other uses that will result in both environmental and economic benefits.

Alfalfa produces more protein per acre than any other crop and is known for its ability to improve soil condition, thus providing value to crops following in the rotation. There is also evidence that alfalfa helps protect surface and groundwater quality by acting as a sponge for excess nitrates and water. A new alfalfa variety has been developed that fixes nitrogen only from the soil, not from the atmosphere, to increase its effectiveness in absorbing nitrates. It also provides a visual clue (yellowing of the foliage) to indicate when soil nitrogen is depleted. New alfalfa varieties have been used to clean up fertilizer spills and residues of atrazine, a corn herbicide. Alfalfa tissue immobilized on silica beads has also been used to filter heavy metals, such as cadmium, chromium, copper, nickel, zinc, and lead from water.

> *Alfalfa produces more protein per acre than any other crop and is known for its ability to improve soil condition, thus providing value to crops following in the rotation.*

Fractionation

Processing alfalfa to obtain value-added products often includes fractionation. There are three different fractionation methods: dry fractionation, wet fractionation, and fractionation by passage of the plant material through the digestive system of ruminant animals.

Dry fractionation is the process of separating the plant into leaf and stem fractions.

Alfalfa leaf meal can effectively replace some of the alfalfa hay, soybean meal, and/or protein supplement in animal rations.

Wet fractionation is the separation of freshly cut herbage into juice and fiber fractions, each of which can be converted into valuable products. The fiber fraction can be used to make paper, or if exposed to appropriate enzymes, the fiber can be converted to sugars, which, in turn, are fermented to industrial chemicals or fuels such as lactic acid or ethanol. Biodegradable plastic can be made from the lactic acid. Products produced from the juice fraction include: food- and feed-grade protein concentrates, industrially valuable enzymes, pigments, antioxidants, and nutraceuticals. *Nutraceutical* is a term that combines "nutrition" and "pharmaceutical" and refers to foods claiming to have a medicinal effect on human health. Such foods are also called *functional foods*.

Passage of the plant material through the digestive system of ruminant animals leaves a high fiber residue. The fiber from alfalfa manure has yielded construction pressboard and water filters capable of removing heavy metals from contaminated water.

Biofuels

Biofuels include ethanol, biodiesel, and other hydrocarbons achieved either through a fermentation or gasification process using biomass. The US Department of Energy reports an annual need for one billion tons of biomass to produce enough biofuel to replace 30 percent of current U.S. petroleum consumption. Perennial crops, including forage crops and trees, account for approximately 377 million tons of that annual production. The primary criteria for any biofuel crop are high yields achieved with low input costs in an environmentally friendly manner. In the past, the focus for biomass production was on poplar trees (*Populus* spp.) but more attention is currently being paid to perennial grasses. Switchgrass (*Panicum virgatum* L.) is one of the main perennial biomass species being evaluated as a dedicated energy crop for cellulosic ethanol production. Other high yielding forages like bermudagrass (*Cynodon* spp.), tall fescue (*Festuca* spp.), red and white clover (*Trifolium pratense* L. and *T. repens* L.), and alfalfa are also good candidates, but comparisons need to be made in terms of production economics and yield of ethanol and biofuel co-products, not simply total tons of biomass per acre. Ethanol produced from any feedstock (corn grain, switchgrass, wheat straw, etc.) is all chemically identical, but cellulosic feed stocks are far better than grain in producing ethanol. They are estimated to produce approximately five times more energy than corn grain and have a broader range of adaptability to poorer soils and regions that cannot support corn production. In order for alfalfa to be competitive as a biomass source, dividing the harvested product into components, such as leaves and stems, and using the leaves as a protein supplement while the stems are used for biofuel production improve the economics for alfalfa. If co-products such as pharmaceuticals are simultaneously extracted from the leaf material, this allows the economics of using alfalfa as a biofuel crop to work even better. An advantage over other crop options is that alfalfa doesn't need a source of nitrogen fertilizer and its ash can be used as a fertilizer and lime source. In addition, another major, short-term advantage is its ability to be used as a rotation crop to supply nitrogen to a subsequent corn crop.

Alfalfa for Electricity Generation

Increasing environmental sensitivity has led to greater consideration of renewable resources as an alternative to fossil fuels. It is widely believed that fossil fuel emissions harm the environment and contribute to global warming. A feasibility study in Minnesota, conducted by the Northern States Power Company and the University of Minnesota, with support from the U.S. Department of Energy and USDA, analyzed the potential of using alfalfa as an environmentally, and economically sustainable, renewable source of energy for the production of electricity.

It was estimated that the program would utilize approximately 750,000 tons (680,250 megagrams) of alfalfa each year. The system separated alfalfa hay into leaf and stem fractions. Leaves were used as a protein feed supplement while the stems were gasified to generate 75 megawatts of electric power. Current low energy costs in this country have limited the use of alfalfa stems to generate electricity from gasification, but the ability to produce a high value co-product may make this approach more economically feasible in the future.

Alfalfa for Protein Production

Potential exists to take advantage of the high quantity and quality of protein in alfalfa. The objective is to extract protein and sell it as a purified product while feeding the extracted leaves and stems to cattle. The extract is 55 percent protein, has a good balance of fat and trace minerals, and is high in xanthophyll content. The amino acid balance is very good for nonruminants and is used for poultry rations to provide protein. Chickens require high xanthophyll in the ration for good skin color and yellow egg yolks (Fig. 19.1). This product is less expensive as a xanthophyll source than the marigold extracts currently used. Protein extract from alfalfa has also been used as a human protein source in Mexico and France.

FIGURE 19.1

Alfalfa extract is high in xanthophylls and is an economically favorable alternative to include in poultry rations for good skin color and yellow egg yolks.

The green alfalfa fiber residue which remains after protein extraction qualifies as a high quality dairy alfalfa feed containing 17 percent protein since the alfalfa is harvested at the bud stage. The product is dried to 10–20 percent moisture and stored in a warehouse to preserve quality.

Alfalfa for Human Consumption

Alfalfa sprouts have been used for human consumption for decades (Fig. 19.2). They are most often used in salads and on sandwiches. Alfalfa sprouts have a high antioxidant activity and phytoestrogen concentration, which may be important in preventing diseases in humans. Alfalfa leaves are a good source of protein and vitamins A, E, and K, and they contain four times as much vitamin C as citrus juice.

Growing Pharmaceuticals

Another potential use of alfalfa is to produce pharmaceuticals. As an example, at the University of Wisconsin, genes have been transferred into alfalfa that allow it to make insulin. Alfalfa could be grown and after the insulin is extracted, the residue could be fed to cattle. This strategy would provide an economic incentive to those growing the crop and encourage increased alfalfa acreage. As mentioned above, alfalfa is also a good source of phytoestrogens, which could also be extracted as a pharmaceutical co-product.

Novel Compounds

> *Alfalfa could be developed to produce phytase, cellulase, antibodies, or edible vaccines.*

Alfalfa could be developed to produce phytase, cellulase, antibodies, or edible vaccines. The enzyme phytase improves phosphorus availability in monogastric animals, such as swine and poultry. Phytase, from

FIGURE 19.2

Alfalfa sprouts are a common addition to salads and sandwiches where their antioxidant activity and phytoestrogens may contribute to disease prevention in humans.

transgenic alfalfa, has already been tested in rations and has the potential to reduce feed costs for producers while at the same time reducing water quality problems caused by phosphorus. It can be fed as leaf meal or as juice dried on ground corn, and the manure has less than half the phosphorus levels of manure from chicks fed inorganic phosphorus supplements.

Researchers in Ontario, Canada, have developed a vaccine against shipping fever, a disease of cattle that occurs when the stress of movement weakens their immune system and they develop viral and then opportunistic bacterial infections. A bacterium that resides in the tonsils is the major cause of the disease. Researchers have genetically modified alfalfa to produce antigens against the bacterium. They plan to feed the alfalfa to calves to see if they will develop immunity to the disease.

Research is also underway to develop alfalfa that produces granules that can be extracted to produce a biodegradable plastic. Such a product would not use petroleum as a base and would not pollute as non-degradable plastic does.

Conclusions

The value of alfalfa is not limited to the cash value of the crop. Production of value-added products can more than double the value of the crop while creating jobs and stimulating the economy in rural areas.

Additional Reading

Bouton, J., 2006. Energy crops and their implications for forages. Pp. 195–199 in: Proceedings, 2006 Western Alfalfa & Forage Conference. December 11–13, Reno, NV.

Martin, N.P. and D.R. Mertens, 2005. Reinventing alfalfa for dairy cattle and novel uses. Pp. 299-311 in: Proceedings, California Alfalfa and Forage Symposium. December 12-14. Visalia, CA.

Russelle, Michael P., 2001. Alfalfa—After an 8000 year journey, the "Queen of forages" stands poised to enjoy renewed popularity. American Scientist Online. 89(3): 252, DOI: 10:1511/2001.3.252

20

Lagoon Water, Manures, and Biosolids Applied to Alfalfa

Roland D. Meyer
Cooperative Extension Specialist Emeritus, Department of Land, Air, and Water Resources, University of California, Davis

Blake L. Sanden
Farm Advisor, University of California Cooperative Extension, Bakersfield, CA

Khaled M. Bali
Farm Advisor, University of California Cooperative Extension, Holtville, CA

Alfalfa is the major forage used for feed in the dairy and other animal industries in California and the United States. It is grown on approximately 10 percent of the irrigated acreage in California and is a major forage crop in many other states. The large numbers of animals as well as a sizeable human population generate substantial amounts of waste materials that need to be utilized or disposed of in an environmentally safe manner. Application to alfalfa is one option for recycling animal wastes and municipal wastes (biosolids).

Advantages and Limitations to Utilization of Manures by Forages

Animal wastes are a valuable resource in the production of a number of crops. Many crops, including alfalfa, require large quantities of nitrogen (N), phosphorus (P), potassium (K), and other nutrients that can be supplied by lagoon water (the wastewater containing liquid and solid manure from a dairy facility) and solid manures. Since alfalfa is a legume and is able to symbiotically fix all or any part of its N requirements, no yield decrease is observed when the N supply from these waste products declines. Alfalfa is particularly well suited to receiving organic waste materials because it can use large amounts of N, and its deep-roots allow utilization of nitrate–nitrogen that has leached to the lower depths of the soil profile. Besides providing nutrients, application of manures and biosolids can increase the organic-matter content of soils, aid in the reclamation of salt-affected soils through increasing water infiltration, and assist in developing soil structure.

> *Alfalfa is particularly well suited to receiving organic waste materials because it can use large amounts of N, and its deep-roots allow utilization of nitrate.*

Although there are clear benefits to recycling animal and municipal wastes with forages, there are limitations in application rate, timing, and distribution that should be considered. Unfortunately, manures may contain weed seeds, and high levels of salts, such as sodium and chloride. In some cases, manures may promote root and crown disease problems, similar to those which occur with excess irrigation water. Sewage sludge or biosolids may contain elevated concentrations of elements such as molybdenum and heavy metals that could contribute to animal health problems.

Nutrient uptake limits should also be considered. The primary nutrient of concern for water quality regulators in California for manure applications to crops is N, because of the potential for nitrate contamination of groundwater. Thus, the upper limits of manure or biosolids application to alfalfa from an environmental point of view are likely to be determined by levels of N uptake by the plant. Nitrogen in the form of nitrate is very mobile and moves with the soil water from manures or biosolids, and with excessively high rates, can be leached beyond the root zone of crops to contaminate groundwater. Thus, for alfalfa, N applications should not exceed the crop uptake levels for N.

Secondarily, P can be of concern in some regions where surface runoff containing high soil sediment loads may occur. Phosphorus can accumulate in soils after years of manure or biosolids applications—but this is not a significant problem where off-site runoff does not occur.

High rates of K applications from manures or biosolids are primarily a concern from an animal feeding perspective. High K concentration in forages produces an ion imbalance with calcium and magnesim which must be corrected in the ration. This can lead to milk fever and other physiological problems. Pregnant dry animals in a herd just prior to calving, or just after calving (often called "close-up" cows), are the most sensitive animals. This sensitive group represents less than 15 percent of the herd at any time, but high K levels in heavily manured forages create a challenge for ration balancing for all animals.

The N contained in lagoon water, manures, and other wastes provides significant economic benefits when applied to corn, cereals, and other non-legume crops, since manures can replace expensive N fertilizers. However, alfalfa growth and yield can be enhanced by the P and perhaps K from wastes, and alfalfa serves as a desirable crop to receive these waste materials due to its high growth rate and large nutrient uptake potential.

Lagoon Water Applications

Many dairies in California have liquid flush systems that move manure from concrete lanes and alleys to lagoons or storage ponds (Fig. 20.1). Some solids are removed from the liquid by mechanical separating devices, settling ponds, or basins. The solids may be hauled and spread on fields surrounding the dairy or adjacent farms, dried and used for bedding or composted, or moved off the dairy to export some of the excess plant nutrients to meet comprehensive nutrient management plans (CNMP's) required by federal and state agencies. Depending on the waste handling system used on the individual dairy, the solids percentage in the lagoon water may vary considerably. In one study, total solids concentrations in lagoon water samples collected from dairies in California ranged from 0.5 to 2.5 percent. Recent sampling indicates that manure waters may be up to 5 percent or more solids.

Lagoon water is stored on the dairy (Fig. 20.1) with piping systems conveying it to mixing chambers or "boxes" where it is mixed with incoming irrigation water and delivered to the fields. In a few cases, the lagoon water may be pumped out, but it must also be delivered to a mixing chamber to ensure adequate mixing with the irrigation water prior to being applied to the field. Even with adequate mixing, once the velocity of the water is reduced as it spreads out in the irrigation check or furrows, the solid particles begin to settle. A higher percentage of the solids are deposited within a few hundred feet of the head of the irrigation checks and a slightly higher rate at the end of the check if considerable tailwater accumulates.

Estimating Applied Nutrients

To estimate the amount of applied nutrients, the piping systems must be equipped with (1) a flow measuring device, and (2) sampling ports to determine nutrient concentrations delivered to each irrigation check while irrigating. The final application amounts can be calculated after laboratory analyses have been received for each irrigation event.

During the summer of 1996, 19 ponds were sampled and found to have total N concentrations in the lagoon water ranging from 115 to 848 ppm (mg kg⁻¹) with ammonium–nitrogen concentrations being 35 to 77 percent of the total N. A more recent sampling study found even higher (2,400 ppm or mg kg⁻¹) concentrations of total N. In the lagoon water applied in one of the case study dairies, the P (P × 2.29 = P_2O_5) content ranged from trace to approximately 35 percent of the total N, and K (K × 1.21 = K_2O) ranged from 50 to 150 percent of the total N. Recent investigations suggest that K concentrations may be twice the N concentrations.

Developing Upper Limits of Applications

Nitrogen and K are the major considerations for lagoon water applications to alfalfa. Since a major fraction of the N, and even more of the K, will be contained in the lagoon water rather than the solids, it may be necessary to use the K concentration in lagoon water to set the upper limit or rate of application to alfalfa. At a minimum, plant K levels should be monitored on alfalfa that receives manures and rations adjusted accordingly. Producing alfalfa that contains higher than 3 percent K may be undesirable when balancing rations, especially for pregnant and newly calved cows.

Applying no more than 50–60 pounds total N and 40–60 pounds K_2O per ton (20–25 kg total N and 17–25 kg K_2O per Mg) of expected alfalfa yield per acre during the growth of each cutting will reduce the likelihood of excessively high K concentrations in the forage, and match crop N uptake. At these rates, excessive N is unlikely to volatilize as ammonia to desiccate leaves or accumulate as nitrate and be leached to groundwater, salts in solution are less likely to damage the alfalfa stand, and the biological oxygen demand (BOD) from suspended organics in the lagoon water will remain sufficiently low so that little or no plant damage will occur.

FIGURE 20.1

Lagoon for liquid dairy waste storage.

Because there is a wide range of low to high magnesium in the soils of California, applying high rates of K can reduce the magnesium concentration in the alfalfa, particularly when there is low magnesium in the soil. This is a major concern for animal feed rations. On the other hand, there are sandy soils where magnesium as well as K levels may be low enough to limit production of high-yielding, high-quality alfalfa. Magnesium applications may be necessary to increase the forage concentrations up to the desired range (>0.25%). Magnesium potassium sulfate, having 18 percent magnesium (and 22% K_2O), is perhaps the most readily available magnesium fertilizer. Epsom salts may also be used. Some dolomite lime sources with relatively high concentrations of magnesium are also available for soils with a low pH (<6.3). Higher application rates of K may be beneficial in areas having high sodium in the soil in order to reduce sodium concentrations in alfalfa. Soil, plant tissue, and forage sampling and analyses discussed in Chapter 6 ("Alfalfa Fertilization Strategies") should be used to monitor soil fertility and forage quality.

FIGURE 20.2

Spreading manure or biosolids at 10 tons per acre.

Solid Manure Applications

Plant-available P, K, and other nutrients in the soil are known to increase following the application of manure. Alfalfa yields are often higher following manure applications, compared to equal rates of mineral fertilizer P and K. It is not well understood why this occurs, whether the manure is supplying other nutrients or if it has an effect on the physical properties of soil, such as water infiltration, soil aggregation which improves aeration and drainage, or if manure affects some other aspects of plant growth. Considerable research has shown that applying manure increases soil organic matter and water infiltration, as well as greatly reduces total infiltration times in the latter part of the alfalfa growing season. When incorporation into the soil is not possible, applications of manures should be made in the fall when the alfalfa becomes dormant, to allow winter rains to move the solids off of the plant crowns.

Research has indicated that alfalfa is capable of taking up significant amounts of nitrate–nitrogen from deeper depths in the soil profile before it is leached to the groundwater following the application of solid manures. Significant reductions in nitrate concentrations were observed in the 0–6 foot (0–180 cm) depth and the 6–12 foot (180–360 cm) depth as well during 2 years of growing alfalfa.

Estimating Applied Nutrients

Whenever applying waste materials such as manures, it is important to determine the amount or weight of material applied per acre and the concentration of nutrients in the manure being applied. Collecting a representative sample from the pile prior to spreading or as it is applied followed by chemical analysis is essential to determine nutrient application rates. Since it is difficult for most spreading equipment (Fig. 20.2) to apply less than 10 tons per acre (22 Mg per ha), higher rates of solid manure should be applied and incorporated into the surface 6–8 inches (15–20 cm) of soil before alfalfa is seeded. Even if lower rates of manure (5–10 tons per acre, 11–22 Mg per ha) can be applied on the soil surface to established stands of alfalfa, this may reduce the effectiveness of herbicides used to control weeds. As with lagoon water, manures often contain weed seeds, and the N applications may encourage grass and other weed growth in alfalfa. Some dry manure may even be picked up during the swathing or windrowing operation, which may have a detrimental effect on the market value of the hay.

Application rates of manure, like those of lagoon water, should not exceed 50–60 pounds total N and 40–60 pounds K_2O per ton (20–25 kg total N, and 17–25 kg K_2O per Mg) of expected alfalfa yield per acre during the growth of each cutting. Maximum rates of solid manure nutrients incorporated into the soil prior to planting alfalfa or applied during the dormant period should not exceed 200–300 pounds N per acre, 200–300 pounds P_2O_5 per acre, and 300–400 pounds K_2O per acre (224–336 kg N per ha, 224–336 kg P_2O_5 per ha, and 336–448 kg K_2O per ha). The lower rate is suggested for sandy or coarse-textured soils, and the higher rate for clay or heavier-textured soils. Approximately 20–35 percent of the N will become available the first year, 5–10 percent the second year, and 2–3 percent for each year thereafter. As indicated earlier, Chapter 6 ("Alfalfa Fertilization Strategies") should be used as a guide to monitor soil fertility and forage quality.

Sewage Sludge or Biosolids Applications

Biosolids or sewage sludge represents another waste product with considerable variation in nutrient concentrations and potential detrimental elements. Nitrogen, P, K, and other nutrient concentrations in biosolids may be nearly in the same range as animal manures but generally have considerably higher concentrations of some micronutrients and other elements, such as zinc, copper, chromium, cadmium, lead, molybdenum, and others. In some areas, like the San Joaquin Valley and Imperial Valley, as well as large areas in several of the western states where molybdenum concentrations in alfalfa and other forages are naturally very high, even to the point of causing animal health problems, additions of this element, if

they result in increased concentrations in the forages, exacerbate an already serious problem. Little research has been conducted to indicate just how serious a potential problem this increase in molybdenum and decrease in copper concentration may be following the application of biosolids.

Preliminary sampling of alfalfa grown on soils that have received multiple applications of biosolids has indicated smaller than expected increases in molybdenum and lower than expected copper concentrations. Sampling of corn and Sudangrass indicated similar trends, with slightly lower than expected forage copper levels. In all cases, copper–molybdenum ratios were near 1:1, rather than the desired 2:1 ratio.

The large amounts of organic matter from biosolids applications increase water infiltration and the rate of reclamation of saline soils, and may in fact aid in the leaching of native mobile ions like molybdenum and boron that can cause plant or animal toxicities.

As is the case with manure, biosolids should be sampled before application to determine the nutrient and metal concentration. This information, along with the amount or weight of material applied per acre, can be used to determine the nutrient and metal application rates. Since it is difficult for most spreading equipment to apply low rates (<10 tons per acre or 22 Mg ha^{-1}) of biosolids, applications are normally made during land preparation for alfalfa seeding and incorporated into the surface 6–8 inches (15–20 cm) of soil. If lower rates of biosolids (5–10 tons per acre or 11–22 Mg ha^{-1}) are applied after establishment, they should be applied in the fall, when the alfalfa becomes dormant, to allow winter rains to move the solids off of the plant crowns.

> *Biosolids generally have considerably higher concentrations of some micronutrients and other elements, such as zinc, copper, chromium, cadmium, lead, molybdenum, and others.*

The benefits of utilizing biosolids in soil reclamation where sodium levels are very high also need to be more clearly documented.

Food processors have taken a firm stand in that they will not accept produce for human consumption grown on soils that have received any biosolids, but many dairies across the United States have no problem feeding forage from biosolids-applied fields to their milking or dry stock. This is usually a market-oriented, risk-based decision and not necessarily based on scientific investigations.

As with manures, biosolids have most of the N in the organic form that is not released in a consistent pattern. Based on a number of field observations, N release rates the first year after application are generally in the 30–35 percent range, rather than the often-suggested 20 percent range. Nitrogen release rates during the second year are generally in the 5–10 percent range; release rates in the third and subsequent years are in the 0–5 percent range. Application rates of biosolids should be based on the N, K, or perhaps even the molybdenum (Mo) and copper concentrations in forages. Follow the guidelines for N and K application rates suggested for solid manure prior to each cutting, or the maximum rates suggested for single applications prior to planting or during dormant periods. Maximum annual rates of molybdenum application should not exceed 0.5–1.0 pound Mo per acre (0.56–1.12 kg ha^{-1}). Forage and plant tissue sampling to monitor nutrient composition represent the best approach to guide biosolids applications (see Chapter 6, "Alfalfa Fertilization Strategies").

Additional Reading

Campbell-Mathews, M., C. Frate, T. Harter, and S. Sather. 2001. Lagoon water composition, sampling and field analysis. Pp. 43–51B in: Proceedings, 2001 California Plant and Soil Conference. Feb. 7–8, Fresno, CA.

Harter, T., M. Campbell-Matthews, and R.D. Meyer. 2001. Shallow groundwater monitoring within animal feeding operations: Issues and pitfalls. In: Proceedings, Western Nutrient Management Conference 4:56–64. March 8–9, Salt Lake City, UT.

Kelling, K.A., and M.A. Schmitt. 1995. Applications of manure to alfalfa: Crop production and environmental implications. Pp. 151–164 in: Proceedings, 25th California Alfalfa Symposium. December 7–8, Modesto, CA.

Mathers, A.C., B.A. Stewart, and B. Blair. 1975. Nitrate–nitrogen removal from soil profiles by alfalfa. J. Environ. Qual. 4:403–405.

Meek, B.D., L. Graham, and T. Donovan. 1982. Long-term effects of manure on soil nitrogen, phosphorus, potassium, sodium, organic matter, and water infiltration rate. Soil Sci. Soc. Am. J. 46:1014–1019.

Meyer, D., and L.J. Schwankl. 2000. Liquid dairy manure utilization in a cropping system: A case study. Pp. 409–423 in: Land application of agricultural, industrial, and municipal by-products. Soil Sci. Soc. Amer. Book Series No. 6. Madison, WI.

Meyer, R.D. 1989. The benefits of managing manures with alfalfa. Pp. 37–42 in: Proceedings, 19th California Alfalfa Symposium. December 6–7, Visalia, CA.

Meyer, R.D., R.L. Phillips, and D.B. Marcum. 1999. Molybdenum, copper, and selenium in alfalfa and other forages. Pp. 134–137 in: Proceedings, 29th California Alfalfa Symposium, December 8–9, Fresno, CA.

Meyer, R.D., B.L. Sanden, and K.M. Bali. 2000. Lagoon water, manures and biosolids applied to alfalfa: Pros and cons. Pp. 107–110 in: Proceedings, 29th National Alfalfa Symposium and 30th California Alfalfa Symposium. December 11–12, Las Vegas, NV.

Meyer, R.D., M. Matthews, J. Deng, and T. Harter. 2001. Dairy lagoon water versus anhydrous ammonia for corn silage production and soil nitrogen management. In: Proceedings, Western Nutrient Management Conference 4:65–73, March 8–9, Salt Lake City, UT.

Phillips, R.L. and R.D. Meyer. 1993. Molybdenum concentration of alfalfa in Kern County, California: 1950 versus 1985. Commun. Soil Sci. Plant Anal. 24(19–20):2725–2731.

Russelle, M.P. 1999. Application of dairy manure to alfalfa—Issues and techniques. Pp. 82–95 in: Proceedings, 29th California Alfalfa Symposium, December 8–9, Fresno, CA.

21

Producing Alfalfa Hay Organically

Rachael F. Long
Farm Advisor, University of California Cooperative Extension, Woodland, CA

Roland D. Meyer
Cooperative Extension Specialist Emeritus, Department of Land, Air, and Water Resources, University of California, Davis

Steve B. Orloff
Farm Advisor, University of California Cooperative Extension, Yreka, CA

Organic alfalfa hay production involves the growing, labeling, and marketing of alfalfa according to National Organic Program (NOP) standards as defined by the U.S. Department of Agriculture (USDA). These standards require that alfalfa be produced with approved inputs given in the national materials list with some brand names listed by the Washington State Department of Agriculture or the Organic Materials Review Institute. Farmers must also take precautions against pesticide drift and other sources of contaminants. In addition, hay handling equipment as well as storage areas must be designated organic or appropriately cleaned between conventional and organic use with documentation noted. Fields on which organic alfalfa is to be produced must be managed organically, with no prohibited substances applied for at least 3 years prior to being certified as organic.

Federal laws regulating organic products require producers to be certified organic through a USDA accredited certifier (public or private) and they must also register with the California Department of Food and Agriculture's Organic Program. This registration is handled through the County Agricultural Commissioner's Office throughout the state. The certification process requires that the producer develop a written organic farm plan, known as the organic system plan (OSP), that describes how the farm is to be managed in accordance with USDA-NOP rules and subsequent approval of the plan by the certifier. In addition, yearly updates to the farm plan are required as well as yearly on-site farm audits by certifiers to ensure compliance with federal regulations.

Despite the extensive recordkeeping needed to produce alfalfa organically, the rise in the demand for feed makes alfalfa an attractive crop for some organic farmers where there can be an average 20 percent or more price premium over conventionally grown alfalfa hay (Fig. 21.1). This need for organic feed is primarily driven by the rise in demand for organic dairy products whereby cows producing organic milk must be fed organic feed. Other markets for organic alfalfa include organic beef and lamb production and hay for horses. Currently about 1 percent of California's total alfalfa hay production is organic, or about 10,000 acres.

Growing alfalfa organically can be quite challenging as compared with conventionally produced alfalfa hay. Unless properly established and managed, there can be a reduction in yield and quality associated with increased weed and pest pressure and main-

taining adequate soil fertility. The purpose of this chapter is to provide information on how to produce alfalfa organically from the establishment to production phase. When in doubt about any farming practice allowed for organic crop production, check with the USDA guidelines, California Department of Food and Agriculture's organic program, or your certifier. For information on costs associated with organic alfalfa production, see http://coststudies.ucdavis.edu, UC Cooperative Extension, "Sample costs to establish and produce organic alfalfa hay in California."

Importance of Stand Establishment

The importance of stand establishment process for organic growers cannot be overemphasized. This includes especially (1) preplant irrigation to reduce weeds, (2) soil preparation and land leveling to improve irrigation efficiency, (3) proper time of planting in early fall to encourage good root development, (4) choice of a pest-resistant variety, and (5) sprinkler irrigation to produce good stands. These methods are all detailed in Chapter 4, "Alfalfa Stand Establishment," and are important for all growers. However, organic growers must have higher levels of management during the stand establishment process, since their subsequent weed and pest control options are fewer. The best protection for an alfalfa crop against pests and diseases is a dense, vigorous alfalfa stand, which has been established at the proper time. This is one of the most important strategies available to organic alfalfa growers to prevent weed intrusion and recover from other pests and crop stresses.

FIGURE 21.1

Organic alfalfa is favored by some growers where there may be a 20% or more price premium over conventionally grown alfalfa hay.

Land Preparation

The basic cultural requirements for alfalfa production are similar whether the crop is grown organically or conventionally. The ground should be worked in the fall, as soon as the previous crop is harvested, to prepare a seedbed. Fields should be disked and landplaned and borders pulled up for irrigation checks. Where better drainage and irrigation water distribution is desired, such as on clay soils, beds should be listed. Extra care should be taken to ensure that fields are leveled and well drained to prevent standing water and subsequent stand loss and weed problems.

Cultivar Selection and Planting

Variety selection is an important step when establishing alfalfa stands. Select the appropriate dormancy type and specific varieties that are resistant to insects and diseases found in your area. The National Alfalfa Alliance maintains a listing of marketed alfalfa varieties, including fall dormancy and pest resistance ratings (http://alfalfa.org). Remember however, alfalfa resistant varieties are not completely pest resistant so additional pest control measures may be needed in years of heavy pest pressure. See Chapter 5, "Choosing an Alfalfa Variety," for additional information. Selecting a variety that has a more nondormant characteristic with faster regrowth will also inhibit weed germination and establishment.

USDA standards require the use of organic seeds. In addition, the National Organic Program regulations prescribe that an organic availability search clause procedure be outlined and approved by the certifier before certification can be granted. This committed procedure must be followed unless approval has been granted to purchase nonorganic seeds. Conventionally grown seeds may be used as long as they are not genetically modified or chemically treated and there is clear documentation of "non-availability" of organic seed from several sources.

Inoculate the seed with the appropriate organically approved nitrogen-fixing bacteria (*Rhizobium* sp.) if alfalfa has not been grown in the area for at least 10 years. Use certified seed,

as it will be nearly weed free. The best time to plant alfalfa is in the fall (September–October) to encourage vigorous stands that outcompete weeds. Seeding rates should be slightly higher than normal, for example, 25–30 pounds per acre (28–34 kg per hectare) to help further suppress weeds.

Fertility Management

Seedling Fields

Prior to planting alfalfa it is important to assess the fertility needs of the crop. See Chapter 6, "Alfalfa Fertilization Strategies," for a more complete discussion of assessing nutrient requirements of alfalfa. The NOP regulations also require the calculation of nutrient needs of the crop and how those needs will be met. The high costs of organic versus synthetic nutrients (4-6 times higher for phosphorus and 2–3 times higher for potassium) makes careful analysis imperative. Sample soils according to the guidelines in Chapter 6 to determine crop needs. Incorporate the recommended amounts of phosphorus and potassium as manure or other organically approved fertilizers into the soil (Table 21.1). If the soil pH is below 6.3, apply an organically approved liming material. For growers transitioning into organic alfalfa production with soils that require large amounts of lime, phosphorus, and potassium, it may be more economical to build up the soil fertility by adding synthetic fertilizers and focus on weed and insect control prior to the 3-year transition period to organic production.

Compared to commercial fertilizers such as 0-46-0, 11-52-0, or 0-0-60, organic manure and compost fertilizers have relatively low concentrations of actual nutrients which can vary, usually 0.5–3% each of nitrogen (N), phosphorus (P_2O_5), and potassium (K_2O) (Table 21.1). In addition, most organically approved materials also have a wide range in moisture content (10–40% or more) so the quantity of nutrients applied must be adjusted based on the actual moisture content. For example, a ton of moist manure or compost may range from only 1,400 pounds (635 kg) of dry weight (30% moisture) up to as much as 1,800 pounds (816 kg) of dry

TABLE 21.1

Status of organic soil amendments and fertilizing materials†

Material[a]	Status[b]	Moisture (%)	CaCO₃ Equiv. (%)[c]	P₂O₅ (%)[c]	K₂O (%)[c]	S (%)[c]
Liming Materials						
Ash, Wood or Fly Ash—Plant and animal sources only. Fly ash is generally 3–50% organic matter. Ash from minerals, manure or prohibited materials (glue, plastics or synthetic substances) is prohibited. Manure ash is prohibited because burning manure is wasteful of organic matter and nutrients.	R	5–20	5–50	0.1–3.0	2.0–20	0.1–3.0
Limestone-mined, calcium carbonate	A[d]	5–10	50–90			
Dolomite-mined calcium, and magnesium carbonate	A[d, e]	5–10	50–95			
Sugarbeet lime	P	5–15	50–85			
Compost						
Compost—(plant and animal materials). Composted plant and animal materials produced through a process that: (i) establishes an initial C:N ratio of between 25:1 and 40:1 and (ii) maintains a temperature of between 131°F and 170°F for 3 days using an in-vessel or static aerated pile system; or (iii) maintains a temperature of between 131°F and 170°F for 15 days using a windrow composting system, during which period the composting materials must be turned a minimum of five times. Acceptable feedstocks include, but are not limited to, animal manure, by-products of agricultural commodities processing, and source-separated yard debris or "clean green."	A	1–50		0.1–2.0	0.3–2.0	0.1–0.3
Compost Tea—extracted from sewage sludge and prohibited synthetic nutrient sources is prohibited.	P					
Manure						
Manure—Composted (See Compost)	A	1–50		0.2–2.5	0.4–3.0	0.1–0.4
Manure—Raw animal—(Also manure or compost tea, slurry, lagoon water)—must be composted unless it is: (i) applied to land used for a crop not intended for human consumption, (ii) incorporated into the soil not less than 120 days prior to the harvest of a product whose edible portion has direct contact with the soil surface or soil particles, or (iii) incorporated into the soil not less than 90 days prior to the harvest of a product whose edible portion does not have direct contact with the soil surface or soil particles. Human waste products and sewage sludge are prohibited. Uncomposted manure can contain high levels of plant and human pathogens, weed seeds, volatile and soluble nitrogen and pesticide residues.	R	1–80		0.5–3.0	0.5–3.0	0.1–0.4
Macro and Secondary Nutrients						
Bone meal	A			10–25		
Guano	A			10–18		
Rock phosphate must not be fortified or processed with synthetic chemicals. Cannot be used in California if it originates from western United States sources.	A[d]			0.5–3.0[f]		
Potassium chloride (KCl) Muriate of potash—Only from mined sources. Shall be used in a manner that prevents excessive chloride in soils.	R[d]				60	
Potassium sulfate—nonsynthetic (synthetic or that produced by acidulation or chemical reaction is prohibited).	A[d]				50–52	18

TABLE 21.1 (continued)

Status of organic soil amendments and fertilizing materials†

Material[a]	Status[b]	Moisture (%)	CaCO₃ Equiv. (%)[c]	P₂O₅ (%)[c]	K₂O (%)[c]	S (%)[c]
Macro and Secondary Nutrients						
Sulfate of potash magnesia or potassium magnesium sulfate (Langbeinite)	A[d]				22	18
Sulfur-Elemental—as plant or soil amendment.	A[d]	5–10				95–99
Gypsum	A[d]	5–10				14–17
Micronutrients						
Synthetic, use restricted to cases where soil/plant nutrient deficiency is documented by soil or plant tissue testing: (i) soluble boron products, (ii) sulfates, carbonates, oxides or silicates of zinc, copper, iron, manganese or sodium molybdate. Ammonium molybdate is prohibited.	R					
Sewage Sludge, Biosolids	P					

† In California, a fertilizer is defined as a material having at least 5% by weight singly or in combination of nitrogen (N), phosphorus (P₂O₅), and potassium (K₂O).

[a] References are the USDA-NOP, 2003, Organic Materials Review Institute Generic Materials List, June 2004, and Washington Department of Agriculture organic materials list, March 2007.

[b] Status designations: **Allowed (A)** include nonsynthetic materials that are not specifically prohibited by NOP Rule Section 205.602 and synthetic materials that are specifically allowed by Section 205.601. **Restricted (R)** substances are allowed in organic production subject to NOP rule use restrictions. **Prohibited (P)** substances in crop production are generally defined in NOP Rule Section 205.105.

[c] Concentration is given on a 100% dry matter basis.

[d] A mined substance of low solubility.

[e] Dolomite contains both calcium and magnesium carbonate and excessive buildup of magnesium may be undesirable particularly on high magnesium soils. It is however, an excellent source of magnesium for soils low in magnesium.

[f] Total phosphorus content may range from approximately 18–25% but citrate and water-soluble phosphorus are much lower. Rock phosphate is almost completely ineffective on alkaline soils (pH greater 7.0) because soil acidity must dissolve the material before the phosphorus becomes available to plants. Also, the heavy metal concentrations prohibit the use of rock phosphate originating from western United States sources.

weight (10% moisture). As a result, if the phosphorus content is 1 percent P₂O₅, then there would be 14 pounds (6.4 kg) P₂O₅ per ton in a 30 percent moisture material, whereas a 10 percent moisture manure or compost would contain 18 pounds (8.2 kg) P₂O₅ per ton. If the manure or compost analysis is reported as phosphorus (P) instead of (P₂O₅) concentration, then multiply P by 2.29 to get the P₂O₅ content. Since suppliers give only estimates of both the moisture content and nutrient content, take several samples of the manure or compost and have them analyzed for moisture and nutrient content to get a more accurate estimate of the nutrients purchased and applied.

Some organic fertilizers contribute substantial amounts of organic matter, which often leads to increased water infiltration into the soil. Organic fertilizers may also improve the physical structure of the soil, which allows more air exchange with plant roots. Where organic sources are used for fertilizers, microbial activity usually increases in the soil, which may help make nutrients and water more available to plants. Because of the slow release of nutrients such as nitrate-nitrogen from the organic sources, alfalfa is a desirable crop because the deep roots take up the nitrates prior to being leached into groundwater. Manure and manure-based composts generally have higher phosphorus and potassium content than green wastes and other composts. The use of dairy and other lagoon waters as well as associated lagoon sludge should be evaluated with the organic certifier as to whether they meet organically approved guidelines.

Established Fields

In established alfalfa stands, plant tissue analyses are valuable tools to monitor the nutritional status of the plants in order to make decisions about fertilization needs. For information on how to take plant tissue samples and interpret the test results, see Chapter 6. Soil fertility and plant nutrient status can be maintained most effectively with animal manures, compost, green waste, and other approved organic fertilizers such as bone meal, guano, potassium sulfate, potassium magnesium sulfate and elemental sulfur. Rock phosphate, which can be used as both a liming material and a phosphorus source on acid soils (below pH 6.5), is quite expensive and usually not cost effective. Rock phosphate is almost completely ineffective on alkaline soils (pH greater than 7.0) because soil acidity must dissolve the material before the phosphorus becomes available for use by plants. The heavy metal concentrations of rock phosphate prohibit the use of this material originating from western United States sources.

Fertilizer application timing may be more important with organic alfalfa production than with conventional production due to the effect that organic fertilizer sources have on promoting weed growth. As a result, some variation in timing of organic fertilizer sources may be necessary depending on predominate weed species and the best time to fertilize alfalfa versus favoring competing weeds. Timing the application of manure or compost after the first or second cutting would give alfalfa the competitive edge to take up fertilizer nutrients rather than fertilizing the weeds providing that summer weeds are not problematic. Since many organic fertilizer sources contain nitrogen, applications during the winter months would be more likely to encourage late winter-spring weed growth prior to the onset of alfalfa growth. Making a second application during August or September when the alfalfa is growing vigorously would also serve to benefit alfalfa over weeds.

Insect Pest Management

Insects can be managed in organic alfalfa production using a variety of tools, including varietal resistance, cultural practices, conservation of natural enemies, and the use of approved organic insecticides (Table 21.2). The need for, and use of, all biological pesticides derived from natural sources is restricted and must be explained in the organic system plan. In addition, the organic system plan must justify that the use of cultural practices and preventive, mechanical, and physical methods are insufficient before organically approved pesticides will be allowed. Following is a discussion of organically approved methods for controlling major insect pests of alfalfa. See Chapter 9, "Managing Insects in Alfalfa," for more detailed descriptions of pest and natural enemy species, pest biology, how to sample, and economic thresholds, or refer to the UC Pest Management Guidelines http://ipm.ucdavis.edu.

Alfalfa Weevils

The Egyptian alfalfa weevil (*Hypera brunneipennis*, Boheman) and the alfalfa weevil (*H. postica*, Gyllenhal) are primarily first cutting pests of established alfalfa. They are considered to be the most serious alfalfa pests for organic growers because the larvae of these pests can severely defoliate stands causing yield and quality losses and there are few control options. Organic pesticides, such as Entrust® (spinosad), will give about 65 percent weevil control compared to conventional insecticides, but may not be economical depending on the weevil pressure. In addition, there are no resistant alfalfa varieties, and natural enemies are not efficacious enough to maintain weevil populations below damaging levels. Early cutting, before weevils reach peak numbers, will help control this pest, but yield of the first cutting will likely be reduced. In addition, larvae that survive the harvest process may concentrate under the windrow and cause extensive damage to alfalfa regrowth and possible stand loss.

Flaming with propane in late winter, just prior to when the alfalfa breaks dormancy, can reduce weevil populations by killing adults as well as the eggs that are deposited in the stems. The charred alfalfa stubble may also be less attractive to adults returning to the alfalfa field to lay eggs during late winter. However, the level of control with propane depends on the weevil pressure and will not be as effective as the use of conventional insecticides. In addition, flaming may not be economically feasible given the high costs of fuel and should be weighed relative to the value of the alfalfa hay.

Winter grazing with sheep (See Chapter 17, "Alfalfa Utilization by Livestock") has also been shown to decrease the number of weevils and increase alfalfa yields (by consuming and trampling eggs and larvae that reside in the plant stems). However, for this option to be viable timing is critical and sheep are often

difficult to obtain, so this practice may be limited. Grazing must occur when weevil eggs are hatching (January to March, depending on the field location) and the fields must be grazed to the ground. The sheep should also be managed carefully to prevent stand loss, especially under wet conditions. There is some suggestion that harrowing for winter weed control in established alfalfa stands may also provide some weevil control, but damage to the alfalfa crowns may occur making them more susceptible to diseases.

Overseeding alfalfa in the fall with grass or legume forages (which are not preferred by weevils) will increase spring yields and help compensate for losses caused by weevil damage to the alfalfa (see Chapter 15, "Managing

TABLE 21.2

Organically approved methods for controlling major insect pests in alfalfa in California[1]

Pest	Status[2]	Comments[3]
Egyptian Alfalfa Weevil		
Early harvest	A	Yield may be reduced.
Grazing or "sheeping off"	A	For maximum effectiveness, grazing must be timed at egg hatch (look for first signs of larvae and plant damage during winter). Animals must be managed carefully to prevent overgrazing and stand loss, especially under wet conditions.
Flaming with propane	A	Timing should occur at egg hatch. Degree of control depends on the severity of the weevil infestation and may not be economical.
Overseeding	A	Alters quality and possibly yield of harvested forage.
Entrust (spinosad) insecticide	R	May not be economical, depending on weevil pressure (65% average control compared with conventional insecticides).
Armyworms and Alfalfa Caterpillars		
Early harvest	A	Yield may be reduced.
Microbial insecticides	R	Most effective on smaller instars (XenTari, Agree).
Conservation of natural enemies	A	Border or strip harvesting.
Aphids		
Varietal resistance	A	See http://alfalfa.org for alfalfa varieties.
Conservation of natural enemies	A	Border or strip harvesting.
Early harvest	A	Yields may be impacted.
Pyrethrum, PyGanic, or Azadirachtin (Neem) insecticide	R	May not be economical.

[1]The need for and use of insecticides derived from natural sources should be explained in the organic system plan. The organic system plan must justify that the use of cultural practices and preventive, mechanical, and physical methods are insufficient before organically approved insecticides are allowed.

[2]Status designations: **Allowed (A)** include nonsynthetic materials that are not specifically prohibited by NOP rule Section 205.602 and synthetic materials that are specifically allowed by Section 205.601. **Restricted (R)** substances are allowed in organic production subject to NOP Rule use restrictions. **Prohibited (P)** substances in crop production are generally defined in NOP Rule Section 205.105.

[3]References are the USDA-NOP, 2003, Organic Materials Review Institute Generic Materials List, June 2004.

Depleted Alfalfa Stands"). However, this practice will change the forage quality and potential market and value of the alfalfa hay. Overseeding may also reduce the vigor of the alfalfa stand, so this practice should only be considered for weakened or older alfalfa stands that are in the final years of production.

Aphids

Most recently released alfalfa varieties have resistance to the pea aphid (*Acyrthosiphon pisum*, Harris), blue alfalfa aphid (*A. kondoi*, Shinji), and spotted alfalfa aphid (*Therioaphis maculata*, Buckton). Organic growers should choose varieties that have the highest level of resistance possible to help control these pests. A fourth aphid species, the cowpea aphid (*Aphis craccivora* Koch), is occasionally found infesting alfalfa, but host plant resistance is not yet available for this pest.

To manage aphids, one should preserve and enhance natural enemies such as ladybugs, lacewings, and parasitic wasps by border or strip cutting (see Chapter 9, "Managing Insects in Alfalfa") to leave habitat and some prey for the beneficial insects so they stay in the field. There is also a naturally occurring fungus that helps control some aphid species during warm, wet periods; however, it is not commercially available. Early harvest, as well as flaming, may help control aphids, but due to the high cost, flaming is not likely to be economically viable. The use of pyrethrum (PyGanic) or azadirachtin (Neemix, Agroneem, or Trilogy) may help control aphids in alfalfa if outbreaks occur, but the degree of control with these materials may not be economical and should be weighed relative to the value of the alfalfa hay.

Caterpillars

The beet armyworm (*Spodoptera exigua*, Hubner), western yellow striped armyworm (*S. praefica* Grote), and the alfalfa caterpillar (*Colias eurytheme* Boisduval) are major pests of alfalfa with outbreaks usually occurring in July and August. Early cutting, before significant damage occurs to the alfalfa, will help manage these pests. Most larvae that survive the cutting process are killed by the hot dry

conditions or preyed upon by birds following harvest so will not damage alfalfa regrowth under the windrows. However, the larger armyworm larvae can migrate to surrounding crops so it may be advisable to plow a ditch between the alfalfa and the adjacent crop and fill it with water to keep them from moving beyond the field. Conservation and enhancement of naturally occurring beneficial insects will also help provide biological control of caterpillar pests. This can be done through strip or border cutting to help retain the beneficial insects in the field as described in Chapter 9. The alfalfa caterpillar, beet armyworm, and western yellow striped armyworms can also be controlled with the microbial insecticides XenTari or Agree (*Bacillus thuringiensis* subsp. *aizawai*) when the insects are in the small larval stages.

Weed Management

Strategies for managing weeds in seedling and established organic alfalfa without herbicides involve a combination of practices including good seedbed preparation, selective grazing, harrowing, flaming with liquid propane, adjusting irrigation and cutting schedules, and overseeding with alternative forages (Table 21.3). For more detailed information on all weed control practices in alfalfa, see Chapter 8, "Weed Management in Alfalfa."

Seedling Fields

Establishing vigorous alfalfa fields is critical for weed management throughout the life of the stand because strong stands help outcompete weeds. Prior to planting, prepare a good seedbed, preferably on well-drained soils, to ensure good seed germination and prevent plant dieback as a result of standing water. Planting alfalfa in rows on beds or on shallow corrugations is commonly practiced in areas where soils lack sufficient drainage. However, some organic growers have found increased weed problems in furrows.

Planting should occur in the fall (September–October) when conditions favor stand establishment. Alfalfa fields planted during winter (December) will grow too slowly,

TABLE 21.3

Organically approved methods for weed control in alfalfa in California

Stage of stand	Status[1]	Comments
Seedling fields		
Time of seeding	A	Seed early fall when summer weeds are not as competitive and before winter weeds germinate for optimum alfalfa vigor.
Early harvest	A	Yield and stand may be impacted, especially under high weed densities.
Grazing or "sheeping off"	A	Must manage sheep carefully to prevent soil compaction and stand loss, especially under wet conditions. Perennial and/or grass weeds less affected.
Interplanting oats with alfalfa	A	Generally lowers nutritional value of harvested forage for the first and second cutting.
Established fields		
Grazing or "sheeping off"	A	Must manage sheep carefully to prevent soil compaction and stand loss, especially under wet conditions.
Flaming with propane	A	Best used for spot treatment of weed-infested areas (such as dodder) due to the high fuel costs.
Adjust irrigation and cutting schedules	A	Most useful for management of summer weeds. Effectiveness depends on soil type and weed pressure.
Overseeding	A	Changes quality of harvested forage.
Tillage	A	Practice occurs when alfalfa is dormant. May injure alfalfa crowns leading to plant disease.

[1]Status designations: **Allowed (A)** include nonsynthetic materials that are not specifically prohibited by NOP Rule Section 205.602 and synthetic materials that are specifically allowed by Section 205.601. **Restricted (R)** substances are allowed in organic production subject to NOP rule use restrictions. **Prohibited (P)** substances in crop production are generally defined in NOP Rule Section 205.105.

allowing winter weeds to take over while those planted late spring will likely be overrun by summer weeds. Fall plantings are especially important for fields infested with field bindweed (*Convolvulus arvensis* L.), perennial grasses, or nutsedge (*Cyperus* spp.) to ensure that the alfalfa becomes well established to help outcompete these weeds when they start growing in the spring. If possible, a more non-dormant variety should be selected to ensure fast regrowth following harvests to further help with weed suppression. Prior to planting, the fields should be irrigated to germinate weeds followed by tillage with a spring-toothed harrow and ring-roller for weed control and seedbed preparation.

Interplanting oats (*Avena sativa* L.) with the alfalfa during stand establishment can suppress weeds without the use of herbicides, and the oats also help reduce soil erosion. The oats should be planted at the same time as the alfalfa at a seeding rate of 15–20 pounds per acre (17–22 kg per hectare). The first several cuttings will be a mixture of oats and alfalfa, which will affect the marketability of the hay (dairy versus other feed). However, losses in quality should be offset by higher yields, and by the third cutting pure alfalfa will be harvested. There should be minimal impact on alfalfa stand density. Curing time for the first cutting will be several days longer than for alfalfa alone.

If weeds become established in seedling stands, fields should be cut close to the ground in the spring to help inhibit weed growth. This will allow the alfalfa to regrow and compete more successfully against existing weeds. In the Low Desert, sheep grazing is sometimes used to remove winter annual weeds in new plantings. Harvest management practices should be followed as outlined in Chapter 13, "Harvest Strategies for Alfalfa," to prevent stand injury caused by cutting or grazing too early or under wet conditions.

Established Fields

Grazing or "sheeping off" during the winter can provide good weed control in established fields (Fig. 21.2), but the sheep must be managed carefully to prevent stand loss, especially under wet conditions. Harrowing also provides some winter weed control, but may cause some stand loss from uprooting and injury of the alfalfa crowns. Flaming can provide some control of seedling weeds, including dodder (*Cuscuta* spp. L), but given the high cost of fuel this practice is best suited for spot treatments of weed-infested areas.

Adjusting irrigation and cutting schedules can also inhibit weeds and enhance stand life. Irrigating alfalfa as close to harvest as possible will allow the alfalfa to regrow more quickly after cutting. Shading will help the alfalfa compete against seedling weeds. Dry soil after harvest also minimizes weed seed germination when the canopy is open. A shorter cutting interval improves forage quality, but reduces alfalfa vigor and encourages weed growth. As a result, alfalfa stands should be properly managed to take into account the tradeoff between time of cutting, yield, forage quality, and stand life.

Overseeding alfalfa stands with annual or perennial grasses or legumes will also help suppress weeds (Fig. 21.3), but is only recommended for weakened or older stands that are in their final years of production. Typically overseeding occurs in the fall after harrowing alfalfa fields to prepare a seedbed and the forage is seeded directly into the stand. Yields are enhanced for spring cuttings, but the forage is mixed, affecting forage quality and markets. For more information on this practice, see Chapter 15, "Managing Depleted Alfalfa Stands."

Disease Management

There are many diseases that cause yield, quality, and stand losses in alfalfa as described in Chapter 10, "Alfalfa Diseases and Management." This chapter focuses on the most significant alfalfa diseases with an emphasis on the use of resistant plant varieties and cultural practices to maintain healthy alfalfa stands. Plant resistant variety information can be found in Chapter 5, "Choosing an Alfalfa Variety," and through the National Alfalfa Alliance, http://alfalfa.org.

FIGURE 21.2

Grazing with sheep can be used to manage weeds in alfalfa stands.

FIGURE 21.3

Interseeding or overseeding oats in alfalfa can be used to help manage insects and weeds, and increase productivity of aging stands.

The major diseases that can affect alfalfa stand establishment include the soilborne fungi *Rhizoctonia spp.*, *Pythium spp.*, and *Phytophthora spp.*, that may cause dieback of seedlings before or soon after they emerge. These diseases are favored by poor growing conditions including too much water, compacted or poorly drained soils, and temperatures unfavorable for alfalfa germination and growth. To manage these diseases, alfalfa should be planted during early fall when conditions are most favorable for alfalfa growth. On heavier soils where waterlogging may occur, growers should consider planting alfalfa on beds to help with drainage. However, this strategy must be balanced by increased weed pressure that may occur in the furrows due to the lack of competition from established alfalfa plants.

One of the major soilborne diseases of established alfalfa is root and crown rot caused by *Phytophthora spp.* Saturated soils are required for this disease, so proper soil preparation (eliminating low spots) and good irrigation management can reduce the opportunity for this fungus to infect roots. Select plant varieties that are resistant to phytophthora, which come in many different dormancy classes. For heavy soils with a potential to waterlog, consider selecting a more dormant variety that begins to grow later in the season when soils dry as alfalfa is most sensitive to root rot when it is actively growing in wet conditions. However, this strategy should be balanced with a reduction in yield associated with more dormant varieties, though hay quality may improve. Growers should also be careful not to stress fields by over or under irrigating or cutting fields too frequently as stressed plants will be more susceptible to diseases.

Other root and crown diseases such as anthracnose and stagonospora can reduce stands. Cultivars resistant to anthracnose are listed in the National Alfalfa Alliance publication. For these diseases, and also many of the foliar diseases such as common leaf spot, spring blackstem, and downy mildew and bacterial caused diseases, crop rotation is helpful in reducing disease pressure. The pathogens causing these diseases survive in alfalfa stems, old leaves and rotting crowns. Rotating out of alfalfa for a minimum of 2 years should reduce the inoculum in the field and delay infection of new plants. Another strategy is to cut and bale younger fields before older ones to reduce the introduction of infected alfalfa debris into the new fields when harvesting. Within reason, when moving from old to new fields, blow out any leaves or stems that are in or on harvest equipment. If leaf spots become widespread, early harvest can minimize defoliation due to the loss of infected leaves.

Sclerotinia stem and crown rot, which is a problem during wet winters, can be managed in established fields by taking a late fall cutting so that there is relatively little canopy during December and January when this disease is most likely to occur. For seedling fields, plantings in February or March will usually avoid this disease but the advantages of a fall planting (quick emergence, less weed competition, higher yields the first year) are lost.

Nematode Management

Plant parasitic nematodes are microscopic roundworms that live in the soil and feed either on or in alfalfa plants, causing extensive chronic yield and quality losses. Although there are many types of nematodes affecting alfalfa production, this chapter focuses on organic management practices for the major root-knot and stem nematodes found in California. For more detailed information on nematodes, including sampling and identification of species, see Chapter 11 on "Parasitic Nematodes in Alfalfa."

Alfalfa roots infected with the root-knot nematode (*Meloidogyne spp.*) have numerous firm galls and may branch excessively. Stem nematodes (*Ditylenchus dispsaci*, Kuhn) cause plants to have shortened, stunted and chlorotic stems with swollen nodes (where leaves attach to stems) and short internodes. The key approach to managing these nematodes is to use resistant plant varieties, which are available in many different dormancy types (refer to the National Alfalfa Alliance at http://alfalfa.org). Be sure to know the nematode species infecting the field because varietal resistance to one nematode species does not necessarily mean the alfalfa will be resistant to another species. For stem nematode control, use certified seed to minimize the chance of contaminating previously uninfested land.

When selecting a site to plant organic alfalfa, select fields that are not infested with nematodes known to be pathogenic to alfalfa. It is also important to wash farm equipment with water to remove soil and plant debris when moving between fields. Avoid using irrigation runoff water from known nematode infested fields to irrigate uncontaminated fields. Delaying cutting until the top 2 to 3 inches of soil is dry will minimize the spread of stem nematode.

For stem nematode control, a 3- to 4-year crop rotation with small grains, cotton, beans, corn, lettuce, melons, carrots, or tomatoes will help control this pest in alfalfa. However, root-knot nematodes have a wide host range in both crops and weeds, so crop rotation is usually not feasible for managing this nematode. The addition of soil amendments prior to planting, including cover crops or composted plant and animal materials, may also help manage nematodes. Such benefits may include improved soil and plant health (reducing nematode stress), enhanced microbial activity including nematode-feeding organisms, and the production of nematode-killing compounds from certain plant breakdown products (such as rapeseed). However, the efficacy of soil amendments on actual nematode mortality and corresponding plant yield is still not well known.

> *For stem nematode control, a 3- to 4-year crop rotation with small grains, cotton, beans, corn, lettuce, melons, carrots, or tomatoes will help control this pest in alfalfa.*

Vertebrate Pest Management

Pocket gophers (*Thomomys* spp.), voles or meadow mice (*Microtus* spp.), and ground squirrels (*Spermophilus* spp.) can be significant pests of alfalfa. Feeding damage, both above and below ground by these rodents, can significantly weaken and often kill alfalfa plants, resulting in yield, forage quality, and stand losses. In addition, the gopher and squirrel burrows and tunnels can cause damage to harvest equipment and disrupt irrigation flows. Since there are no rodenticides available for use in organic alfalfa production, management practices primarily focus on cultural and mechanical practices for rodent control. For more detailed information on the biology of gophers, squirrels, and voles as well as other vertebrate pests found in alfalfa, see Chapter 12, "Integrated Management of Vertebrate Pests in Alfalfa."

If there were problems with rodents in previous crops, consider rotating with cereal crops (barley, wheat, oats, ryegrass, or sudangrass), which may reduce gopher activity. Prior to planting alfalfa, check the field and the surrounding landscape to determine possible sources of vertebrate pests. Remove unmanaged cover along fencerows, roadsides, and ditch banks where rodents often hide and build up to prevent them from dispersing into new alfalfa fields. During ground preparation, deep tillage can be used to disrupt or destroy ground squirrel burrows prior to planting alfalfa. However, gophers can survive cultivation and deep tillage, so they should be trapped where activity is observed prior to planting.

In established alfalfa, flood irrigation nearly eliminates ground squirrels (except perhaps on field edges) and can significantly decrease gopher numbers, possibly reducing the potential for large populations to rebuild. Reducing the amount of vegetative cover during the winter months by mowing and sheep grazing will aid in reducing voles. Shooting, trapping, and the use of owl boxes and perches to attract raptors, as well as encouraging other birds such as egrets and herons to forage in alfalfa, may also help improve the control of rodents.

Additional Reading

Canevari, W.M., D.H. Putnam, W.T. Lanini, *R.F. Long, S.B. Orloff, B.A. Reed, R.N. Vargas.* 2000. Overseeding and companion cropping in alfalfa. University of California Division of Agriculture and Natural Resources, Oakland. Publication 21594.

CDFA-OP. California Department of Food and Agriculture, California Organic Program, http://www.cdfa.ca.gov/is/i_&_c/organic .html.

Long, R., S. Orloff, R. Meyer. 2007. Sample costs to produce organic alfalfa hay in California. University of California Cooperative Extension. http://coststudies .ucdavis.edu.

National Alfalfa Alliance. http://alfalfa.org.

OMRI. Organic Materials Review Institute, http://www.omri.org.

UC IPM. University of California integrated pest management guidelines for alfalfa. http://www.ipm.ucdavis.edu/PMG/select-newpest.alfalfa-hay.html.

USDA. U.S. Department of Agriculture National Organic Program (NOP) regulations. http:// www.ams.usda.gov/nop/.

WSDA. Washington State Department of Agriculture organic materials lists and material registration. http://agr.wa.gov/ FoodAnimal/Organic/MaterialsLists.htm.

22

Alfalfa Seed Production in California

Shannon C. Mueller
Farm Advisor, University of California Cooperative Extension, Fresno, CA

California is an ideal location for production of high quality alfalfa seed. Although seed production has declined in recent decades, this state remains the primary producer in the United States. Nondormant varieties (fall dormancy [FD] ratings of 7–10) are the dominant varieties grown for seed in the Mediterranean and Desert zones of California, particularly Fresno, Kings, and Imperial Counties.

Alfalfa seed produced throughout the world is primarily used for forage production. Seed is planted to produce alfalfa for grazing, greenchop, silage, baled hay, cubes, or pellets to support the livestock industry, including dairy, beef, horses, goats, and sheep. A very small fraction of the total production is used by the sprout industry. This chapter provides an overview of alfalfa seed production techniques in California.

Scope of the Seed Industry

Approximately 80 million pounds (36.3 million kg) of alfalfa seed are produced in the United States each year (Fig. 22.1). Eighty-five percent of that total is produced in the five western states—California, Idaho, Oregon, Washington, and Nevada. U.S. acreage ranged from 60 to 75 thousand acres (24 to 30 thousand hectares) between 2002 and 2006, but was greater than 150,000 acres (60,000 ha) during the 1990s. The balance of the seed

FIGURE 22.1

Alfalfa seed production for the five western states.

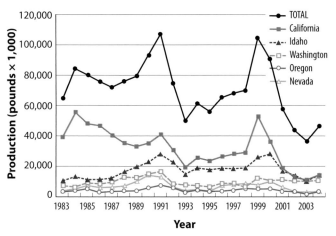

FIGURE 22.2

Alfalfa seed acreage for the five western states.

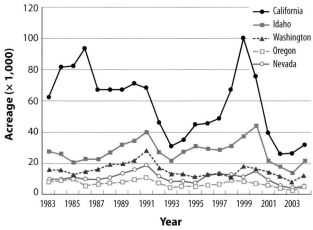

FIGURE 22.3

Alfalfa seed yield for the five western states.

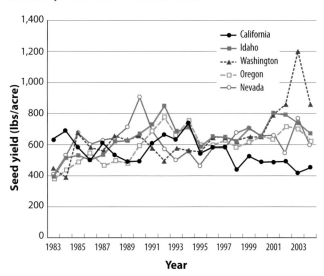

comes primarily from Arizona, Utah, Montana, and Wyoming. Seed production systems in each of these states are tailored to balance the climate and soil conditions with management to optimize seed yield and quality.

Historically, California has been the largest supplier of alfalfa seed in the United States. However, due to changes in economics, environmental constraints, and regulatory issues, acreage in California has declined (Fig. 22.2). As acreage decreased in California, expansion in Idaho and other northwestern states maintained U.S. supplies at a nearly constant level. Production on a per-acre basis has been fairly steady within a given seed-producing region (Fig. 22.3). Production in California is located in the central San Joaquin Valley (Fresno and Kings Counties), the Imperial Valley, and in Yolo County, near Sacramento.

Ninety-five percent of the seed produced in California is of nondormant varieties (FD 7–10). A significant percentage of California's production is exported. The Pacific Northwest produces seed of semidormant (FD 5–6) and dormant (FD 2–4) varieties. Seed of a specific dormancy class is normally produced in its area of adaptation to prevent genetic shifts.

Stand Establishment

Site Selection

Alfalfa seed production is well adapted to the arid climates of the western United States. A warm, dry production and harvest season is important to maximize seed yield and quality. Alfalfa seed production is best suited to deep, well-drained soils; heavier clay or loam soils are preferred over lighter, sandy soils. Seed fields in California are irrigated, and heavy soils, characterized by high water holding capacity, are more easily managed for seed production. Soils should be low in alkali and in soluble salts; however, salt-tolerant varieties can produce high seed yields in saline soils. Alfalfa seed can be grown on soils with a shallow water table (3–4 feet [0.9-1.2 m] from the surface) if special care is taken with respect to irrigation and field management.

Time of Seeding

Properly timed production practices are the key to high seed yield and quality. Successful seed production begins with proper stand establishment. The majority of seed alfalfa stands are established in the fall. The recommended planting dates are the same as for alfalfa forage production (mid-September through October in the central San Joaquin Valley); however, growers are often forced by constraints of their crop rotations to schedule later planting dates. If planting takes place during the winter months (November–January), alfalfa seed germinates and emerges slowly, giving winter weeds a competitive advantage, thereby hampering stand establishment. Spring (February) establishment of alfalfa seed fields is possible, but the seed harvest is later and yield for that year will be lower. Recommended land preparation procedures used for planting alfalfa hay in the area should be followed when establishing stands for seed production. See Chapter 4, "Stand Establishment," for specific information regarding planting recommendations.

Solid Versus Row Planting

Where alfalfa stands are dedicated to seed production, growers most often plant in rows. If the grower plans to take forage from the field as well as a seed crop, then solid plantings will give higher forage yields. A grower must consider the difficulties imposed by managing a field for both seed and forage, as compared to the individual crop options. Dense stands maximize hay production, but typically produce lower seed yields than thinner stands. In addition, chemicals used in the production of the seed crop often limit the future use of the field for forage production. In some areas, certified seed production requires that the field be planted in rows to enable assessment of volunteer alfalfa control.

Row-planted fields may be flat planted or planted on beds (Fig. 22.4). Bed planting is usually more successful than flat planting because early cultivation for weed control is possible, and it permits furrow rather than flood irrigation. The distance between the rows or beds is usually determined by the growth potential in

FIGURE 22.4

Alfalfa seed production in rows on a bedded production system.

that location, which is influenced by soil texture, water availability, variety, and length of the growing season. If the plants tend to grow vigorously in a given area, wider row spacing (40 inches [102 cm]) may be preferred over a narrower spacing (30 inches [76 cm]) used when smaller plants are produced.

A number of interacting factors contribute to higher yield and quality from thinner, row-planted stands:

- Water management is enhanced when seed fields are planted on beds.

- Honey bee pollination is improved in thinner stands since bees have better access to bloom.

- The efficacy of pesticide applications increases due to better spray penetration within the canopy.

- Volunteer alfalfa and weed control is easier to assess and carry out.

- Desiccation in preparation for harvest is optimized.

- There is less lodging of the canopy, which improves overall seed quality.

TABLE 22.1

First and second year alfalfa seed yields from plant spacing trial, Mendota, CA; all treatments were on beds in 30" (76 cm) rows

Planting Date, Variety, and Seeding Treatment	Spacing (inches)[1]	Yield (pounds/acre)[1] 1990	1991
Fall Planted (11/5/89) Variety: CUF 101			
Unthinned Control	Unthinned[2]	621	1,397
Thinned	Thinned[2]	647	1,473
Spaced	4	740	1,482
Spaced	8	684	1,418
Spaced	12	727	1,378
Spaced	18	726	1,382
	LSD (0.05)[3]	ns	ns
	CV (%)[3]	7.27	7.10
Spring Planted (3/1/90) Variety: WL 605			
Unthinned Control	Unthinned	487 b	1,321
Thinned	Thinned	567 ab	1,349
Spaced	4	607 a	1,395
Spaced	8	644 a	1,371
Spaced	12	653 a	1,294
Spaced	18	639 a	1,311
	LSD (0.05)	93.7	ns
	CV (%)	8.59	4.82
Comparisons[3]			
Fall Planted—Unthinned vs. thinned and spaced plantings	Significance	*[3]	ns
Spring Planted—Unthinned vs. thinned and spaced plantings	Significance	**	ns
Fall Planted—Unthinned and thinned vs. spaced plantings	Significance	**	ns
Spring Planted—Unthinned and thinned vs. spaced plantings	Significance	**	ns

[1] To convert inches to cm, multiply times 2.54. To convert lb/acre to kg/ha, multiply by 1.12.

[2] Unthinned = 1.5 lbs/acre seed (approx. 15 plants/foot). Thinned = 1.5 lbs/acre seed in solid planted rows that were later thinned to alternating areas of 6 inches of planted space and 6 to 12 inches where plants are removed.

[3] LSD = Least Significant Difference at P≤0.05. Values followed by the same letter are not significantly different; C.V. = Coefficient of Variation. Comparisons are orthogonal comparisons: * = Significant at P=0.05, **=Significant at P = 0.01, ns = nonsignificant by F-test.

Plant Population (Seeding Rate)

The density of plants in the entire field, or within an individual row, has a direct effect on alfalfa seed yield. Improved water use efficiency, pest control, and pollination are thought to be factors contributing to higher yields in thinner stands. In addition, higher seed yields may be associated with higher levels of carbohydrate reserves in plants. Plants with high root reserves produce more stems, more pods per stem, and more seeds per pod than plants with reduced carbohydrate concentrations.

Stand density can be controlled either by reducing the seeding rate or by thinning the stand once plants emerge. There are risks associated with both of these approaches. Low seeding rates have a higher risk of stand failure if adverse conditions prevail. On the other hand, weather conditions may prevent equipment or crews from entering the field at the optimum time for thinning, which may impact seed yield. Planting at very low seeding rates requires pelleted seed and precision planting equipment. Excellent alfalfa stands for seed production have been successfully established with 0.5 to 0.75 pounds (0.2–0.3 kg) of seed per acre or less in row plantings, and 6 to 10 pounds (2.7–4.5 kg) of seed per acre in solid stands.

The plant density required to optimize seed yield depends on row spacing and soil type, which influence growth and final size of the alfalfa plant. In a 1990 trial on a clay loam soil, solid row plantings and conventionally thinned plantings were compared with plots planted using precision equipment to place individual seeds from 4 to 18 inches (10–46 cm) apart. Fall and spring planting dates were evaluated. All rows were planted on beds spaced 30 inches (76 cm) apart. In the first year, plantings with seed spaced from 4 to 18 inches apart produced higher yields than solid plantings or thinned plantings (Table 22.1). Differences in water use efficiency and maturity were also noted. In the second year of the trial, there were no significant differences in seed yield when spaced plantings were compared with solid or hand-thinned plantings.

Seeding Methods

When planting, seed depth should not exceed 0.5 inch (1.3 cm). Alfalfa seed is small and has only a limited amount of reserves to carry the seedling through to emergence. Poor stand establishment with uneven emergence and skipped areas will result if the seed is planted too deep or into a poorly prepared seedbed. If the field does not have a history of alfalfa production, inoculation of the seed with the proper *Rhizobium* bacteria is desirable prior to planting to ensure adequate nodulation for nitrogen fixation.

Seed may either be planted to moisture or irrigated following planting. The surface layer of soil must stay moist to promote uniform germination and seedling establishment.

Cultural Practices

Thinning of Stands

Using traditional management practices, thinner stands are an advantage in seed production. The common practice has been to plant a solid row and later thin the row to alternating areas of 6 inches (15 cm) of planted space and 6 to 12 inches (15–30 cm) where plants are removed using a hoe or by cross disking. First-year stands are thinned when the seedlings are in the two- to four-trifoliolate leaf stage. Mechanical thinning can be used if the stand is uniform with three to five plants per foot. However, hand hoeing is preferred if the stand is not uniform since large skips in the row can be avoided. In established stands, most growers thin in the fall, after harvest, by cross disking or "cross-blocking." Since the adoption of alfalfa leafcutting bees (*Megachile rotundata* (F.)) for pollination in the central San Joaquin Valley, most growers do not believe it is necessary to thin alfalfa seed fields to achieve maximum yields.

Clipback

Once the stand is established, fields are clipped in the spring (early April in the central San Joaquin Valley) to initiate the seed production season. The clipping may be a forage harvest, chopping, chemical clipping, or taken by grazing sheep, depending on grower preference and previous pesticide use in the field. The field should be coming into bloom at the time of clipback, or initial seed set may be reduced due to the negative impact on root reserves. The purpose of clipback is to encourage plants to come into bloom uniformly and to synchronize bloom with the period in the season when pollinators are most active. Spring clipping also removes growth that has overwintered, and cleans up the field for herbicide applications. Clipback can be followed by light harrowing and row cultivation to control weeds and volunteer alfalfa from the previous harvest. Many growers also cultipack fields immediately after clipback to conserve moisture, firm seed beds, and smooth fields to reduce soil contamination at harvest.

> *The purpose of clipback is to encourage plants to come into bloom uniformly and to synchronize bloom with the period in the season when pollinators are most active.*

Following clipback, regrowth is initiated and the plant blooms approximately 35 to 45 days later. Properly timed and uniformly scheduled within an area, clipback is also used as a cultural method for controlling the alfalfa seed chalcid (*Bruchophagus roddi* Gussakovsky). If all fields are close to the same stage of maturity due to a uniform clipback schedule, seed is not at a susceptible stage of development when peak emergence of chalcid occurs. Early April clipping interrupts the chalcid life cycle and has reduced damage to seed crops by chalcid to less than 0.5 percent from a high of 16 percent in the early 1960s.

Fertilization

Soil tests can provide an indication of the fertility status of a field prior to planting. Specific fertilizer recommendations for seed alfalfa production in the western United States are not currently available. Fertility is considered adequate if the crop is grown in rotation with other crops where fertility is adequate. If a field is known to be deficient in a particular nutrient, apply necessary fertilizers before planting. Most researchers have been unable to detect increases in seed yield as a result of soil or foliar applications of fertilizer containing either major or minor elements.

Supplying Water

In the central San Joaquin Valley, alfalfa grown for seed requires 3.5 to 4 acre-feet (0.43–0.49 ha-m) of water per year as irrigation or effective rainfall. However, the timing of irrigation is a critical aspect of seed production and differs significantly from alfalfa forage production.

First-year seed fields may require less water than established stands because soil moisture often remains after harvest of the previous crop, and the alfalfa has a less-well-developed root system during the establishment year. Approximately 3 acre-feet (0.37 ha-m) of water should be adequate for a first-year stand. Both the timing and amount of water applied in an irrigation can greatly affect the condition of the field and subsequent seed production.

When water is available, fall, winter, and early spring irrigations are applied to fill the soil profile and help moderate summer irrigation extremes. During the season, controlled moisture stress is considered an important component in the water management of alfalfa for seed production. In the Central Valley, two to three flushes of bloom are typically produced from the crown, pollinated, matured, and harvested at one time in early fall. Irrigation must be properly timed during each of the bloom cycles to promote slow continuous growth, bloom, and seed set without severely stressing the plant. If the plants are severely stressed, growth and flower production stops. If too much water is applied,

> *When water is available, fall, winter, and early spring irrigations are applied to fill the soil profile and help moderate summer irrigation extremes.*

vegetative production is promoted and seed set suffers. Late in the season, adequate moisture must be available to mature the seed crop, but then soil moisture must be depleted or plants will not dry down sufficiently in preparation for harvest. Most irrigation systems are surface systems—flood or furrow—but some seed is grown under sprinkler irrigation. Drip irrigation systems are rare in alfalfa seed fields.

Irrigation Timing

There are few tools available that allow growers to better time their irrigation events. Gypsum blocks, tensiometers, and neutron probes provide good indications of soil water status, but they may not function properly in the moisture range where growers attempt to pollinate seed fields. They also do not work in areas with shallow water tables. In an irrigation trial conducted in the central San Joaquin Valley from 1988 through 1990, maximum seed yields were associated with treatments that allowed midday plant leaf water potential (LWP) to drop to –2.5 megapascals (MPa) (–25 bars) before irrigation. Later in the season, LWP can be allowed to drop to –3.0 (MPa) (–30 bars) or lower during the preharvest dry-down period.

When timing irrigation, growers take pollinator activity into consideration. Irrigating immediately before introducing honey bees to a field or during peak pollinator activity could be devastating to seed production potential. Honey bees are not as active in recently irrigated fields because of a reduction in the available sugars in the nectar. Growers often stress alfalfa fields to encourage honey bees to pollinate the bloom. When reaching the point where irrigation is necessary, they may time a pesticide application in conjunction with their irrigation to minimize the length of time that honey bees are repelled from the field. Alfalfa leafcutting bees do not show this same reluctance to enter recently irrigated fields.

Weed and Pest Management

Weed Management

In addition to concerns about competition from unwanted plants, weed management in alfalfa seed fields is important because there are strict requirements regarding the purity of certified seed. No primary or secondary noxious weeds are permitted in certified seed fields. From stand establishment through the final cleaning and conditioning process, the goal is to eliminate weeds. In the field, growers use a combination of herbicides, mechanical cultivation, and weeding crews to remove weeds. Volunteer alfalfa plants in certified seed fields should be treated as weeds.

During conditioning, a variety of screening and separation techniques are used to remove foreign material. However, depending on the level of contamination, substantial quantities of alfalfa seed can be lost in the cleaning process, so it is more efficient and economical to control weeds in the field, or at least prevent them from going to seed.

Dodder Control

Dodder (*Cuscuta* spp., primarily *C. indecora* Choisy, *C. campestris* Yunck and *C. planiflora* Ten.) can be a particularly troublesome weed in alfalfa seed fields (Fig. 22.5). There is zero tolerance for dodder seeds in certified alfalfa seed. Dodder is a parasite that lives off the host plant; it has no direct connection to the soil once it has attached itself to the host. To control dodder once it has attached, you must destroy and remove the above-ground portions of the plant. Currently registered herbicides can only control dodder prior to emergence and attachment. However, dodder continues to germinate throughout the production season, when residual activity of herbicides declines. Spot burning, or clipping and carrying dodder-infested plants out of the field, will control late-emerging dodder that attaches to the alfalfa seed plant. Often, the alfalfa is killed in an area during the dodder control process, giving weeds a greater opportunity to encroach.

FIGURE 22.5

Dodder in alfalfa seed.

Dodder seed is one of the most difficult weed seeds to remove during the cleaning process since it is approximately the same size as alfalfa seed. Removal requires a recleaning of the alfalfa seed with a magnetic separator to remove dodder seeds, which usually increases the loss of alfalfa seed from 2 to 15 percent. If dodder seed is not removed, the lot cannot be certified.

Insect Pests

A number of arthropod pests have an impact on the yield or quality of alfalfa seed, or both. Major pests include lygus bugs (*Lygus* spp.), spider mites (*Tetranychus* spp.), and alfalfa seed chalcid (*Bruchophagus roddi*) (Figs. 22.6–22.8). Occasionally stink bugs (*Chlorochroa sayi* Stal and *Euschistus conspersus* Unler) and armyworms (*Spodoptera* spp.) may require control measures. Resistant cultivars of alfalfa have been effective in controlling pea aphid (*Acyrthosiphon pisum* Harris), blue alfalfa aphid (*Acyrthosiphon kondoi* Shinji), and spotted alfalfa aphid (*Therioaphis maculata* Buckton). For this reason, they are only considered to be major pests on susceptible varieties grown for seed in California. The cowpea aphid (*Aphis craccivora* Koch.), which is a shiny, black aphid, has been a sporadic summer pest in black eye beans (*Vigna unguiculata* (L.) Walp), but showed up in high numbers in Desert and San Joaquin Valley alfalfa fields during spring 1999. Hundreds of aphids can develop on a single

FIGURE 22.6

Lygus bug damage to alfalfa. (a) Lygus bug adult, and (b) stem showing stripping at the top of the plant caused by lygus bug feeding.

FIGURE 22.7

Spider mite damage to alfalfa. (a) Close-up photo of leaf damage caused by spider mites, and (b) webbing over leaves and stems caused by spider mites.

FIGURE 22.8

Alfalfa seed chalcid adult (bottom left), and damage from exit hole in seed (center) and pod (right), as compared to an undamaged alfalfa seed (left).

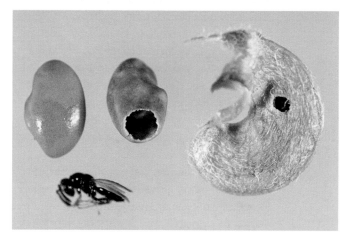

plant, producing large amounts of honeydew and desiccating green tissue. Efforts are underway to develop host plant resistance to this aphid in new alfalfa cultivars.

Beneficial insects in alfalfa seed fields include minute pirate bugs (*Orius* spp.), big-eyed bugs (*Geocoris* spp.), damsel bugs (*Nabis* spp.), and lacewings (primarily *Chrysoperla* spp.). Spiders and ladybird beetles also contribute to management of various pest species. Adults and nymphs of these predators feed on insect eggs and small insects such as thrips, mites, aphids, whiteflies, and small caterpillars.

Insect Monitoring and Pesticide Use

Growers or pest control advisors monitor most pest and beneficial insect populations once or twice each week throughout the season. Both population counts and stage of insect development are used to determine management strategies. Continuous monitoring of predators and pests in the field can result in reduced use of chemicals and improved timing of pesticide applications.

Typically, an insecticide is applied in May before bees are placed in the seed field. During bloom and pollination, multiple applications of pesticides are usually required. To protect pollinating insects, pesticide applicators need to apply chemicals according to their written labels. They should be particularly aware of special instructions, including locations of bee colonies, to avoid or treat with different chemicals, night application start and stop time limits, and inspection of fields for bee activity just before aerial application. Nearly all chemicals used for pest control purposes in seed alfalfa are capable of killing pollinators by direct contact. Visual inspection of colonies must be made to determine if bees are on the outside of the colony boxes before applying insecticides in an area. The condition of colonies, air temperature, and field conditions will vary greatly, so visual inspection before starting a pesticide treatment is the best way to avoid direct contact between pesticides and bees. These same guidelines are recommended for all pesticide applications in regions where seed is grown.

Lygus Control

Lygus bugs (*Lygus* spp.) are among the most significant pest species in alfalfa seed production in California. These pests occur throughout the season, moving between a variety of crops in a region as they become unsuitable hosts due to maturity or harvest. They are by far the most difficult insects to manage in alfalfa seed fields; when present in high numbers they may completely destroy the crop. Both adults and nymphs feed on the alfalfa plant, attacking reproductive parts and causing premature drop of buds and flowers (stripping), seed deformation, and reduced seed viability. Control of the lygus bug is essential to the economic production of alfalfa seed. Action thresholds vary with the stage of crop development (Table 22.2).

Lygus bugs overwinter as adults on a number of winter annuals, in the crowns of alfalfa plants, and in plant debris. The adults become active in the spring, mate, and lay eggs immediately. Approximately 12 to 30 days are required from the time an egg hatches until the insect reaches the adult stage. During this developmental process, lygus bugs pass through five growth stages called instars. All nymphs (immatures) are wingless, so only the adults are capable of flight. Temperature is a major factor in lygus bug development. High temperatures shorten the time required for lygus bugs to pass through the developmental stages. In general, nymphs remain in each of the first four stages of development for 2 to 7 days and remain in the fifth stage for 4 to 10 days. With an average generation time of 6 weeks, there are usually about five generations per year in Central California. If winter and spring are very warm and rainfall patterns have

TABLE 22.2

Treatment thresholds for lygus bugs in alfalfa seed fields.

Alfalfa Growth Stage	Treatment Threshold for Lygus Bugs (lygus bugs/sweep)
Early season (pre-bee)	2–6
Bloom and seed set	8–10
Seed maturation	10–15

provided a continuous food supply, a greater number of generations per year can be produced. The greatest period of lygus bug activity is from June through August.

Degree days can be used to forecast seasonal lygus bug development, especially hatch and migration dates. The dates are forecast using weather averages and predict the beginning of hatch and migration, which will continue for several weeks. This information is available to growers and pest control advisors through the UC-IPM Web site (http://www.ipm.ucdavis.edu/).

> *Treatment can be delayed until egg hatch is complete but should take place before the nymphs reach the fourth and fifth instar.*

Lygus bug populations are monitored using a sweep net. During summer, most pesticide applications are targeted toward lygus bugs. Treatment thresholds are based on the average number of lygus bug nymphs and adults present in 10 to 20 sets of two 180-degree sweeps (see Chapter 9, "Managing Insects in Alfalfa," for an illustration of sweeping). Pesticide applications should be timed to coincide with the hatching of lygus bug brood. Treatment can be delayed until egg hatch is complete but should take place before the nymphs reach the fourth and fifth instar. Older instars and adults are more difficult to control with insecticides than are younger instars. Attempts to develop alfalfa germplasm with resistance to lygus bugs continue. Detailed information on scouting and pest control options is available in the *Pest Management Strategic Plan for Western U.S. Alfalfa and Clover Seed Production*, which can be found online at http://groups.ucanr.org/alfalfaseed/WestAlfalfaCloverSeed.pdf.

Few materials are available for the control of lygus bug in alfalfa seed fields. Because of the limited number of options, and the high potential for the development of resistance, it is critical to maintain the efficacy of currently registered chemicals. Lygus bugs are quickly able to develop resistance to chemicals applied to control them because of several characteristics:

- They have a short life cycle with many generations per year.
- They have a wide host range.
- They are exposed to many insecticide applications each year, not only in seed alfalfa but also in other susceptible crops.

Furthermore, insecticide applications generally eliminate or greatly reduce naturally occurring beneficial organisms, such as parasitic wasps and predatory insects that help keep the pest population somewhat in check.

The best insurance against development of insecticide resistance is rotating chemical controls and maintaining the insect's natural enemies in the field. If control by insecticides is necessary, the best way to reduce resistance development, and in some cases even allow pest populations to become more susceptible, is to alternate insecticides, paying particular attention to the *class* of each insecticide (e.g., pyrethroid or organophosphate) and rotating between classes.

Spider Mites

Each year, alfalfa seed growers in California experience significant problems due to infestations of spider mites. Enclosing stems, leaves, and flowers in sheets of fine webbing and feeding off the lower leaf surface, spider mites can cause considerable damage by interfering with pollination. Consequently, they can reduce yields, or if there is a heavy infestation, kill the entire plant (Fig. 22.7). Spider mites commonly found in California's alfalfa seed fields are twospotted (*Tetranychus urticae* Koch), pacific (*T. pacificus* McGregor), and strawberry (*T. turkestani* Ugarov & Nikolski) spider mites.

Damage caused by spider mites worsens during hot weather. A complete generation of the microscopic mites can be produced in as little as ten days when temperatures are high (> 90°F [32°C]). The hot, dry climate of the San Joaquin Valley allows mites to flourish. Damage resulting from spider mite infestations can be substantial. Growers must monitor their fields weekly, examining leaf surfaces to detect the presence of spider mites and watching for the appearance of webbing. Ideally, fields should be treated as soon as an infestation is discovered, unless it appears too late in the season to cause economic damage (i.e., when the seed crop is already made and the field is beginning to dry down).

Alfalfa Seed Chalcid

Alfalfa seed chalcid (*B. roddi*) damage varies from year to year and from field to field. All life stages of the chalcid—eggs, larvae, and pupae—develop within the seed and are protected from insecticides applied to the field. Adults emerge continuously from seed in the field and from adjacent areas, making attempts to manage chalcid populations with insecticides expensive and ineffective. Cultural control strategies, such as clipping fields in the spring (early April) to set the crop early and uniformly, controlling volunteer alfalfa plants in and around seed fields, and irrigating and cultivating fields after harvest to promote rotting of seed and decomposition of debris left in the field, all aid in suppressing chalcid populations. For the most effective results, these practices should be scheduled on a regional basis.

Other Insect Pests

Although the above-mentioned species are the major pests that affect seed production, several common insect pests in alfalfa hay may also affect seed fields. These include the alfalfa weevil (*Hypera postica* Gyllenhal) and Egyptian alfalfa weevil (*H. brunneipennis* Boheman), pea aphid, blue alfalfa aphid, spotted alfalfa aphid, cowpea aphid, and several species of Lepidoptera that occur in summer and fall. Please see Chapter 9, "Managing Insects in Alfalfa," for a thorough review of these pests.

Insect Management Strategies

There are a limited number of options for managing insect pest populations in seed alfalfa fields.

Biological Control. Biological control involves the use of naturally occurring or released predators and parasites. In most cases, biological control can't be relied upon in and of itself to provide economic insect control in seed fields. Recently, a small, native, parasitic wasp, *Peristenus* spp., which attacks lygus bug nymphs, was identified in the Pacific Northwest. Further research may develop strategies whereby *Peristenus* may be used to help suppress lygus bug populations in areas where they overwinter, on early spring hosts, or in other untreated crops.

Cultural Control. Cultural management is of limited effectiveness in controlling most pests in alfalfa seed fields. When strategies are available, they should be used in conjunction with other management methods. The most effective example of cultural control of an insect is the combination of early clipback and fall management strategies used to suppress alfalfa seed chalcid populations.

Chemical Control. Chemical control is currently the most effective and widely used pest management option, but it is not without problems. Chemicals must be carefully selected and applied to kill the target pest without harming pollinators. During bloom, insecticides are applied at night to lessen the impact on pollinators. Most chemicals are applied by air to avoid damaging bloom and seed set by driving through the field. There are few materials available to control the most damaging insect pests in seed alfalfa fields. For that reason, resistance management is an important consideration. Maintaining the susceptibility of insect populations to chemicals is critical. Growers

> *During bloom, insecticides are applied at night to lessen the impact on pollinators.*

and pest control advisors should take into consideration the population of beneficial insects in the field, use selective materials first if possible, and monitor resistance to make informed pest management decisions.

Disease and Nematode Control. Seed alfalfa growers benefit from the pest resistance bred into varieties for forage production. In addition, since stands are often planted on beds in rows, or at lower population densities than forage production stands, diseases are less of an issue.

Pollination

Alfalfa flowers require tripping and cross-pollination for maximum seed yields. Three types of pollinators are used in seed production in the western United States: honey bees (*Apis mellifera* L.), alfalfa leafcutting bees (*Megachile rotundata*), and alkali bees (*Nomia melanderi* Ck11.) (Fig. 22.9).

Honey Bees

In California, most alfalfa seed producers use honey bees (*A. mellifera*) for pollination. They are inexpensive but are relatively inefficient pollinators. Honey bee inefficiency is due to the fact that only a small percentage of the foraging bees are active pollen collectors. In addition, they prefer most other blooming crops to alfalfa and avoid the tripping mechanism that results in cross-pollination. Due to their inefficiency, honey bees require a long season to pollinate the seed crop. For that reason, they can be used in California, but cannot compete with more efficient, but expensive, pollinators used in other seed producing states. Researchers have attempted to improve the attractiveness of alfalfa to honey bees through plant breeding to enhance seed production, while apiculturists have simultaneously attempted to breed bees with a higher propensity to collect pollen. Both groups of researchers have been successful, but the industry has yet to widely adopt these strategies to improve alfalfa seed pollination.

Honey bees are usually placed in or around seed fields when they are between one-third and one-half bloom. This typically occurs about 45 days following clipback in the central San Joaquin Valley. Timing placement is important; bees placed before adequate bloom is present may leave the alfalfa in search of greater pollen and nectar resources elsewhere. When the bees' requirements can be satisfied by better or more easily worked blossoms, they show no interest in alfalfa pollen. It may be advantageous to place a second set of bees in the alfalfa seed field 3 to 4 weeks after the first colonies are placed to enhance pollination activity as the field comes into full bloom.

FIGURE 22.9

Pollinators used in alfalfa seed production in the western United States: (a) honey bees, (b) leafcutting bees, and (c) alkali bees.

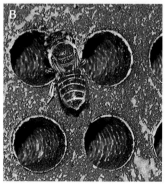

Pollinator activity is impacted by production practices such as irrigation and pesticide applications, as well as weather conditions. It takes 20 to 25 days, depending on temperature, to mature seed after pollination. It takes approximately 14 days to progress from the green pod stage to physiological maturity. Given this information, bees should be removed from fields about 30 days before the projected harvest date (allowing 7 days for desiccation). Blossoms pollinated beyond that point would not reach maturity by harvest.

Although pollinator populations (colony strength) and rental fees vary, most growers use two to three strong colonies per acre at a cost of about $35 per colony. Many rental fees are based on colony strength, which can be evaluated by the County Agricultural Commissioner or an independent consultant. A fee to cover the cost will be assessed to the party requesting the inspection and certification.

Leafcutting Bees

Growers in the Pacific Northwest rely on alfalfa leafcutting bees (*M. rotundata*) for seed pollination. Since 1990, many growers in the central San Joaquin Valley of California have come to appreciate the benefits of incorporating leafcutting bees into their pollination systems. Compared to honey bees, leafcutting bees are more efficient, but they are also often more expensive and require a greater degree of management. They are more efficient because each female in the population (approximately one-third of the total population) actively gathers pollen and nectar to provision her nest. Growers use 1 to 4 gallons (3.78 to 15.12 liters—9.35 to 37.4 liters per ha) of bees (10,000 bees per gallon [2,646 per liter]) per acre. Higher labor requirements, significant annual fluctuations in bee prices, the need for incubation, housing, and nest material, as well as a greater sensitivity to pesticides currently limit the exclusive use of leafcutting bees in California. However, leafcutting bees can be used in combination with honey bees, and many growers are taking advantage of this combined pollinator approach to maximize seed yields.

Alkali Bees

Seed growers in a small area of Washington State use alkali bees (*N. melanderi*), which are solitary, soil-nesting bees. Bee beds (nesting sites) are difficult to manage in California cropping systems and, as a consequence, alkali bees are no longer used for commercial pollination here.

Dessication and Harvest

Alfalfa seed fields must be dried before harvest to efficiently separate the seed from the pod and residual plant material. Irrigation is terminated late in the season in preparation for harvest. Once the plants dry to a certain point, the grower prepares the seed crop for harvest by either cutting and windrow curing or chemically desiccating the standing crop.

The Windrow Curing Process

Once the majority of the seed is mature (two-thirds or three-fourths of the pods have changed from green to dark brown in color), a swather cuts the alfalfa at the base of the plant and lays it in windrows on the stubble to air dry in the field. Alfalfa seed should be swathed during periods of high humidity or heavy dew. If windrowing is done under dry conditions, as much as one-half of the seed can be lost. Any green seed that remains on the plant will continue to ripen (mature) in the windrow. Windrows are ready for threshing when the moisture content of the plant is from 12 to 18 percent. In California, windrow curing is most common in the desert regions of the south. In the San Joaquin Valley, low humidity and strong winds during harvest make windrow curing a risky venture. Windrow losses can exceed 50 percent in fields subject to strong winds during curing.

Chemical Desiccation

For spray curing to be effective, the seed field must be mature, open, and erect. Desiccants are usually applied to fields 7 to 10 days before harvest. The chemicals dry the leaves and the stems of the plant without inducing defoliation. One application can sufficiently desiccate a light field in approximately 5 days. Heavier plant growth may require two sequential applications of a desiccant to prepare the field adequately for harvest. Unlike the windrow curing process, immature green pods that come in contact with the desiccant will not develop viable seed. It is important that residual soil moisture be utilized prior to desiccation or the plant will continue to regrow from the crown, interfering with harvest. When the plants are dry, the standing crop can be directly harvested using a combine.

Harvest Technique

Harvest begins when seeds are mature and pods and plant material are thoroughly dried. A standard combine is used to pick up the crop in the windrow, or harvest the whole plant standing in the field and thresh the seed from the pod. To minimize the loss of seed, properly adjusted lifter guards should be used in row-planted stands. A short, vertical cutter bar attached to one side of the platform or header also helps reduce header losses by cutting through foliage and avoiding tearing pods from the stems. A reel is considered necessary only in very light seed crops. All equipment must be carefully adjusted to achieve separation of the very small alfalfa seeds from a large amount of plant material without damaging them. Damaged seed will not germinate. Losses during harvest depend on a number of factors, such as field conditions, crop conditions, machine adjustments, and operation. To minimize seed losses and obtain high-quality seed, machine adjustments and operation must match the field and crop conditions. The seed is transferred from the combine into boxes on trucks and is then taken to the conditioning facility for cleaning and bagging.

Seed Conditioning

Conditioning removes soil, weed seeds, and other debris from the alfalfa seed. This is accomplished by equipment that uses differ-

ences in physical characteristics of alfalfa seed and the nonseed fraction, such as particle size, shape, density, and surface texture. Separating machines include (1) air-screen cleaners, (2) specific gravity separators, (3) velvet roll seed separators, and (4) magnetic separators. All equipment is thoroughly cleaned between seed lots.

When a high hard-seed percentage occurs, a process called scarification is performed to lower the hard-seed content. Seed can be scarified by chemically or mechanically scratching the seed coat to allow for moisture penetration. Generally, this is not required for seed of nondormant varieties; however, dormant varieties have a higher hard-seed percentage, and scarification improves germination of those lots.

All seed lots are tested for purity, germination, and noxious weed content before marketing.

Crop Residue Management

Crop residue following harvest (straw, chaff, and shattered seed) must be managed to eliminate overwintering sites for alfalfa insect pests and prepare the field for subsequent production. Typically, the combine leaves the straw in windrows. Following harvest, the straw is chopped and scattered throughout the field. Subsequent cultivation followed by irrigation facilitates the decomposition process. In some cases, growers may burn the residue in the field. Years ago, the residue was baled and removed, or grazing sheep were brought in to clean up the debris, but many of the currently registered chemicals for pest control and desiccation restrict treated plant material from entering the food chain.

Volunteer alfalfa that germinates and emerges from seed dropped during harvest must be controlled to maintain the genetic characteristics of the variety and also to reduce populations of alfalfa seed chalcid. Irrigating the field following harvest will aid in germinating good seed or rotting the chalcid-infested seed. Volunteer alfalfa and any weeds that emerge may be controlled by cultivation and/or chemical treatments.

In some areas, the regrowth following harvest may be taken as a forage cutting either in fall or spring. Removal of the regrowth improves the efficacy of soil-active herbicides, helps control some insect pests, brings income to the grower, and allows for optimum timing of the crop production season.

Seed Certification

Typically, about 60 percent of the alfalfa seed produced in California is certified. Certification is required for export, and highly recommended for domestic use. Certified alfalfa seed production requires that the grower meet specific standards, regulated by state and federal seed-certifying agencies. Inspectors from the state Crop Improvement Association look at each field at least once during the growing season to make sure it meets the requirements for certification.

Before establishing a new stand of alfalfa for seed production, the proximity to adjacent alfalfa fields should be taken into consideration. Isolation requirements for certified seed production are based on the size of the certified field and the percentage of the field within 165 feet of another variety of alfalfa. If 10 percent or less of the certified field is within the 165-foot isolation zone, no isolation is required. If more than 10 percent of the field is within the isolation zone, that part of the field must not be harvested as certified seed. This requirement is based on the assumption that seed from the entire field will be mechanically mixed during harvest and cleaning operations, and in this process will dilute the small percentage of off-type seed that may be produced in the area closest to adjacent fields of different varieties. With the recent introduction of genetically modified alfalfa varieties, isolation standards are being reviewed to make sure they result in acceptable levels of adventitious presence, since some markets are sensitive to genetically-modified traits.

Fields must be free from prohibited noxious weeds, and sweet clover may not exceed 10 plants per acre. Restricted noxious weeds must be controlled, and any such infestation (including common weeds that are difficult to separate, such as dodder and Johnsongrass) will be described on the field inspection report. Every field should be rogued to remove any plants of another crop or variety. Some noxious weeds that must be controlled are Russian knapweed (*Acroptilon repens* [L.] DC), white horsenettle (*Solanum elaeagnifolium* Cav.), alkali mallow (*Malvella leprosa* [Ortega] Krapov), and field bindweed (*Convolvulus arvensis* L.).

Fields may be refused certification due to poor growth, poor stand, disease, insect damage, and/or any other condition that prevents accurate inspection or creates doubt as to the identity of the variety.

Additional Reading

Alfalfa Seed Production Research Board. 1975. Proceedings of the Biennial Alfalfa Seed Production Symposium. http://alfalfaseed.ucdavis.edu/.

Dobrenz, A.K., and M.A. Massengale. 1966. Change in carbohydrates in alfalfa (*Medicago sativa* L.) roots during the period of floral initiation and seed development. Crop Sci. 6:604–607.

Marble, V.L. 1976. Producing alfalfa seed in California. University of California Division of Agriculture and Natural Resources, Oakland, CA. Leaflet 2383.

Rincker, C.M., V.L. Marble, D.E. Brown, and C.A. Johansen, 1988. Seed production practices. Pp. 985–1022 in: A.A. Hanson, D.K. Barnes, and R.R. Hill, Jr., eds. Alfalfa and alfalfa improvement. American Society of Agronomy, Madison, WI. Publication 29.

Western Integrated Pest Management Center. 2004. Pest management strategic plan for western U.S. alfalfa and clover seed production. http://groups.ucanr.org/alfalfaseed/WestAlfalfaCloverSeed.pdf.

23

Alfalfa Marketing and Economics

Karen Klonsky
Cooperative Extension Specialist, Department of Agricultural and Resource Economics, University of California, Davis

Barbara Reed
Farm Advisor, University of California Cooperative Extension, Orland, CA

Daniel H. Putnam
Forage Extension Specialist, Department of Plant Sciences University of California, Davis

Historically, and in some regions, alfalfa has been viewed as a "low value" rotation or pasture crop, of economic importance primarily as a supplement to other higher value row and specialty crops. However, in recent decades, alfalfa has become a valuable and profitable crop in its own right, competing successfully with many higher-value specialty crops, especially in California. Many growers approach this crop as a serious business enterprise, with careful consideration of costs, value, and markets. The value of alfalfa in California has approached $1 billion in recent years, and it has competed economically with many other specialty and row crop options in the state.

Alfalfa is an extremely versatile crop. It is widely grown in many environments and in many types of farming systems. It can be harvested and packaged into several sizes and shapes of bales and cubes, or cut for silage, grown for seed, or used for pasture. It can be fed to a wide variety of livestock. Income from alfalfa will vary by the forms marketed, forage quality, market outlets, yield, and the supply and demand situation for each market category. Since there is a tradeoff between quality and yield, growers must consider optimizing the crop quality (and therefore price), as well as tonnage per unit area (see Chapter 13, "Harvest Strategies for Alfalfa," for a detailed discussion of the yield–quality tradeoff).

Alfalfa is a crop that can be used on-farm, with milk or meat as the primary economic return, or sold to other livestock producers. Although nationwide most alfalfa is consumed on-farm, in California and other western areas, the vast majority of hay is sold on the open market as a cash crop. The primary markets are dairy, horse, and beef, with minor markets for sheep, goats, zoo animals, export, and other uses (e.g., pellets for pets, alfalfa tablets).

Alfalfa Markets in California

An estimation of alfalfa sales to different market segments in California is provided in Table 23.1. It is clear that dairy production markets dominate, with horses an increasingly important component of the market. Secondary markets are domestic beef, small ruminants, and export. Specialty markets, such as certified organic hay or certified weed-free hay, are a small but increasing component of the alfalfa market (current estimates rank organic hay at less than 0.5 percent of the California alfalfa market). There is no systematic data collected that would provide accurate information regarding use by various alfalfa consumers, so keep in mind that the data herein, although

based on the best available sources, are estimates.

Dairy Markets

Dairy producers are unquestionably the most important purchasers of alfalfa hay in California, and indeed the nation. California has 1.8 million dairy cows and is home to some of the most intensive dairy operations in the world, particularly in the southern San Joaquin Valley. The dairy market is characterized by emphasis on quality, as defined by low-fiber, weed free, leafy, high-protein hay products. It is driven primarily by the needs of high-producing dairy cows, since milk production is enhanced with high-quality hay.

The dairy market is segmented into several quality categories: Supreme, Premium, Good, Fair, and Utility grades (see Chapter 16, "Forage Quality and Testing," for a complete discussion and definition of hay quality categories). Dairy markets favor what is termed "dairy-quality" (Supreme and Premium) hay; the cutoff for high-producing dairy cows is typically between 25 and 29 percent acid detergent fiber (ADF, equivalent to 54.5–58 percent total digestible nutrients or TDN on a 90 percent dry matter basis). Dairies also utilize considerable quantities of medium (Good and Fair) and even low (Fair and Utility) quality hay for lower-producing animals and "dry" (nonlactating) cows, calves, and heifers. The dairy markets largely function with "supply and demand" curves for each of these hay quality categories, affecting price.

Hay for high-producing dairy cows is frequently analyzed by laboratories, sometimes even two or three times, by sellers, brokers, buyers, and nutritionists. Domestic dairy markets, particularly the "dairy-quality" categories,

TABLE 23.1

Estimation of alfalfa hay consumption in California and alfalfa hay entering and leaving California, expressed as a percentage of production

Category	Estimated Percentage Utilization*
Dairy (including milk cows, heifers, dry cows)	75–85%
Horse	10–15%
Beef	5–10%
Small Ruminant	1%
Export from State*	1–2%
Imported into State	8–12%

* Total utilization in state may exceed 100 percent, since imports into California from neighboring states often exceed exports to foreign countries. Estimates by authors.

have the dominant effect on demand, price, and quality definition. These quality categories have changed to some degree over the years (see Chapter 16, "Forage Quality and Testing"), and no single regulatory body determines dairy quality definitions. Hay quality guidelines are published by USDA Hay Market News, but quality factors are generally loosely decided by industry habit and practice, and can be freely modified by individual buyers and sellers, depending on their needs and the realities of the market.

Horse Markets

Alfalfa and alfalfa–grass mixtures are the most important hay crops for the California and U.S. horse industry, and weed-free, bright green alfalfa or grass–alfalfa mixes are in high demand by horse owners. There are probably 6–7 million horses in the United States, and some authors have estimated that there are over 650,000 horses in California. Collectively, horses make up a large and expanding sector. The horse hay market is characterized by a large number of small buyers, each with their own views on quality and value. Feed stores often play a significant role in determining price and quality. This market is much more subjective than dairy markets. Buyers do not value lab tests to the same degree, and weed-free (especially free of poisonous or noxious weeds), non-moldy, dust-free hay is especially valued. Alfalfa competes to some degree with perennial grasses and oat hay for the horse dollar. Demand for bright green, weed-free alfalfa that is mold-free and well-conditioned, or alfalfa–grass mixtures of medium or even high fiber content has been strong, and prices have often exceeded dairy prices.

Beef, Sheep, Goats

Beef, sheep, and goat markets are similar in some respects to dairy markets, because all of these classes of animals are ruminants, and similar quality considerations are in force. However, beef, sheep, and goat markets typically put less emphasis on high-quality alfalfa

than is the case for high-producing dairy cows, with the exception of dairy goats. Medium- and lower-quality hay is frequently acceptable for nonlactating and meat-producing animals in these classes. Beef producers tend to be highly sensitive to price because of the low margins of that industry and will often accept lower-quality hay or compare alfalfa with other types of hay that are adequate for maintenance or weight gain. Grazing of winter alfalfa growth by sheep through a cash transaction is a significant component of the alfalfa system in the

Beef, sheep, and goat markets typically put less emphasis on high-quality alfalfa than is the case for high-producing dairy cows, with the exception of dairy goats.

southern areas of California. This provides a benefit for herdsmen and growers alike, since haying is difficult during winter months. Dairy goats are a small but increasing component of the miscellaneous markets for high-quality alfalfa hay.

Exports

Pacific Rim nations, including Japan, Korea, and Taiwan, are major importers of California alfalfa hay and cubes. Although cubing has historically been important, double-compressed hay has dominated exports in recent years. Hay is hydraulically compressed to about 25 pounds per cubic foot by specialty equipment—this provides superior packing geometry and ease of handling compared with cubes. About 80 percent of California's exports are compressed bales (excluding nonalfalfa hays) and 20 percent cubes—similar to exports from the Pacific Northwest. California exports include hays produced in neighboring states, particularly Utah and Nevada.

The vast majority of both baled and cubed alfalfa goes to dairies in Japan. The Korean market averages about one-quarter to one-third of the Japanese market. Products are shipped overseas in 40-foot cargo containers.

Double-compressed hay is typically cut from larger bales and packaged in compressed small bales (e.g., 30–50 lb or 14–23 kg) for delivery to Japanese dairy farmers for direct hand-feeding.

TABLE 23.2

Imports of hay bales and cubes from neighboring states 2004–2006 (short tons)

State	Package	2004	2005	2006
Arizona	Bales	208,651	186,000	112,198
	Cubes	264	176	65
Nevada	Bales	290,089	283,323	291,040
	Cubes	16,103	8,047	6,449
Utah	Bales	197,748	325,769	279,912
	Cubes	85,741	83,877	90,994
Oregon	Bales	56,353	80,073	67,429
	Cubes	*	*	*
Idaho	Bales	10,295	18,155	15,661
	Cubes	4,692	*	*

*None reported

Source: USDA, AMS, Livestock and Grain Market News, Moses Lake, WA.
Alfalfa Hay: California Market Summary, 2004, 2005, 2006

Many countries have stringent import regulations. Containers are fumigated before shipment to their destination. Agricultural inspectors in the destination country may reject loads with pests or foreign contamination (noxious weeds). If the shipment is rejected it may be destroyed or returned to the United States, and the buyer can seek price relief from the seller based on issues with quality, foreign matter, damage, or changes in market conditions (price). Export figures from California include some hay and a large volume of cubes from Nevada and Utah entering California but destined for export (see California Department of Food and Agriculture [CDFA] for information on exports, www.calagexports.com).

Hay Moving In and Out of California

Alfalfa hay and cubes are shipped into California for the dairy, horse, and export markets (Table 23.2, Fig. 23.1). Due to the presence of millions of dairy and beef cows, horses, sheep, and goats, California is a "sink"

FIGURE 23.1

Tonnage of alfalfa hay imported from neighboring states into California, 1987–2005, also expressed as percentage of CA production. Data adapted from Hoyt (2006 Western Alfalfa & Forage Conference Proceedings, see http://alfalfa.ucdavis.edu), based on CDFA border stations, USDA–Hay Market News Service, and USDA-NASS production data.

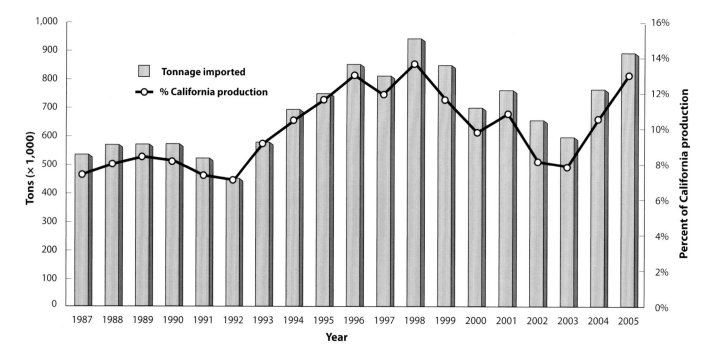

for much of the hay produced in neighboring states, particularly Nevada and Utah, but also Oregon, Arizona, and sometimes Idaho. This imported hay increases supply by an average of nearly 10 percent over the state's production (Fig. 23.1), significantly impacting market price. Alfalfa hay imported from other countries is not significant, although a small quantity may enter occasionally from Mexico. The highest-quantity alfalfa enters from Nevada, followed by Arizona (Table 23.2). Utah is the largest supplier of cubes. Some of this "imported" hay, especially the cubes, is trans-shipped from California ports to overseas ports.

Packaging Methods for Different Markets

Alfalfa is marketed in California in several forms. The predominant method of harvest is baled hay production, with a small minority of production in greenchop, silage, cubes, or grazing (see Chapter 14, "Harvesting, Curing, and Preservation of Alfalfa," and Chapter 18, "Alfalfa Grazing Management"). The yield advantages and costs of production for harvest operations for bales, cubes, and silage differ significantly.

Bales

Baled alfalfa packages are produced in a range of forms, but the predominant form is rectangular bales of various sizes (see Chapter 13, "Harvest Strategies for Alfalfa," and Chapter 14, "Harvesting, Curing, and Preservation of Alfalfa"). Growers in California and other western states very rarely use round bales, due to the stacking and shipping disadvantages of these packages. The traditional "small" square bale with three ties weighs about 125 pounds (57 kg), in contrast to the eastern United States, where "small" rectangular bales are largely 40–60 pound (18–27 kg) two-tie bales (although some of the latter is used for the horse market in the West as well). Large, rectangular bales have become very important in the past two decades. These rectangular bales

range from 750 to 2,000 pounds (340–907 kg). The dairy industry is the primary user of large, baled alfalfa, but the smaller 125-pound (57-kg) bales have greater flexibility for market purposes. Large bales have superior trucking and handling characteristics but are at greater risk of hay fires or mold because of the low surface area for escape of moisture. Their primary application is for larger feedlot operations.

Cubes and Pellets

Alfalfa cubes are a minor-use package used in California for horses, dairy, or export. Both mobile and stationary cubers are used, but stationary cubing units are more important. Cubes or pellets are popular with the horse industry because of convenience, reduced feed waste, ease of handling, and reduced respiratory problems. Alfalfa cubes for horses are mechanically compressed into 1.25 × 2-inch (3 × 5-cm) cubes that are not as dense as those produced for cattle. Manufacturers of cubes must provide guaranteed levels of protein, fat, and fiber. Cubing facilities can accept hay at a higher moisture content compared to moisture levels when hay is baled, shortening field drying time. The drying and cubing process dramatically decreases the moisture level and the opportunity for mold to develop. Some companies may offer cubes that provide a combination of Timothy or other cool-season grasses and alfalfa, targeting the horse market.

The predominant package for California alfalfa is baled hay production, with a small minority of greenchop, silage, cubes, or grazing.

Silage and Greenchop

Most alfalfa silage and greenchop is grown within a few miles of its use, with the dairy producer as the predominant grower as well as end user. However, there is some marketing of alfalfa as silage or greenchop through contracts or other agreements. The added cost of hauling moisture limits the distance that alfalfa silage will be transported from point of harvest for market purposes. The advantages and disadvantages of silage and greenchop are discussed in Chapter 14, "Harvesting, Curing, and Preservation of Alfalfa."

Relationship of Markets to Forage Quality

The USDA Agricultural Marketing Service tracks the prices paid for different quality grades of alfalfa in California. The categories of Supreme, Premium, Good, Fair, and Utility are described in Table 23.3 and are tracked by market subregion within California in Table 23.4. Differences in prices between regions are primarily a function of distance from dairy markets—production in the Imperial Valley and other Low Desert areas takes place 100–200 miles (160–320 km) from the Chino milk shed and a greater distance from the dairy concentrations in the lower San Joaquin Valley. Intermountain production in California and Nevada is mostly shipped south to the mar-

kets in the Central Valley. The highest prices and greatest premiums based on quality are realized in the San Joaquin and Sacramento Valleys; farm hay prices are lower in the Intermountain and Southern Desert regions. Year-to-year variation in price is affected by supply and demand factors, including milk price, alfalfa acreage, weather, and exports. However, alfalfa price is strongly influenced by forage quality in all years (Fig. 23.2). For a more in-depth discussion of alfalfa quality, refer to Chapter 16, "Forage Quality and Testing."

Market Behavior

Alfalfa hay is one of the most freely traded agricultural commodities in the United States, and more hay is commercially traded in California than in any other state. Alfalfa does not have government price support, nor even formal market-quality standards or market regulation. The market-quality factors described here are guidelines, and buyers and sellers are free to adhere to or ignore those guidelines, or develop additional criteria. Thousands of buyers and sellers determine price and service (e.g., storage, financing, and delivery) based on mutual agreement. Buyers differ in their requirements. Therefore, each alfalfa producer must develop a business strategy for alfalfa production to make production and marketing decisions that best fit their overall farm business plan.

TABLE 23.3

USDA hay quality guidelines for nationwide market news reporting adopted in 2002 for domestic livestock use and not more than 10 percent grass[1]

Category	ADF	NDF	RFV[2]	TDN[3]	TDN (90% DM)[4]	CP
			%			
Supreme	<27	<34	>185	>62	>55.9	>22
Premium	27–29	34–36	170–185	60.5–62	54.5–55.9	20–22
Good	29–32	36–40	150–170	58–60.5	52.5–54.5	18–20
Fair	32–35	40–44	130–150	56–58	50.5–52.5	16–18
Utility	>35	>44	<100	<56	<50.5	<16

Source: 2006 USDA, AMS, Livestock, Hay and Grain Market News, Moses Lake, WA. Alfalfa Hay: 2006 California Market Summary

[1] Guidelines are used along with visual appearance to determine quality. All figures are expressed on 100% DM, except as noted.

[2] RFV is calculated from ADF and NDF: RFV = [88.9 − (.779 × %ADF)] × [(120÷%NDF)÷1.29]

[3] TDN = [82.38 − (0.7515 × ADF)] according to Bath and Marble, 1989.

[4] TDN (90% DM) = TDN × 0.9.

Abbreviations: ADF = Acid Detergent Fiber. NDF = Neutral Detergent Fiber. RFV = Relative Feeding Value. TDN = Total Digestible Nutrients. DM = Dry Matter. CP = Crude Protein.

Business Strategies

There are several potential business strategies for alfalfa hay production that growers might employ to meet market expectations. They include the low-cost production strategy, product-quality differentiation or niche-marketing strategy, and provision of additional service strategy. Most growers will predominantly follow one of these strategies, with consideration of one or both of the others.

Low-cost, High-yield Production Strategy

A grower can choose to simply produce maximum yields and compete with other growers primarily on price. This strategy is the least complex and historically the primary strategy employed by growers. There is little question that controlling costs and maximizing yields are the fundamentals of alfalfa economics. However, over time, most growers have had to pay much more attention to quality or other factors to differentiate their hay in the market to maximize ranch profits, even when high crop yield remains the primary goal.

FIGURE 23.2

Average prices due to differences in forage quality, 10-year period, all California markets. *Source:* USDA, AMS, Livestock, Hay and Grain Market News, Moses Lake, WA. Alfalfa Hay: California Market Summary.

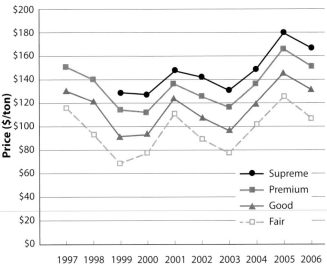

Quality Differentiation Strategy

Another marketing strategy is to differentiate the alfalfa products by quality or targeted market use, thereby creating a unique perception about the products for buyers. Although "quality" is most often associated with the dairy

TABLE 23.4

Differences between regions in price structure due to hay quality category (10-year average, 1997–2006)

| Region | Hay Quality Category | | | |
| | Supreme | Premium | Good | Fair |
	($/ton)			
Southern California				
Imperial Valley	121.00	115.24	100.29	86.35
Blythe/Parker	120.14	114.52	99.38	82.56
Chino/LA	148.37	140.34	125.65	110.74
Mojave Desert	129.11	123.01	111.86	93.52
San Joaquin Valley				
Kern County	139.45	128.07	110.01	92.57
Tulare/Visalia/Hanford	163.54	149.42	129.83	109.13
Hanford/Corcoran/Tulare	146.25	132.62	113.75	94.08
Fresno/Madera Counties	145.24	129.77	108.48	92.27
Los Banos/Dos Palos	147.21	136.66	116.92	96.98
Escalon/Modesto/Turlock	161.69	148.94	130.23	109.20
Delta/Sacramento Valley/North Coast				
Tracy/Patterson/Stockton	145.99	134.13	113.05	94.25
Sacramento Valley	135.74	125.97	106.04	83.81
Petaluma	163.57	151.49	129.29	109.81
Intermountain				
Northern Mountain	124.42	116.24	103.56	85.79

Source: USDA, AMS, Livestock, Hay and Grain Market News, Moses Lake, WA. Alfalfa Hay: California Market Summary, various issues.

industry, with its demand for low-fiber, high-protein hay (as judged by laboratory tests), quality can also be more broadly interpreted for different markets. Consistent with this strategy is the development of a small but well-defined market niche to get top dollar for a consistently high-quality product. This might mean developing a reputation for green, weed-free alfalfa (or alfalfa–grass mixtures) grown for horses, or a specific grind or package designed for the export market. Specialty differentiation may include designation such as "certified weed-free" hay (available in some areas), certified organic hay (a rapidly growing market), hay grown in a region with a reputation for quality, marketing a specific cube product that includes grasses for horses, or "low-potassium" hay that is suited for close-up dairy cows (milk-producing cows just before and just after giving birth). Growers frequently market first cutting (sometimes second cutting) and fall clippings separately from lower-quality summer harvests as a method to differentiate quality. It should be noted that these growers who focus on quality also pay close attention to yields.

Additional Services Strategy

A third strategy is to discover methods to provide a service to the customer along with the forage product. This might entail investing in storage facilities so that hay is available to customers on demand (lessening weather risk to the buyer), meeting specific baling requirements (e.g., precise weight or bale dimensions), developing favorable payment or delivery contracts, offering quality warrantees, or allowing the customer to harvest the alfalfa themselves for silage. Some growers have offered silage-making services, including storage and daily delivery, or greenchop delivery marketing services as part of their overall marketing strategy.

Many farmers use a combination of these strategies. These marketing strategies for the alfalfa enterprise must be integrated with the rest of the farm business with respect to resource use, business growth, risk management, cash flow, capital investment, and the personal vision of the farmer.

Cash Flow Characteristics of Alfalfa

Many farmers value the favorable cash-flow characteristics of alfalfa in their crop mix, which provides steady, season-long income, while waiting for the cash returns from other crops that are harvested only once per year. This is a key economic attribute of alfalfa grown in rotation with specialty crops, row or grain crops, or integrated with cow–calf operations. The stability of the alfalfa production systems, with their relatively low risk and predictable cash flow, is quite attractive to many farmers. Some grow higher-risk crops, such as tomatoes or lettuce, that generally have more volatile prices than alfalfa. All of these annual crops are harvested only once compared to alfalfa, which is harvested 4–10 times per year, generating cash flow over several months or throughout the year if hay products are stored.

> *Many farmers value the favorable cash-flow characteristics of alfalfa in their crop mix, which provides steady, season-long income while other crops are harvested only once per year.*

Additionally, alfalfa may provide economic benefits through crop rotation, which benefits a following crop, lowers the nitrogen requirement, improves water infiltration, and provides excellent soil tilth and weed management for rotation crops (See Chapter 1, "Alfalfa Production Systems in California"). The bottom-line profitability of the alfalfa operation, by definition, depends on the income generated and the costs of production for the crop itself. The economic performance of the alfalfa enterprise is then integrated into the whole farm business performance.

Marketing Through Contracts, Associations, or Brokers

There are a range of advantages and disadvantages to marketing through intermediaries such as individual brokers or hay grower associations. There are thousands of registered individual hay brokers licensed in California who have a widely varying range of reputations for performance and honesty. Hay brokering is often performed by the hay growers or dairy operators themselves, or by third-party brokers.

The San Joaquin Valley Hay Growers Association (in business for over 60 years) and High Mountain Hay Growers are examples of associations that market hay for grower owner-members; these associations represent the growers and fulfill the role of intermediary. Associations may provide services in addition to brokering hay, such as insurance benefits, testing of hay, better prices on seed or fertilizer supplies, guarantees that all hay will be sold, and guarantees that a seller will be paid. Because development of a market requires considerable time and knowledge of issues like forage quality and market preference, in many cases growers may prefer to work through brokers or join associations that have invested time in developing this expertise. On the other hand, growers must give up a portion of the value of their crop for this expertise and run the risk that brokers may seek market advantages that do not necessarily accrue to the producer.

Other marketing arrangements, such as forward contracting with buyers for a given price or pre-payments, have been tried. These arrangements have the advantages of making supply and price more predictable, and thus may be advantageous to both buyer and seller. Various types of contracts have been tried, for example, delivery of a certain quantity of alfalfa hay of a specific quality on a regular schedule. A key stumbling block is often the unpredictable influence of season or weather on forage quality (or yield), which must be addressed in the contracting arrangements.

Production Costs and Budgets

Alfalfa is unique among field crops. Once established, it is harvested for several years and several times throughout each of those years. Thus, there are two parts to any cost analysis for alfalfa production. The first part is the costs associated with stand establishment before any harvest takes place. Second, the annual cost of production include annual cultural costs, harvest costs, business overhead costs, and capital recovery for equipment, land, and stand establishment amortized over the life of the stand.

> *Alfalfa is unique among field crops. Once established, it is harvested for several years and several times throughout each of those years.*

Cost Studies

Cost studies are useful as a first approximation of the relative costs of producing a crop. From these data, growers can adjust estimated costs of their own operation. The Department of Agricultural and Resource Economics at UC Davis, in cooperation with UC Cooperative Extension Farm Advisors, has produced several cost and return studies for alfalfa production under a variety of conditions throughout the state (Table 23.5). Each study includes detailed information about typical production practices, input costs, expected yields and prices, and a list of equipment and costs, as well as a monthly calendar of operations and cash flow. Because costs and returns vary so much from farm to farm and year to year, these should be viewed as examples of what one would expect, not absolute values. Tables 23.6 and 23.7 provide an example of a cost study for alfalfa from the study "Costs to Establish and Produce Alfalfa—Sacramento 2003." All studies, including updates, are available at http://coststudies.ucdavis.edu.

TABLE 23.5

Alfalfa cost and return studies available for California production. New and updated costs studies can be found at http://coststudies.ucdavis.edu/

County/Region	Year	Production Conditions
Intermountain (North)	2007	Wheel line and center pivot irrigation
Intermountain (North)	2007	Center pivot irrigation
Sacramento Valley (N. Central)	2003	400 acres, flood irrigation
Sacramento Valley (N. Central)	2007	Organic production practices
San Joaquin Valley (S. Central)	2003	50-acre unit, flood irrigation
San Joaquin Valley (S. Central)	2003	300-acre unit, hay and haylage, flood irrigation
Imperial County (South)	2004	Bed planted irrigation method
Imperial County (South)	2004	Flat field (check flood irrigation)

Source: Department of Agricultural and Resource Economics, University of California, Davis (http://coststudies.ucdavis.edu)

Stand Establishment Costs

University of California cost and return studies estimate that costs to establish a stand of alfalfa can vary from $300 to $750 per acre ($741 to $1,853/ha), including the cultural costs, taxes and insurance, and ownership costs of equipment and land. The costs vary substantially due to the specifics of the extent of land preparation before planting and how much of the land preparation is done by the owner/operator vs. custom operators. The land preparation will vary depending on soil conditions, the irrigation system, and the previous crop. For example, flood irrigation using checks will require more land preparation than sprinkler irrigation, but labor or pumping costs might be greater for sprinklers, depending on type of sprinkler.

The cost of stand establishment must be amortized over the life of the stand when calculating annual costs of production. Stand life tends to decrease from north to south in California, starting at a high of 5 to 8 years in the northern mountain areas and decreasing to an expected 3 years in Imperial County. The majority of California alfalfa fields in Mediterranean and desert zones last from 3 to 5 years.

Annual Cultural Costs

Once established, annual cultural costs, including irrigation, pest control, and fertilization, will range from about $150 per acre to $300 per acre ($370 to $740/ha). The largest source of variation is the cost of water. Water cost per acre foot (ha/m) varies, depending on the source of water and the irrigation district and degree of pumping required. Also, the amount of water used varies, depending on the climate, with approximately 2.5 acre feet per acre (760 mm) applied in the Intermountain North, 4.5 acre feet per acre (1,370 mm) in the San Joaquin Valley, and 7 acre feet per acre (2,130 mm) in the Imperial Valley.

Land costs vary significantly across the state and contribute to the large variation in total costs. The type of irrigation system also affects costs; sprinkler and center pivot systems are more expensive than flood irrigation systems due to the capital investment required. The cost per acre tends to be higher for smaller fields than for larger fields because the equipment and building costs are spread out over a smaller number of acres.

Harvesting Costs

Harvesting costs typically range from $100 to $200 per acre ($247 to $496/ha) per year, depending on the number of cuttings and whether an operator owns harvesting equipment. Generally, the number of cuttings increases from north to south through the state. The number of cuttings in the northern part of the state is three to four per year, six to eight cuttings in the Central Valley, and in the

TABLE 23.6

Cost per acre to establish alfalfa, Sacramento Valley, 2003. This is provided as an example of how to calculate costs, and should be adjusted for each situation

Operation	Operation Time (Hrs/A)	Cash and Labor Cost per Acre				
		Labor Cost	Fuel, Lube & Repairs	Material Cost	Custom/ Rent	Total Cost
CULTURAL:						
Disc Stubble (2 times)	0.27	4	8	0	0	12
Chisel Field	0.19	3	5	0	0	8
Laser Level 1 time each/7 years	0.00	0	0	0	11	11
Disc	0.10	1	3	0	0	4
Triplane (3 times)	0.36	6	7	0	0	13
Border Preparation (3 times)	0.09	1	1	0	0	2
Fertilize (11-52-0) 33% Cost	0.00	0	0	16	2	18
Fertilize (Sulfur)	0.00	0	0	11	6	17
Plant (including seed)	0.26	4	3	54	0	61
Harrow and Ring Roll	0.09	1	1	0	0	2
Irrigate—Sprinkle	0.80	8	0	12	0	20
Weed (including herbicide)	0.07	1	0	46	0	47
Pickup truck	0.12	2	1	0	0	3
ATV Use	0.12	2	0	0	0	2
TOTAL CULTURAL COSTS	2.47	33	29	139	19	220
Interest on operating capital @ 7.14%						4
TOTAL OPERATING COSTS/ACRE		33	29	139	19	224
CASH OVERHEAD:*						
Liability Insurance						1
Office Expense						34
Property Taxes						1
Property Insurance						1
Investment Repairs						3
TOTAL CASH OVERHEAD COSTS						40
TOTAL CASH COSTS/ACRE						264

NON-CASH OVERHEAD *(Investments)	Per producing acre	— Annual Cost — Capital Recovery	
Irrigation—Hand Line Sprinkler	4	1	1
Forklift	7	1	1
Buildings	20	2	2
Shop Tools	4	0	0
Fuel Tanks	1	0	0
Hay Barn	98	9	9
Equipment	125	16	16
TOTAL NON-CASH OVERHEAD COSTS	259	29	29
TOTAL ESTABLISHMENT COSTS/ACRE			**293**

Source: http://coststudies.ucdavis.edu.

TABLE 23.7

Cost per acre to produce alfalfa, Sacramento Valley, 2003

Operation	Operation Time (Hrs/A)	Cash and Labor Cost per Acre				
		Labor Cost	Fuel, Lube & Repairs	Material Cost	Custom/ Rent	Total Cost
CULTURAL:						
Summer Weed Control (Treflan)	0.06	1	0	21	0	22
Insect: Aphid/Weevil (Warrior)	0.00	0	0	11	9	20
Irrigation	1.26	12	0	96	0	108
Insect–Worm (Lannate)	0.00	0	0	20	9	29
Insect–Worm (Steward)	0.00	0	0	13	9	22
Fertilize 1 time every 2 years (11-52-0)	0.00	0	0	16	3	19
Winter Weed Control (Velpar/Karmex)	0.00	0	0	27	9	36
Pickup Truck	0.40	6	3	0	0	9
ATV Use	0.24	4	1	0	0	5
TOTAL CULTURAL COSTS	1.96	23	4	204	39	270
HARVEST:						
Harvest	0.00	0	0	0	196	196
TOTAL HARVEST COSTS	0.00	0	0	0	196	196
Interest on operating capital @ 7.14%						12
TOTAL OPERATING COSTS/ACRE		23	4	204	235	478

CASH OVERHEAD:	
Liability Insurance	0
Office Expense	35
Crop Share 20% of Gross	140
Property Taxes	1
Property Insurance	1
Investment Repairs	3
TOTAL CASH OVERHEAD COSTS	180
TOTAL CASH COSTS/ACRE	658

NON-CASH OVERHEAD:	Per producing acre	— Annual Cost — Capital Recovery	
Buildings	21	2	2
Hay Barn	123	11	11
Forklift	7	1	1
Fuel Tanks	1	0	0
Shop Tools	5	0	0
Alfalfa Establishment Costs	264	77	77
Equipment	25	4	4
TOTAL NON-CASH OVERHEAD COSTS	445	94	95
TOTAL YEARLY PRODUCTION COSTS/ACRE			**753**

Source: http://coststudies.ucdavis.edu.

Imperial Valley, growers typically make nine harvests, but could harvest up to twelve times per year (including winter grazing). The current practice of green chopping throughout the winter in the southern San Joaquin Valley has increased the number of harvests there to eight or ten. Custom operator costs for swathing, raking, baling, and "road siding" (moving bales from the field to a stack) vary, depending on the size of the field being harvested, the proximity to the custom operator, and the tonnage. The current range is $30–$38 per ton ($33–$42 per MT) for custom harvest. Many harvesting companies swath, rake, bale, and roadside the harvested hay for a single fee. In this case, fees are based on a per-ton (or MT) basis, with a minimum of 1 ton (0.907 MT) of hay per acre. Some companies charge by individual operations. Individually, swathing and raking are charged on a per-acre (ha) basis, and baling and road-siding are charged on a per-ton (MT) basis.

Obviously, with nine cuttings per year, Imperial Valley harvest costs are much higher than costs in Siskiyou County, which averages three cuttings per year. However, each cutting in the Intermountain regions can be as high as three tons per acre (6.7 MT per ha) for the first or second cutting, whereas in the rest of the state, one to two tons per acre (2.2 to 4.4 MT/ha) per cutting is more typical. The per-acre annual yields vary tremendously throughout California, from 4.5 to 14 tons per acre (10.1 to 31 MT/ha) depending on location, quality of the stand establishment, weed and insect pressures, and the age of the stand. Average yields in California are between 6.5 to 7.5 tons per acre (14.6 to 16.8 MT/ha).

Statistics on hay prices are maintained by the USDA-Market News Service, and can be found at: http://www.ams.usda.gov/lsmnpubs/hsum.htm.

Statistics on alfalfa and other hay production from the United States are maintained by the USDA-National Agricultural Statistics Service, and can be found at: http://www.nass.usda.gov.

Additional Reading

Bath, D. L., and V. L. Marble. 1989. Testing alfalfa for its feeding value. University of California, Cooperative Extension, Division of Agriculture and Natural Resources, Oakland. Leaflet 21457-WREP 109.

Klonsky, K., et al. Cost and returns studies. Department of Agricultural and Resource Economics, University of California, Davis. http://coststudies.ucdavis.edu/.

Klonsky, K., S. Blank, K. Fuller, 2007. Alfalfa hay harvesting costs. In: Proceedings, 37th California Alfalfa & Forage Symposium, Monterey, CA. December 17-19. UC Cooperative Extension, Agronomy Research and Information Center, Plant Sciences Department, Davis.

Dark bands on antennae
...Pea Aphid

Antennae uniform color
...Blue Alfalfa Aphid

24

Diagnostic Key to Problems in Alfalfa

Charles G. Summers
Entomologist, University of California
Kearney Agricultural Center, Parlier, CA

This key is written as a quick guide to some of the common problems, including insects, diseases, vertebrate pests, herbicide injury, and mineral deficiencies, found in alfalfa. The focus of this chapter is on alfalfa grown for forage, not for seed, and will therefore not key out problems particular to seed alfalfa, such as seed chalcid or lygus bugs. This key is based, wherever possible, on diagnostic damage symptoms, thus it is unnecessary to find the actual organism causing the injury. Further detailed descriptions of these symptoms can be found in respective chapters on these pests and plant stresses.

Not all problems that may be encountered in alfalfa are included. Diseases or insects that are not common may not be identified by this key.

This key may be used to identify several symptoms observed simultaneously in the field. It is highly likely that growers are confronted with two or more problems at the same time. For example, alfalfa weevil feeding damage and common leaf spot or stemphylium leaf spot frequently occur together. These symptoms may be identified by repeatedly going through the key. For example, if leaflets are identified as "chewed or eaten" in late winter or spring, this will likely be alfalfa weevil damage. But, leaf spots may also be present. In a second pass through the key, this time identifying leaflets as "are not chewed or eaten" (Couplet II), you will end up at either "common leaf spot" and/or "stemphylium leaf spot" to identify this symptom.

If you are unable to diagnose your problem(s) using this key, please refer to the respective chapters in this volume for more details, or contact your local farm advisor.

Additional information is also available at the UC IPM Web site (http://www.ipm.ucdavis.edu/PMG/selectnewpest .alfalfa-hay.html) and at http://alfalfa.ucdavis.edu.

Diagnostic Key

I. Leaflets or entire stem(s) chewed or eaten.

   A. Leaflets skeletonized or stem epidermis stripped.

      1. Stem epidermis "stripped."

. . . . *Adult Alfalfa or Egyptian Alfalfa Weevil* [Chapter 9]

      2. Leaflets skeletonized; veins eaten.

        a. Leaflets skeletonized in winter or early spring.

Alfalfa Weevil or Egyptian Alfalfa Weevil [Chapter 9]

        b. Leaflets skeletonized in summer.

          i. Damage associated with webbing in terminals.

. . . . *Alfalfa Webworm* [Chapter 9]

          ii. Damage not associated with webbing.

. . . .*Alfalfa Caterpillar* [Chapter 9]

      3. Leaflet skeletonized, but veins remain intact (summer).

. . . . *Armyworms* [Chapter 9]

B. Entire stem chewed or cut off.

1. Few stems cut off at base of plant, stems frequently found lying on ground, C-shaped larvae often found at base of the plant.

. . . . *Cutworm* [Chapter 9]

2. Stem generally not cut off, but entire plant eaten.

a. Entire plant consumed, generally around margin of field, only stubble or sometimes chewed stems remaining. Droppings are frequently apparent.

. . . *Rabbits, Hares, or Deer* [Chapter 12]

b. Tips of stems or shoots consumed.

i. Well-worn trails in field.

. . . . *Meadow Mice* [Chapter 12]

ii. Burrows inside or outside of the field or along field edges.

. . . . *Belding Ground Squirrel* or *California Ground Squirrel* [Chapter 12]

California. Burrows out of field.

Belding. Burrows in field.

c. Plant or stems not consumed. Taproot chewed off. Plant(s) frequently seen wilting. Plants easily pulled from soil.

. . . . *Gopher Damage* [Chapter 12]

II. Leaflets or stems not chewed or eaten.

A. Leaves green, plants not wilted.

  1. Leaflets deformed.

    a. Plants not stunted.

      i. Leaflets cupped, appear clasped together.

. . . .*Eptam Injury* [Chapter 8]

Moderate   Severe

      ii. Leaflets long and narrow—leaf strapping.

. . . .*Butyrac (2,4-DB)* [Chapter 8]

      iii. Leaflets distorted and wrinkled, distortions often appear to arise from the midrib.

. . . . *Thrips* [Chapter 9]

      iv. Leaflets distorted in the terminal, grayish fuzzy appearance on underside, winter or spring.

. . *Systemic Downey Mildew* [Chapter 10]

    b. Plants stunted.

      i. Aphids present.

         a. Aphids green.

            i. Dark bands on antennae.

. . . . *Pea Aphid* [Chapter 9]

           ii. Antennae uniform color.

. . . .*Blue Alfalfa Aphid* [Chapter 9]

 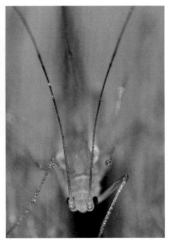

b. Aphids not green.

   i. Aphids black.

   . . . .*Cowpea Aphid* [Chapter 9]

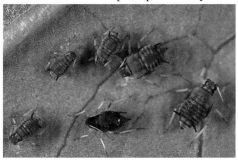

   ii. Aphids yellowish, five or six rows of black spots on back.

   . . . . . *Spotted Alfalfa Aphid* [Chapter 9]

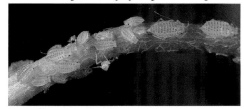

ii. Aphids not present.

   a. Leaflets small and crinkled.

   . . . .*Roundup Injury* [Chapter 8]

   b. Plants severely stunted, internodes greatly shortened, dead stem buds. Plants may also be white.

   . . . *Alfalfa Stem Nematode* [Chapter 11]

2. Leaves not deformed, plants not stunted.

   a. Shortened internodes near top of plant. Upper leaflets rolled inward. V-shaped necrotic area at tip of leaflets.

   . . . . *Verticillium Wilt* [Chapter 10]

   b. Taproot with "gouges" cut across much of the surface.

   . . . . . .*Clover Root Curculio* [Chapter 9]

3. Leaves not deformed. Plants not stunted. Roots swollen with galls or nodules.

   a. Roots with galls or swollen areas that cannot be dislodged by rubbing.

   . . . . . *Root-Knot Nematode* [Chapter 11]

   b. Roots with knots or nodules that are easily dislodged. Pink color shows when nodules are rubbed between fingers.

   . . . *Nitrogen-Fixing Nodules* [Chapter 4]

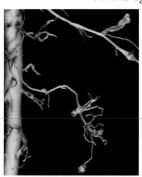

Root-Knot Nematode   Nitrogen-Fixing Nodules

B. Leaves green, plants wilted.

1. Seedling plants, fewer than two to four true leaves.

. . . . *Damping Off* [Chapter 10]

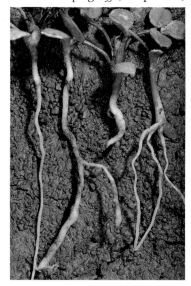

2. Mature plants, more than two to four true leaves.

a. Plant with very dark, bluish-green leaves; soil dry.

. . . . *Moisture Stress* [Chapter 7]

b. Terminal portion of plant wilted, leaves appear water soaked, later becoming yellow or white.

. . . . *Frost Injury* [Chapter 10]

C. Leaflets yellow or reddish, lacking normal green color. Leaflets not spotted; plants not wilted.

1. Leaflets yellowish or reddish, but not spotted.

a. Leaflets yellowish or reddish, wedge-shaped area at tip of leaflet.

. . . . *Potato Leafhopper* [Chapter 9]

b. Leaflet yellowish and/or reddish, but lacking wedge-shaped area at tip of leaf. Few or no leafhoppers present.

. . . .*Boron Deficiency* [Chapter 6]

c. Leaflet yellowish and/or reddish, lacking wedge shaped area at tip of leaf. Stem girdled at base.

. . . . *Three Cornered Alfalfa Hopper* [Chapter 9]

2. Leaves yellowish, but not reddish; not spotted.

a. Overall yellowing on all plants, most commonly observed in spring.

. . . . . . *Sulfur or Molybdenum Deficiency* [Chapter 6]

Sulfur Deficiency   Molybdenum Deficiency

b. Stunted yellow plants interspersed with normal green plants.

. . . .*Nitrogen Deficiency* [Chapter 6]

D. Leaflets yellow and/or spotted; plants not wilted.

1. Spots white.

a. Spots small.

i. Spots roughly circular and found over entire leaflet surface. Webbing on underside of leaflet.

. . . . *Mites* [Chapter 9]

ii. Spots roughly circular, but confined to leaf margin, particularly near tip of leaflet. No webbing.

. . . . . *Potassium Deficiency* [Chapter 6]

b. Spots large.

i. Spots irregular in shape, found over entire leaflet.

. . . .*Paraquat Injury* [Chapter 8]

ii. Spots irregular in shape, mainly interveinal.

. . . .*Ozone Injury* [Chapter 10]

2. Spots yellow or black.

   a. Spots yellow.

      i. Spots yellow; underside of leaflet gray or tan; "fuzzy" appearance.

          . . . . *Downy Mildew* [Chapter 10]

      ii. Spots bright yellow, interveinal and elongated on scattered plants.

          . . . . . *Alfalfa Mosaic Virus* [Chapter 10]

      iii. Interveinal chlorosis widespread, found on majority of plants.

          . . . . *Velpar, Karmex, Sencor Injury* [Chapter 8]

3. Spots tan or brown.

   a. Small, circular brown spots with a darker brown raised center; on upper side of leaflets.

       . . . . . . *Common Leaf Spot* [Chapter 10]

   b. Variably sized spots with a tan center and dark brown border—on upper surface of the leaflet.

       . . . *Stemphylium Leaf Spot* [Chapter 10]

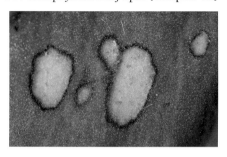

   c. Lesions associated with leaf margins giving appearance of concentric rings. Multiple raised fruiting bodies within individual lesions. Oblong stem lesions also containing multiple fruiting bodies.

       . . . . . *Stagonospora Crown and Root Rot* [Chapter 10]

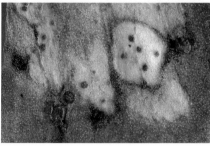

4. Small black spots on leaves and stems. Spots on stems often coalesce to make portions of the stem black.

       . . . .*Spring Black Stem* [Chapter 10]

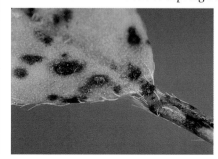

E. Leaflets yellow, not spotted; plants wilted.

1. Stems with "fluffy" white mycelial growth near crown, most common in cool, wet weather.

. . . . *Sclerotinia Stem and Crown Rot* [Chapter 10]

2. Stems without "fluffy" mycelial growth, crowns or roots rotted or deformed.

   a. Bluish-black discoloration of crown often joining reddish streaks inside root. Bleached and bent stems frequently found scattered throughout the field.

   . . . . *Anthracnose* [Chapter 10]

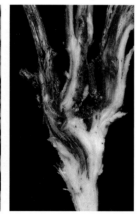

   b. Reddish-orange to yellow streaks spreading from dead areas internally. Rot often starts in lower part of root.

   . . . *Phytophthora Root Rot* [Chapter 10]

c. Elliptical-shaped sunken lesions, tan in the center and dark on the edges (in hot, wet conditions); lesions black in cool season.

. . *Rhizoctonia Root Canker* [Chapter 10]

d. Off-color foliage and wilting, even though the soil is wet. Roots may rot and have a putrid odor when removed from the soil. Maximum temperature >100°F (32°C).

. . . . *Scald* [Chapter 10]

e. Center core of root dark reddish brown, as seen in longitudinal section.

. . . . *Fusarium Wilt* [Chapter 10]

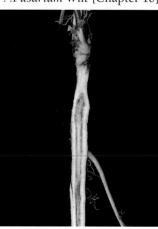

Index

Page numbers followed by *f* refer to figures; page numbers followed by *t* refer to tables.